CU00819481

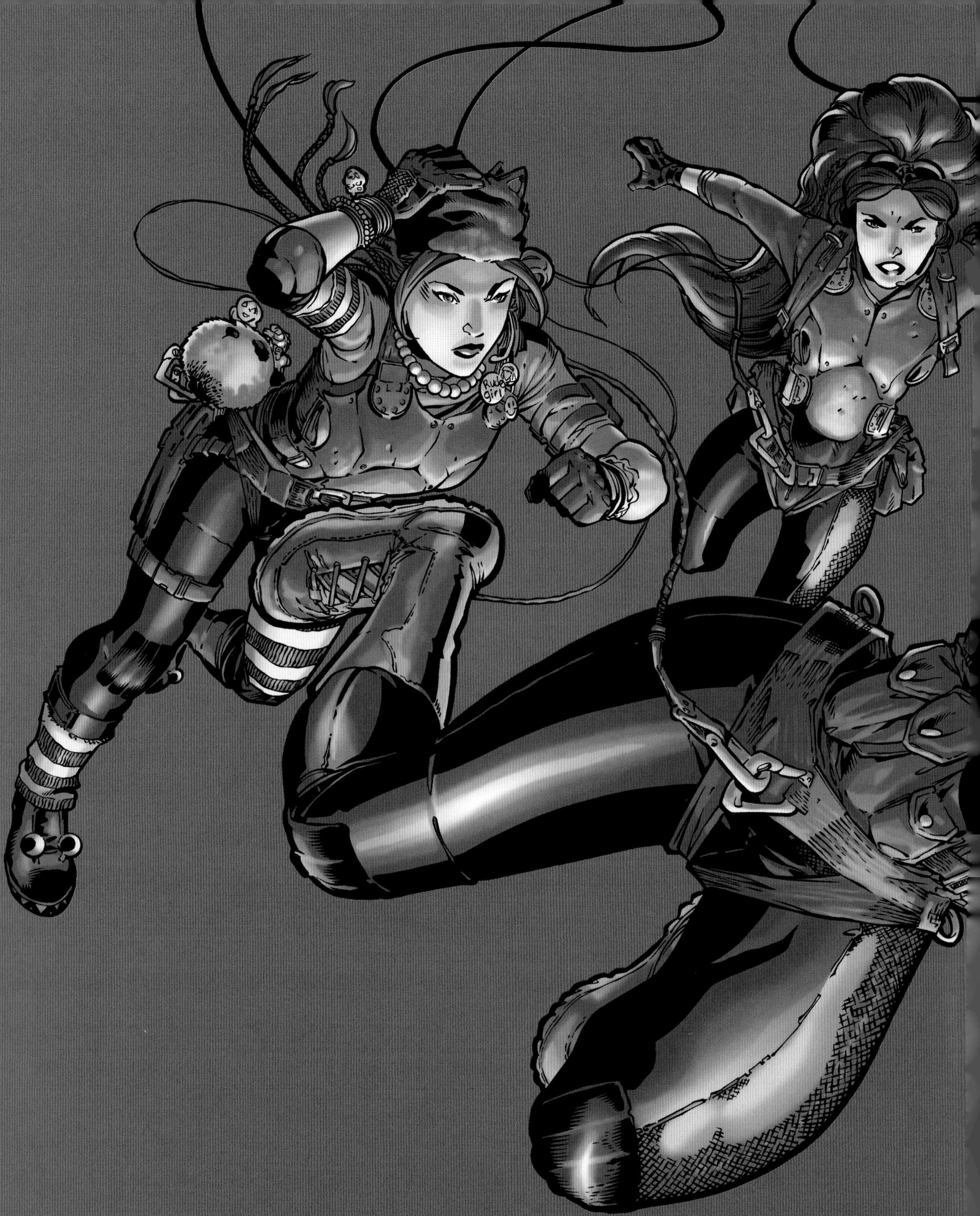

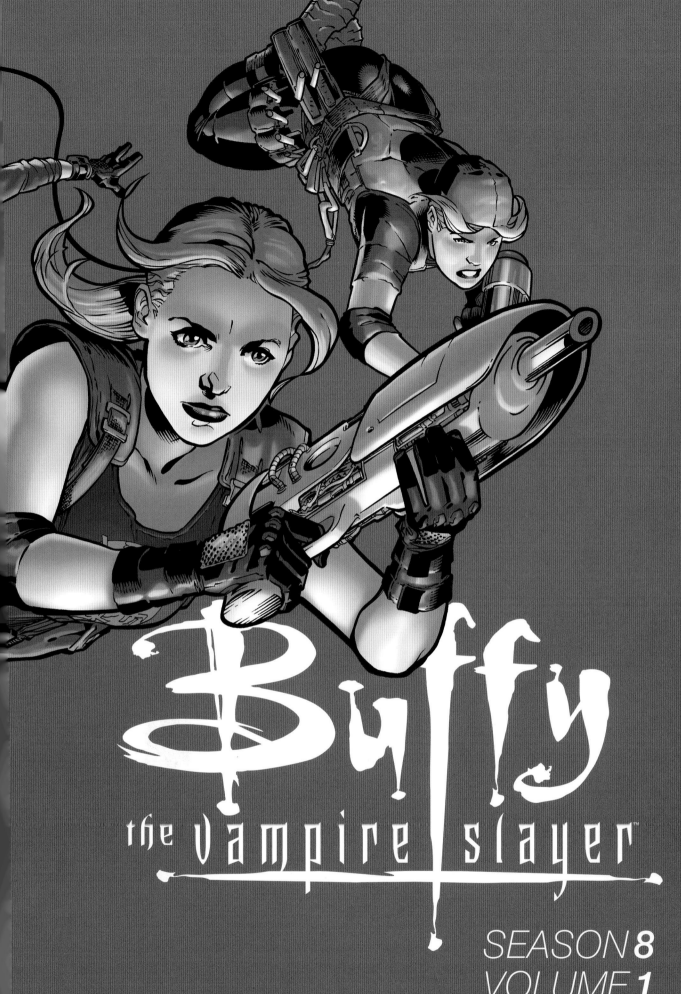

Buffy
the Vampire Slayer

SEASON 8
VOLUME 1

DARK HORSE BOOKS

President and Publisher
MIKE RICHARDSON

Designer
JUSTIN COUCH

Editors
SCOTT ALLIE
and SIERRA HAHN

Assistant Editor
FREDDYE LINS

Cover Art
JO CHEN

Published by
DARK HORSE BOOKS

A division of
DARK HORSE COMICS, INC.
10956 SE Main Street
Milwaukie, Oregon 97222

DarkHorse.com

First edition: May 2012
ISBN 978-1-59582-888-0
10 9 8 7 6 5 4 3 2 1

Special thanks to Debbie Olshan at Twentieth Century Fox,
Michael Boretz, Crystal Shand, Jarrod and Robin Balzer,
Rachel Edidin, and Katie Moody.

To find a comic shop in your area, call the
Comic Shop Locator Service: (888) 266-4226.

This volume reprints Buffy the Vampire Slayer Season 8 #1–#10
and "Buffy the Vampire Slayer: Always Darkest" from MySpace Dark
Horse Presents #24.

NEIL HANKERSON Executive Vice President • TOM WEDDLE Chief Financial
Officer • RANDY STRADLEY Vice President of Publishing • MICHAEL MARTENS
Vice President of Book Trade Sales • ANITA NELSON Vice President of Business
Affairs • DAVID SCROGGY Vice President of Product Development • DALE LAFOUNTAIN Vice
President of Information Technology • DARLENE VOGEL Senior Director of Print, Design,
and Production • KEN LIZZI General Counsel • MATT PARKINSON Senior Director of
Marketing • DAVEY ESTRADA Editorial Director • SCOTT ALLIE Senior Managing
Editor • CHRIS WARNER Senior Books Editor • DIANA SCHUTZ Executive Editor
CARY GRAZZINI Director of Print and Development • LIA RIBACCHI Art Director

Printed at Midas Printing International, Ltd., Huizhou, China

TABLE OF CONTENTS

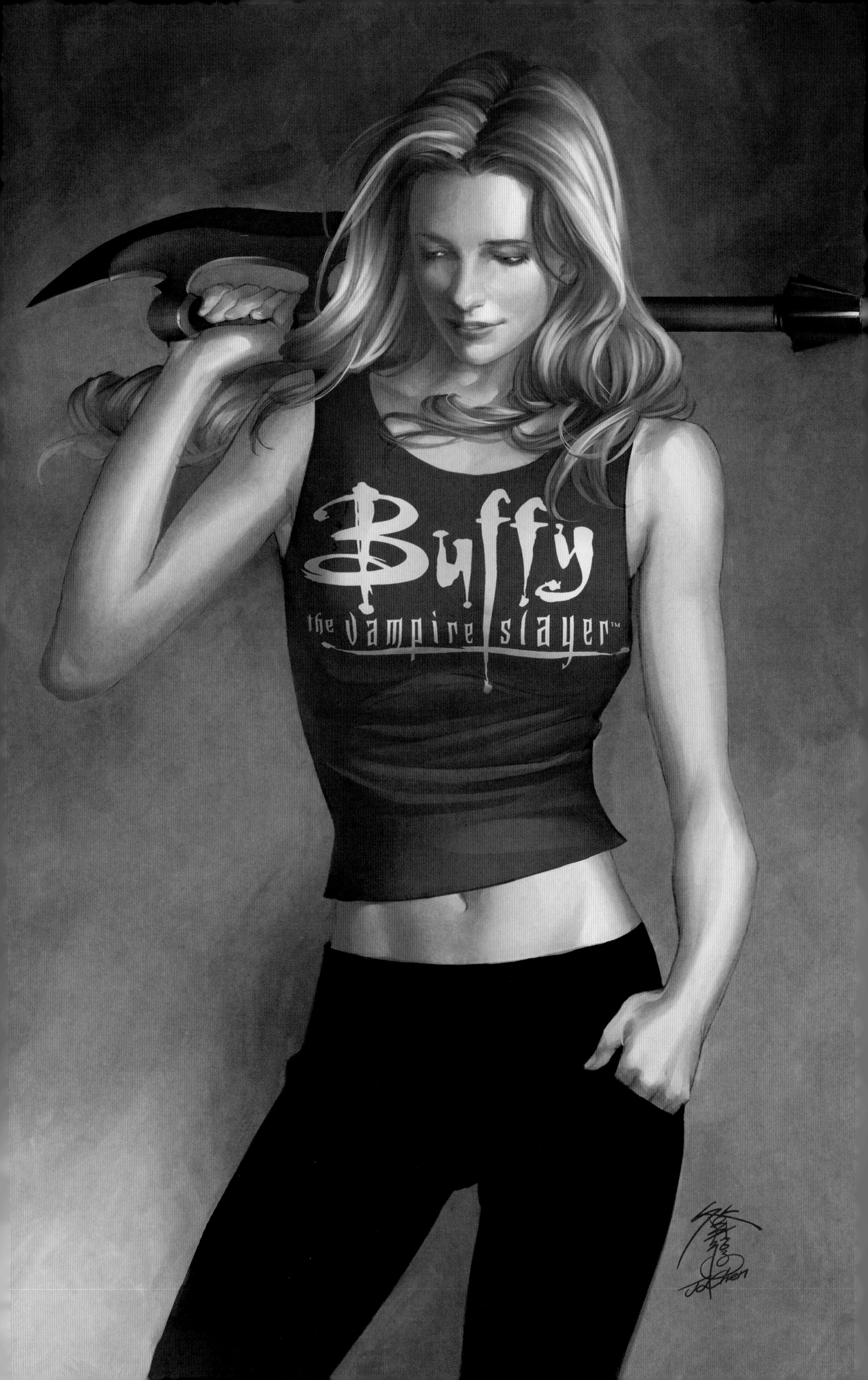
Buffy
the Vampire Slayer™

The LONG WAY HOME

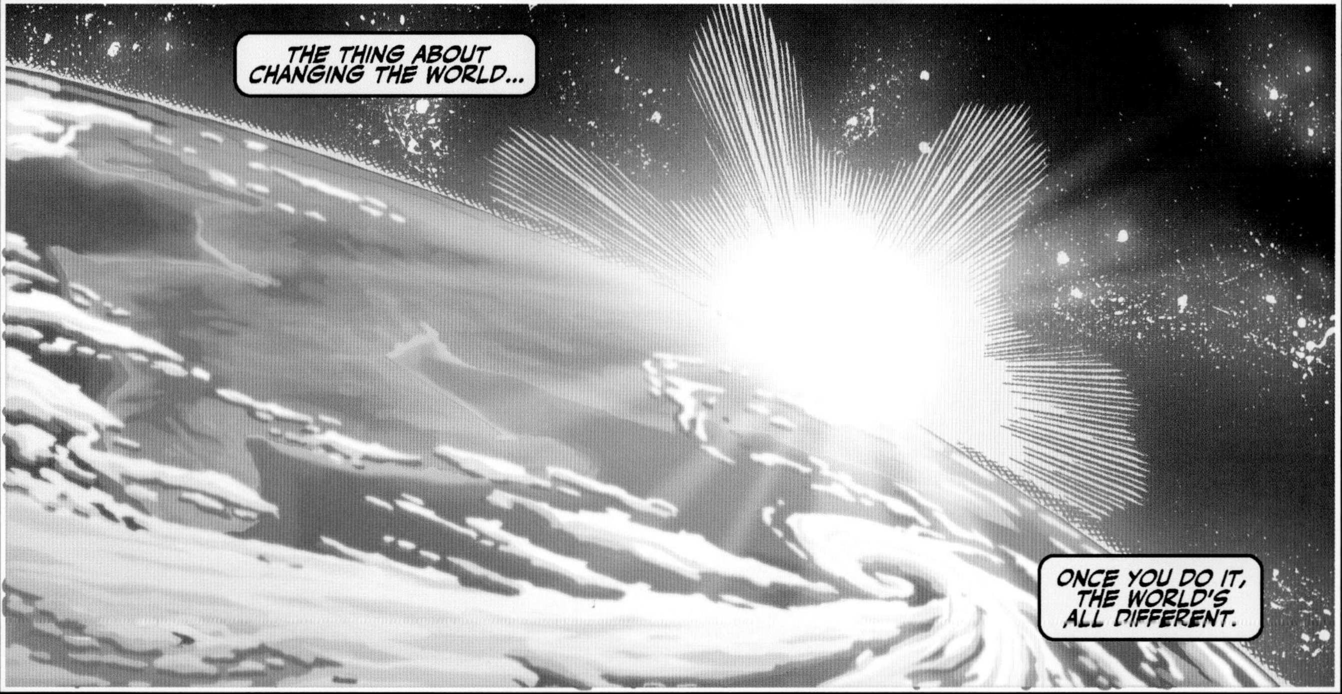
THE THING ABOUT CHANGING THE WORLD...
ONCE YOU DO IT, THE WORLD'S ALL DIFFERENT.

Part One

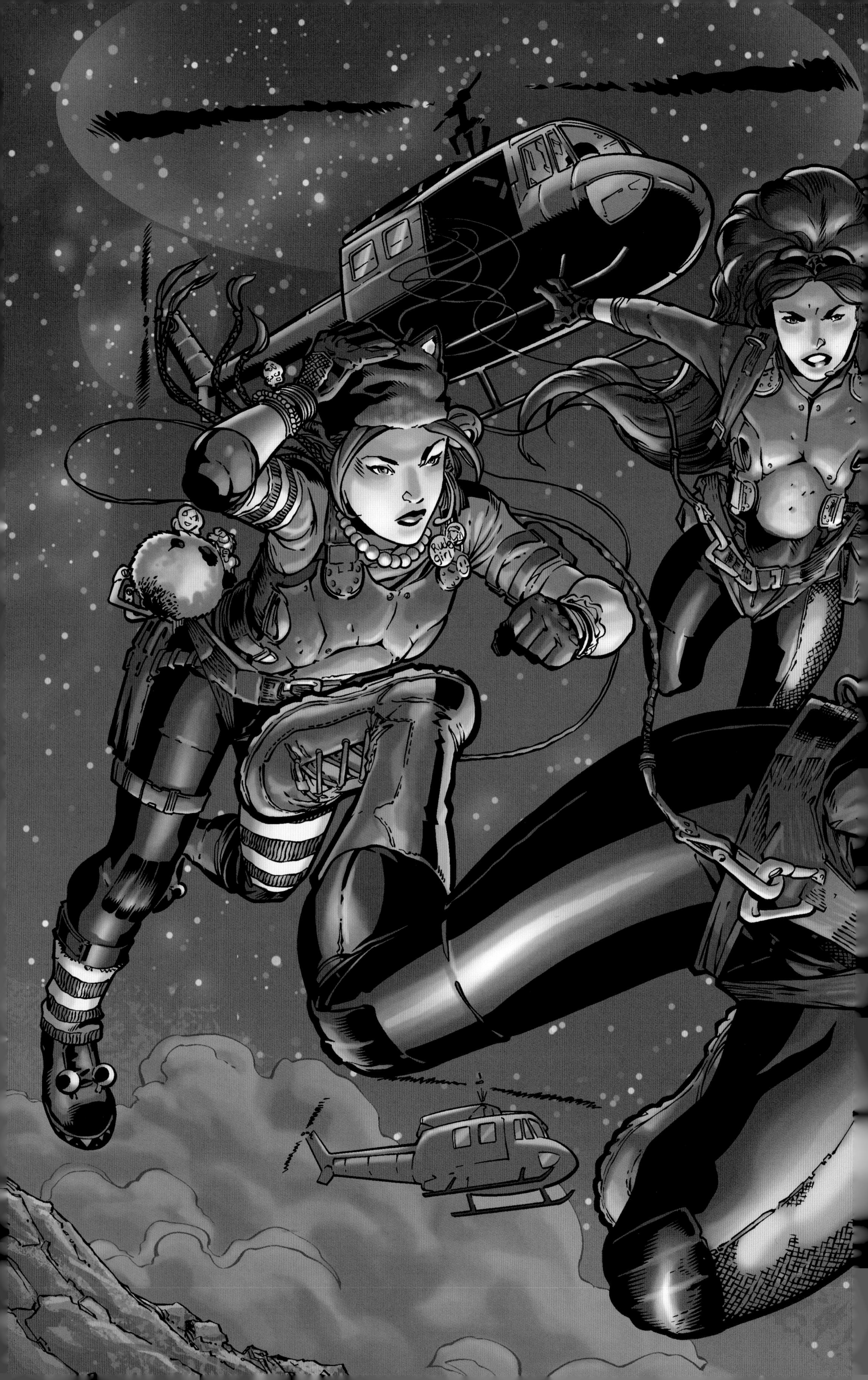
Rude girl

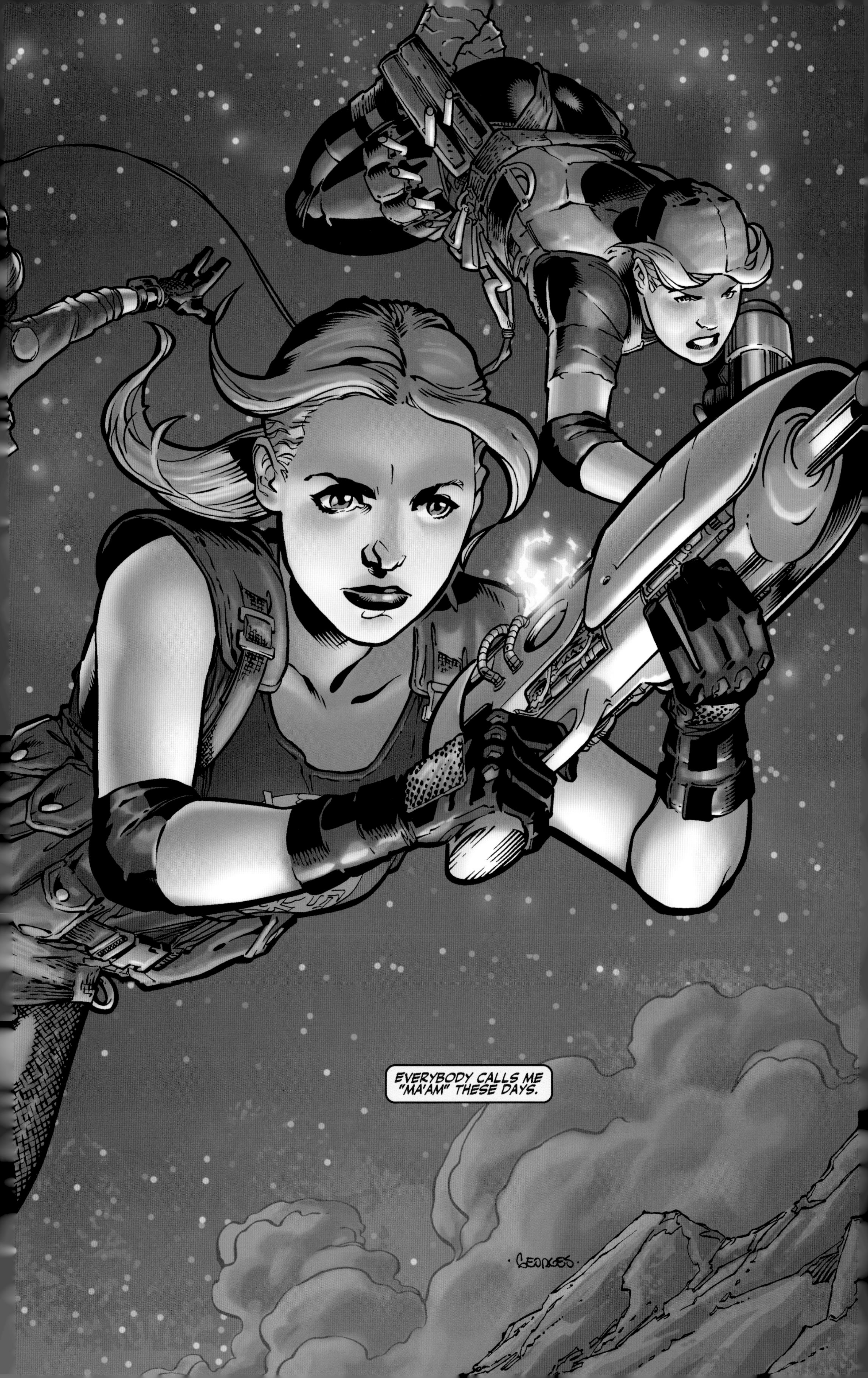
EVERYBODY CALLS ME "MA'AM" THESE DAYS.

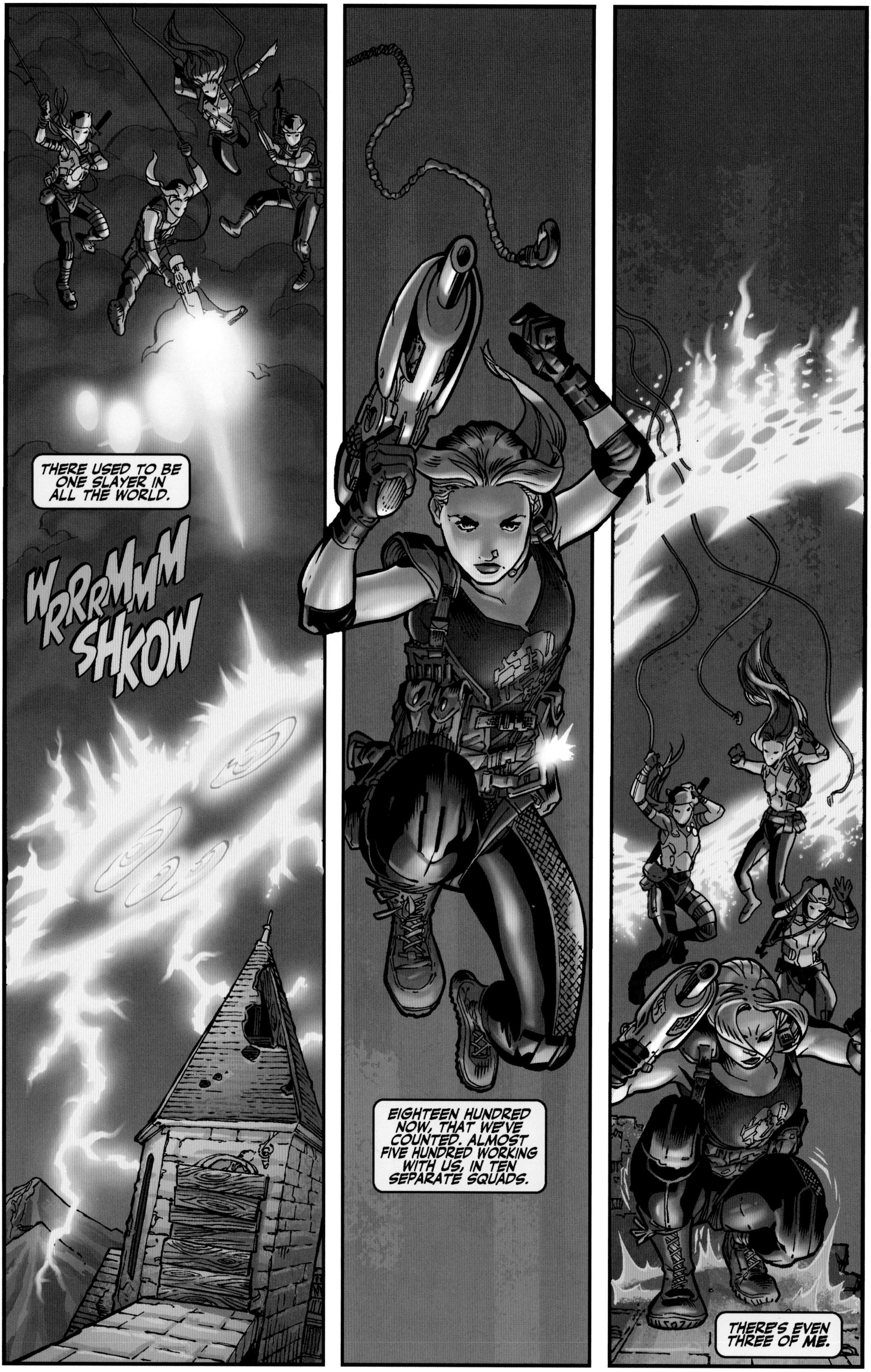
THERE USED TO BE ONE SLAYER IN ALL THE WORLD.
WRRRMMM SHKOW
EIGHTEEN HUNDRED NOW, THAT WE'VE COUNTED. ALMOST FIVE HUNDRED WORKING WITH US, IN TEN SEPARATE SQUADS.
THERE'S EVEN THREE OF ME.

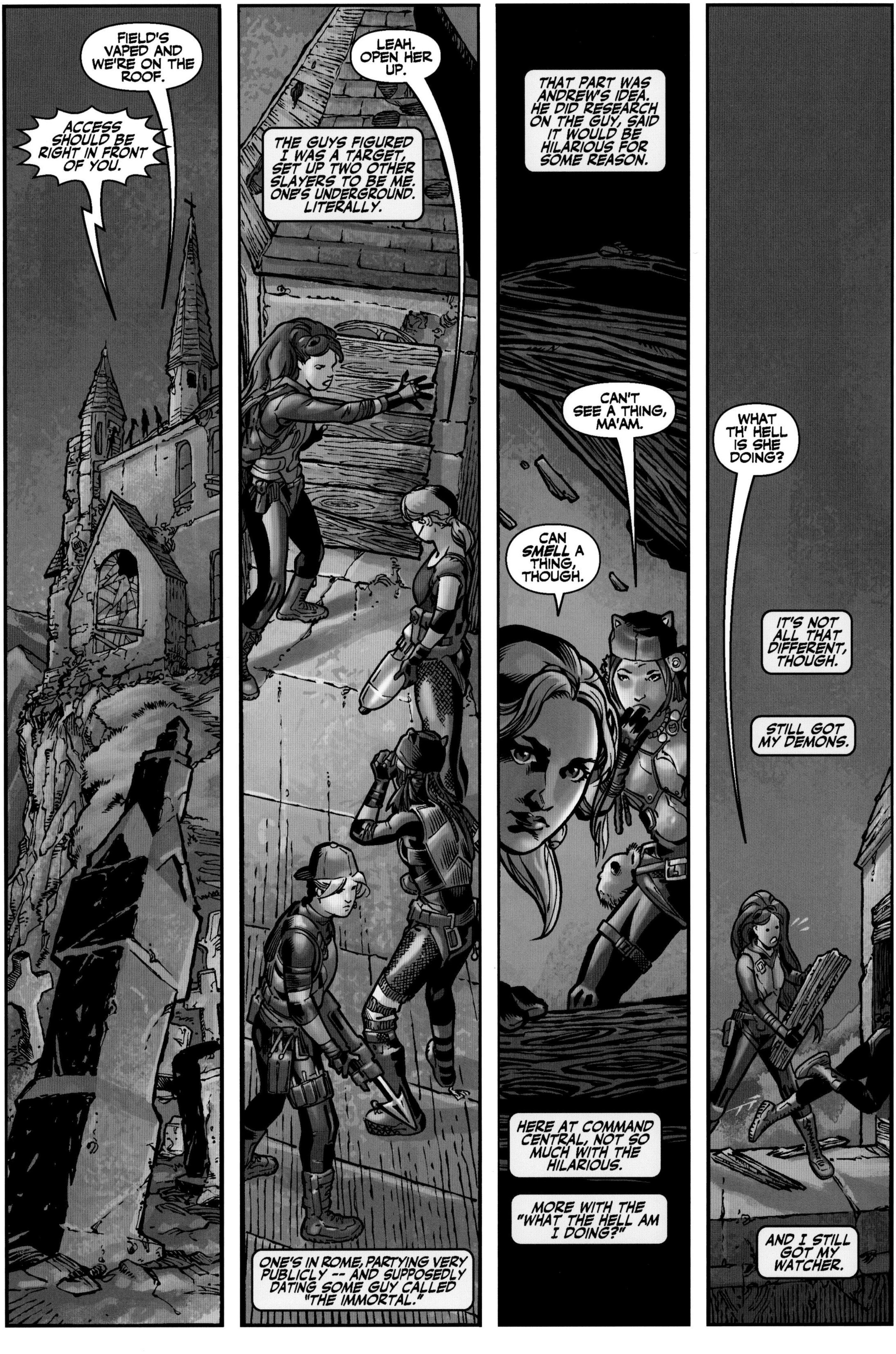
FIELD'S VAPED AND WE'RE ON THE ROOF.
ACCESS SHOULD BE RIGHT IN FRONT OF YOU.
LEAH. OPEN HER UP.
THE GUYS FIGURED I WAS A TARGET, SET UP TWO OTHER SLAYERS TO BE ME. ONE'S UNDERGROUND. LITERALLY.
ONE'S IN ROME, PARTYING VERY PUBLICLY -- AND SUPPOSEDLY DATING SOME GUY CALLED "THE IMMORTAL."
THAT PART WAS ANDREW'S IDEA. HE DID RESEARCH ON THE GUY, SAID IT WOULD BE HILARIOUS FOR SOME REASON.
CAN'T SEE A THING, MA'AM.
CAN SMELL A THING, THOUGH.
HERE AT COMMAND CENTRAL, NOT SO MUCH WITH THE HILARIOUS.
MORE WITH THE "WHAT THE HELL AM I DOING?"
WHAT TH' HELL IS SHE DOING?
IT'S NOT ALL THAT DIFFERENT, THOUGH.
STILL GOT MY DEMONS.
AND I STILL GOT MY WATCHER.

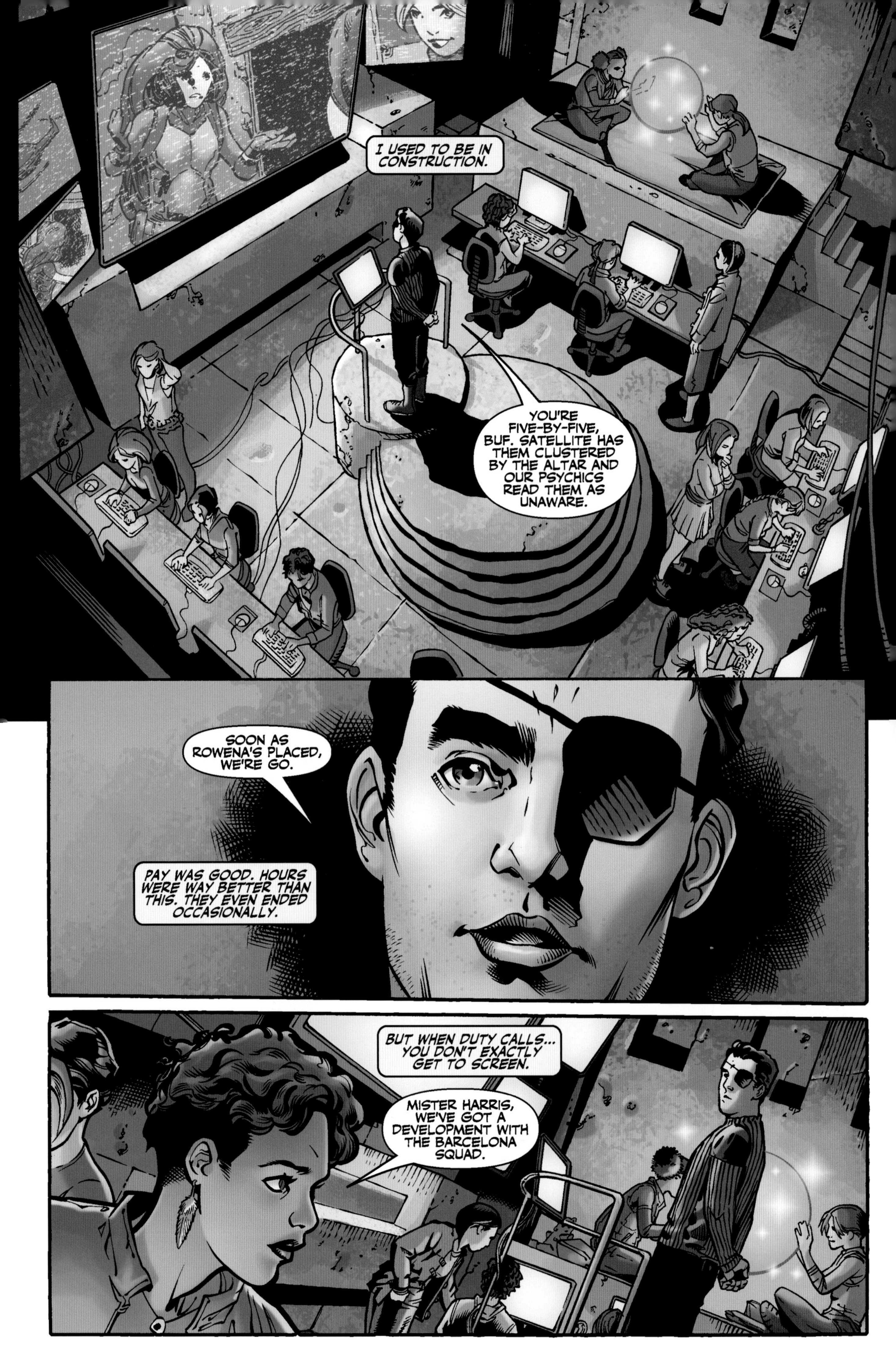
I USED TO BE IN CONSTRUCTION.
YOU'RE FIVE-BY-FIVE, BUF. SATELLITE HAS THEM CLUSTERED BY THE ALTAR AND OUR PSYCHICS READ THEM AS UNAWARE.
SOON AS ROWENA'S PLACED, WE'RE GO.
PAY WAS GOOD. HOURS WERE WAY BETTER THAN THIS. THEY EVEN ENDED OCCASIONALLY.
BUT WHEN DUTY CALLS... YOU DON'T EXACTLY GET TO SCREEN.
MISTER HARRIS, WE'VE GOT A DEVELOPMENT WITH THE BARCELONA SQUAD.

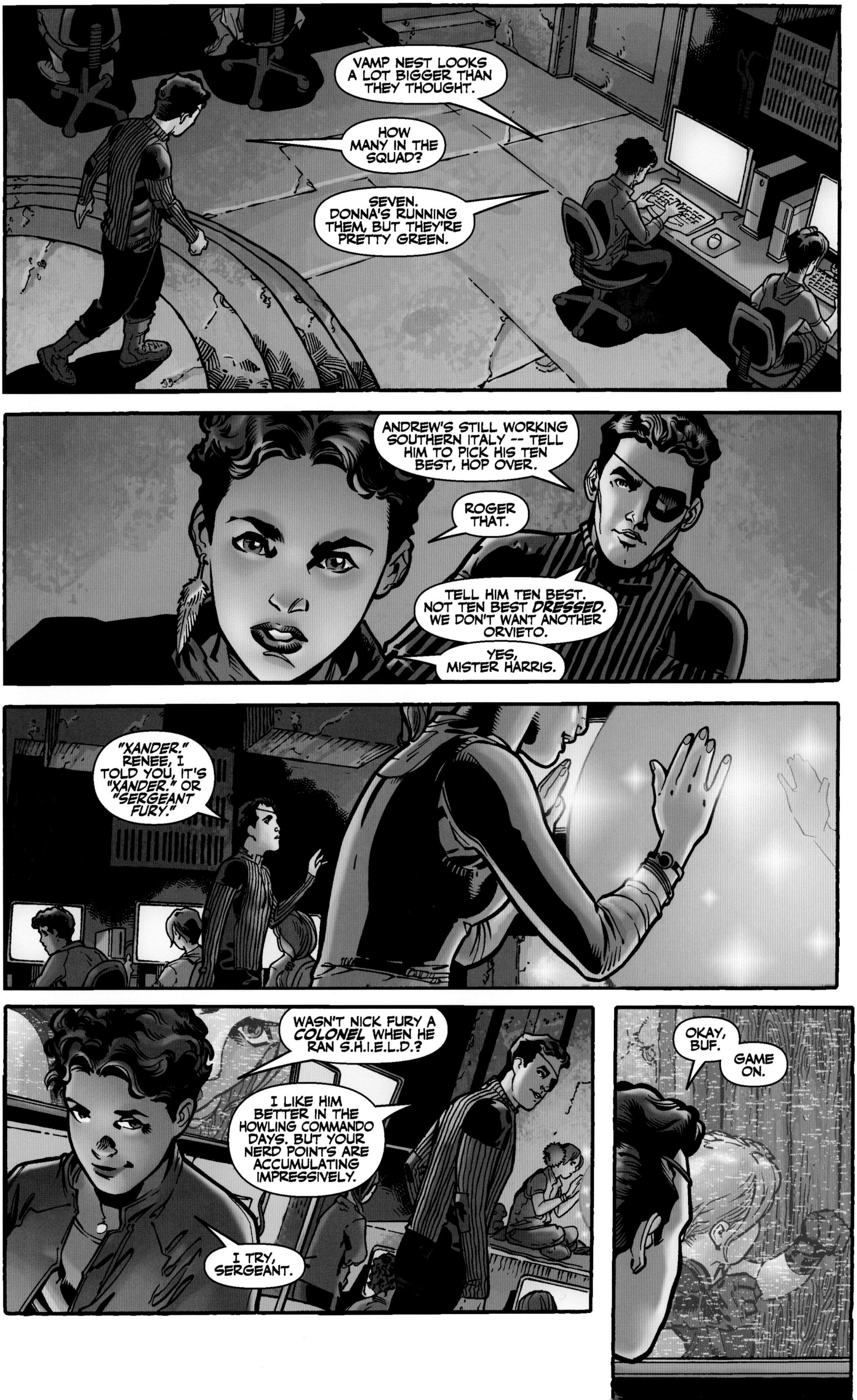
VAMP NEST LOOKS A LOT BIGGER THAN THEY THOUGHT.
HOW MANY IN THE SQUAD?
SEVEN. DONNA'S RUNNING THEM, BUT THEY'RE PRETTY GREEN.
ANDREW'S STILL WORKING SOUTHERN ITALY -- TELL HIM TO PICK HIS TEN BEST, HOP OVER.
ROGER THAT.
TELL HIM TEN BEST. NOT TEN BEST *DRESSED*. WE DON'T WANT ANOTHER ORVIETO.
YES, MISTER HARRIS.
"XANDER." RENEE, I TOLD YOU, IT'S "XANDER." OR "SERGEANT FURY."
WASN'T NICK FURY A *COLONEL* WHEN HE RAN S.H.I.E.L.D.?
I LIKE HIM BETTER IN THE HOWLING COMMANDO DAYS. BUT YOUR NERD POINTS ARE ACCUMULATING IMPRESSIVELY.
I TRY, SERGEANT.
OKAY, BUF.
GAME ON.

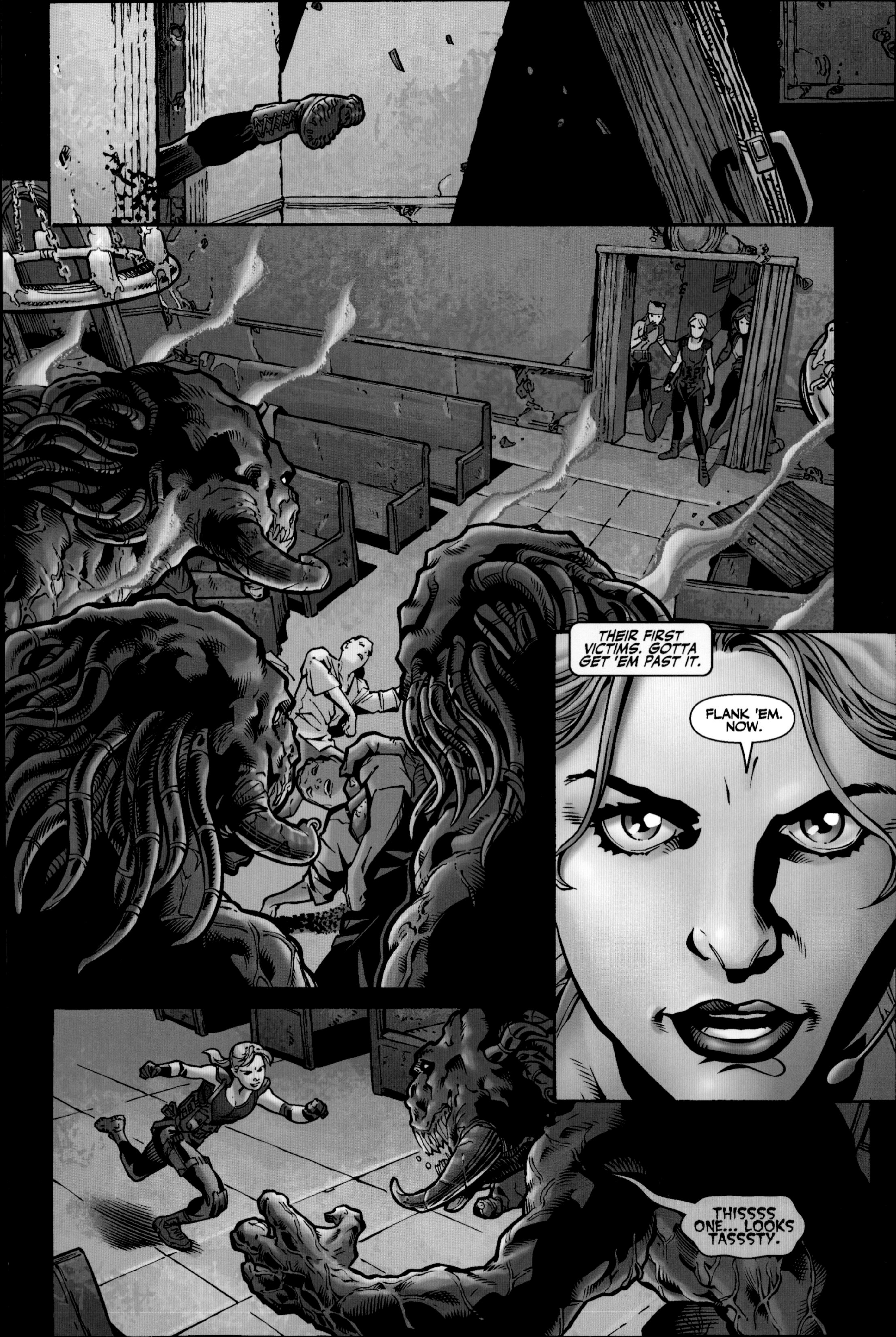
THEIR FIRST VICTIMS. GOTTA GET 'EM PAST IT.
FLANK 'EM. NOW.
THISSSS ONE... LOOKS TASSSTY.

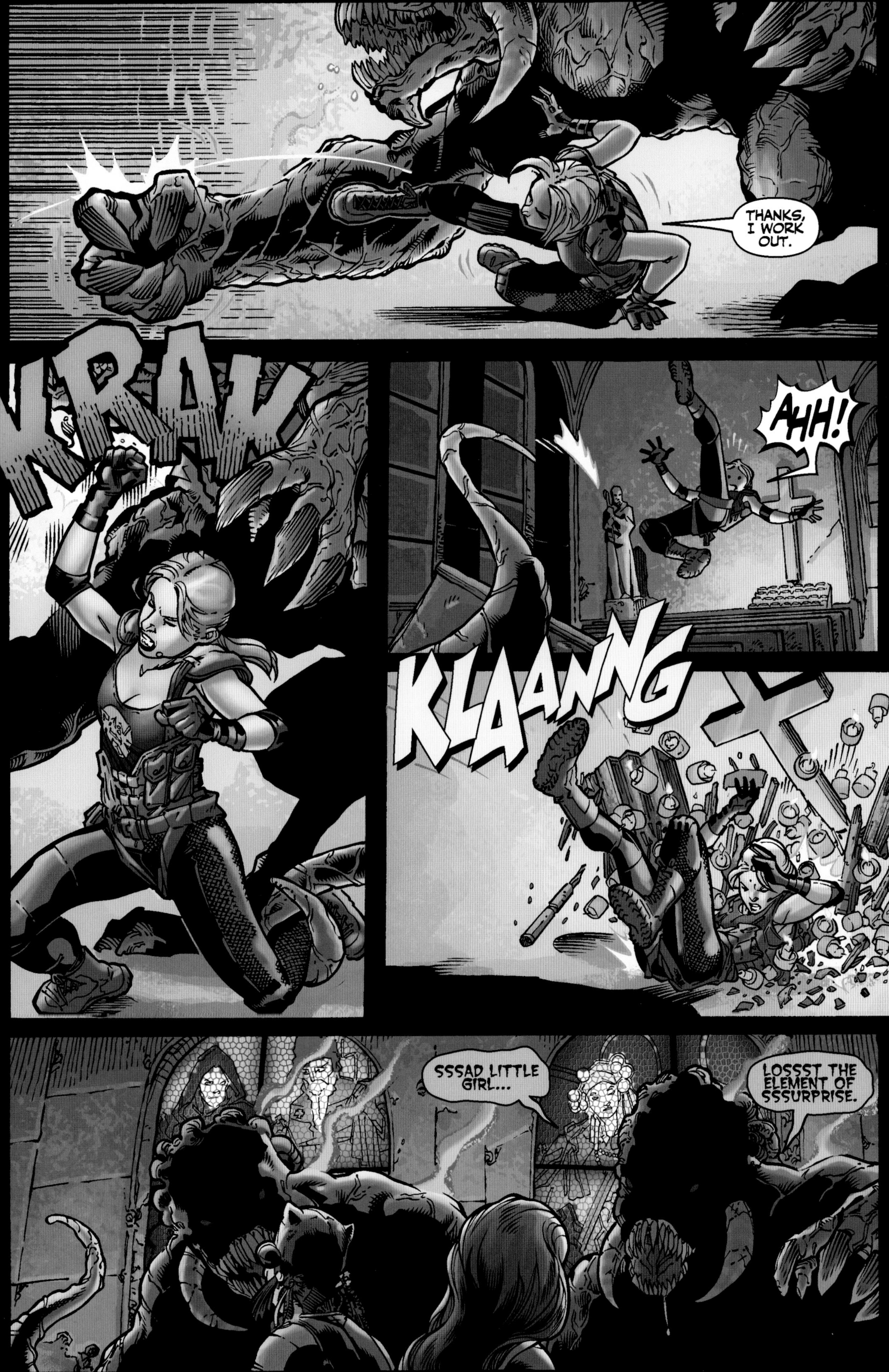
THANKS, I WORK OUT.
KRAK
AHH!
KLAANNG
SSSAD LITTLE GIRL...
LOSSST THE ELEMENT OF SSSURPRISE.

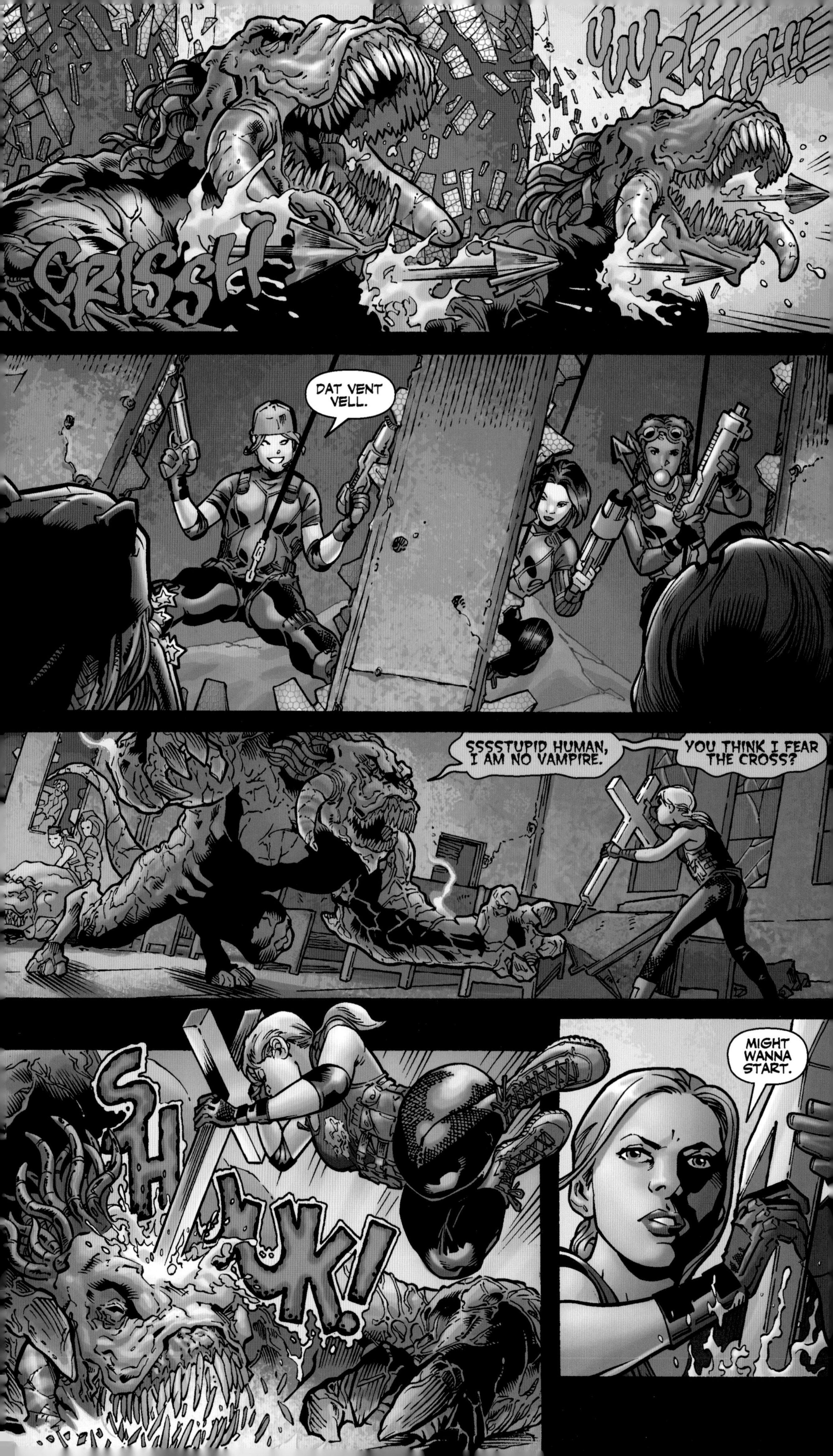
UWRUUGH!!
CRISSH
DAT VENT VELL.
SSSSTUPID HUMAN, I AM NO VAMPIRE.
YOU THINK I FEAR THE CROSS?
SHUNK!
MIGHT WANNA START.

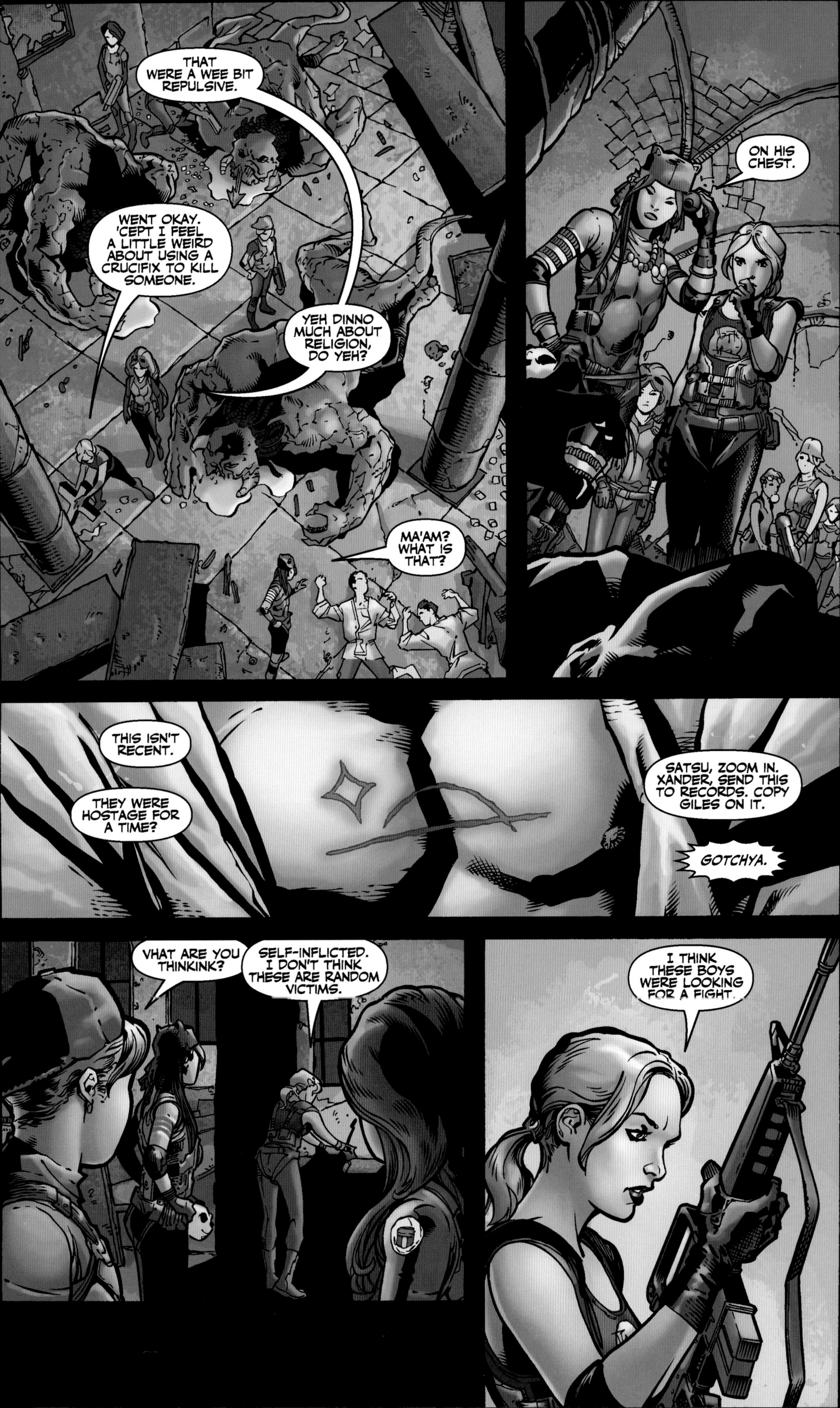
THAT WERE A WEE BIT REPULSIVE.
WENT OKAY. 'CEPT I FEEL A LITTLE WEIRD ABOUT USING A CRUCIFIX TO KILL SOMEONE.
YEH DINNO MUCH ABOUT RELIGION, DO YEH?
MA'AM? WHAT IS THAT?
ON HIS CHEST.
THIS ISN'T RECENT.
THEY WERE HOSTAGE FOR A TIME?
SATSU, ZOOM IN. XANDER, SEND THIS TO RECORDS. COPY GILES ON IT.
GOTCHYA.
VHAT ARE YOU THINKINK?
SELF-INFLICTED. I DON'T THINK THESE ARE RANDOM VICTIMS.
I THINK THESE BOYS WERE LOOKING FOR A FIGHT.

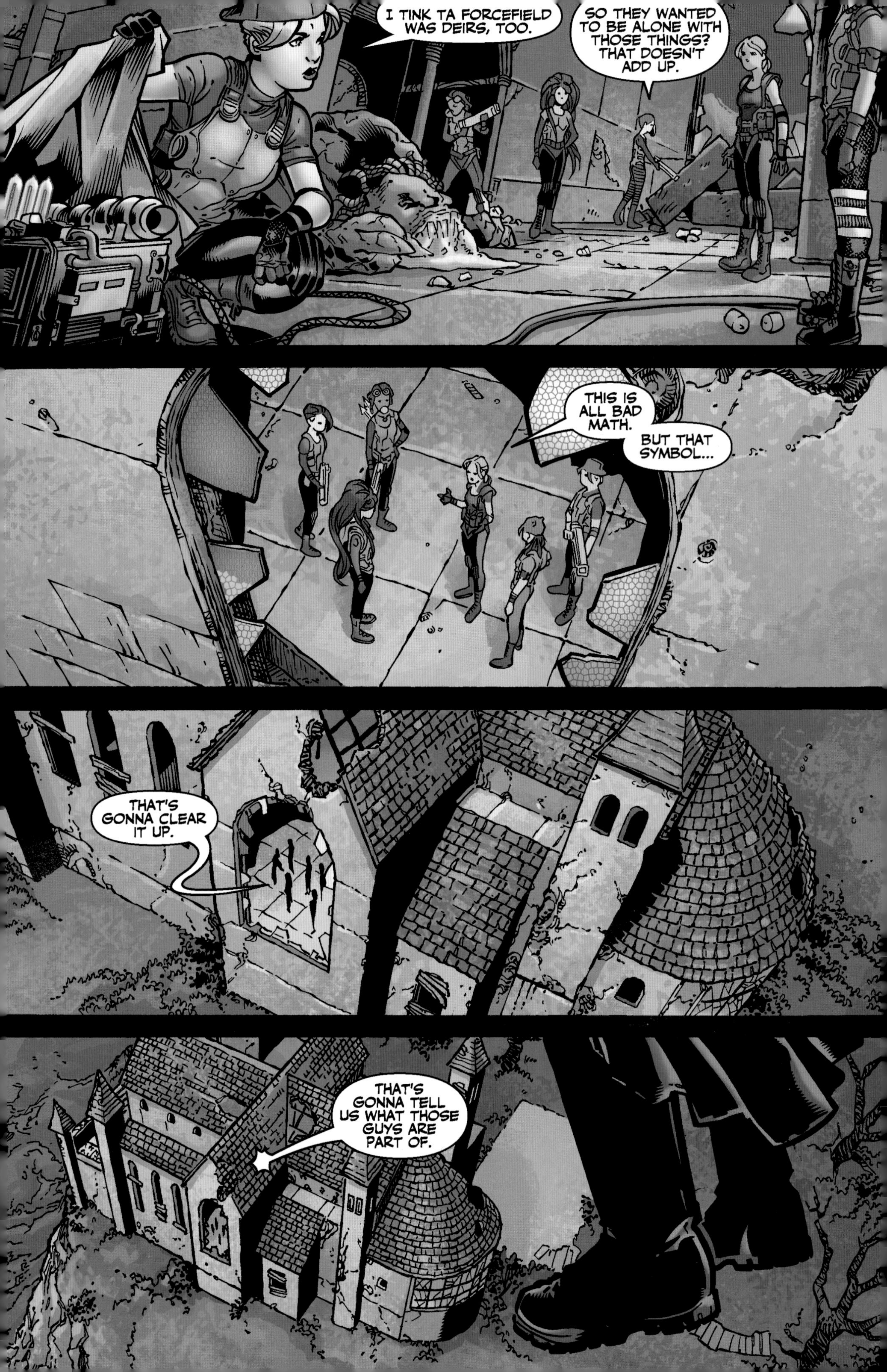
I TINK TA FORCEFIELD WAS DEIRS, TOO.
SO THEY WANTED TO BE ALONE WITH THOSE THINGS? THAT DOESN'T ADD UP.
THIS IS ALL BAD MATH.
BUT THAT SYMBOL...
THAT'S GONNA CLEAR IT UP.
THAT'S GONNA TELL US WHAT THOSE GUYS ARE PART OF.

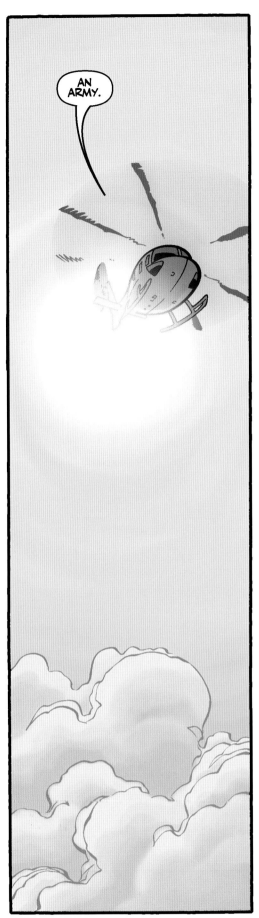

AN ARMY.

YOU DON'T THINK THAT'S OVERSTATING IT, GENERAL VOLL?

OUR INTEL SAYS THEY'RE TOO LOOSELY AFFILIATED TO... I MEAN, THEY'RE SCATTERED IN THOSE --

"SQUADS," RIGHT. TERRORISTS CALL 'EM "CELLS."

WE GO AHEAD WITH THIS, WE GOTTA BE TOGETHER ON EXACTLY WHAT WE'RE FACING. AND THAT'S AN ARMY.

THEY GOT POWER, THEY GOT RESOURCES, AND THEY GOT A HARD-LINE IDEOLOGY THAT DOES NOT JIBE WITH AMERICAN INTERESTS.

WORST OF ALL, THEY GOT A LEADER.

CHARISMATIC, UNCOMPROMISING, AND COMPLETELY DESTRUCTIVE.

I MEAN, FOR THE LOVE OF GOD...

19

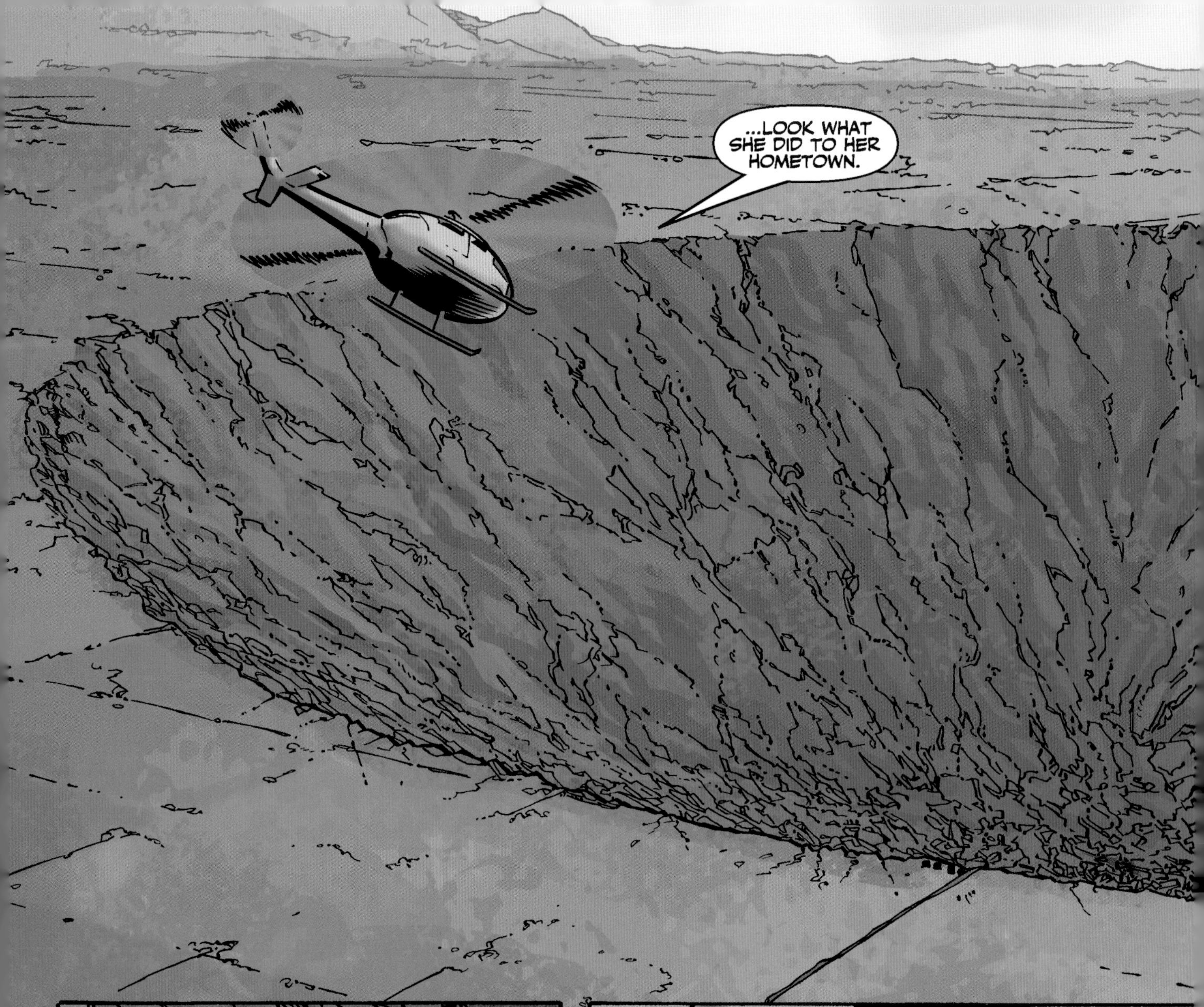
...LOOK WHAT SHE DID TO HER HOMETOWN.

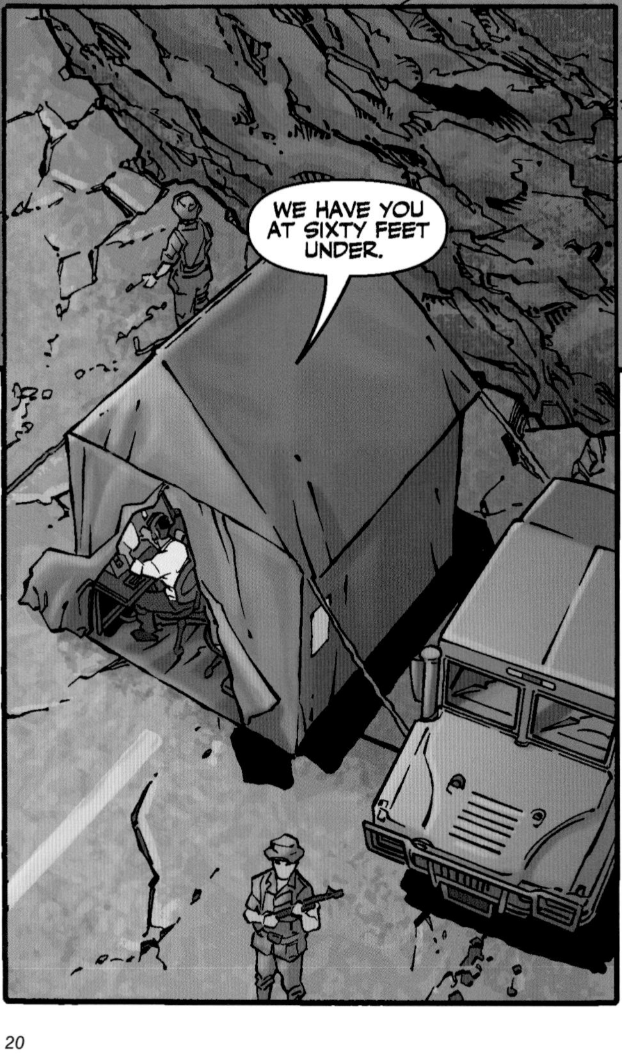
WE HAVE YOU AT SIXTY FEET UNDER.

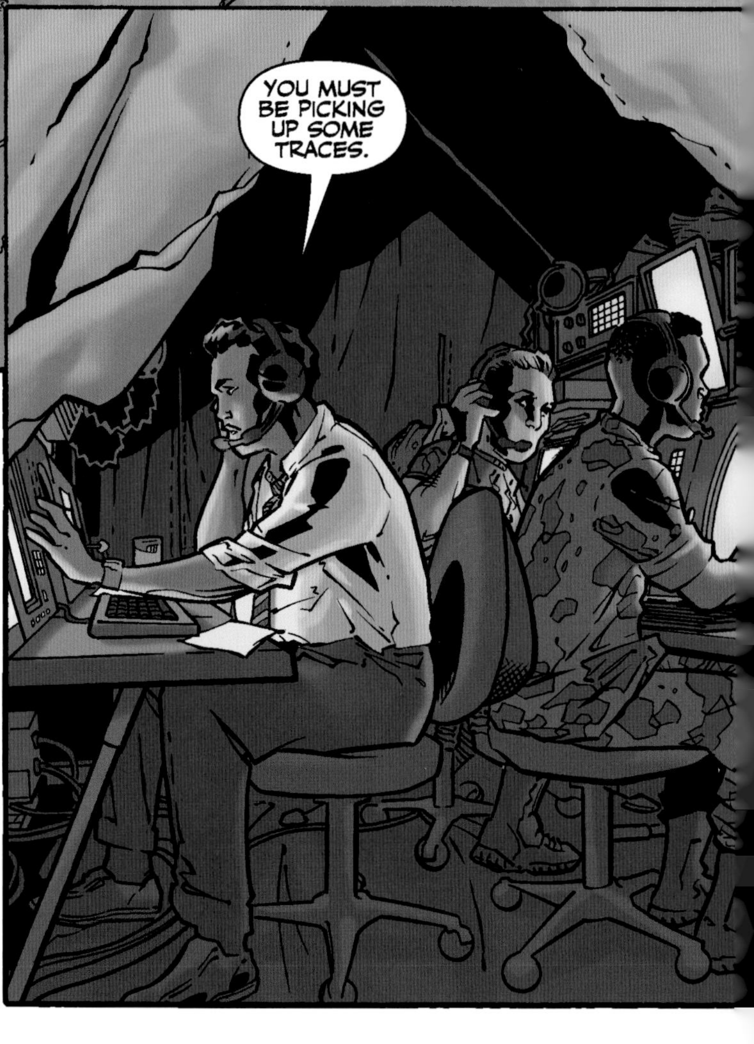
YOU MUST BE PICKING UP SOME TRACES.

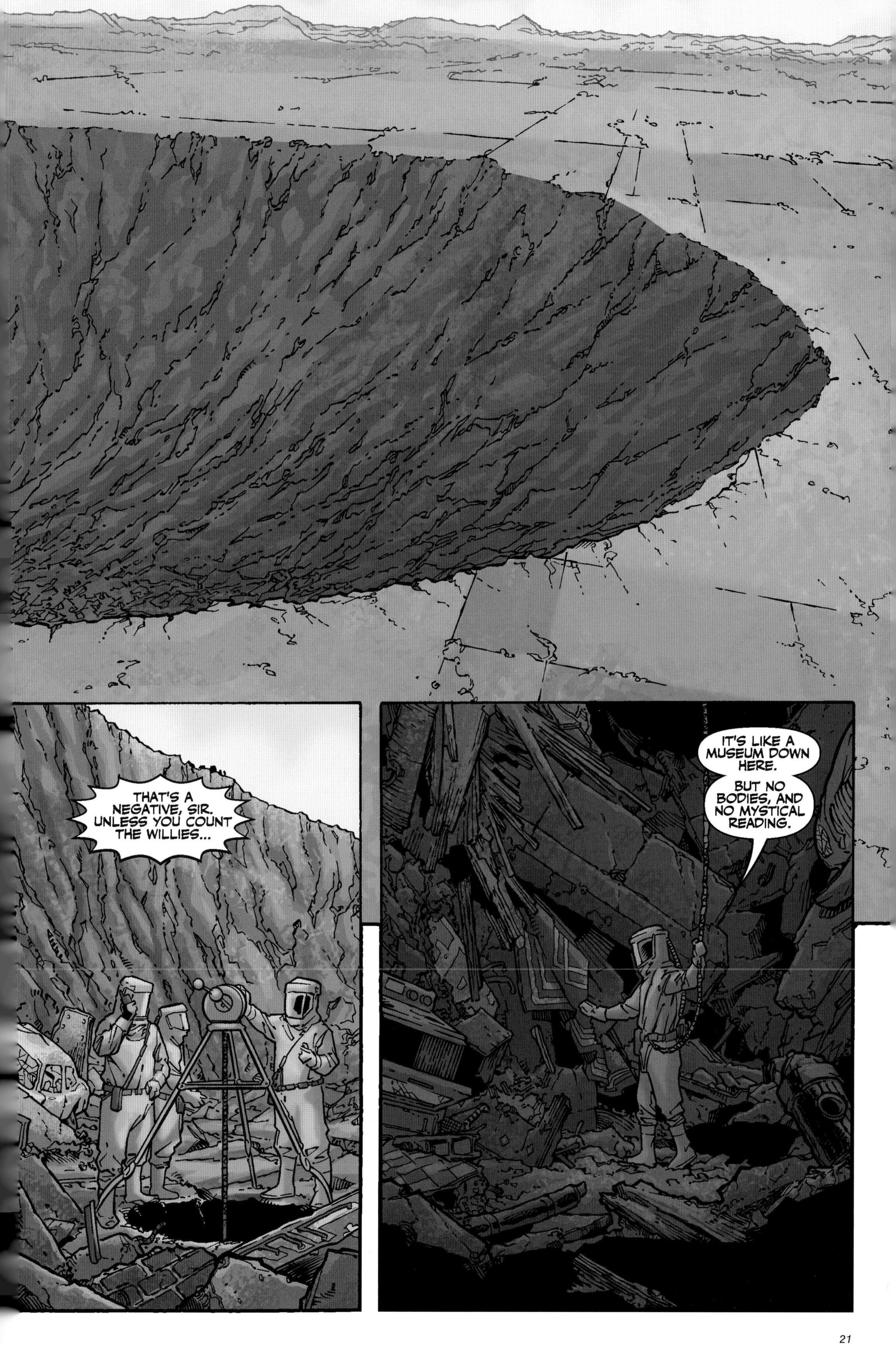
THAT'S A NEGATIVE, SIR. UNLESS YOU COUNT THE WILLIES...
IT'S LIKE A MUSEUM DOWN HERE.
BUT NO BODIES, AND NO MYSTICAL READING.

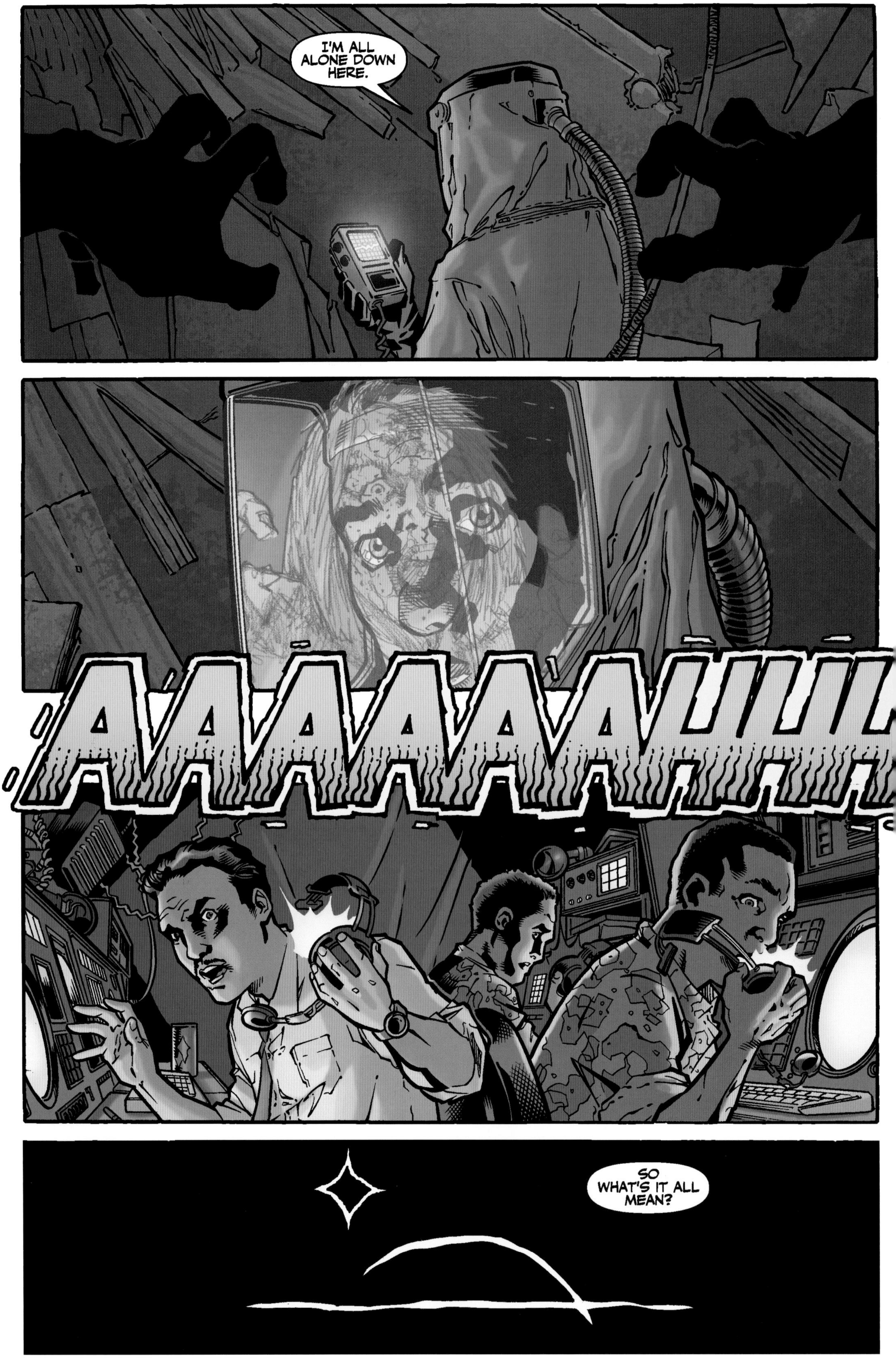
I'M ALL ALONE DOWN HERE.
AAAAAAAHHH
SO WHAT'S IT ALL MEAN?

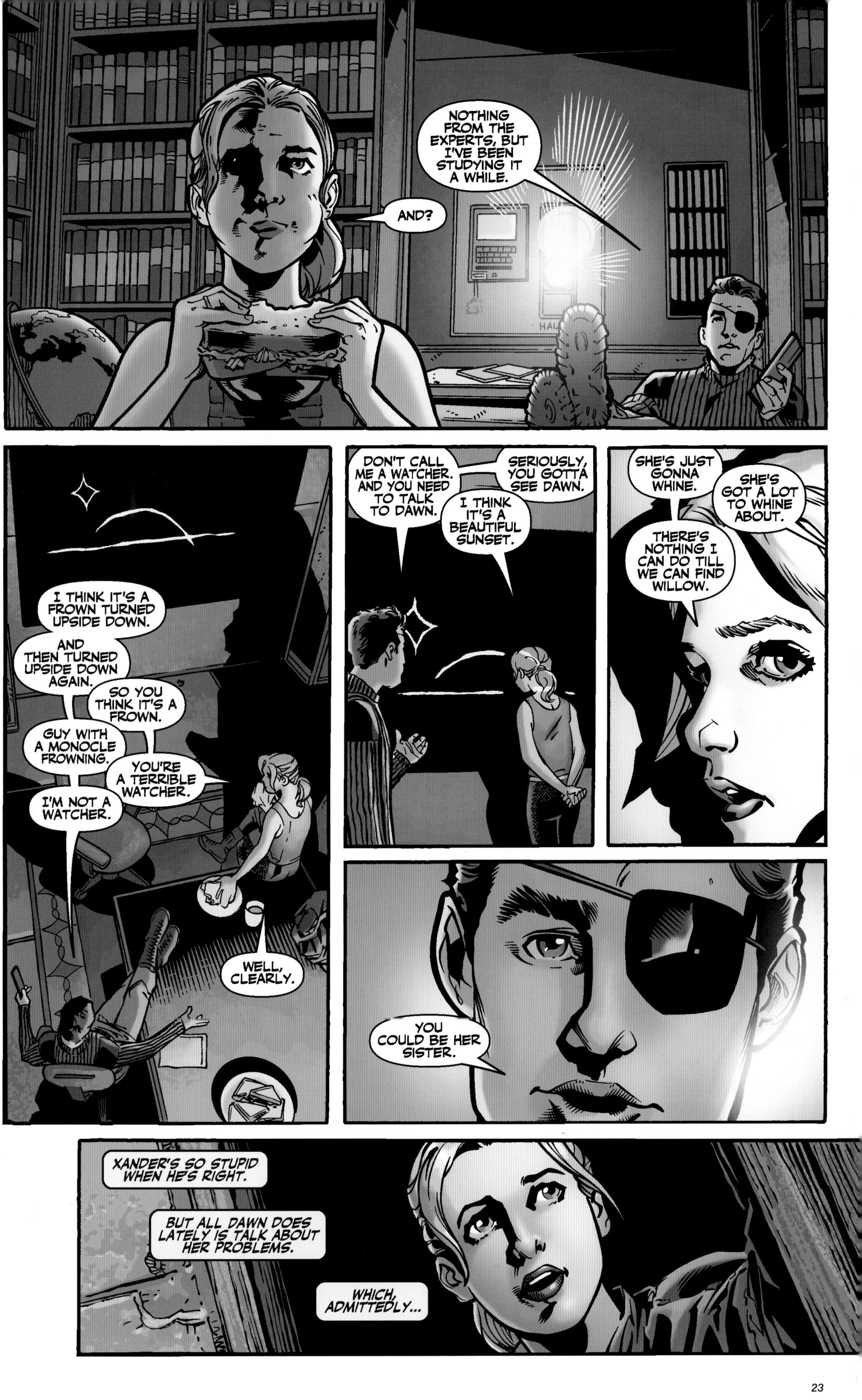
NOTHING FROM THE EXPERTS, BUT I'VE BEEN STUDYING IT A WHILE.
AND?
I THINK IT'S A FROWN TURNED UPSIDE DOWN.
AND THEN TURNED UPSIDE DOWN AGAIN.
SO YOU THINK IT'S A FROWN.
GUY WITH A MONOCLE FROWNING.
YOU'RE A TERRIBLE WATCHER.
I'M NOT A WATCHER.
WELL, CLEARLY.
SERIOUSLY, YOU GOTTA SEE DAWN.
DON'T CALL ME A WATCHER. AND YOU NEED TO TALK TO DAWN.
I THINK IT'S A BEAUTIFUL SUNSET.
SHE'S JUST GONNA WHINE.
SHE'S GOT A LOT TO WHINE ABOUT.
THERE'S NOTHING I CAN DO TILL WE CAN FIND WILLOW.
YOU COULD BE HER SISTER.
XANDER'S SO STUPID WHEN HE'S RIGHT.
BUT ALL DAWN DOES LATELY IS TALK ABOUT HER PROBLEMS.
WHICH, ADMITTEDLY...

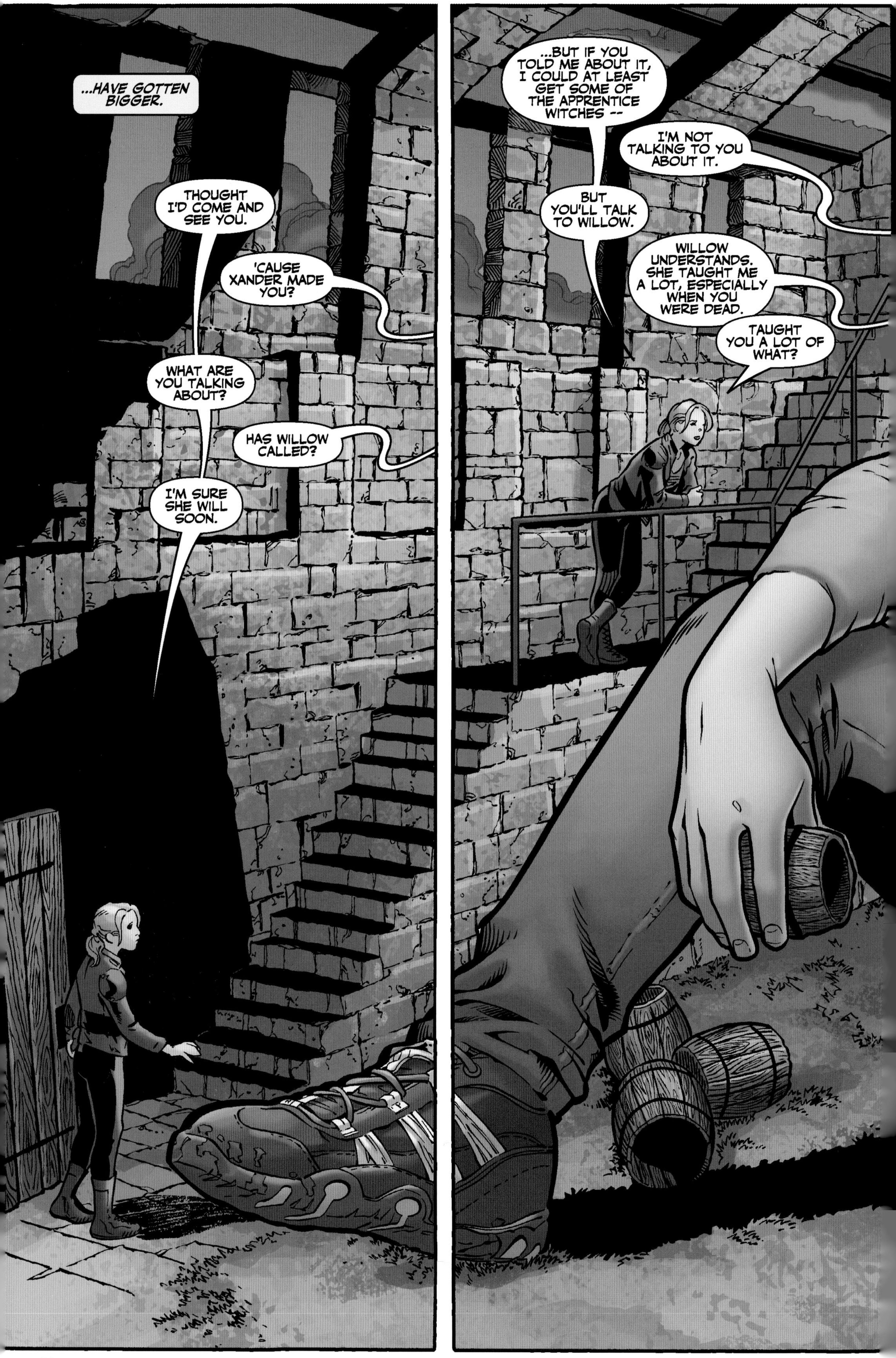
...HAVE GOTTEN BIGGER.
THOUGHT I'D COME AND SEE YOU.
'CAUSE XANDER MADE YOU?
WHAT ARE YOU TALKING ABOUT?
HAS WILLOW CALLED?
I'M SURE SHE WILL SOON.
...BUT IF YOU TOLD ME ABOUT IT, I COULD AT LEAST GET SOME OF THE APPRENTICE WITCHES --
I'M NOT TALKING TO YOU ABOUT IT.
BUT YOU'LL TALK TO WILLOW.
WILLOW UNDERSTANDS. SHE TAUGHT ME A LOT, ESPECIALLY WHEN YOU WERE DEAD.
TAUGHT YOU A LOT OF WHAT?

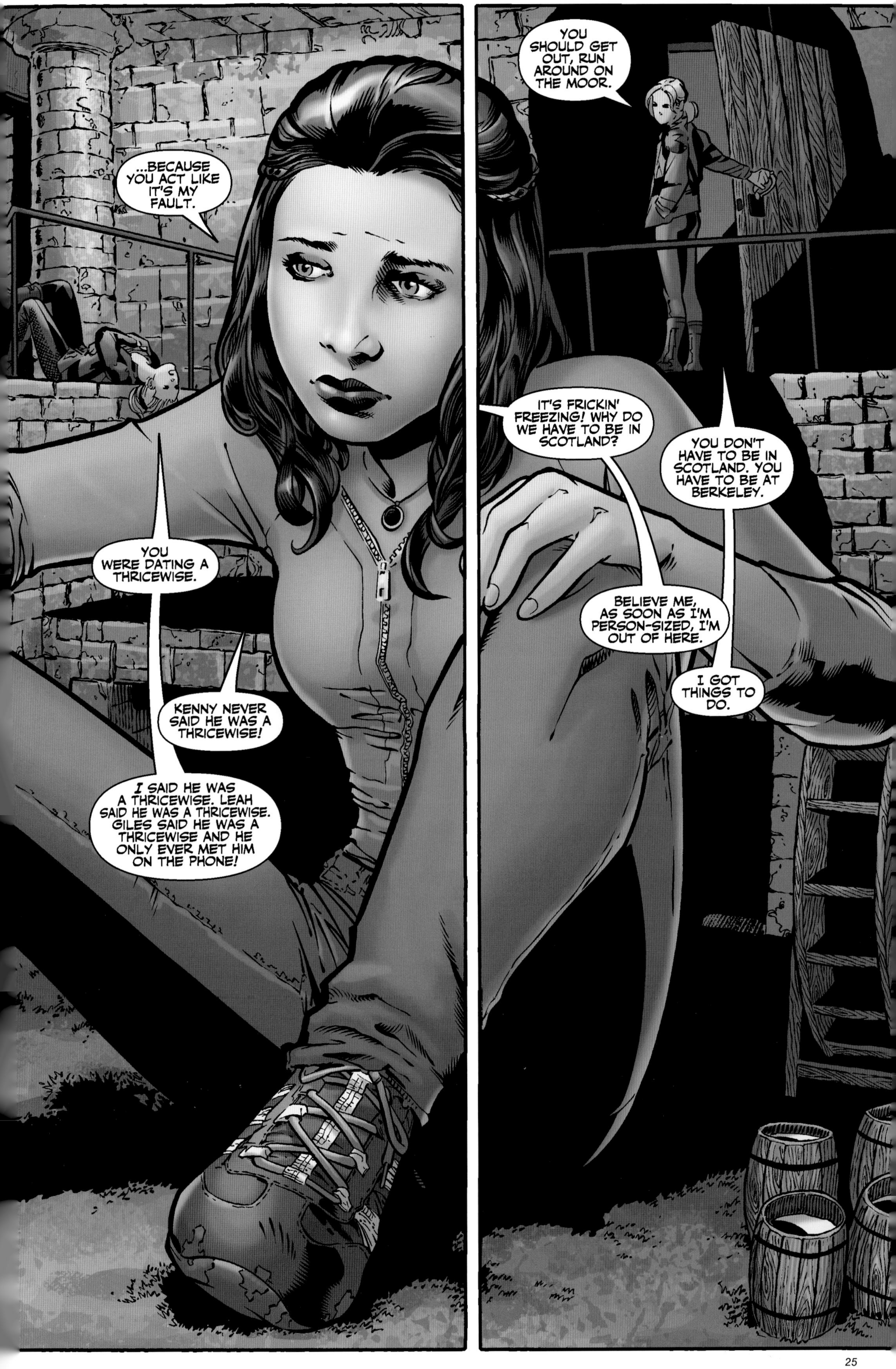
...BECAUSE YOU ACT LIKE IT'S MY FAULT.
YOU WERE DATING A THRICEWISE.
KENNY NEVER SAID HE WAS A THRICEWISE!
I SAID HE WAS A THRICEWISE. LEAH SAID HE WAS A THRICEWISE. GILES SAID HE WAS A THRICEWISE AND HE ONLY EVER MET HIM ON THE PHONE!
YOU SHOULD GET OUT, RUN AROUND ON THE MOOR.
IT'S FRICKIN' FREEZING! WHY DO WE HAVE TO BE IN SCOTLAND?
BELIEVE ME, AS SOON AS I'M PERSON-SIZED, I'M OUT OF HERE.
YOU DON'T HAVE TO BE IN SCOTLAND. YOU HAVE TO BE AT BERKELEY.
I GOT THINGS TO DO.

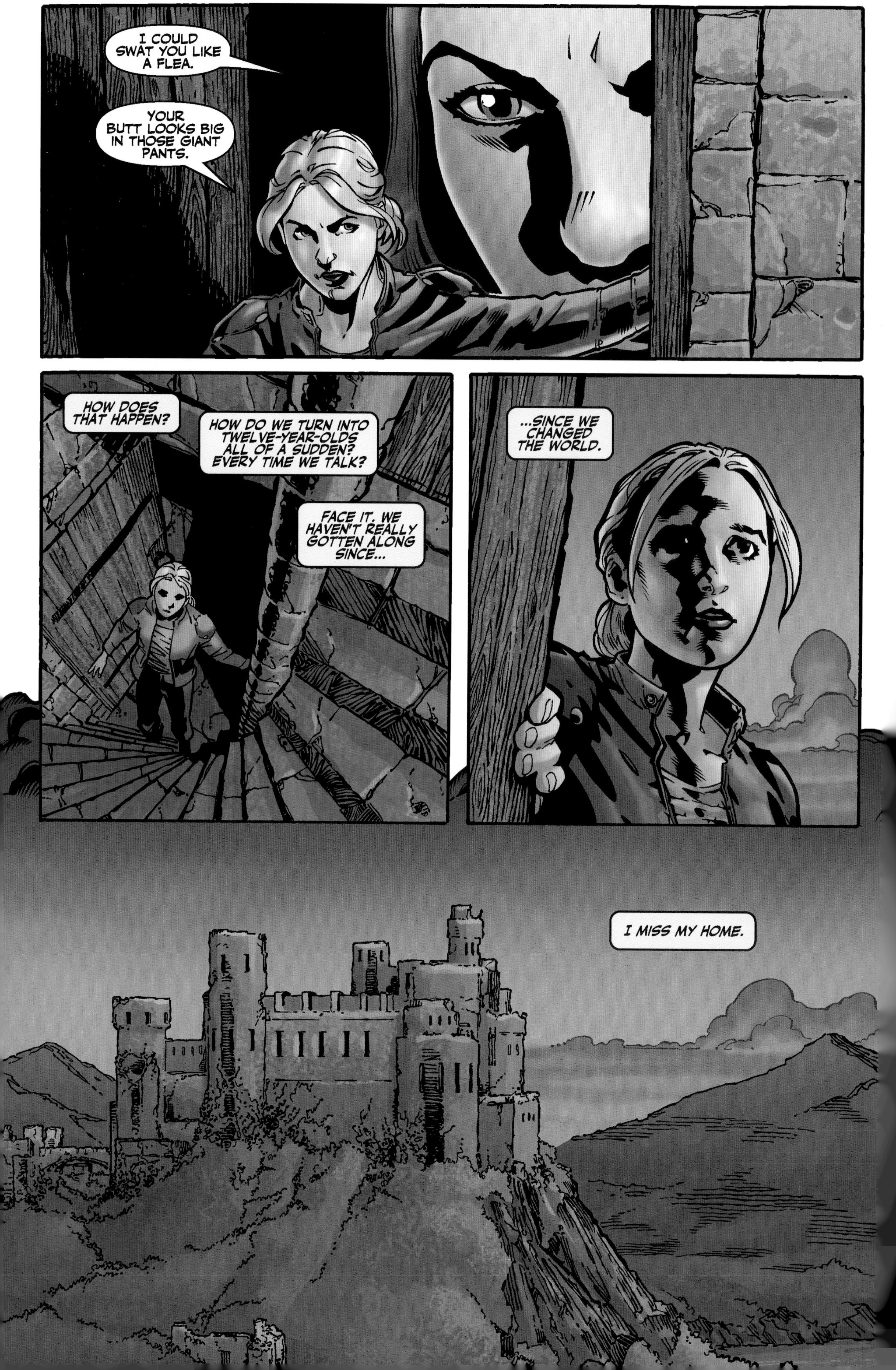
I COULD SWAT YOU LIKE A FLEA.
YOUR BUTT LOOKS BIG IN THOSE GIANT PANTS.
HOW DOES THAT HAPPEN?
HOW DO WE TURN INTO TWELVE-YEAR-OLDS ALL OF A SUDDEN? EVERY TIME WE TALK?
FACE IT. WE HAVEN'T REALLY GOTTEN ALONG SINCE...
...SINCE WE CHANGED THE WORLD.
I MISS MY HOME.

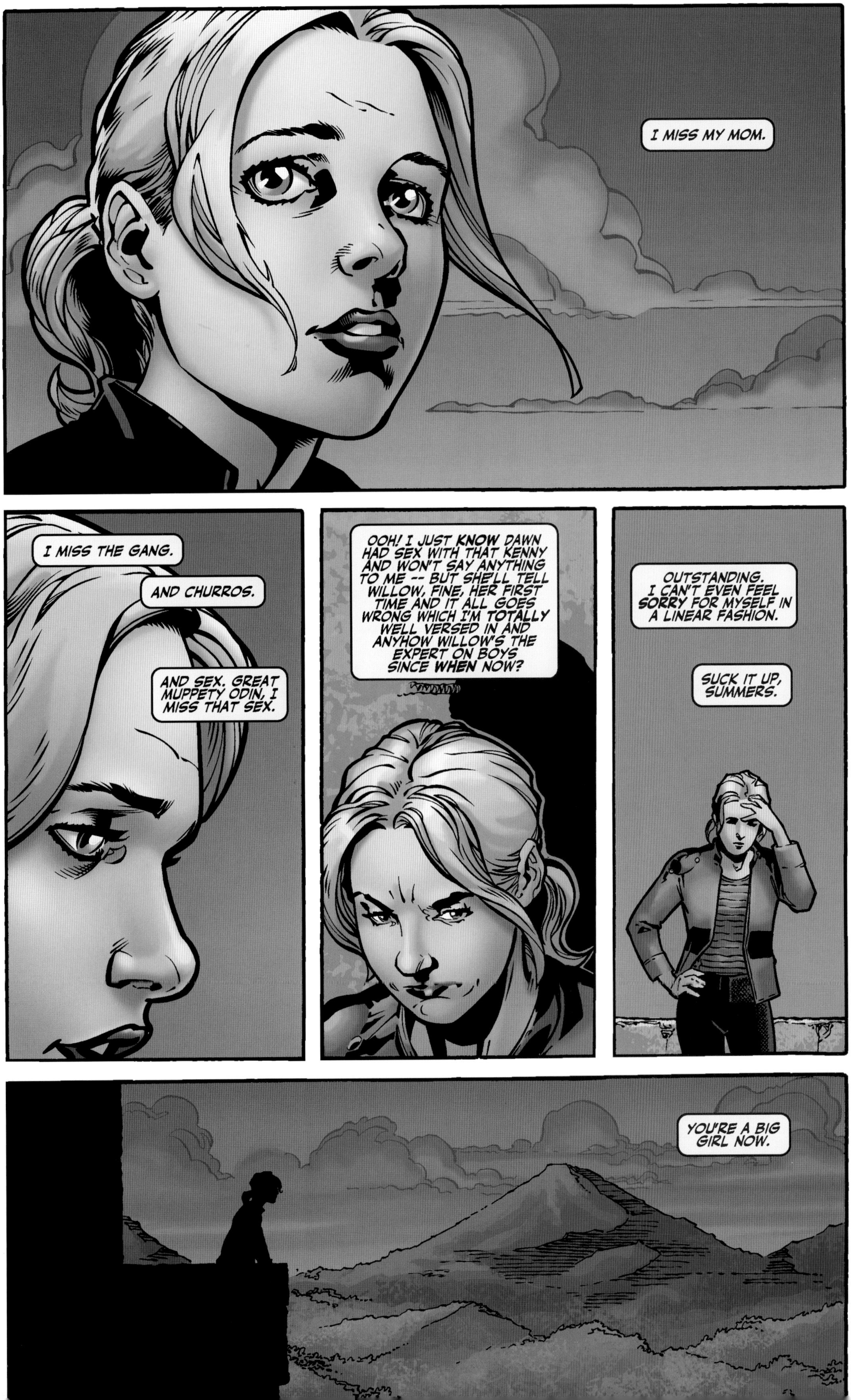
I MISS MY MOM.
I MISS THE GANG.
AND CHURROS.
AND SEX. GREAT MUPPETY ODIN, I MISS THAT SEX.
OOH! I JUST KNOW DAWN HAD SEX WITH THAT KENNY AND WON'T SAY ANYTHING TO ME -- BUT SHE'LL TELL WILLOW. FINE, HER FIRST TIME AND IT ALL GOES WRONG WHICH I'M TOTALLY WELL VERSED IN AND ANYHOW WILLOW'S THE EXPERT ON BOYS SINCE WHEN NOW?
OUTSTANDING. I CAN'T EVEN FEEL SORRY FOR MYSELF IN A LINEAR FASHION.
SUCK IT UP, SUMMERS.
YOU'RE A BIG GIRL NOW.

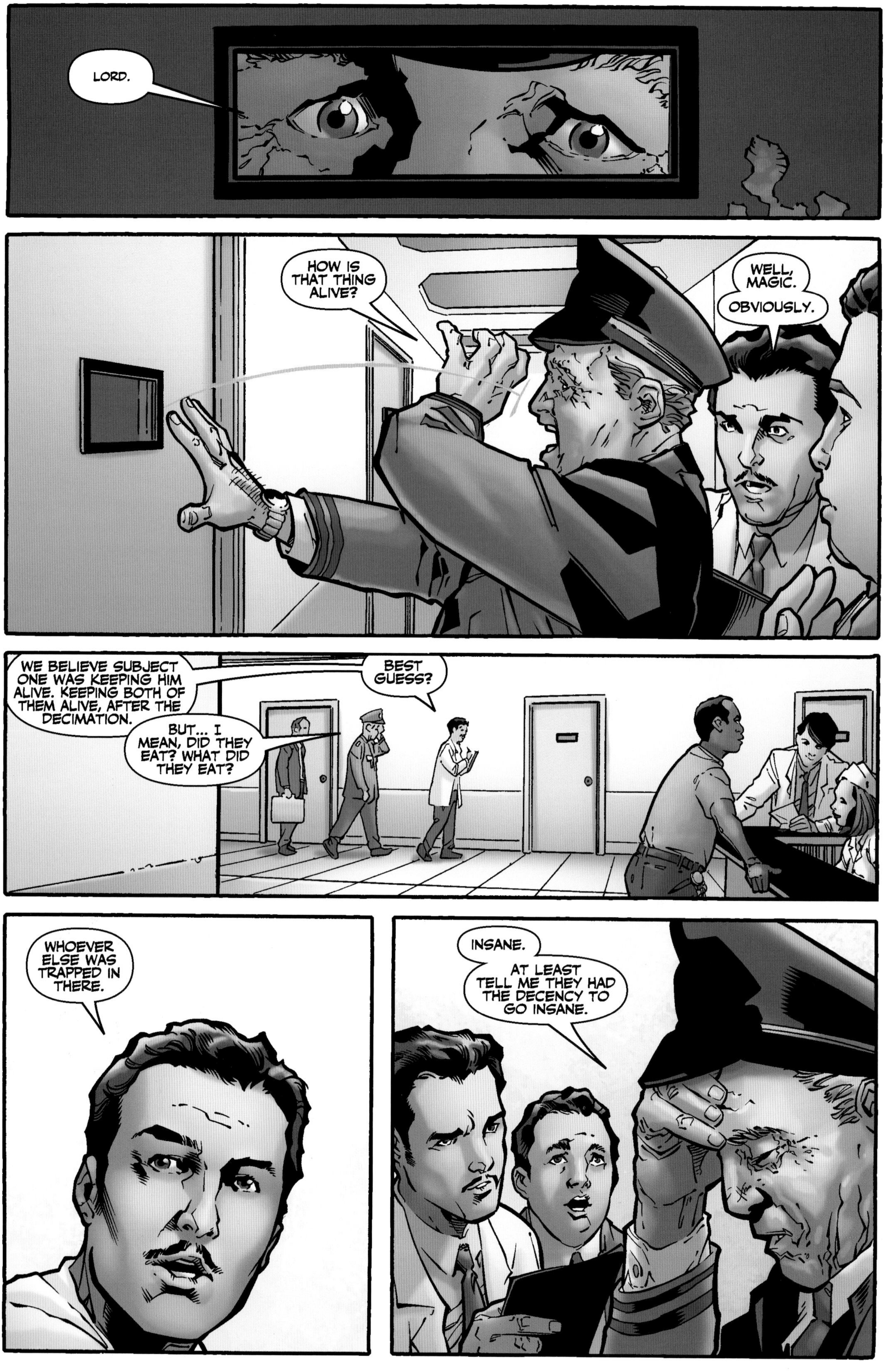
LORD.
HOW IS THAT THING ALIVE?
WELL, MAGIC.
OBVIOUSLY.
WE BELIEVE SUBJECT ONE WAS KEEPING HIM ALIVE. KEEPING BOTH OF THEM ALIVE, AFTER THE DECIMATION.
BEST GUESS?
BUT... I MEAN, DID THEY EAT? WHAT DID THEY EAT?
WHOEVER ELSE WAS TRAPPED IN THERE.
INSANE.
AT LEAST TELL ME THEY HAD THE DECENCY TO GO INSANE.

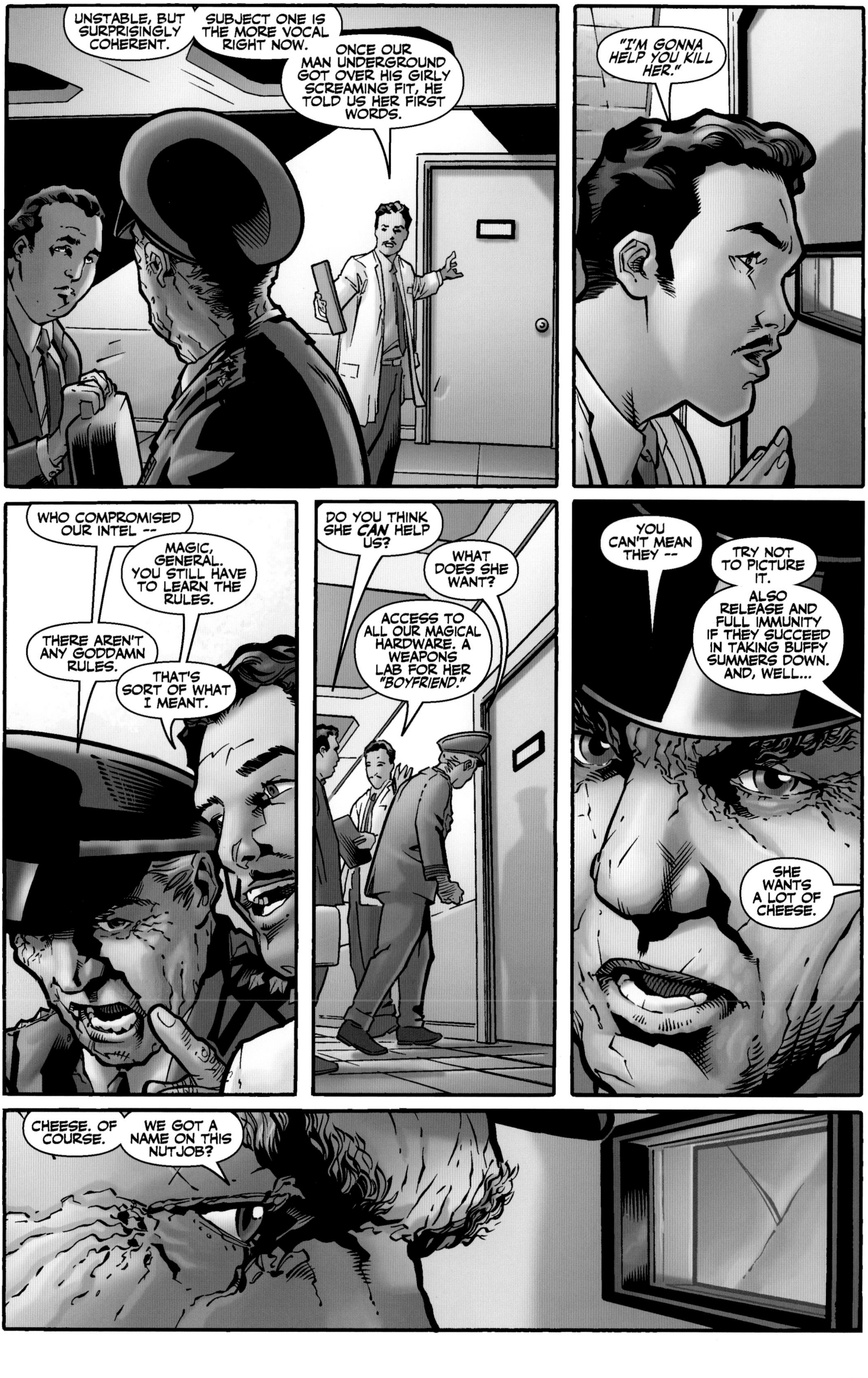
UNSTABLE, BUT SURPRISINGLY COHERENT.
SUBJECT ONE IS THE MORE VOCAL RIGHT NOW.
ONCE OUR MAN UNDERGROUND GOT OVER HIS GIRLY SCREAMING FIT, HE TOLD US HER FIRST WORDS.
"I'M GONNA HELP YOU KILL HER."
WHO COMPROMISED OUR INTEL --
MAGIC, GENERAL. YOU STILL HAVE TO LEARN THE RULES.
THERE AREN'T ANY GODDAMN RULES.
THAT'S SORT OF WHAT I MEANT.
DO YOU THINK SHE *CAN* HELP US?
WHAT DOES SHE WANT?
ACCESS TO ALL OUR MAGICAL HARDWARE. A WEAPONS LAB FOR HER *"BOYFRIEND."*
YOU CAN'T MEAN THEY --
TRY NOT TO PICTURE IT.
ALSO RELEASE AND FULL IMMUNITY IF THEY SUCCEED IN TAKING BUFFY SUMMERS DOWN. AND, WELL...
SHE WANTS A LOT OF CHEESE.
CHEESE. OF COURSE.
WE GOT A NAME ON THIS NUTJOB?

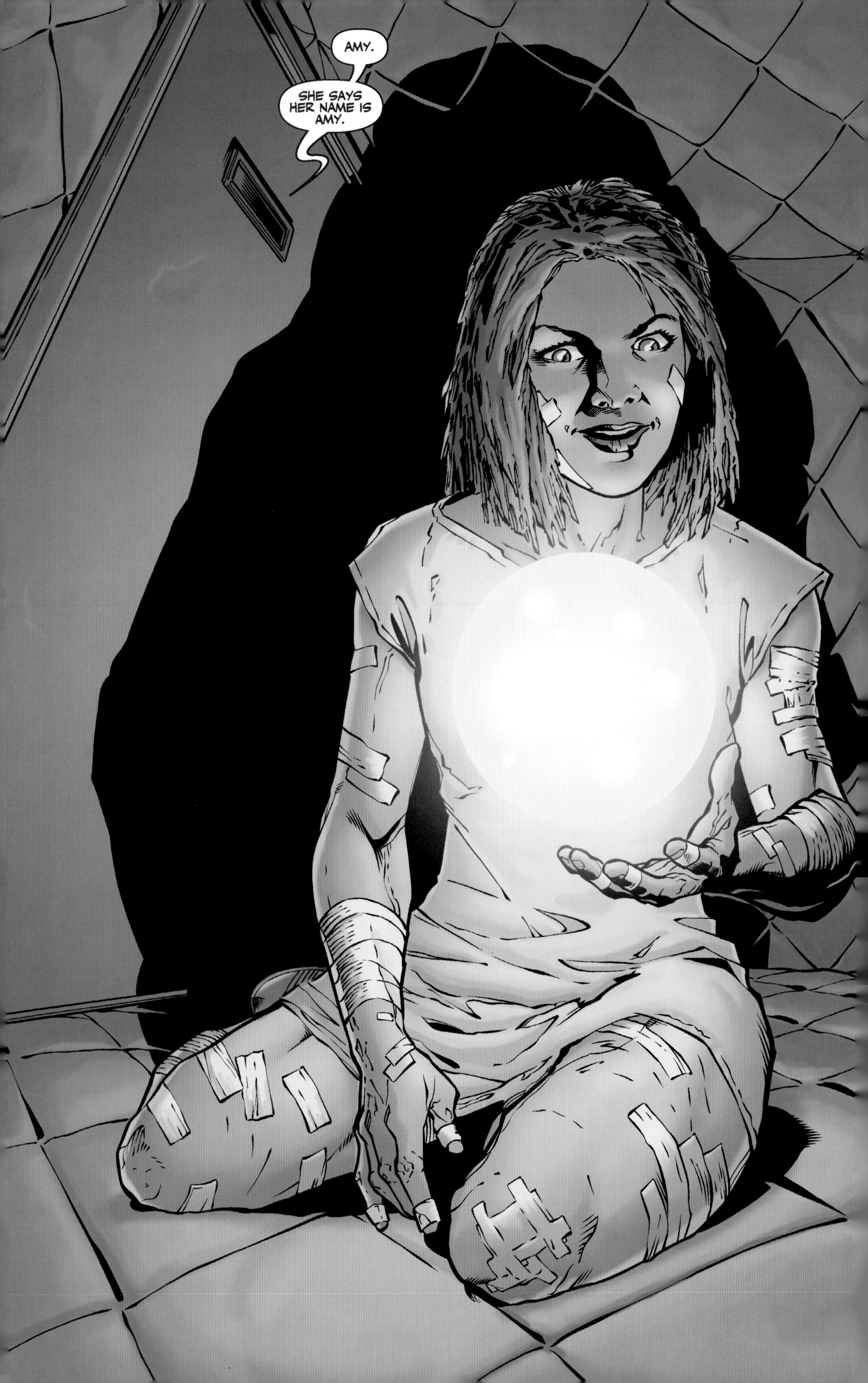
AMY.
SHE SAYS HER NAME IS AMY.

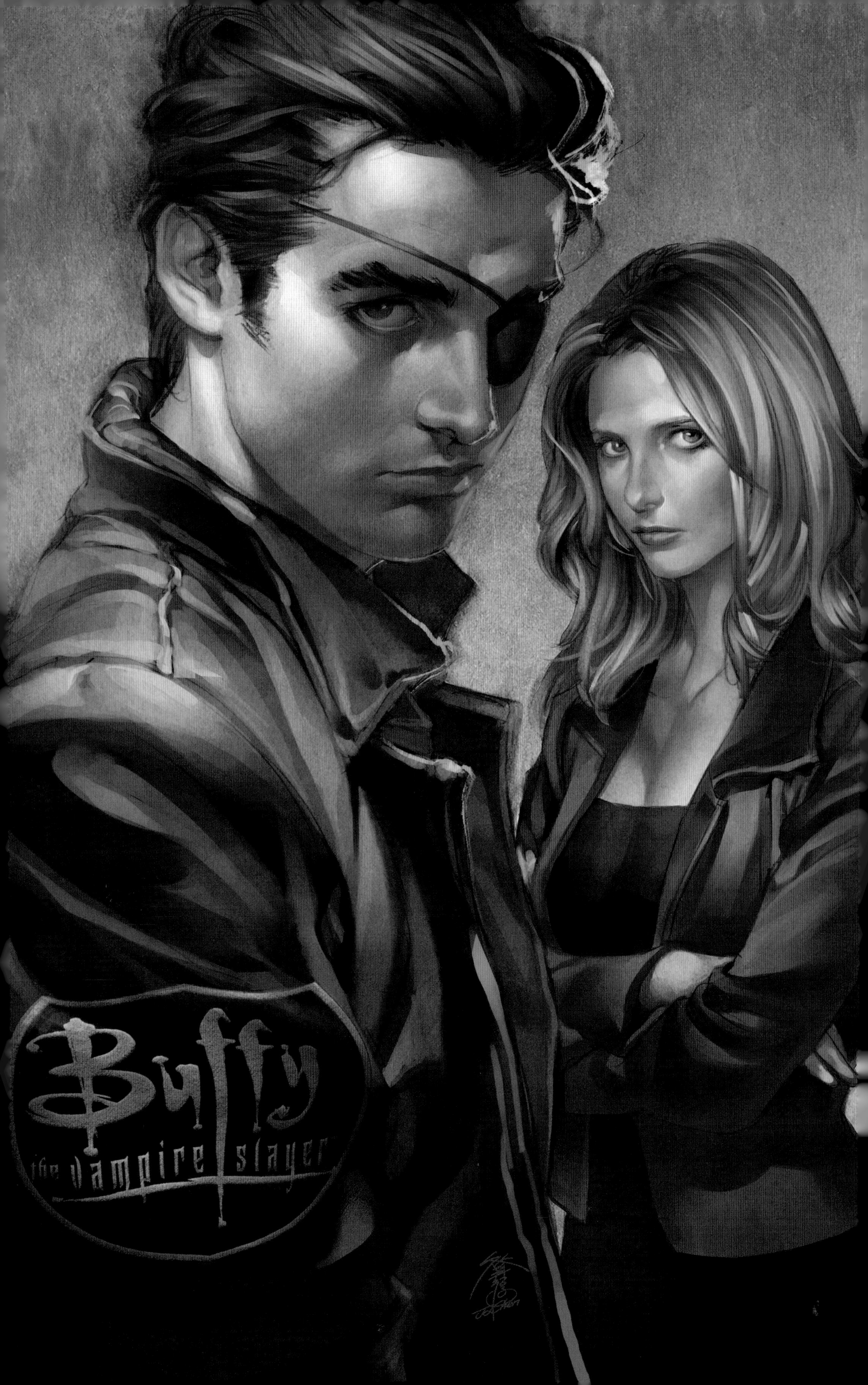
Buffy
the vampire slayer

The LONG WAY HOME

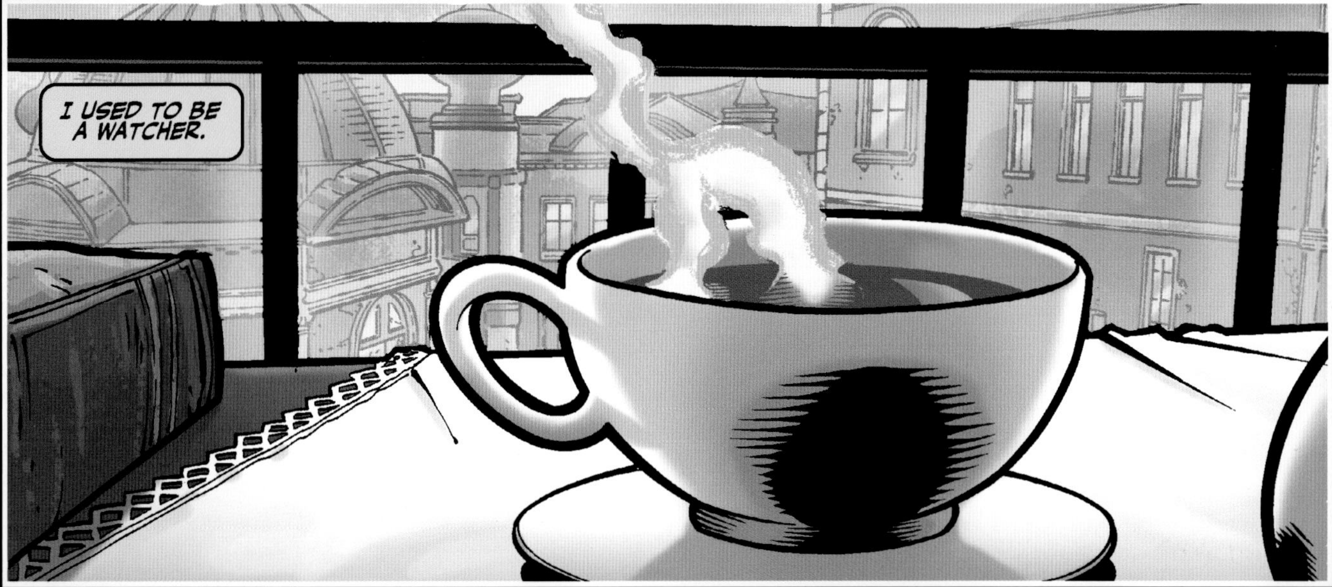
I USED TO BE A WATCHER.

Part Two

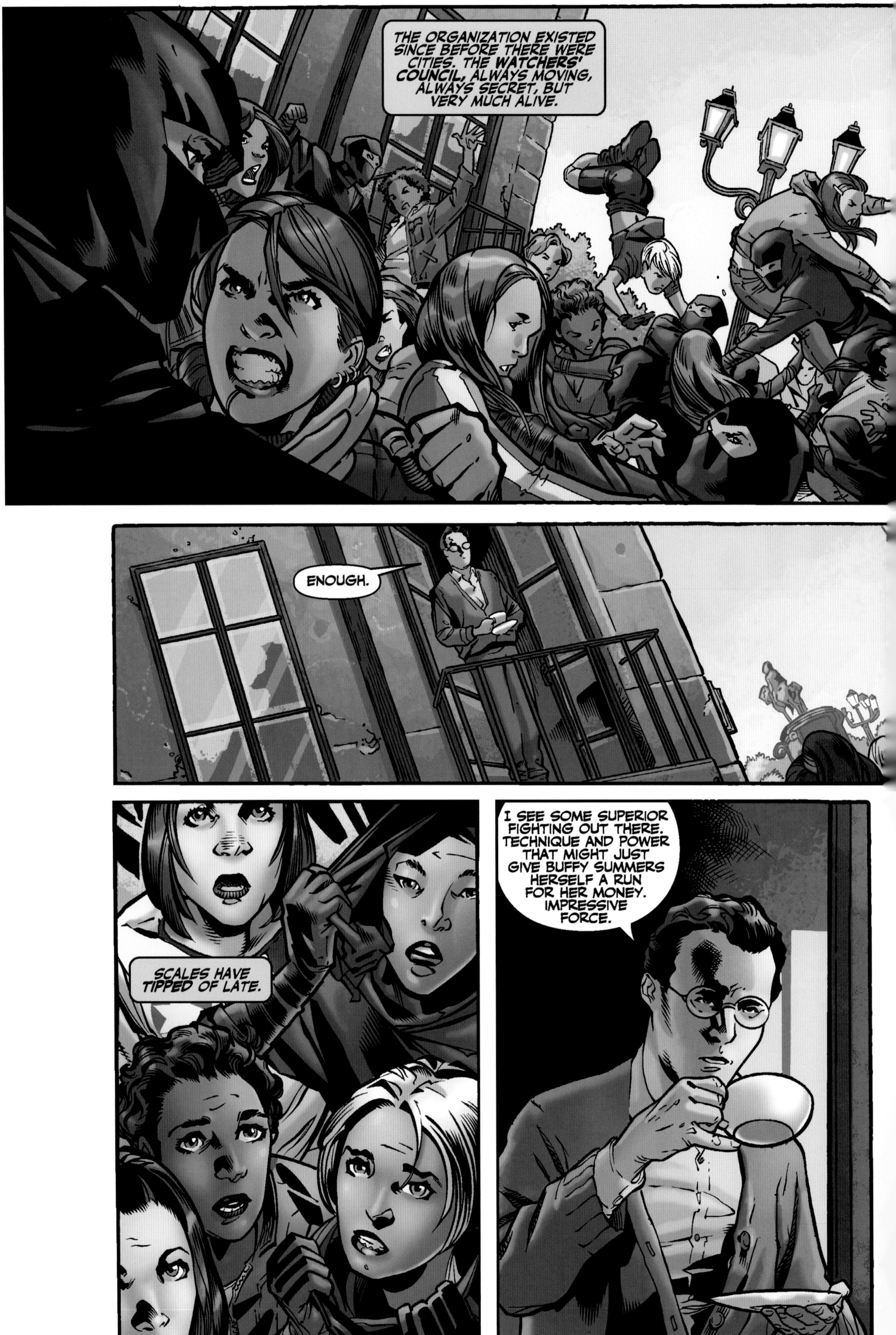
THE ORGANIZATION EXISTED SINCE BEFORE THERE WERE CITIES. THE WATCHERS' COUNCIL, ALWAYS MOVING, ALWAYS SECRET, BUT VERY MUCH ALIVE.
ENOUGH.
SCALES HAVE TIPPED OF LATE.
I SEE SOME SUPERIOR FIGHTING OUT THERE. TECHNIQUE AND POWER THAT MIGHT JUST GIVE BUFFY SUMMERS HERSELF A RUN FOR HER MONEY. IMPRESSIVE FORCE.

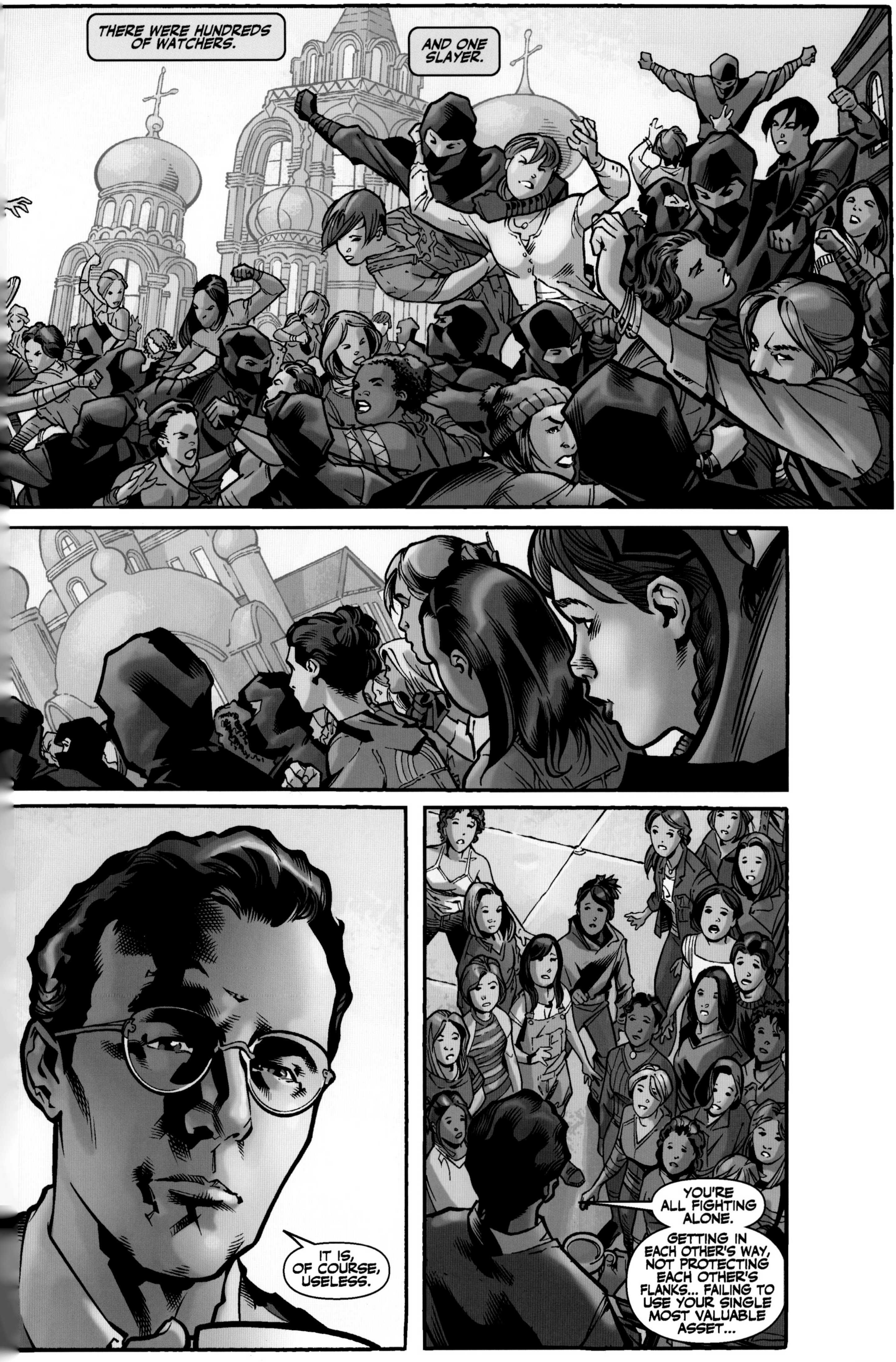
THERE WERE HUNDREDS OF WATCHERS.
AND ONE SLAYER.
IT IS, OF COURSE, USELESS.
YOU'RE ALL FIGHTING ALONE.
GETTING IN EACH OTHER'S WAY, NOT PROTECTING EACH OTHER'S FLANKS... FAILING TO USE YOUR SINGLE MOST VALUABLE ASSET...

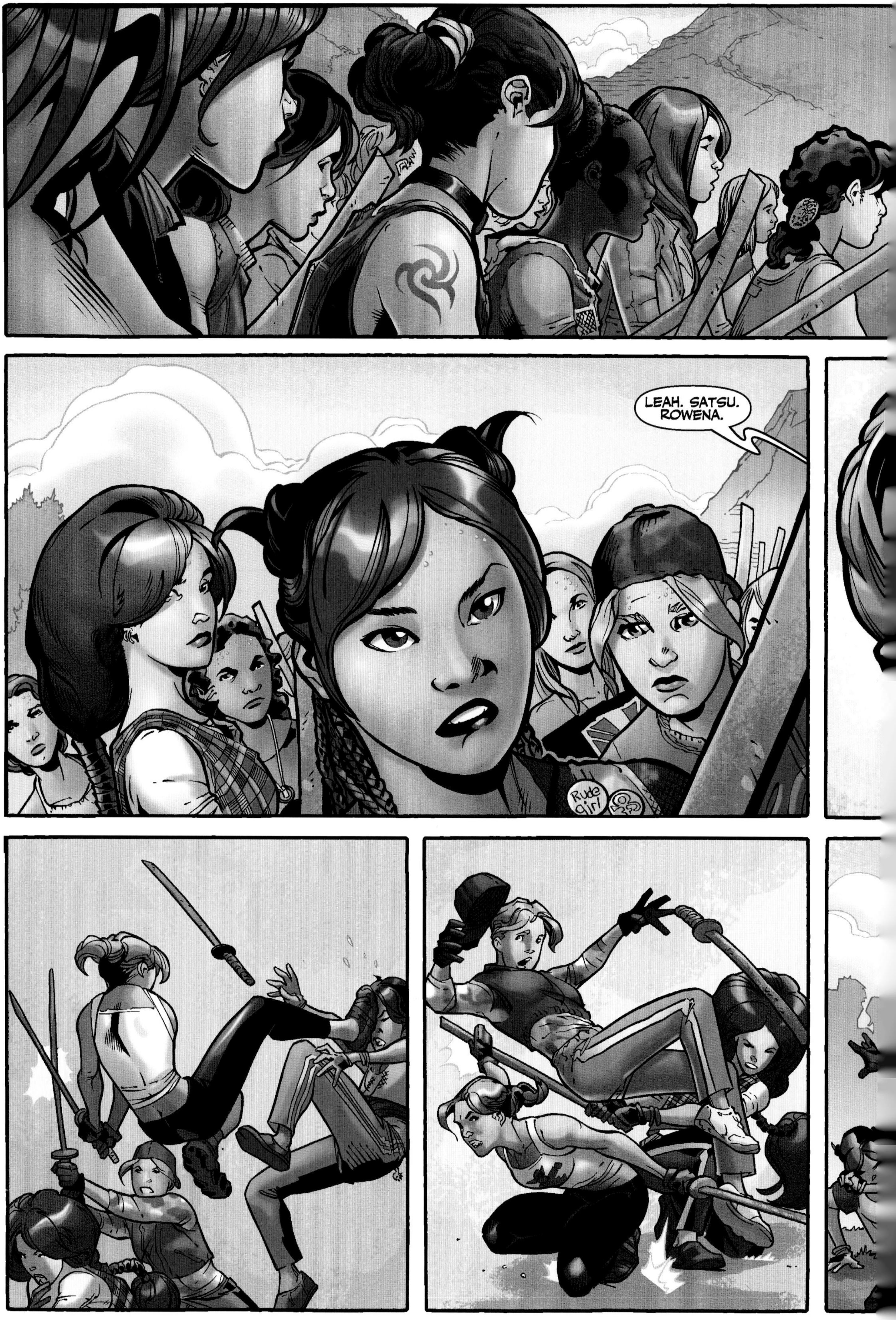
LEAH. SATSU. ROWENA.
Rude girl

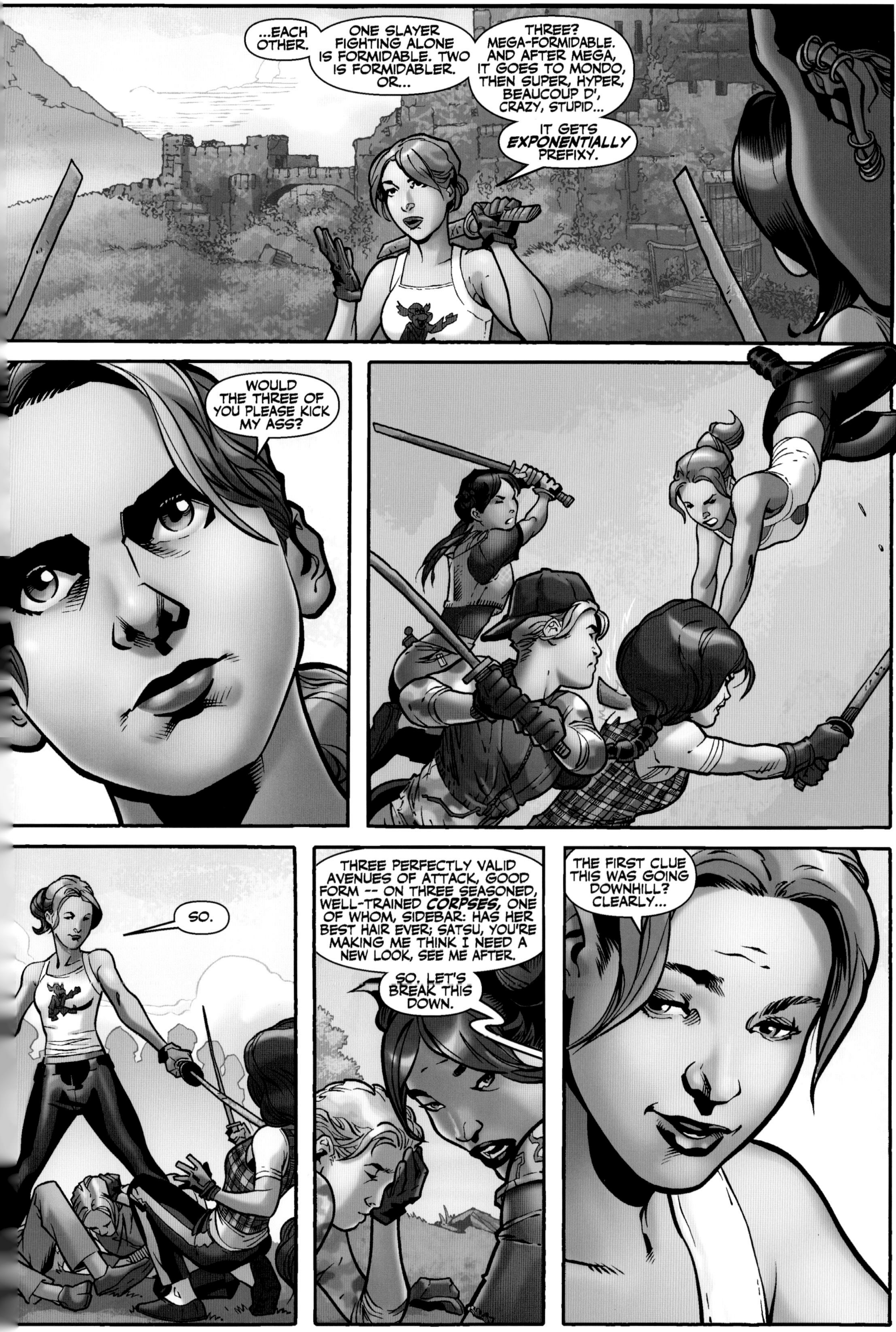
...EACH OTHER.
ONE SLAYER FIGHTING ALONE IS FORMIDABLE. TWO IS FORMIDABLER. OR...
THREE? MEGA-FORMIDABLE. AND AFTER MEGA, IT GOES TO MONDO, THEN SUPER, HYPER, BEAUCOUP D', CRAZY, STUPID...
IT GETS *EXPONENTIALLY* PREFIXY.
WOULD THE THREE OF YOU PLEASE KICK MY ASS?
SO.
THREE PERFECTLY VALID AVENUES OF ATTACK, GOOD FORM -- ON THREE SEASONED, WELL-TRAINED *CORPSES,* ONE OF WHOM, SIDEBAR: HAS HER BEST HAIR EVER; SATSU, YOU'RE MAKING ME THINK I NEED A NEW LOOK, SEE ME AFTER.
SO. LET'S BREAK THIS DOWN.
THE FIRST CLUE THIS WAS GOING DOWNHILL? CLEARLY...

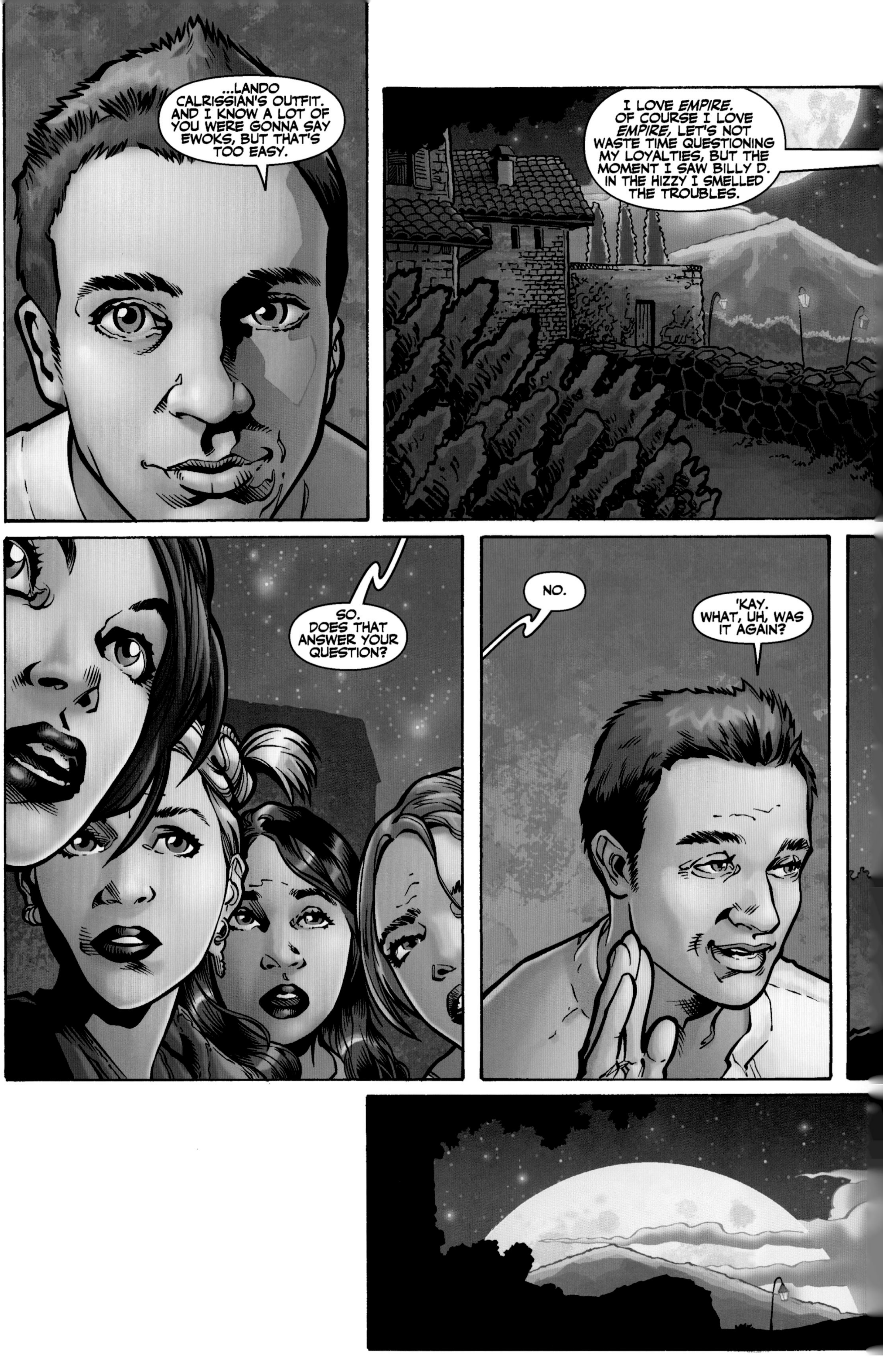
...LANDO CALRISSIAN'S OUTFIT. AND I KNOW A LOT OF YOU WERE GONNA SAY EWOKS, BUT THAT'S TOO EASY.
I LOVE *EMPIRE*. OF COURSE I LOVE *EMPIRE*, LET'S NOT WASTE TIME QUESTIONING MY LOYALTIES, BUT THE MOMENT I SAW BILLY D. IN THE HIZZY I SMELLED THE TROUBLES.
SO. DOES THAT ANSWER YOUR QUESTION?
NO.
'KAY. WHAT, UH, WAS IT AGAIN?

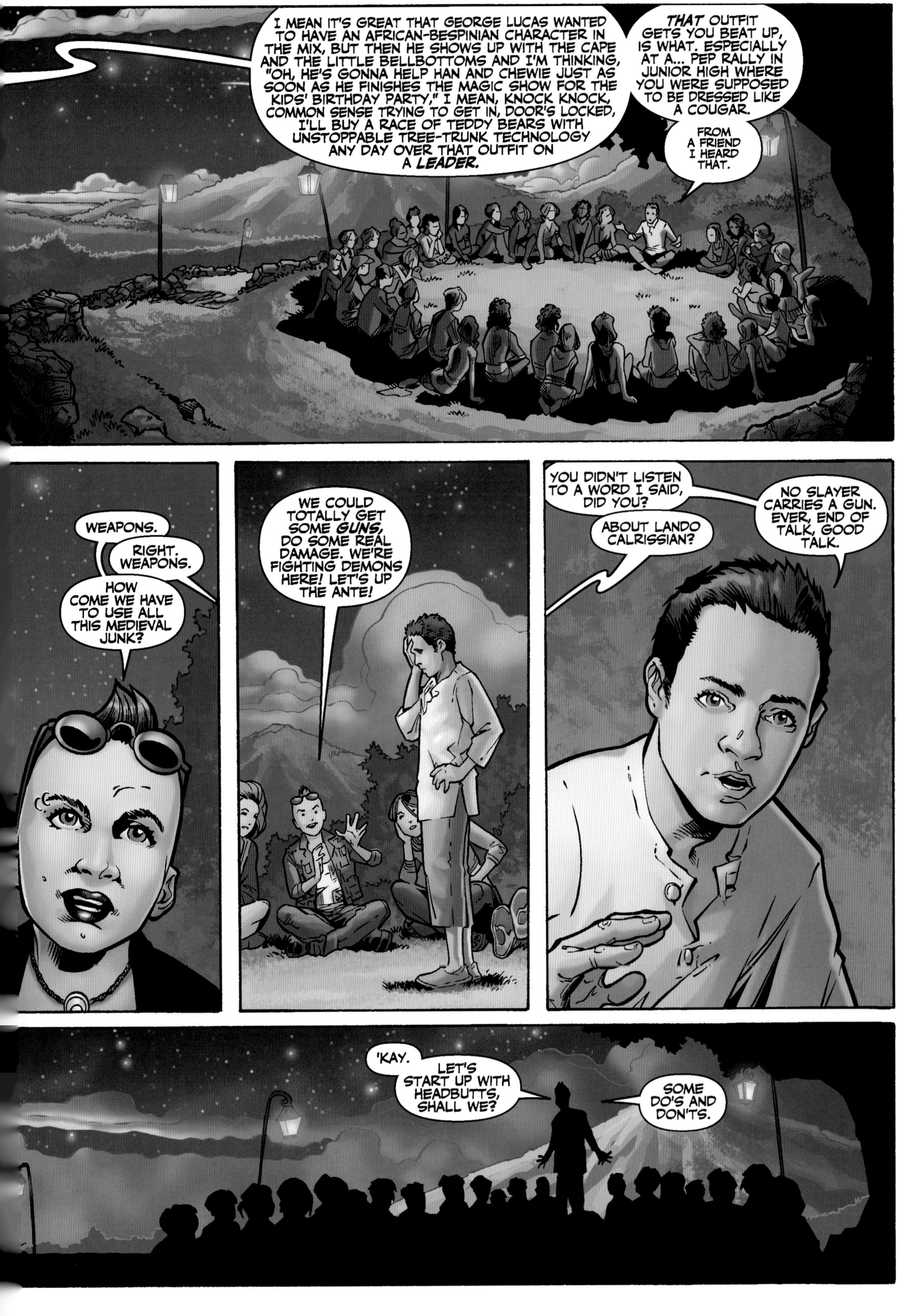
I MEAN IT'S GREAT THAT GEORGE LUCAS WANTED TO HAVE AN AFRICAN-BESPINIAN CHARACTER IN THE MIX, BUT THEN HE SHOWS UP WITH THE CAPE AND THE LITTLE BELLBOTTOMS AND I'M THINKING, "OH, HE'S GONNA HELP HAN AND CHEWIE JUST AS SOON AS HE FINISHES THE MAGIC SHOW FOR THE KIDS' BIRTHDAY PARTY," I MEAN, KNOCK KNOCK, COMMON SENSE TRYING TO GET IN, DOOR'S LOCKED, I'LL BUY A RACE OF TEDDY BEARS WITH UNSTOPPABLE TREE-TRUNK TECHNOLOGY ANY DAY OVER THAT OUTFIT ON A LEADER.
THAT OUTFIT GETS YOU BEAT UP, IS WHAT. ESPECIALLY AT A... PEP RALLY IN JUNIOR HIGH WHERE YOU WERE SUPPOSED TO BE DRESSED LIKE A COUGAR.
FROM A FRIEND I HEARD THAT.
WEAPONS.
RIGHT. WEAPONS.
HOW COME WE HAVE TO USE ALL THIS MEDIEVAL JUNK?
WE COULD TOTALLY GET SOME GUNS, DO SOME REAL DAMAGE. WE'RE FIGHTING DEMONS HERE! LET'S UP THE ANTE!
YOU DIDN'T LISTEN TO A WORD I SAID, DID YOU?
ABOUT LANDO CALRISSIAN?
NO SLAYER CARRIES A GUN. EVER, END OF TALK, GOOD TALK.
'KAY.
LET'S START UP WITH HEADBUTTS, SHALL WE?
SOME DO'S AND DON'TS.

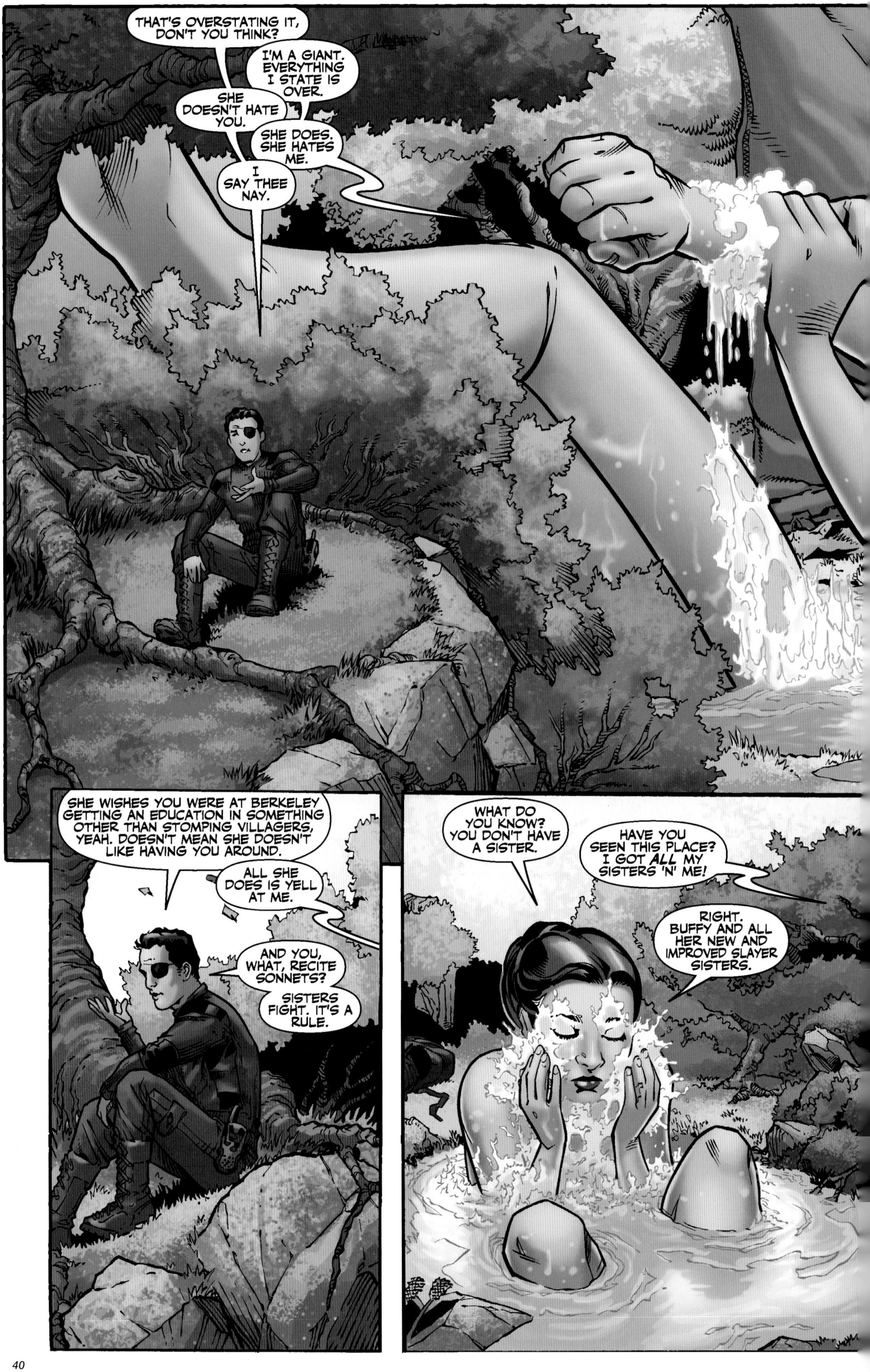

THAT'S OVERSTATING IT, DON'T YOU THINK?
I'M A GIANT. EVERYTHING I STATE IS OVER.
SHE DOESN'T HATE YOU.
SHE DOES. SHE HATES ME.
I SAY THEE NAY.
SHE WISHES YOU WERE AT BERKELEY GETTING AN EDUCATION IN SOMETHING OTHER THAN STOMPING VILLAGERS, YEAH. DOESN'T MEAN SHE DOESN'T LIKE HAVING YOU AROUND.
ALL SHE DOES IS YELL AT ME.
AND YOU, WHAT, RECITE SONNETS?
SISTERS FIGHT. IT'S A RULE.
WHAT DO YOU KNOW? YOU DON'T HAVE A SISTER.
HAVE YOU SEEN THIS PLACE? I GOT ALL MY SISTERS 'N' ME!
RIGHT. BUFFY AND ALL HER NEW AND IMPROVED SLAYER SISTERS.

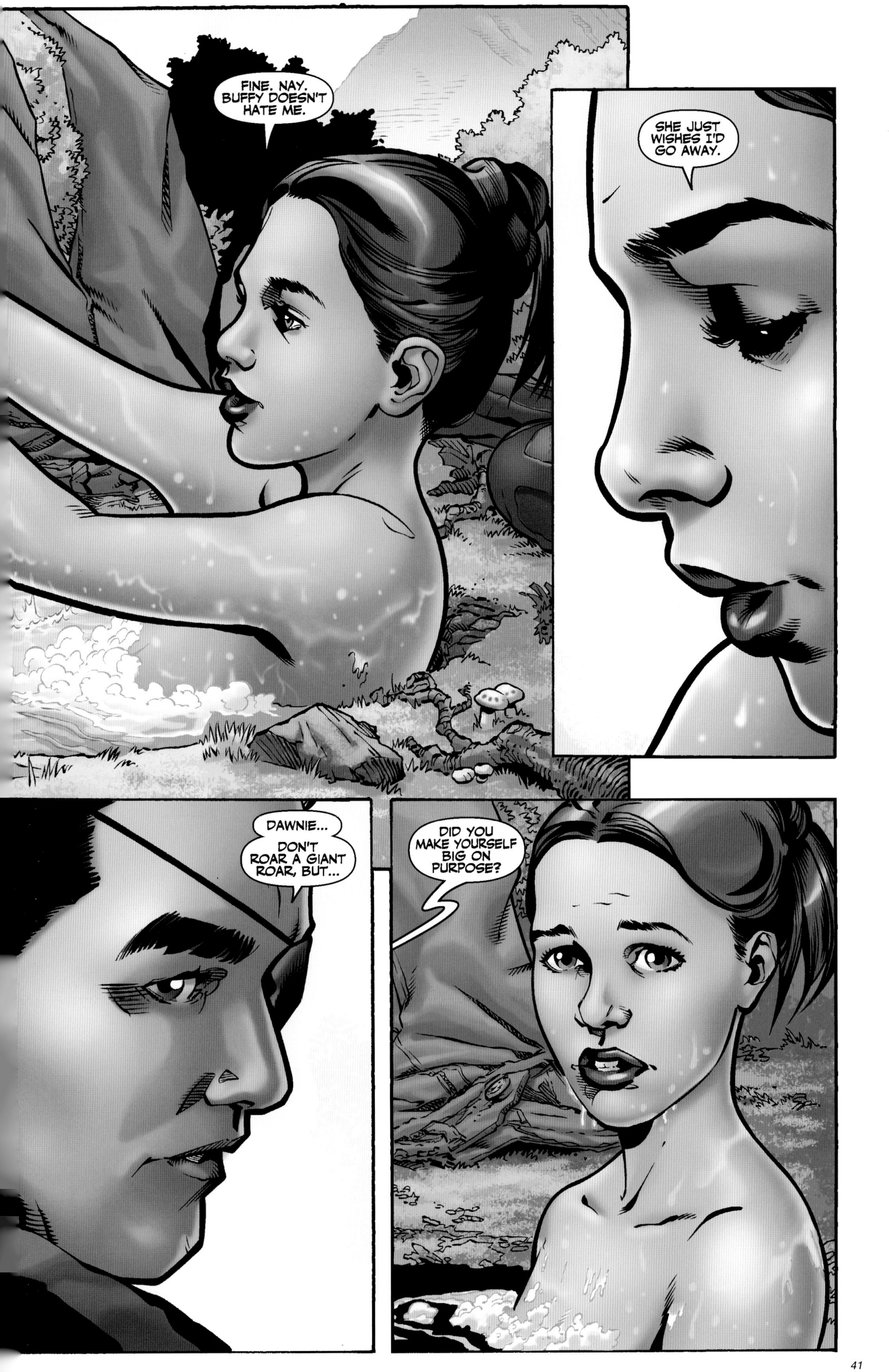
FINE. NAY. BUFFY DOESN'T HATE ME.
SHE JUST WISHES I'D GO AWAY.
DAWNIE... DON'T ROAR A GIANT ROAR, BUT...
DID YOU MAKE YOURSELF BIG ON PURPOSE?

SPLOOOSH

YOU KNOW I ONLY HAVE TWO OF THESE OUTFITS.

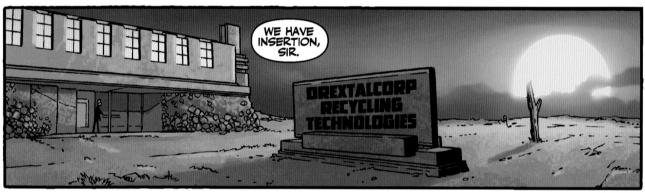

WE HAVE INSERTION, SIR.

DREXTALCORP RECYCLING TECHNOLOGIES

OUR OP SHOULD BE IN AND OUT BY TONIGHT.

SHOULD.

CORP

DREX

YOU KNOW HOW MUCH GOOD "SHOULD" DOES ME?

YOU'RE GONNA SAY "NOT MUCH."

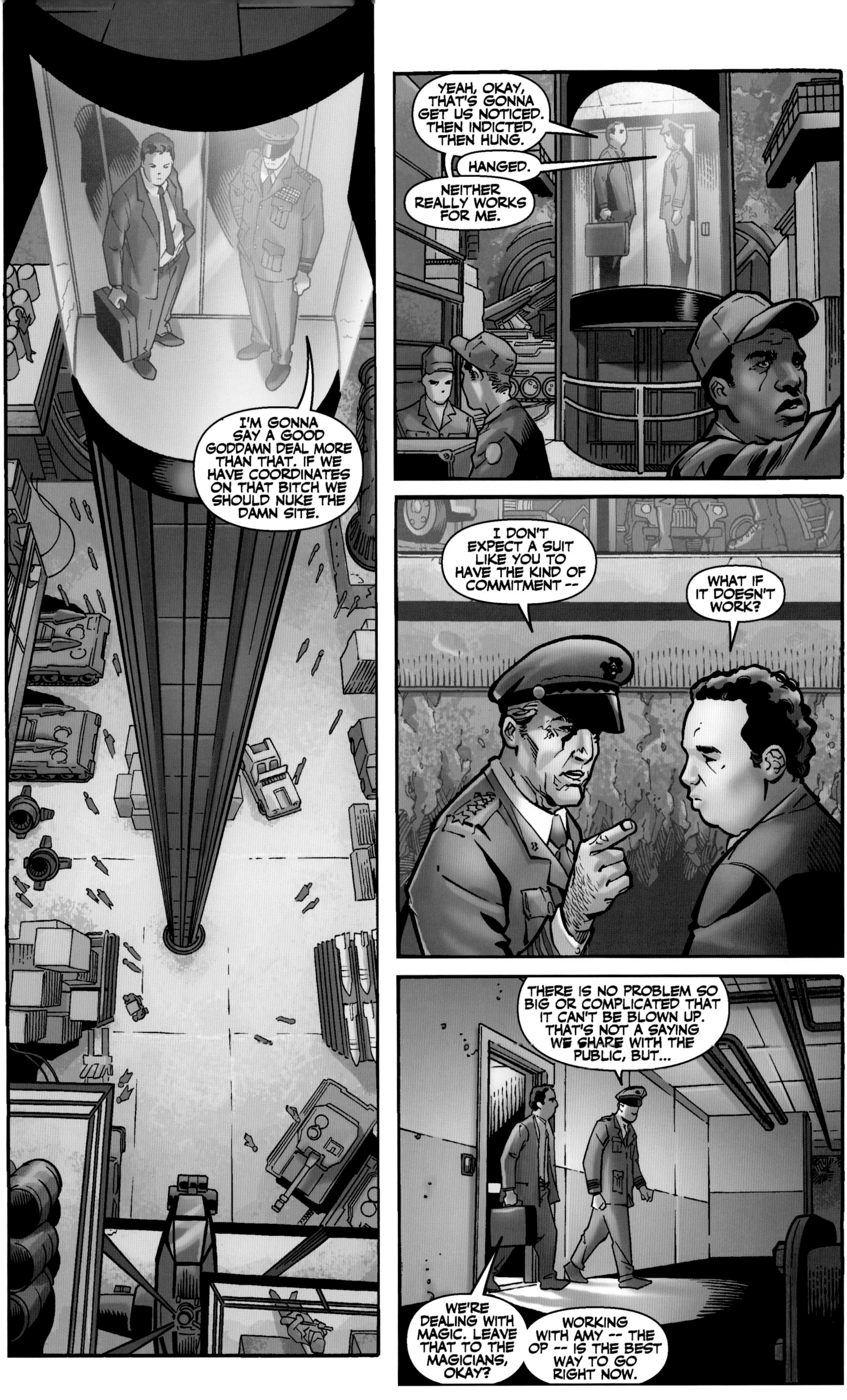
I'M GONNA SAY A GOOD GODDAMN DEAL MORE THAN THAT. IF WE HAVE COORDINATES ON THAT BITCH WE SHOULD NUKE THE DAMN SITE.
YEAH, OKAY, THAT'S GONNA GET US NOTICED. THEN INDICTED, THEN HUNG.
HANGED.
NEITHER REALLY WORKS FOR ME.
I DON'T EXPECT A SUIT LIKE YOU TO HAVE THE KIND OF COMMITMENT --
WHAT IF IT DOESN'T WORK?
THERE IS NO PROBLEM SO BIG OR COMPLICATED THAT IT CAN'T BE BLOWN UP. THAT'S NOT A SAYING WE SHARE WITH THE PUBLIC, BUT...
WE'RE DEALING WITH MAGIC. LEAVE THAT TO THE MAGICIANS, OKAY?
WORKING WITH AMY -- THE OP -- IS THE BEST WAY TO GO RIGHT NOW.

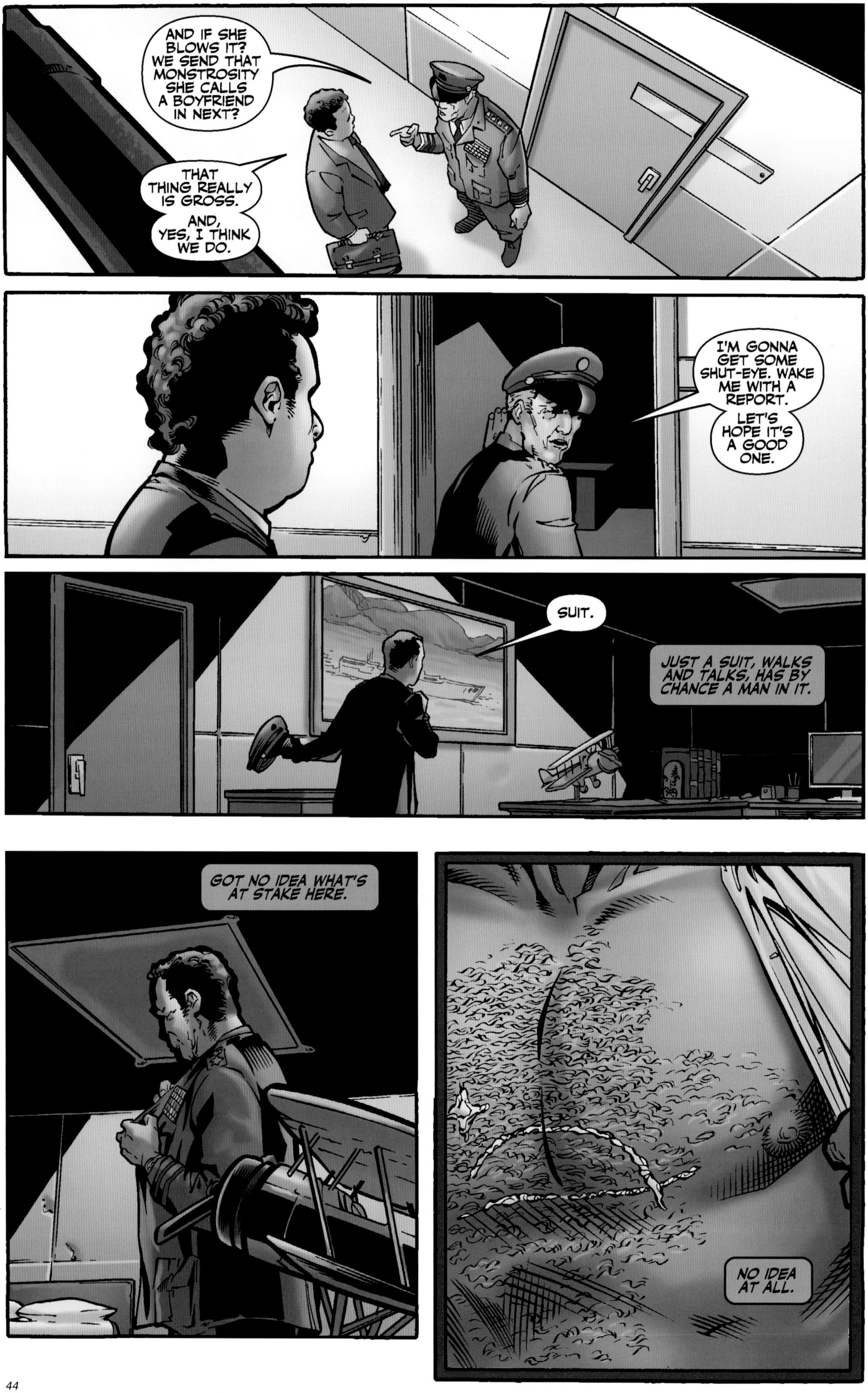
AND IF SHE BLOWS IT? WE SEND THAT MONSTROSITY SHE CALLS A BOYFRIEND IN NEXT?
THAT THING REALLY IS GROSS.
AND, YES, I THINK WE DO.
I'M GONNA GET SOME SHUT-EYE. WAKE ME WITH A REPORT.
LET'S HOPE IT'S A GOOD ONE.
SUIT.
JUST A SUIT, WALKS AND TALKS, HAS BY CHANCE A MAN IN IT.
GOT NO IDEA WHAT'S AT STAKE HERE.
NO IDEA AT ALL.

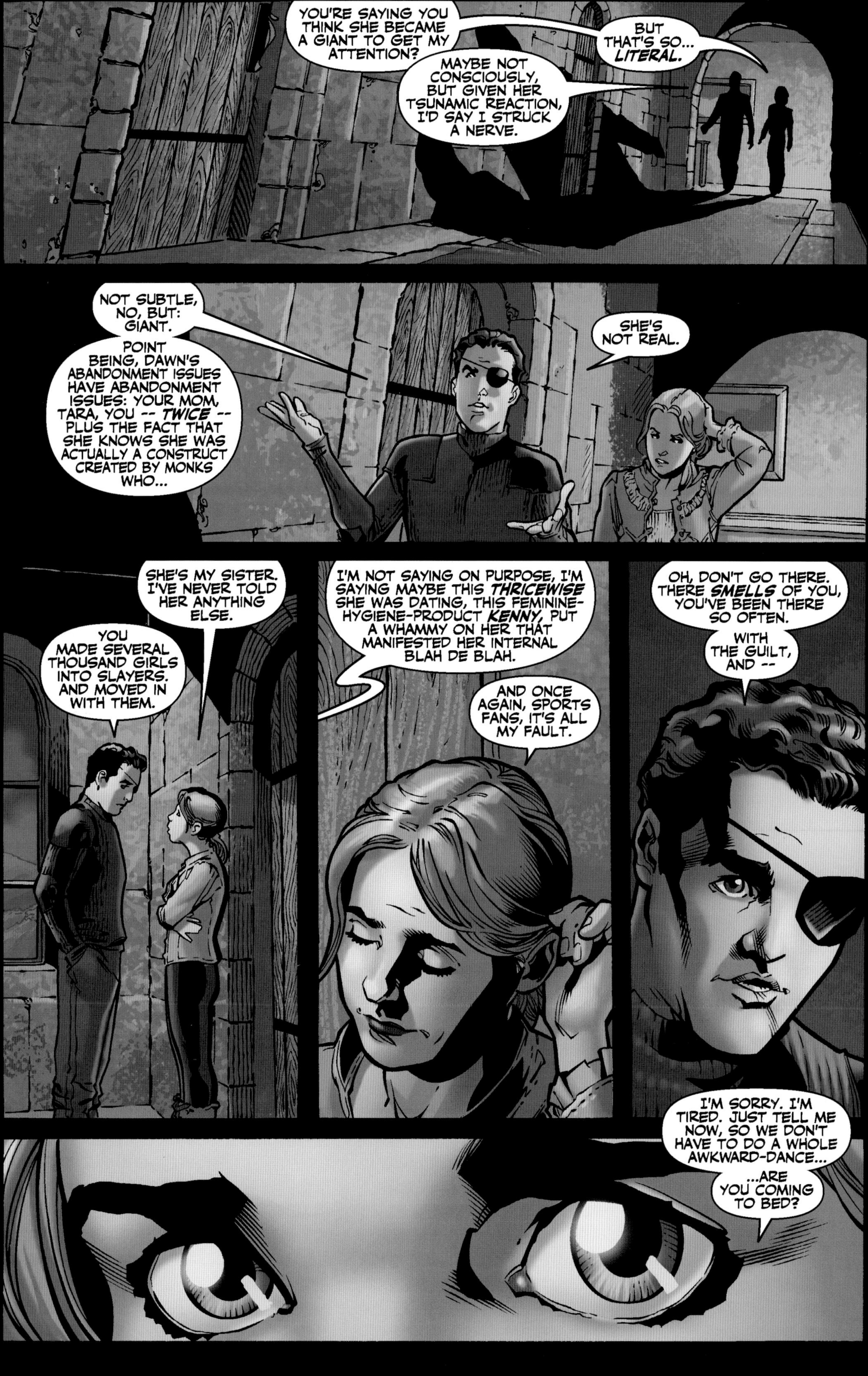
YOU'RE SAYING YOU THINK SHE BECAME A GIANT TO GET MY ATTENTION?
BUT THAT'S SO... LITERAL.
MAYBE NOT CONSCIOUSLY, BUT GIVEN HER TSUNAMIC REACTION, I'D SAY I STRUCK A NERVE.
NOT SUBTLE, NO, BUT: GIANT.
POINT BEING, DAWN'S ABANDONMENT ISSUES HAVE ABANDONMENT ISSUES: YOUR MOM, TARA, YOU -- TWICE -- PLUS THE FACT THAT SHE KNOWS SHE WAS ACTUALLY A CONSTRUCT CREATED BY MONKS WHO...
SHE'S NOT REAL.
SHE'S MY SISTER. I'VE NEVER TOLD HER ANYTHING ELSE.
YOU MADE SEVERAL THOUSAND GIRLS INTO SLAYERS. AND MOVED IN WITH THEM.
I'M NOT SAYING ON PURPOSE, I'M SAYING MAYBE THIS THRICEWISE SHE WAS DATING, THIS FEMININE-HYGIENE-PRODUCT KENNY, PUT A WHAMMY ON HER THAT MANIFESTED HER INTERNAL BLAH DE BLAH.
AND ONCE AGAIN, SPORTS FANS, IT'S ALL MY FAULT.
OH, DON'T GO THERE. THERE SMELLS OF YOU, YOU'VE BEEN THERE SO OFTEN.
WITH THE GUILT, AND --
I'M SORRY. I'M TIRED. JUST TELL ME NOW, SO WE DON'T HAVE TO DO A WHOLE AWKWARD-DANCE...
...ARE YOU COMING TO BED?

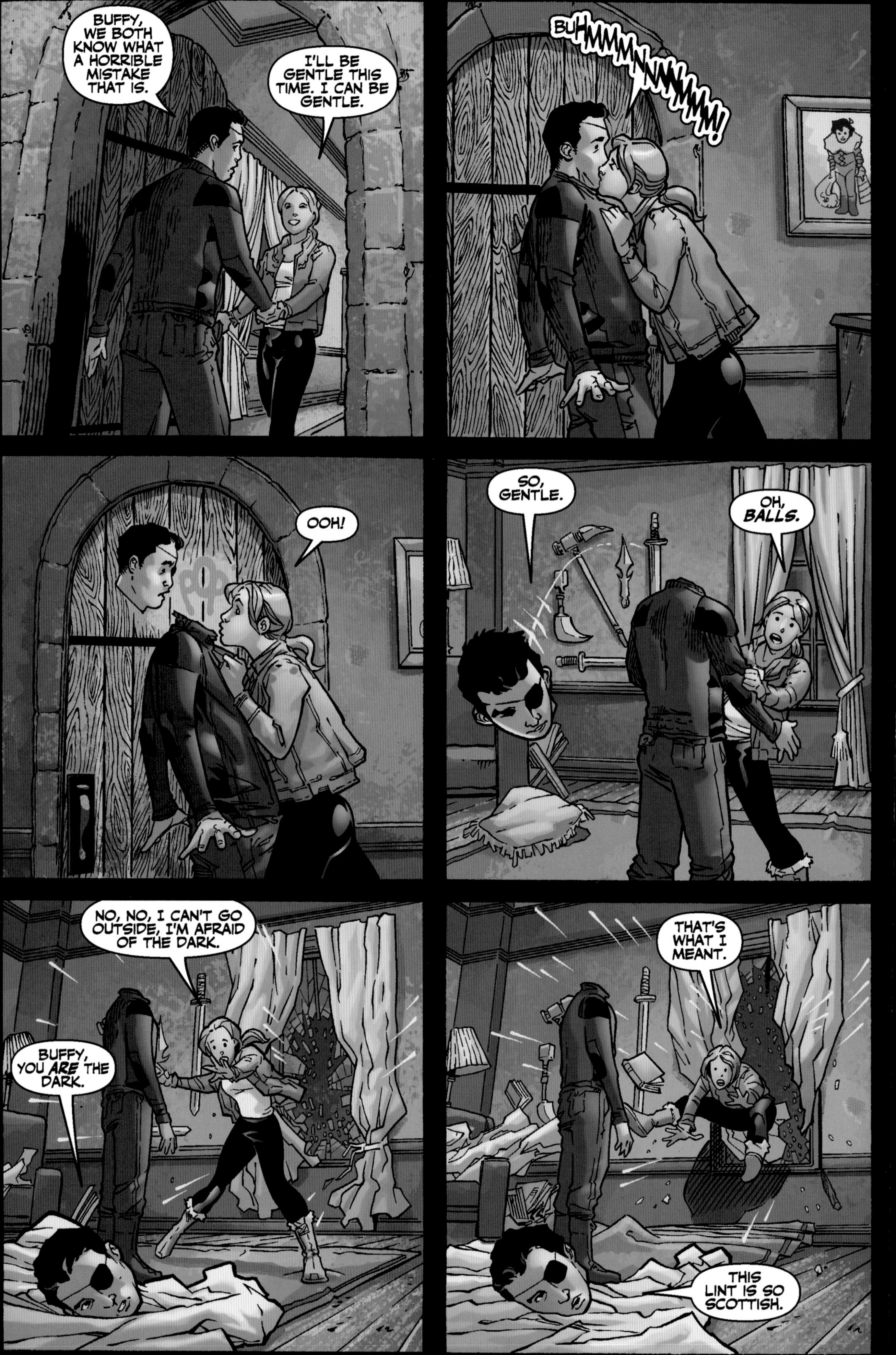
BUFFY, WE BOTH KNOW WHAT A HORRIBLE MISTAKE THAT IS.
I'LL BE GENTLE THIS TIME. I CAN BE GENTLE.
BUHMMMNNNMMM!
OOH!
SO, GENTLE.
OH, *BALLS.*
NO, NO, I CAN'T GO OUTSIDE, I'M AFRAID OF THE DARK.
BUFFY, YOU *ARE* THE DARK.
THAT'S WHAT I MEANT.
THIS LINT IS SO SCOTTISH.

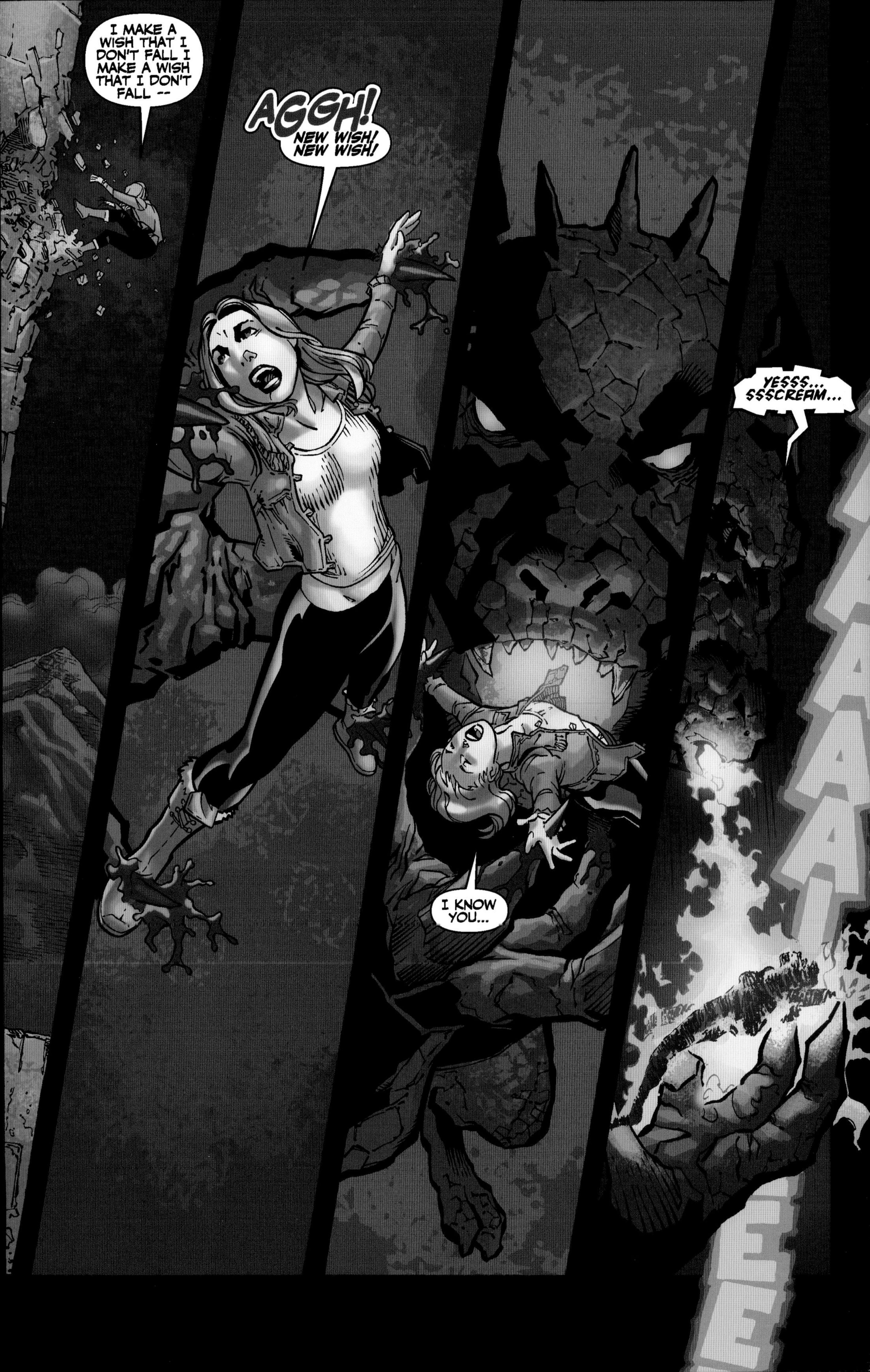
I MAKE A WISH THAT I DON'T FALL I MAKE A WISH THAT I DON'T FALL --
AGGH!
NEW WISH! NEW WISH!
I KNOW YOU...
YESSS... SSSCREAM...

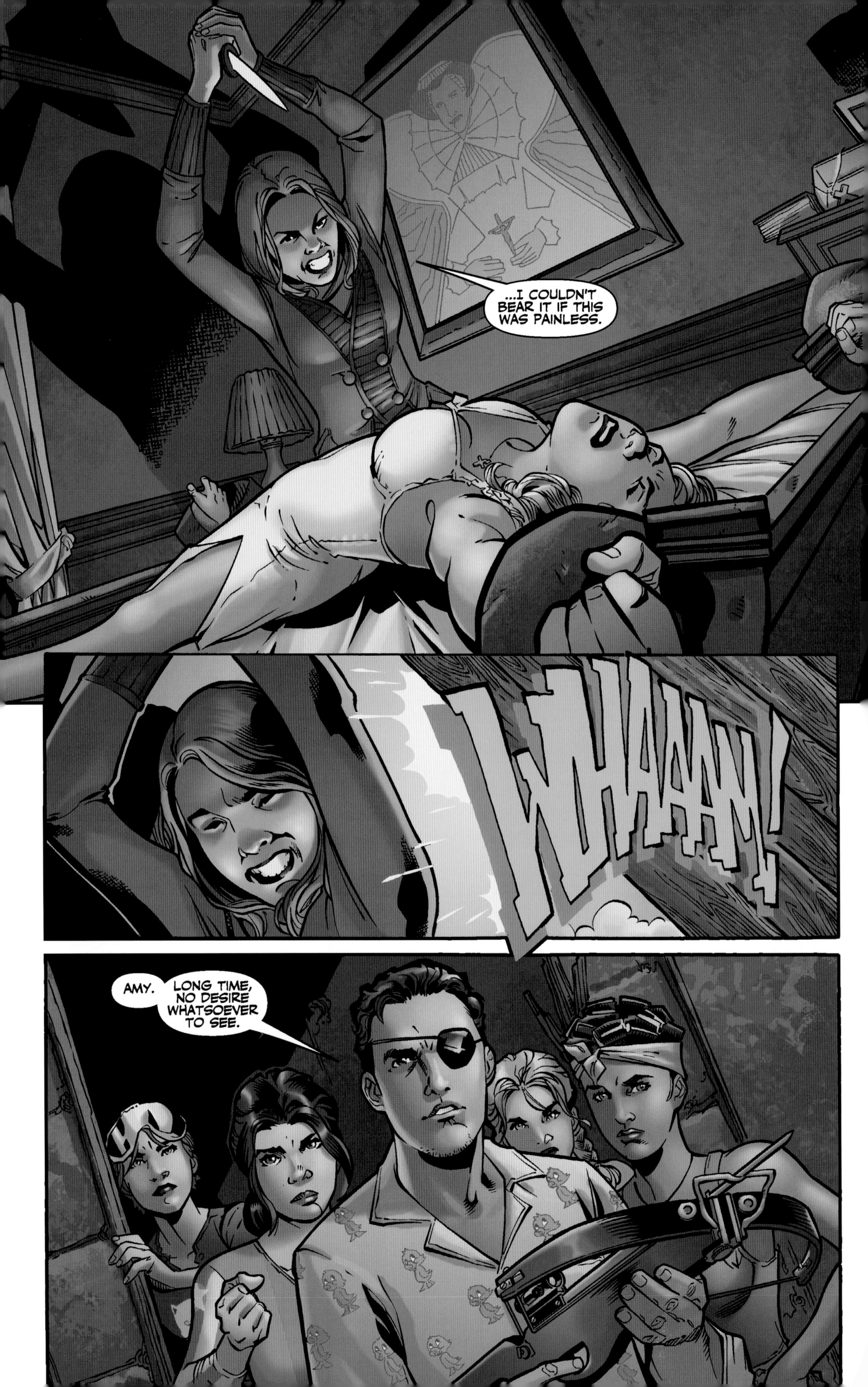
...I COULDN'T BEAR IT IF THIS WAS PAINLESS.
WHAAAM!
AMY.
LONG TIME, NO DESIRE WHATSOEVER TO SEE.

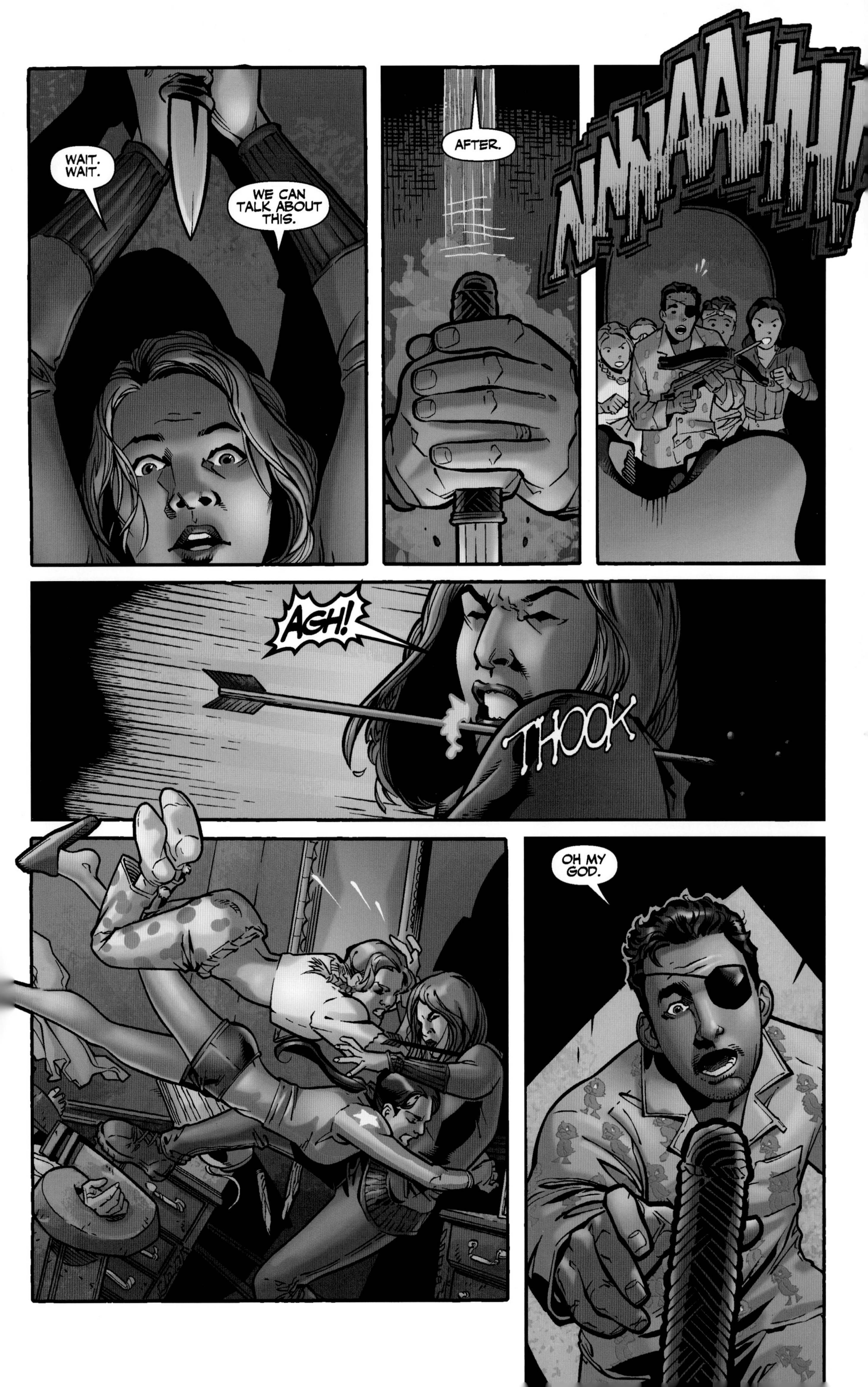
WAIT. WAIT.
WE CAN TALK ABOUT THIS.
AFTER.
AHHAAHH!
AGH!
THOOK
OH MY GOD.

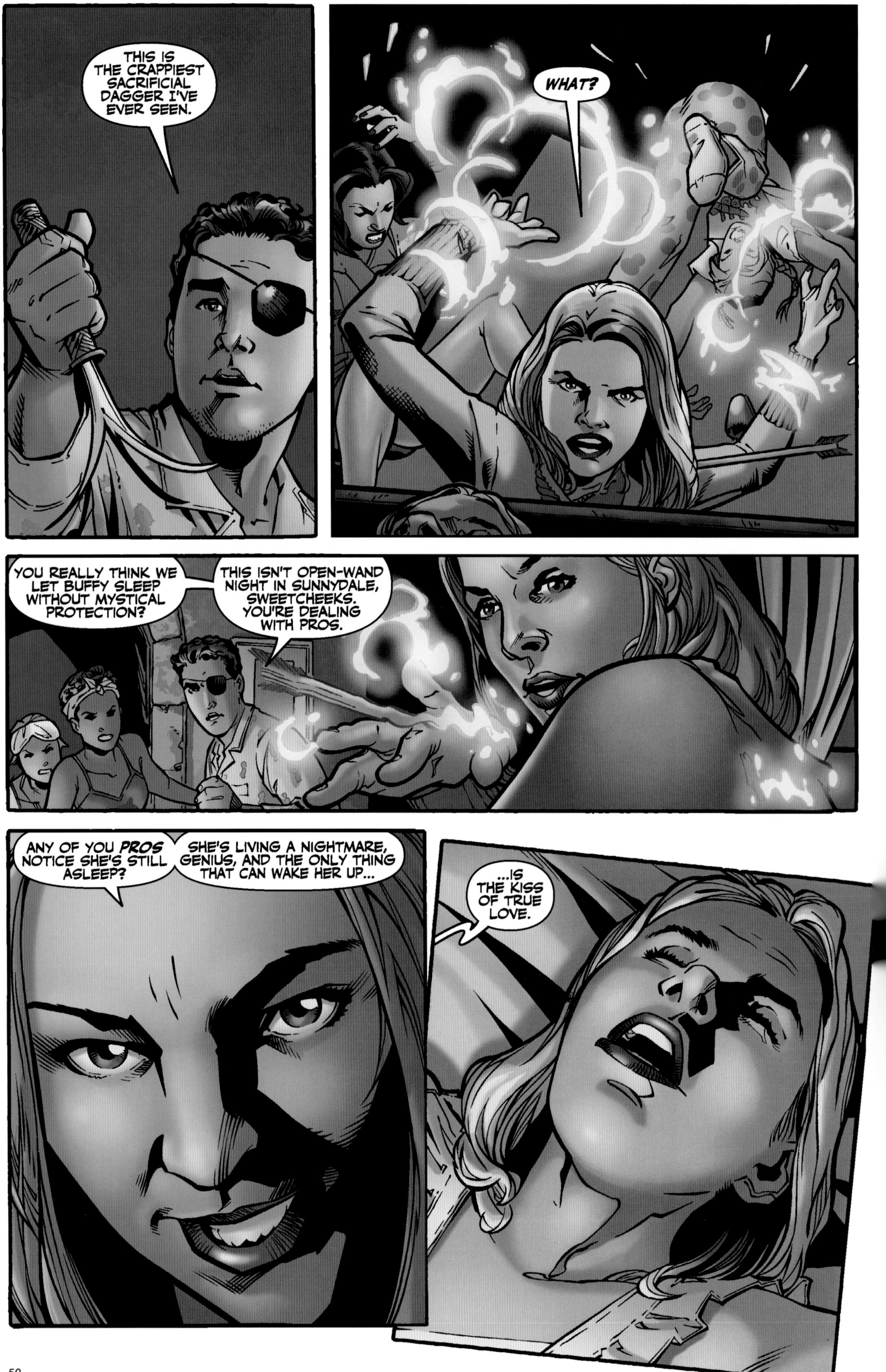
THIS IS THE CRAPPIEST SACRIFICIAL DAGGER I'VE EVER SEEN.
WHAT?
YOU REALLY THINK WE LET BUFFY SLEEP WITHOUT MYSTICAL PROTECTION?
THIS ISN'T OPEN-WAND NIGHT IN SUNNYDALE, SWEETCHEEKS. YOU'RE DEALING WITH PROS.
ANY OF YOU PROS NOTICE SHE'S STILL ASLEEP?
SHE'S LIVING A NIGHTMARE, GENIUS, AND THE ONLY THING THAT CAN WAKE HER UP...
...IS THE KISS OF TRUE LOVE.

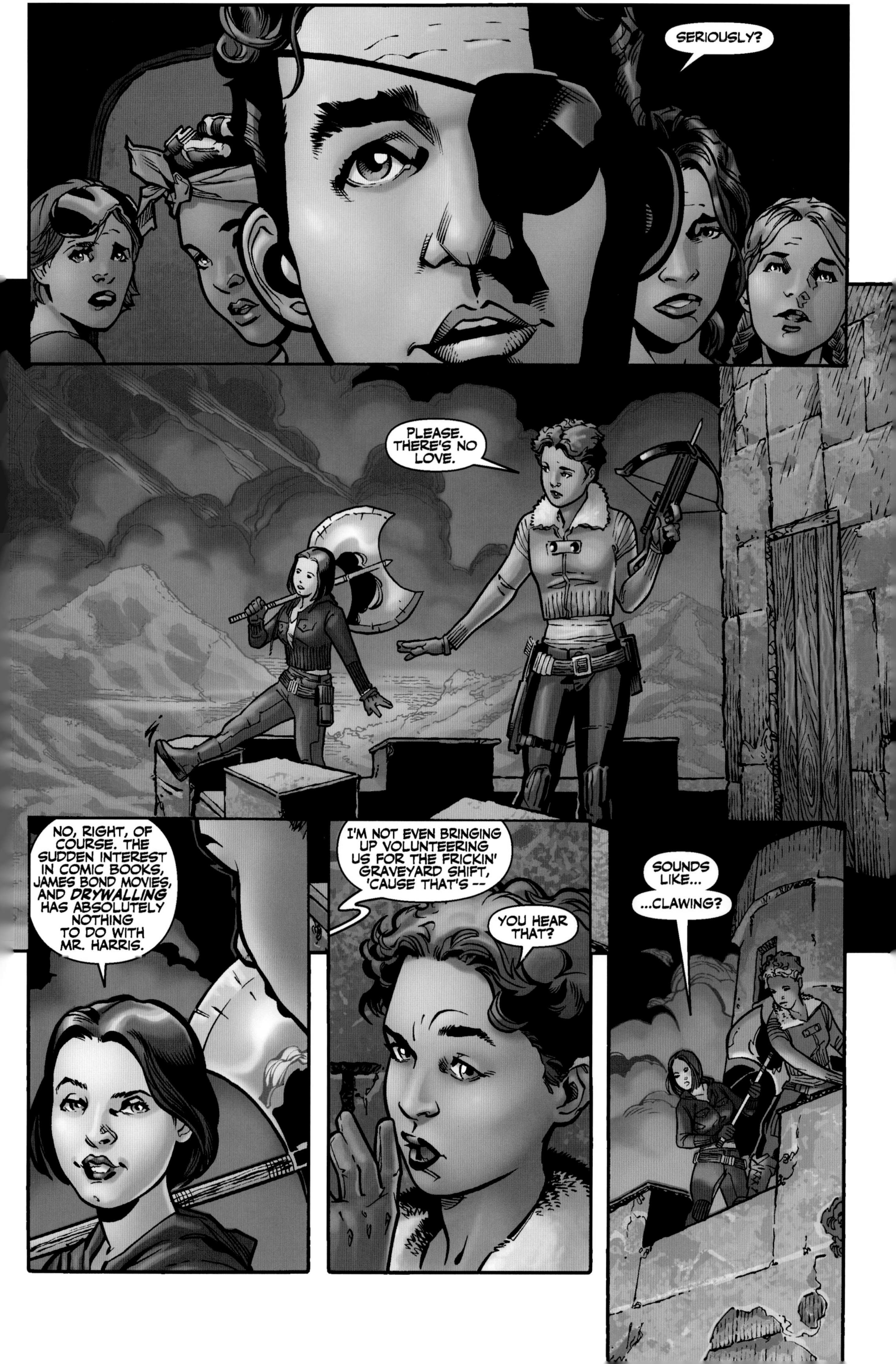
SERIOUSLY?
PLEASE. THERE'S NO LOVE.
NO, RIGHT, OF COURSE. THE SUDDEN INTEREST IN COMIC BOOKS, JAMES BOND MOVIES, AND *DRYWALLING* HAS ABSOLUTELY NOTHING TO DO WITH MR. HARRIS.
I'M NOT EVEN BRINGING UP VOLUNTEERING US FOR THE FRICKIN' GRAVEYARD SHIFT, 'CAUSE THAT'S --
YOU HEAR THAT?
SOUNDS LIKE...
...CLAWING?

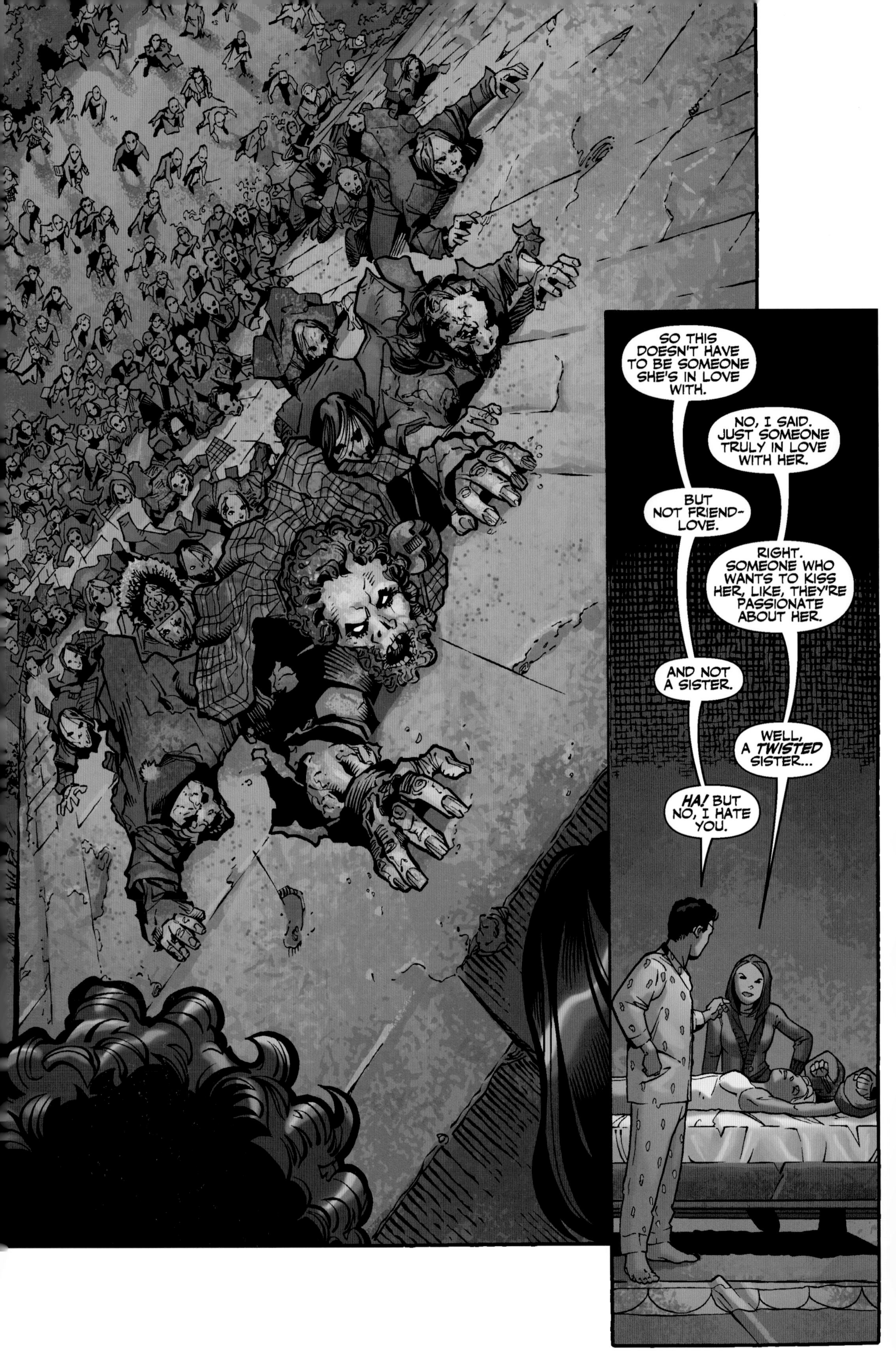
SO THIS DOESN'T HAVE TO BE SOMEONE SHE'S IN LOVE WITH.
NO, I SAID. JUST SOMEONE TRULY IN LOVE WITH HER.
BUT NOT FRIEND-LOVE.
RIGHT. SOMEONE WHO WANTS TO KISS HER, LIKE, THEY'RE PASSIONATE ABOUT HER.
AND NOT A SISTER.
WELL, A *TWISTED* SISTER...
HA! BUT NO, I HATE YOU.

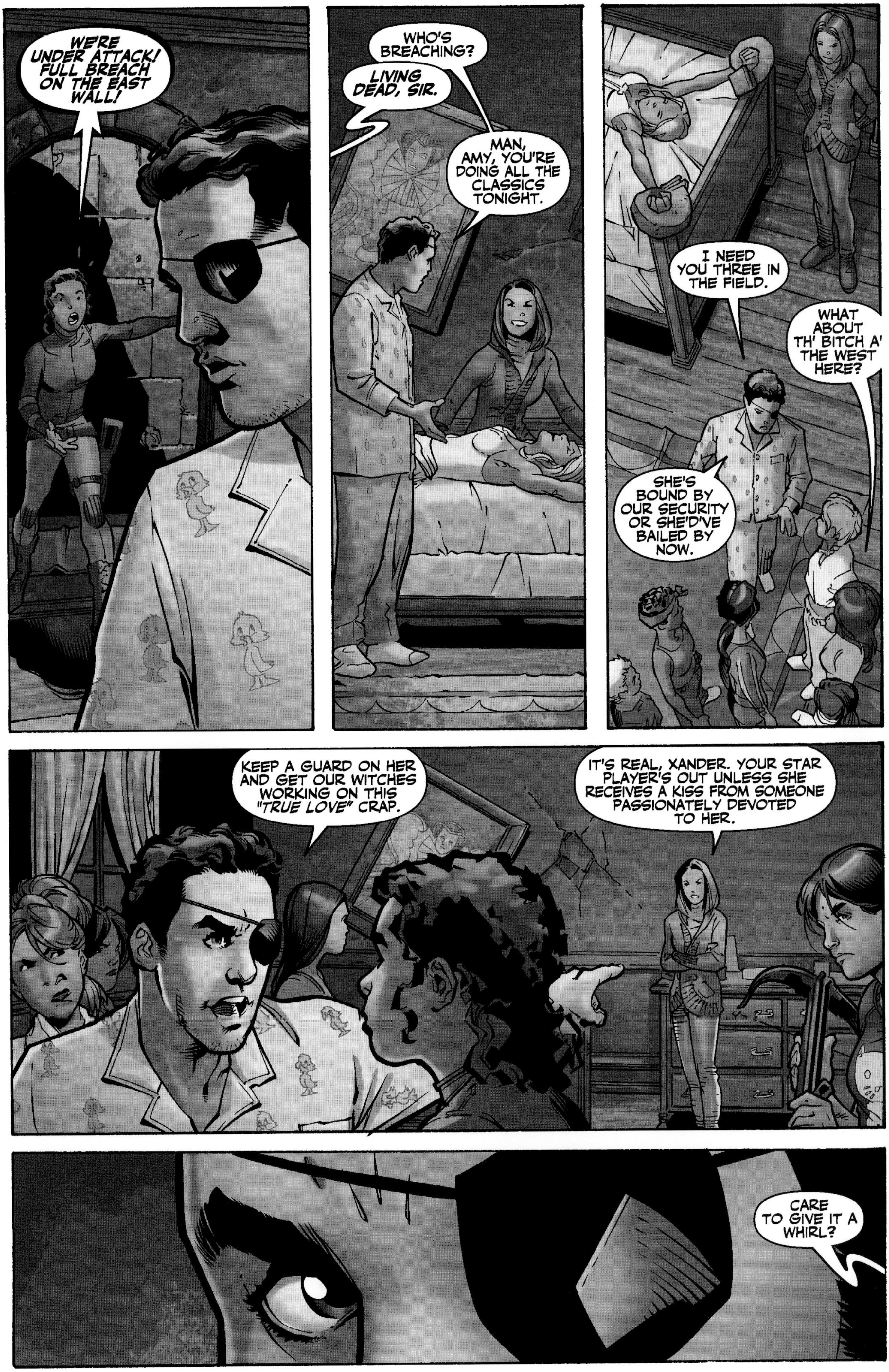
WE'RE UNDER ATTACK! FULL BREACH ON THE EAST WALL!
WHO'S BREACHING?
LIVING DEAD, SIR.
MAN, AMY, YOU'RE DOING ALL THE CLASSICS TONIGHT.
I NEED YOU THREE IN THE FIELD.
WHAT ABOUT TH' BITCH A' THE WEST HERE?
SHE'S BOUND BY OUR SECURITY OR SHE'D'VE BAILED BY NOW.
KEEP A GUARD ON HER AND GET OUR WITCHES WORKING ON THIS "TRUE LOVE" CRAP.
IT'S REAL, XANDER. YOUR STAR PLAYER'S OUT UNLESS SHE RECEIVES A KISS FROM SOMEONE PASSIONATELY DEVOTED TO HER.
CARE TO GIVE IT A WHIRL?

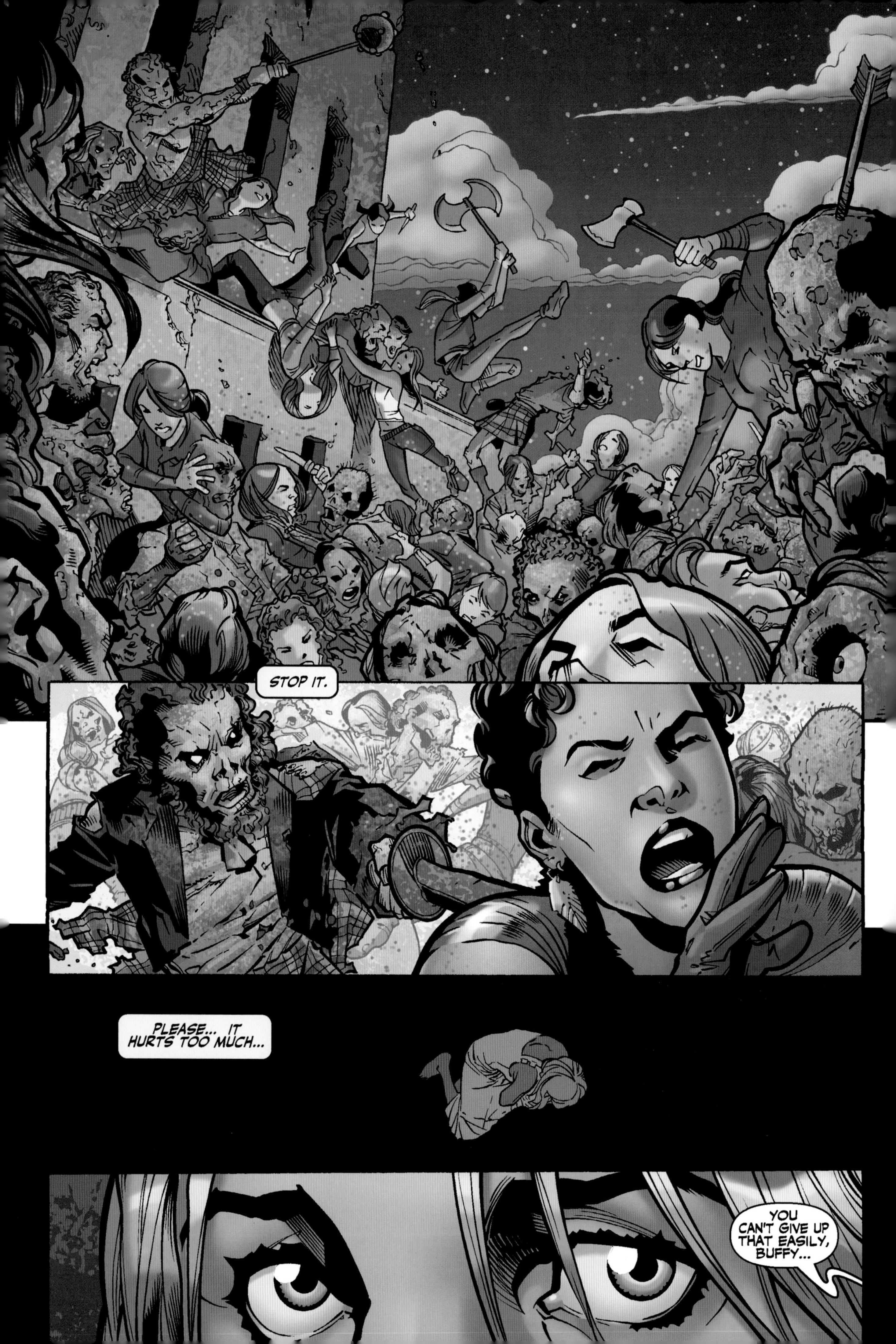
STOP IT.
PLEASE... IT HURTS TOO MUCH...
YOU CAN'T GIVE UP THAT EASILY, BUFFY...

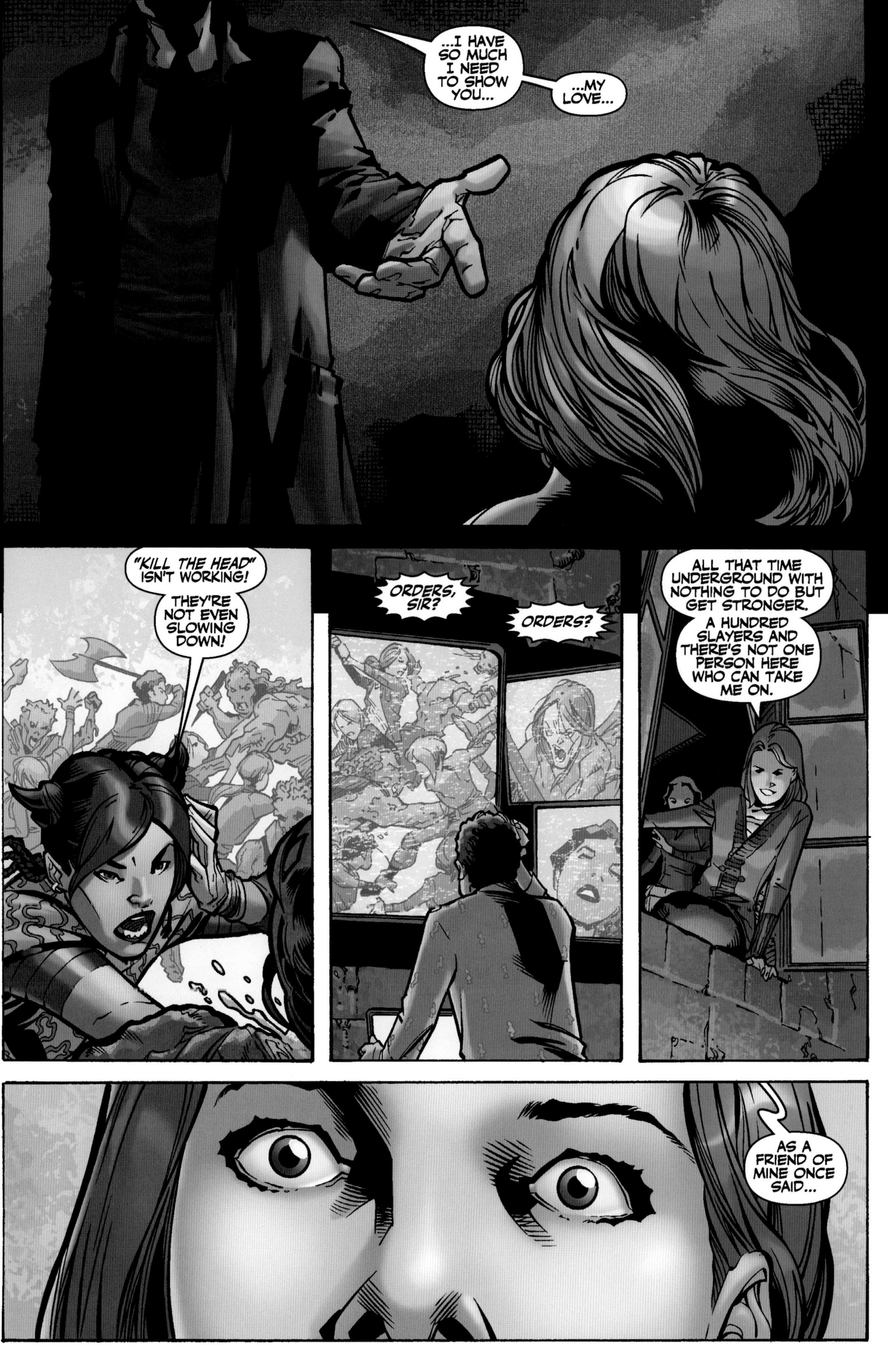
...I HAVE SO MUCH I NEED TO SHOW YOU...
...MY LOVE...
"KILL THE HEAD" ISN'T WORKING!
THEY'RE NOT EVEN SLOWING DOWN!
ORDERS, SIR?
ORDERS?
ALL THAT TIME UNDERGROUND WITH NOTHING TO DO BUT GET STRONGER.
A HUNDRED SLAYERS AND THERE'S NOT ONE PERSON HERE WHO CAN TAKE ME ON.
AS A FRIEND OF MINE ONCE SAID...

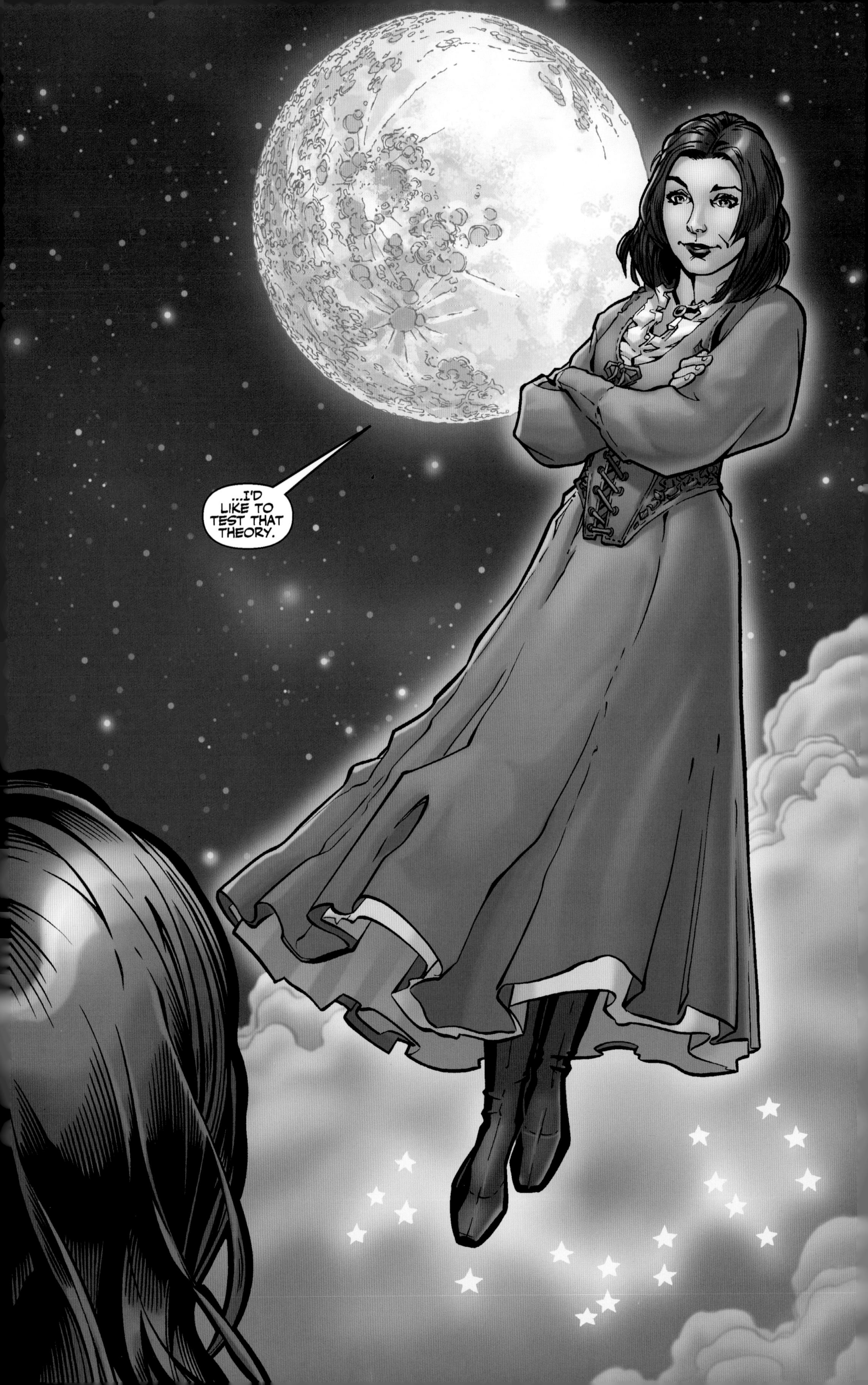
...I'D LIKE TO TEST THAT THEORY.

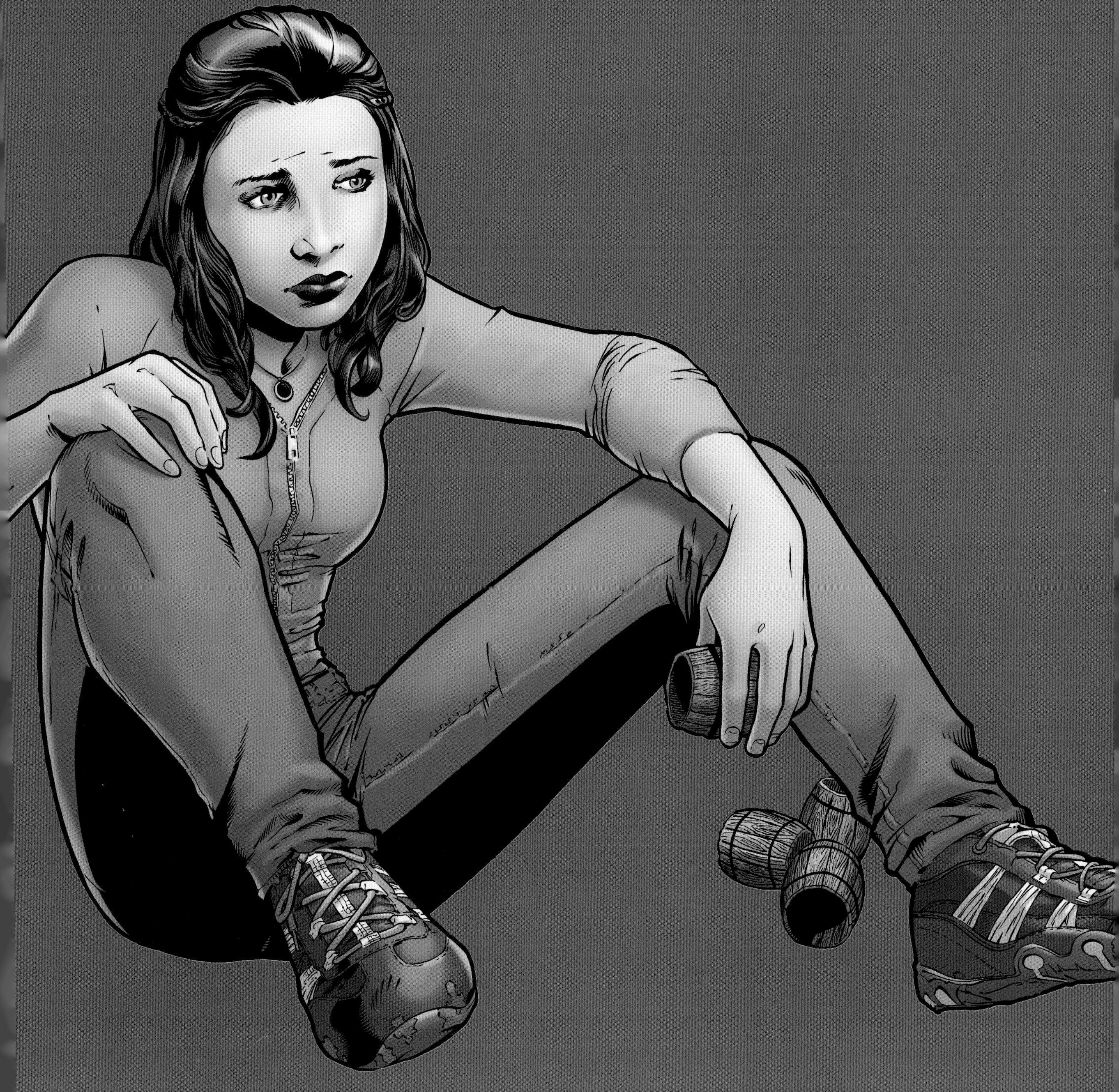

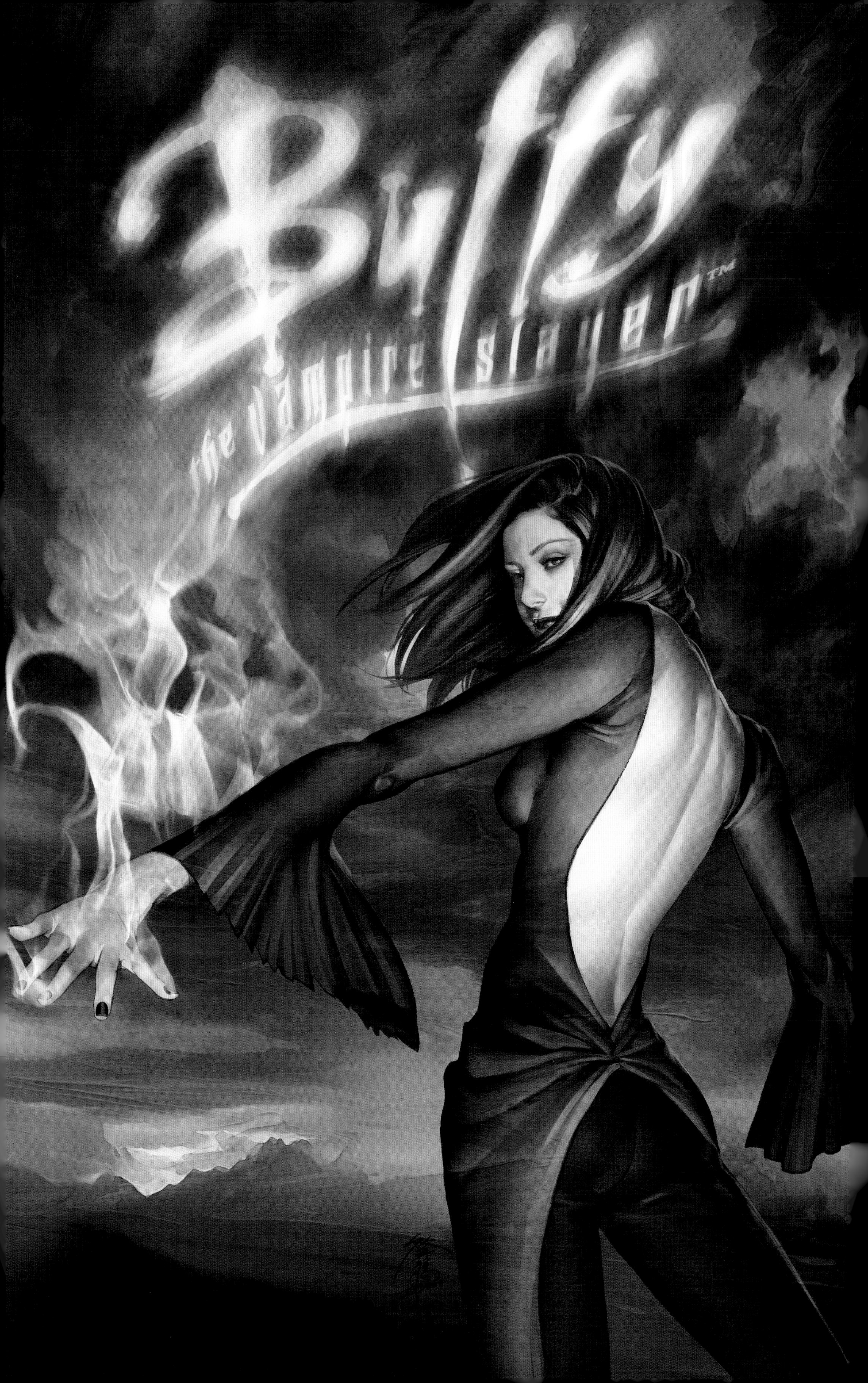
Buffy
the Vampire Slayer™

The LONG WAY HOME

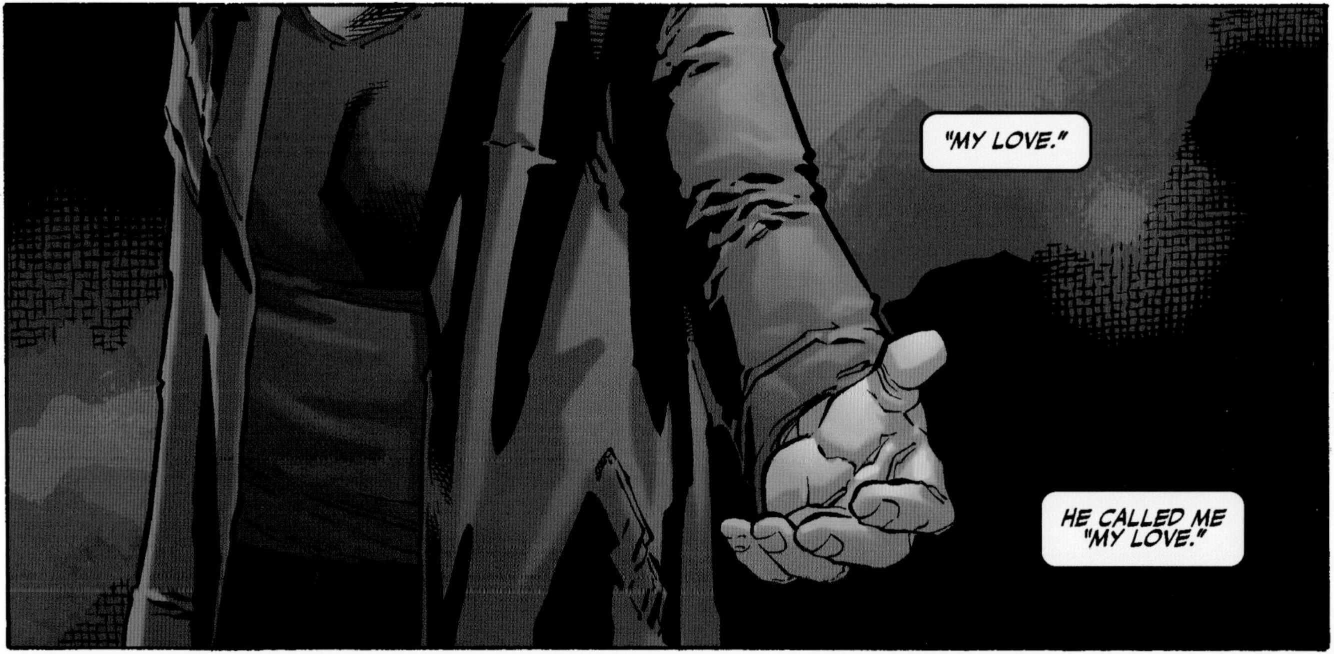
"MY LOVE."
HE CALLED ME "MY LOVE."

Part Three

AND THEN I THREW UP IN MY MOUTH A LITTLE.

ETHAN RAYNE?

IN THE FLESH, MY LOVE.

AND AGAIN, A SLIGHT BARFLEX. YOU *HAVE* TO STOP CALLING ME THAT.

IT'S AN EXPRESSION, PET. LIKE *"PET."*

ALSO NOT OKAY. HOW DID YOU GET IN MY DREAM?

WE HAVEN'T OODLES OF TIME.

YOU'RE A CHAOS-WORSHIPING WANNABE SORCERER WHO TAKES UP NONE COUNT IT *NONE* OF MY SUBCONSCIOUS. WHICH MEANS YOU *FORCED* YOUR WAY INTO MY DREAM.

I JUST HITCHED A RIDE. AND WE'RE NOT IN YOUR DREAM.

WE'RE IN YOUR DREAM*SPACE.*

SPLAINY. DREAMSPACE?

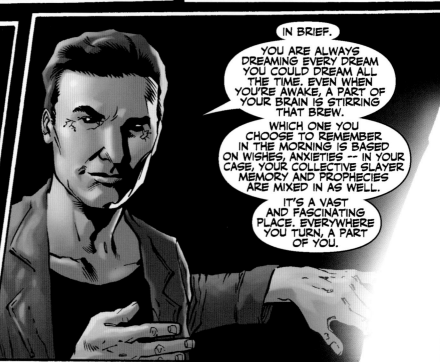

IN BRIEF.

YOU ARE ALWAYS DREAMING EVERY DREAM YOU COULD DREAM ALL THE TIME. EVEN WHEN YOU'RE AWAKE, A PART OF YOUR BRAIN IS STIRRING THAT BREW.

WHICH ONE YOU CHOOSE TO REMEMBER IN THE MORNING IS BASED ON WISHES, ANXIETIES -- IN YOUR CASE, YOUR COLLECTIVE SLAYER MEMORY AND PROPHECIES ARE MIXED IN AS WELL.

IT'S A VAST AND FASCINATING PLACE. EVERYWHERE YOU TURN, A PART OF YOU.

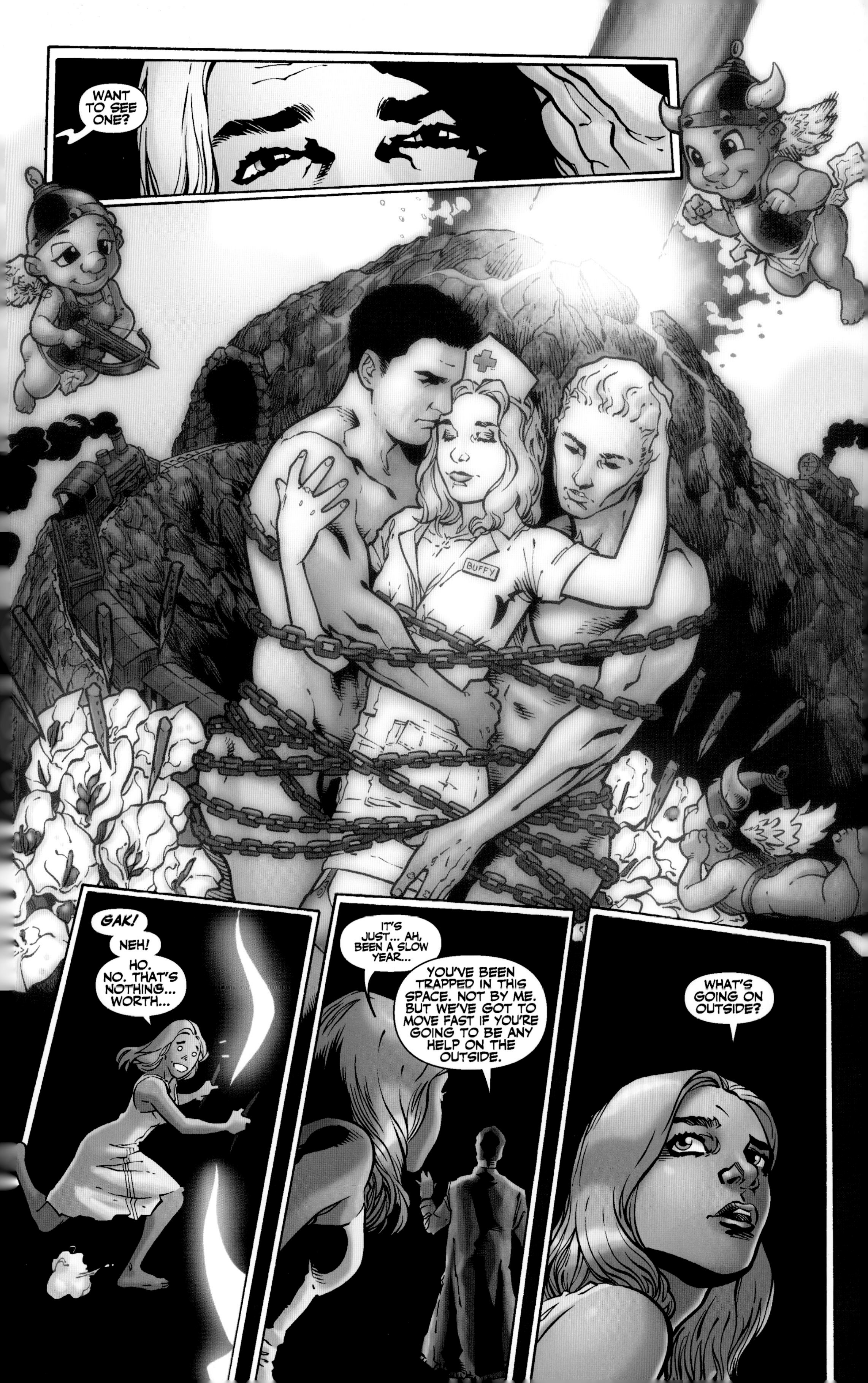
WANT TO SEE ONE?
BUFFY
GAK!
NEH!
HO. NO. THAT'S NOTHING... WORTH...
IT'S JUST... AH, BEEN A SLOW YEAR...
YOU'VE BEEN TRAPPED IN THIS SPACE. NOT BY ME. BUT WE'VE GOT TO MOVE FAST IF YOU'RE GOING TO BE ANY HELP ON THE OUTSIDE.
WHAT'S GOING ON OUTSIDE?

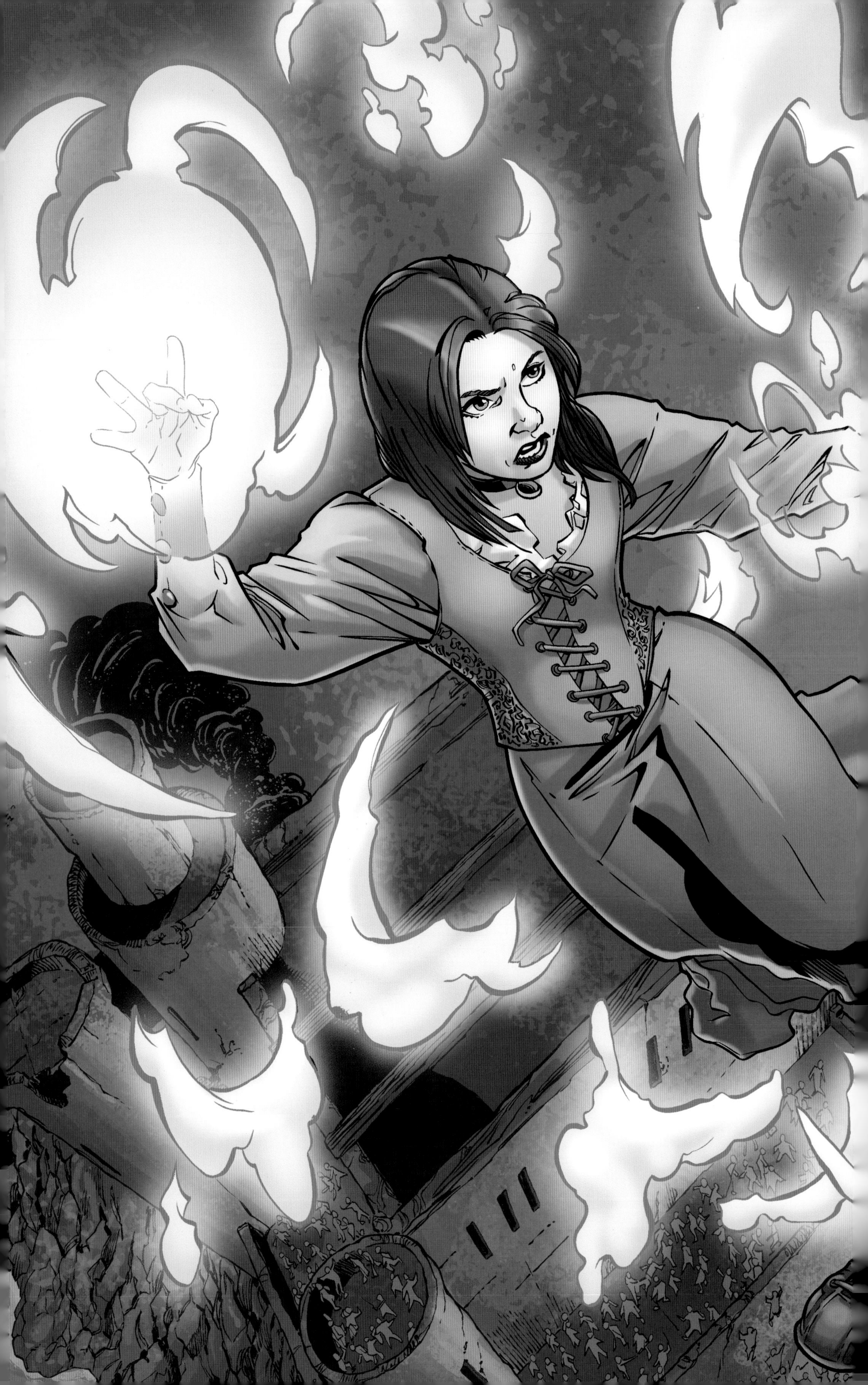

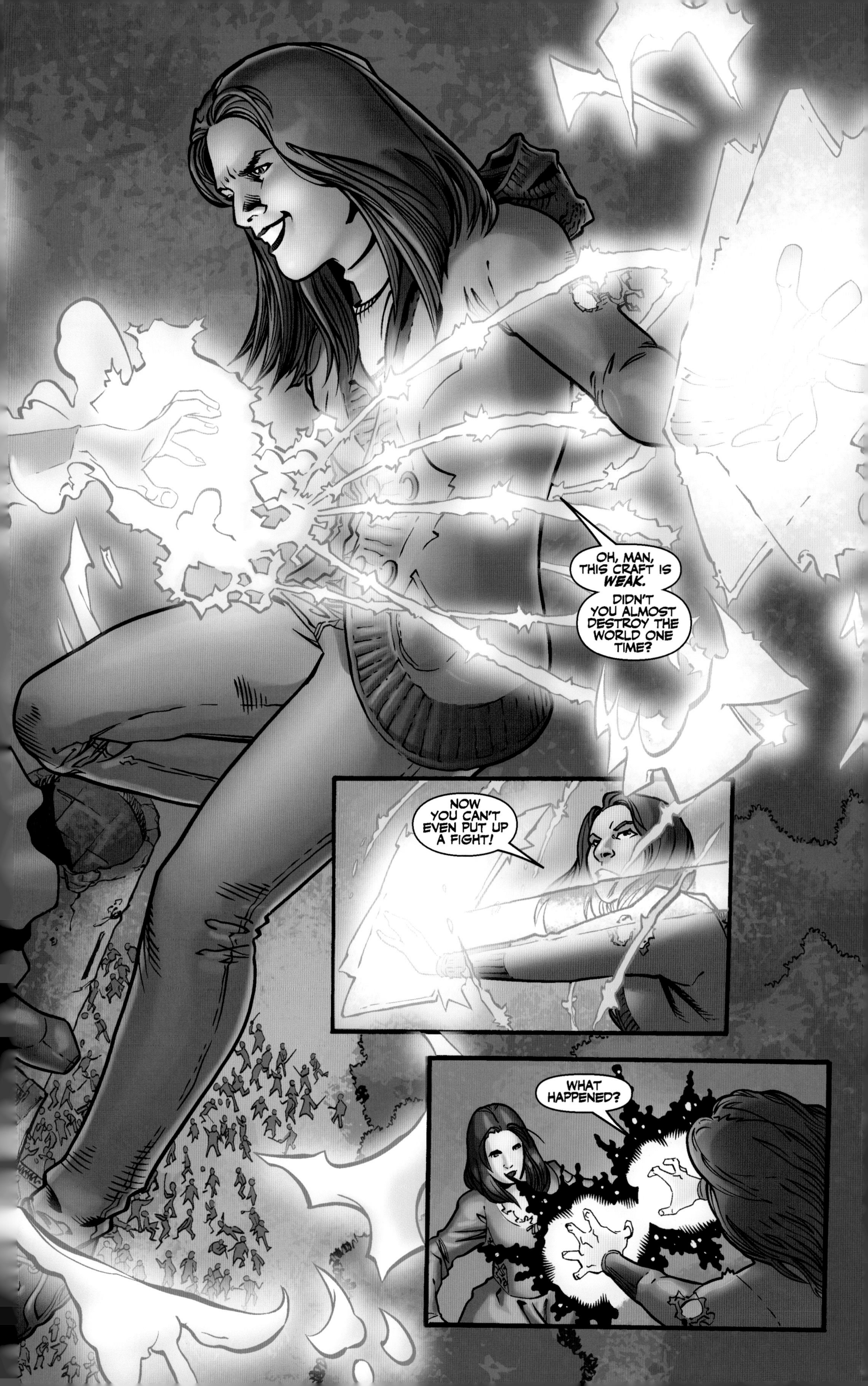
OH, MAN, THIS CRAFT IS ***WEAK.***
DIDN'T YOU ALMOST DESTROY THE WORLD ONE TIME?
NOW YOU CAN'T EVEN PUT UP A FIGHT!
WHAT HAPPENED?

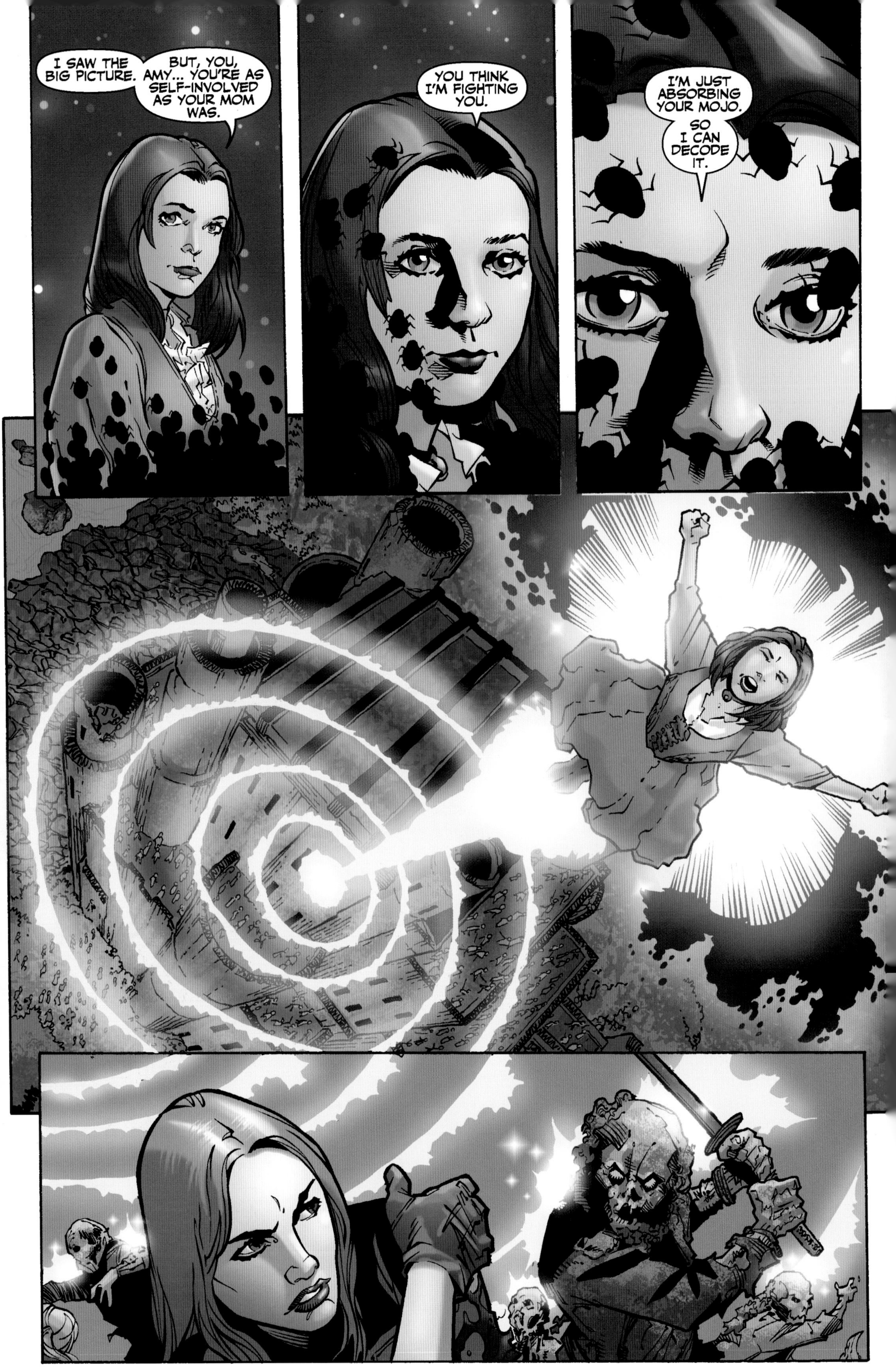

I SAW THE BIG PICTURE.
BUT, YOU, AMY... YOU'RE AS SELF-INVOLVED AS YOUR MOM WAS.
YOU THINK I'M FIGHTING YOU.
I'M JUST ABSORBING YOUR MOJO.
SO I CAN DECODE IT.

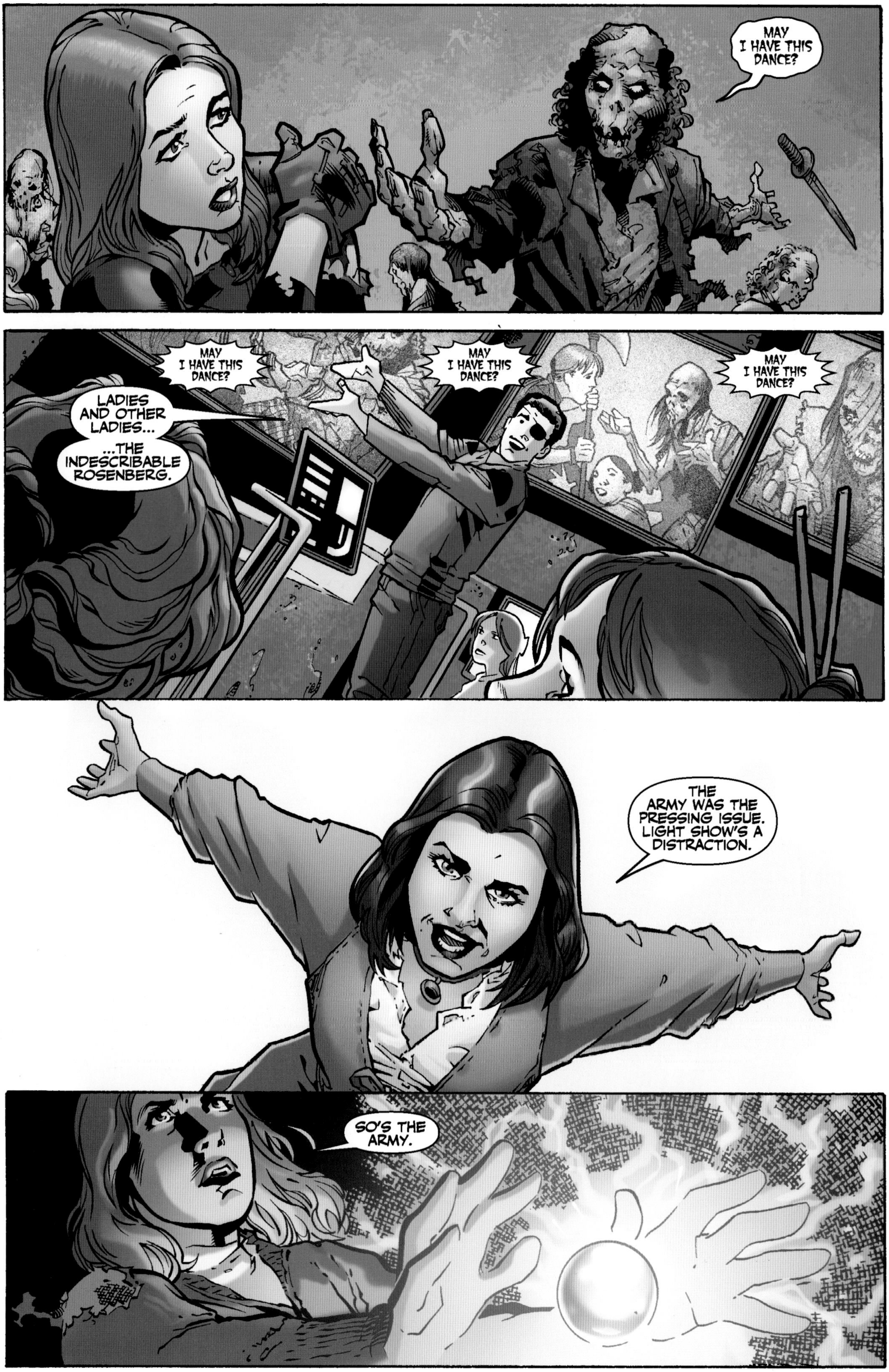
MAY I HAVE THIS DANCE?
MAY I HAVE THIS DANCE?
MAY I HAVE THIS DANCE?
MAY I HAVE THIS DANCE?
LADIES AND OTHER LADIES...
...THE INDESCRIBABLE ROSENBERG.
THE ARMY WAS THE PRESSING ISSUE. LIGHT SHOW'S A DISTRACTION.
SO'S THE ARMY.

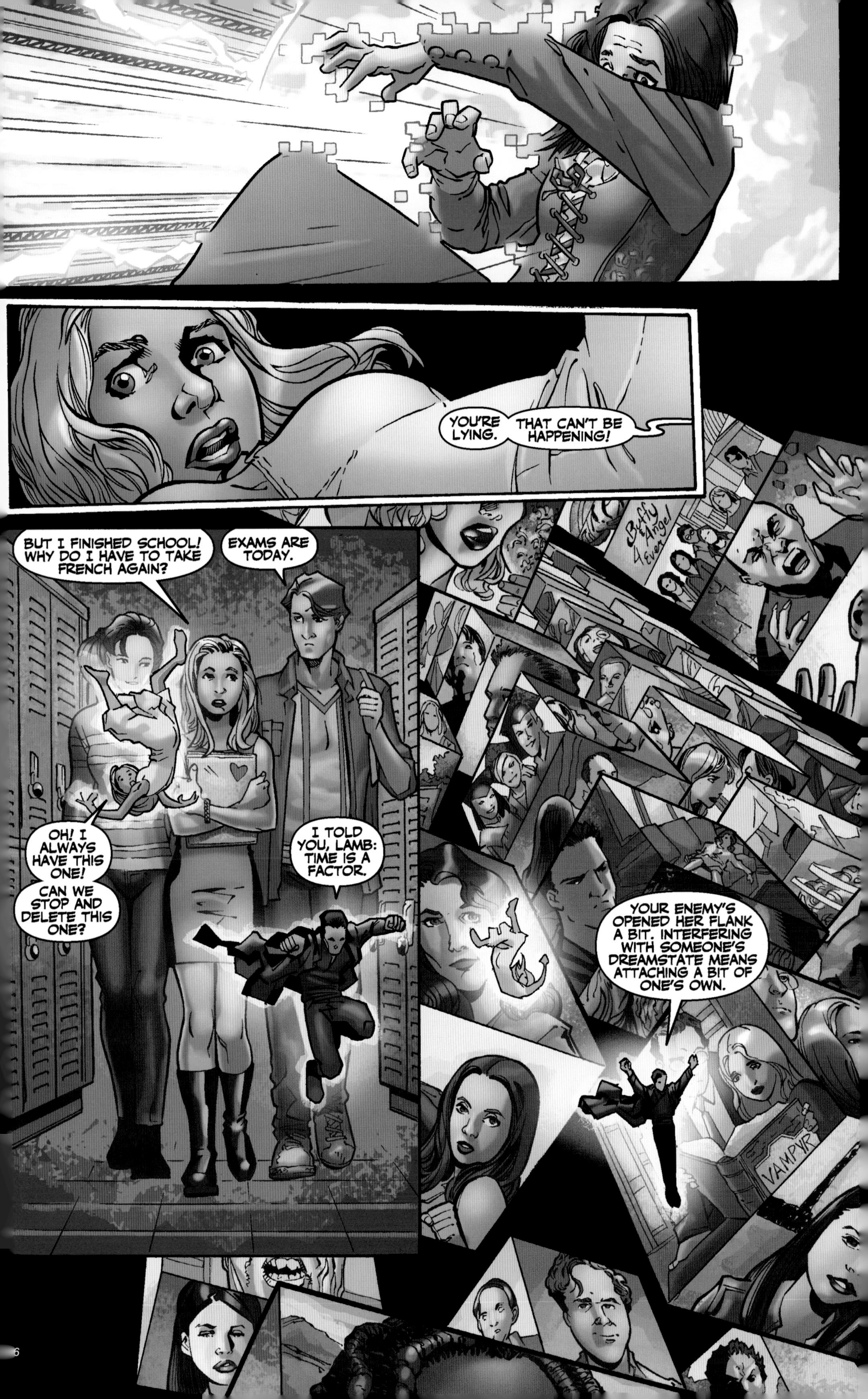
YOU'RE LYING.
THAT CAN'T BE HAPPENING!
BUT I FINISHED SCHOOL! WHY DO I HAVE TO TAKE FRENCH AGAIN?
EXAMS ARE TODAY.
Buffy & Angel 4 Ever
OH! I ALWAYS HAVE THIS ONE!
CAN WE STOP AND DELETE THIS ONE?
I TOLD YOU, LAMB: TIME IS A FACTOR.
YOUR ENEMY'S OPENED HER FLANK A BIT. INTERFERING WITH SOMEONE'S DREAMSTATE MEANS ATTACHING A BIT OF ONE'S OWN.
VAMPYR

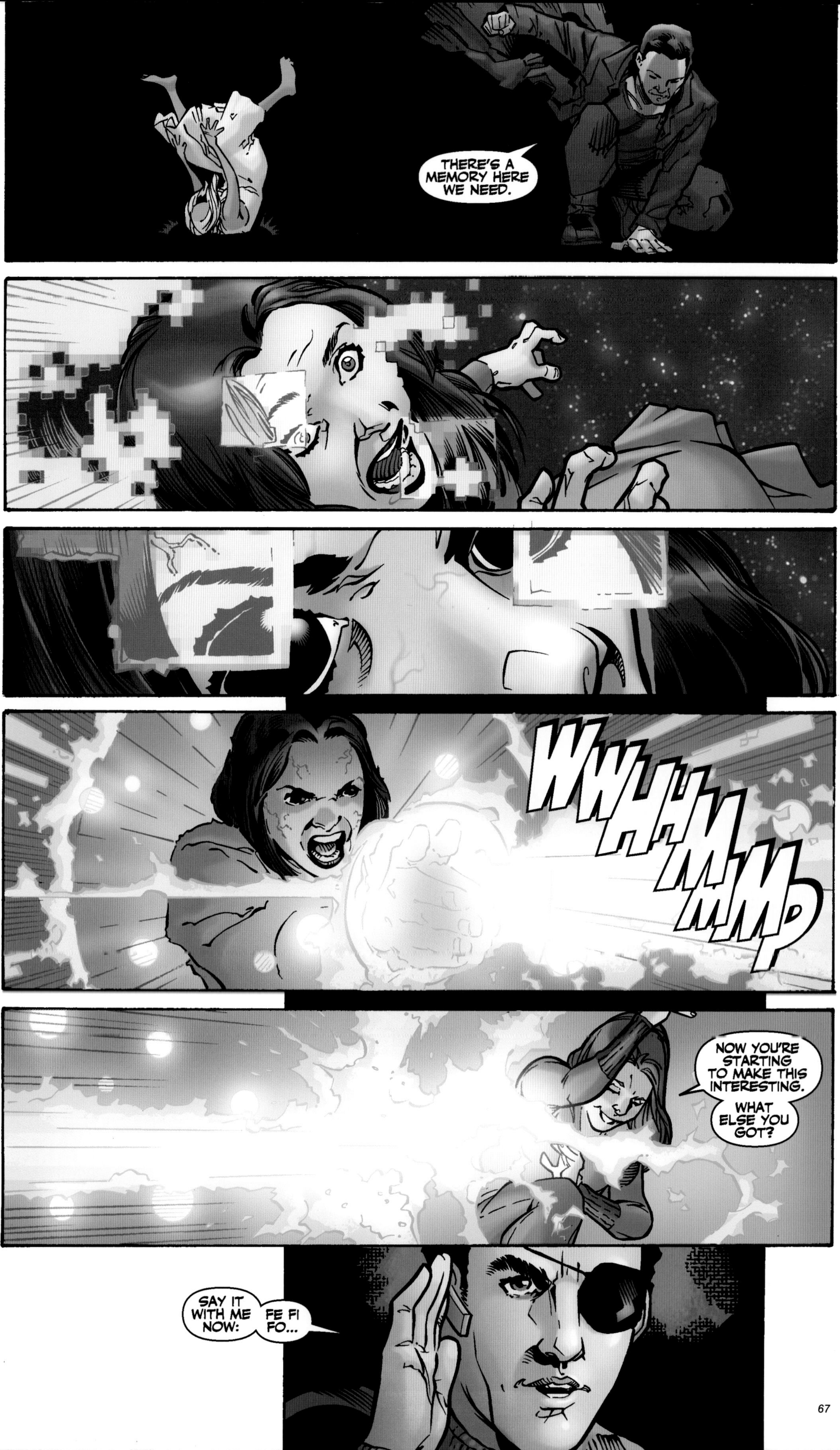
THERE'S A MEMORY HERE WE NEED.
WWHHMMMP
NOW YOU'RE STARTING TO MAKE THIS INTERESTING.
WHAT ELSE YOU GOT?
SAY IT WITH ME NOW:
FE FI FO...

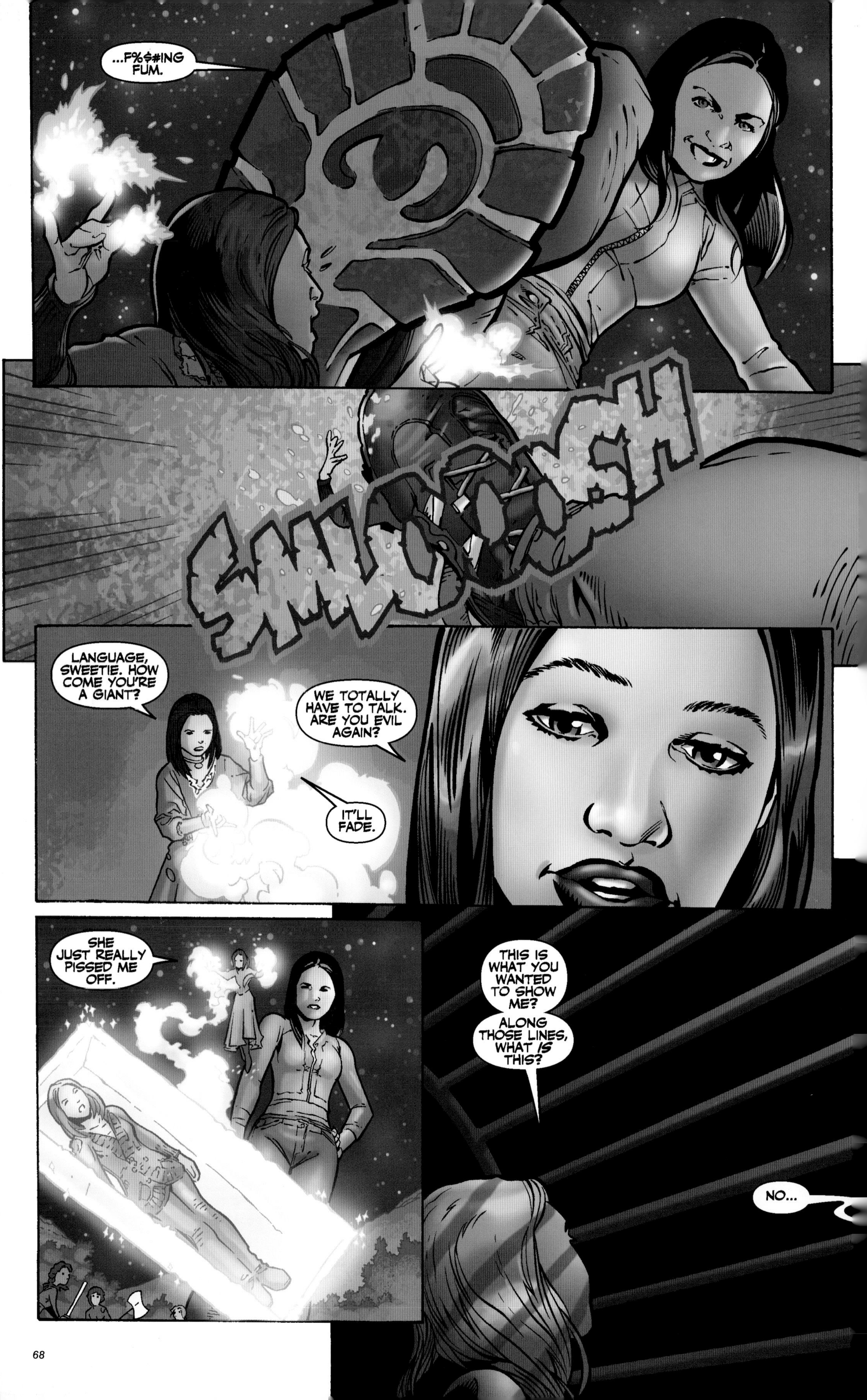
...F%$#ING FUM.
SMWOOOSH
LANGUAGE, SWEETIE. HOW COME YOU'RE A GIANT?
WE TOTALLY HAVE TO TALK. ARE YOU EVIL AGAIN?
IT'LL FADE.
SHE JUST REALLY PISSED ME OFF.
THIS IS WHAT YOU WANTED TO SHOW ME?
ALONG THOSE LINES, WHAT *IS* THIS?
NO...

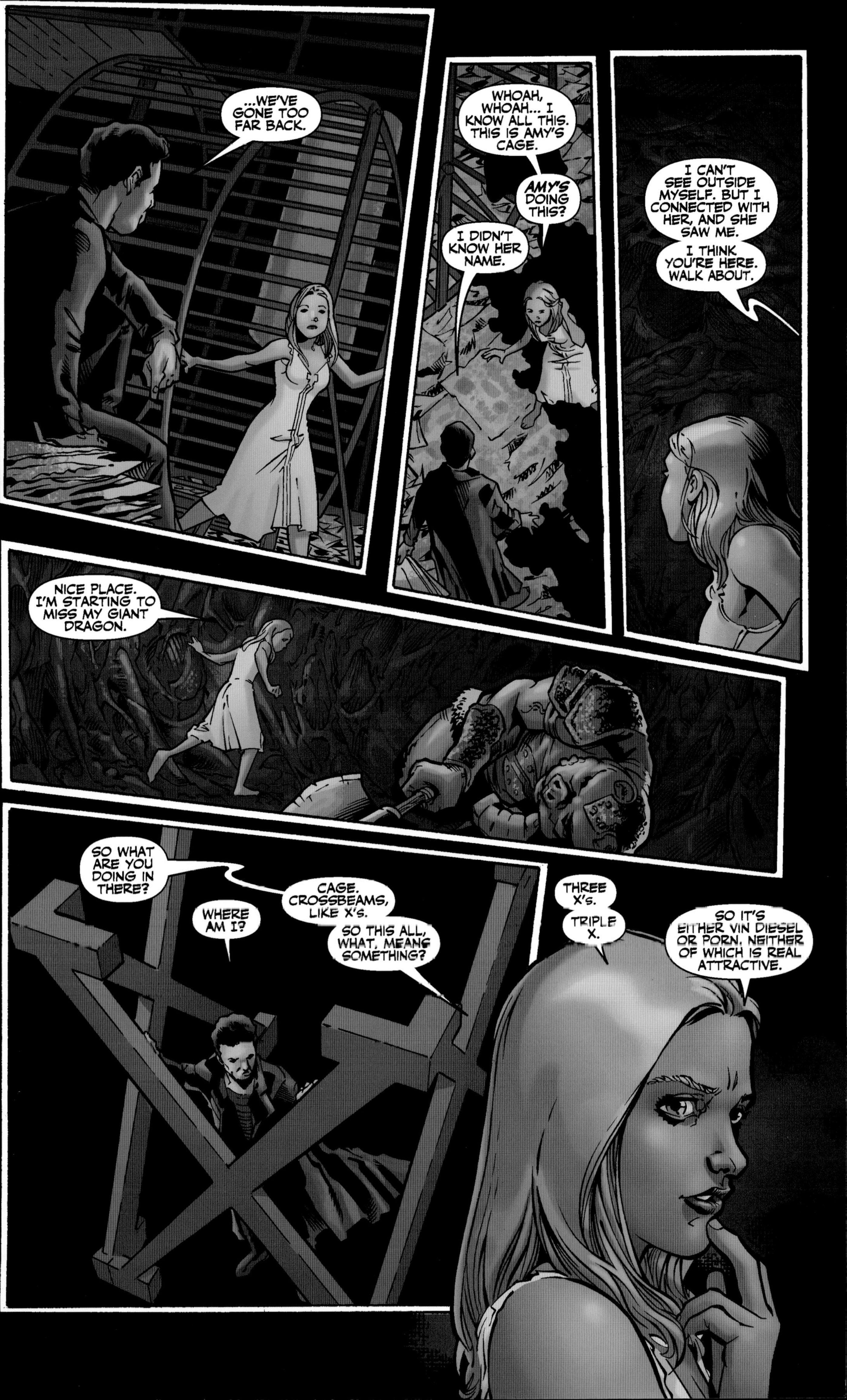
...WE'VE GONE TOO FAR BACK.
WHOAH, WHOAH... I KNOW ALL THIS. THIS IS AMY'S CAGE.
AMY'S DOING THIS?
I DIDN'T KNOW HER NAME.
I CAN'T SEE OUTSIDE MYSELF. BUT I CONNECTED WITH HER, AND SHE SAW ME.
I THINK YOU'RE HERE. WALK ABOUT.
NICE PLACE. I'M STARTING TO MISS MY GIANT DRAGON.
SO WHAT ARE YOU DOING IN THERE?
WHERE AM I?
CAGE. CROSSBEAMS, LIKE X's.
SO THIS ALL, WHAT, MEANS SOMETHING?
THREE X's.
TRIPLE X.
SO IT'S EITHER VIN DIESEL OR PORN. NEITHER OF WHICH IS REAL ATTRACTIVE.

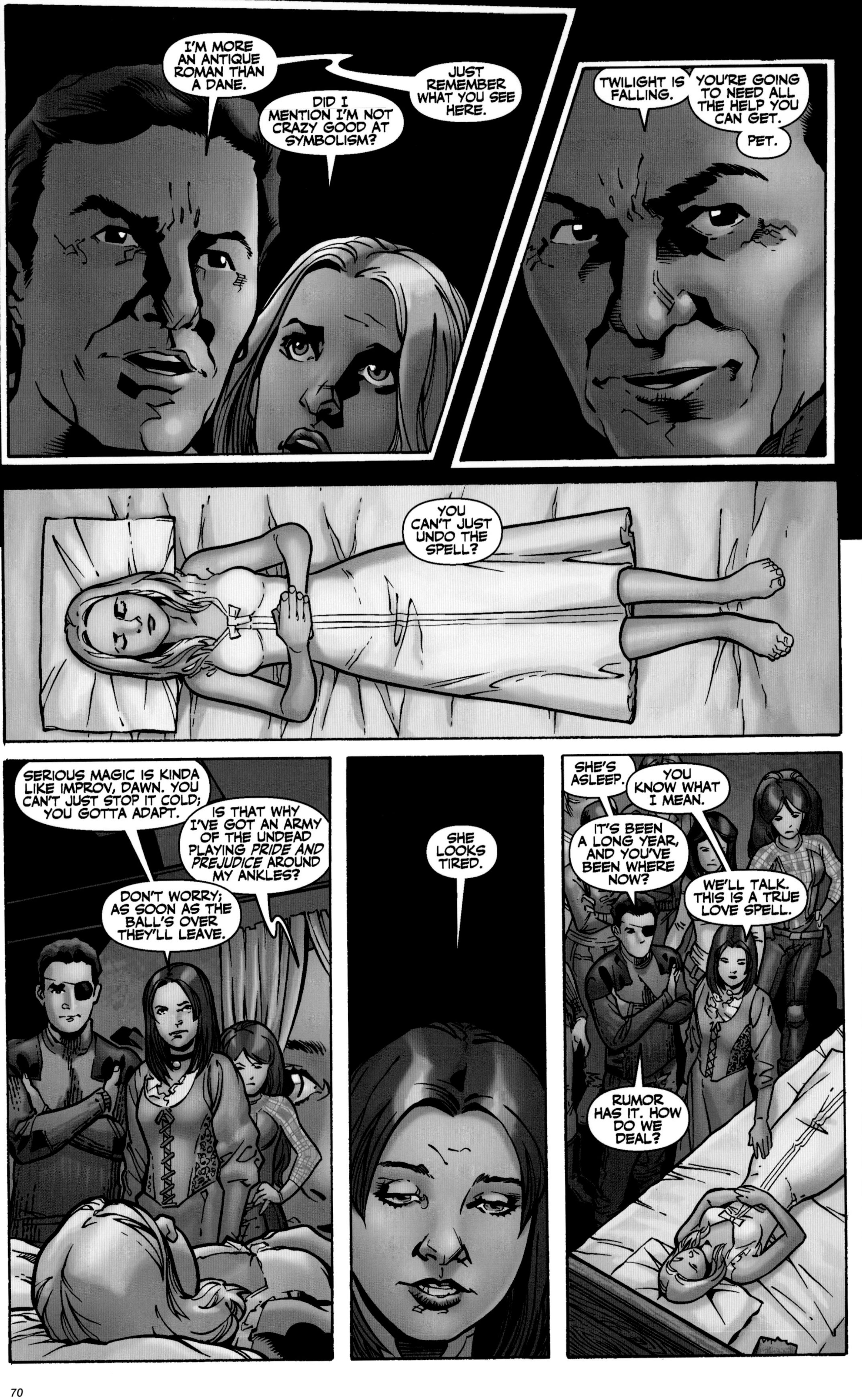
I'M MORE AN ANTIQUE ROMAN THAN A DANE.
JUST REMEMBER WHAT YOU SEE HERE.
DID I MENTION I'M NOT CRAZY GOOD AT SYMBOLISM?
TWILIGHT IS FALLING.
YOU'RE GOING TO NEED ALL THE HELP YOU CAN GET.
PET.
YOU CAN'T JUST UNDO THE SPELL?
SERIOUS MAGIC IS KINDA LIKE IMPROV, DAWN. YOU CAN'T JUST STOP IT COLD; YOU GOTTA ADAPT.
IS THAT WHY I'VE GOT AN ARMY OF THE UNDEAD PLAYING *PRIDE AND PREJUDICE* AROUND MY ANKLES?
DON'T WORRY; AS SOON AS THE BALL'S OVER THEY'LL LEAVE.
SHE LOOKS TIRED.
SHE'S ASLEEP.
YOU KNOW WHAT I MEAN.
IT'S BEEN A LONG YEAR, AND YOU'VE BEEN WHERE NOW?
WE'LL TALK. THIS IS A TRUE LOVE SPELL.
RUMOR HAS IT. HOW DO WE DEAL?

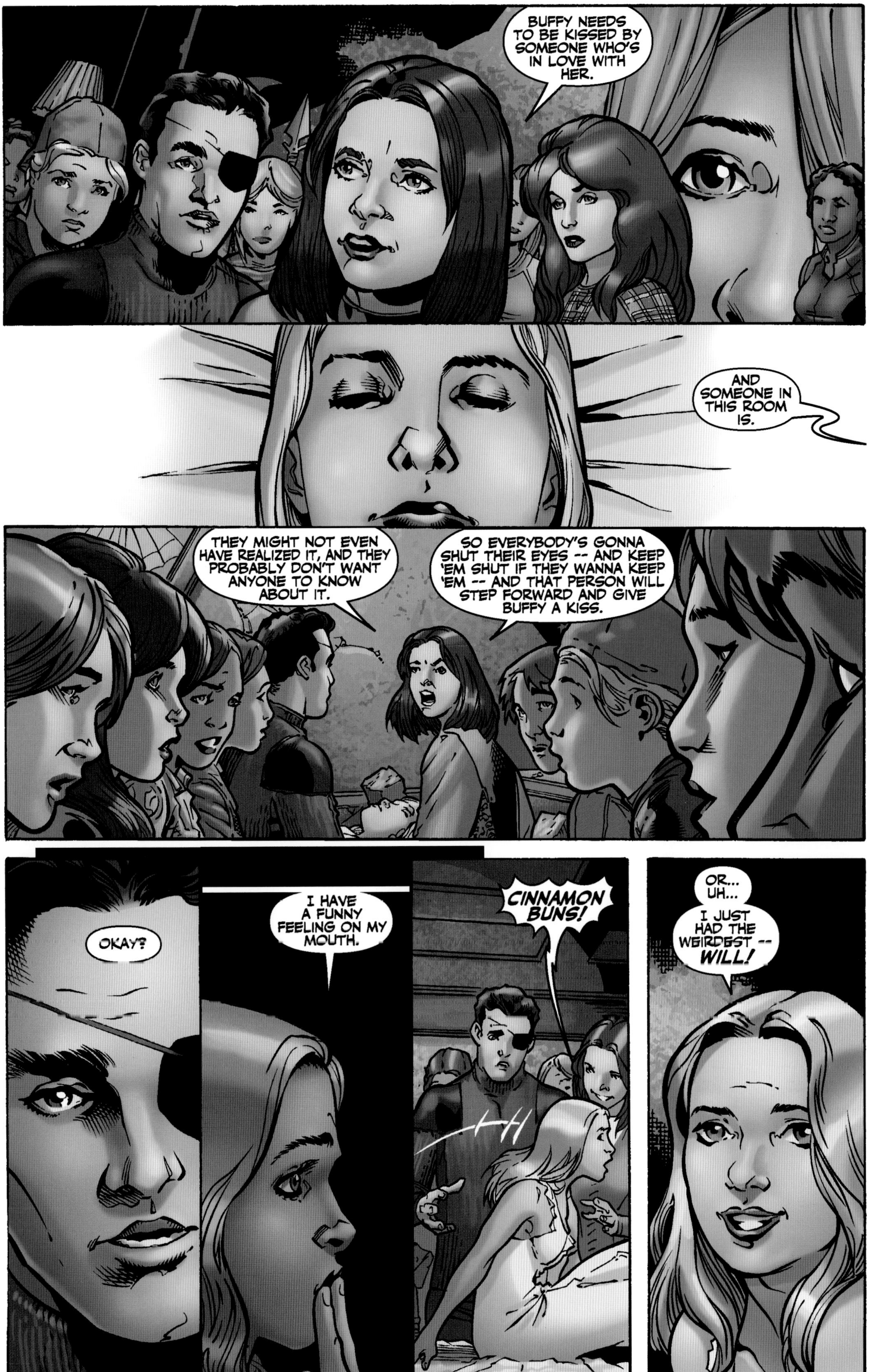
BUFFY NEEDS TO BE KISSED BY SOMEONE WHO'S IN LOVE WITH HER.
AND SOMEONE IN THIS ROOM IS.
THEY MIGHT NOT EVEN HAVE REALIZED IT, AND THEY PROBABLY DON'T WANT ANYONE TO KNOW ABOUT IT.
SO EVERYBODY'S GONNA SHUT THEIR EYES -- AND KEEP 'EM SHUT IF THEY WANNA KEEP 'EM -- AND THAT PERSON WILL STEP FORWARD AND GIVE BUFFY A KISS.
OKAY?
I HAVE A FUNNY FEELING ON MY MOUTH.
CINNAMON BUNS!
OR... UH... I JUST HAD THE WEIRDEST -- WILL!

WE ARE NOT AMUSED.

NO ONE'S EXACTLY GIGGLING ON THIS SIDE OF THE FENCE EITHER.

THREE OF OUR BROOD SLAIN!

THEY BROKE PROTOCOL.

THEY WERE LURED OUT THERE!

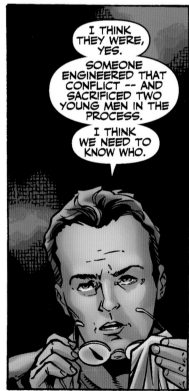

I THINK THEY WERE, YES.

SOMEONE ENGINEERED THAT CONFLICT -- AND SACRIFICED TWO YOUNG MEN IN THE PROCESS.

I THINK WE NEED TO KNOW WHO.

THIS SYMBOL IS MEANINGLESS TO US.

AND WE ARE NOT CONVINCED THIS IS NOT SOME SLAYER TRICK. WE HAVE EVER BEEN ENEMIES.

AND EVER SHALL BE. WE'LL COME TO GRIPS ONE DAY, BUT ON A DAY WE CHOOSE. WE'LL NOT BE LED THERE LIKE CATTLE.

RIGHT NOW, INFORMATION BENEFITS US BOTH. IF YOU LEARN ANYTHING...

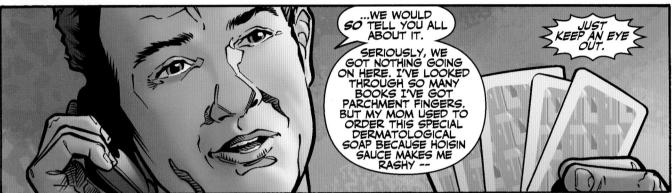

...WE WOULD SO TELL YOU ALL ABOUT IT.

SERIOUSLY, WE GOT NOTHING GOING ON HERE. I'VE LOOKED THROUGH SO MANY BOOKS I'VE GOT PARCHMENT FINGERS. BUT MY MOM USED TO ORDER THIS SPECIAL DERMATOLOGICAL SOAP BECAUSE HOISIN SAUCE MAKES ME RASHY --

JUST KEEP AN EYE OUT.

OH, WE'RE ON ALERT. YOU THINK AMY'S ATTACK AND THE SYMBOL ARE LINKED?

JUST A WHOLE LOTTA QUESTION MARKS COMING UP AT THE SAME TIME. WANTED TO MAKE SURE YOU'RE NOT SEEING ANY ACTION.

I WISH! WE'RE JUST TRYING TO THINK OF GAMES TO STAY AWAKE. IT'S DULLSVILLE, ITALY.

SOUNDS GOOD ENOUGH TO ME.

NO, TRUST ME...

...YOU'D BE BORED STIFF.

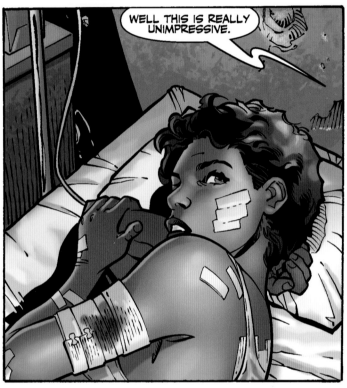

WELL THIS IS REALLY UNIMPRESSIVE.

ONE ATTACK BY THE UNDEAD AND RENEE HAS TO TAKE A NAP, "OH I'M ALL RUN THROUGH WITH A BROADSWORD, I HAVE TO LIE AROUND AND HEAL..."

BACK IN *MY* DAY, WHICH WAS ABOUT A WEEK AND A HALF AGO, WE TOOK OUR LUMPS AND WE GOT BACK UP AND WE CRIED LIKE BABIES AND QUIT AND THEN PUT ON WEIGHT.

I SHOULD'VE SEEN 'EM COMING.

THEY SHOULDA NEVER GOT OVER THAT WALL. WE LOST GIRLS BECAUSE OF --

OH, ARE YOU STILL TALKING?

YOU MESS UP, BUFFY'LL KICK YOUR ASS. ASSUMING SHE'S NOT IN A MYSTICAL COMA, IN WHICH CASE I OR A QUALIFIED REPRESENTATIVE WILL KICK YOUR ASS.

YOU RAISED THE CALL AND YOU STOOD YOUR GROUND. IT WAS SOLID SOLDIERING, SO SHUT UP AND HEAL.

YOU'RE SO BUTCH.

ALMOST A KIND OF MASCULINE VIBE, DON'T YOU THINK?

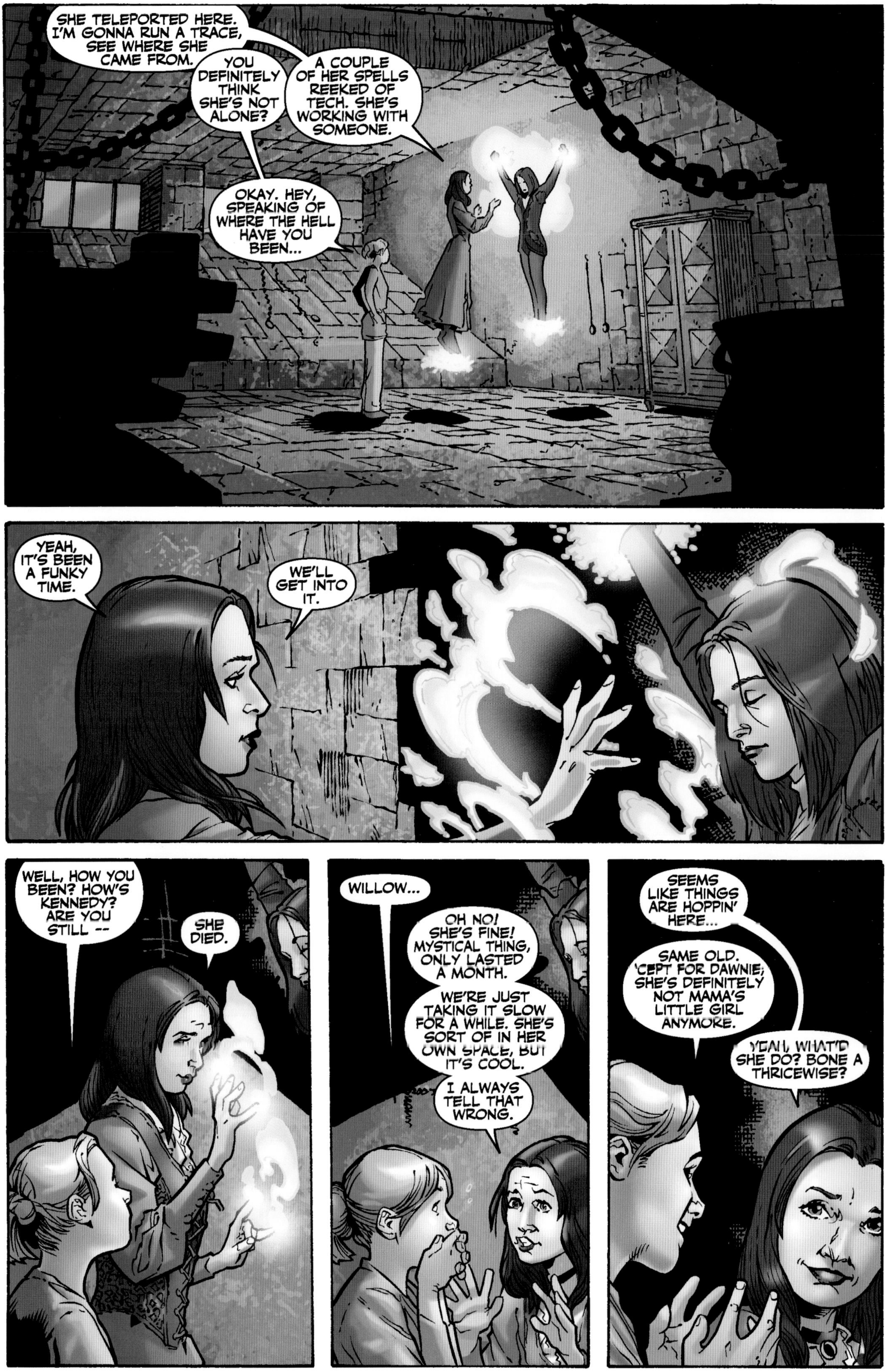

SHE TELEPORTED HERE. I'M GONNA RUN A TRACE, SEE WHERE SHE CAME FROM.
YOU DEFINITELY THINK SHE'S NOT ALONE?
A COUPLE OF HER SPELLS REEKED OF TECH. SHE'S WORKING WITH SOMEONE.
OKAY. HEY, SPEAKING OF WHERE THE HELL HAVE YOU BEEN...
YEAH, IT'S BEEN A FUNKY TIME.
WE'LL GET INTO IT.
WELL, HOW YOU BEEN? HOW'S KENNEDY? ARE YOU STILL --
SHE DIED.
WILLOW...
OH NO! SHE'S FINE! MYSTICAL THING, ONLY LASTED A MONTH.
WE'RE JUST TAKING IT SLOW FOR A WHILE. SHE'S SORT OF IN HER OWN SPACE, BUT IT'S COOL.
I ALWAYS TELL THAT WRONG.
SEEMS LIKE THINGS ARE HOPPIN' HERE...
SAME OLD. 'CEPT FOR DAWNIE; SHE'S DEFINITELY NOT MAMA'S LITTLE GIRL ANYMORE.
YEAH, WHAT'D SHE DO? BONE A THRICEWISE?

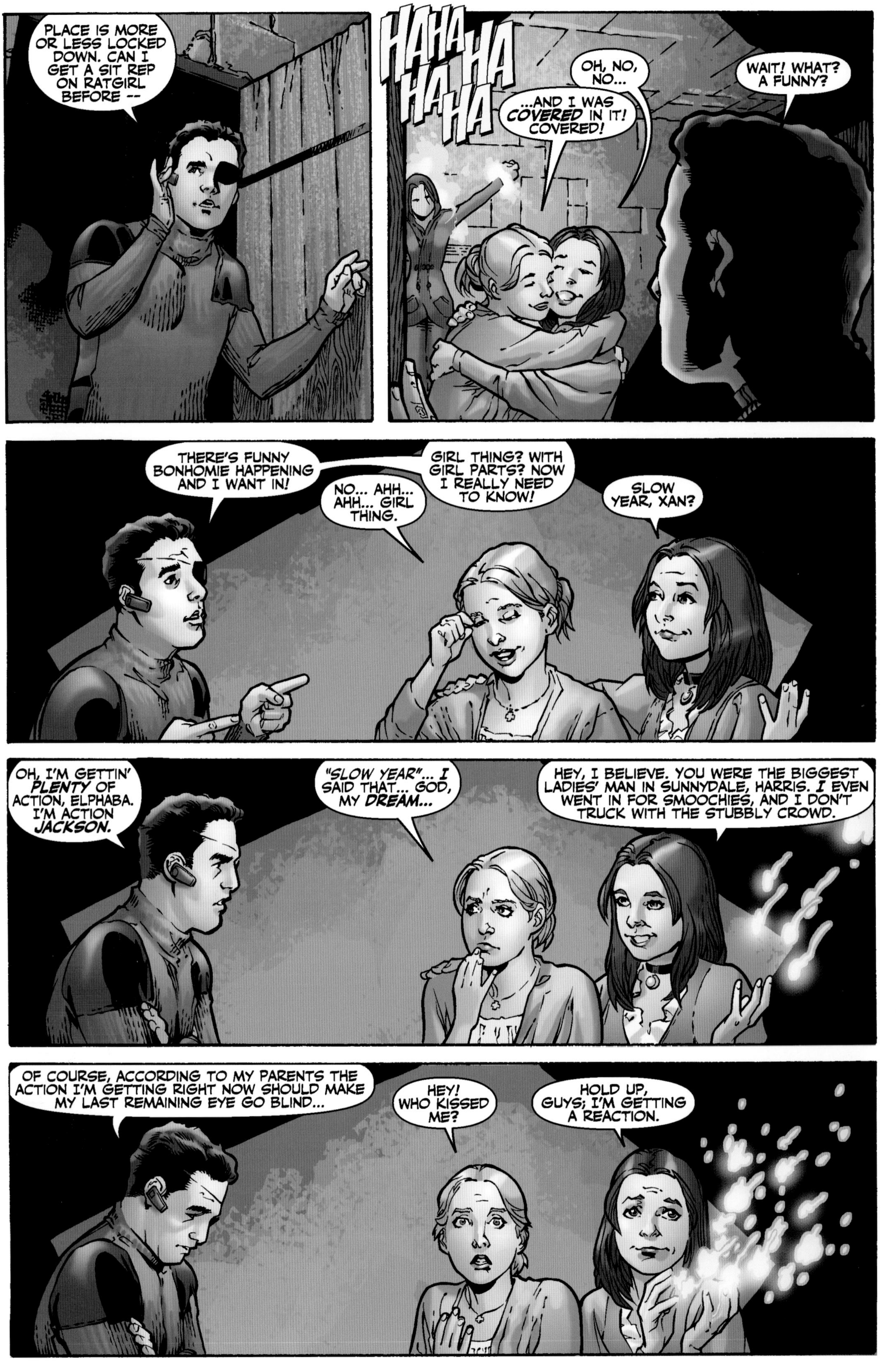
PLACE IS MORE OR LESS LOCKED DOWN. CAN I GET A SIT REP ON RATGIRL BEFORE --
HAHAHA HAHAHA
OH, NO, NO...
...AND I WAS COVERED IN IT! COVERED!
WAIT! WHAT? A FUNNY?
THERE'S FUNNY BONHOMIE HAPPENING AND I WANT IN!
NO... AHH... AHH... GIRL THING.
GIRL THING? WITH GIRL PARTS? NOW I REALLY NEED TO KNOW!
SLOW YEAR, XAN?
OH, I'M GETTIN' PLENTY OF ACTION, ELPHABA. I'M ACTION JACKSON.
"SLOW YEAR"... I SAID THAT... GOD, MY DREAM...
HEY, I BELIEVE. YOU WERE THE BIGGEST LADIES' MAN IN SUNNYDALE, HARRIS. I EVEN WENT IN FOR SMOOCHIES, AND I DON'T TRUCK WITH THE STUBBLY CROWD.
OF COURSE, ACCORDING TO MY PARENTS THE ACTION I'M GETTING RIGHT NOW SHOULD MAKE MY LAST REMAINING EYE GO BLIND...
HEY! WHO KISSED ME?
HOLD UP, GUYS; I'M GETTING A REACTION.

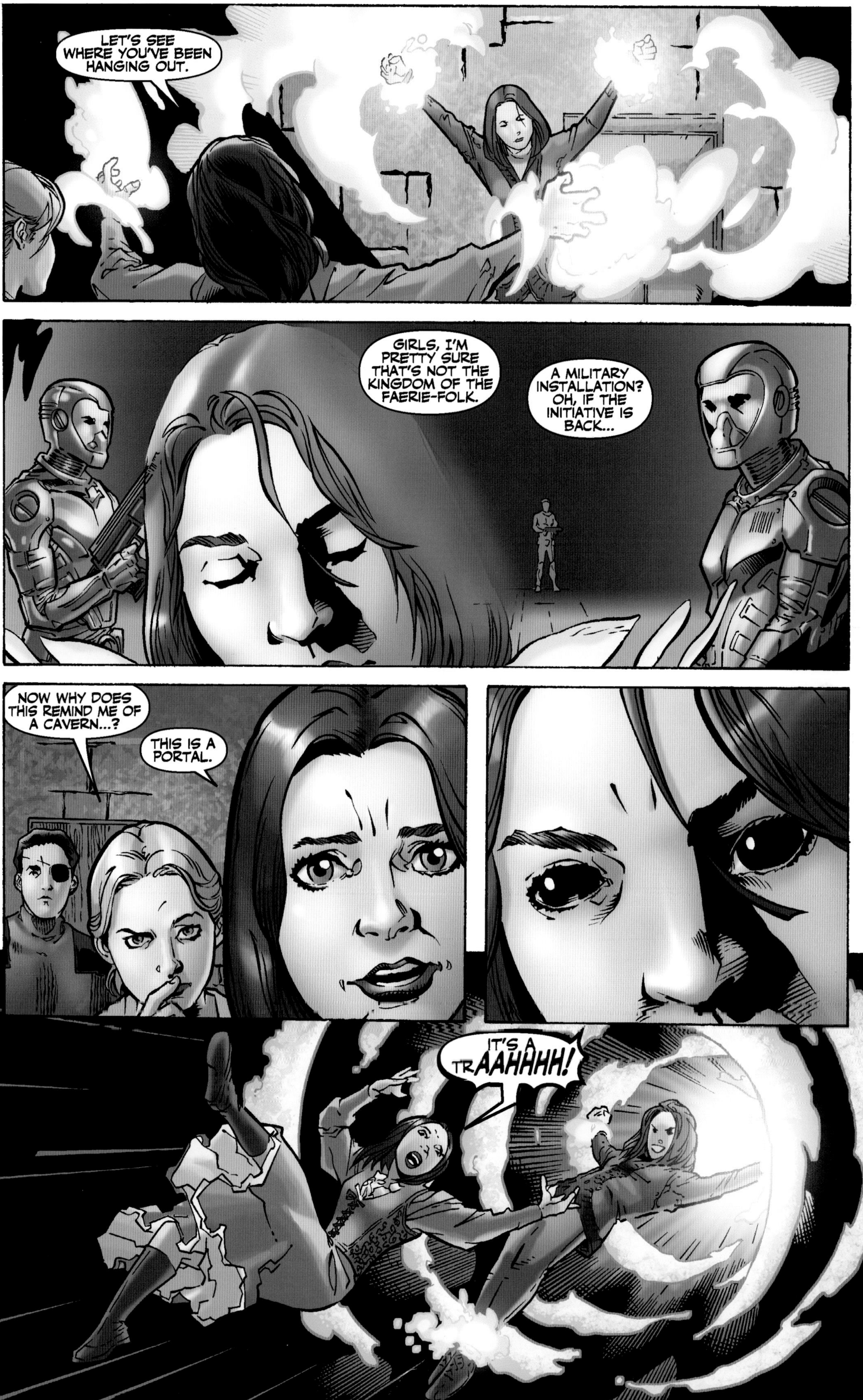
LET'S SEE WHERE YOU'VE BEEN HANGING OUT.
GIRLS, I'M PRETTY SURE THAT'S NOT THE KINGDOM OF THE FAERIE-FOLK.
A MILITARY INSTALLATION? OH, IF THE INITIATIVE IS BACK...
NOW WHY DOES THIS REMIND ME OF A CAVERN...?
THIS IS A PORTAL.
IT'S A TRAAHHHH!

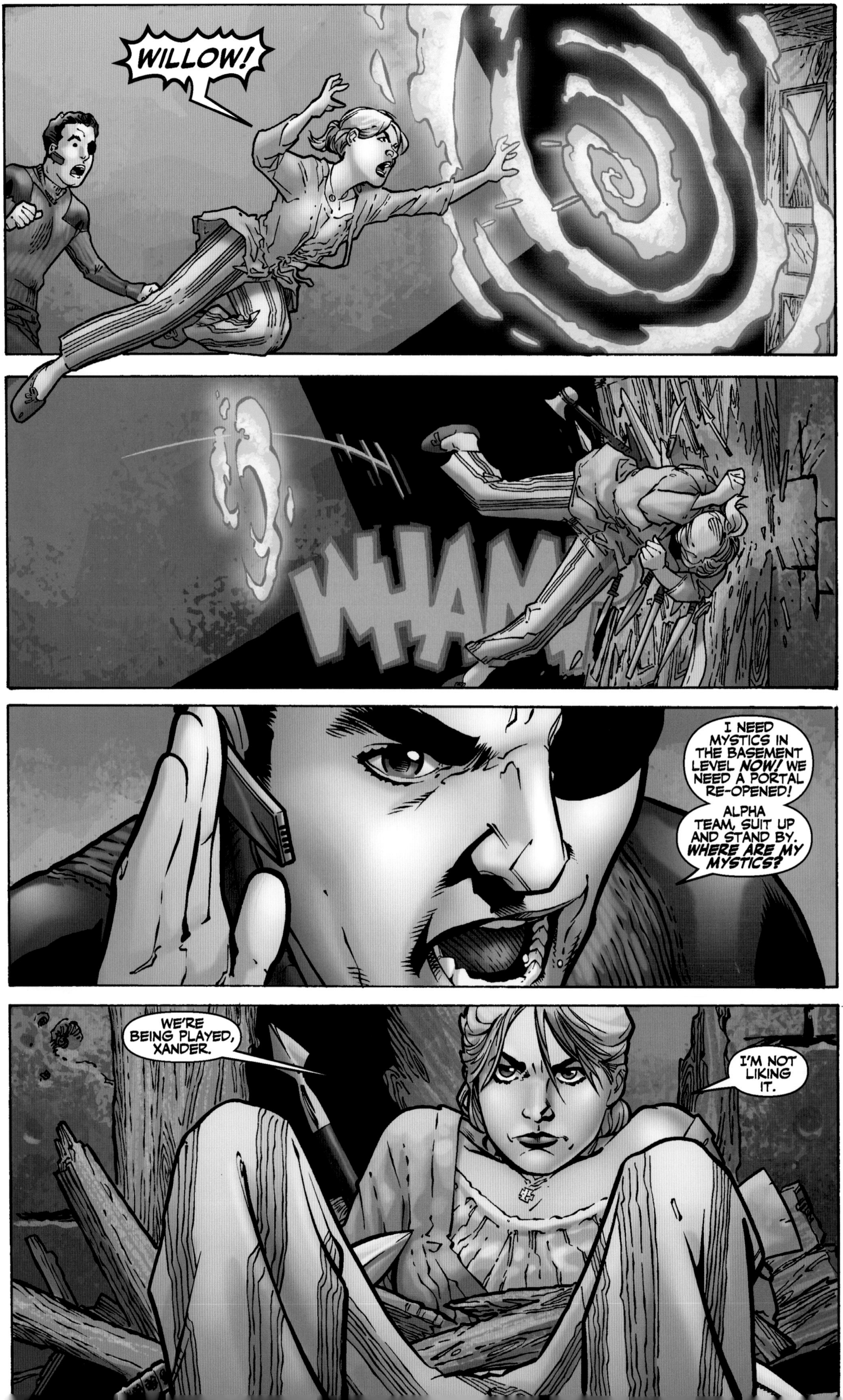
WILLOW!
WHAM
I NEED MYSTICS IN THE BASEMENT LEVEL NOW! WE NEED A PORTAL RE-OPENED!
ALPHA TEAM, SUIT UP AND STAND BY. WHERE ARE MY MYSTICS?
WE'RE BEING PLAYED, XANDER.
I'M NOT LIKING IT.

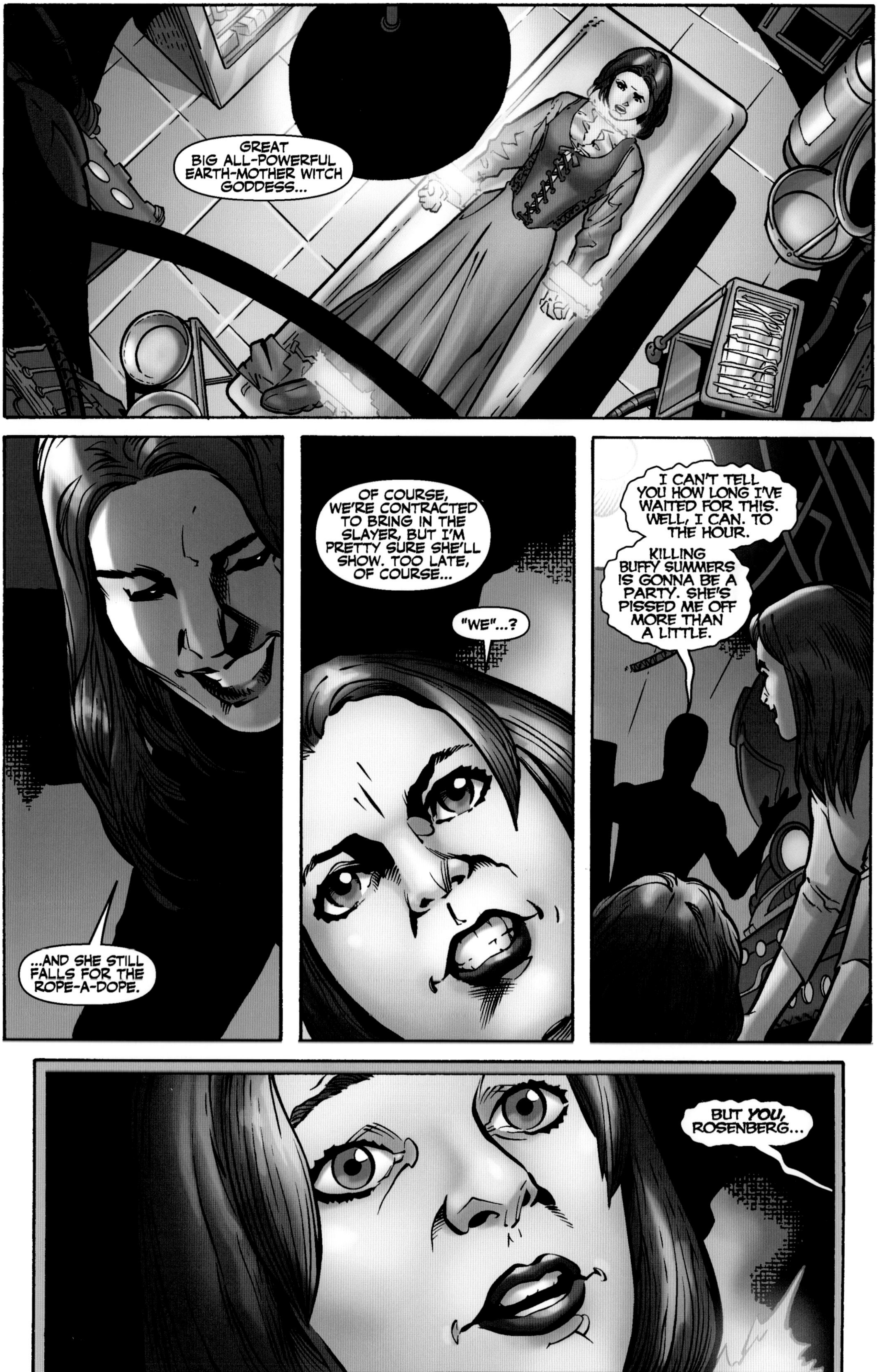
GREAT BIG ALL-POWERFUL EARTH-MOTHER WITCH GODDESS...
...AND SHE STILL FALLS FOR THE ROPE-A-DOPE.
OF COURSE, WE'RE CONTRACTED TO BRING IN THE SLAYER, BUT I'M PRETTY SURE SHE'LL SHOW. TOO LATE, OF COURSE...
"WE"...?
I CAN'T TELL YOU HOW LONG I'VE WAITED FOR THIS. WELL, I CAN. TO THE HOUR.
KILLING BUFFY SUMMERS IS GONNA BE A PARTY. SHE'S PISSED ME OFF MORE THAN A LITTLE.
BUT YOU, ROSENBERG...

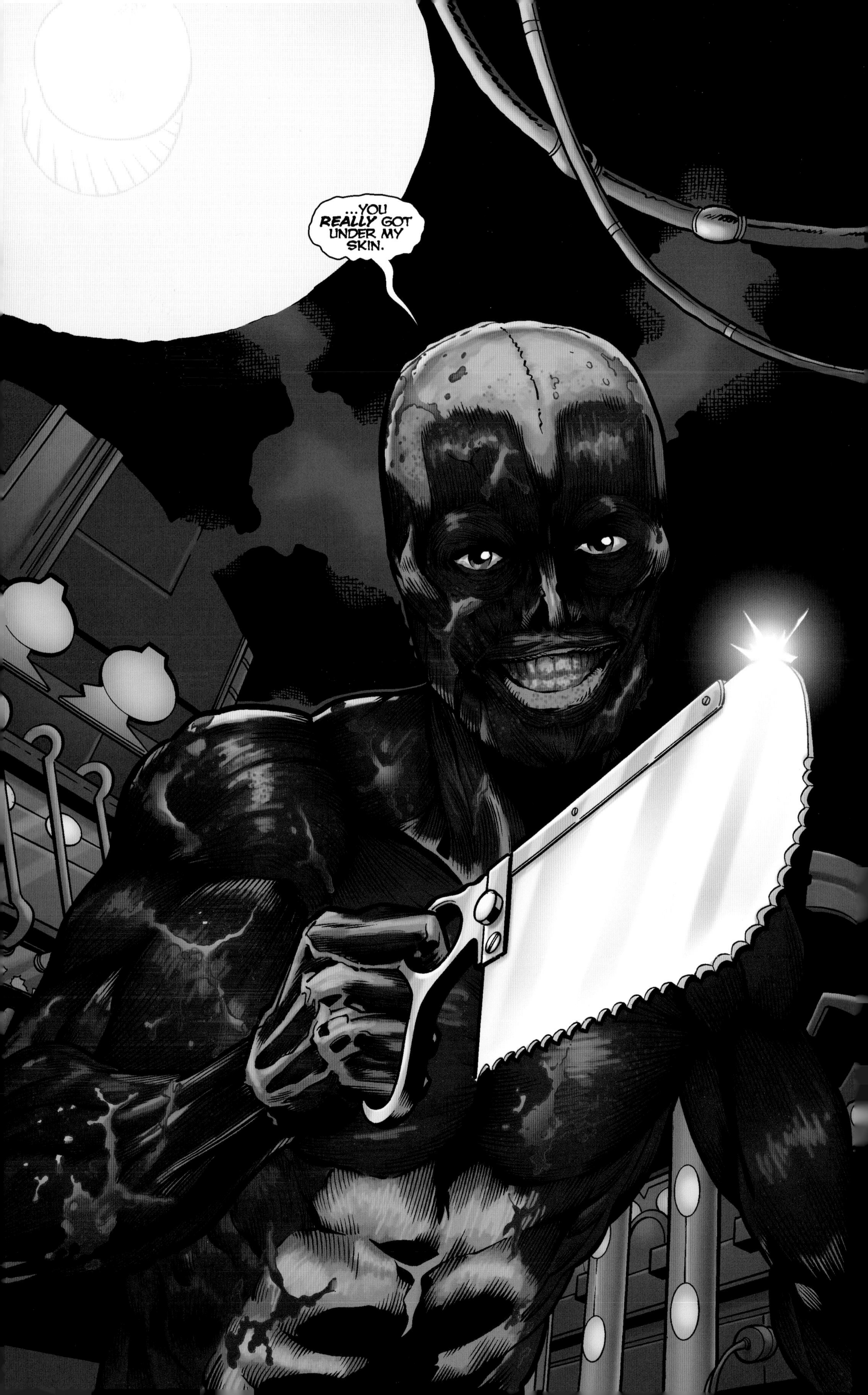
...YOU REALLY GOT UNDER MY SKIN.

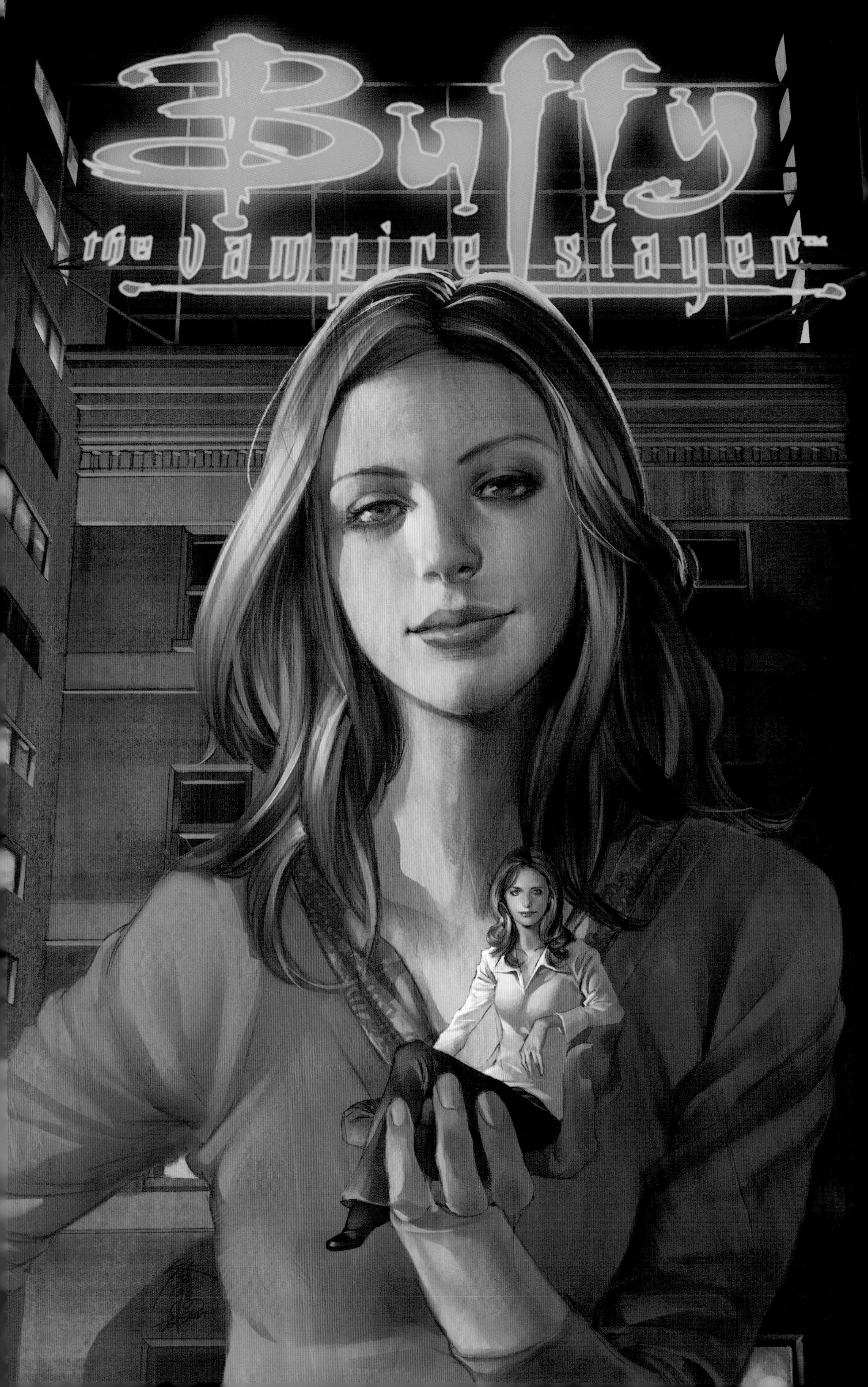
Buffy
the vampire slayer™

The LONG WAY HOME

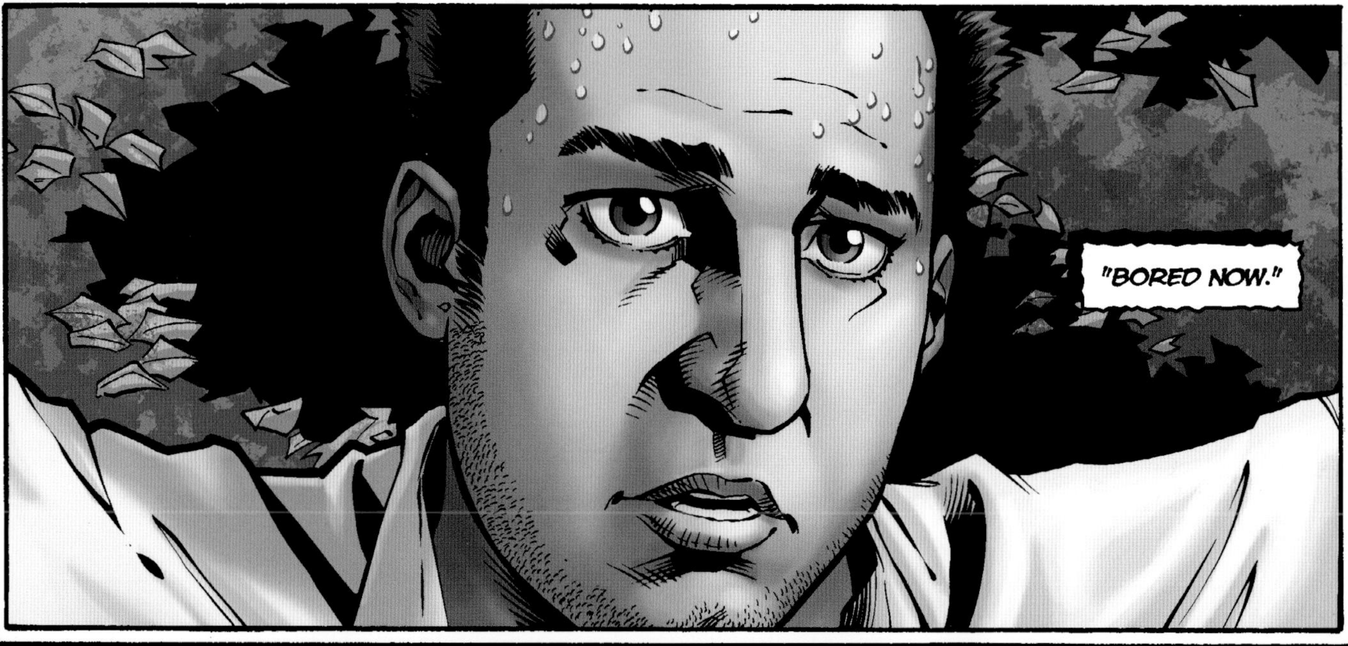
"BORED NOW."

Part Four

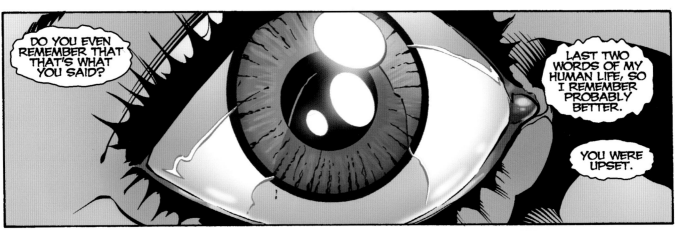

DO YOU EVEN REMEMBER THAT THAT'S WHAT YOU SAID?

LAST TWO WORDS OF MY HUMAN LIFE, SO I REMEMBER PROBABLY BETTER.

YOU WERE UPSET.

KINDA SPIRALING, IS WHAT THEY SAY.

WHICH IS, HEY--I'M NOT EXCUSING WHERE I WAS AT, SO DON'T THINK--

I MEAN YOU-- IF AMY HADN'T BEEN WATCHING YOU, SHE WOULD NEVER HAVE STARTED WATCHING ME.

WATCHING OVER ME.

"DO YOU KNOW SHE HAD MAYBE A FOUR-SECOND WINDOW AFTER MY SKIN CAME OFF BEFORE I DIED OF SHOCK ALONE?

"THAT FLASH-PAPER DISAPPEARING TRICK WAS PRETTY HOKEY, WE KID ABOUT THAT, BUT THINKING ON YOUR FEET? THIS IS THE GIRL.

"HER MAGIC IS MY SKIN."

THAT TIME WE CAME UP WITH THE SPELL FOR YOU AND YOUR NEW GIRLFRIEND--

--AND HEY, THAT WAS QUICK, I WAS STILL LEARNING TO WALK AGAIN AND YOU'RE ALREADY IN THE FRESH TRIM...

I REMEMBER THINKING AND IT COMES UP AGAIN IN THIS SITUATION, I JUST HAVE TO WONDER...

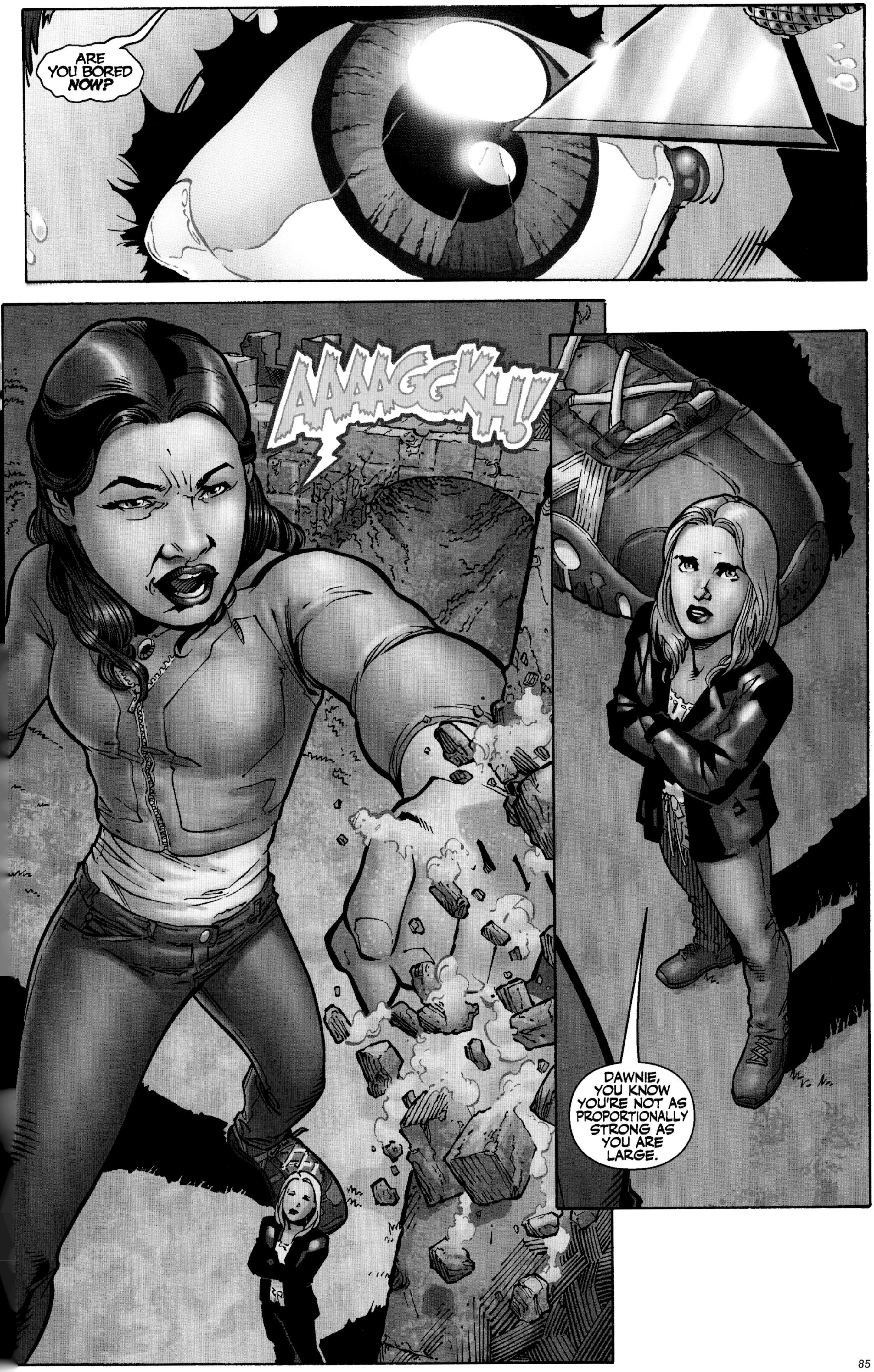
ARE YOU BORED NOW?
AAAAGGKH!!
DAWNIE, YOU KNOW YOU'RE NOT AS PROPORTIONALLY STRONG AS YOU ARE LARGE.

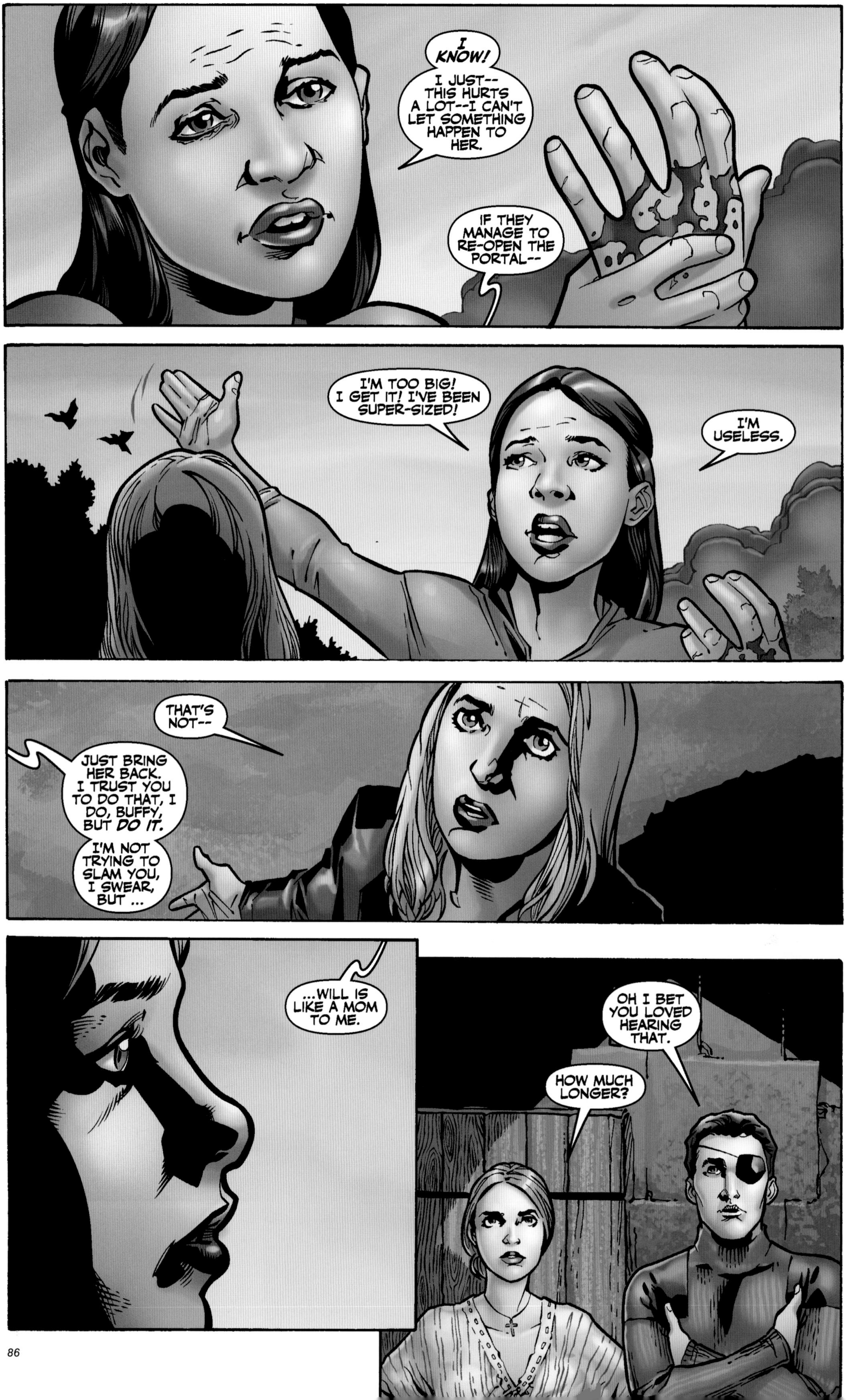
I KNOW!
I JUST-- THIS HURTS A LOT--I CAN'T LET SOMETHING HAPPEN TO HER.
IF THEY MANAGE TO RE-OPEN THE PORTAL--
I'M TOO BIG! I GET IT! I'VE BEEN SUPER-SIZED!
I'M USELESS.
THAT'S NOT--
JUST BRING HER BACK. I TRUST YOU TO DO THAT, I DO, BUFFY, BUT DO IT.
I'M NOT TRYING TO SLAM YOU, I SWEAR, BUT ...
...WILL IS LIKE A MOM TO ME.
OH I BET YOU LOVED HEARING THAT.
HOW MUCH LONGER?

XANDER...

I'M NOT A FIGHTER, I GOT NO MAGIC. IF THERE'S ANY KIND OF SATELLITE BOUNCE I'M YOUR EYES AND EARS, THAT'S IT.

TELEPORTATION'S NOT AN EXACT MAGIC, BUFFY. AND GOOD AS THESE GIRLS ARE, WE'RE NOT SPORTIN' A GILES, SO...

THEY SAY A COUPLE HOURS. PORTAL ECHO BIG ENOUGH FOR ... MAYBE ONE OR TWO GUYS, TOPS.

WHAT CAN I DO?

IT'S WILL. WE PLAY IT SMART.

AND WE REMEMBER SHE'S STRONGER THAN ALL OF US.

FIGURE OUT WHO YOUR MOVING BUDDY IS.

AND THEREIN LIES, IT'S VERY OPERATIC, YOUR DOWNFALL.

YOU'RE JUST SO STRONG.

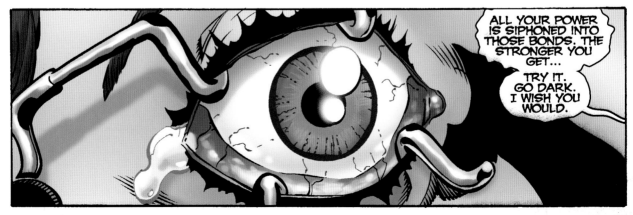

ALL YOUR POWER IS SIPHONED INTO THOSE BONDS. THE STRONGER YOU GET...

TRY IT. GO DARK. I WISH YOU WOULD.

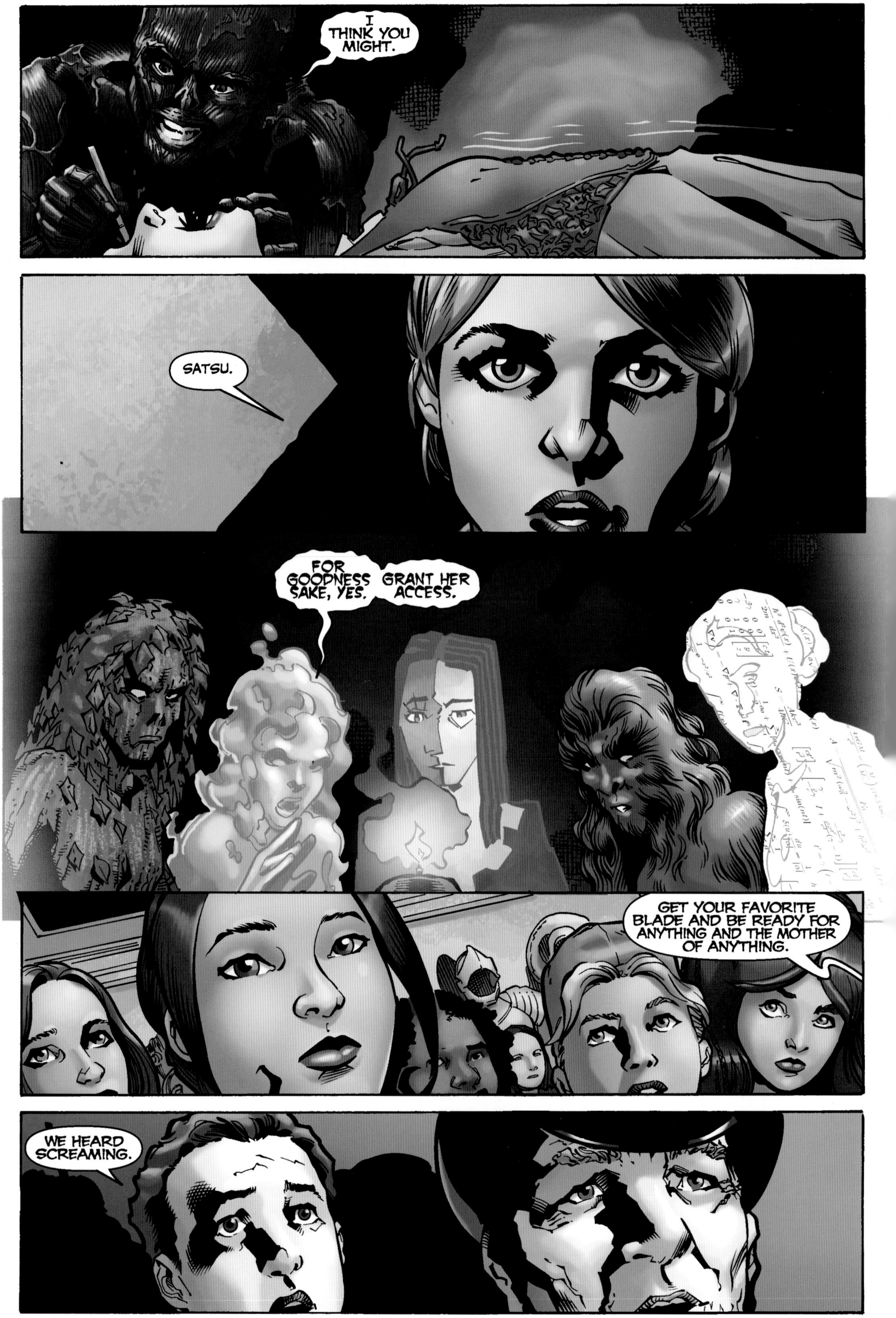
I THINK YOU MIGHT.
SATSU.
FOR GOODNESS SAKE, YES.
GRANT HER ACCESS.
GET YOUR FAVORITE BLADE AND BE READY FOR ANYTHING AND THE MOTHER OF ANYTHING.
WE HEARD SCREAMING.

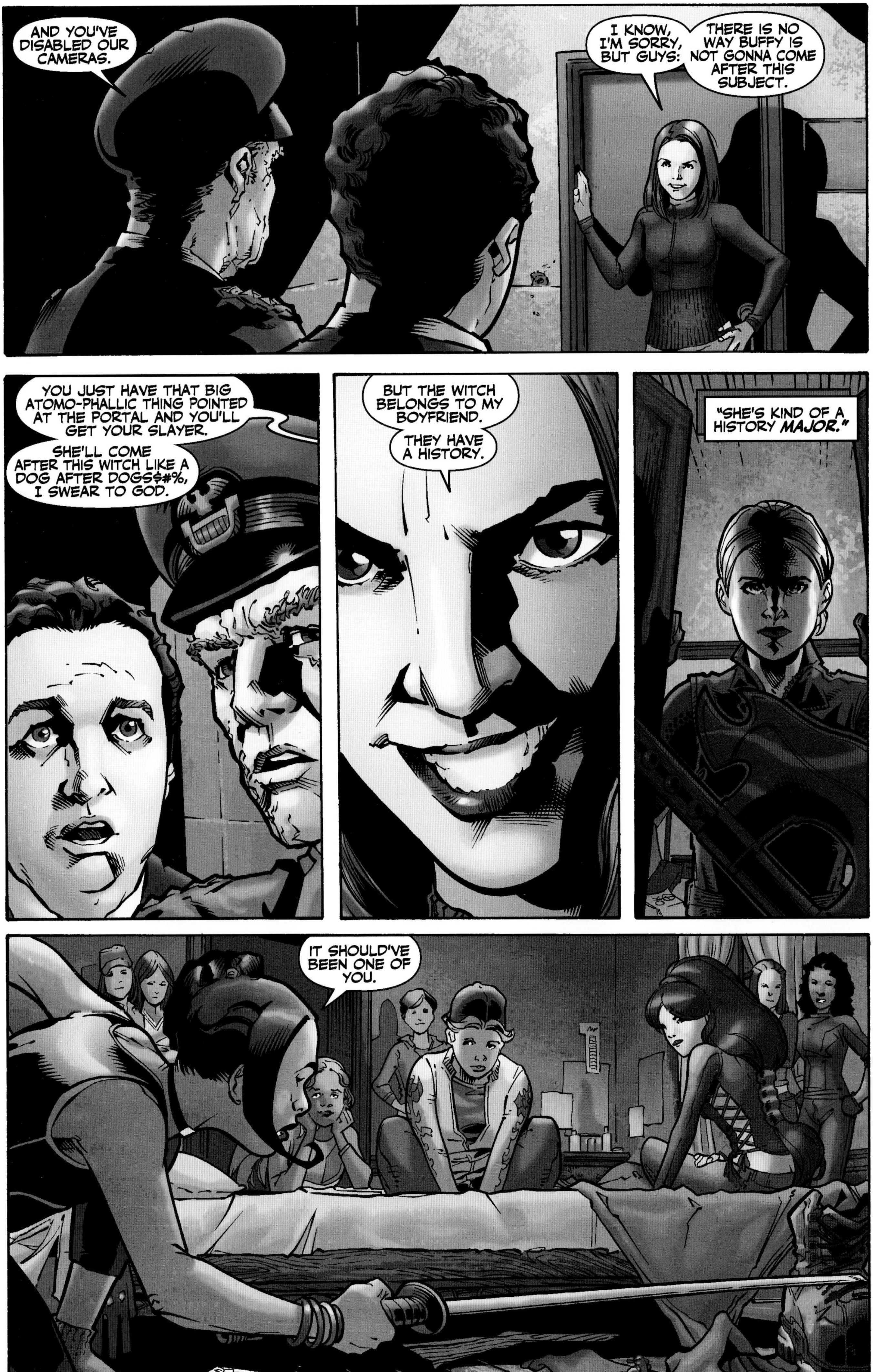
AND YOU'VE DISABLED OUR CAMERAS.
I KNOW, I'M SORRY, BUT GUYS:
THERE IS NO WAY BUFFY IS NOT GONNA COME AFTER THIS SUBJECT.
YOU JUST HAVE THAT BIG ATOMO-PHALLIC THING POINTED AT THE PORTAL AND YOU'LL GET YOUR SLAYER.
SHE'LL COME AFTER THIS WITCH LIKE A DOG AFTER DOGS$#%, I SWEAR TO GOD.
BUT THE WITCH BELONGS TO MY BOYFRIEND.
THEY HAVE A HISTORY.
"SHE'S KIND OF A HISTORY MAJOR."
IT SHOULD'VE BEEN ONE OF YOU.

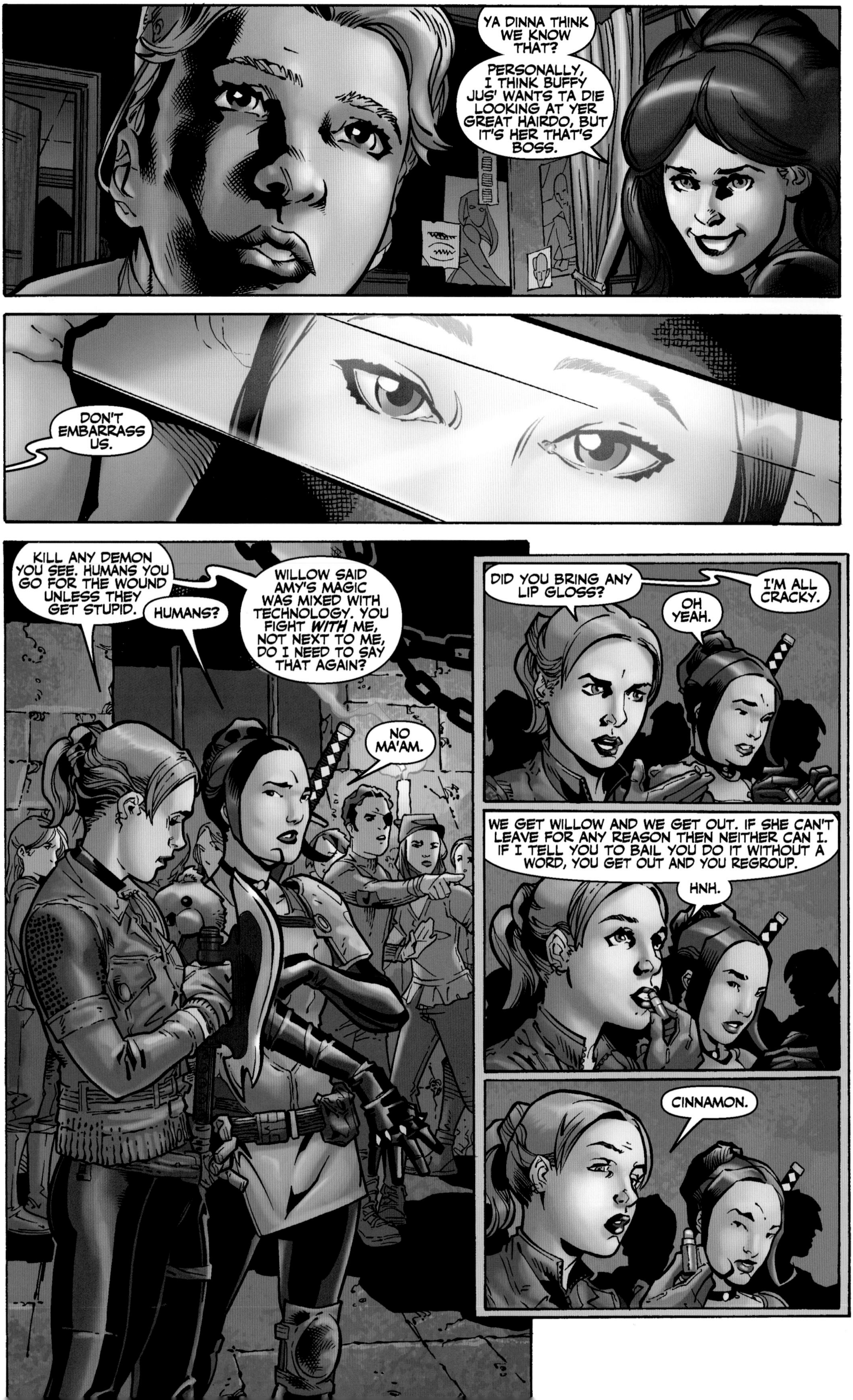
YA DINNA THINK WE KNOW THAT?
PERSONALLY, I THINK BUFFY JUS' WANTS TA DIE LOOKING AT YER GREAT HAIRDO, BUT IT'S HER THAT'S BOSS.
DON'T EMBARRASS US.
KILL ANY DEMON YOU SEE. HUMANS YOU GO FOR THE WOUND UNLESS THEY GET STUPID.
HUMANS?
WILLOW SAID AMY'S MAGIC WAS MIXED WITH TECHNOLOGY. YOU FIGHT WITH ME, NOT NEXT TO ME, DO I NEED TO SAY THAT AGAIN?
NO MA'AM.
DID YOU BRING ANY LIP GLOSS?
I'M ALL CRACKY.
OH YEAH.
WE GET WILLOW AND WE GET OUT. IF SHE CAN'T LEAVE FOR ANY REASON THEN NEITHER CAN I. IF I TELL YOU TO BAIL YOU DO IT WITHOUT A WORD, YOU GET OUT AND YOU REGROUP.
HNH.
CINNAMON.

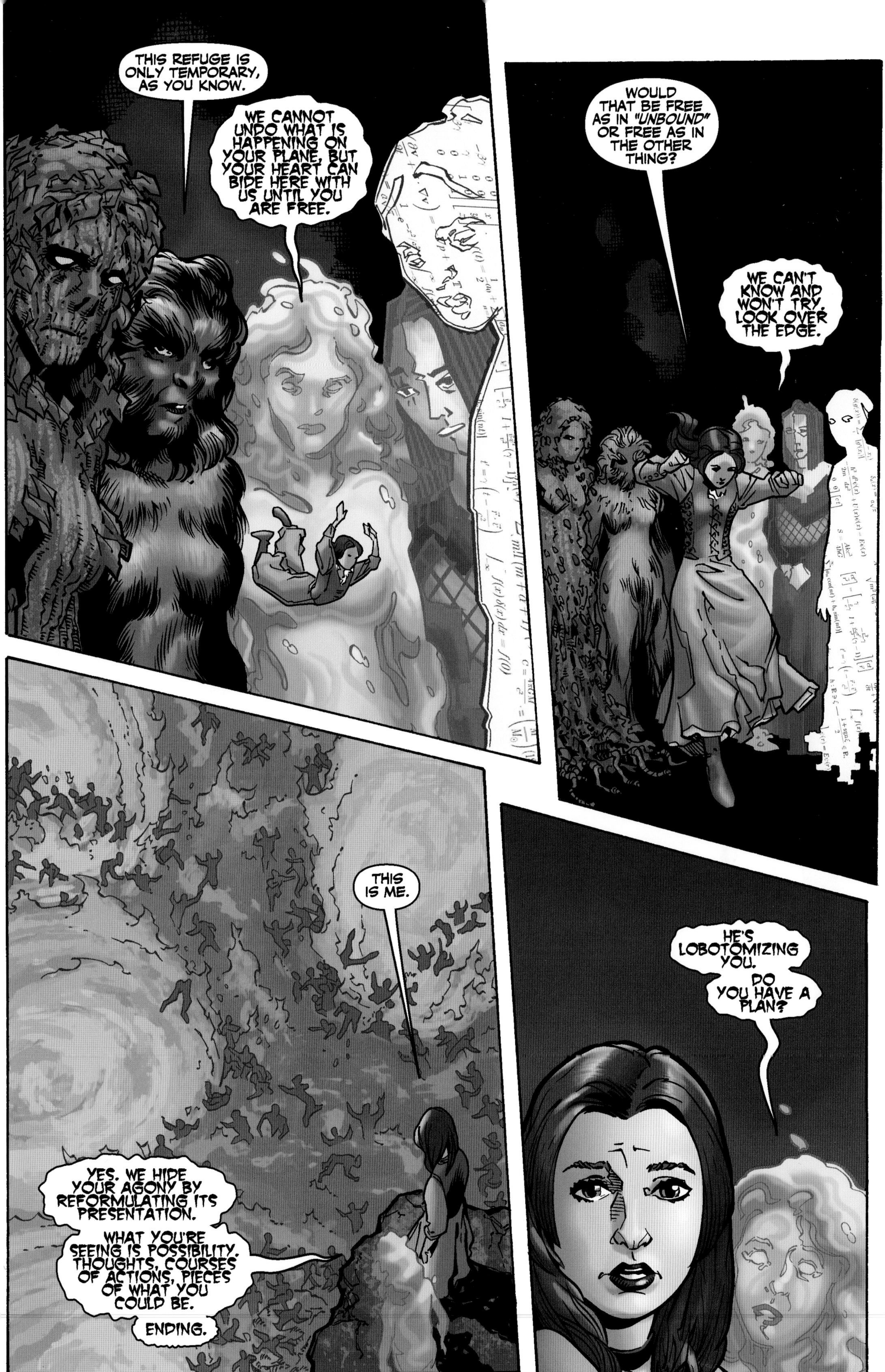
THIS REFUGE IS ONLY TEMPORARY, AS YOU KNOW.
WE CANNOT UNDO WHAT IS HAPPENING ON YOUR PLANE, BUT YOUR HEART CAN BIDE HERE WITH US UNTIL YOU ARE FREE.
WOULD THAT BE FREE AS IN "UNBOUND" OR FREE AS IN THE OTHER THING?
WE CAN'T KNOW AND WON'T TRY. LOOK OVER THE EDGE.
THIS IS ME.
YES. WE HIDE YOUR AGONY BY REFORMULATING ITS PRESENTATION.
WHAT YOU'RE SEEING IS POSSIBILITY. THOUGHTS, COURSES OF ACTIONS, PIECES OF WHAT YOU COULD BE.
ENDING.
HE'S LOBOTOMIZING YOU.
DO YOU HAVE A PLAN?

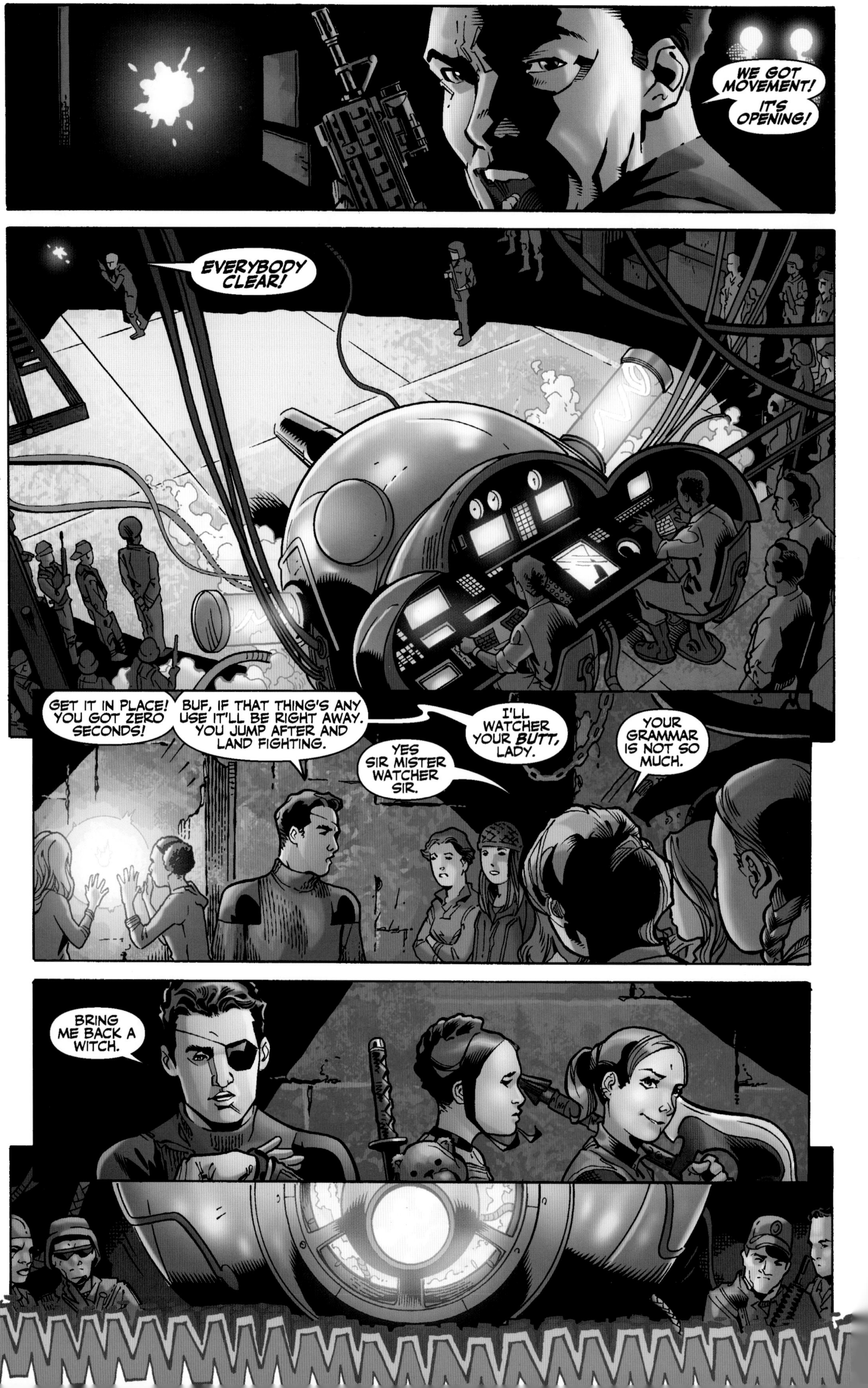
WE GOT MOVEMENT! IT'S OPENING!
EVERYBODY CLEAR!
GET IT IN PLACE! YOU GOT ZERO SECONDS!
BUF, IF THAT THING'S ANY USE IT'LL BE RIGHT AWAY. YOU JUMP AFTER AND LAND FIGHTING.
YES SIR MISTER WATCHER SIR.
I'LL WATCHER YOUR BUTT, LADY.
YOUR GRAMMAR IS NOT SO MUCH.
BRING ME BACK A WITCH.

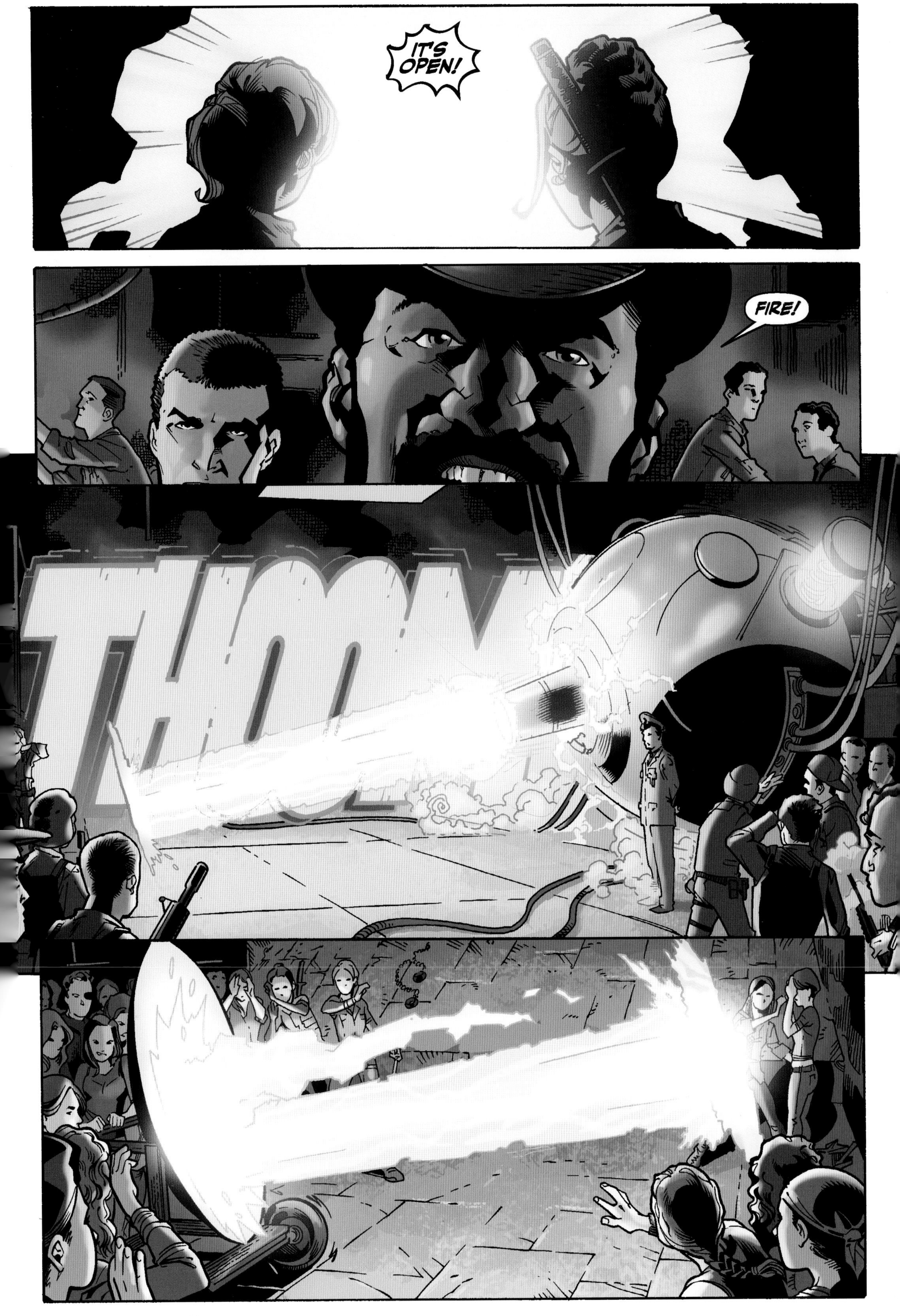
IT'S OPEN!
FIRE!

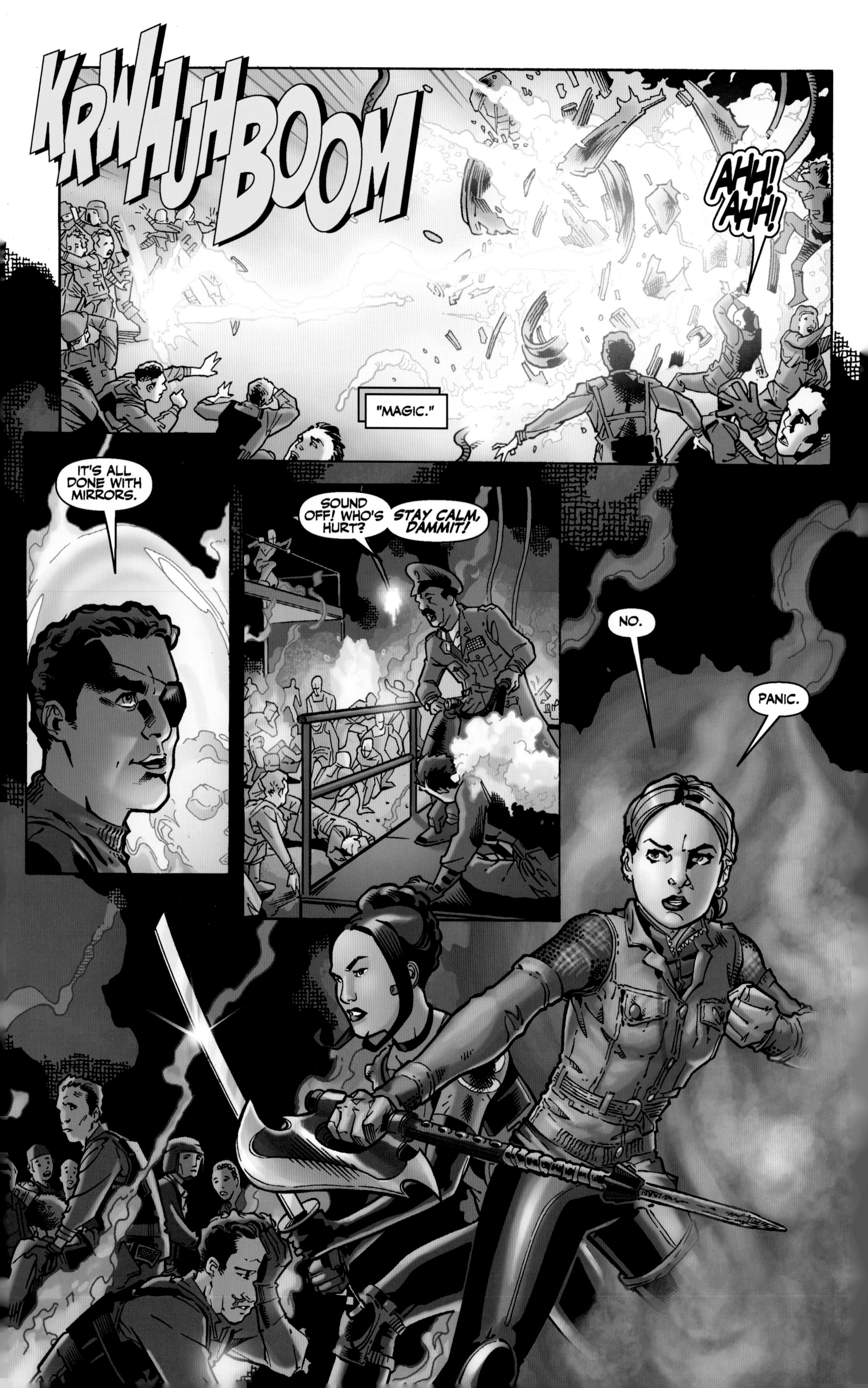
KRWHUHBOOM
AHH! AHH!
"MAGIC."
IT'S ALL DONE WITH MIRRORS.
SOUND OFF! WHO'S HURT?
STAY CALM, DAMMIT!
NO.
PANIC.

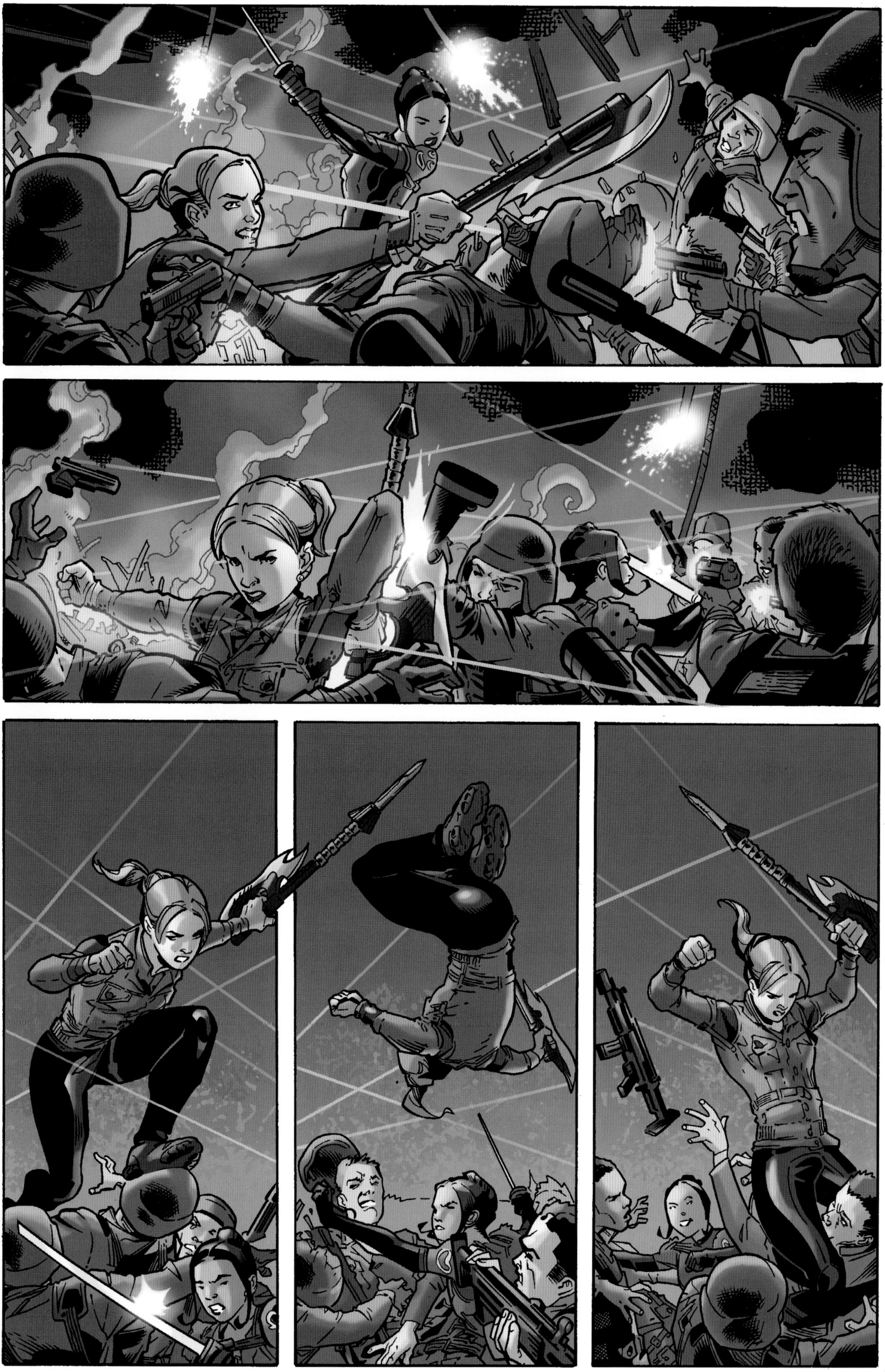

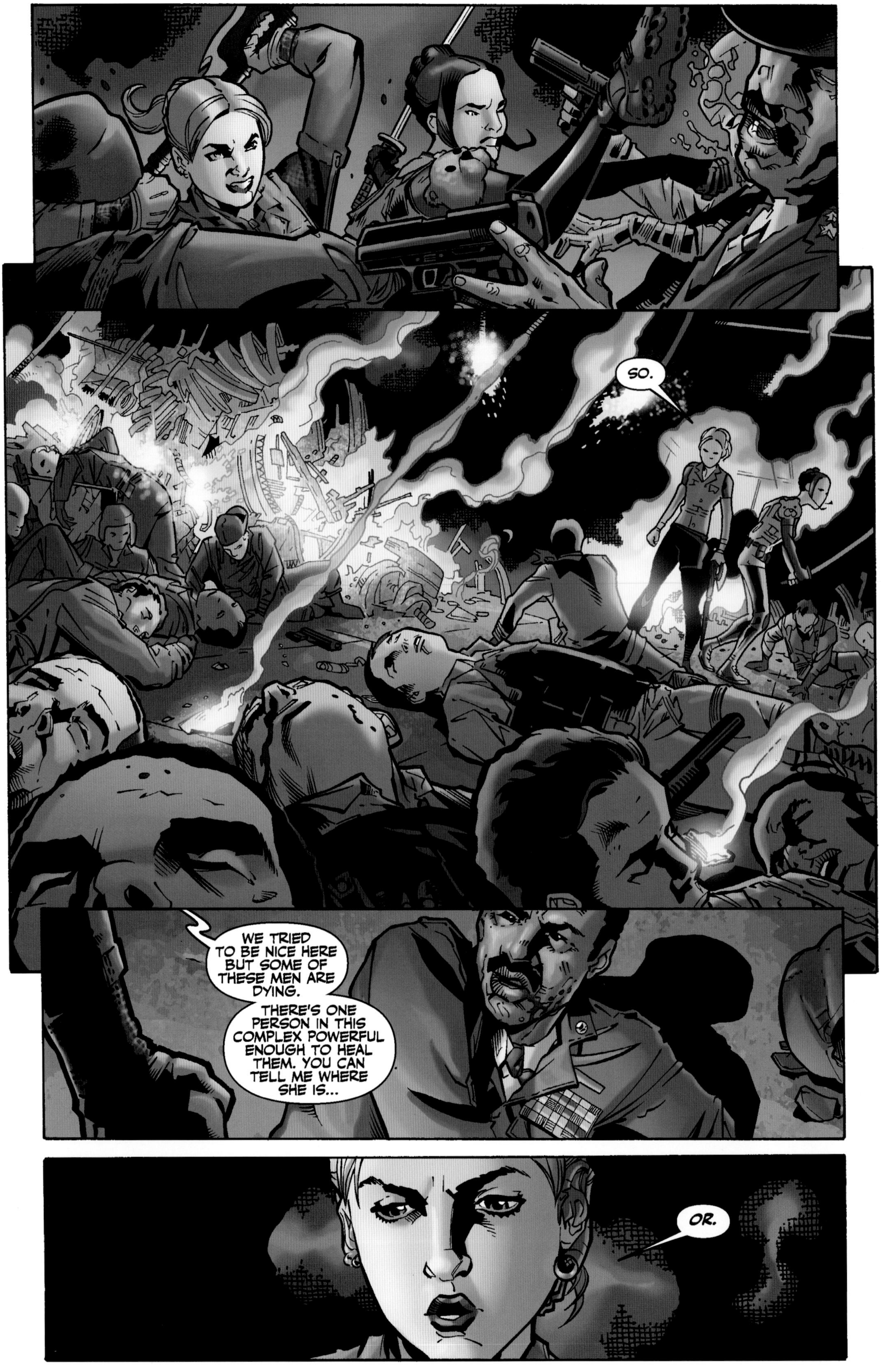
SO.
WE TRIED TO BE NICE HERE BUT SOME OF THESE MEN ARE DYING.
THERE'S ONE PERSON IN THIS COMPLEX POWERFUL ENOUGH TO HEAL THEM. YOU CAN TELL ME WHERE SHE IS...
OR.

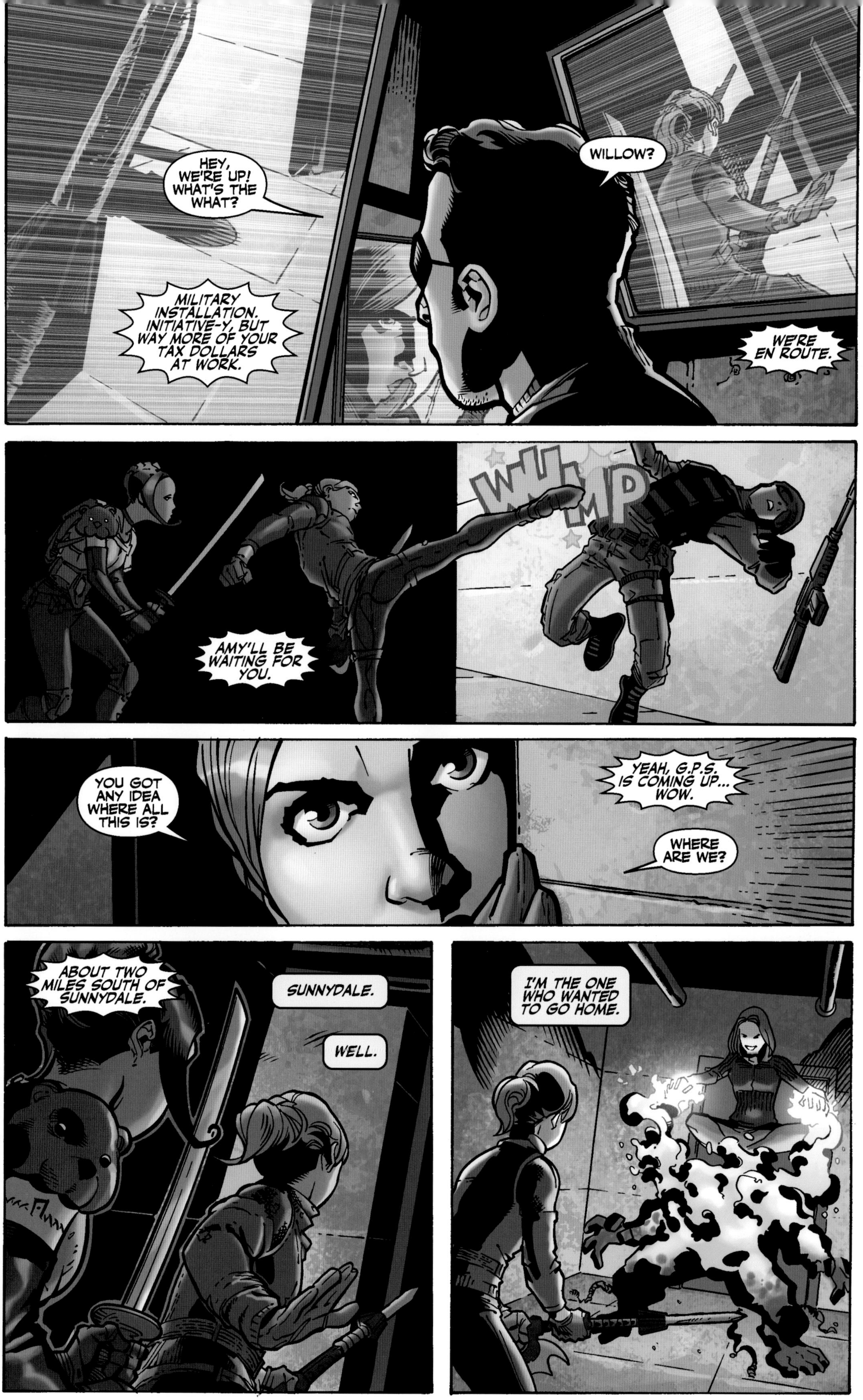

HEY, WE'RE UP! WHAT'S THE WHAT?
WILLOW?
MILITARY INSTALLATION. INITIATIVE-Y, BUT WAY MORE OF YOUR TAX DOLLARS AT WORK.
WE'RE EN ROUTE.
AMY'LL BE WAITING FOR YOU.
WHMP
YOU GOT ANY IDEA WHERE ALL THIS IS?
YEAH, G.P.S. IS COMING UP... WOW.
WHERE ARE WE?
ABOUT TWO MILES SOUTH OF SUNNYDALE.
SUNNYDALE.
WELL.
I'M THE ONE WHO WANTED TO GO HOME.

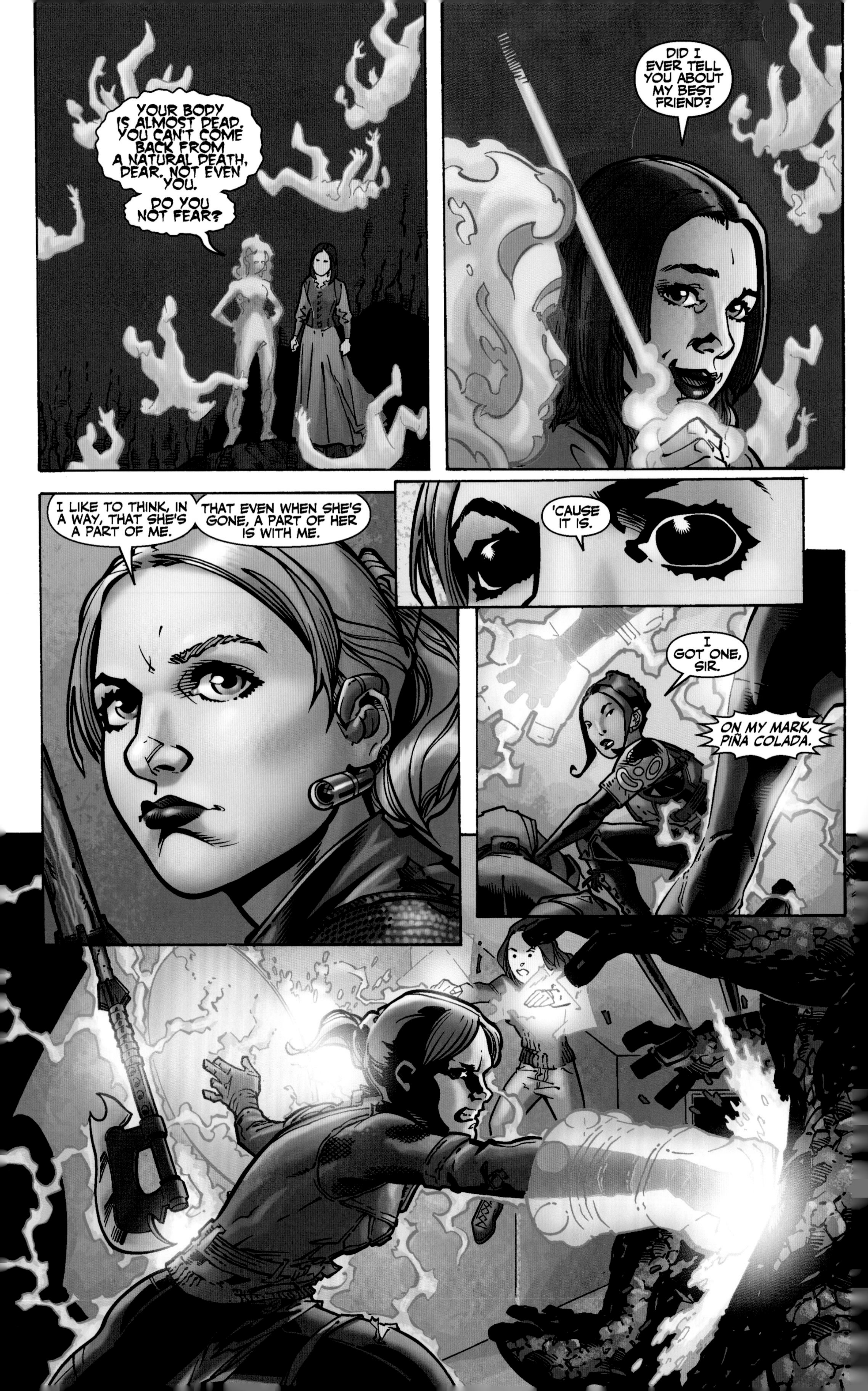
YOUR BODY IS ALMOST DEAD. YOU CAN'T COME BACK FROM A NATURAL DEATH, DEAR. NOT EVEN YOU.
DO YOU NOT FEAR?
DID I EVER TELL YOU ABOUT MY BEST FRIEND?
I LIKE TO THINK, IN A WAY, THAT SHE'S A PART OF ME.
THAT EVEN WHEN SHE'S GONE, A PART OF HER IS WITH ME.
'CAUSE IT IS.
I GOT ONE, SIR.
ON MY MARK, PIÑA COLADA.

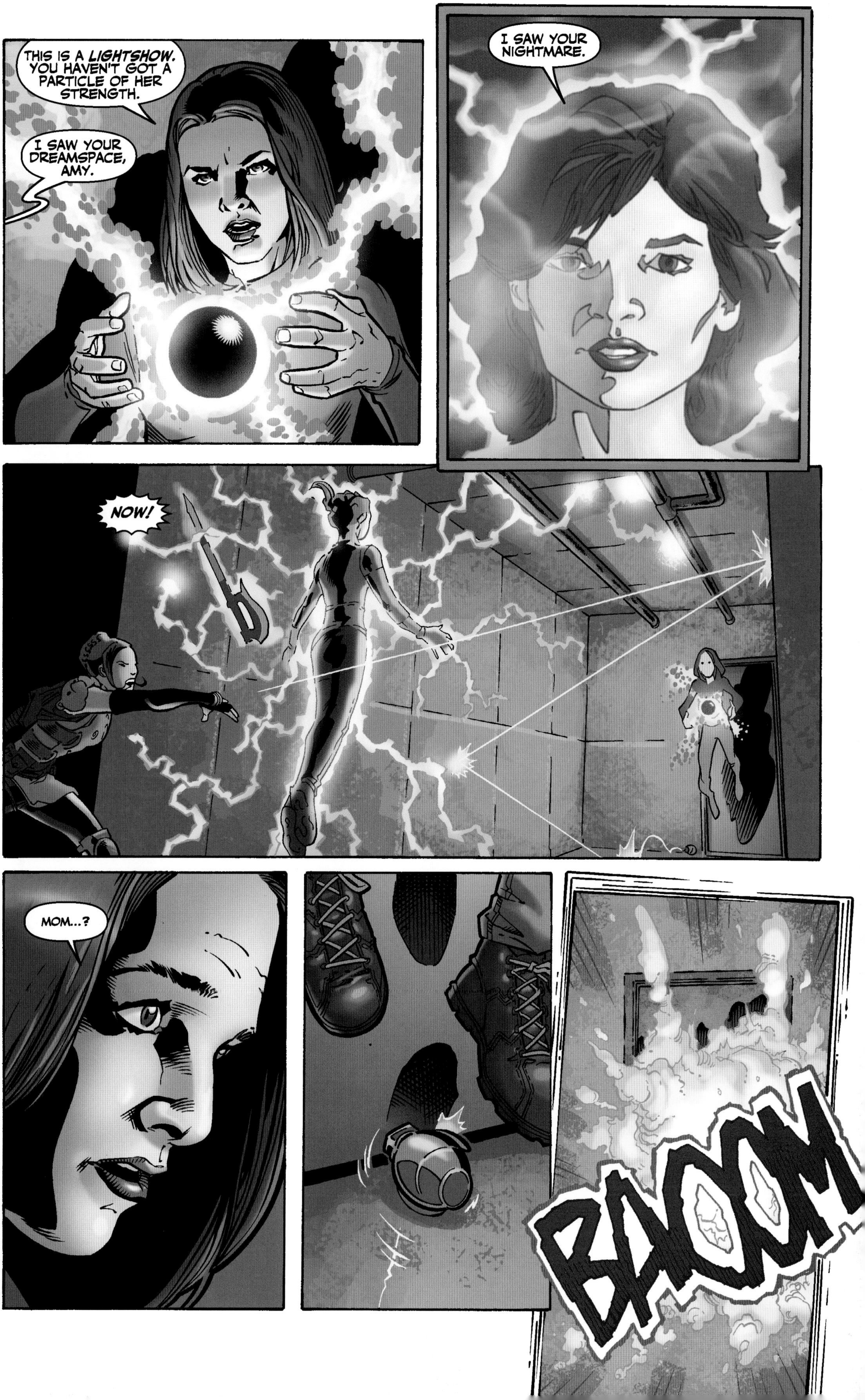
THIS IS A LIGHTSHOW. YOU HAVEN'T GOT A PARTICLE OF HER STRENGTH.
I SAW YOUR DREAMSPACE, AMY.
I SAW YOUR NIGHTMARE.
NOW!
MOM...?
BAOOM

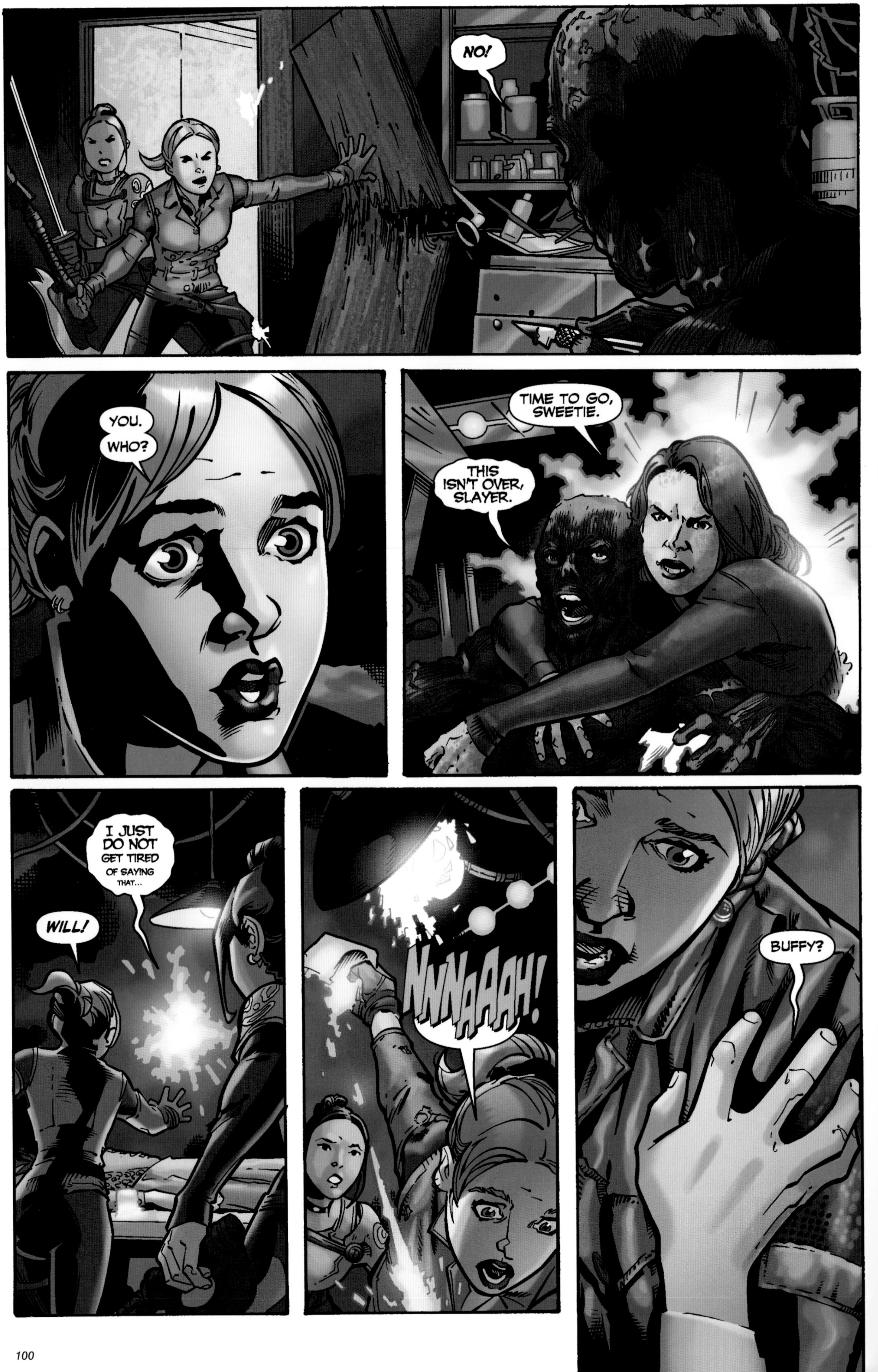
NO!
YOU.
WHO?
TIME TO GO, SWEETIE.
THIS ISN'T OVER, SLAYER.
I JUST DO NOT GET TIRED OF SAYING THAT...
WILL!
NNNAAAH!
BUFFY?

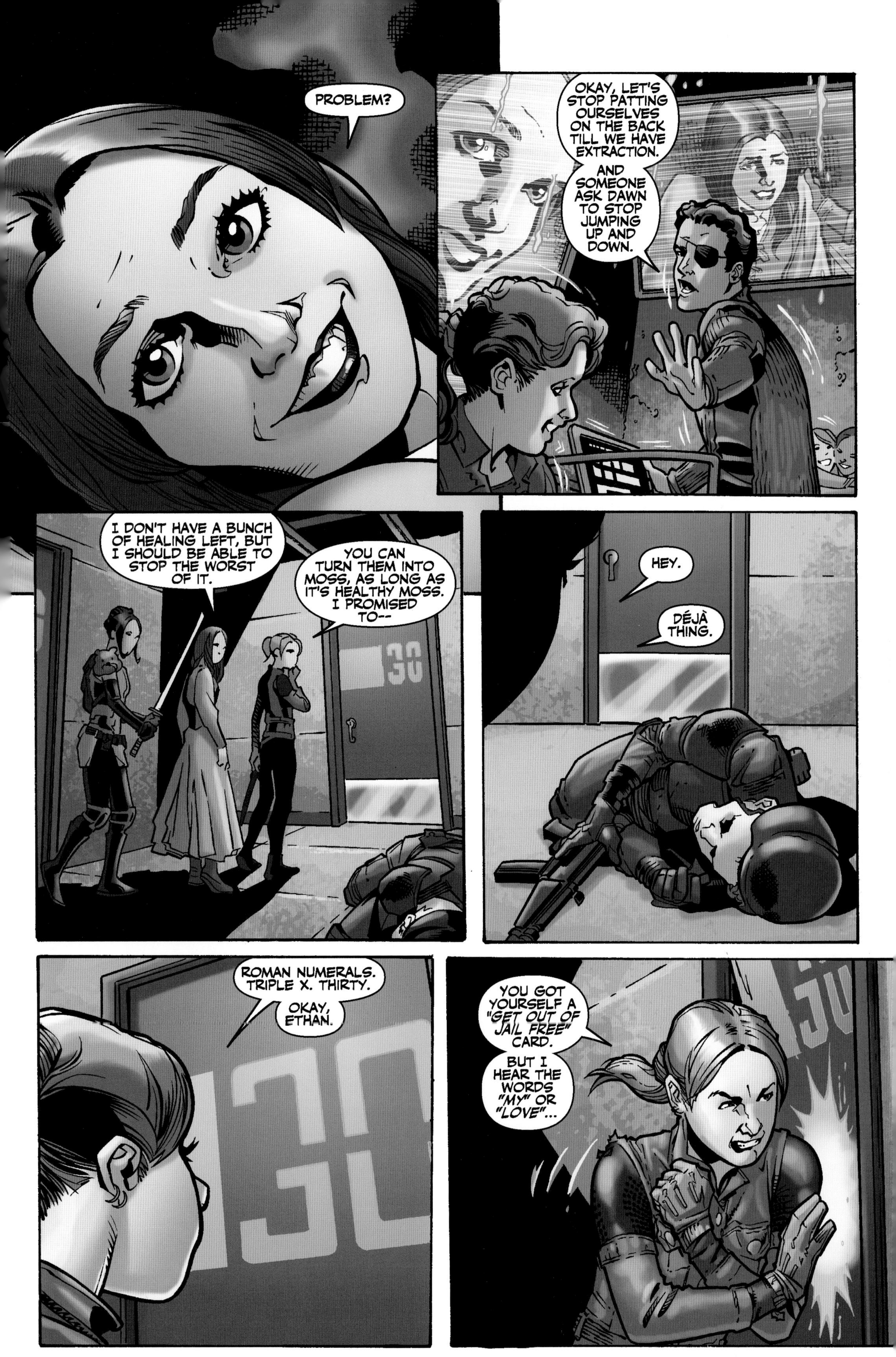
PROBLEM?
OKAY, LET'S STOP PATTING OURSELVES ON THE BACK TILL WE HAVE EXTRACTION.
AND SOMEONE ASK DAWN TO STOP JUMPING UP AND DOWN.
I DON'T HAVE A BUNCH OF HEALING LEFT, BUT I SHOULD BE ABLE TO STOP THE WORST OF IT.
YOU CAN TURN THEM INTO MOSS, AS LONG AS IT'S HEALTHY MOSS. I PROMISED TO--
HEY.
DÉJÀ THING.
ROMAN NUMERALS. TRIPLE X. THIRTY.
OKAY, ETHAN.
YOU GOT YOURSELF A "GET OUT OF JAIL FREE" CARD.
BUT I HEAR THE WORDS "MY" OR "LOVE"...

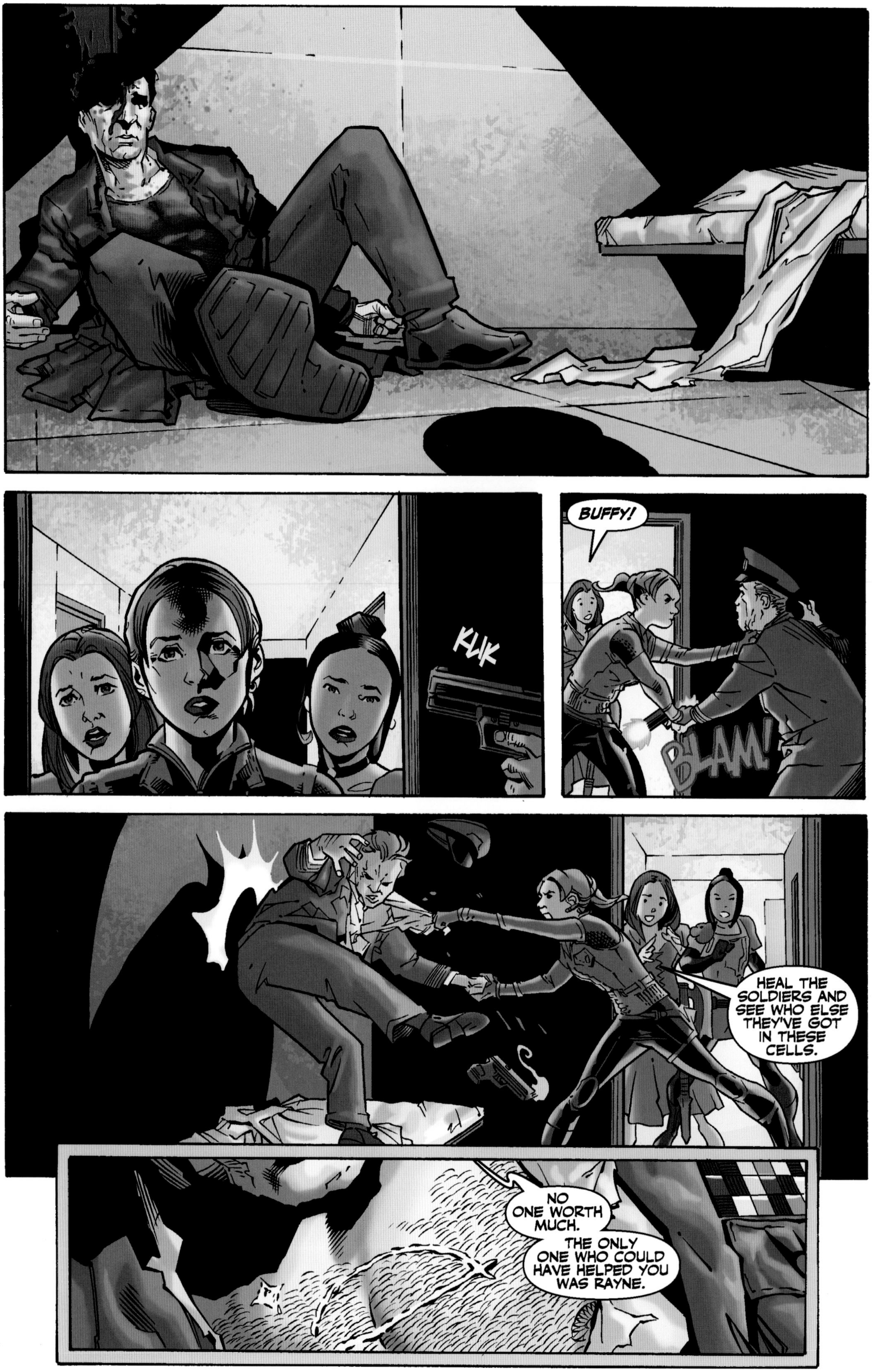
KLIK
BUFFY!
BLAM!
HEAL THE SOLDIERS AND SEE WHO ELSE THEY'VE GOT IN THESE CELLS.
NO ONE WORTH MUCH.
THE ONLY ONE WHO COULD HAVE HELPED YOU WAS RAYNE.

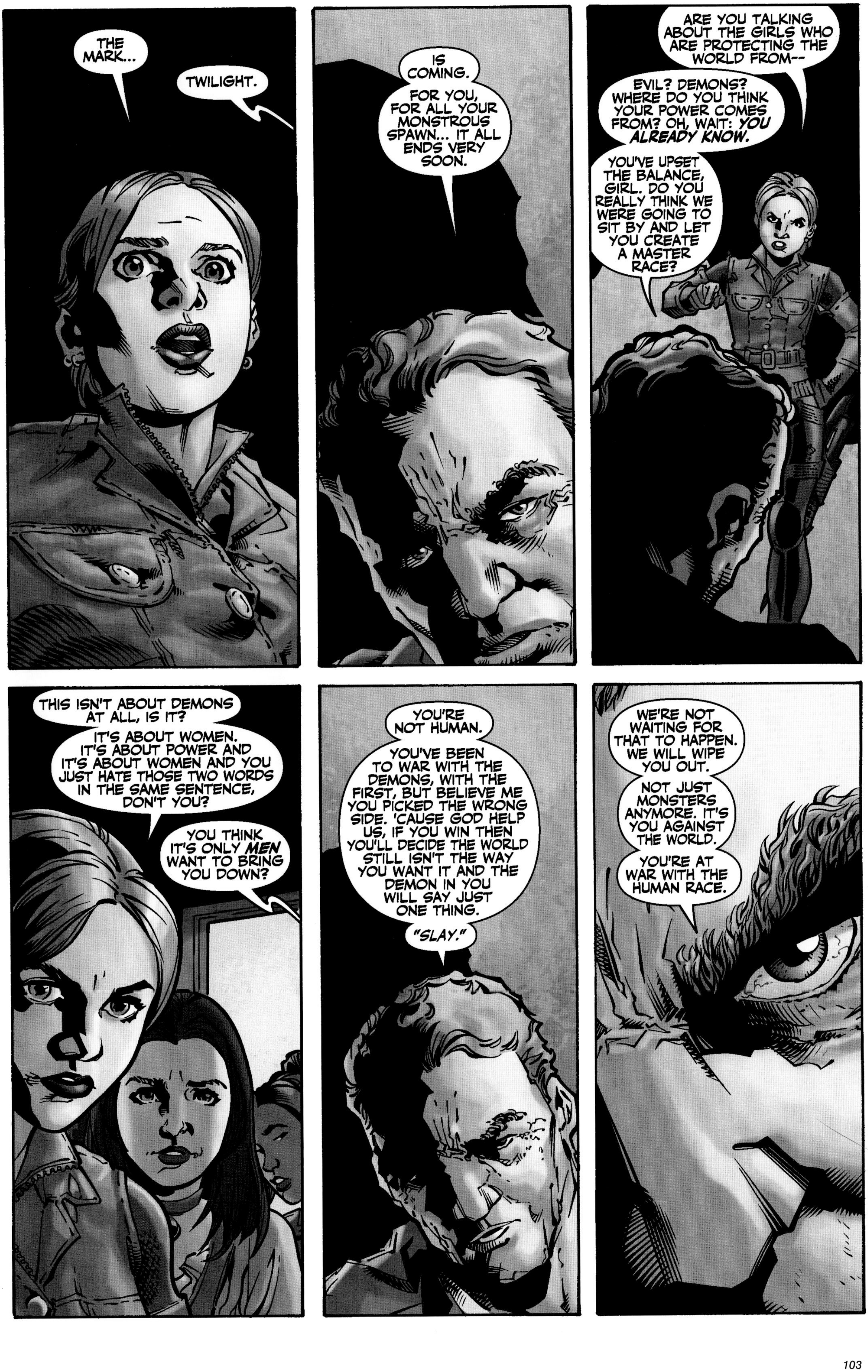
THE MARK...
TWILIGHT.
IS COMING.
FOR YOU, FOR ALL YOUR MONSTROUS SPAWN... IT ALL ENDS VERY SOON.
ARE YOU TALKING ABOUT THE GIRLS WHO ARE PROTECTING THE WORLD FROM--
EVIL? DEMONS? WHERE DO YOU THINK YOUR POWER COMES FROM? OH, WAIT: *YOU ALREADY KNOW.*
YOU'VE UPSET THE BALANCE, GIRL. DO YOU REALLY THINK WE WERE GOING TO SIT BY AND LET YOU CREATE A MASTER RACE?
THIS ISN'T ABOUT DEMONS AT ALL, IS IT?
IT'S ABOUT WOMEN. IT'S ABOUT POWER AND IT'S ABOUT WOMEN AND YOU JUST HATE THOSE TWO WORDS IN THE SAME SENTENCE, DON'T YOU?
YOU THINK IT'S ONLY *MEN* WANT TO BRING YOU DOWN?
YOU'RE NOT HUMAN.
YOU'VE BEEN TO WAR WITH THE DEMONS, WITH THE FIRST, BUT BELIEVE ME YOU PICKED THE WRONG SIDE. 'CAUSE GOD HELP US, IF YOU WIN THEN YOU'LL DECIDE THE WORLD STILL ISN'T THE WAY YOU WANT IT AND THE DEMON IN YOU WILL SAY JUST ONE THING.
"SLAY."
WE'RE NOT WAITING FOR THAT TO HAPPEN. WE WILL WIPE YOU OUT.
NOT JUST MONSTERS ANYMORE. IT'S YOU AGAINST THE WORLD.
YOU'RE AT WAR WITH THE HUMAN RACE.

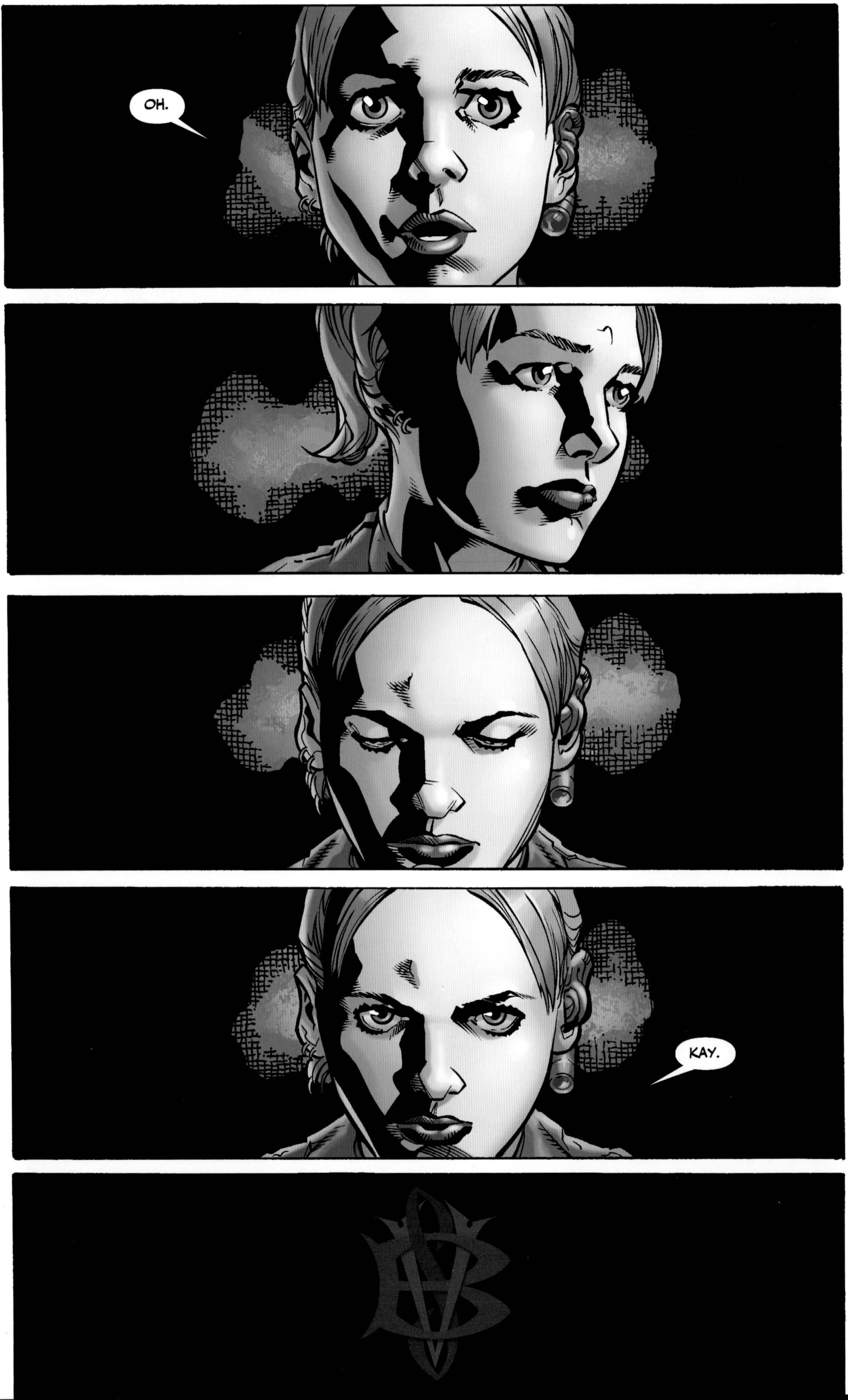
OH.
KAY.

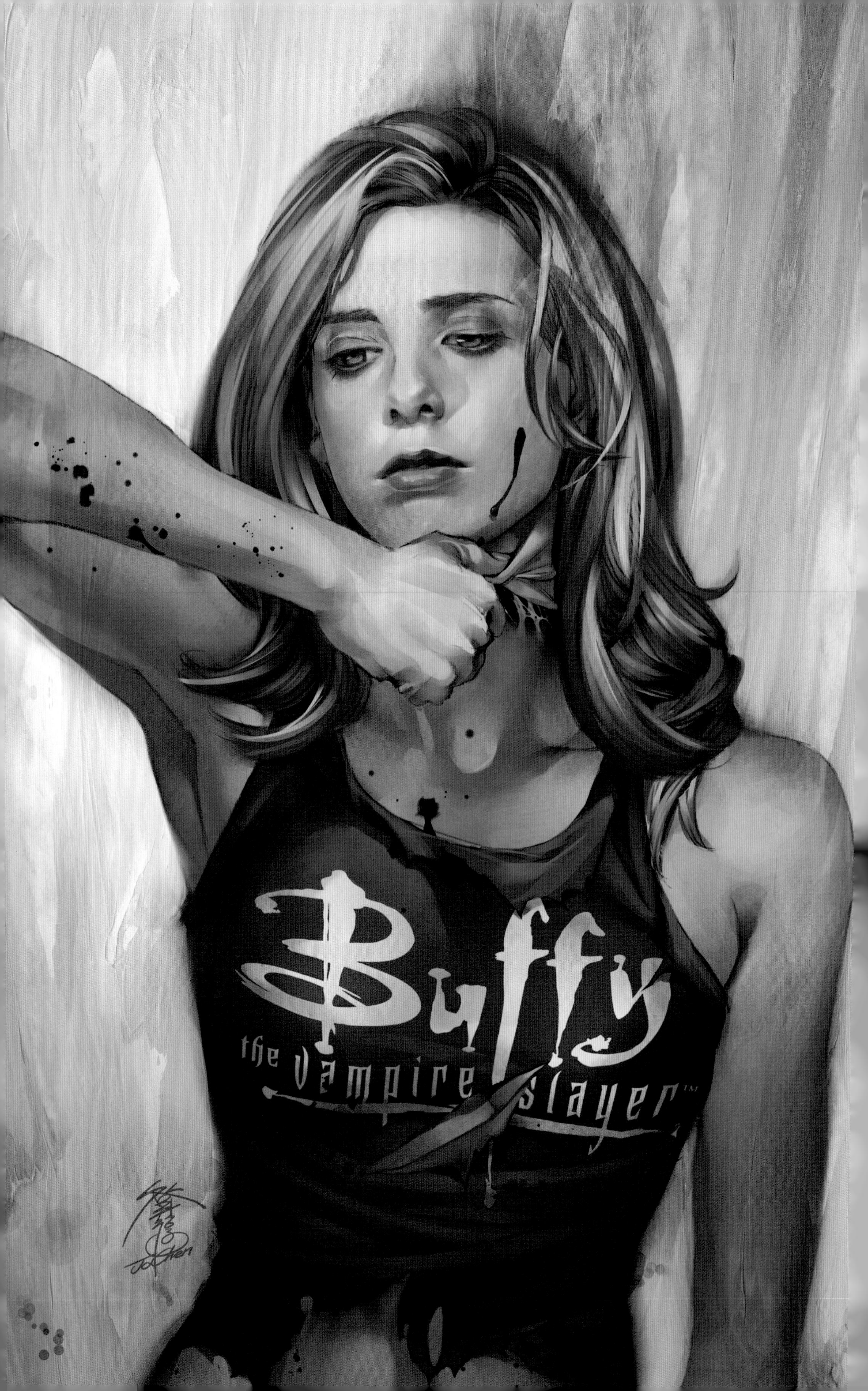
Buffy
the Vampire Slayer™

The CHAIN

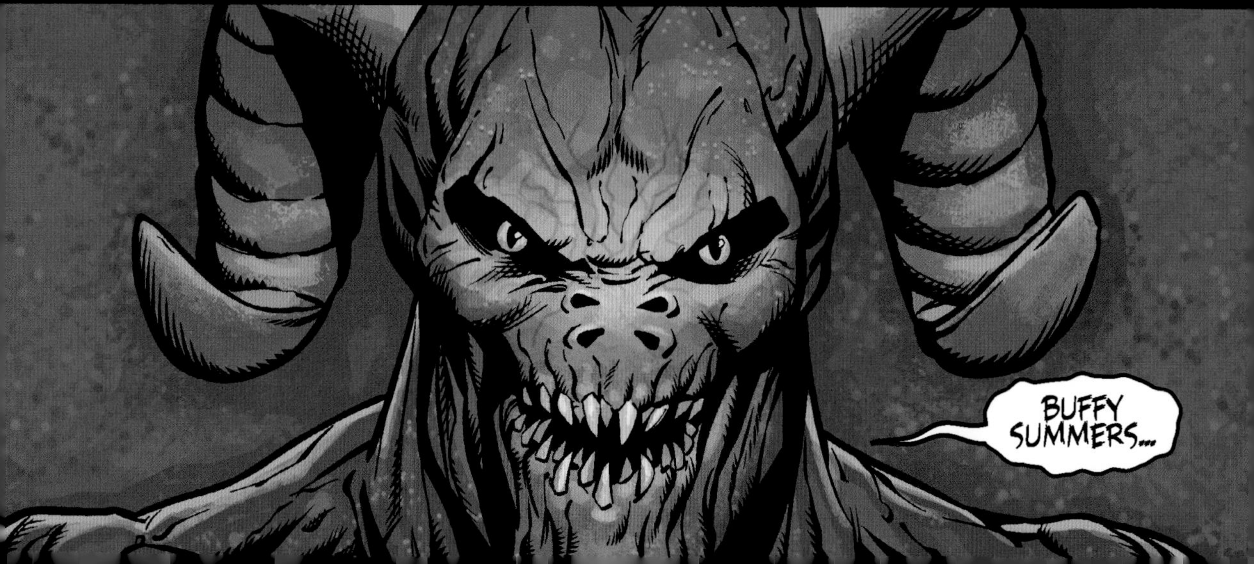
BUFFY SUMMERS...

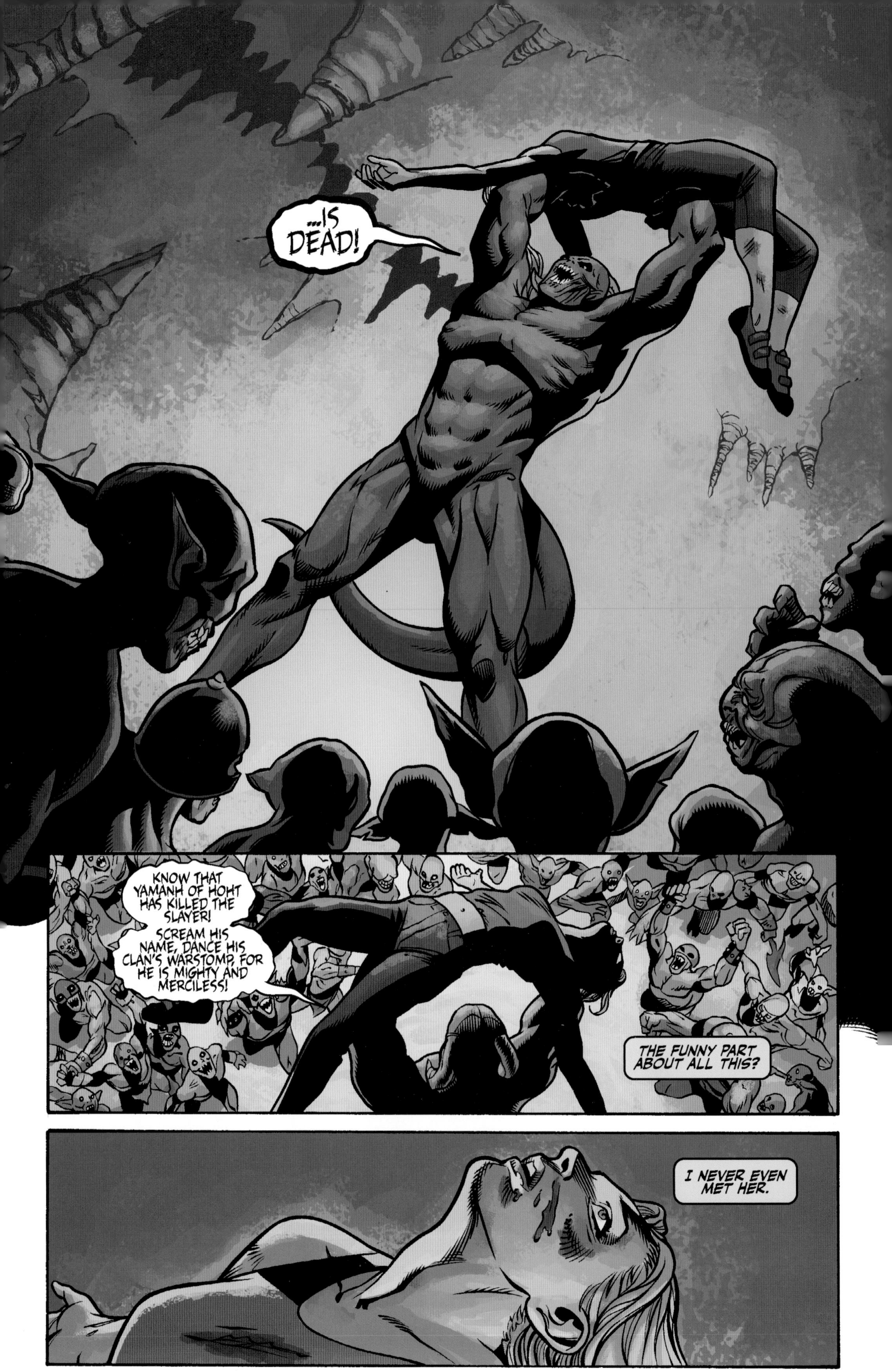
...IS DEAD!
KNOW THAT YAMANH OF HOHT HAS KILLED THE SLAYER!
SCREAM HIS NAME, DANCE HIS CLAN'S WARSTOMP, FOR HE IS MIGHTY AND MERCILESS!
THE FUNNY PART ABOUT ALL THIS?
I NEVER EVEN MET HER.

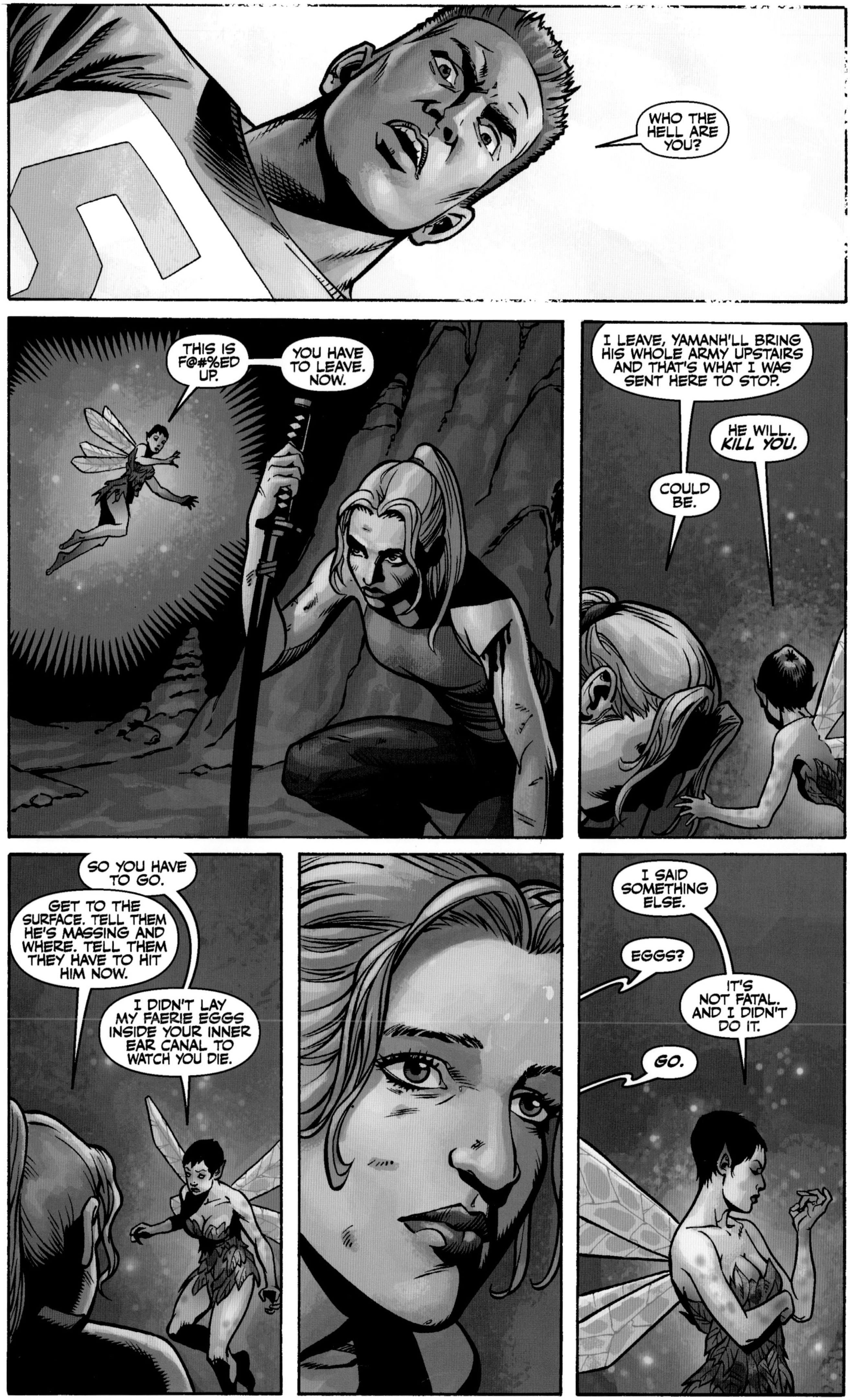
WHO THE HELL ARE YOU?
THIS IS F@#%ED UP.
YOU HAVE TO LEAVE. NOW.
I LEAVE, YAMANH'LL BRING HIS WHOLE ARMY UPSTAIRS AND THAT'S WHAT I WAS SENT HERE TO STOP.
HE WILL. KILL YOU.
COULD BE.
SO YOU HAVE TO GO.
GET TO THE SURFACE. TELL THEM HE'S MASSING AND WHERE. TELL THEM THEY HAVE TO HIT HIM NOW.
I DIDN'T LAY MY FAERIE EGGS INSIDE YOUR INNER EAR CANAL TO WATCH YOU DIE.
I SAID SOMETHING ELSE.
EGGS?
IT'S NOT FATAL. AND I DIDN'T DO IT.
GO.

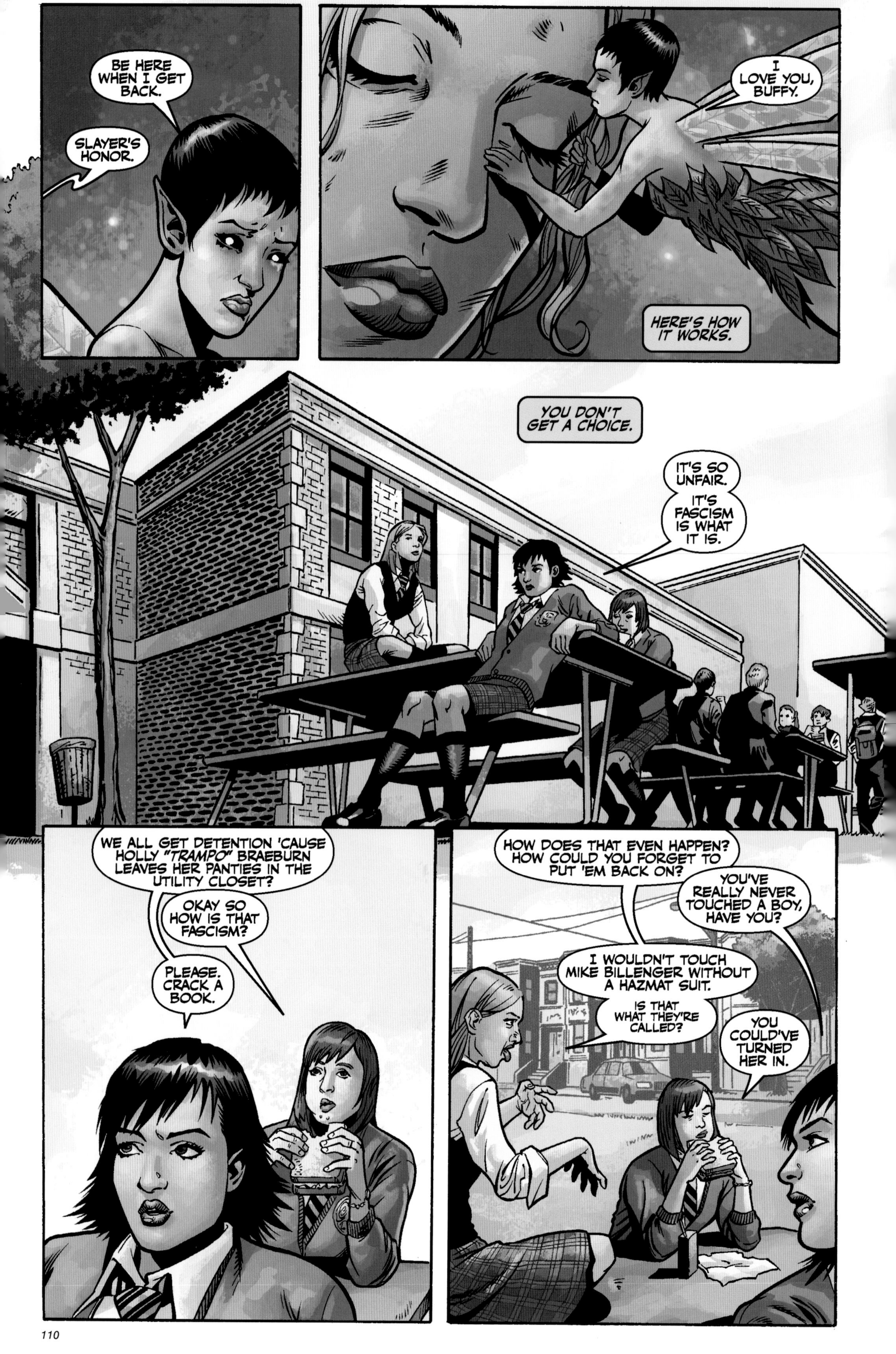
BE HERE WHEN I GET BACK.
SLAYER'S HONOR.
I LOVE YOU, BUFFY.
HERE'S HOW IT WORKS.
YOU DON'T GET A CHOICE.
IT'S SO UNFAIR.
IT'S FASCISM IS WHAT IT IS.
WE ALL GET DETENTION 'CAUSE HOLLY *"TRAMPO"* BRAEBURN LEAVES HER PANTIES IN THE UTILITY CLOSET?
OKAY SO HOW IS THAT FASCISM?
PLEASE. CRACK A BOOK.
HOW DOES THAT EVEN HAPPEN? HOW COULD YOU FORGET TO PUT 'EM BACK ON?
YOU'VE REALLY NEVER TOUCHED A BOY, HAVE YOU?
I WOULDN'T TOUCH MIKE BILLENGER WITHOUT A HAZMAT SUIT.
IS THAT WHAT THEY'RE CALLED?
YOU COULD'VE TURNED HER IN.

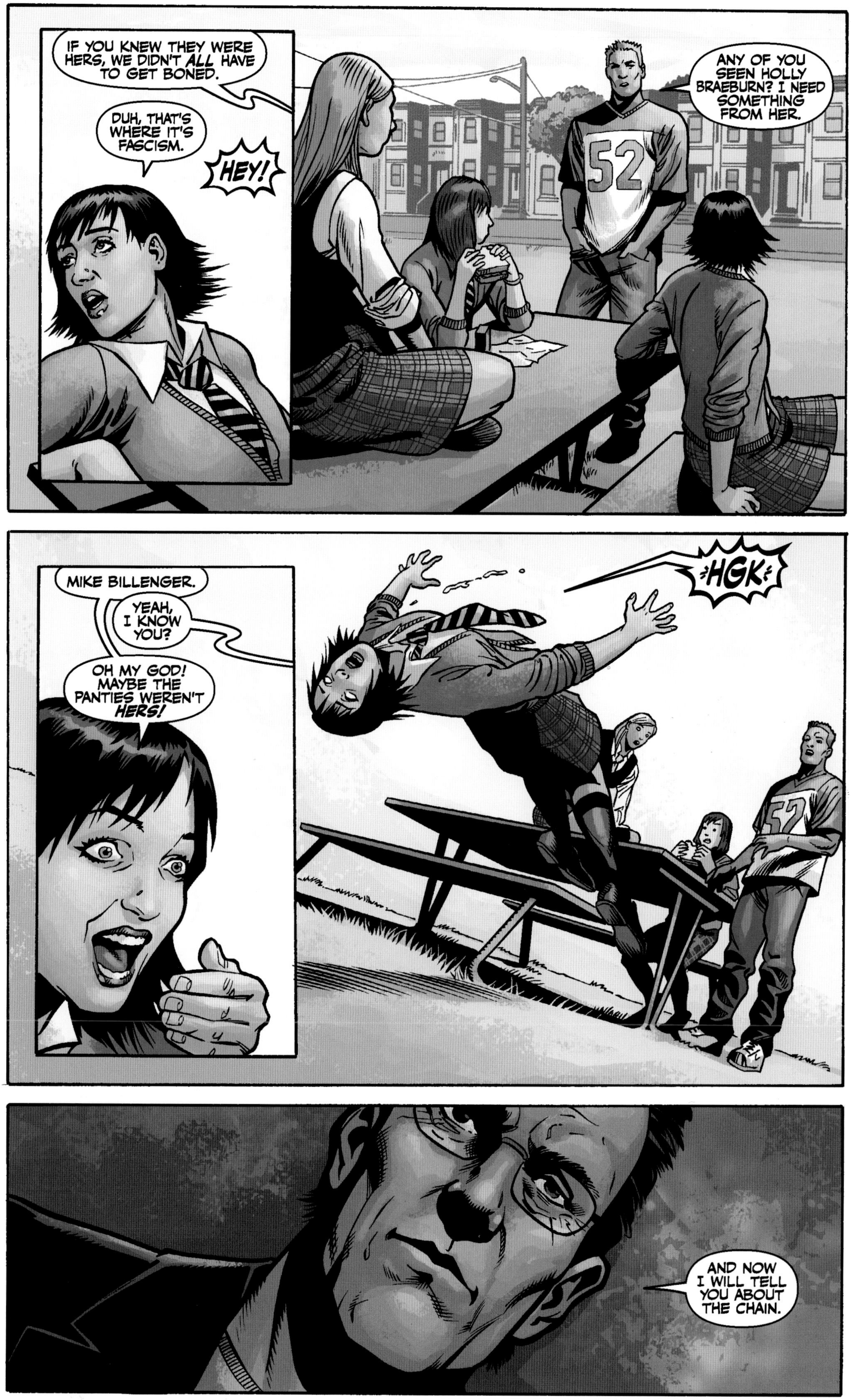
IF YOU KNEW THEY WERE HERS, WE DIDN'T ALL HAVE TO GET BONED.
DUH, THAT'S WHERE IT'S FASCISM.
HEY!
ANY OF YOU SEEN HOLLY BRAEBURN? I NEED SOMETHING FROM HER.
52
MIKE BILLENGER.
YEAH, I KNOW YOU?
OH MY GOD! MAYBE THE PANTIES WEREN'T HERS!
HGK
52
AND NOW I WILL TELL YOU ABOUT THE CHAIN.

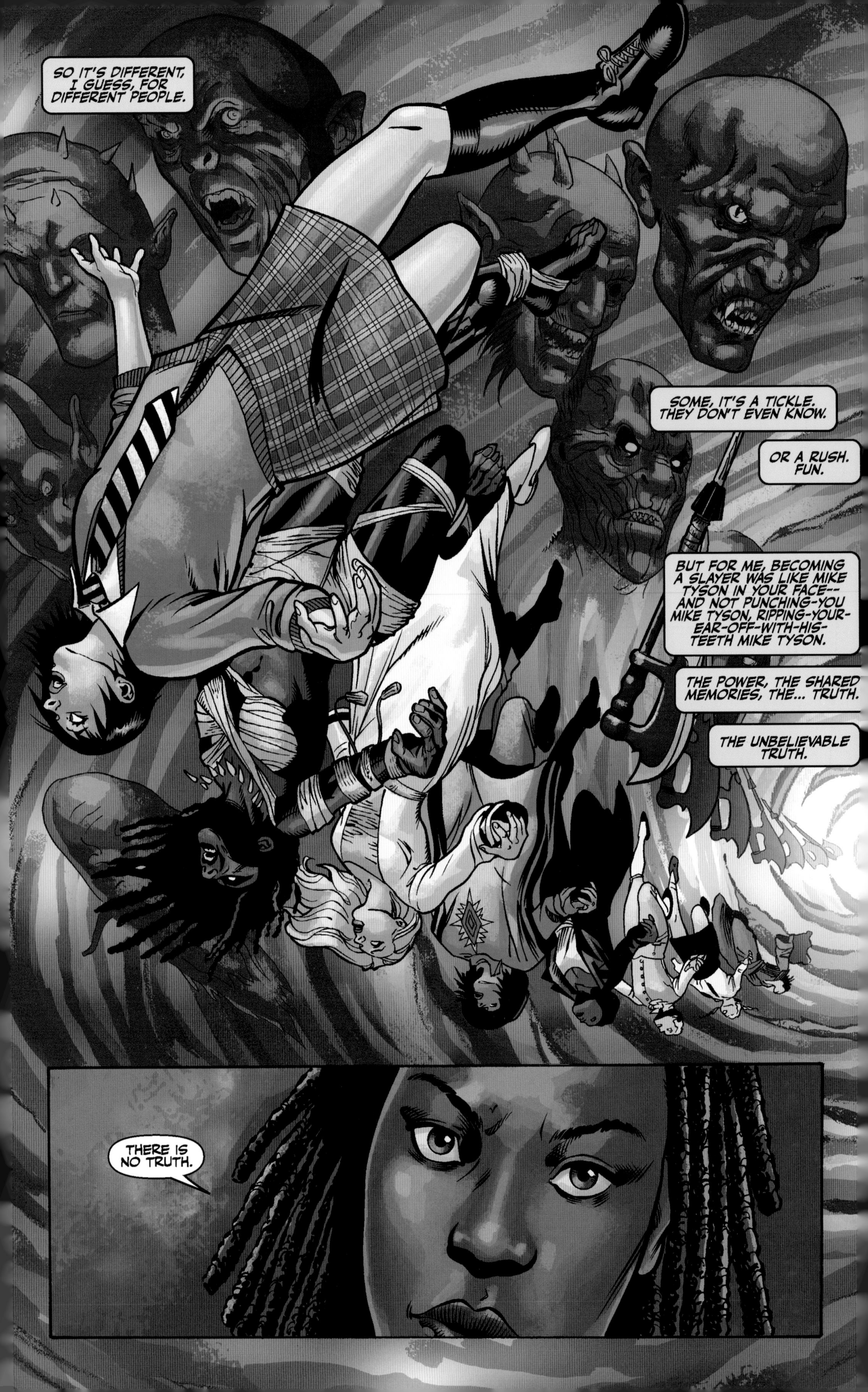
SO IT'S DIFFERENT, I GUESS, FOR DIFFERENT PEOPLE.
SOME, IT'S A TICKLE. THEY DON'T EVEN KNOW.
OR A RUSH. FUN.
BUT FOR ME, BECOMING A SLAYER WAS LIKE MIKE TYSON IN YOUR FACE-- AND NOT PUNCHING-YOU MIKE TYSON, RIPPING-YOUR-EAR-OFF-WITH-HIS-TEETH MIKE TYSON.
THE POWER, THE SHARED MEMORIES, THE... TRUTH.
THE UNBELIEVABLE TRUTH.
THERE IS NO TRUTH.

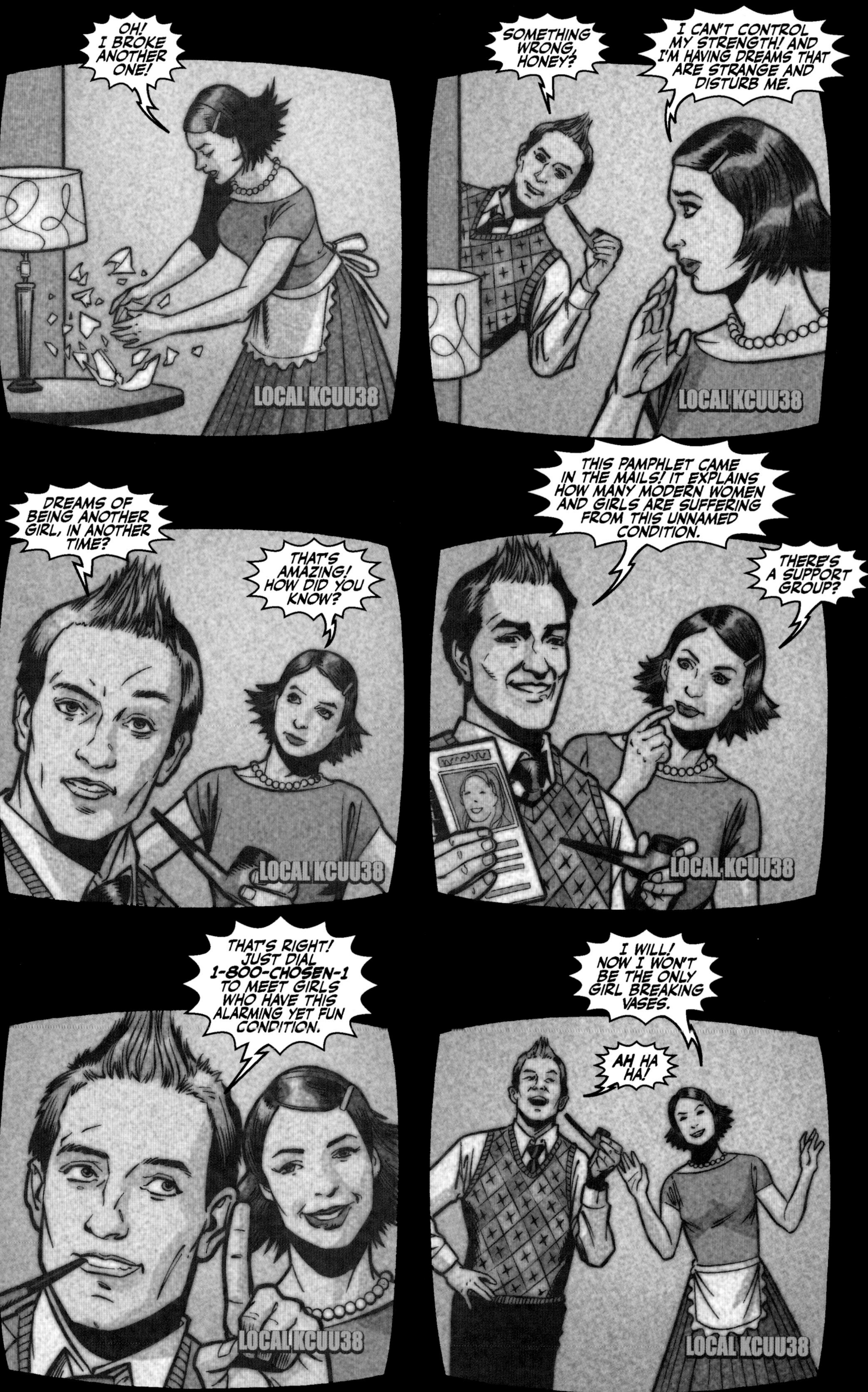
OH! I BROKE ANOTHER ONE!
LOCAL KCUU38
SOMETHING WRONG, HONEY?
I CAN'T CONTROL MY STRENGTH! AND I'M HAVING DREAMS THAT ARE STRANGE AND DISTURB ME.
LOCAL KCUU38
DREAMS OF BEING ANOTHER GIRL, IN ANOTHER TIME?
THAT'S AMAZING! HOW DID YOU KNOW?
LOCAL KCUU38
THIS PAMPHLET CAME IN THE MAILS! IT EXPLAINS HOW MANY MODERN WOMEN AND GIRLS ARE SUFFERING FROM THIS UNNAMED CONDITION.
THERE'S A SUPPORT GROUP?
LOCAL KCUU38
THAT'S RIGHT! JUST DIAL 1-800-CHOSEN-1 TO MEET GIRLS WHO HAVE THIS ALARMING YET FUN CONDITION.
LOCAL KCUU38
I WILL! NOW I WON'T BE THE ONLY GIRL BREAKING VASES.
AH HA HA!
LOCAL KCUU38

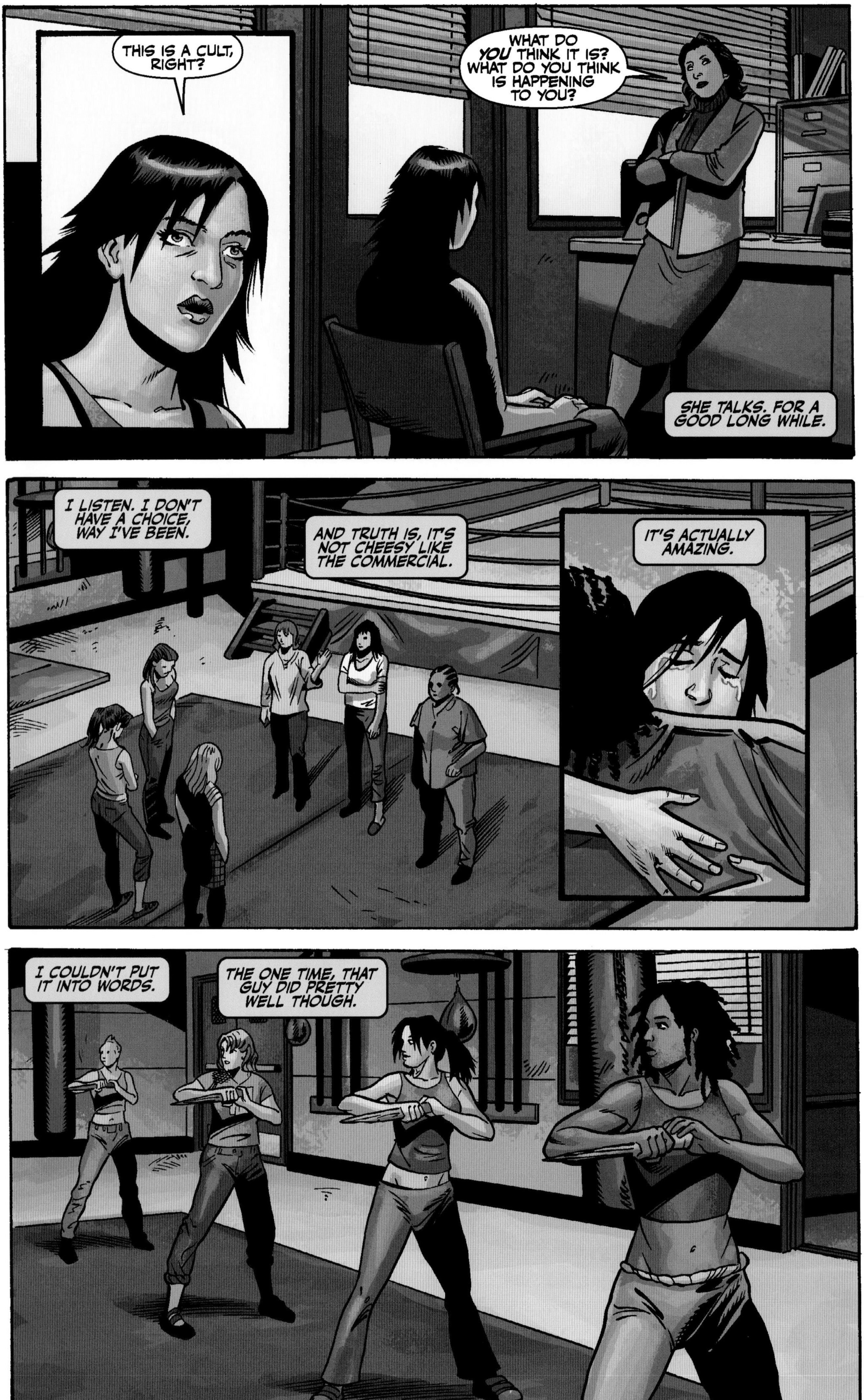
THIS IS A CULT, RIGHT?
WHAT DO YOU THINK IT IS? WHAT DO YOU THINK IS HAPPENING TO YOU?
SHE TALKS. FOR A GOOD LONG WHILE.
I LISTEN. I DON'T HAVE A CHOICE, WAY I'VE BEEN.
AND TRUTH IS, IT'S NOT CHEESY LIKE THE COMMERCIAL.
IT'S ACTUALLY AMAZING.
I COULDN'T PUT IT INTO WORDS.
THE ONE TIME, THAT GUY DID PRETTY WELL THOUGH.

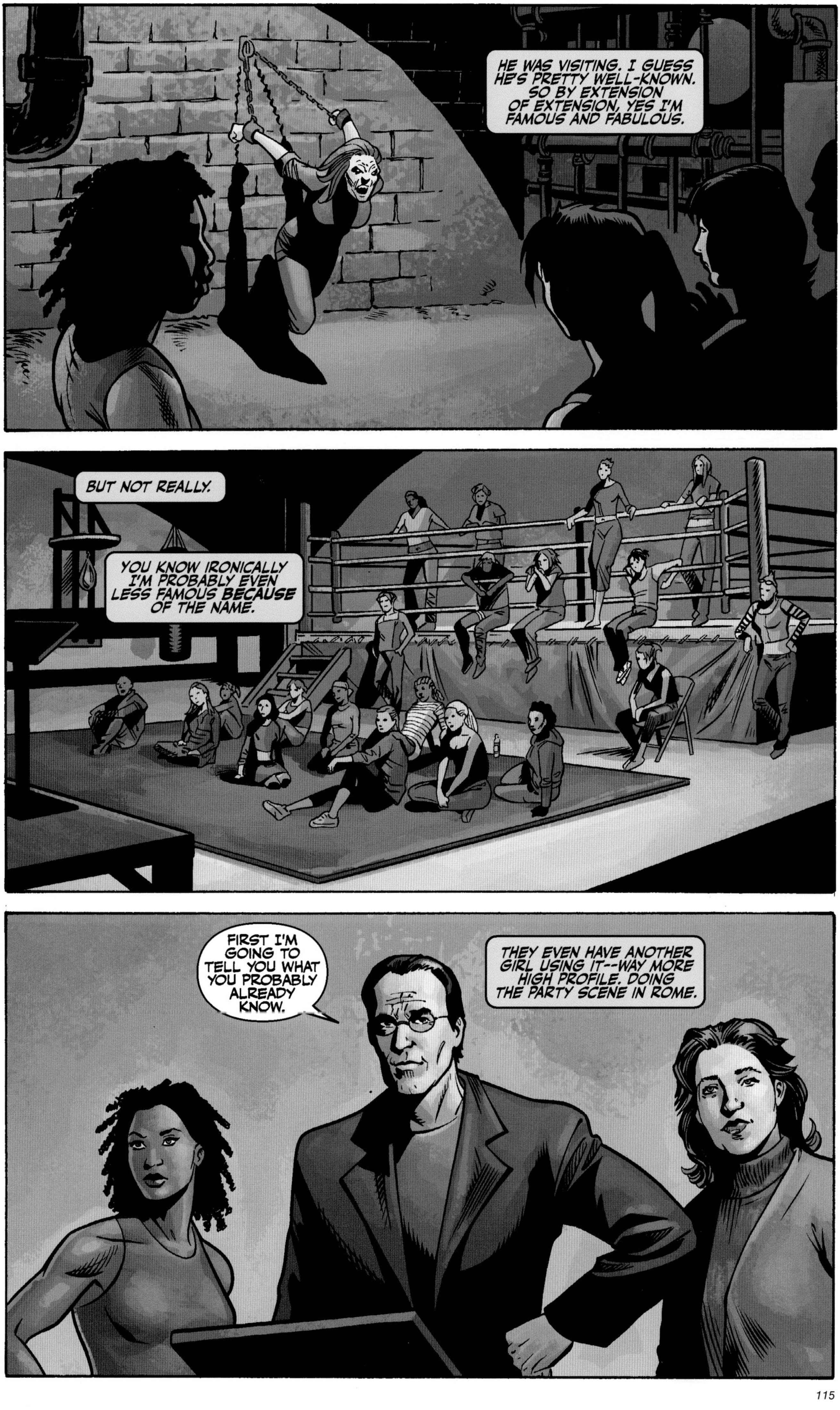
HE WAS VISITING. I GUESS HE'S PRETTY WELL-KNOWN. SO BY EXTENSION OF EXTENSION, YES I'M FAMOUS AND FABULOUS.
BUT NOT REALLY.
YOU KNOW IRONICALLY I'M PROBABLY EVEN LESS FAMOUS BECAUSE OF THE NAME.
FIRST I'M GOING TO TELL YOU WHAT YOU PROBABLY ALREADY KNOW.
THEY EVEN HAVE ANOTHER GIRL USING IT--WAY MORE HIGH PROFILE. DOING THE PARTY SCENE IN ROME.

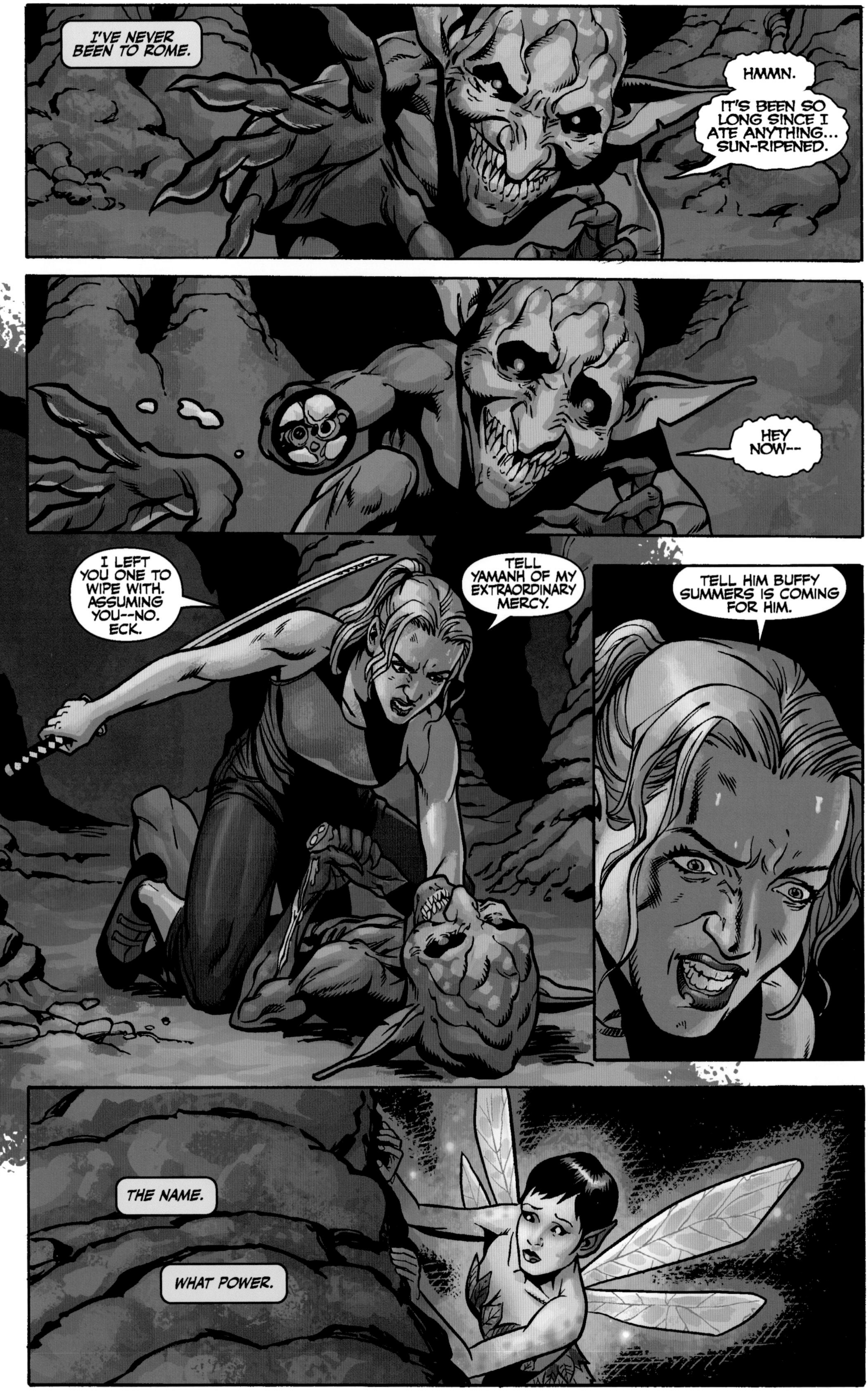
I'VE NEVER BEEN TO ROME.
HMMN.
IT'S BEEN SO LONG SINCE I ATE ANYTHING... SUN-RIPENED.
HEY NOW--
I LEFT YOU ONE TO WIPE WITH. ASSUMING YOU--NO. ECK.
TELL YAMANH OF MY EXTRAORDINARY MERCY.
TELL HIM BUFFY SUMMERS IS COMING FOR HIM.
THE NAME.
WHAT POWER.

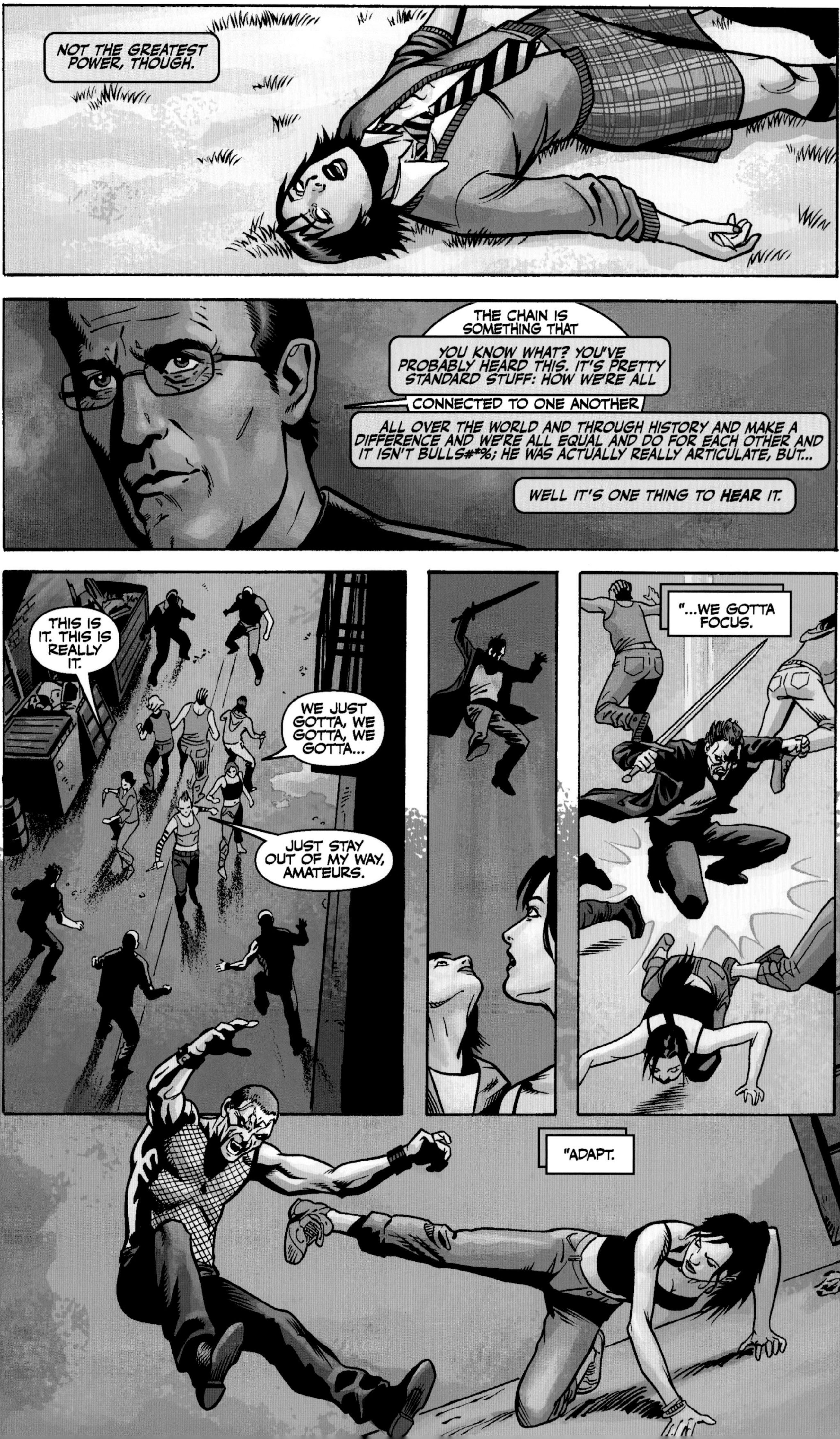
NOT THE GREATEST POWER, THOUGH.
THE CHAIN IS SOMETHING THAT
YOU KNOW WHAT? YOU'VE PROBABLY HEARD THIS. IT'S PRETTY STANDARD STUFF: HOW WE'RE ALL
CONNECTED TO ONE ANOTHER
ALL OVER THE WORLD AND THROUGH HISTORY AND MAKE A DIFFERENCE AND WE'RE ALL EQUAL AND DO FOR EACH OTHER AND IT ISN'T BULLS#*%; HE WAS ACTUALLY REALLY ARTICULATE, BUT...
WELL IT'S ONE THING TO HEAR IT.
THIS IS IT. THIS IS REALLY IT.
WE JUST GOTTA, WE GOTTA, WE GOTTA...
JUST STAY OUT OF MY WAY, AMATEURS.
"...WE GOTTA FOCUS.
"ADAPT.

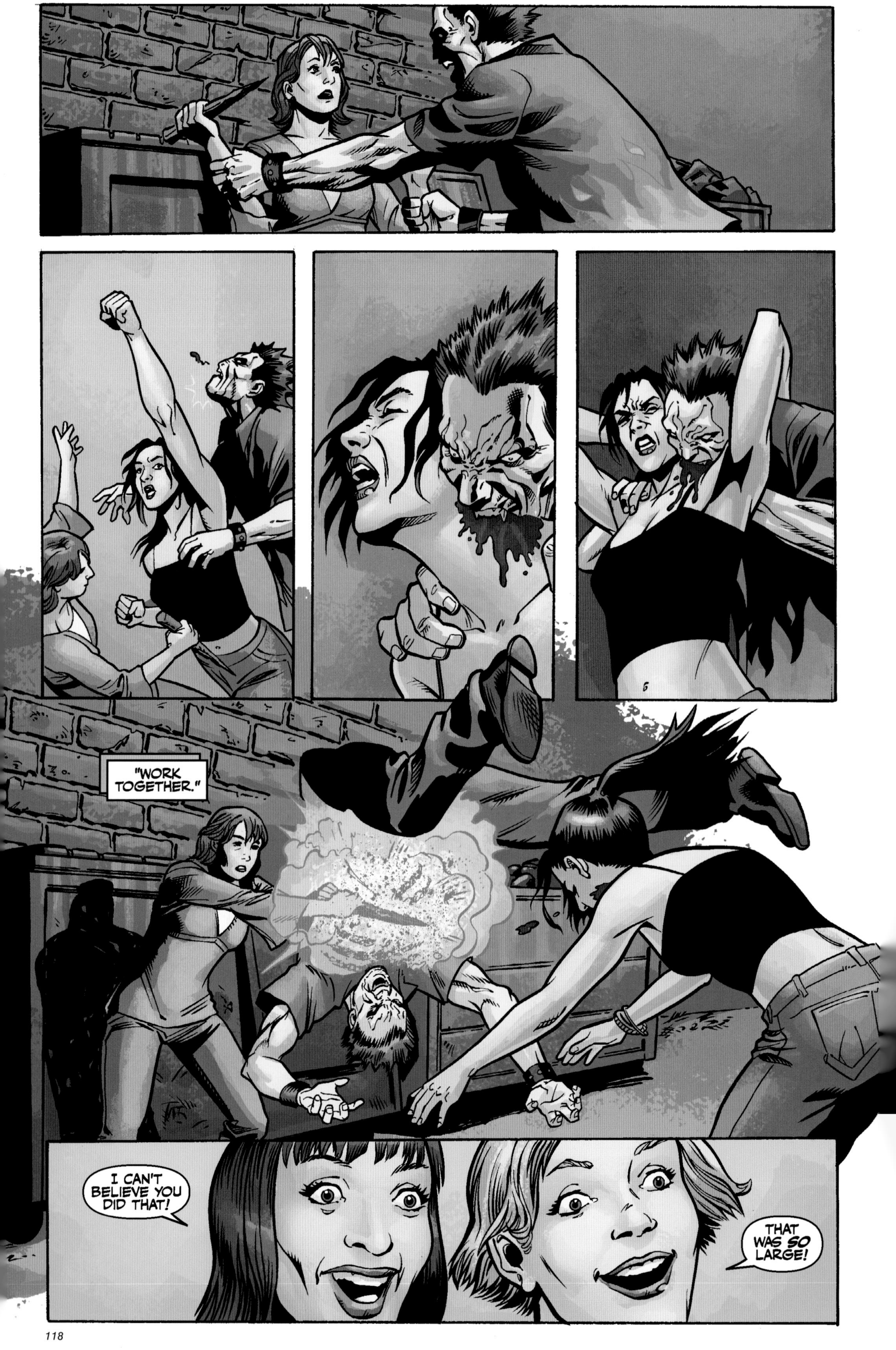
"WORK TOGETHER."
I CAN'T BELIEVE YOU DID THAT!
THAT WAS SO LARGE!

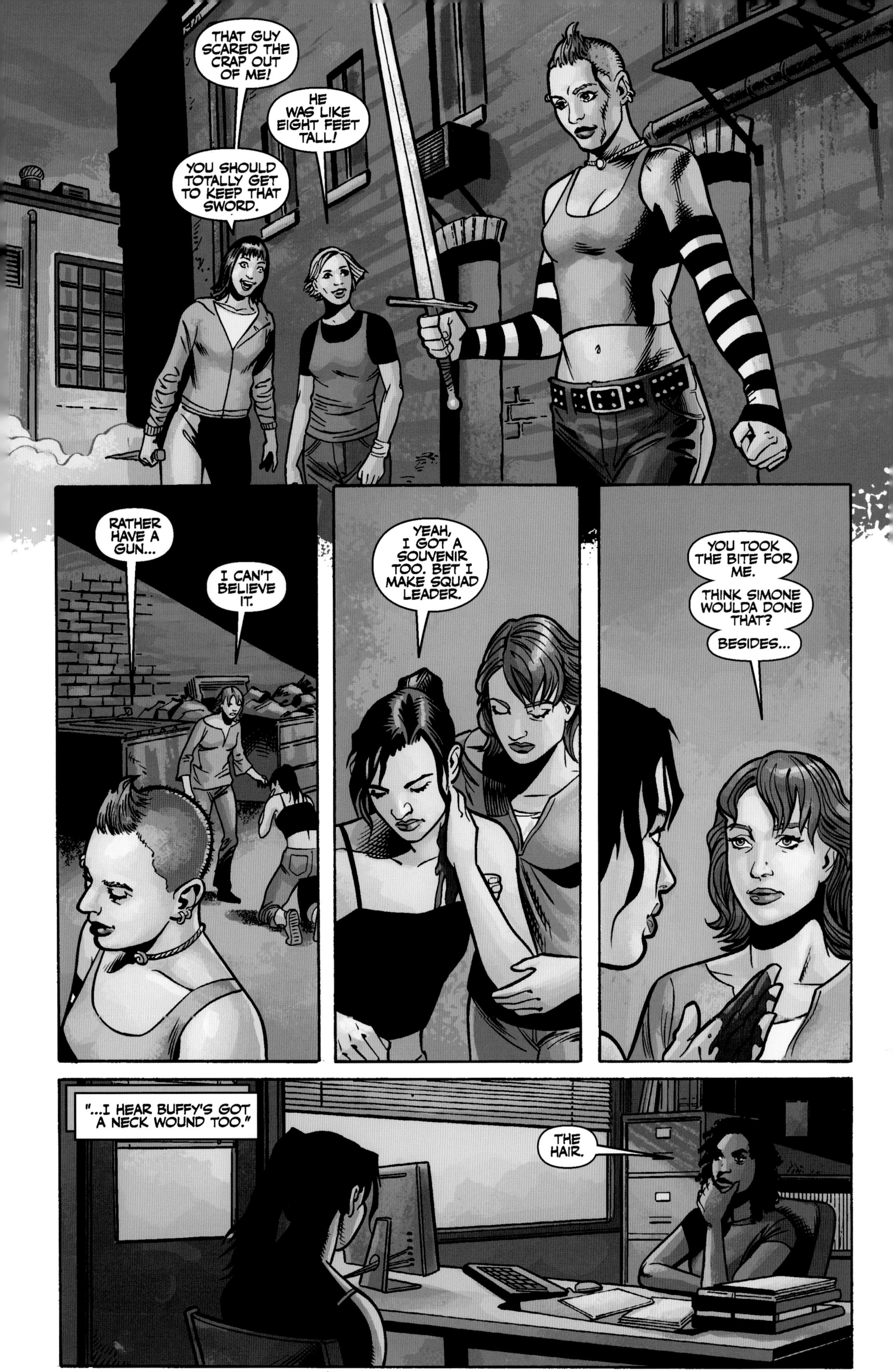
THAT GUY SCARED THE CRAP OUT OF ME!
YOU SHOULD TOTALLY GET TO KEEP THAT SWORD.
HE WAS LIKE EIGHT FEET TALL!
RATHER HAVE A GUN...
I CAN'T BELIEVE IT.
YEAH, I GOT A SOUVENIR TOO. BET I MAKE SQUAD LEADER.
YOU TOOK THE BITE FOR ME.
THINK SIMONE WOULDA DONE THAT?
BESIDES...
"...I HEAR BUFFY'S GOT A NECK WOUND TOO."
THE HAIR.

NEED A SERIOUS DYE JOB, AND YOU'D HAVE TO MAINTAIN IT YOURSELF.

BODY TYPE, HEIGHT ARE GOOD... HAVE TO PAD THE BRA A LITTLE, BUT... WE'RE COUNTING ON THESE GUYS NEVER TO HAVE ACTUALLY SEEN HER.

YOU GET WHAT ALL THIS IS?

YOU WANT ME TO BE BUFFY.

SOUNDS A LOT MORE GLAM THAN IT IS. WE'D BE SENDING YOU UNDERGROUND. UNDER ACTUAL GROUND.

NO ONE UP HERE CAN KNOW YOU'RE HER, NO ONE DOWN THERE CAN KNOW YOU'RE NOT.

IT'S DEEP COVER AND IT'S UNBELIEVABLY DANGEROUS. WE KNOW NEXT TO NOTHING ABOUT THE UNDER-COMMUNITY, EXCEPT THEY'RE STRONG AND THEY MIGHT BE HEADED UP. YAMANH'S THE NAME DOWN THERE.

IF YOU KNOW HIS NAME...

... THEN HE PROBABLY KNOWS HERS, SO YEAH, A DECOY MIGHT KEEP HIM OCCUPIED, MIGHT DO SOME INTERNAL DAMAGE.

I'M LOOKIN' AT YOU FOR THIS SO I GOTTA FIGURE YOU WANT THE TRUTH.

AS IN...

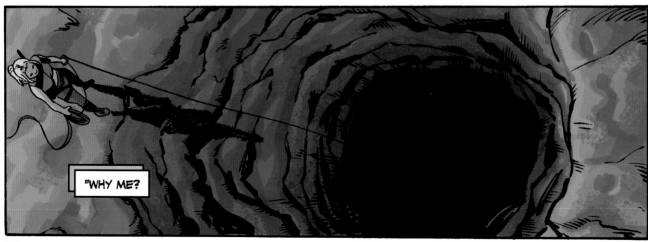

"WHY ME?

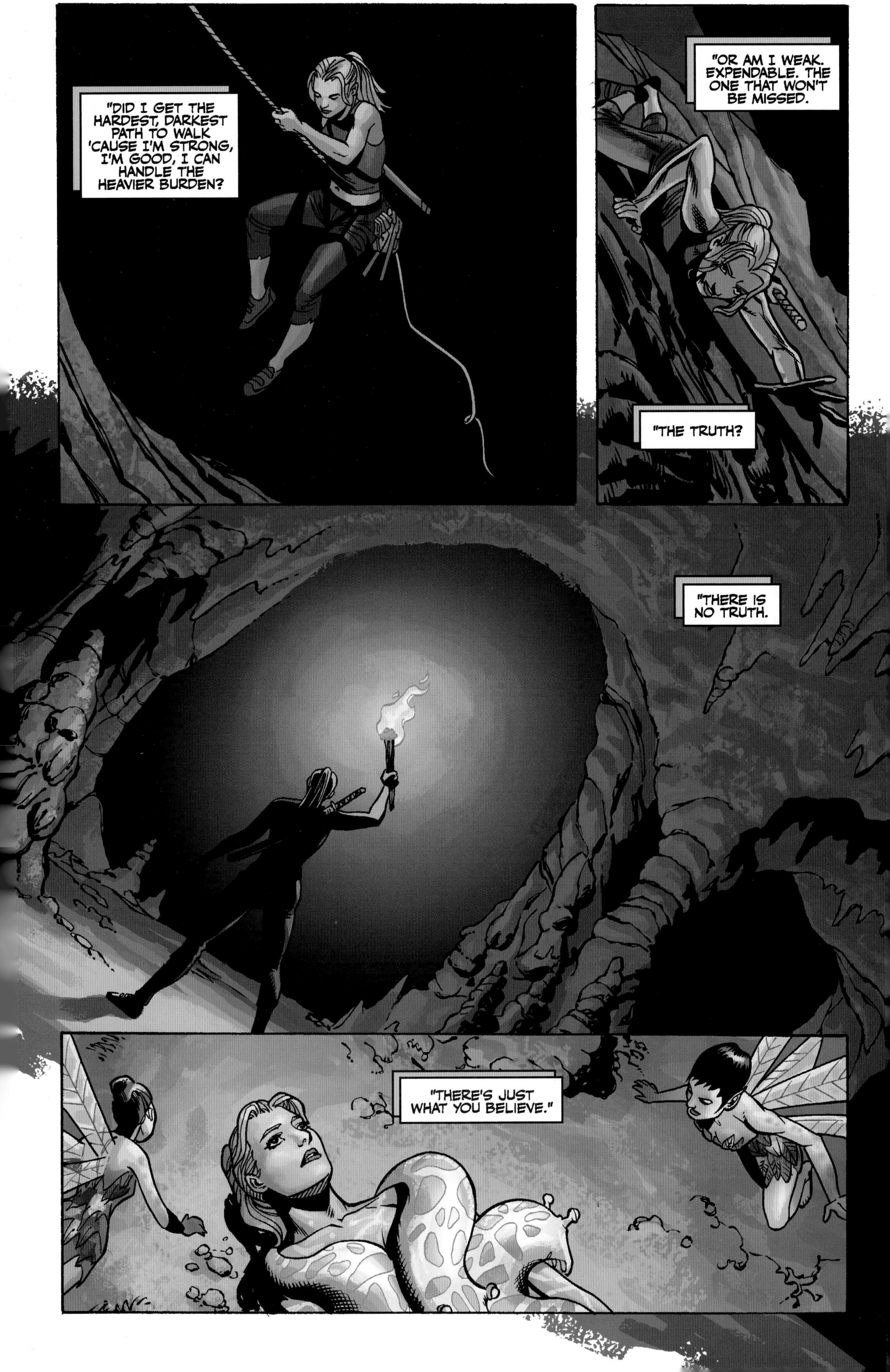
"DID I GET THE HARDEST, DARKEST PATH TO WALK 'CAUSE I'M STRONG, I'M GOOD, I CAN HANDLE THE HEAVIER BURDEN?
"OR AM I WEAK. EXPENDABLE. THE ONE THAT WON'T BE MISSED.
"THE TRUTH?
"THERE IS NO TRUTH.
"THERE'S JUST WHAT YOU BELIEVE."

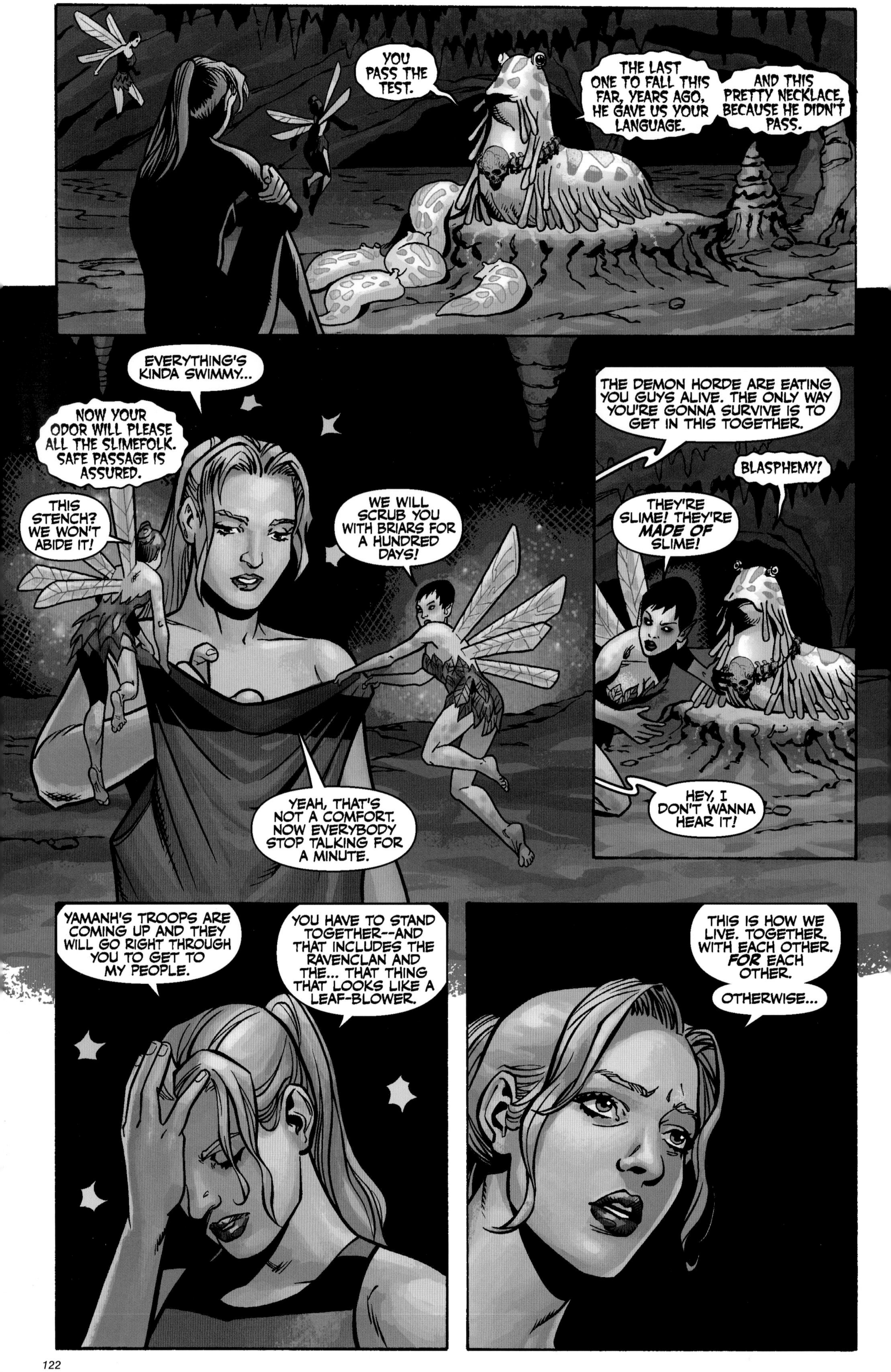
YOU PASS THE TEST.
THE LAST ONE TO FALL THIS FAR, YEARS AGO, HE GAVE US YOUR LANGUAGE.
AND THIS PRETTY NECKLACE, BECAUSE HE DIDN'T PASS.
EVERYTHING'S KINDA SWIMMY...
NOW YOUR ODOR WILL PLEASE ALL THE SLIMEFOLK. SAFE PASSAGE IS ASSURED.
THIS STENCH? WE WON'T ABIDE IT!
WE WILL SCRUB YOU WITH BRIARS FOR A HUNDRED DAYS!
YEAH, THAT'S NOT A COMFORT. NOW EVERYBODY STOP TALKING FOR A MINUTE.
THE DEMON HORDE ARE EATING YOU GUYS ALIVE. THE ONLY WAY YOU'RE GONNA SURVIVE IS TO GET IN THIS TOGETHER.
BLASPHEMY!
THEY'RE SLIME! THEY'RE *MADE OF* SLIME!
HEY, I DON'T WANNA HEAR IT!
YAMANH'S TROOPS ARE COMING UP AND THEY WILL GO RIGHT THROUGH YOU TO GET TO MY PEOPLE.
YOU HAVE TO STAND TOGETHER--AND THAT INCLUDES THE RAVENCLAN AND THE... THAT THING THAT LOOKS LIKE A LEAF-BLOWER.
THIS IS HOW WE LIVE. TOGETHER. WITH EACH OTHER. *FOR* EACH OTHER.
OTHERWISE...

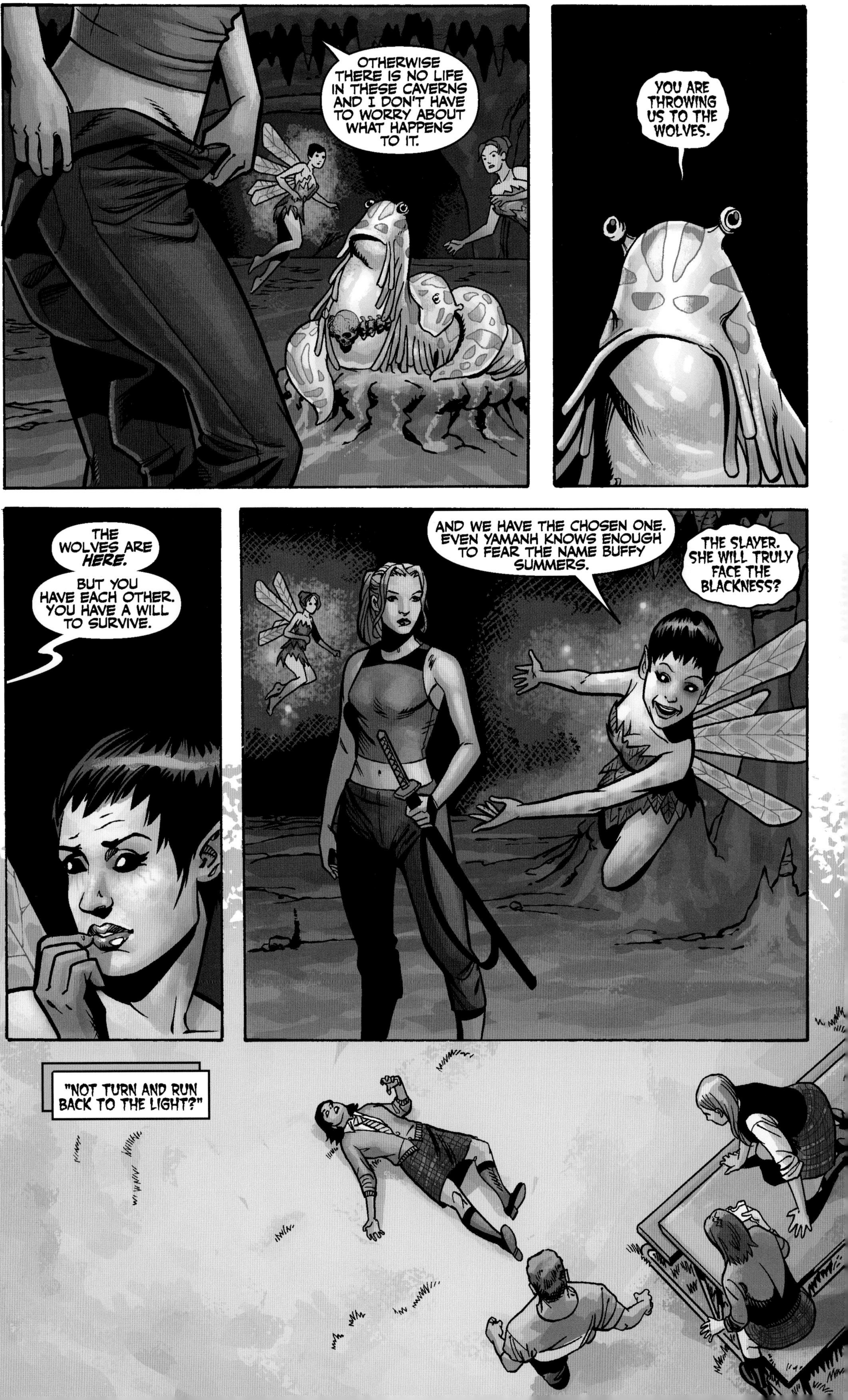
OTHERWISE THERE IS NO LIFE IN THESE CAVERNS AND I DON'T HAVE TO WORRY ABOUT WHAT HAPPENS TO IT.
YOU ARE THROWING US TO THE WOLVES.
THE WOLVES ARE HERE.
BUT YOU HAVE EACH OTHER. YOU HAVE A WILL TO SURVIVE.
AND WE HAVE THE CHOSEN ONE. EVEN YAMANH KNOWS ENOUGH TO FEAR THE NAME BUFFY SUMMERS.
THE SLAYER. SHE WILL TRULY FACE THE BLACKNESS?
"NOT TURN AND RUN BACK TO THE LIGHT?"

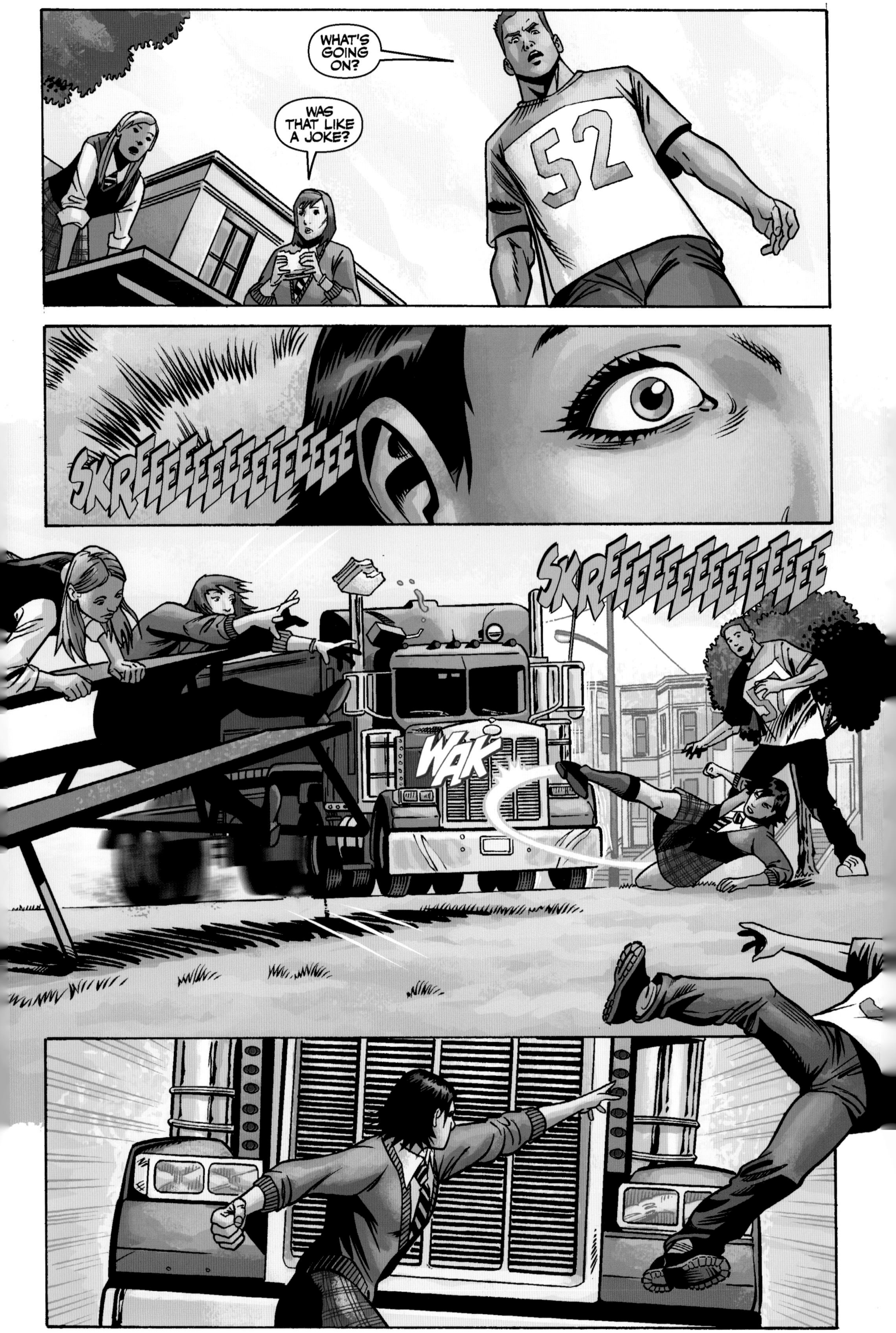
WHAT'S GOING ON?
WAS THAT LIKE A JOKE?
SKREEEEEEEEEEEEEE
SKREEEEEEEEEEEEEE
WAK

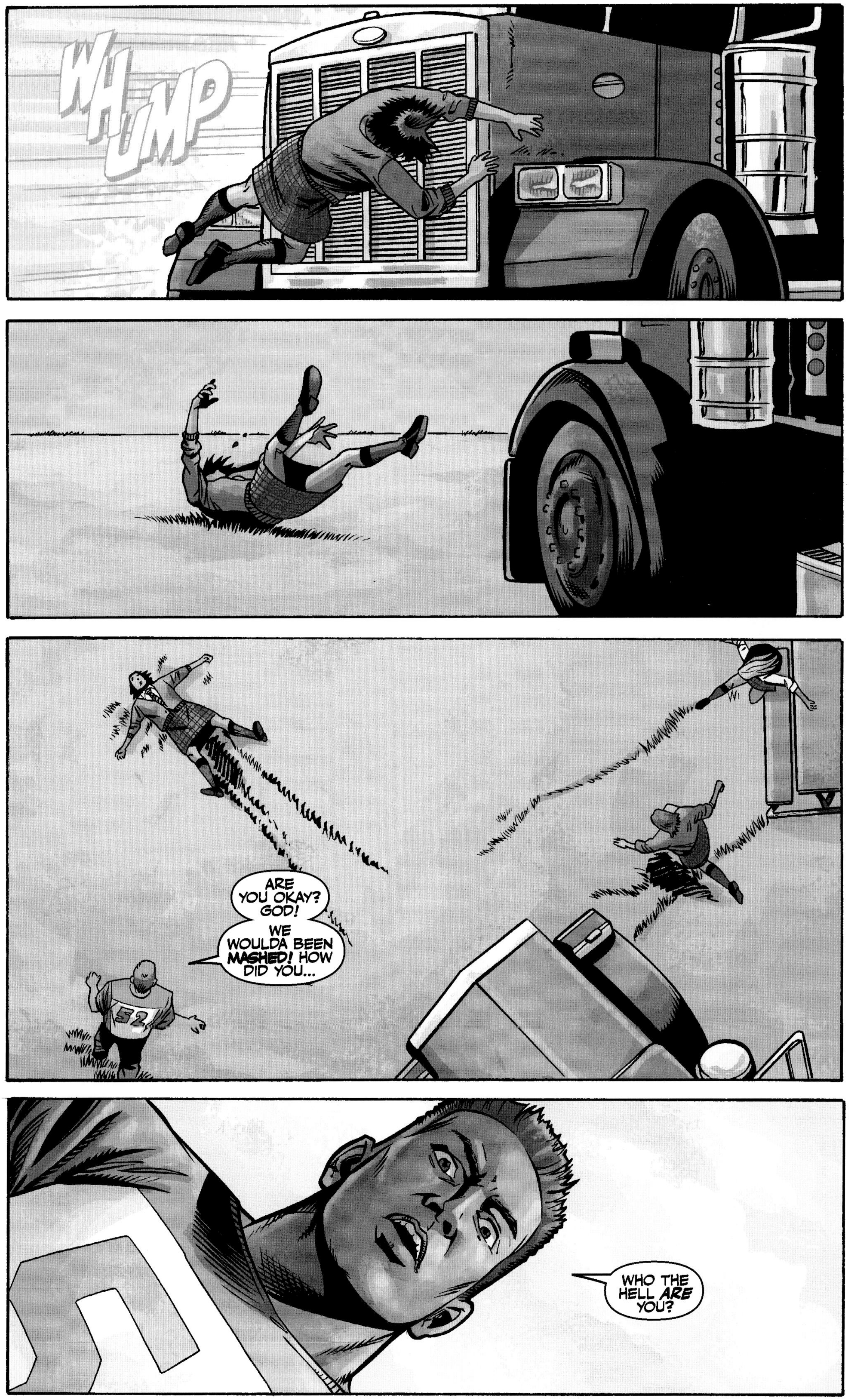
WHUMP
ARE YOU OKAY? GOD!
WE WOULDA BEEN MASHED! HOW DID YOU...
52
WHO THE HELL ARE YOU?

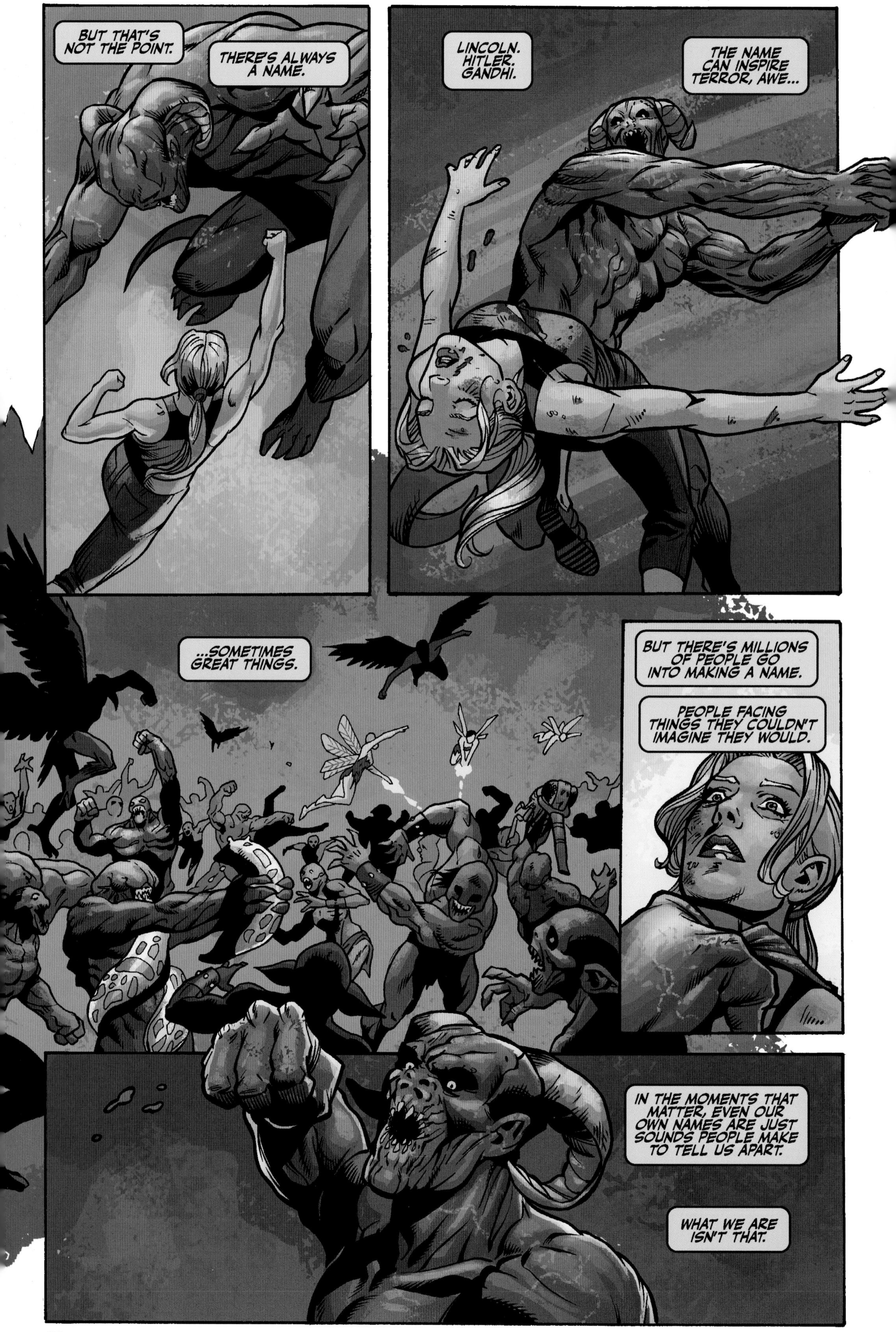
BUT THAT'S NOT THE POINT.
THERE'S ALWAYS A NAME.
LINCOLN. HITLER. GANDHI.
THE NAME CAN INSPIRE TERROR, AWE...
...SOMETIMES GREAT THINGS.
BUT THERE'S MILLIONS OF PEOPLE GO INTO MAKING A NAME.
PEOPLE FACING THINGS THEY COULDN'T IMAGINE THEY WOULD.
IN THE MOMENTS THAT MATTER, EVEN OUR OWN NAMES ARE JUST SOUNDS PEOPLE MAKE TO TELL US APART.
WHAT WE ARE ISN'T THAT.

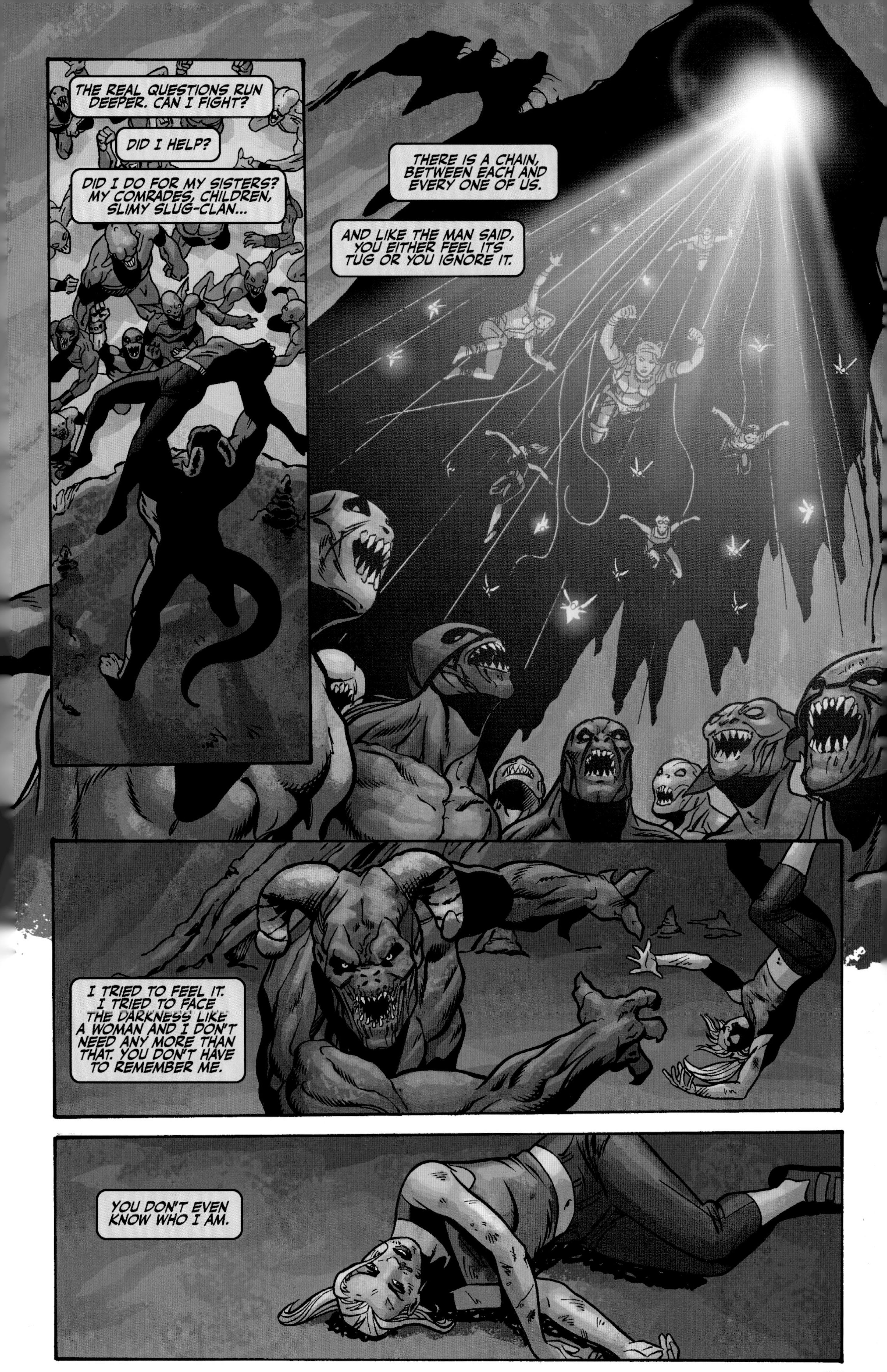
THE REAL QUESTIONS RUN DEEPER. CAN I FIGHT?
DID I HELP?
DID I DO FOR MY SISTERS? MY COMRADES, CHILDREN, SLIMY SLUG-CLAN...
THERE IS A CHAIN, BETWEEN EACH AND EVERY ONE OF US.
AND LIKE THE MAN SAID, YOU EITHER FEEL ITS TUG OR YOU IGNORE IT.
I TRIED TO FEEL IT. I TRIED TO FACE THE DARKNESS LIKE A WOMAN AND I DON'T NEED ANY MORE THAN THAT. YOU DON'T HAVE TO REMEMBER ME.
YOU DON'T EVEN KNOW WHO I AM.

BUT I DO.

FOR
JANIE
KLEINMAN

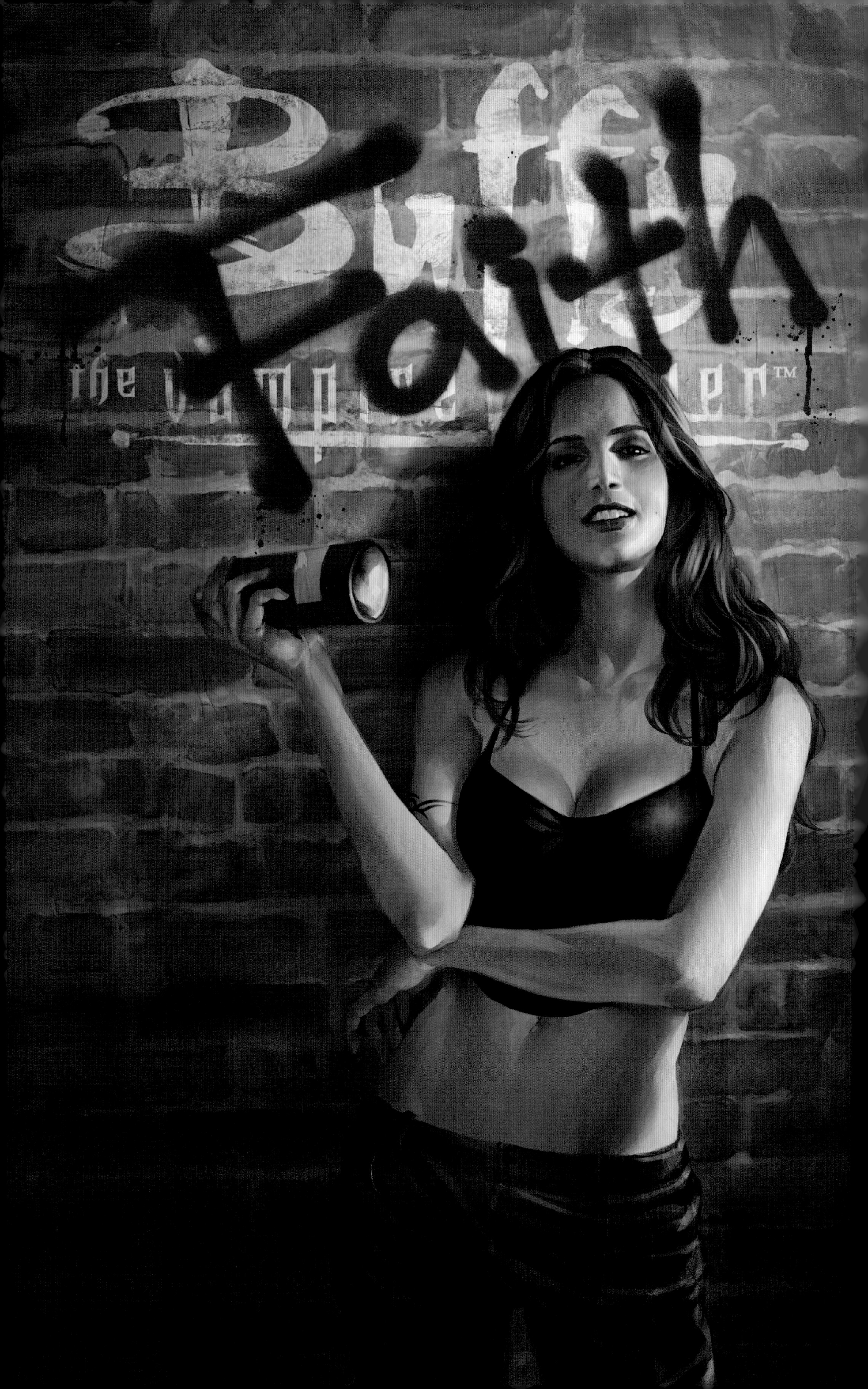
Buffy
Faith

NO FUTURE FOR YOU

PART ONE

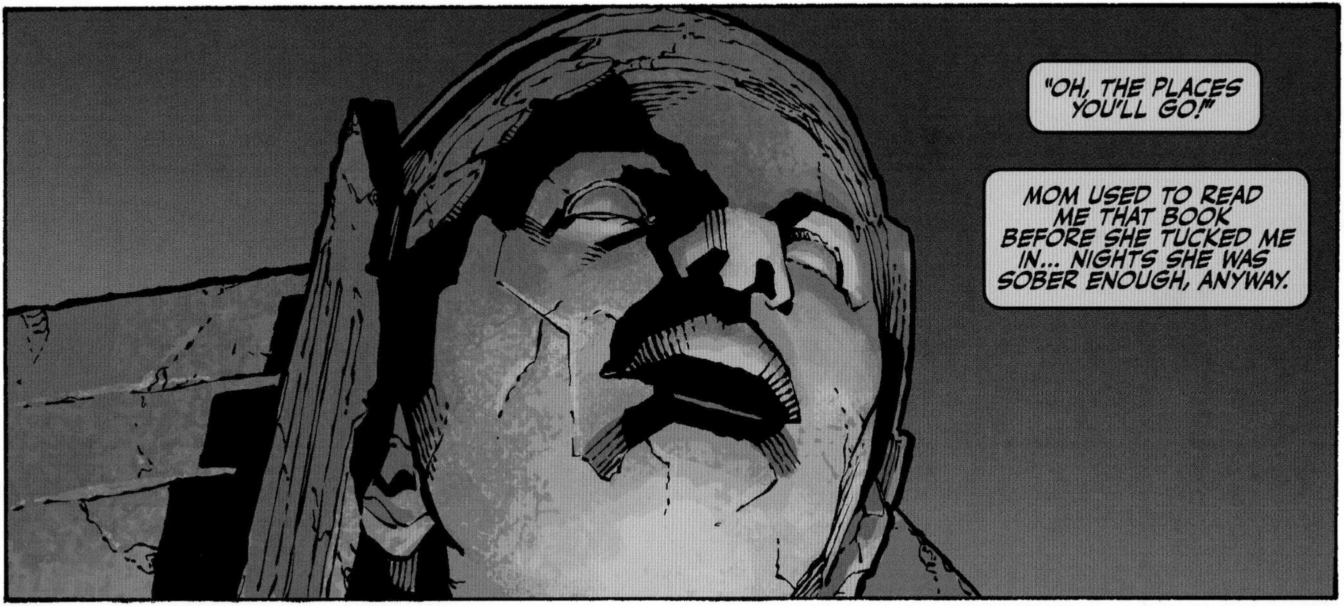
"OH, THE PLACES YOU'LL GO!"
MOM USED TO READ ME THAT BOOK BEFORE SHE TUCKED ME IN... NIGHTS SHE WAS SOBER ENOUGH, ANYWAY.

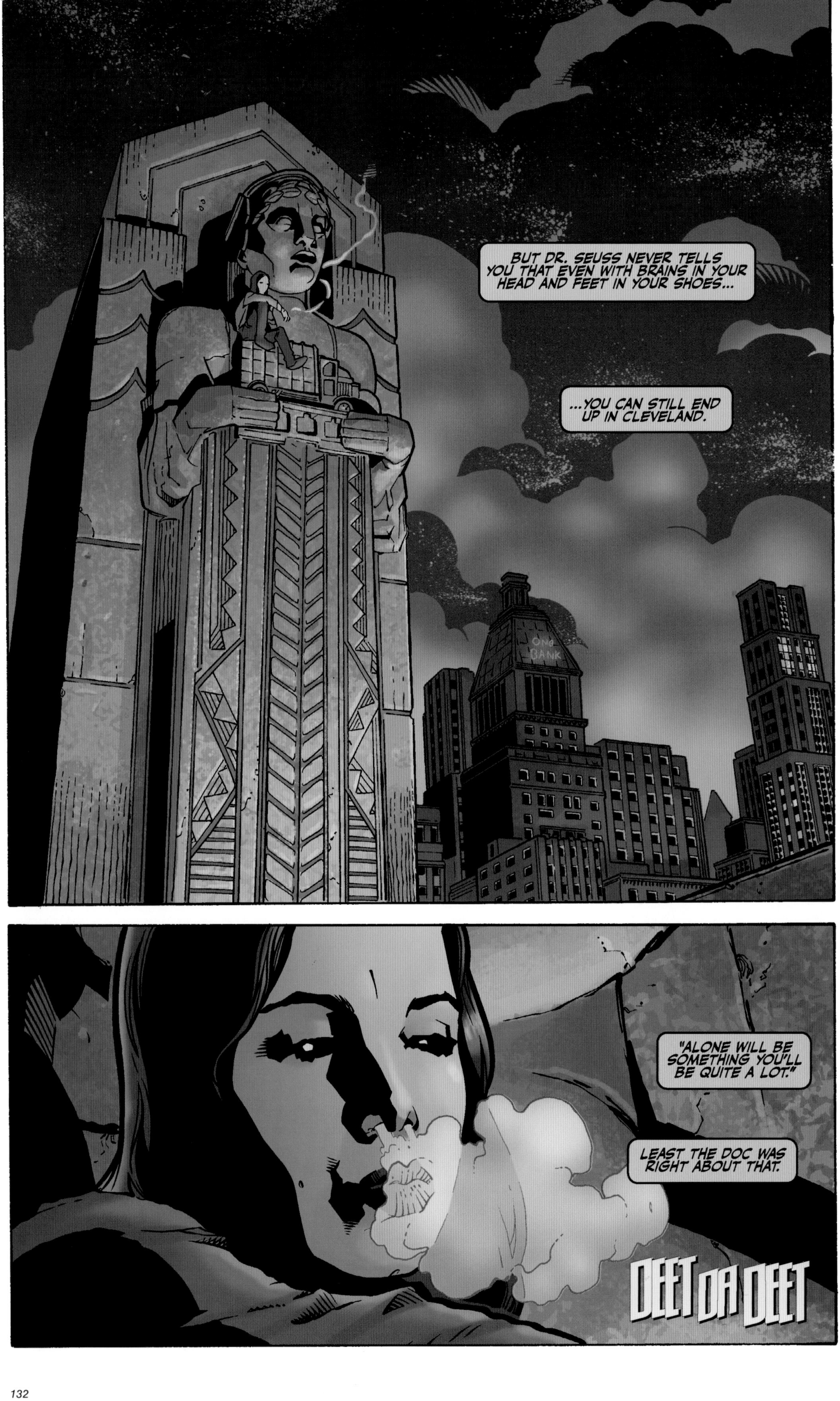
BUT DR. SEUSS NEVER TELLS YOU THAT EVEN WITH BRAINS IN YOUR HEAD AND FEET IN YOUR SHOES...
...YOU CAN STILL END UP IN CLEVELAND.
"ALONE WILL BE SOMETHING YOU'LL BE QUITE A LOT."
LEAST THE DOC WAS RIGHT ABOUT THAT.
DEET DA DEET

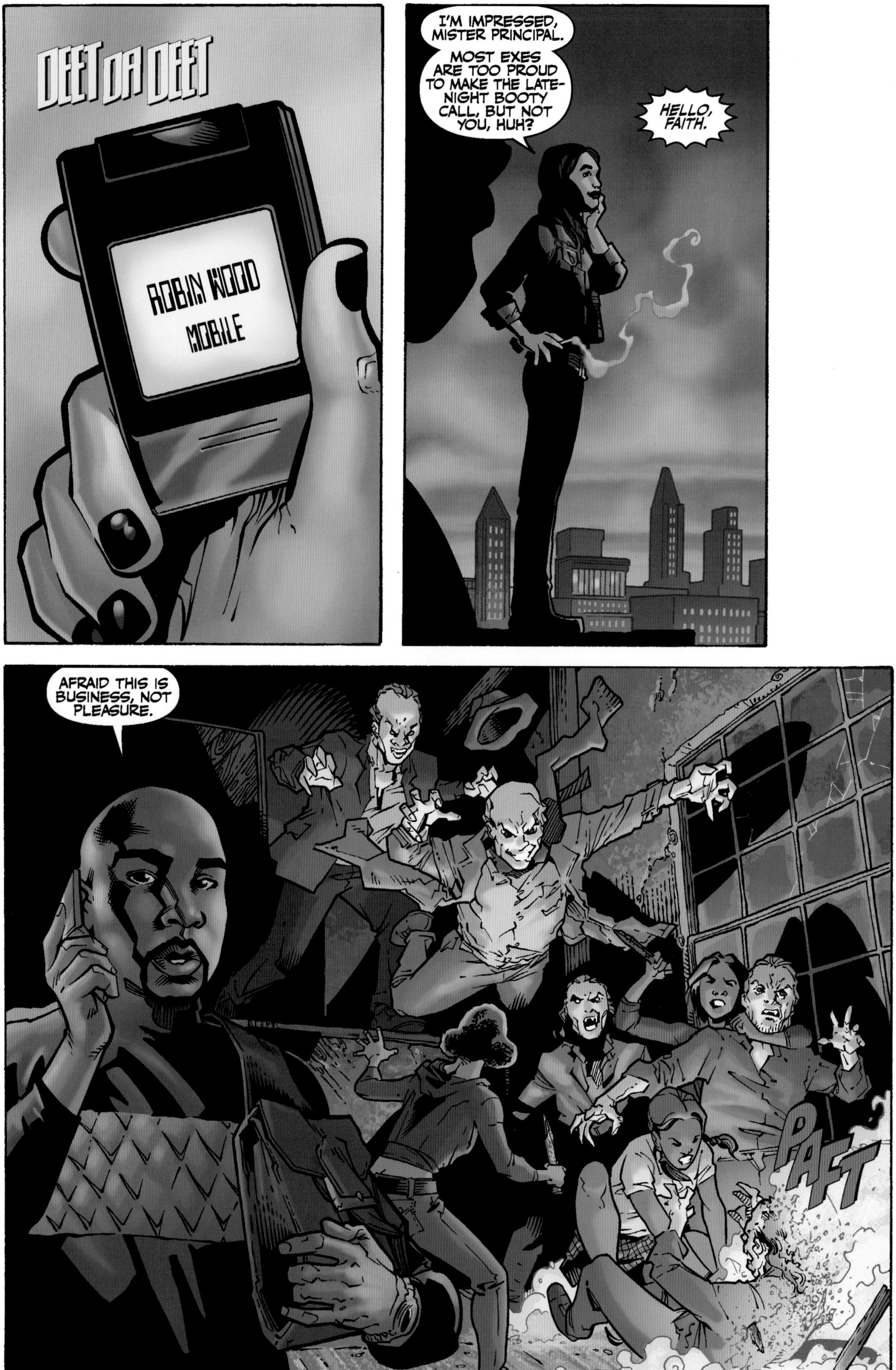
DEET DA DEET
ROBIN WOOD
MOBILE
I'M IMPRESSED, MISTER PRINCIPAL.
MOST EXES ARE TOO PROUD TO MAKE THE LATE-NIGHT BOOTY CALL, BUT NOT YOU, HUH?
HELLO, FAITH.
AFRAID THIS IS BUSINESS, NOT PLEASURE.
PAFT

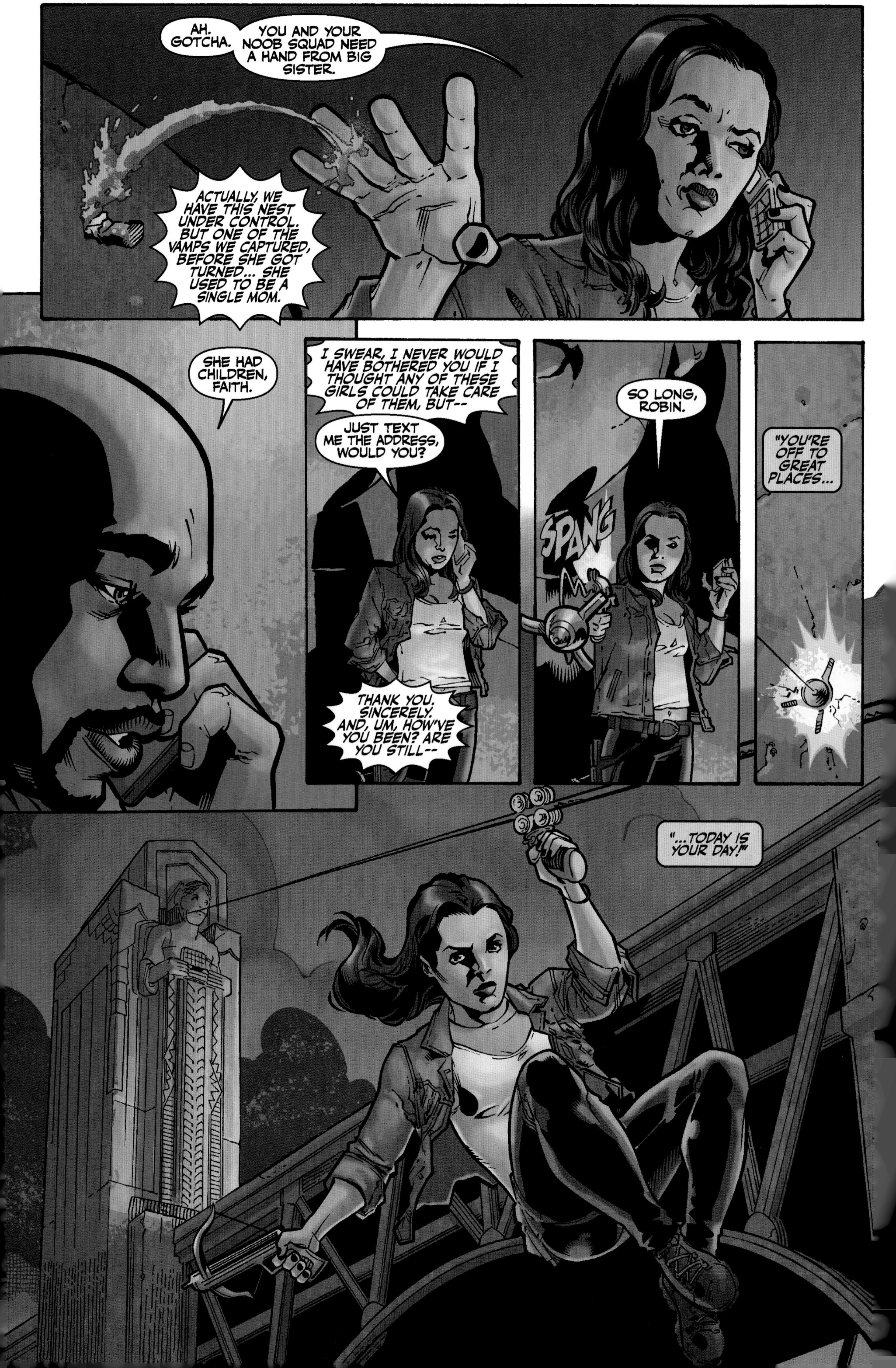
AH. GOTCHA.
YOU AND YOUR NOOB SQUAD NEED A HAND FROM BIG SISTER.
ACTUALLY, WE HAVE THIS NEST UNDER CONTROL. BUT ONE OF THE VAMPS WE CAPTURED, BEFORE SHE GOT TURNED... SHE USED TO BE A SINGLE MOM.
SHE HAD CHILDREN, FAITH.
I SWEAR, I NEVER WOULD HAVE BOTHERED YOU IF I THOUGHT ANY OF THESE GIRLS COULD TAKE CARE OF THEM, BUT--
JUST TEXT ME THE ADDRESS, WOULD YOU?
THANK YOU. SINCERELY. AND, UM, HOW'VE YOU BEEN? ARE YOU STILL--
SO LONG, ROBIN.
SPANG
"YOU'RE OFF TO GREAT PLACES...
"...TODAY IS YOUR DAY!"

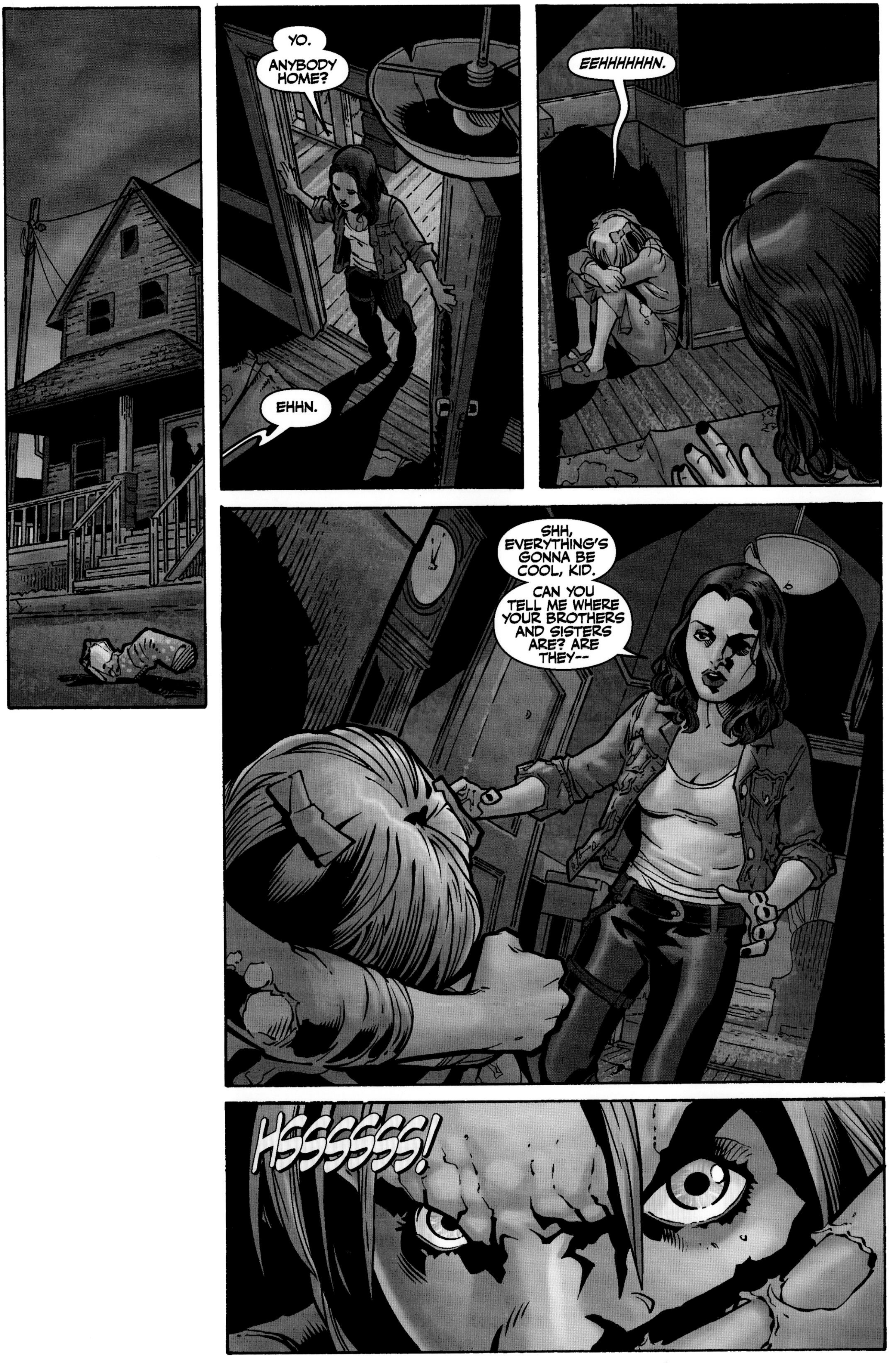
YO. ANYBODY HOME?
EHHN.
EEHHHHHHN.
SHH, EVERYTHING'S GONNA BE COOL, KID.
CAN YOU TELL ME WHERE YOUR BROTHERS AND SISTERS ARE? ARE THEY--
HSSSSSS!

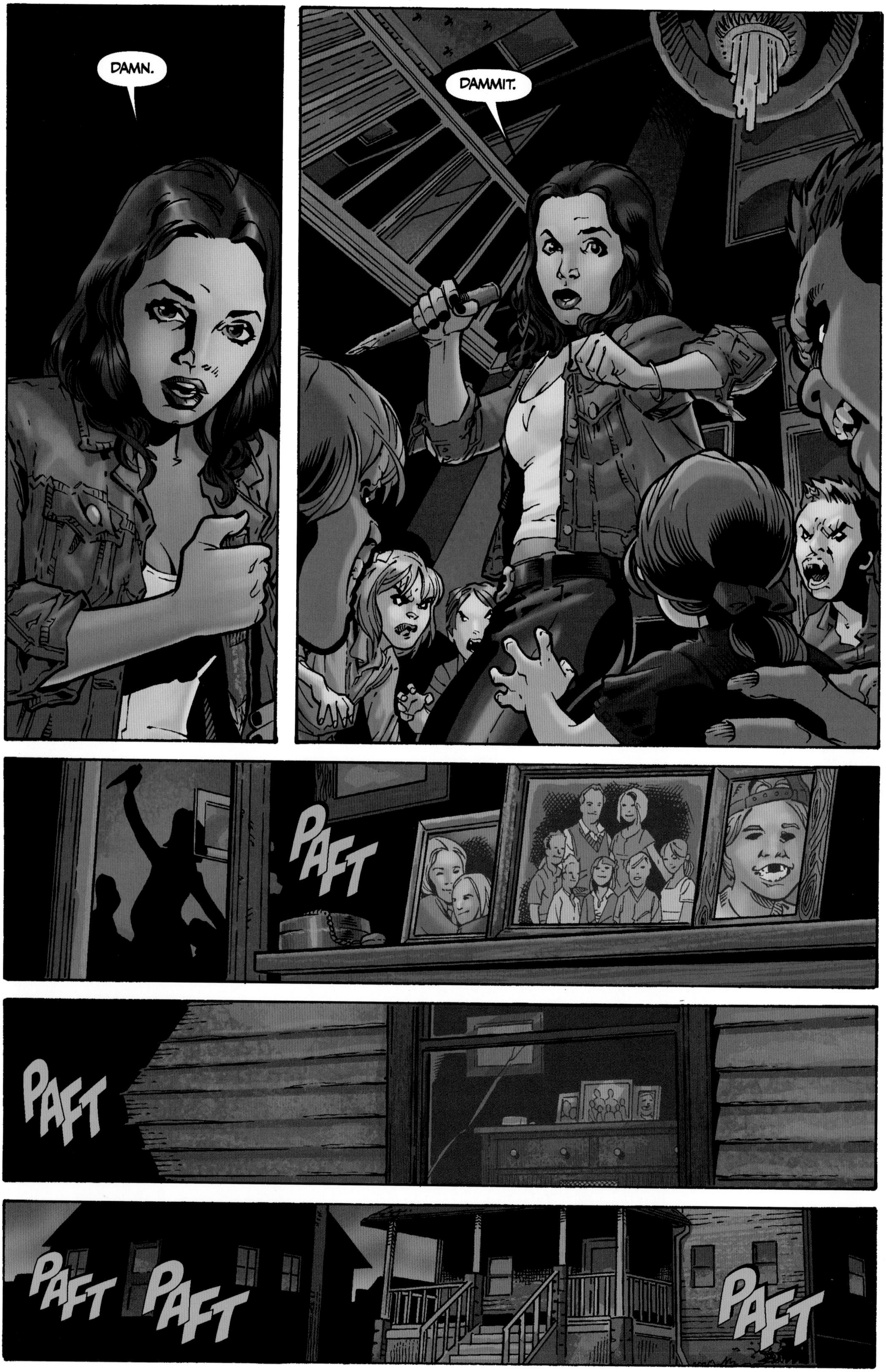
DAMN.
DAMMIT.
PAFT
PAFT
PAFT
PAFT
PAFT

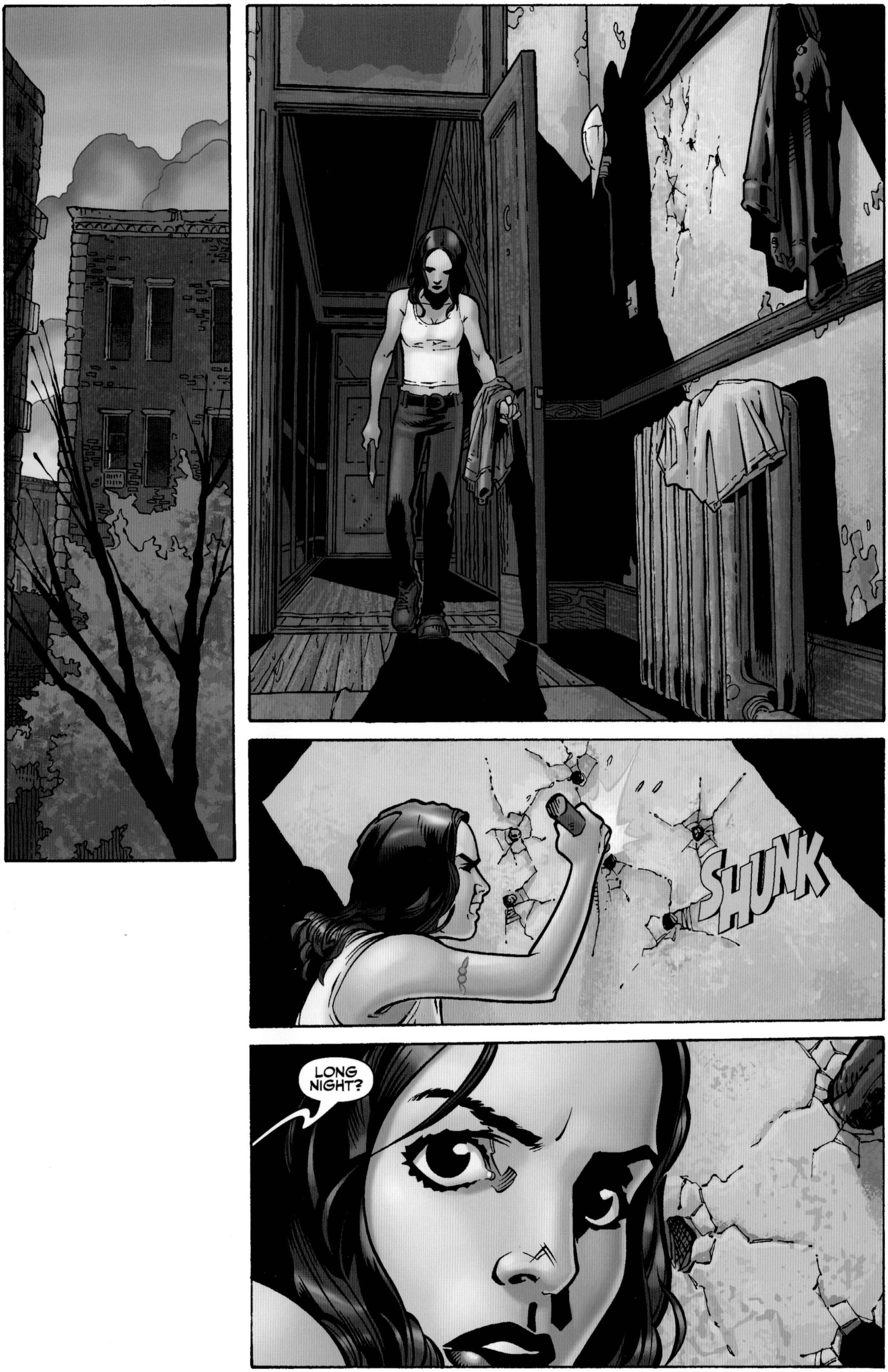
SHUNK
LONG NIGHT?

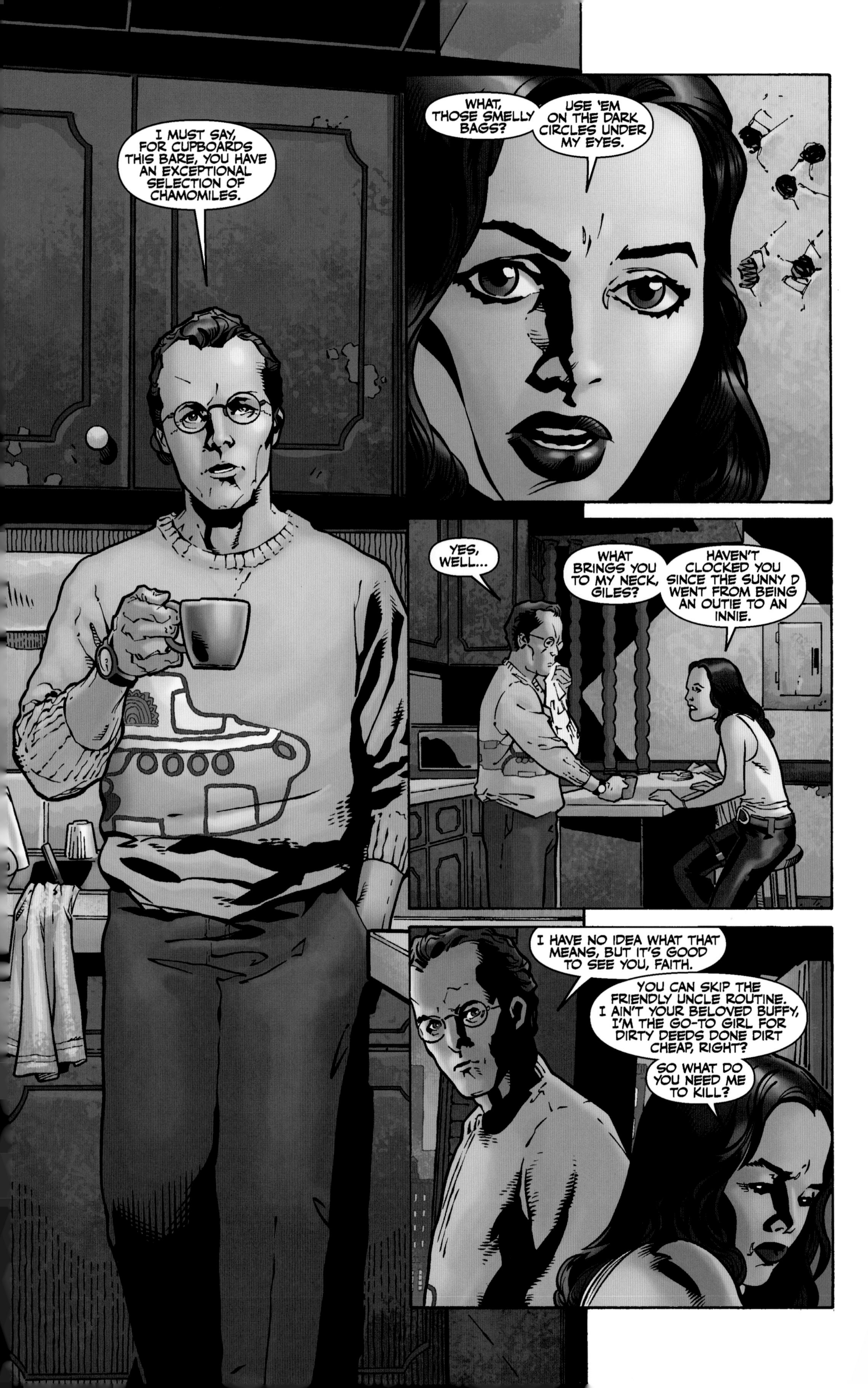
I MUST SAY, FOR CUPBOARDS THIS BARE, YOU HAVE AN EXCEPTIONAL SELECTION OF CHAMOMILES.
WHAT, THOSE SMELLY BAGS?
USE 'EM ON THE DARK CIRCLES UNDER MY EYES.
YES, WELL...
WHAT BRINGS YOU TO MY NECK, GILES?
HAVEN'T CLOCKED YOU SINCE THE SUNNY D WENT FROM BEING AN OUTIE TO AN INNIE.
I HAVE NO IDEA WHAT THAT MEANS, BUT IT'S GOOD TO SEE YOU, FAITH.
YOU CAN SKIP THE FRIENDLY UNCLE ROUTINE. I AIN'T YOUR BELOVED BUFFY, I'M THE GO-TO GIRL FOR DIRTY DEEDS DONE DIRT CHEAP, RIGHT?
SO WHAT DO YOU NEED ME TO KILL?

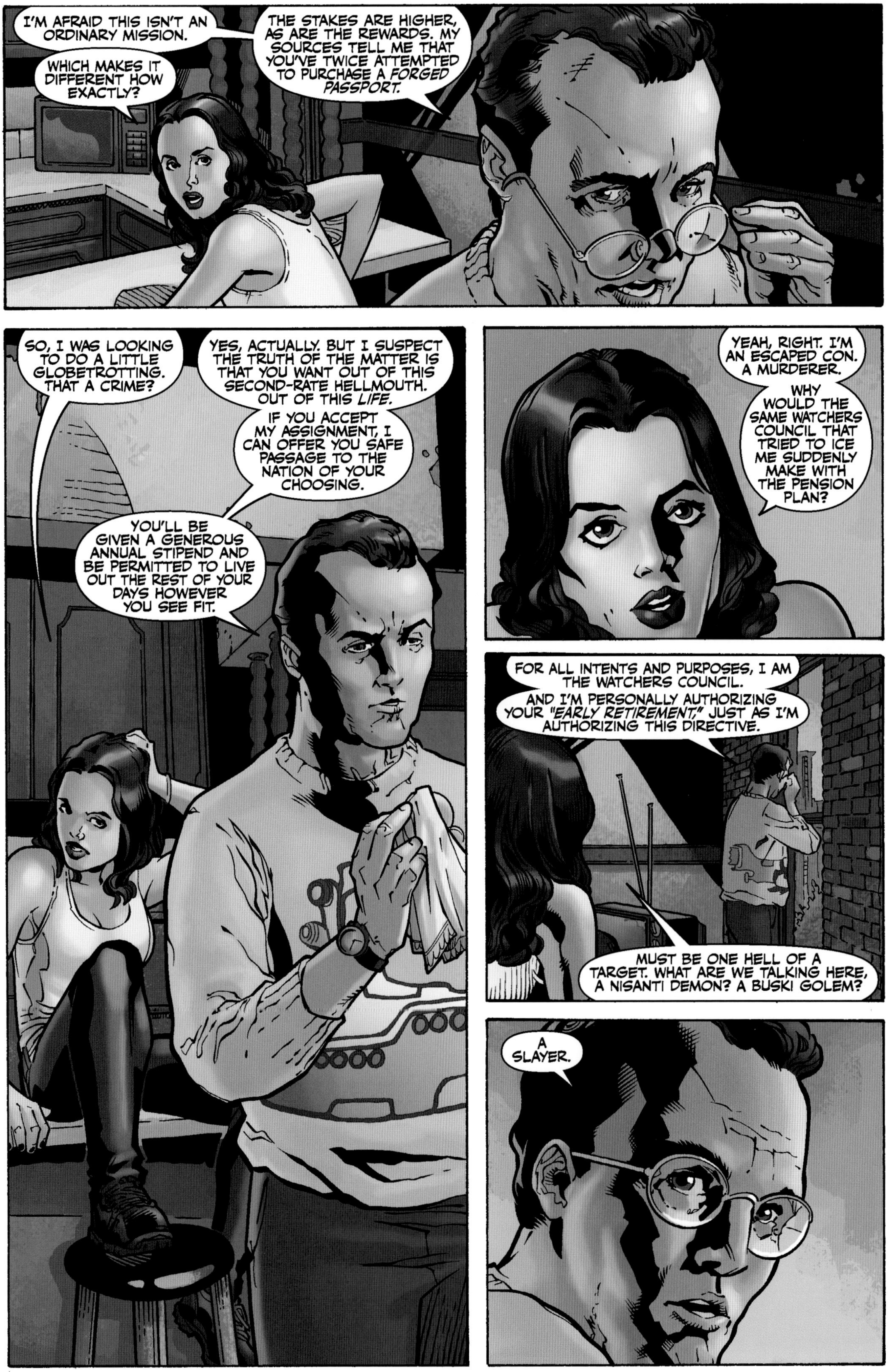
I'M AFRAID THIS ISN'T AN ORDINARY MISSION.
WHICH MAKES IT DIFFERENT HOW EXACTLY?
THE STAKES ARE HIGHER, AS ARE THE REWARDS. MY SOURCES TELL ME THAT YOU'VE TWICE ATTEMPTED TO PURCHASE A *FORGED PASSPORT.*
SO, I WAS LOOKING TO DO A LITTLE GLOBETROTTING. THAT A CRIME?
YES, ACTUALLY. BUT I SUSPECT THE TRUTH OF THE MATTER IS THAT YOU WANT OUT OF THIS SECOND-RATE HELLMOUTH. OUT OF THIS *LIFE.*
IF YOU ACCEPT MY ASSIGNMENT, I CAN OFFER YOU SAFE PASSAGE TO THE NATION OF YOUR CHOOSING.
YOU'LL BE GIVEN A GENEROUS ANNUAL STIPEND AND BE PERMITTED TO LIVE OUT THE REST OF YOUR DAYS HOWEVER YOU SEE FIT.
YEAH, RIGHT. I'M AN ESCAPED CON. A MURDERER.
WHY WOULD THE SAME WATCHERS COUNCIL THAT TRIED TO ICE ME SUDDENLY MAKE WITH THE PENSION PLAN?
FOR ALL INTENTS AND PURPOSES, I AM THE WATCHERS COUNCIL.
AND I'M PERSONALLY AUTHORIZING YOUR *"EARLY RETIREMENT,"* JUST AS I'M AUTHORIZING THIS DIRECTIVE.
MUST BE ONE HELL OF A TARGET. WHAT ARE WE TALKING HERE, A NISANTI DEMON? A BUSKI GOLEM?
A SLAYER.

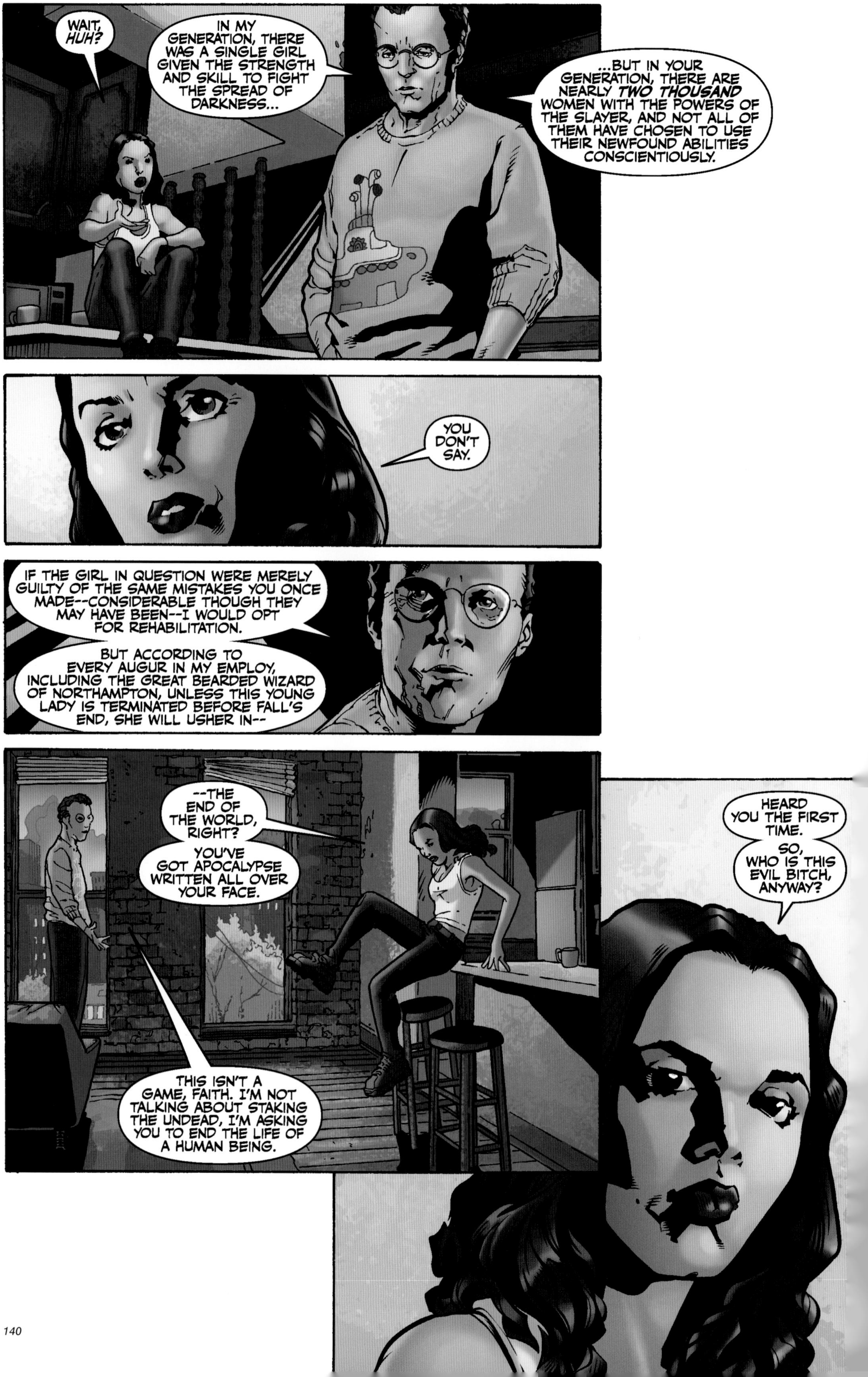
WAIT, HUH?
IN MY GENERATION, THERE WAS A SINGLE GIRL GIVEN THE STRENGTH AND SKILL TO FIGHT THE SPREAD OF DARKNESS...
...BUT IN YOUR GENERATION, THERE ARE NEARLY TWO THOUSAND WOMEN WITH THE POWERS OF THE SLAYER, AND NOT ALL OF THEM HAVE CHOSEN TO USE THEIR NEWFOUND ABILITIES CONSCIENTIOUSLY.
YOU DON'T SAY.
IF THE GIRL IN QUESTION WERE MERELY GUILTY OF THE SAME MISTAKES YOU ONCE MADE--CONSIDERABLE THOUGH THEY MAY HAVE BEEN--I WOULD OPT FOR REHABILITATION.
BUT ACCORDING TO EVERY AUGUR IN MY EMPLOY, INCLUDING THE GREAT BEARDED WIZARD OF NORTHAMPTON, UNLESS THIS YOUNG LADY IS TERMINATED BEFORE FALL'S END, SHE WILL USHER IN--
--THE END OF THE WORLD, RIGHT?
YOU'VE GOT APOCALYPSE WRITTEN ALL OVER YOUR FACE.
THIS ISN'T A GAME, FAITH. I'M NOT TALKING ABOUT STAKING THE UNDEAD, I'M ASKING YOU TO END THE LIFE OF A HUMAN BEING.
HEARD YOU THE FIRST TIME.
SO, WHO IS THIS EVIL BITCH, ANYWAY?

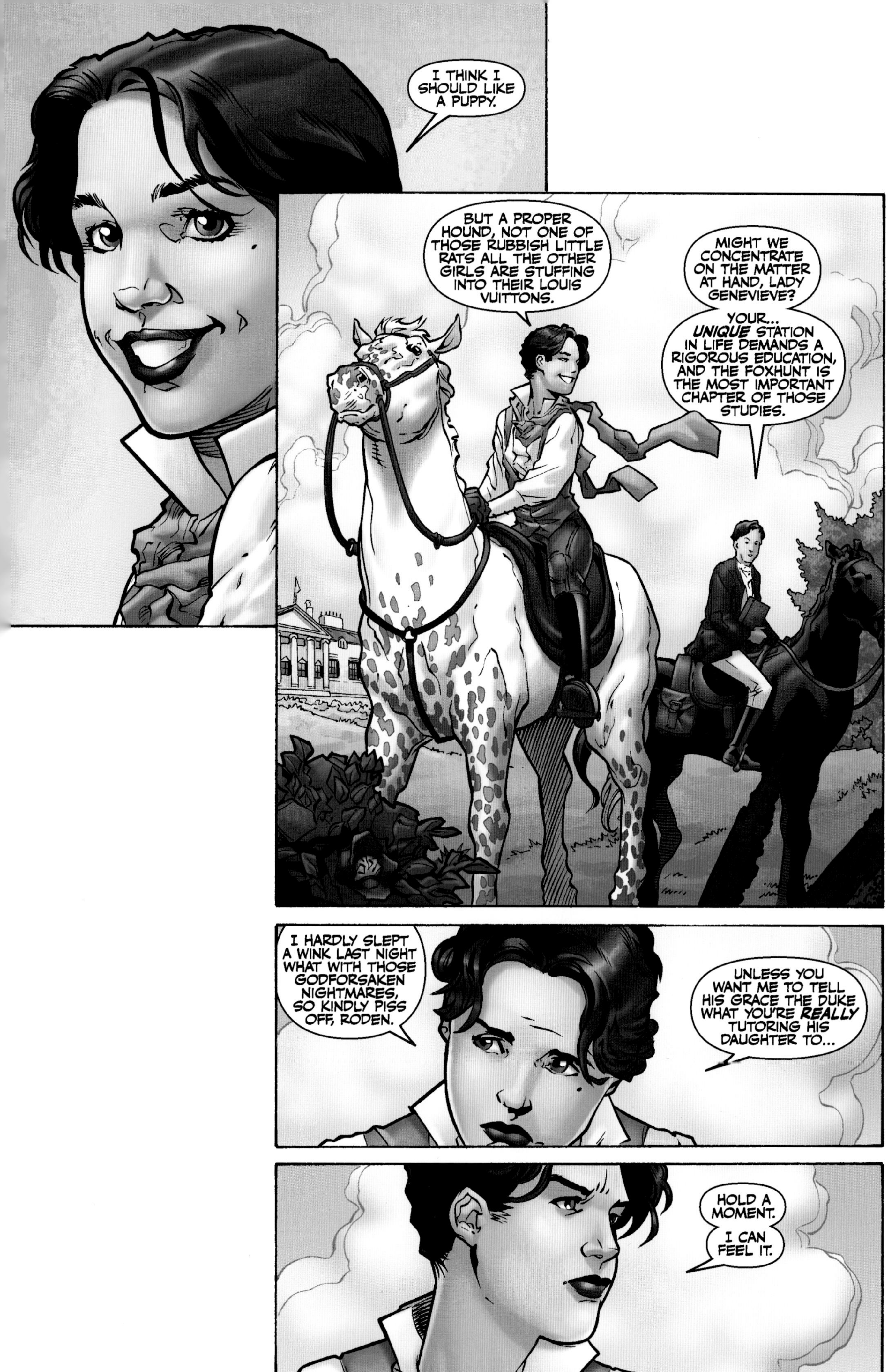
I THINK I SHOULD LIKE A PUPPY.
BUT A PROPER HOUND, NOT ONE OF THOSE RUBBISH LITTLE RATS ALL THE OTHER GIRLS ARE STUFFING INTO THEIR LOUIS VUITTONS.
MIGHT WE CONCENTRATE ON THE MATTER AT HAND, LADY GENEVIEVE?
YOUR... UNIQUE STATION IN LIFE DEMANDS A RIGOROUS EDUCATION, AND THE FOXHUNT IS THE MOST IMPORTANT CHAPTER OF THOSE STUDIES.
I HARDLY SLEPT A WINK LAST NIGHT WHAT WITH THOSE GODFORSAKEN NIGHTMARES, SO KINDLY PISS OFF, RODEN.
UNLESS YOU WANT ME TO TELL HIS GRACE THE DUKE WHAT YOU'RE REALLY TUTORING HIS DAUGHTER TO...
HOLD A MOMENT.
I CAN FEEL IT.

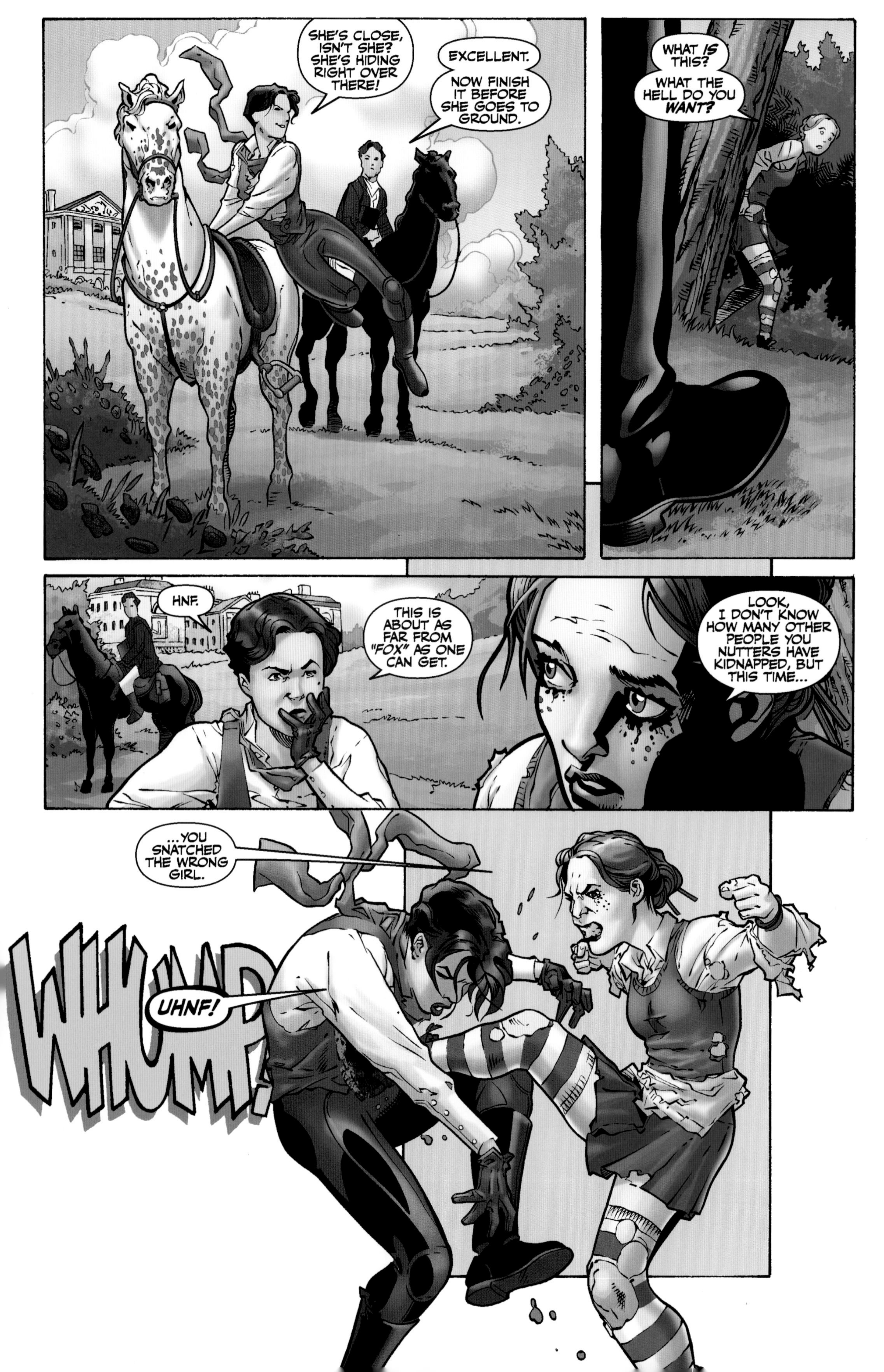
SHE'S CLOSE, ISN'T SHE? SHE'S HIDING RIGHT OVER THERE!
EXCELLENT.
NOW FINISH IT BEFORE SHE GOES TO GROUND.
WHAT *IS* THIS?
WHAT THE HELL DO YOU *WANT?*
HNF.
THIS IS ABOUT AS FAR FROM "FOX" AS ONE CAN GET.
LOOK, I DON'T KNOW HOW MANY OTHER PEOPLE YOU NUTTERS HAVE KIDNAPPED, BUT THIS TIME...
...YOU SNATCHED THE WRONG GIRL.
WHUMP!
UHNF!

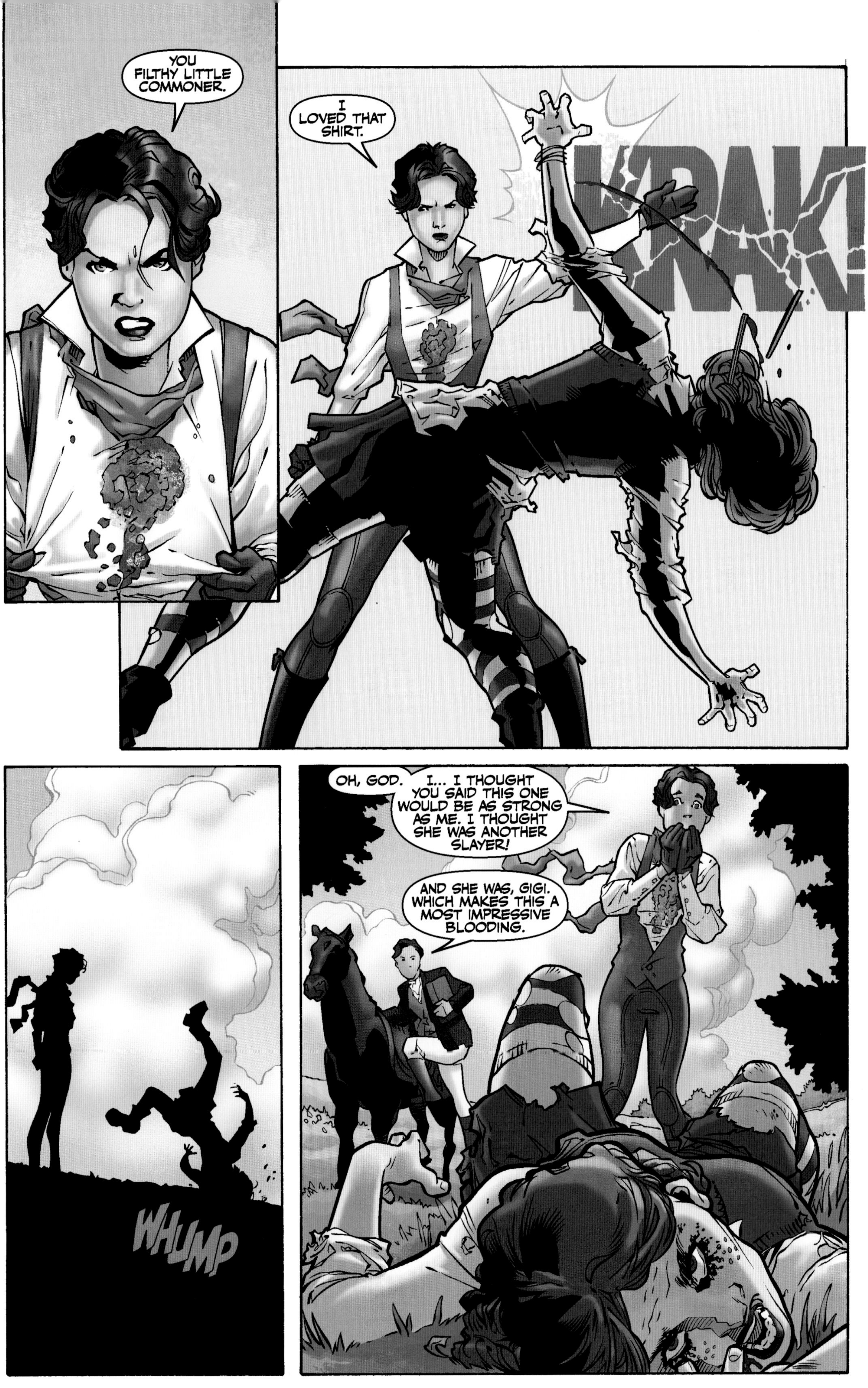
YOU FILTHY LITTLE COMMONER.
I LOVED THAT SHIRT.
KRAK!
WHUMP
OH, GOD.
I... I THOUGHT YOU SAID THIS ONE WOULD BE AS STRONG AS ME. I THOUGHT SHE WAS ANOTHER SLAYER!
AND SHE WAS, GIGI. WHICH MAKES THIS A MOST IMPRESSIVE BLOODING.

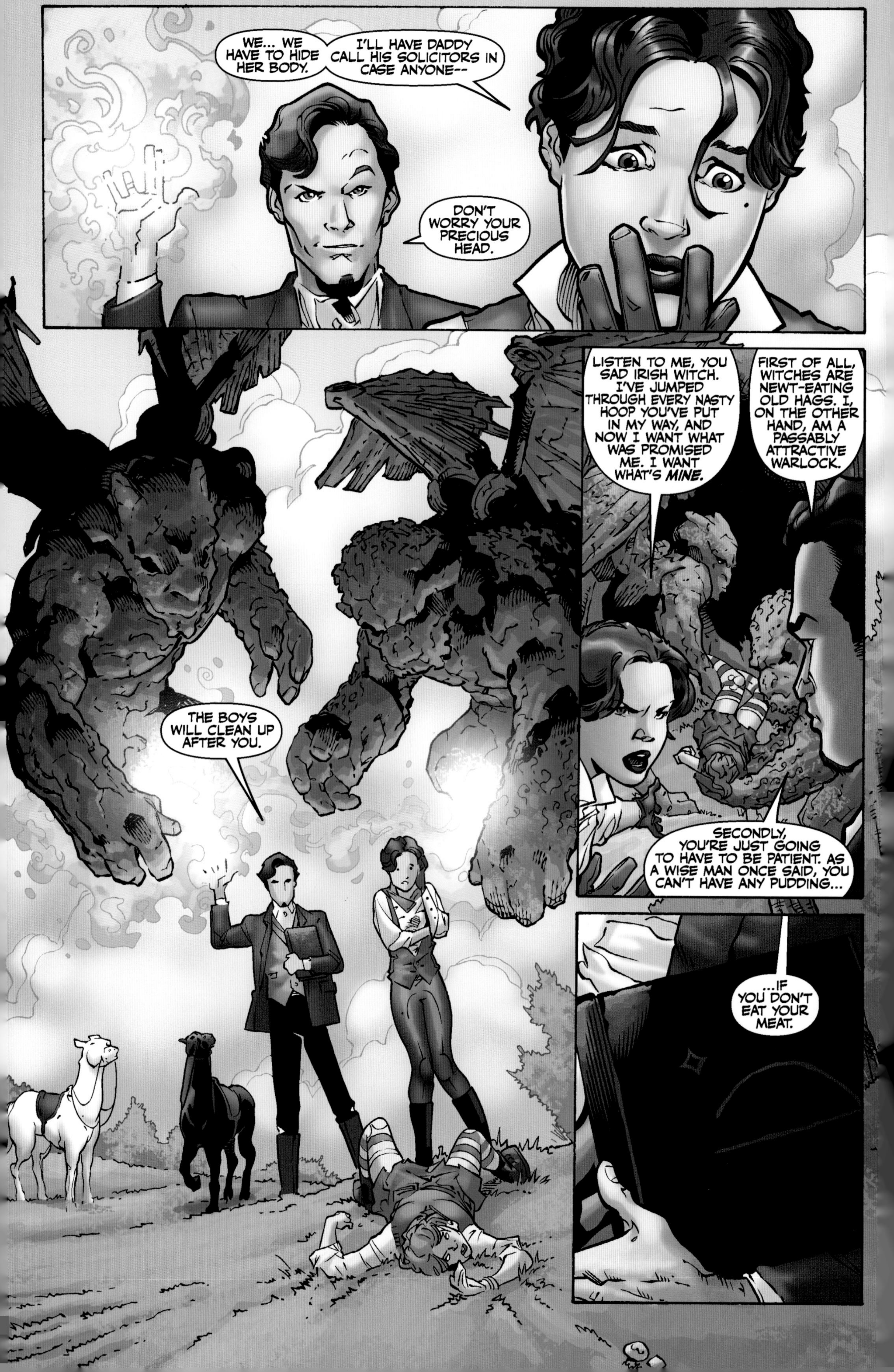
WE... WE HAVE TO HIDE HER BODY.
I'LL HAVE DADDY CALL HIS SOLICITORS IN CASE ANYONE--
DON'T WORRY YOUR PRECIOUS HEAD.
THE BOYS WILL CLEAN UP AFTER YOU.
LISTEN TO ME, YOU SAD IRISH WITCH. I'VE JUMPED THROUGH EVERY NASTY HOOP YOU'VE PUT IN MY WAY, AND NOW I WANT WHAT WAS PROMISED ME. I WANT WHAT'S MINE.
FIRST OF ALL, WITCHES ARE NEWT-EATING OLD HAGS. I, ON THE OTHER HAND, AM A PASSABLY ATTRACTIVE WARLOCK.
SECONDLY, YOU'RE JUST GOING TO HAVE TO BE PATIENT. AS A WISE MAN ONCE SAID, YOU CAN'T HAVE ANY PUDDING...
...IF YOU DON'T EAT YOUR MEAT.

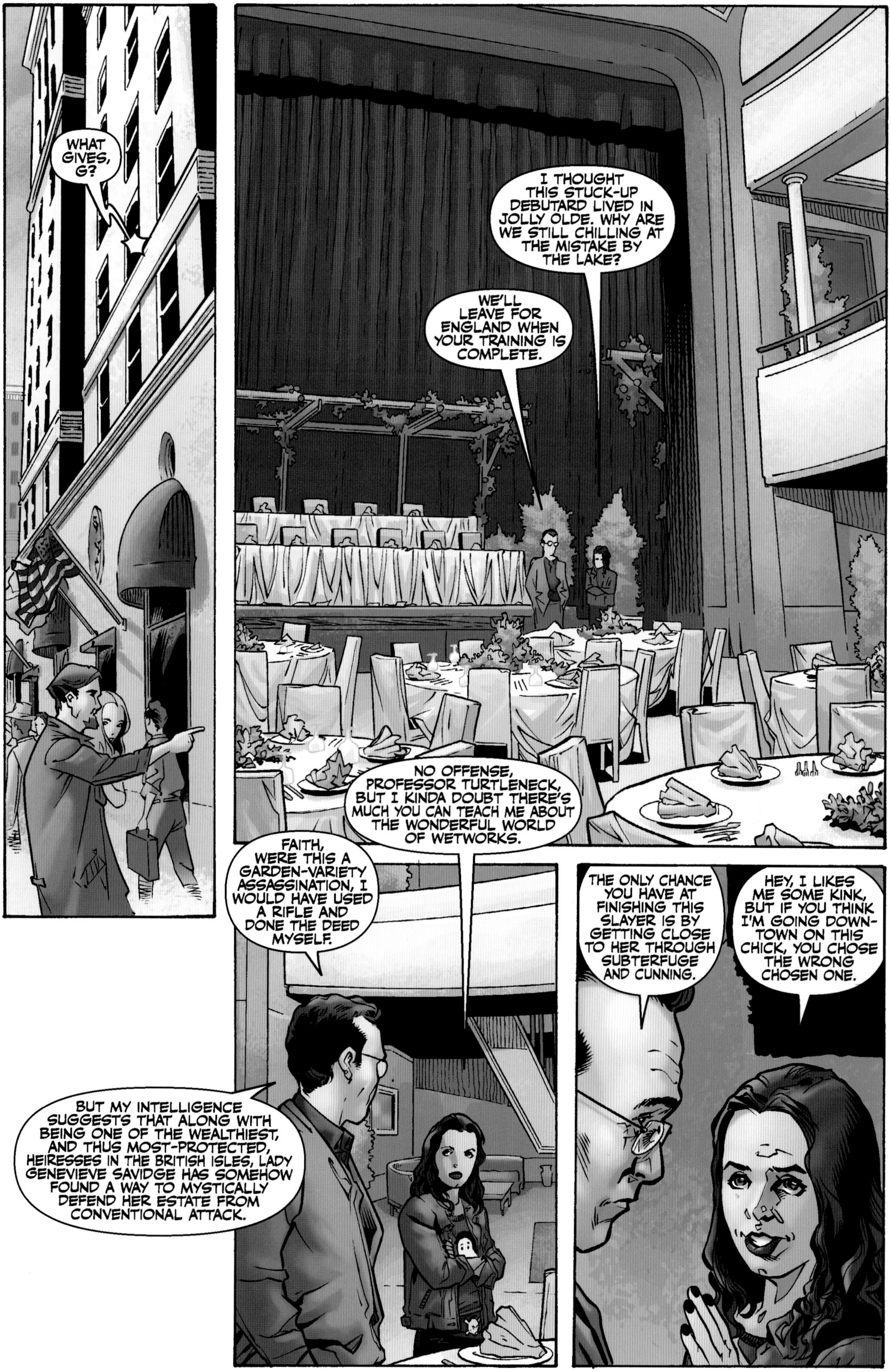
WHAT GIVES, G?
I THOUGHT THIS STUCK-UP DEBUTARD LIVED IN JOLLY OLDE. WHY ARE WE STILL CHILLING AT THE MISTAKE BY THE LAKE?
WE'LL LEAVE FOR ENGLAND WHEN YOUR TRAINING IS COMPLETE.
NO OFFENSE, PROFESSOR TURTLENECK, BUT I KINDA DOUBT THERE'S MUCH YOU CAN TEACH ME ABOUT THE WONDERFUL WORLD OF WETWORKS.
FAITH, WERE THIS A GARDEN-VARIETY ASSASSINATION, I WOULD HAVE USED A RIFLE AND DONE THE DEED MYSELF.
BUT MY INTELLIGENCE SUGGESTS THAT ALONG WITH BEING ONE OF THE WEALTHIEST, AND THUS MOST-PROTECTED, HEIRESSES IN THE BRITISH ISLES, LADY GENEVIEVE SAVIDGE HAS SOMEHOW FOUND A WAY TO MYSTICALLY DEFEND HER ESTATE FROM CONVENTIONAL ATTACK.
THE ONLY CHANCE YOU HAVE AT FINISHING THIS SLAYER IS BY GETTING CLOSE TO HER THROUGH SUBTERFUGE AND CUNNING.
HEY, I LIKES ME SOME KINK, BUT IF YOU THINK I'M GOING DOWNTOWN ON THIS CHICK, YOU CHOSE THE WRONG CHOSEN ONE.

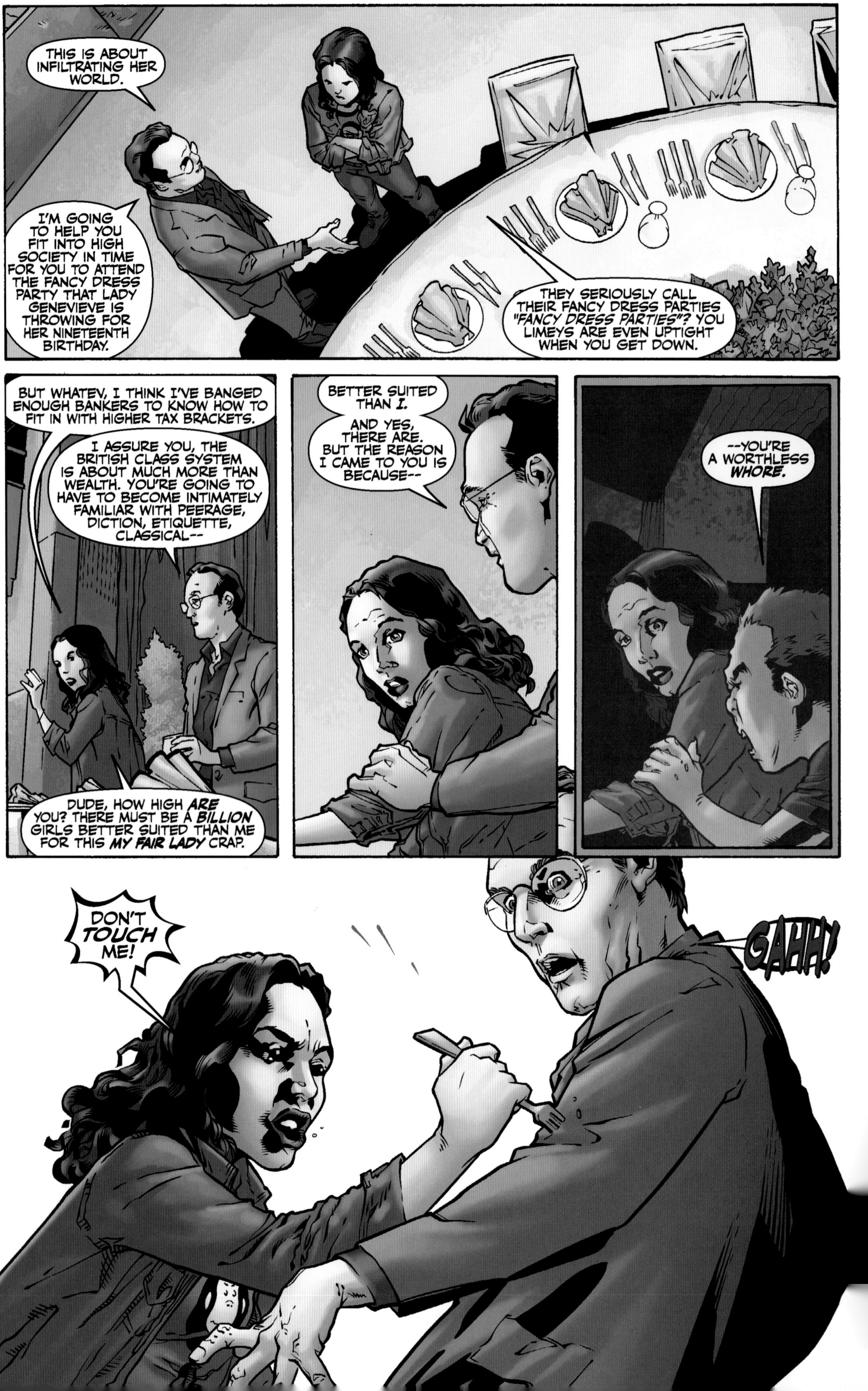

THIS IS ABOUT INFILTRATING HER WORLD.
I'M GOING TO HELP YOU FIT INTO HIGH SOCIETY IN TIME FOR YOU TO ATTEND THE FANCY DRESS PARTY THAT LADY GENEVIEVE IS THROWING FOR HER NINETEENTH BIRTHDAY.
THEY SERIOUSLY CALL THEIR FANCY DRESS PARTIES "FANCY DRESS PARTIES"? YOU LIMEYS ARE EVEN UPTIGHT WHEN YOU GET DOWN.
BUT WHATEV, I THINK I'VE BANGED ENOUGH BANKERS TO KNOW HOW TO FIT IN WITH HIGHER TAX BRACKETS.
I ASSURE YOU, THE BRITISH CLASS SYSTEM IS ABOUT MUCH MORE THAN WEALTH. YOU'RE GOING TO HAVE TO BECOME INTIMATELY FAMILIAR WITH PEERAGE, DICTION, ETIQUETTE, CLASSICAL--
DUDE, HOW HIGH ARE YOU? THERE MUST BE A BILLION GIRLS BETTER SUITED THAN ME FOR THIS MY FAIR LADY CRAP.
BETTER SUITED THAN I.
AND YES, THERE ARE. BUT THE REASON I CAME TO YOU IS BECAUSE--
--YOU'RE A WORTHLESS WHORE.
DON'T TOUCH ME!
GAHH!

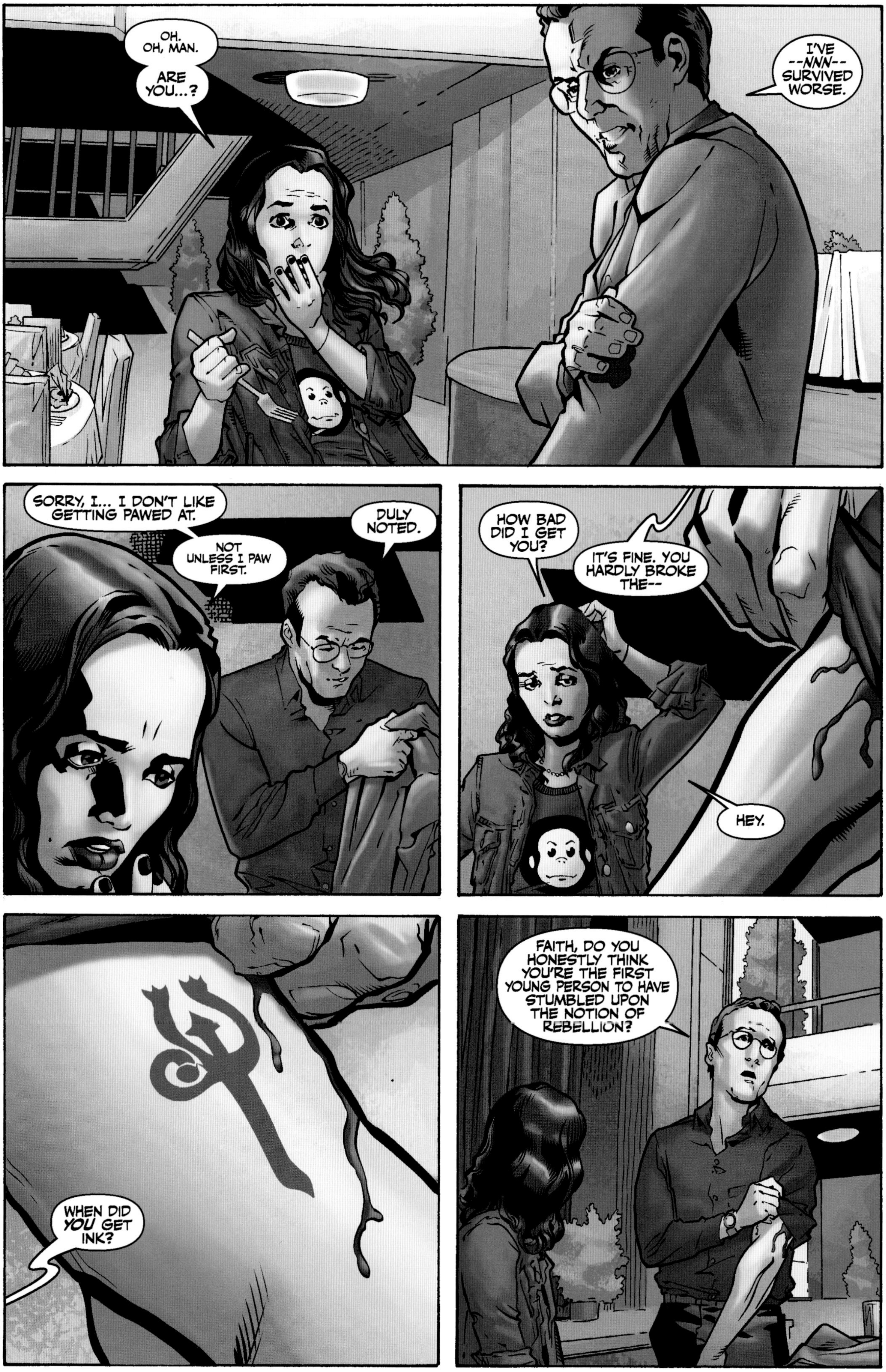
OH.
OH, MAN.
ARE YOU...?
I'VE --NNN-- SURVIVED WORSE.
SORRY, I... I DON'T LIKE GETTING PAWED AT.
NOT UNLESS I PAW FIRST.
DULY NOTED.
HOW BAD DID I GET YOU?
IT'S FINE. YOU HARDLY BROKE THE--
HEY.
WHEN DID *YOU* GET INK?
FAITH, DO YOU HONESTLY THINK YOU'RE THE FIRST YOUNG PERSON TO HAVE STUMBLED UPON THE NOTION OF REBELLION?

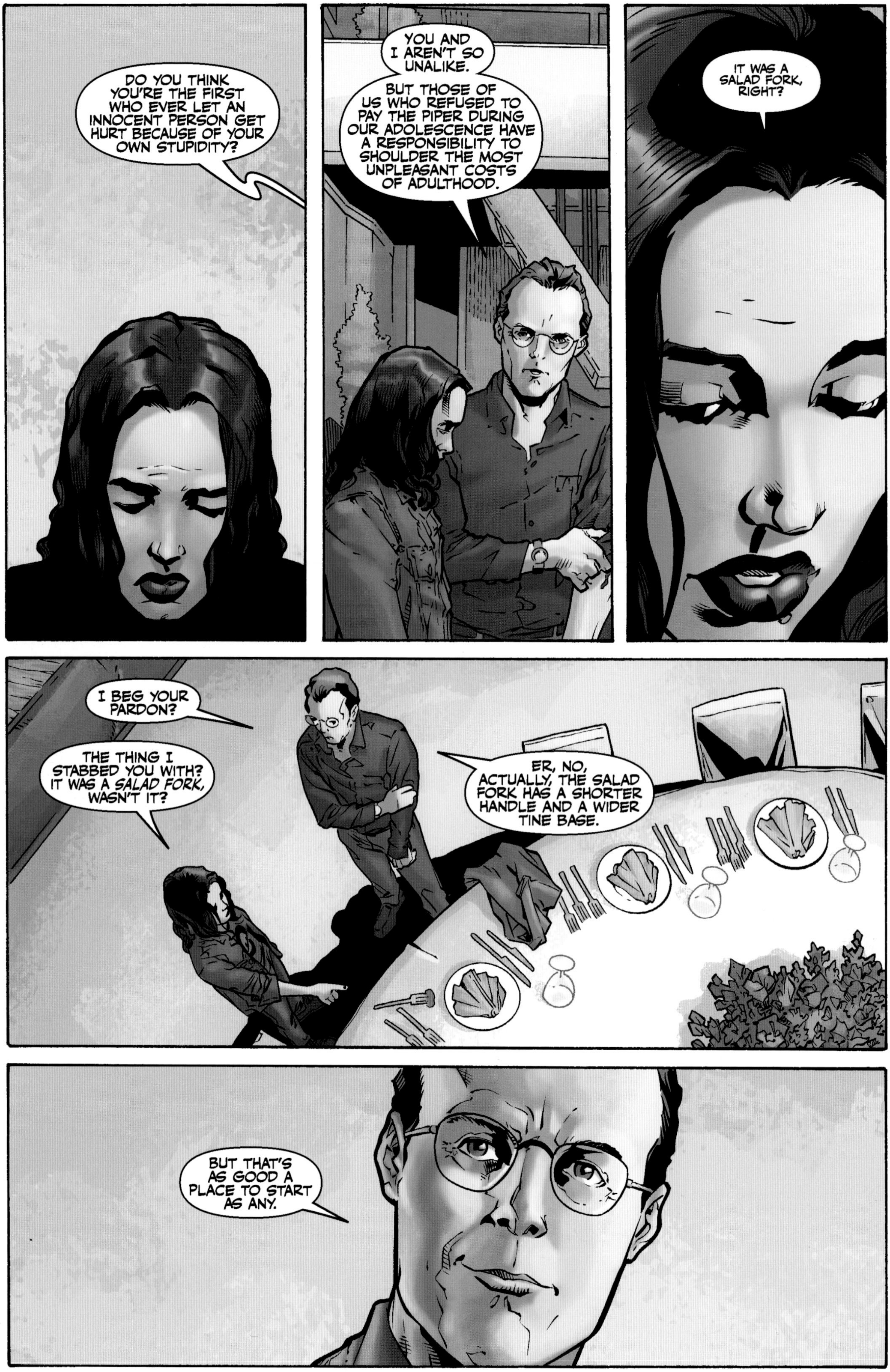
DO YOU THINK YOU'RE THE FIRST WHO EVER LET AN INNOCENT PERSON GET HURT BECAUSE OF YOUR OWN STUPIDITY?
YOU AND I AREN'T SO UNALIKE.
BUT THOSE OF US WHO REFUSED TO PAY THE PIPER DURING OUR ADOLESCENCE HAVE A RESPONSIBILITY TO SHOULDER THE MOST UNPLEASANT COSTS OF ADULTHOOD.
IT WAS A SALAD FORK, RIGHT?
I BEG YOUR PARDON?
THE THING I STABBED YOU WITH? IT WAS A *SALAD FORK*, WASN'T IT?
ER, NO, ACTUALLY, THE SALAD FORK HAS A SHORTER HANDLE AND A WIDER TINE BASE.
BUT THAT'S AS GOOD A PLACE TO START AS ANY.

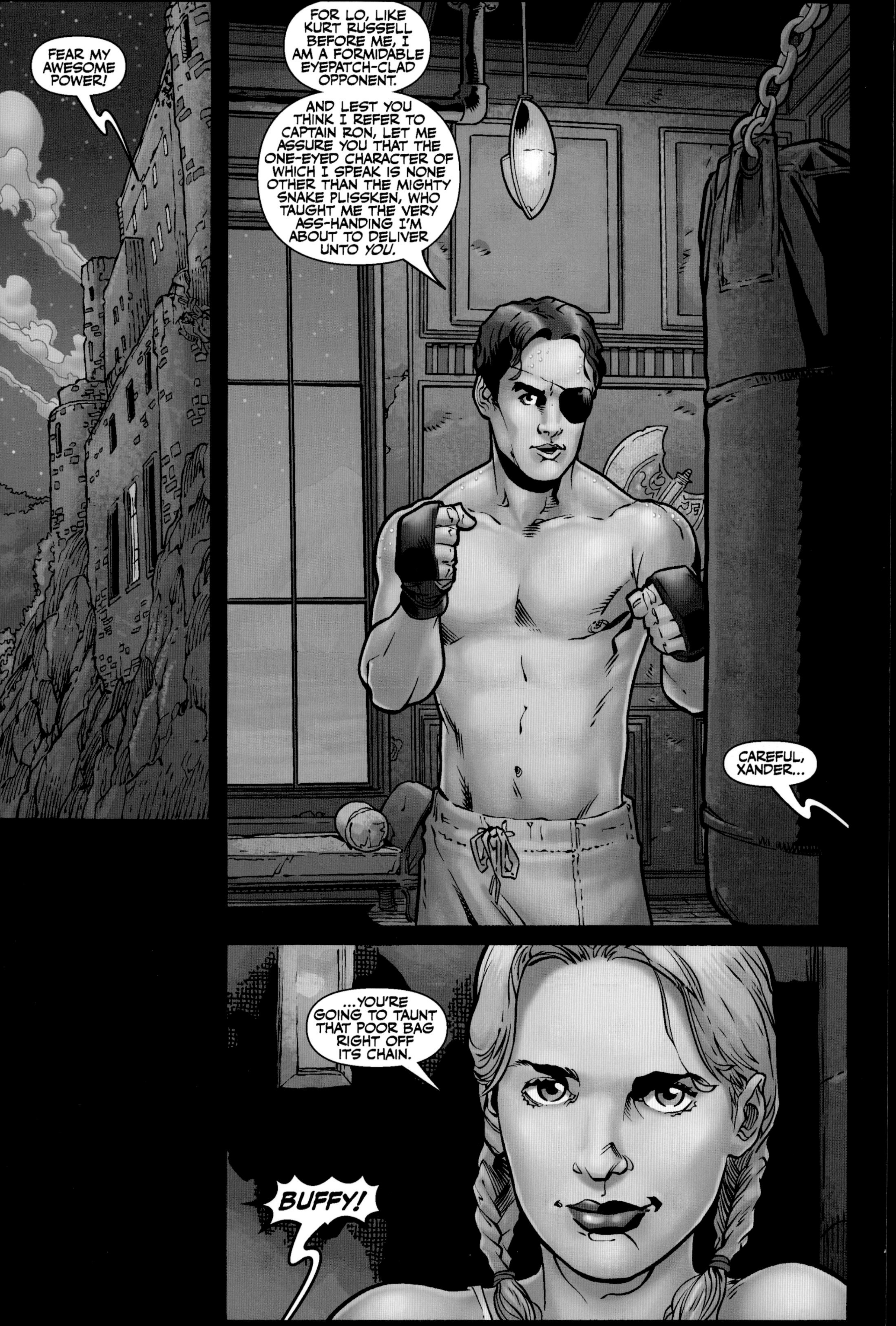
FEAR MY AWESOME POWER!
FOR LO, LIKE KURT RUSSELL BEFORE ME, I AM A FORMIDABLE EYEPATCH-CLAD OPPONENT.
AND LEST YOU THINK I REFER TO CAPTAIN RON, LET ME ASSURE YOU THAT THE ONE-EYED CHARACTER OF WHICH I SPEAK IS NONE OTHER THAN THE MIGHTY SNAKE PLISSKEN, WHO TAUGHT ME THE VERY ASS-HANDING I'M ABOUT TO DELIVER UNTO *YOU*.
CAREFUL, XANDER...
...YOU'RE GOING TO TAUNT THAT POOR BAG RIGHT OFF ITS CHAIN.
BUFFY!

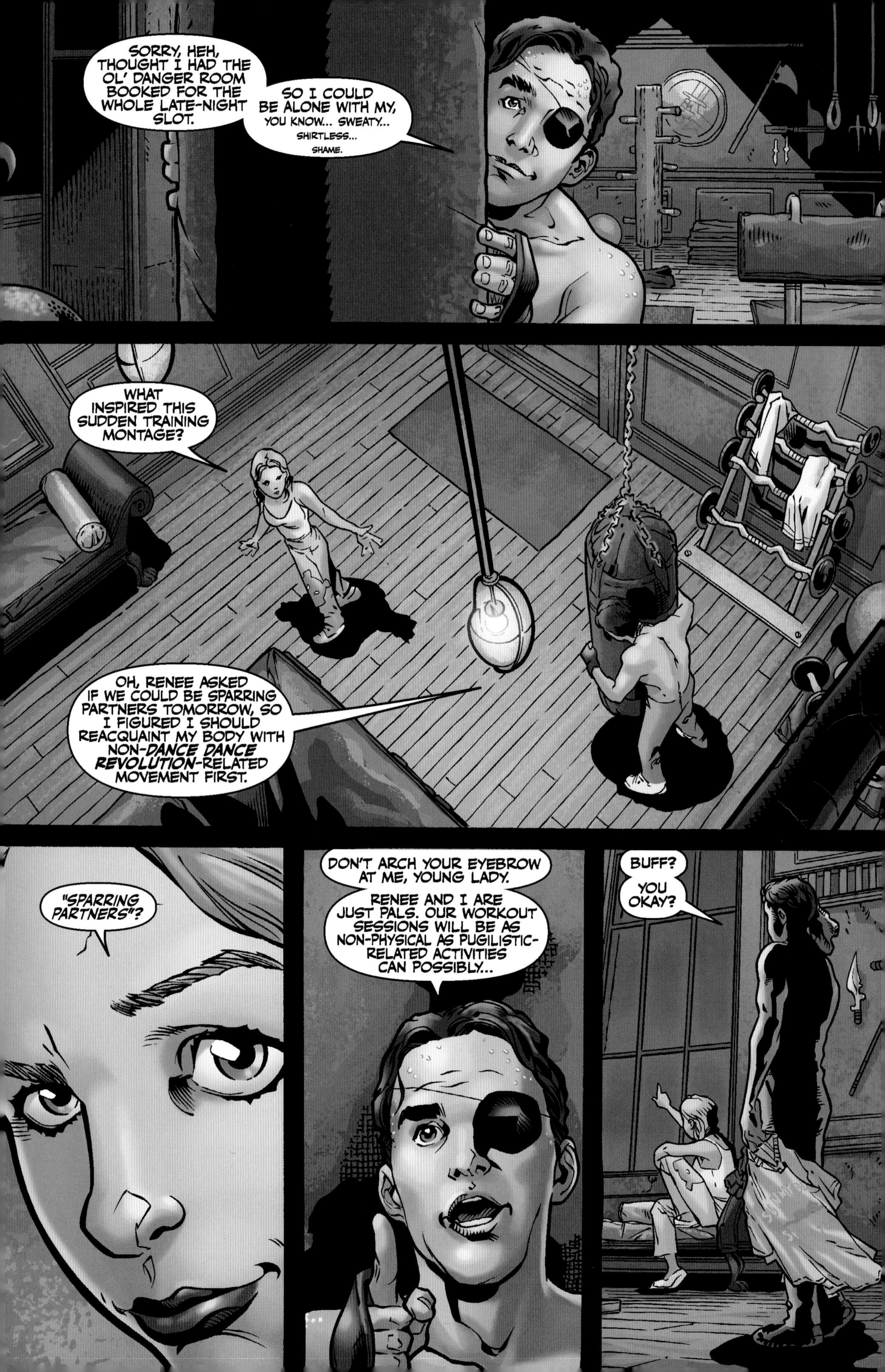
SORRY, HEH, THOUGHT I HAD THE OL' DANGER ROOM BOOKED FOR THE WHOLE LATE-NIGHT SLOT.
SO I COULD BE ALONE WITH MY, YOU KNOW... SWEATY... SHIRTLESS... SHAME.
WHAT INSPIRED THIS SUDDEN TRAINING MONTAGE?
OH, RENEE ASKED IF WE COULD BE SPARRING PARTNERS TOMORROW, SO I FIGURED I SHOULD REACQUAINT MY BODY WITH NON-*DANCE DANCE REVOLUTION*-RELATED MOVEMENT FIRST.
"SPARRING PARTNERS"?
DON'T ARCH YOUR EYEBROW AT ME, YOUNG LADY.
RENEE AND I ARE JUST PALS. OUR WORKOUT SESSIONS WILL BE AS NON-PHYSICAL AS PUGILISTIC-RELATED ACTIVITIES CAN POSSIBLY...
BUFF?
YOU OKAY?

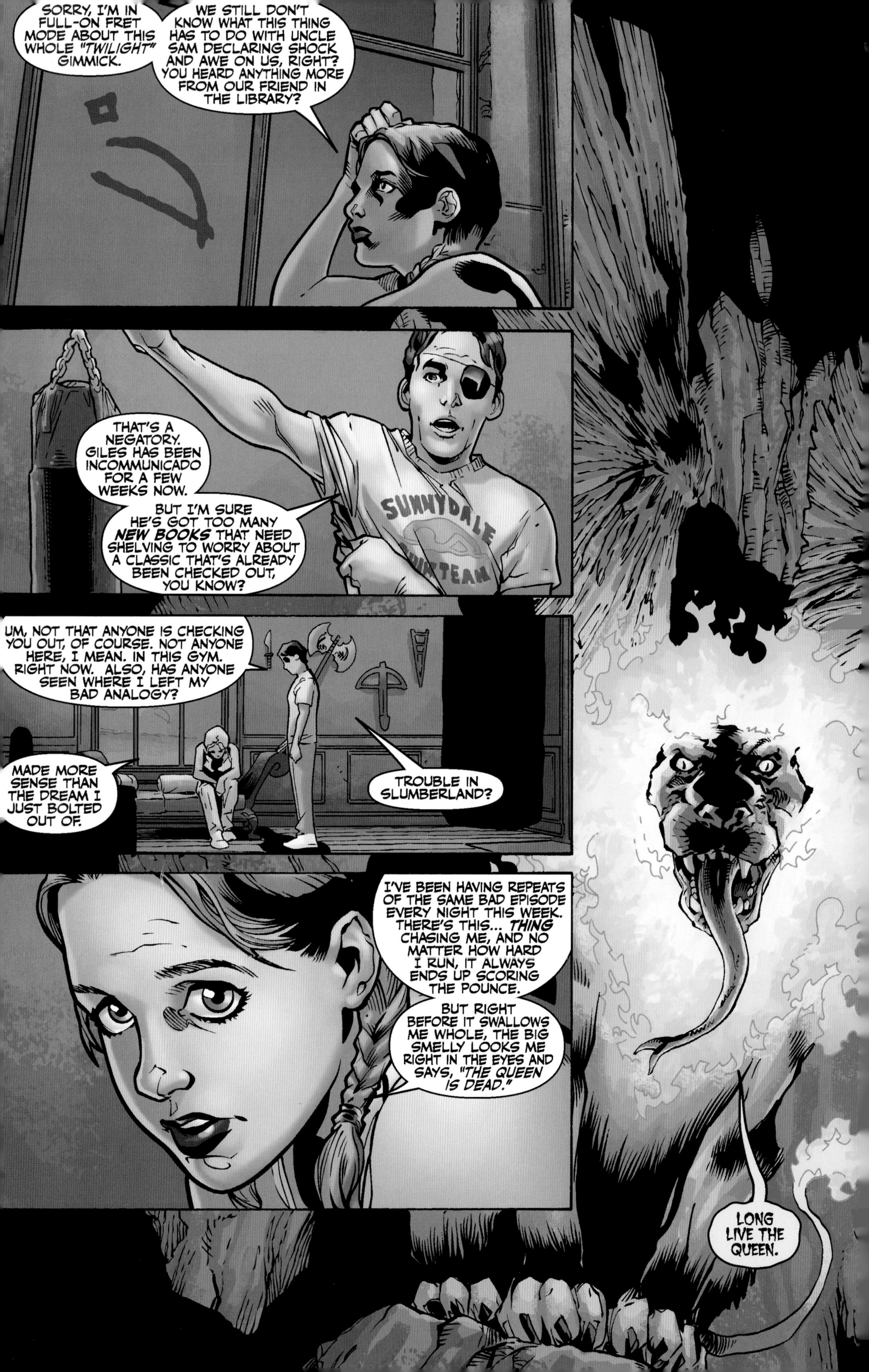
SORRY, I'M IN FULL-ON FRET MODE ABOUT THIS WHOLE "TWILIGHT" GIMMICK.
WE STILL DON'T KNOW WHAT THIS THING HAS TO DO WITH UNCLE SAM DECLARING SHOCK AND AWE ON US, RIGHT? YOU HEARD ANYTHING MORE FROM OUR FRIEND IN THE LIBRARY?
THAT'S A NEGATORY. GILES HAS BEEN INCOMMUNICADO FOR A FEW WEEKS NOW.
BUT I'M SURE HE'S GOT TOO MANY NEW BOOKS THAT NEED SHELVING TO WORRY ABOUT A CLASSIC THAT'S ALREADY BEEN CHECKED OUT, YOU KNOW?
SUNNYDALE
UM, NOT THAT ANYONE IS CHECKING YOU OUT, OF COURSE. NOT ANYONE HERE, I MEAN. IN THIS GYM. RIGHT NOW. ALSO, HAS ANYONE SEEN WHERE I LEFT MY BAD ANALOGY?
MADE MORE SENSE THAN THE DREAM I JUST BOLTED OUT OF.
TROUBLE IN SLUMBERLAND?
I'VE BEEN HAVING REPEATS OF THE SAME BAD EPISODE EVERY NIGHT THIS WEEK. THERE'S THIS... THING CHASING ME, AND NO MATTER HOW HARD I RUN, IT ALWAYS ENDS UP SCORING THE POUNCE.
BUT RIGHT BEFORE IT SWALLOWS ME WHOLE, THE BIG SMELLY LOOKS ME RIGHT IN THE EYES AND SAYS, "THE QUEEN IS DEAD."
LONG LIVE THE QUEEN.

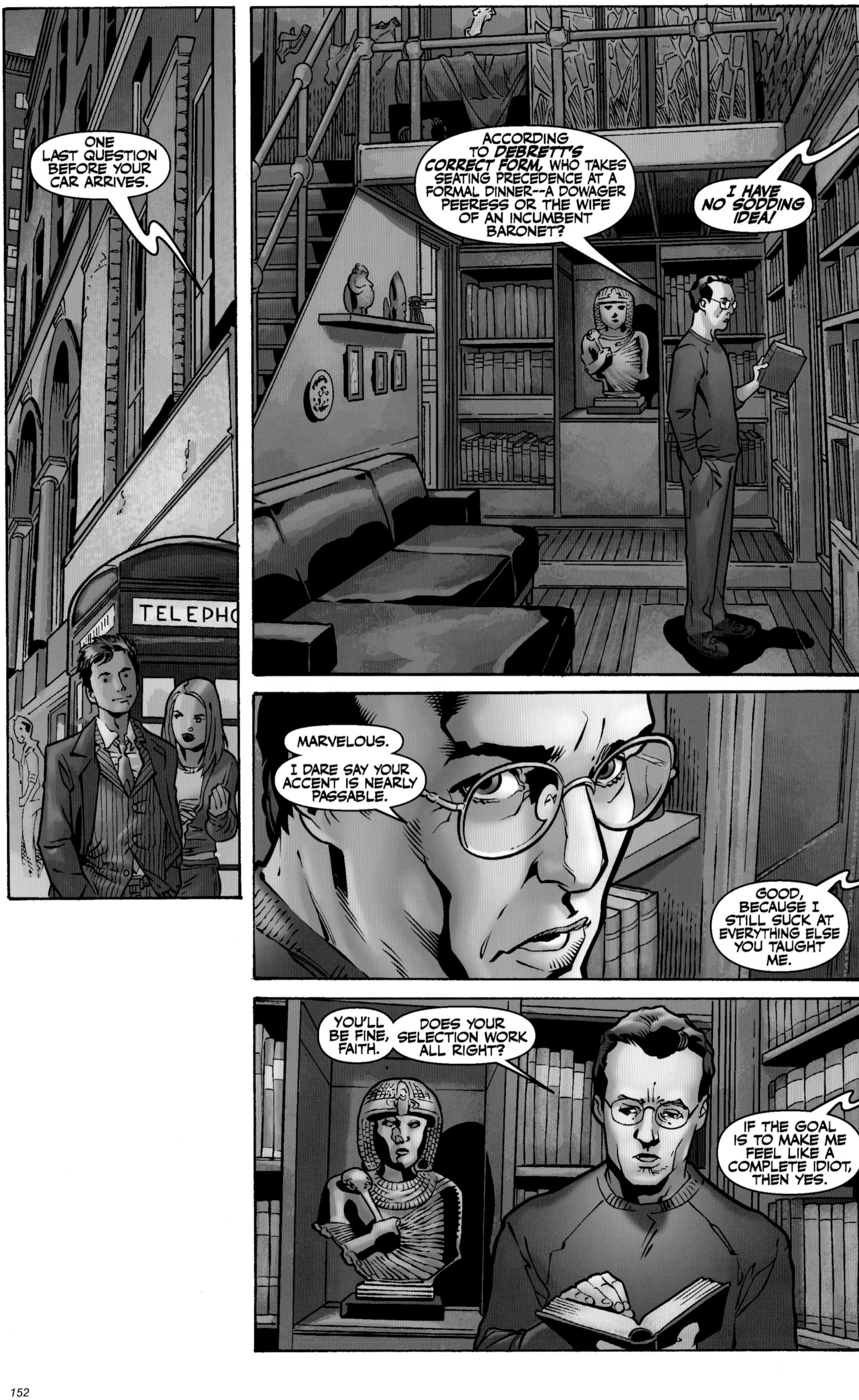
ONE LAST QUESTION BEFORE YOUR CAR ARRIVES.
TELEPHO
ACCORDING TO DEBRETT'S CORRECT FORM, WHO TAKES SEATING PRECEDENCE AT A FORMAL DINNER--A DOWAGER PEERESS OR THE WIFE OF AN INCUMBENT BARONET?
I HAVE NO SODDING IDEA!
MARVELOUS.
I DARE SAY YOUR ACCENT IS NEARLY PASSABLE.
GOOD, BECAUSE I STILL SUCK AT EVERYTHING ELSE YOU TAUGHT ME.
YOU'LL BE FINE, FAITH.
DOES YOUR SELECTION WORK ALL RIGHT?
IF THE GOAL IS TO MAKE ME FEEL LIKE A COMPLETE IDIOT, THEN YES.

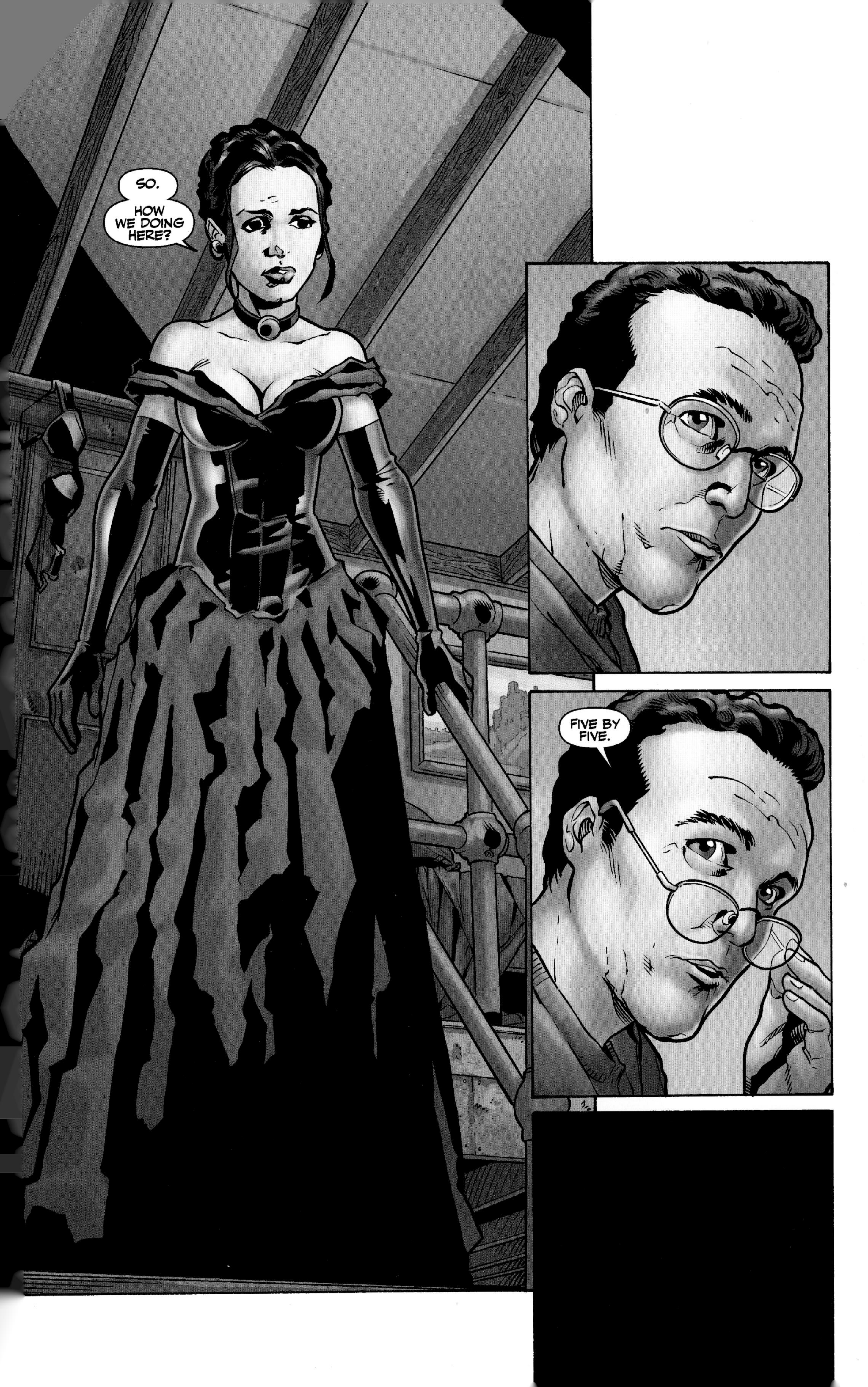
SO.
HOW WE DOING HERE?
FIVE BY FIVE.

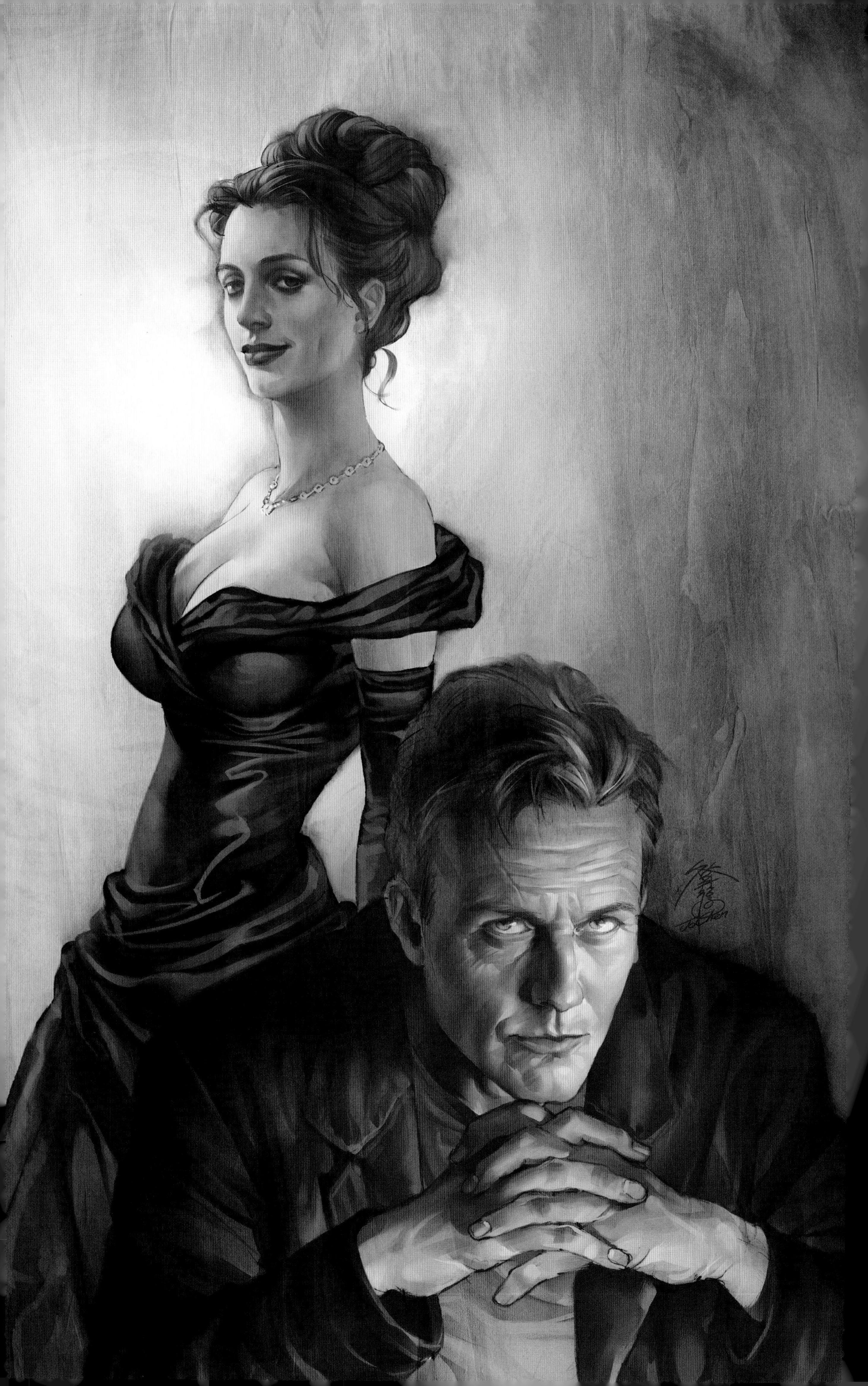

NO FUTURE FOR YOU

PART TWO

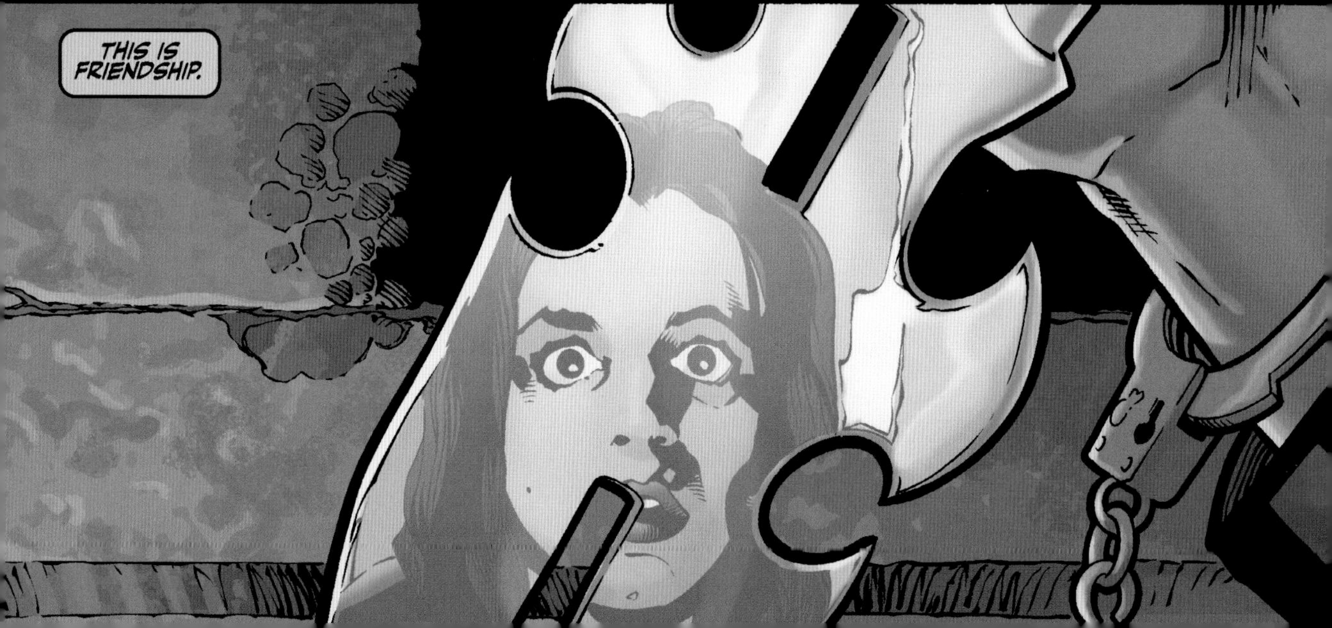
THIS IS FRIENDSHIP.

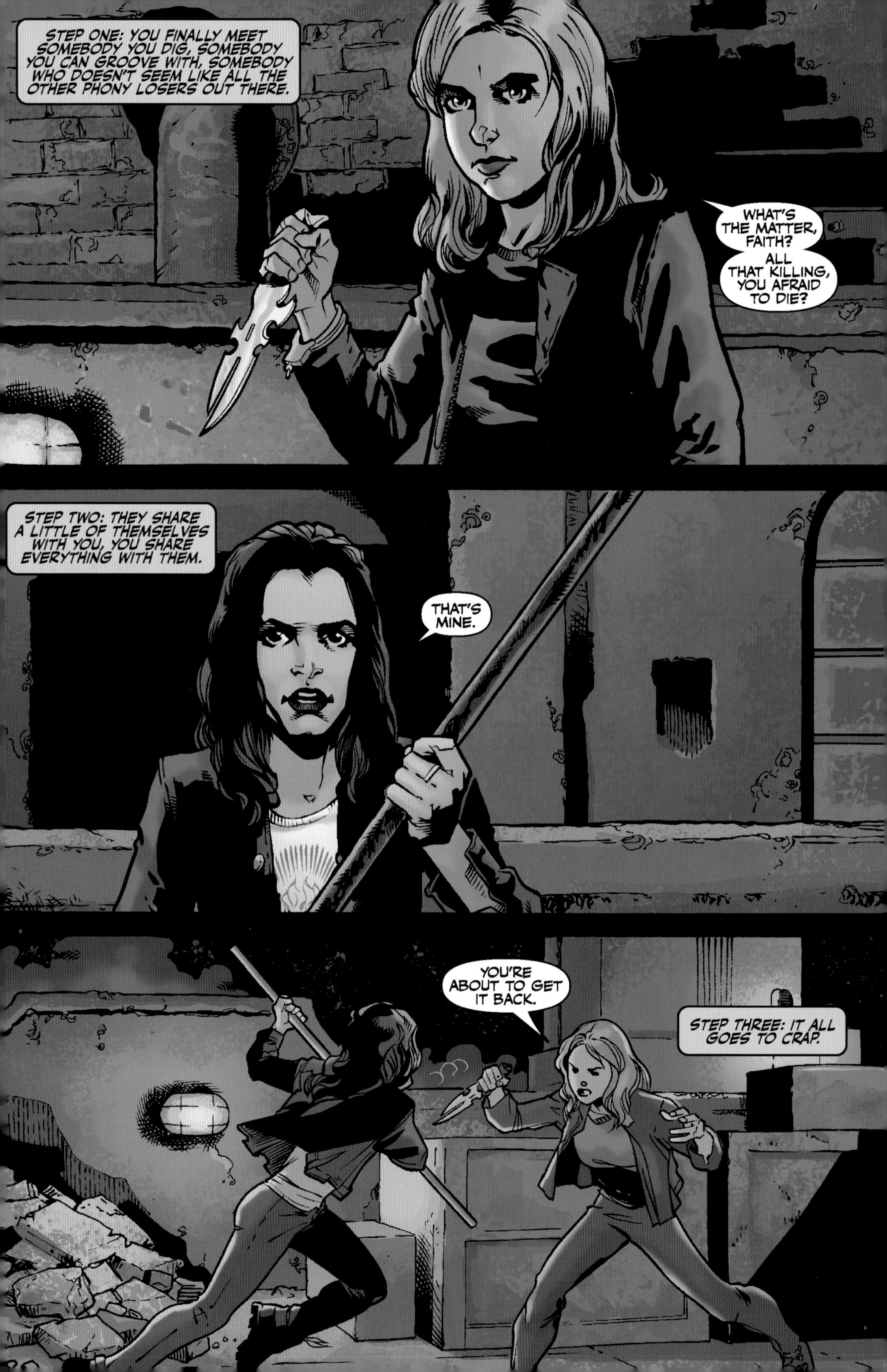
STEP ONE: YOU FINALLY MEET SOMEBODY YOU DIG, SOMEBODY YOU CAN GROOVE WITH, SOMEBODY WHO DOESN'T SEEM LIKE ALL THE OTHER PHONY LOSERS OUT THERE.
WHAT'S THE MATTER, FAITH?
ALL THAT KILLING, YOU AFRAID TO DIE?
STEP TWO: THEY SHARE A LITTLE OF THEMSELVES WITH YOU, YOU SHARE EVERYTHING WITH THEM.
THAT'S MINE.
YOU'RE ABOUT TO GET IT BACK.
STEP THREE: IT ALL GOES TO CRAP.

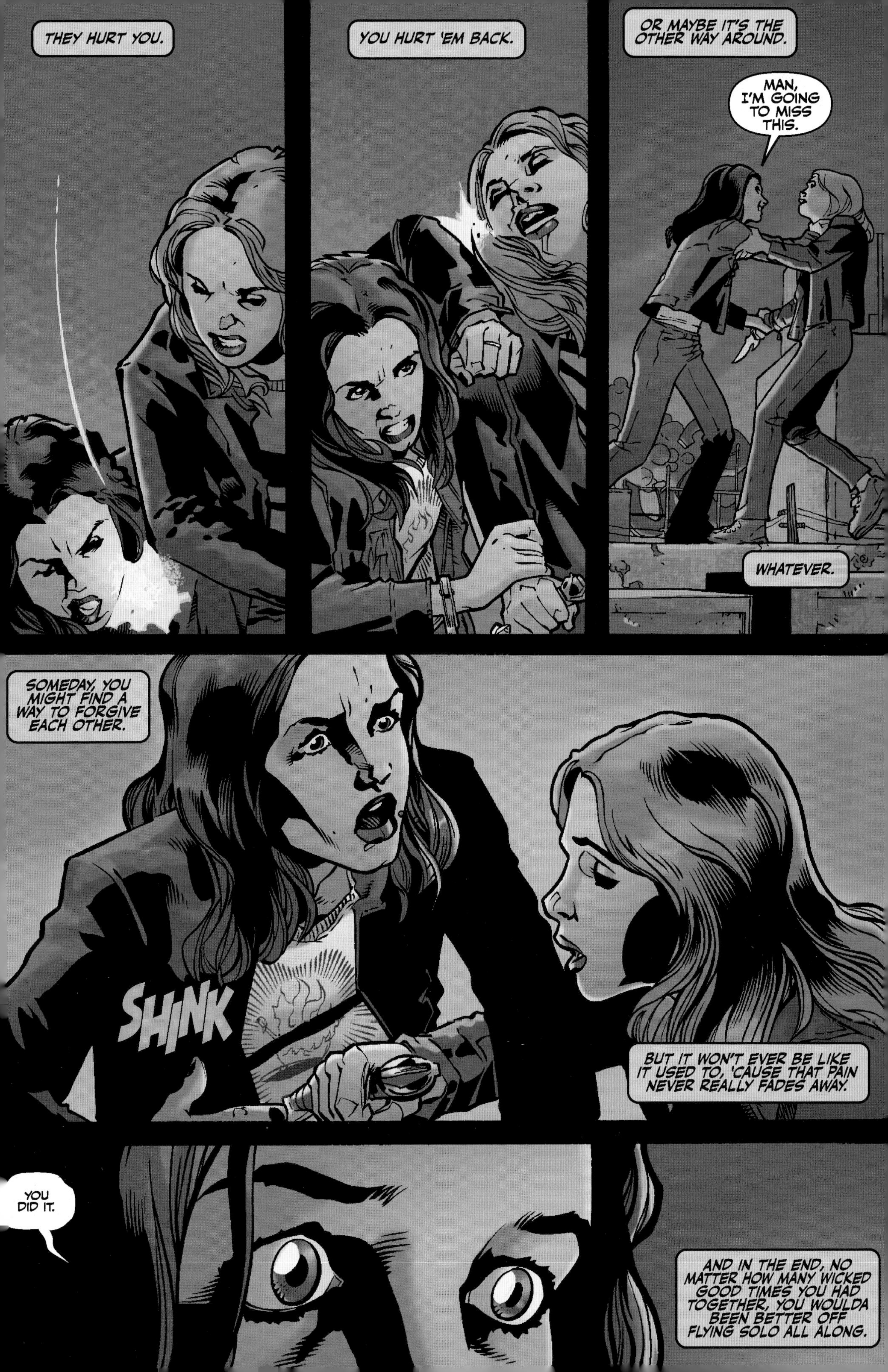

THEY HURT YOU.
YOU HURT 'EM BACK.
OR MAYBE IT'S THE OTHER WAY AROUND.
MAN, I'M GOING TO MISS THIS.
WHATEVER.
SOMEDAY, YOU MIGHT FIND A WAY TO FORGIVE EACH OTHER.
SHINK
BUT IT WON'T EVER BE LIKE IT USED TO, 'CAUSE THAT PAIN NEVER REALLY FADES AWAY.
YOU DID IT.
AND IN THE END, NO MATTER HOW MANY WICKED GOOD TIMES YOU HAD TOGETHER, YOU WOULDA BEEN BETTER OFF FLYING SOLO ALL ALONG.

ANYWAY, LIVE AND LEARN.

ALMOST DIE AND LEARN WAY MORE.

FAITH, ARE YOU ONLINE?

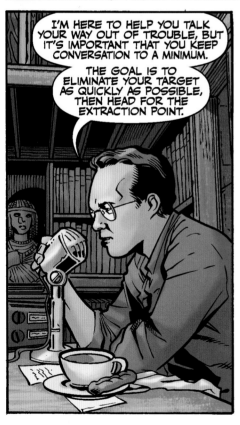

I'M HERE TO HELP YOU TALK YOUR WAY OUT OF TROUBLE, BUT IT'S IMPORTANT THAT YOU KEEP CONVERSATION TO A MINIMUM.

THE GOAL IS TO ELIMINATE YOUR TARGET AS QUICKLY AS POSSIBLE, THEN HEAD FOR THE EXTRACTION POINT.

I KNOW HOW DIFFICULT THIS MUST BE FOR YOU, BUT ONCE IT'S FINISHED, YOUR SLAYING DAYS ARE OVER AND YOU CAN--

SORRY, GILES.

I'VE GOT ENOUGH VOICES IN MY HEAD ALREADY.

PARDON ME!

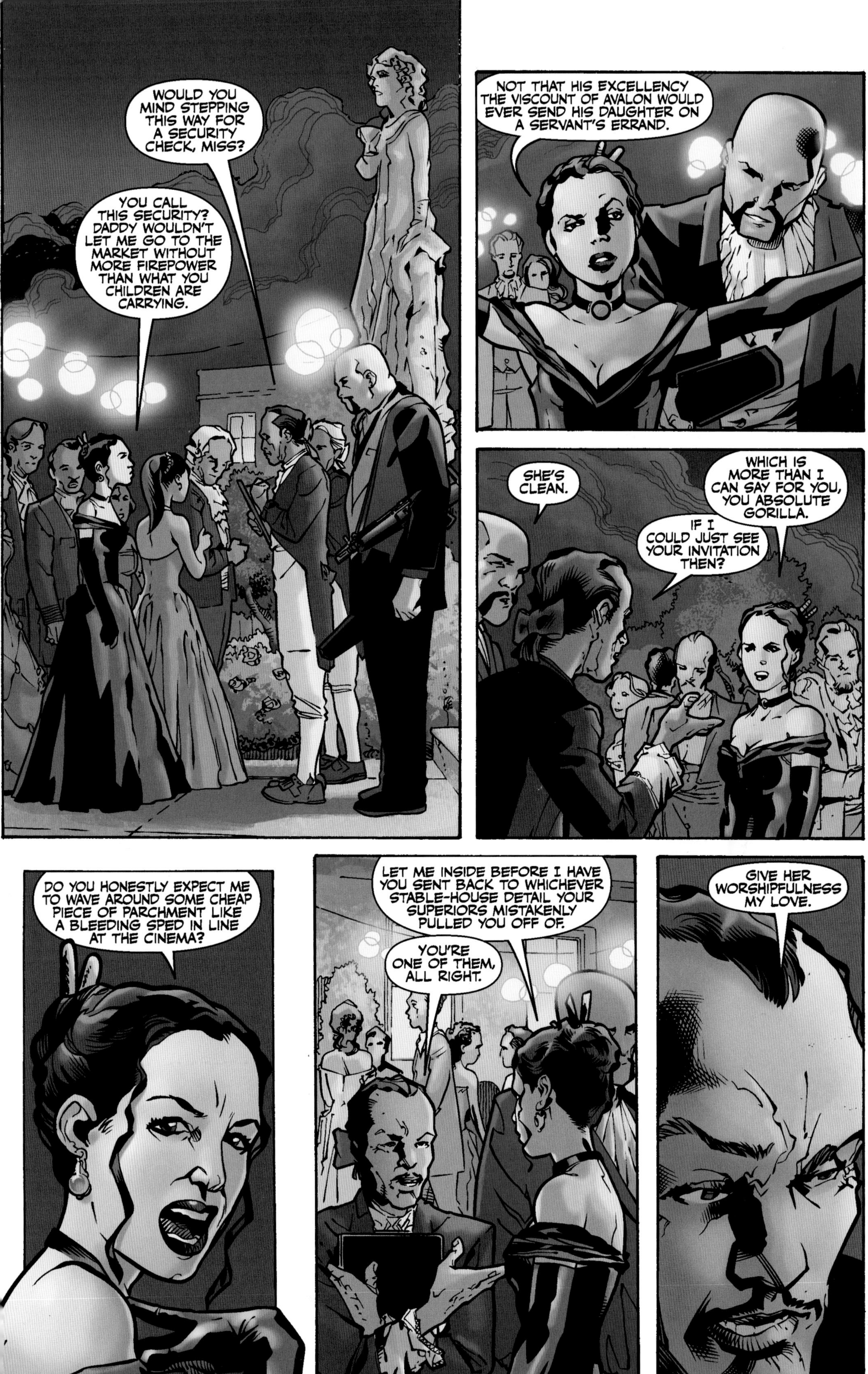
WOULD YOU MIND STEPPING THIS WAY FOR A SECURITY CHECK, MISS?
YOU CALL THIS SECURITY? DADDY WOULDN'T LET ME GO TO THE MARKET WITHOUT MORE FIREPOWER THAN WHAT YOU CHILDREN ARE CARRYING.
NOT THAT HIS EXCELLENCY THE VISCOUNT OF AVALON WOULD EVER SEND HIS DAUGHTER ON A SERVANT'S ERRAND.
SHE'S CLEAN.
WHICH IS MORE THAN I CAN SAY FOR YOU, YOU ABSOLUTE GORILLA.
IF I COULD JUST SEE YOUR INVITATION THEN?
DO YOU HONESTLY EXPECT ME TO WAVE AROUND SOME CHEAP PIECE OF PARCHMENT LIKE A BLEEDING SPED IN LINE AT THE CINEMA?
LET ME INSIDE BEFORE I HAVE YOU SENT BACK TO WHICHEVER STABLE-HOUSE DETAIL YOUR SUPERIORS MISTAKENLY PULLED YOU OFF OF.
YOU'RE ONE OF THEM, ALL RIGHT.
GIVE HER WORSHIPFULNESS MY LOVE.

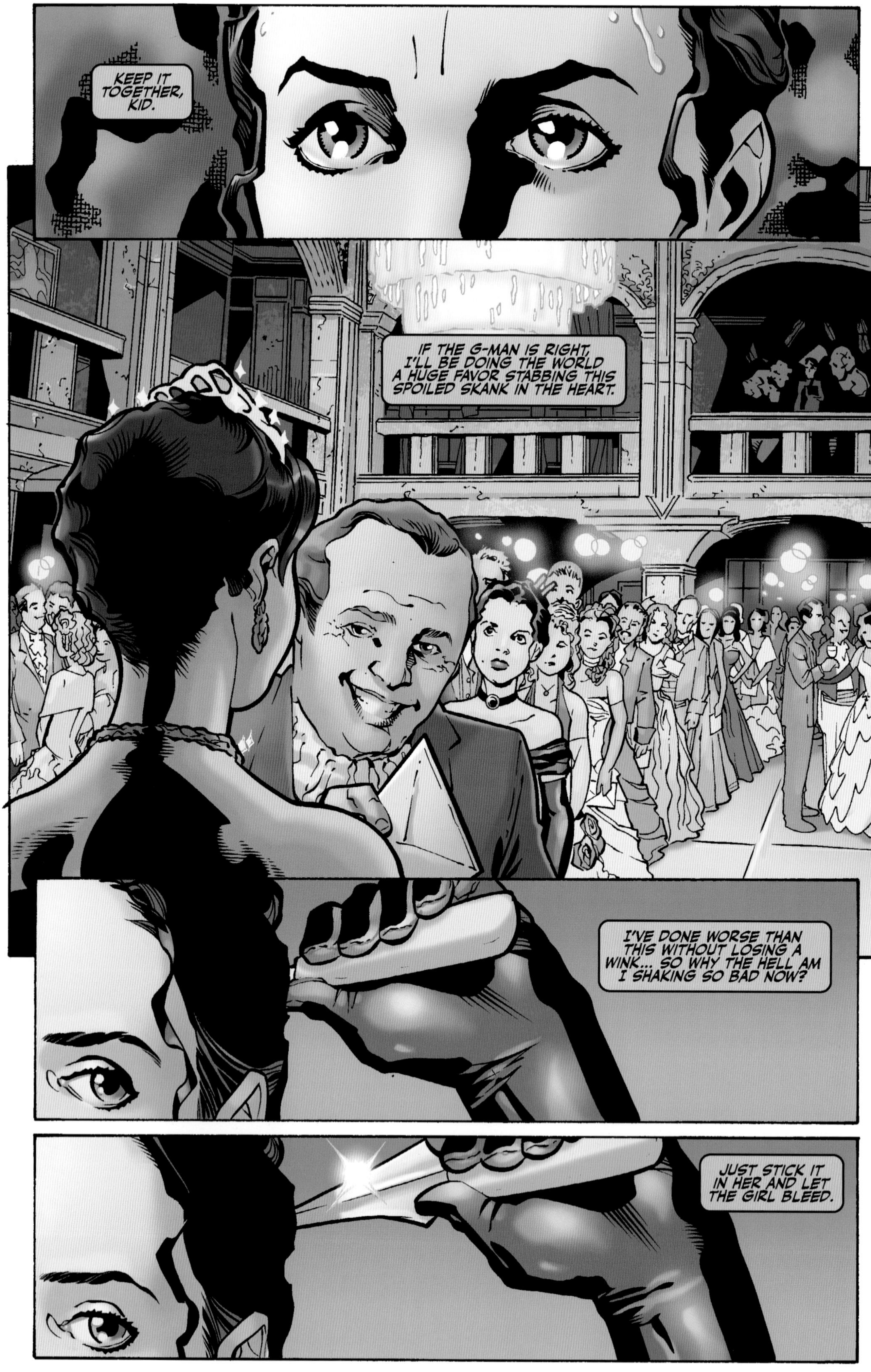
KEEP IT TOGETHER, KID.
IF THE G-MAN IS RIGHT, I'LL BE DOING THE WORLD A HUGE FAVOR STABBING THIS SPOILED SKANK IN THE HEART.
I'VE DONE WORSE THAN THIS WITHOUT LOSING A WINK... SO WHY THE HELL AM I SHAKING SO BAD NOW?
JUST STICK IT IN HER AND LET THE GIRL BLEED.

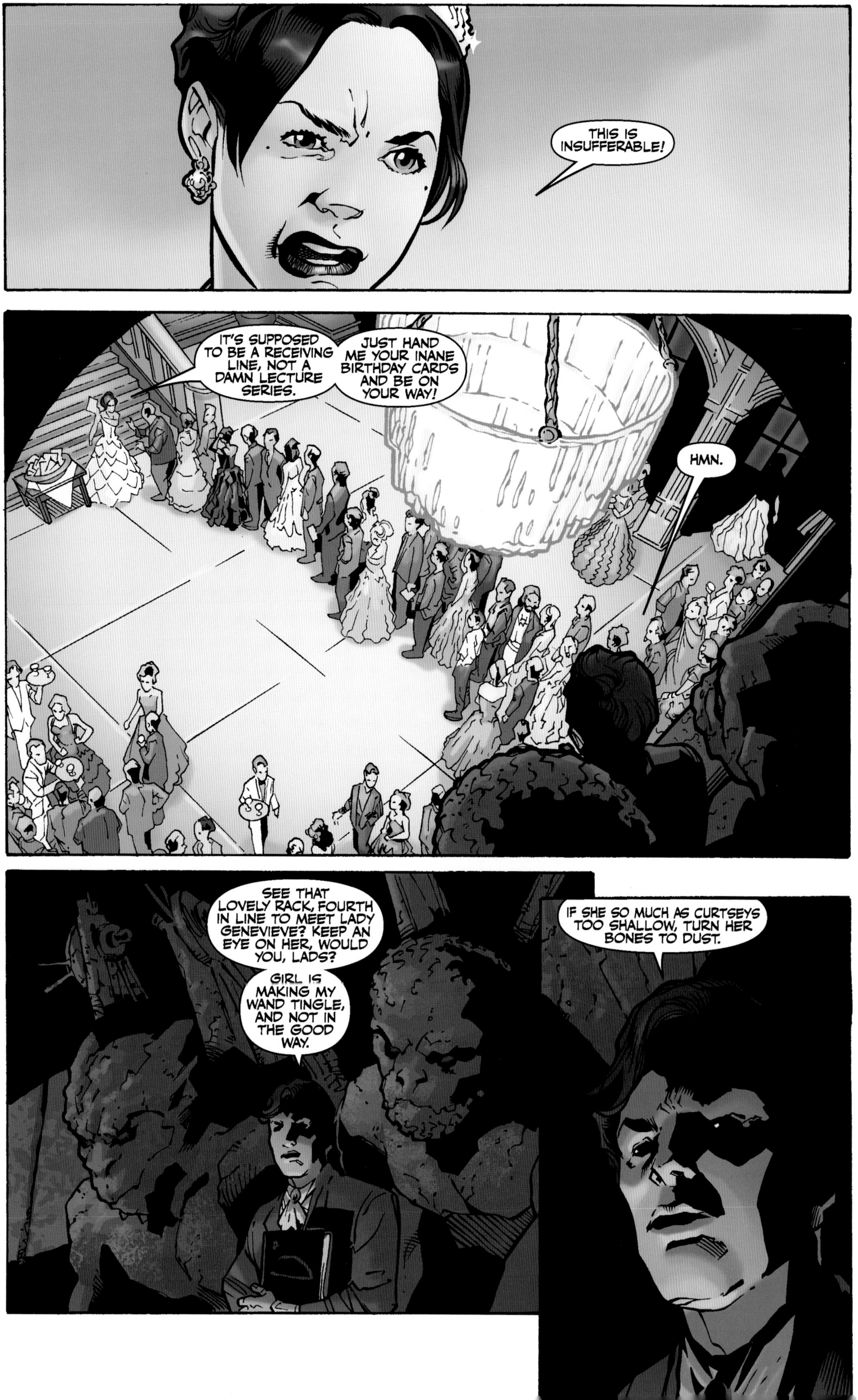
THIS IS INSUFFERABLE!
IT'S SUPPOSED TO BE A RECEIVING LINE, NOT A DAMN LECTURE SERIES.
JUST HAND ME YOUR INANE BIRTHDAY CARDS AND BE ON YOUR WAY!
HMN.
SEE THAT LOVELY RACK, FOURTH IN LINE TO MEET LADY GENEVIEVE? KEEP AN EYE ON HER, WOULD YOU, LADS?
GIRL IS MAKING MY WAND TINGLE, AND NOT IN THE GOOD WAY.
IF SHE SO MUCH AS CURTSEYS TOO SHALLOW, TURN HER BONES TO DUST.

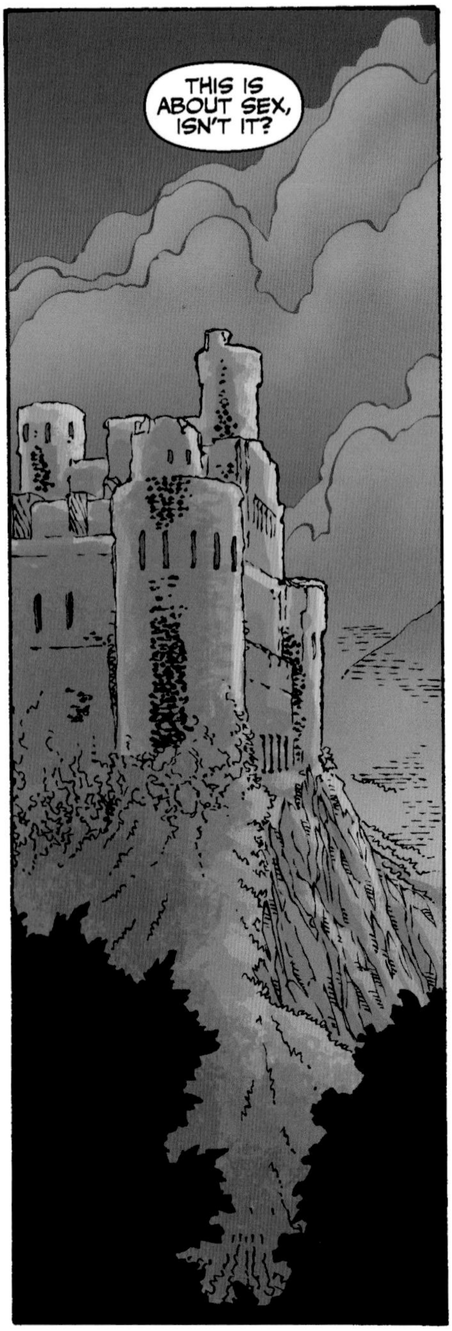
THIS IS ABOUT SEX, ISN'T IT?

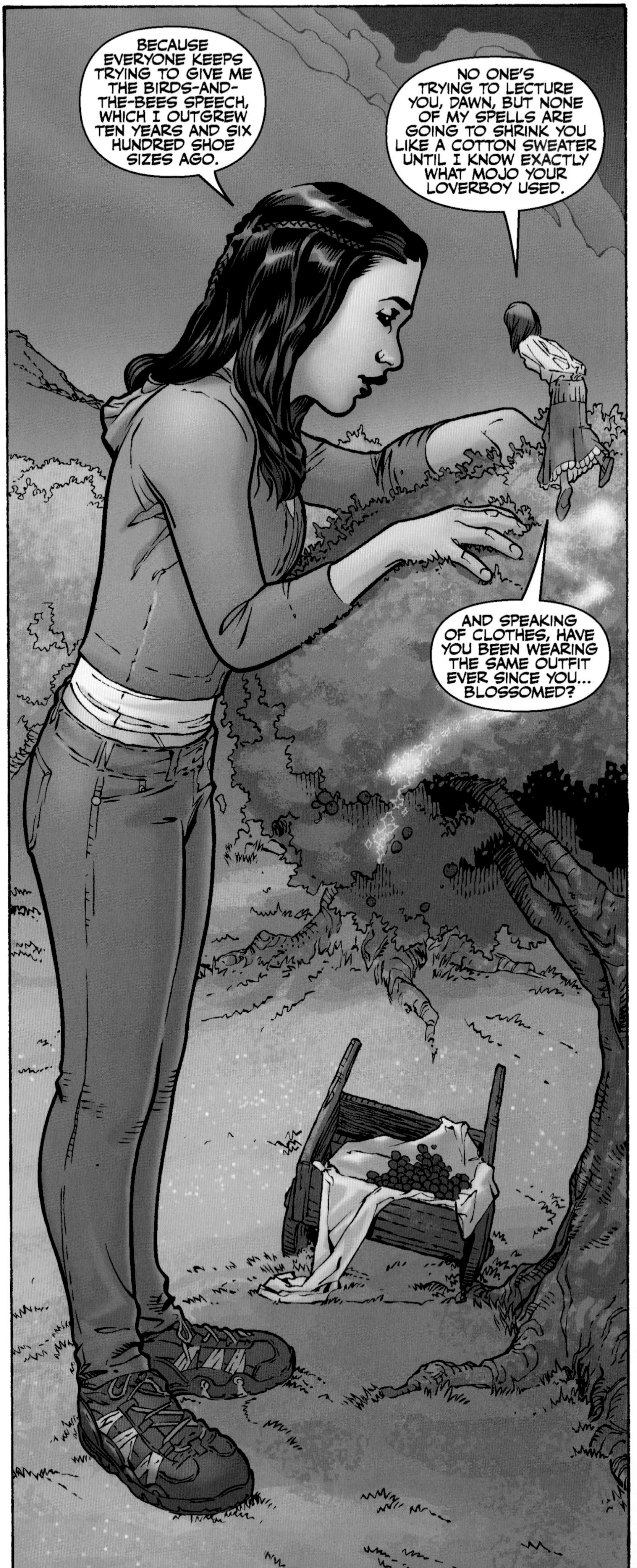
BECAUSE EVERYONE KEEPS TRYING TO GIVE ME THE BIRDS-AND-THE-BEES SPEECH, WHICH I OUTGREW TEN YEARS AND SIX HUNDRED SHOE SIZES AGO.
NO ONE'S TRYING TO LECTURE YOU, DAWN, BUT NONE OF MY SPELLS ARE GOING TO SHRINK YOU LIKE A COTTON SWEATER UNTIL I KNOW EXACTLY WHAT MOJO YOUR LOVERBOY USED.
AND SPEAKING OF CLOTHES, HAVE YOU BEEN WEARING THE SAME OUTFIT EVER SINCE YOU... BLOSSOMED?

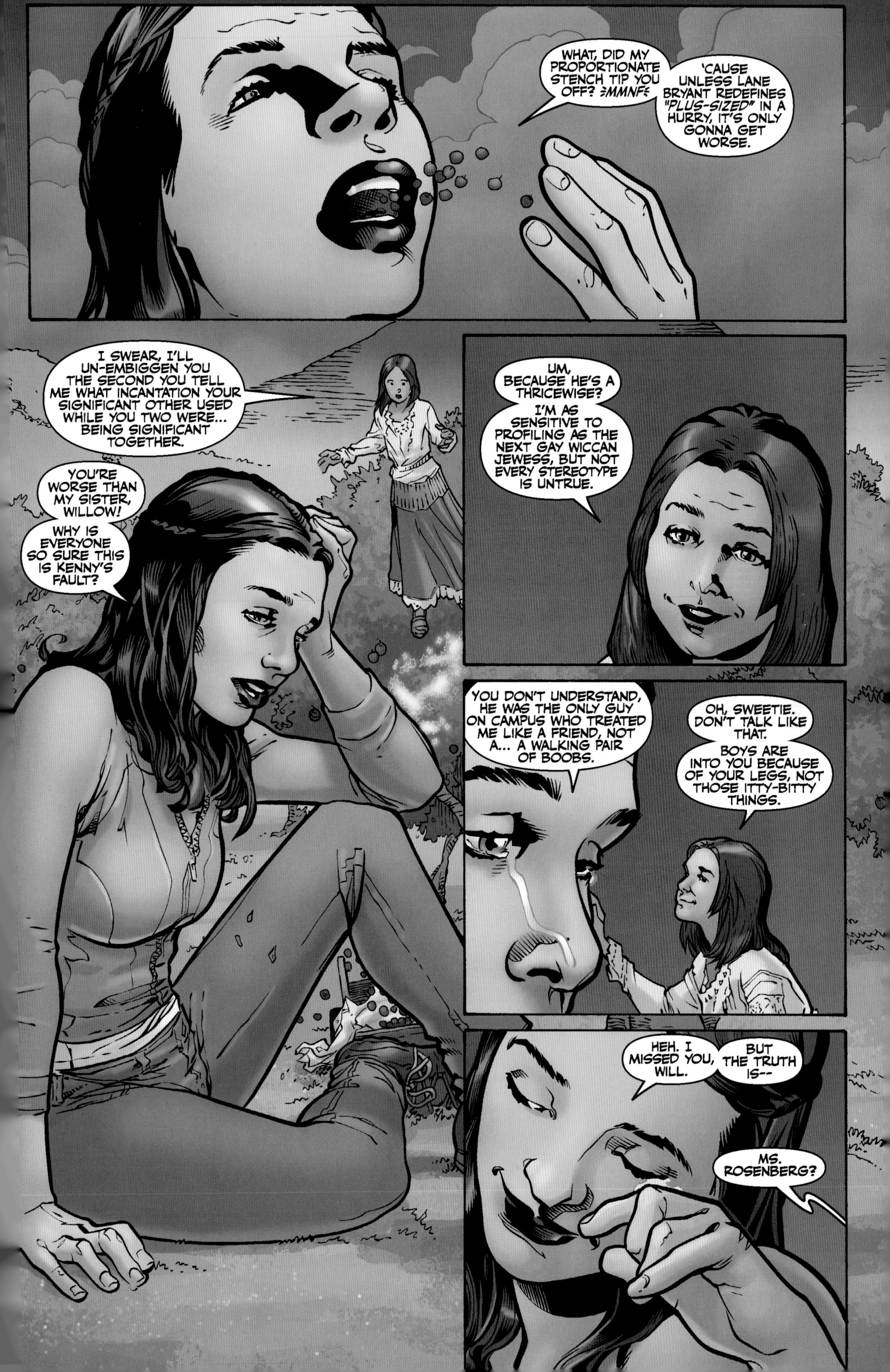

WHAT, DID MY PROPORTIONATE STENCH TIP YOU OFF? *MMNF*
'CAUSE UNLESS LANE BRYANT REDEFINES "PLUS-SIZED" IN A HURRY, IT'S ONLY GONNA GET WORSE.
I SWEAR, I'LL UN-EMBIGGEN YOU THE SECOND YOU TELL ME WHAT INCANTATION YOUR SIGNIFICANT OTHER USED WHILE YOU TWO WERE... BEING SIGNIFICANT TOGETHER.
YOU'RE WORSE THAN MY SISTER, WILLOW!
WHY IS EVERYONE SO SURE THIS IS KENNY'S FAULT?
UM, BECAUSE HE'S A THRICEWISE?
I'M AS SENSITIVE TO PROFILING AS THE NEXT GAY WICCAN JEWESS, BUT NOT EVERY STEREOTYPE IS UNTRUE.
YOU DON'T UNDERSTAND, HE WAS THE ONLY GUY ON CAMPUS WHO TREATED ME LIKE A FRIEND, NOT A... A WALKING PAIR OF BOOBS.
OH, SWEETIE. DON'T TALK LIKE THAT.
BOYS ARE INTO YOU BECAUSE OF YOUR LEGS, NOT THOSE ITTY-BITTY THINGS.
HEH. I MISSED YOU, WILL.
BUT THE TRUTH IS--
MS. ROSENBERG?

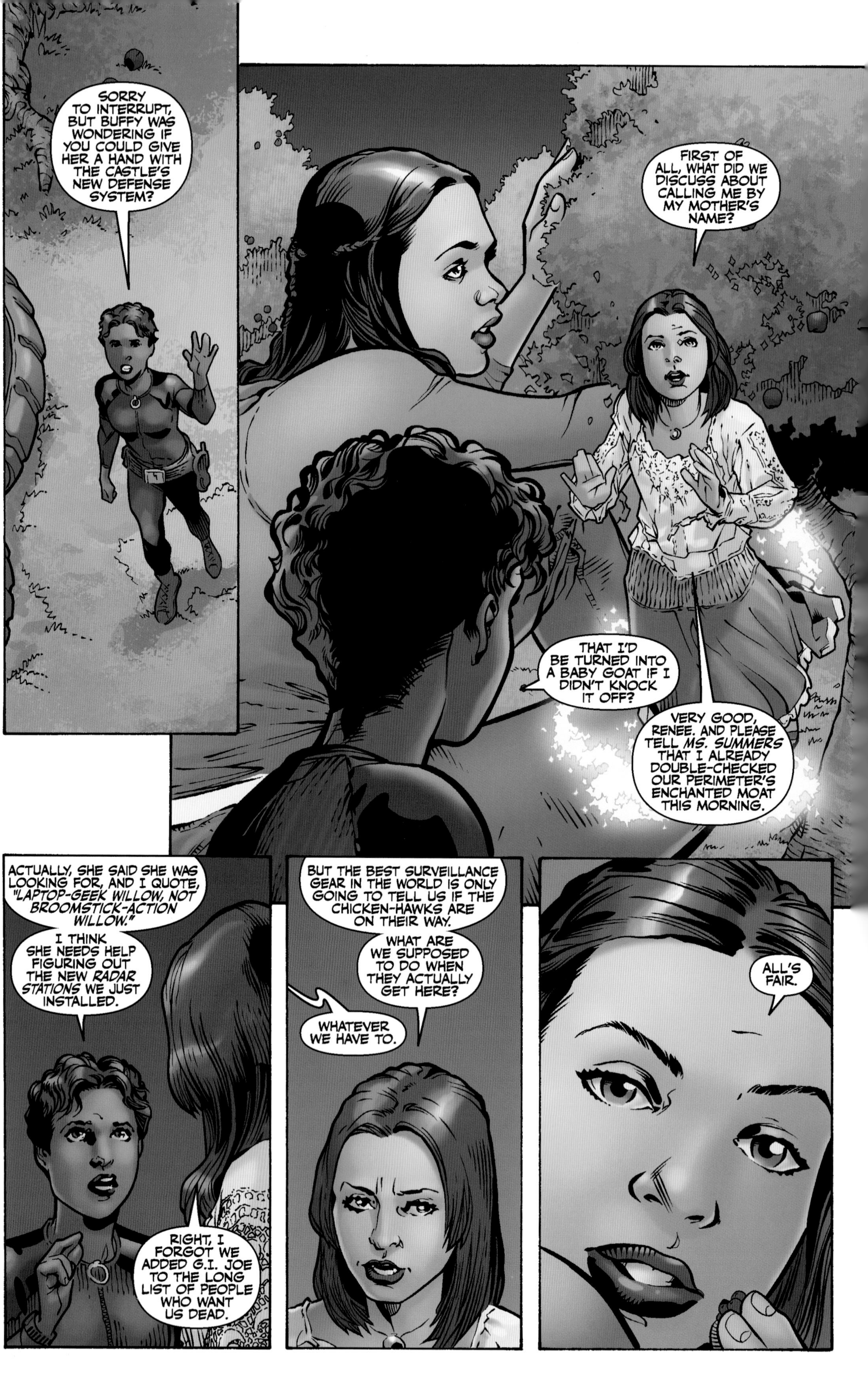
SORRY TO INTERRUPT, BUT BUFFY WAS WONDERING IF YOU COULD GIVE HER A HAND WITH THE CASTLE'S NEW DEFENSE SYSTEM?
FIRST OF ALL, WHAT DID WE DISCUSS ABOUT CALLING ME BY MY MOTHER'S NAME?
THAT I'D BE TURNED INTO A BABY GOAT IF I DIDN'T KNOCK IT OFF?
VERY GOOD, RENEE. AND PLEASE TELL MS. SUMMERS THAT I ALREADY DOUBLE-CHECKED OUR PERIMETER'S ENCHANTED MOAT THIS MORNING.
ACTUALLY, SHE SAID SHE WAS LOOKING FOR, AND I QUOTE, "LAPTOP-GEEK WILLOW, NOT BROOMSTICK-ACTION WILLOW."
I THINK SHE NEEDS HELP FIGURING OUT THE NEW RADAR STATIONS WE JUST INSTALLED.
RIGHT, I FORGOT WE ADDED G.I. JOE TO THE LONG LIST OF PEOPLE WHO WANT US DEAD.
BUT THE BEST SURVEILLANCE GEAR IN THE WORLD IS ONLY GOING TO TELL US IF THE CHICKEN-HAWKS ARE ON THEIR WAY.
WHAT ARE WE SUPPOSED TO DO WHEN THEY ACTUALLY GET HERE?
WHATEVER WE HAVE TO.
ALL'S FAIR.

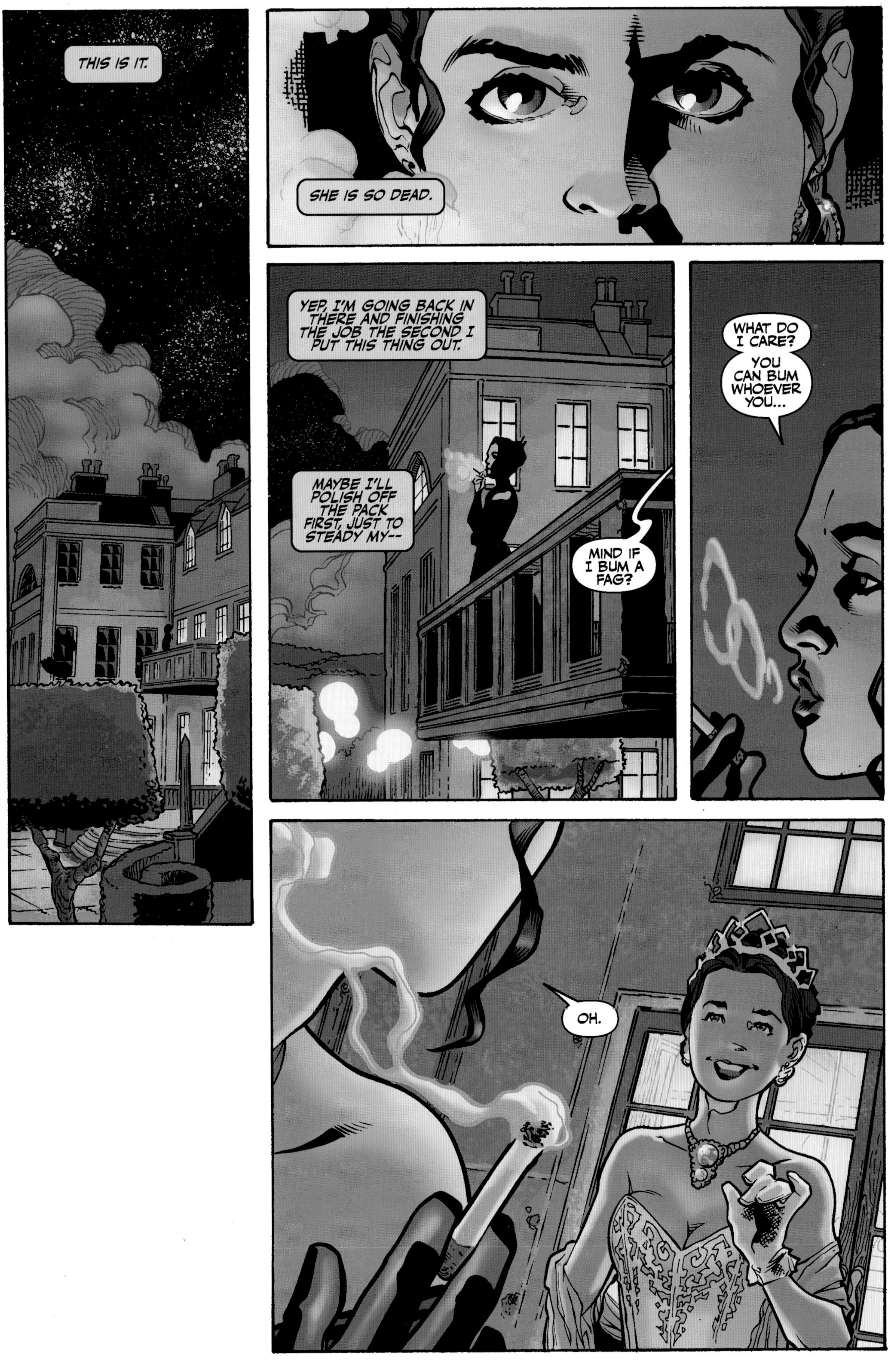
THIS IS IT.
SHE IS SO DEAD.
YEP, I'M GOING BACK IN THERE AND FINISHING THE JOB THE SECOND I PUT THIS THING OUT.
MAYBE I'LL POLISH OFF THE PACK FIRST, JUST TO STEADY MY--
MIND IF I BUM A FAG?
WHAT DO I CARE?
YOU CAN BUM WHOEVER YOU...
OH.

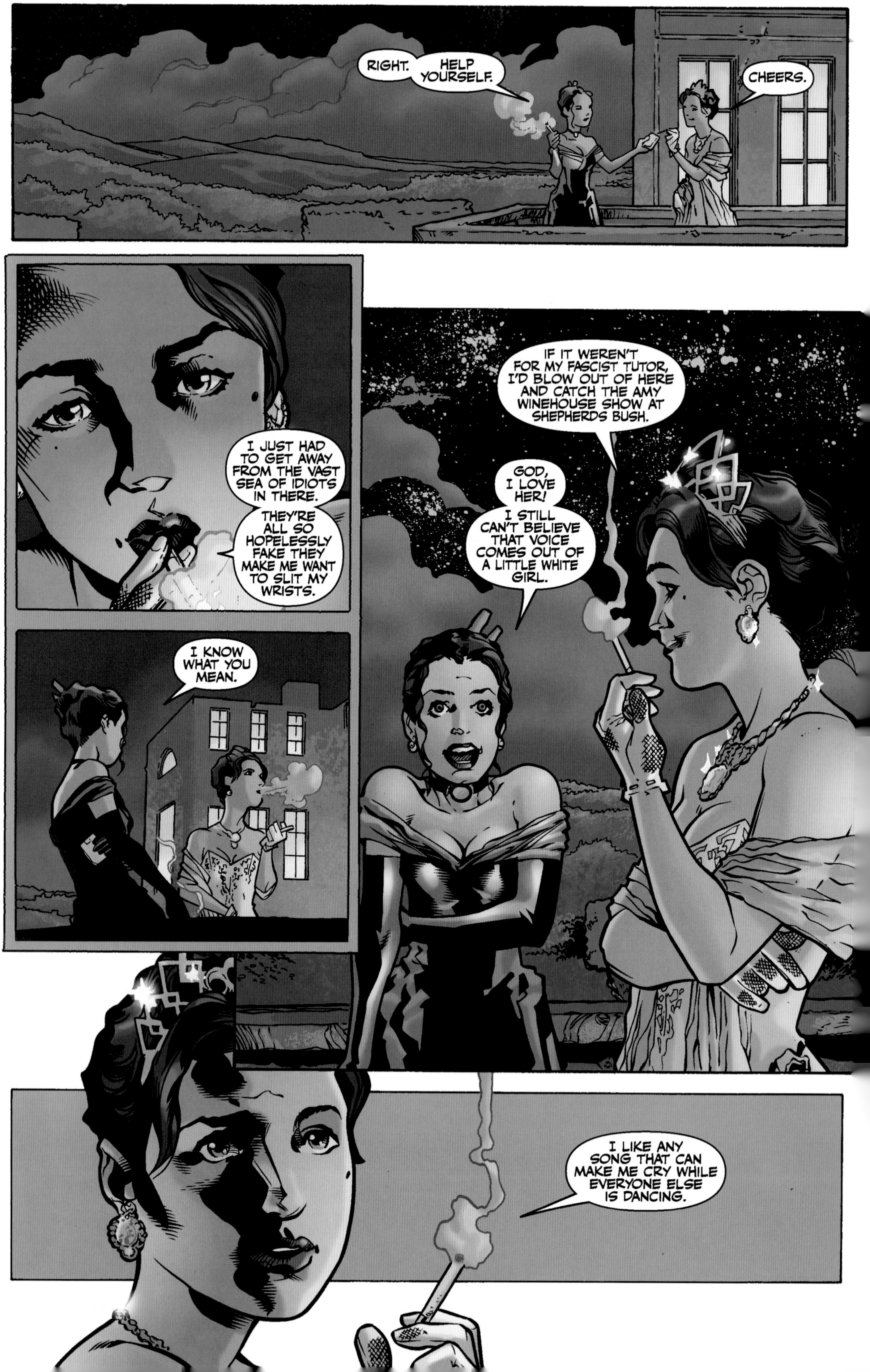

RIGHT.
HELP YOURSELF.
CHEERS.
I JUST HAD TO GET AWAY FROM THE VAST SEA OF IDIOTS IN THERE.
THEY'RE ALL SO HOPELESSLY FAKE THEY MAKE ME WANT TO SLIT MY WRISTS.
I KNOW WHAT YOU MEAN.
IF IT WEREN'T FOR MY FASCIST TUTOR, I'D BLOW OUT OF HERE AND CATCH THE AMY WINEHOUSE SHOW AT SHEPHERDS BUSH.
GOD, I LOVE HER!
I STILL CAN'T BELIEVE THAT VOICE COMES OUT OF A LITTLE WHITE GIRL.
I LIKE ANY SONG THAT CAN MAKE ME CRY WHILE EVERYONE ELSE IS DANCING.

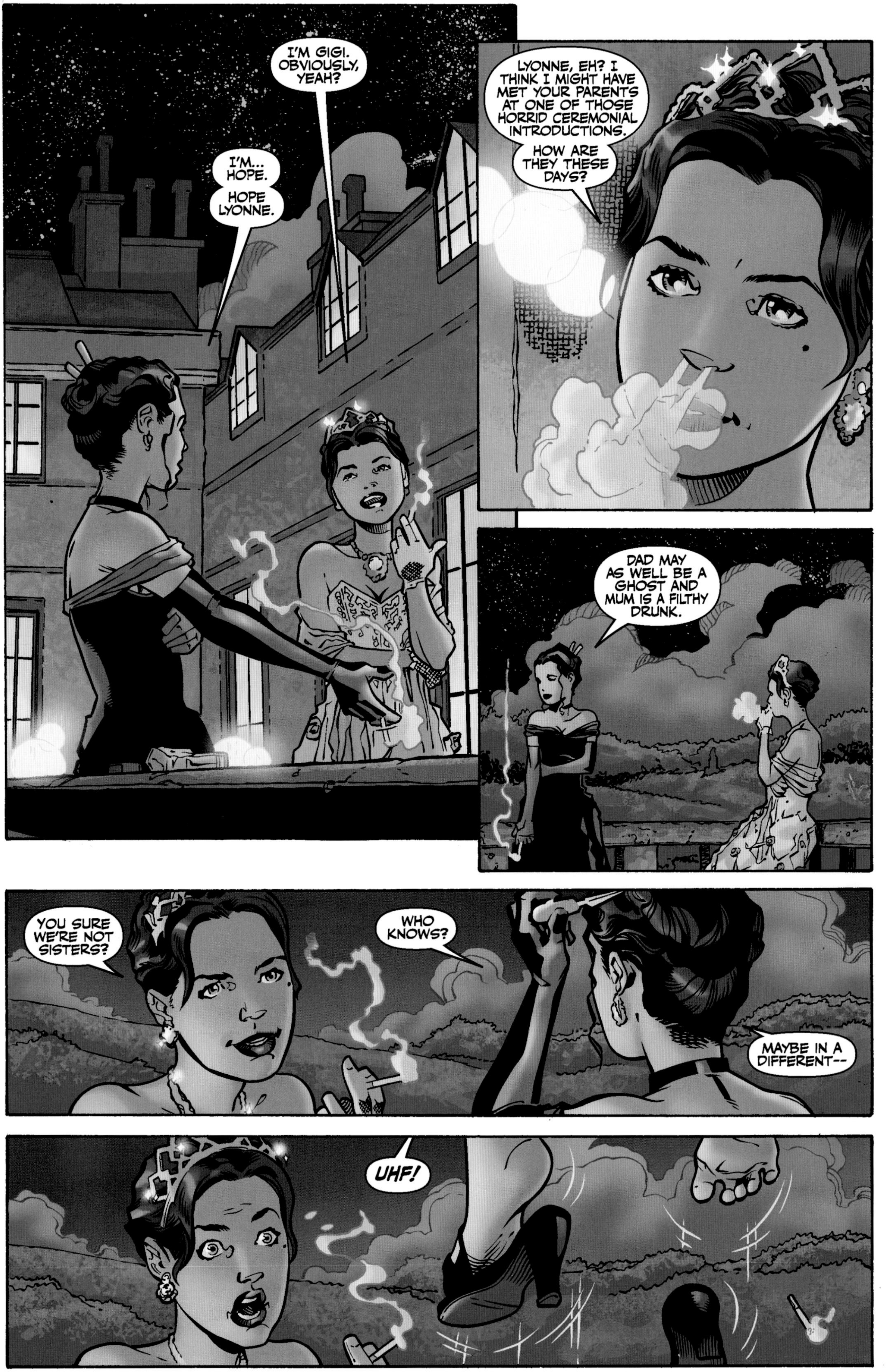
I'M... HOPE.
HOPE LYONNE.
I'M GIGI. OBVIOUSLY, YEAH?
LYONNE, EH? I THINK I MIGHT HAVE MET YOUR PARENTS AT ONE OF THOSE HORRID CEREMONIAL INTRODUCTIONS.
HOW ARE THEY THESE DAYS?
DAD MAY AS WELL BE A GHOST AND MUM IS A FILTHY DRUNK.
YOU SURE WE'RE NOT SISTERS?
WHO KNOWS?
MAYBE IN A DIFFERENT--
UHF!

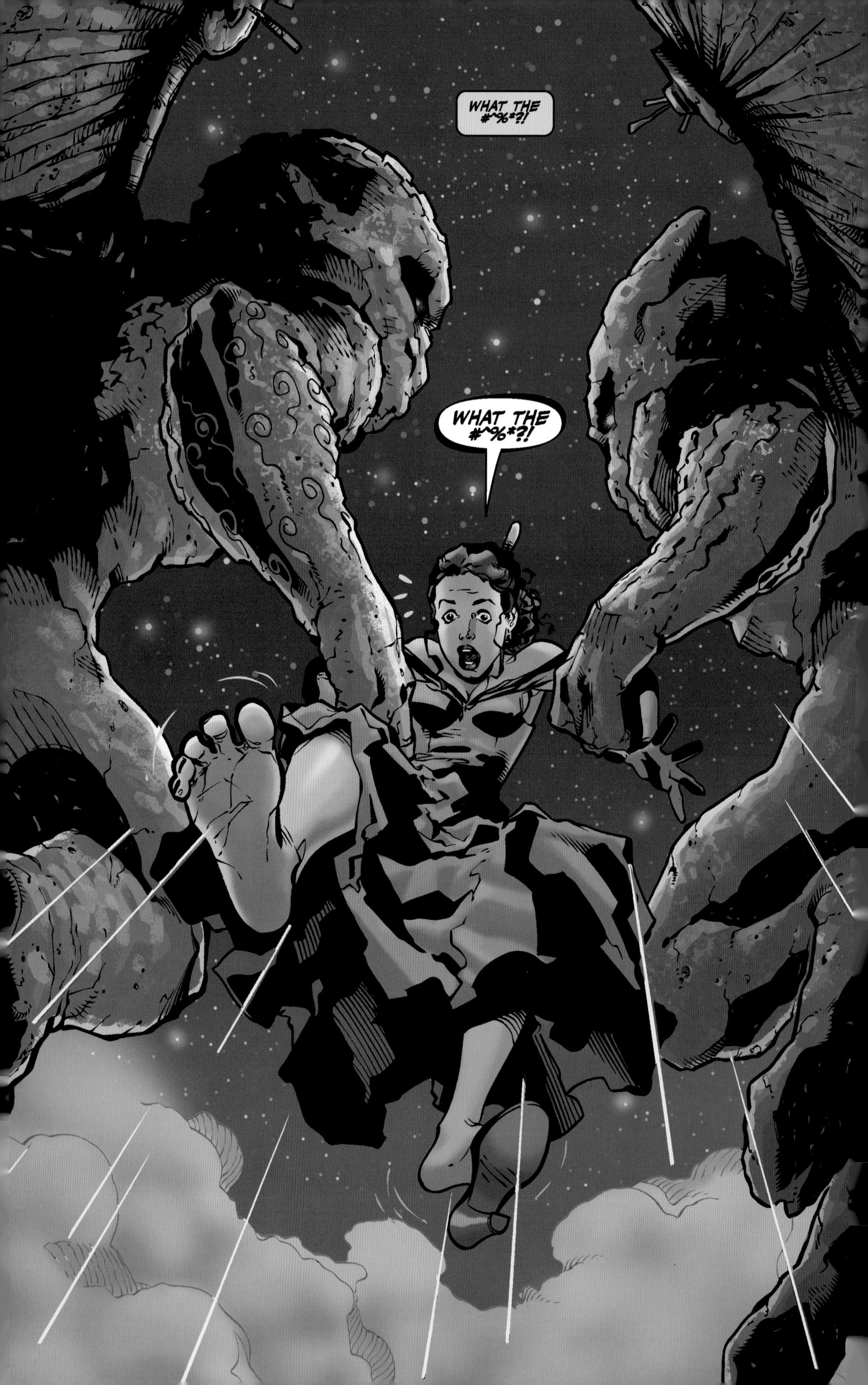
WHAT THE #~%*?!
WHAT THE #~%*?!

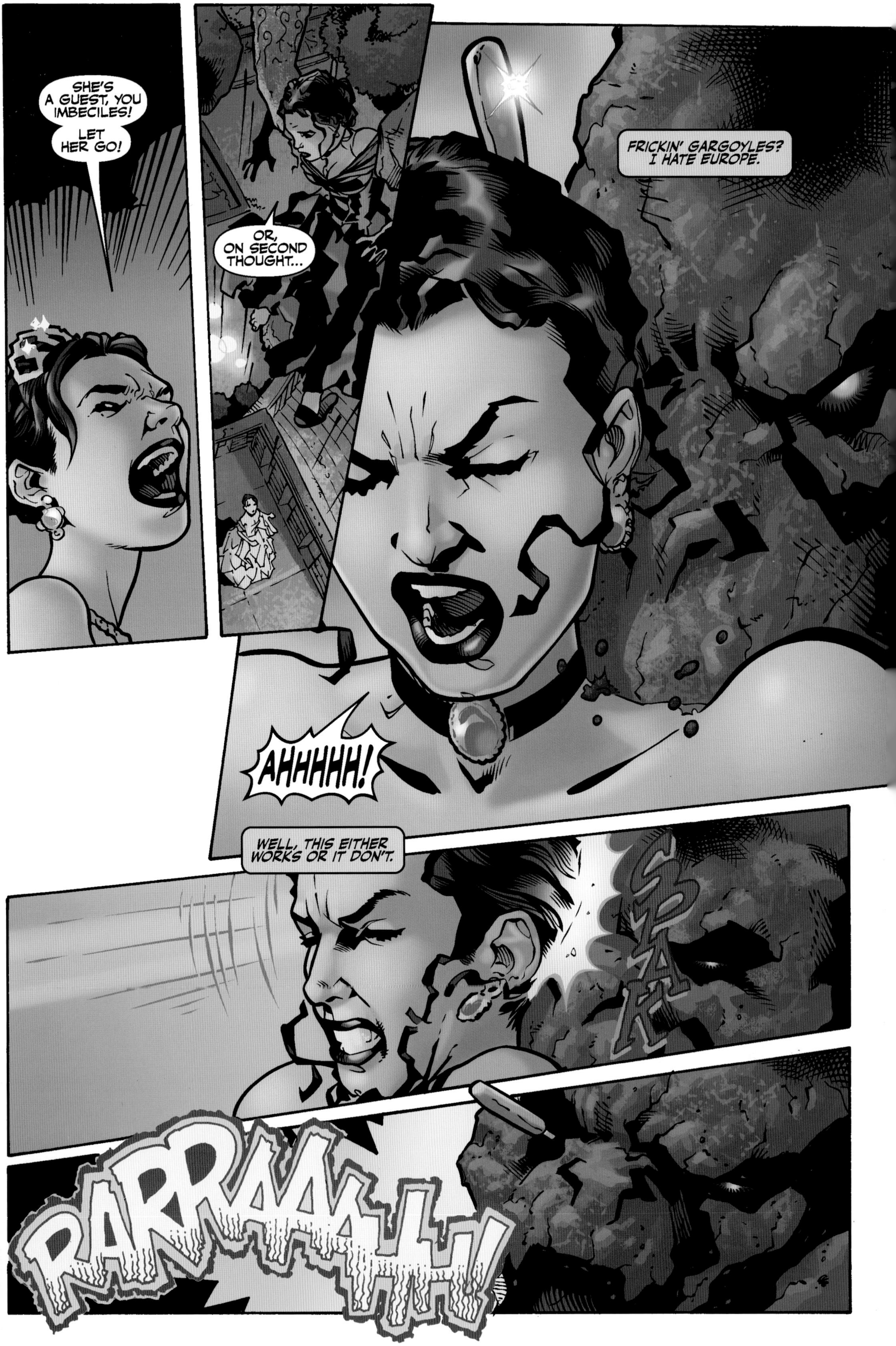
SHE'S A GUEST, YOU IMBECILES!
LET HER GO!
OR, ON SECOND THOUGHT...
FRICKIN' GARGOYLES? I HATE EUROPE.
AHHHHH!
WELL, THIS EITHER WORKS OR IT DON'T.
SMACK
RARRAAAHH!

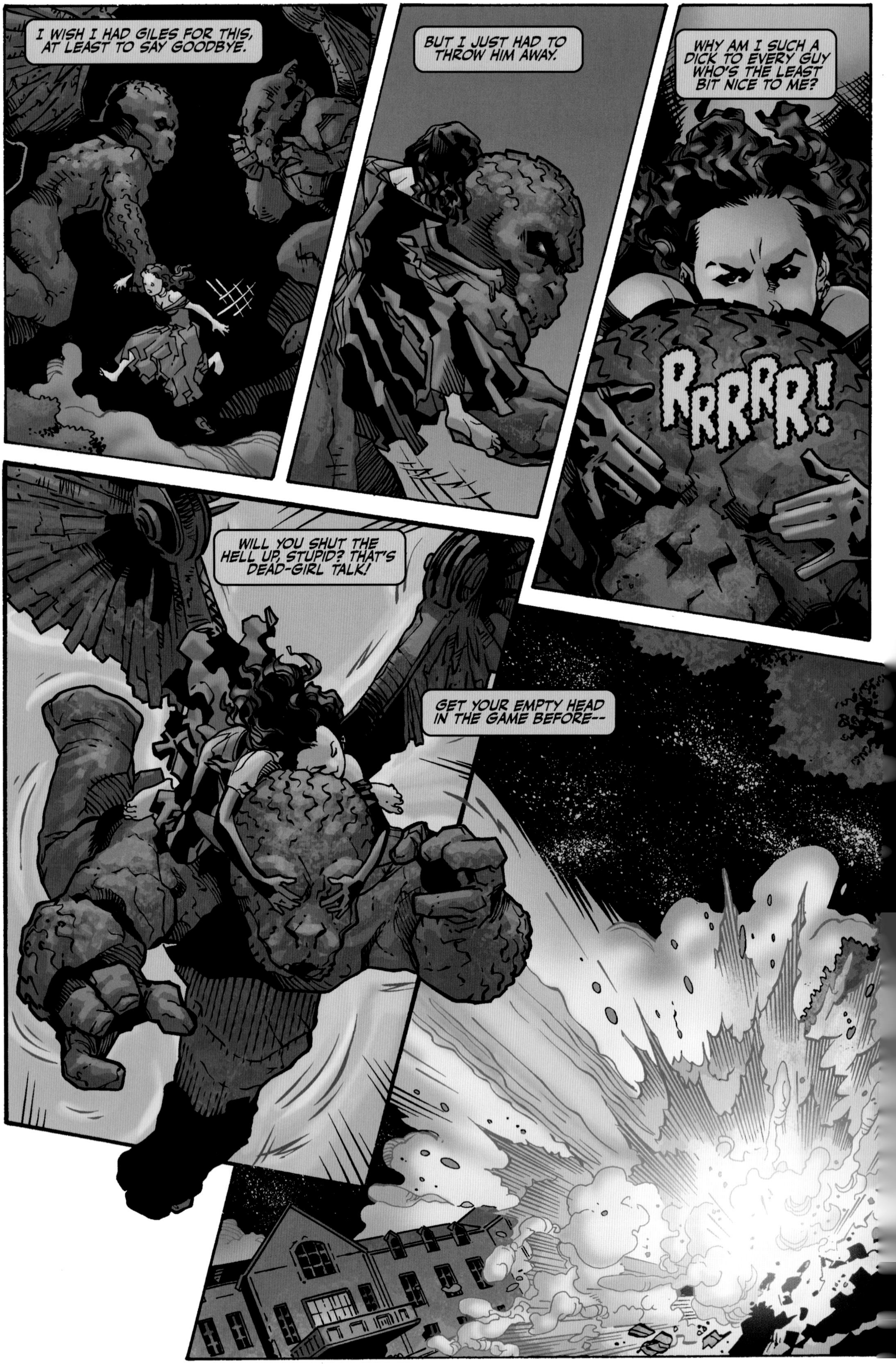
I WISH I HAD GILES FOR THIS, AT LEAST TO SAY GOODBYE.
BUT I JUST HAD TO THROW HIM AWAY.
WHY AM I SUCH A DICK TO EVERY GUY WHO'S THE LEAST BIT NICE TO ME?
RRRRR!
WILL YOU SHUT THE HELL UP, STUPID? THAT'S DEAD-GIRL TALK!
GET YOUR EMPTY HEAD IN THE GAME BEFORE--

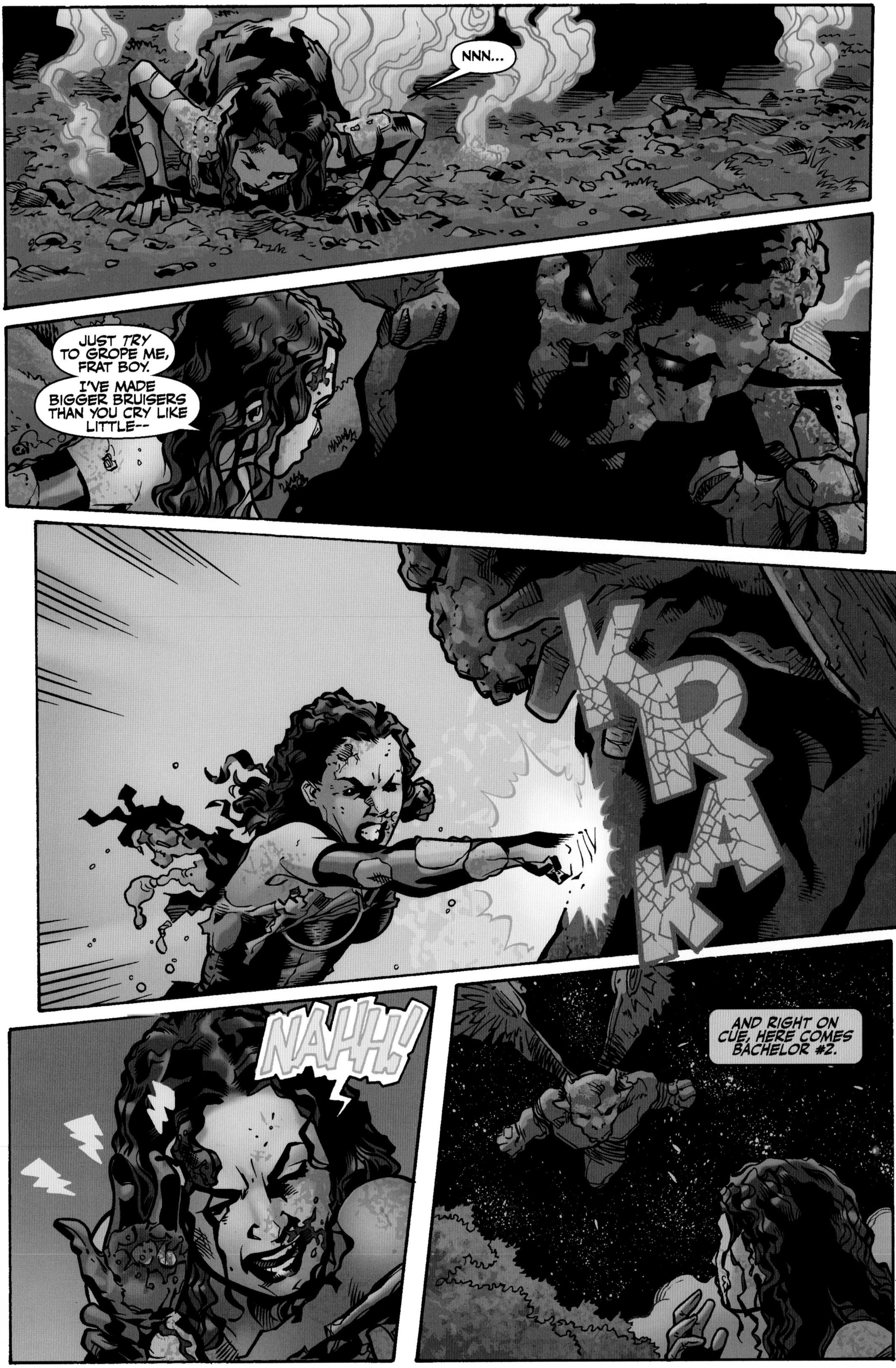
NNN...
JUST TRY TO GROPE ME, FRAT BOY.
I'VE MADE BIGGER BRUISERS THAN YOU CRY LIKE LITTLE--
KRAKA
NAHH!
AND RIGHT ON CUE, HERE COMES BACHELOR #2.

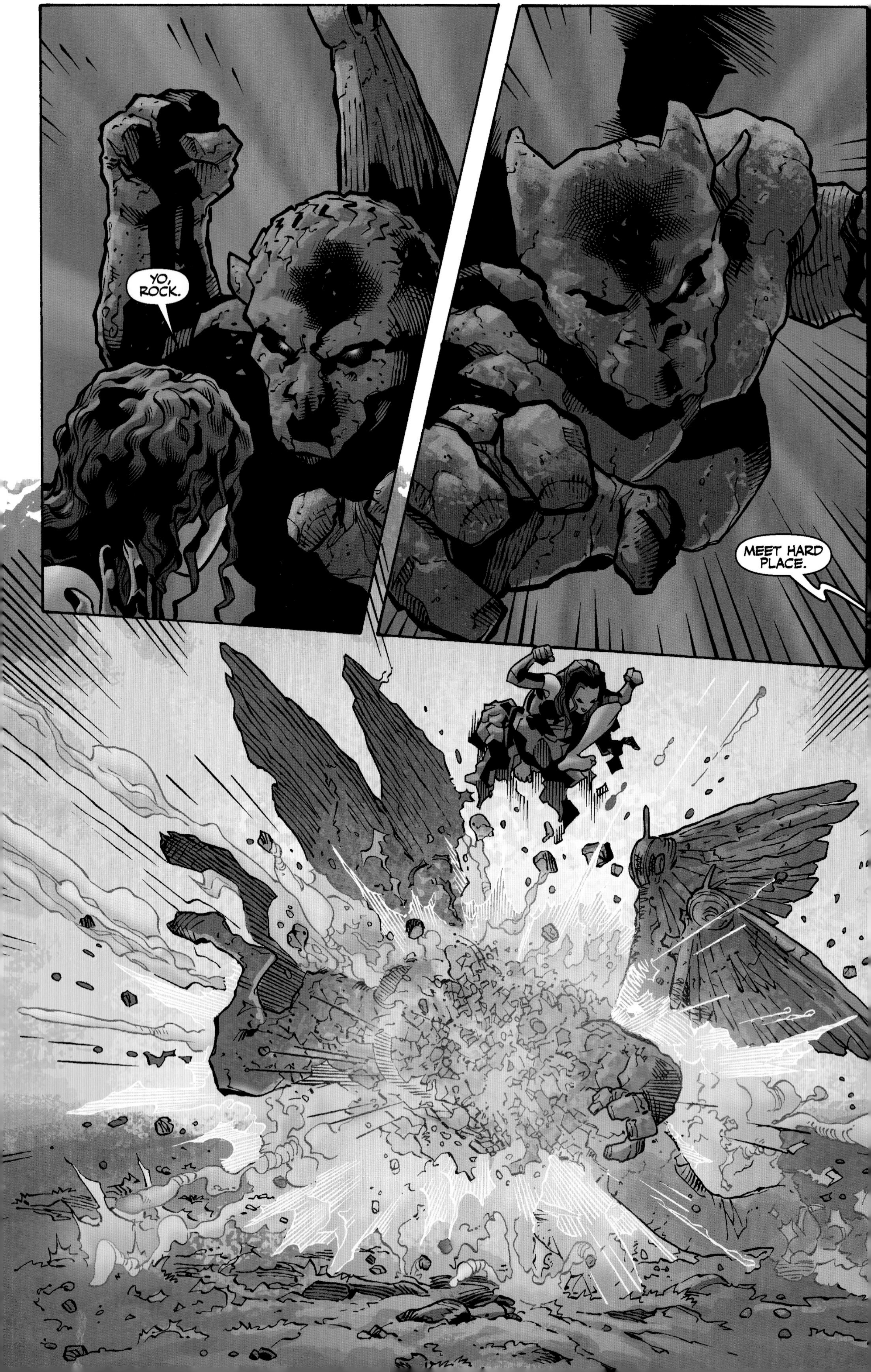
YO, ROCK.
MEET HARD PLACE.

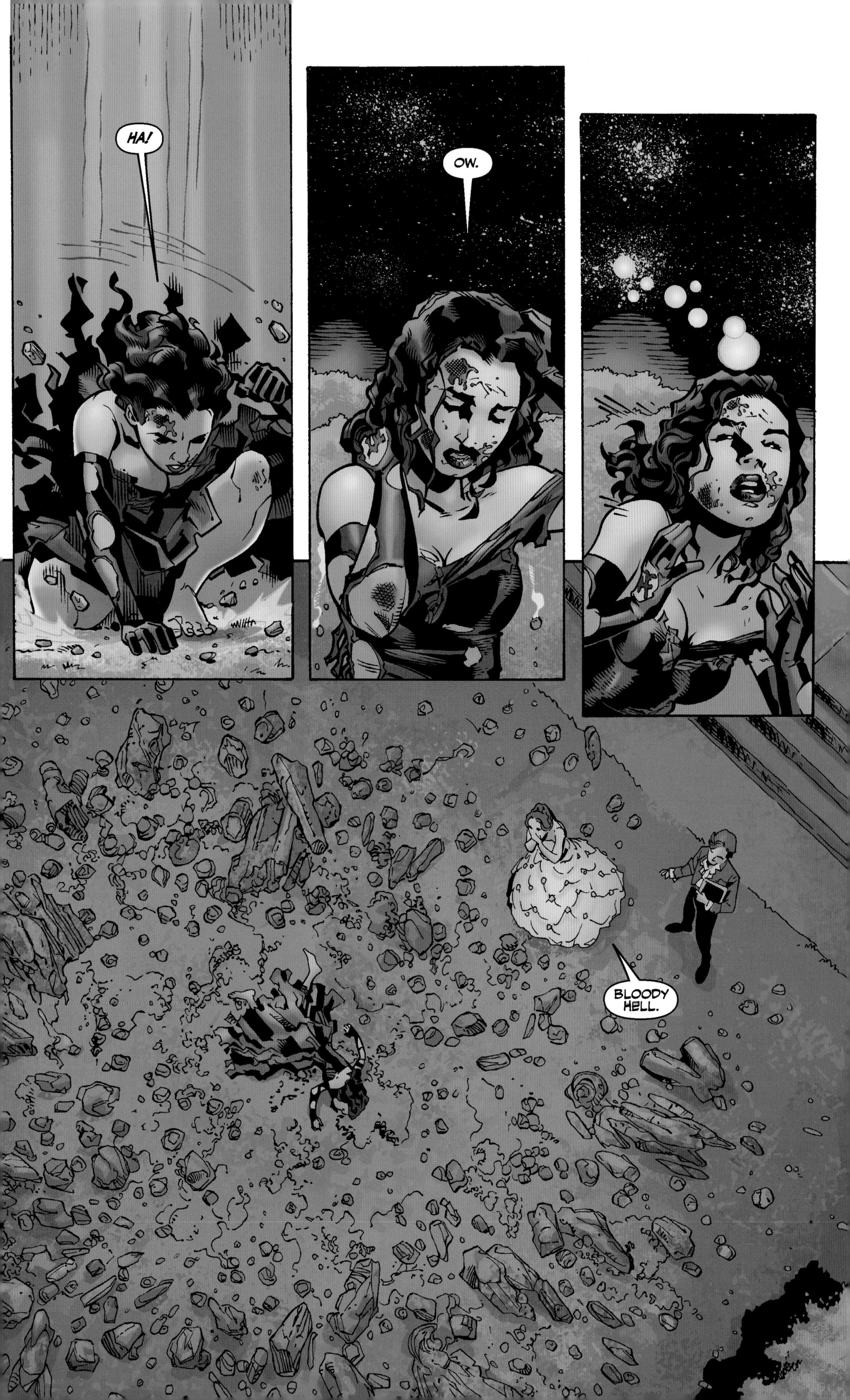
HA!
OW.
BLOODY HELL.

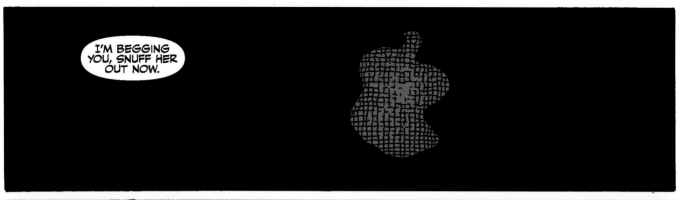

I'M BEGGING YOU, SNUFF HER OUT NOW.

NO, SHE ISN'T ONE OF YOUR DISPOSABLE STREET URCHINS. THIS SLAYER IS A FELLOW BLUE BLOOD.

SHE'S A VISCOUNT'S KID, NOT A SODDING PRINCESS!

PRECISELY. THE WHOLE POINT OF THIS LITTLE SOIREE WAS IDENTIFYING POSSIBLE THREATS TO MY IMPENDING CORONATION, WHICH A LOWLY BANKER'S DAUGHTER CLEARLY IS NOT.

NOT A THREAT? ARE YOU MAD? SHE TURNED MY BOYS TO RUBBLE!

AFTER THEY ATTACKED HER UNPROVOKED. AND SHE WAS BRILLIANT. I COULD USE SOMEONE LIKE HER AT MY SIDE.

TRUST ME, THIS GIRL AND I ARE ON THE SAME WAVELENGTH.

ONE CIGARETTE AND YOU'RE READY TO MAKE HER YOUR BEST MATE? YOU DON'T EVEN KNOW--

HUSH, SHE'S COMING AROUND.

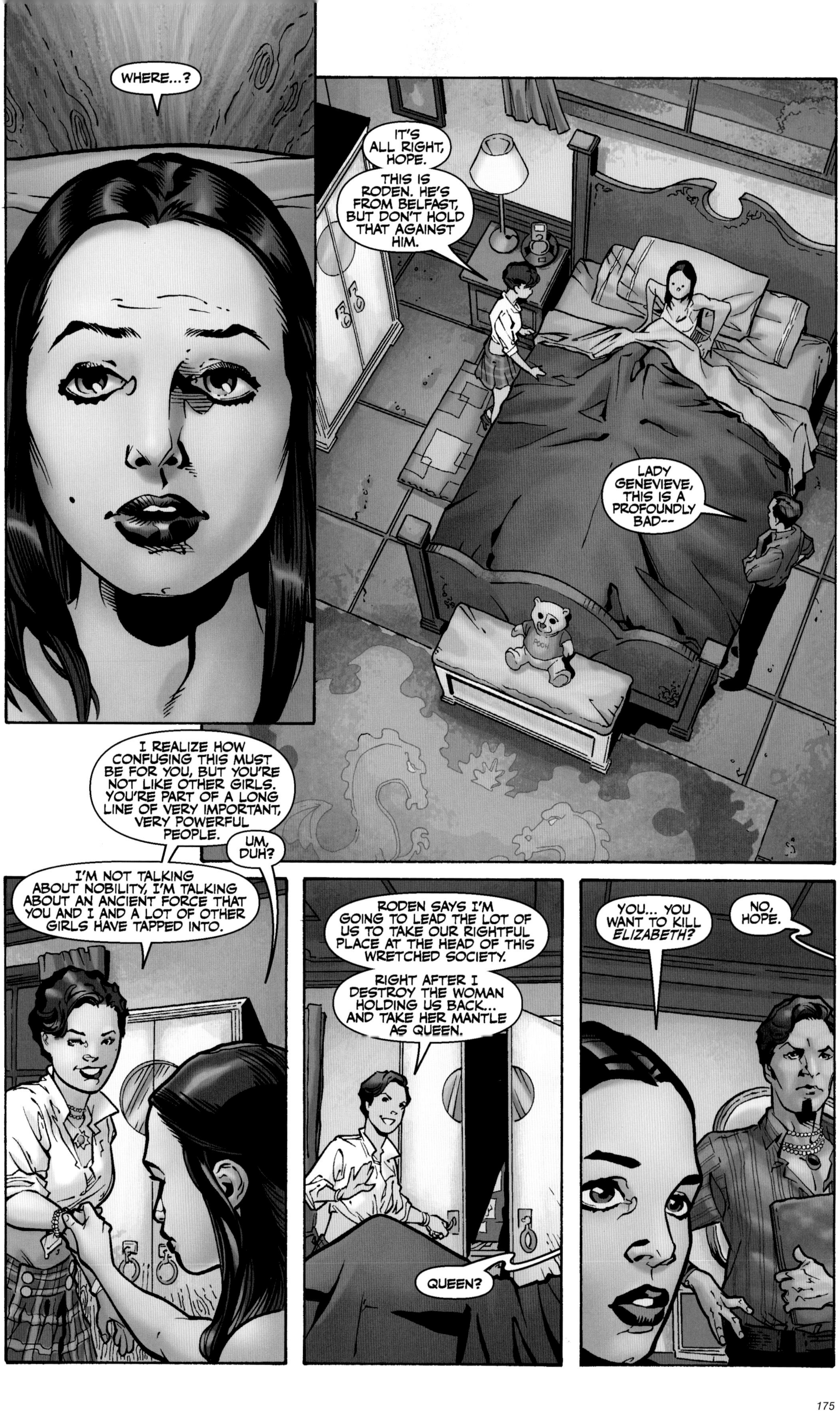
WHERE...?
IT'S ALL RIGHT, HOPE.
THIS IS RODEN. HE'S FROM BELFAST, BUT DON'T HOLD THAT AGAINST HIM.
LADY GENEVIEVE, THIS IS A PROFOUNDLY BAD--
I REALIZE HOW CONFUSING THIS MUST BE FOR YOU, BUT YOU'RE NOT LIKE OTHER GIRLS. YOU'RE PART OF A LONG LINE OF VERY IMPORTANT, VERY POWERFUL PEOPLE.
UM, DUH?
I'M NOT TALKING ABOUT NOBILITY, I'M TALKING ABOUT AN ANCIENT FORCE THAT YOU AND I AND A LOT OF OTHER GIRLS HAVE TAPPED INTO.
RODEN SAYS I'M GOING TO LEAD THE LOT OF US TO TAKE OUR RIGHTFUL PLACE AT THE HEAD OF THIS WRETCHED SOCIETY.
RIGHT AFTER I DESTROY THE WOMAN HOLDING US BACK... AND TAKE HER MANTLE AS QUEEN.
QUEEN?
YOU... YOU WANT TO KILL *ELIZABETH?*
NO, HOPE.

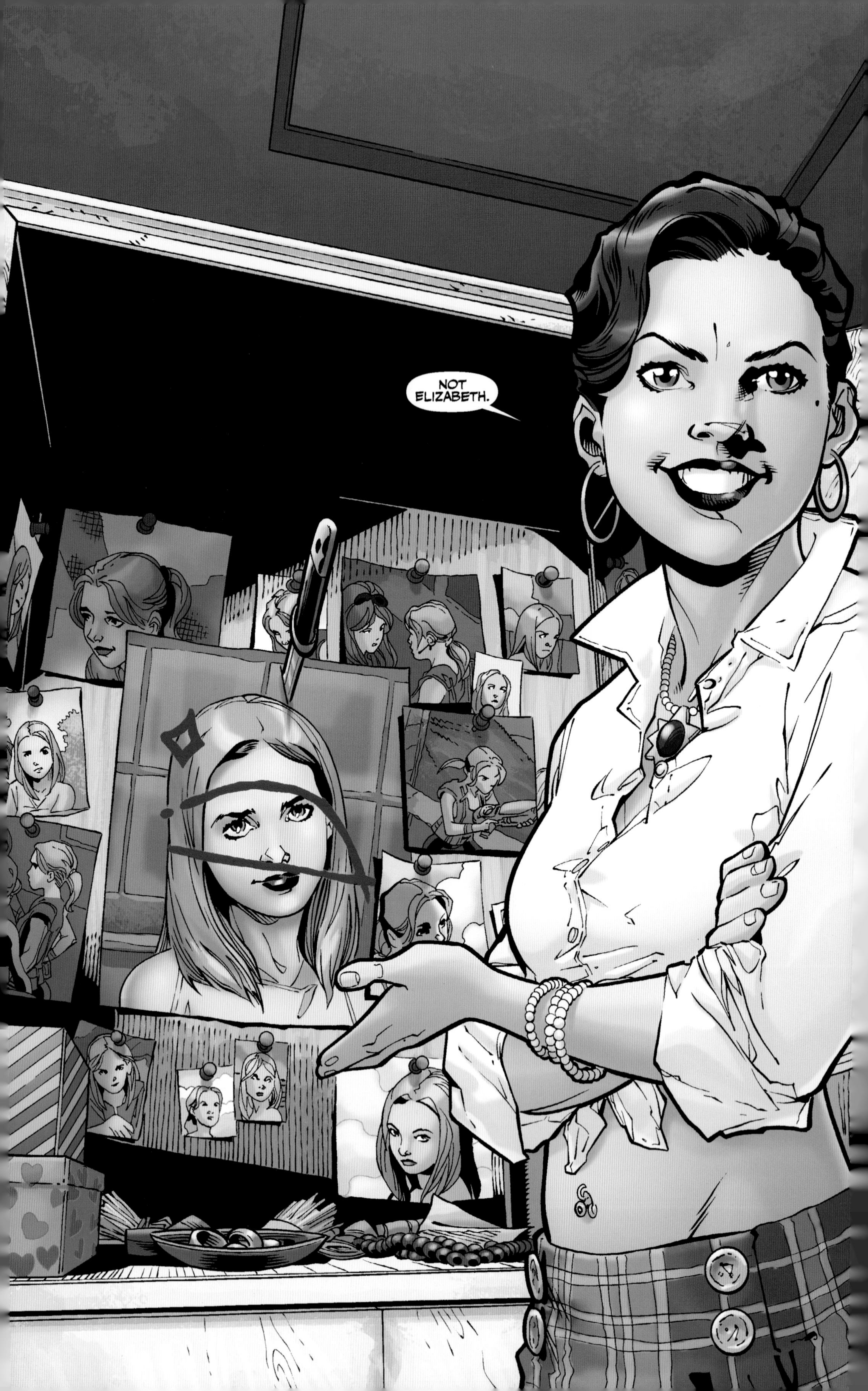
NOT ELIZABETH.

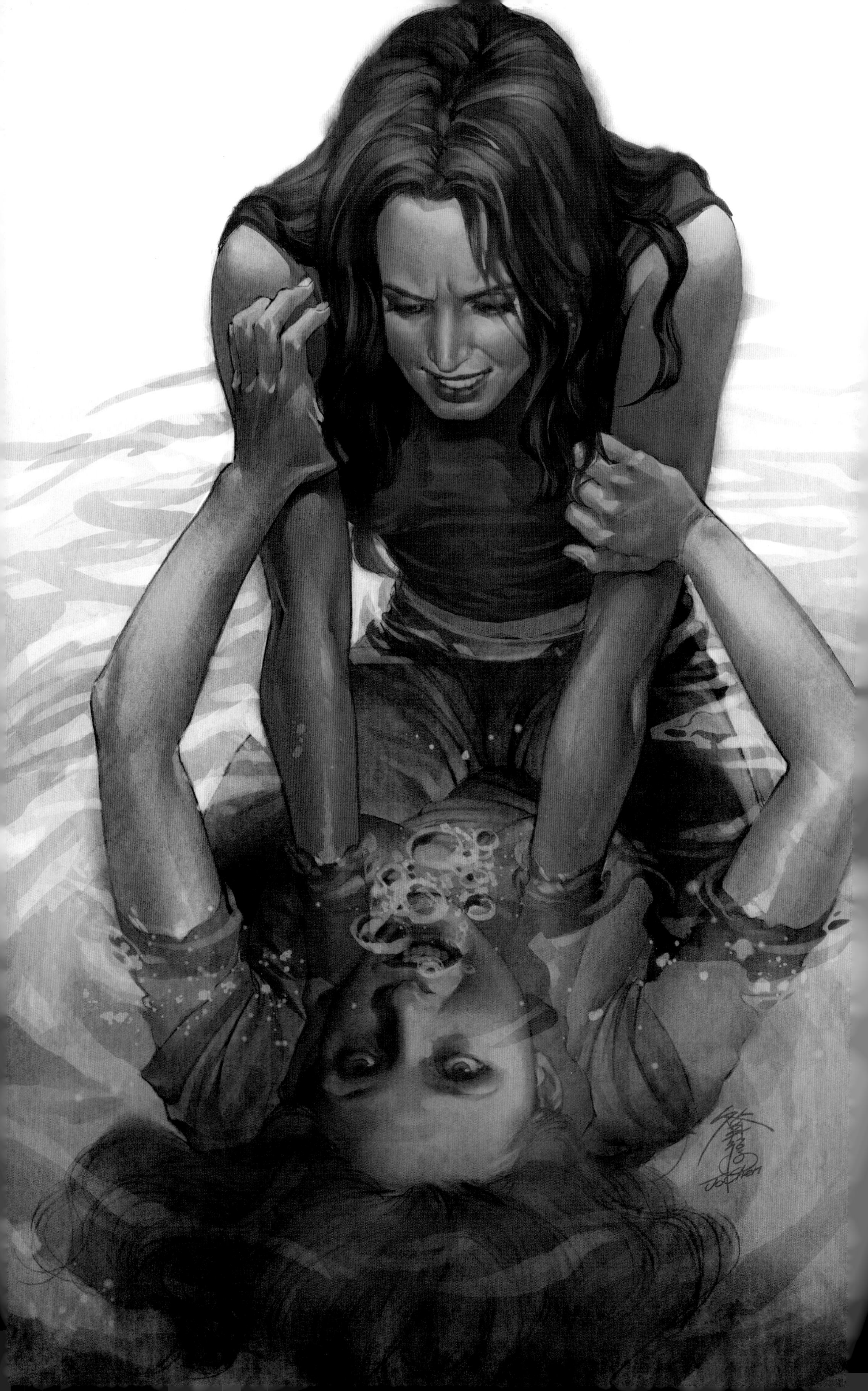

NO FUTURE FOR YOU

PART THREE

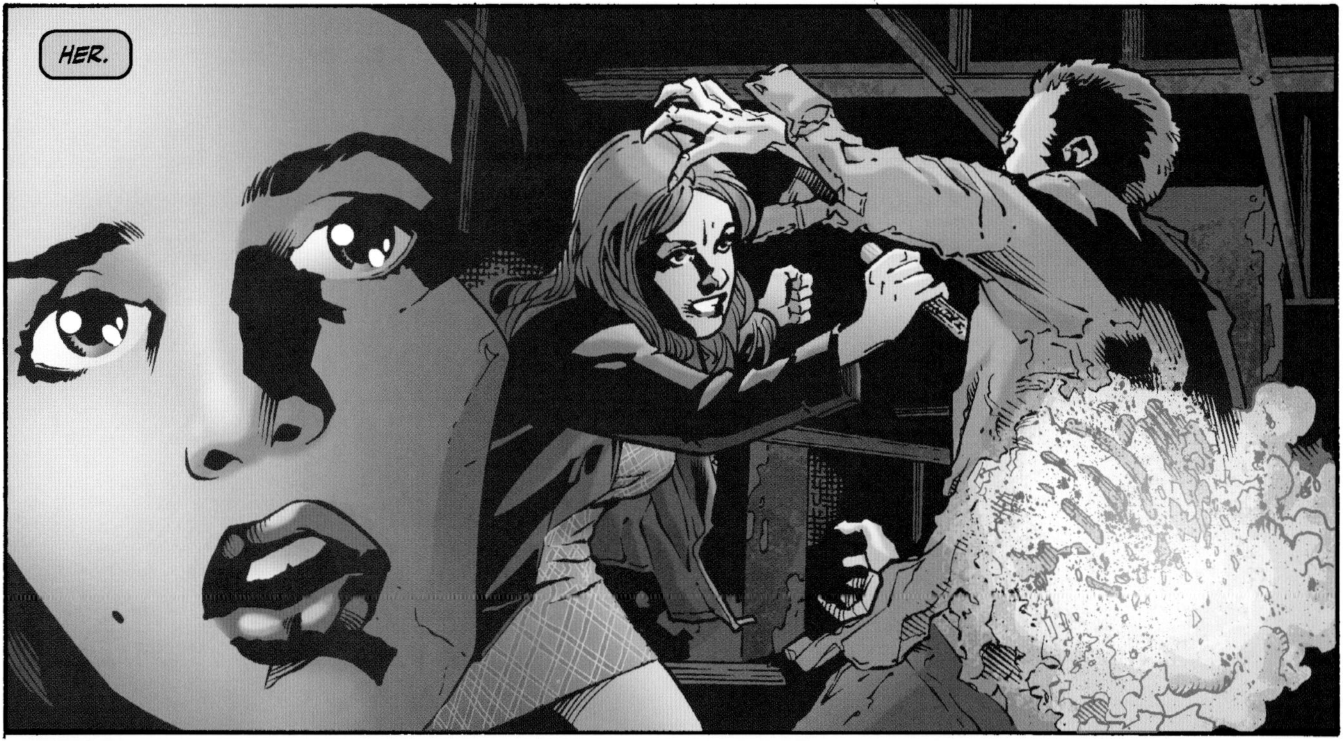
HER.

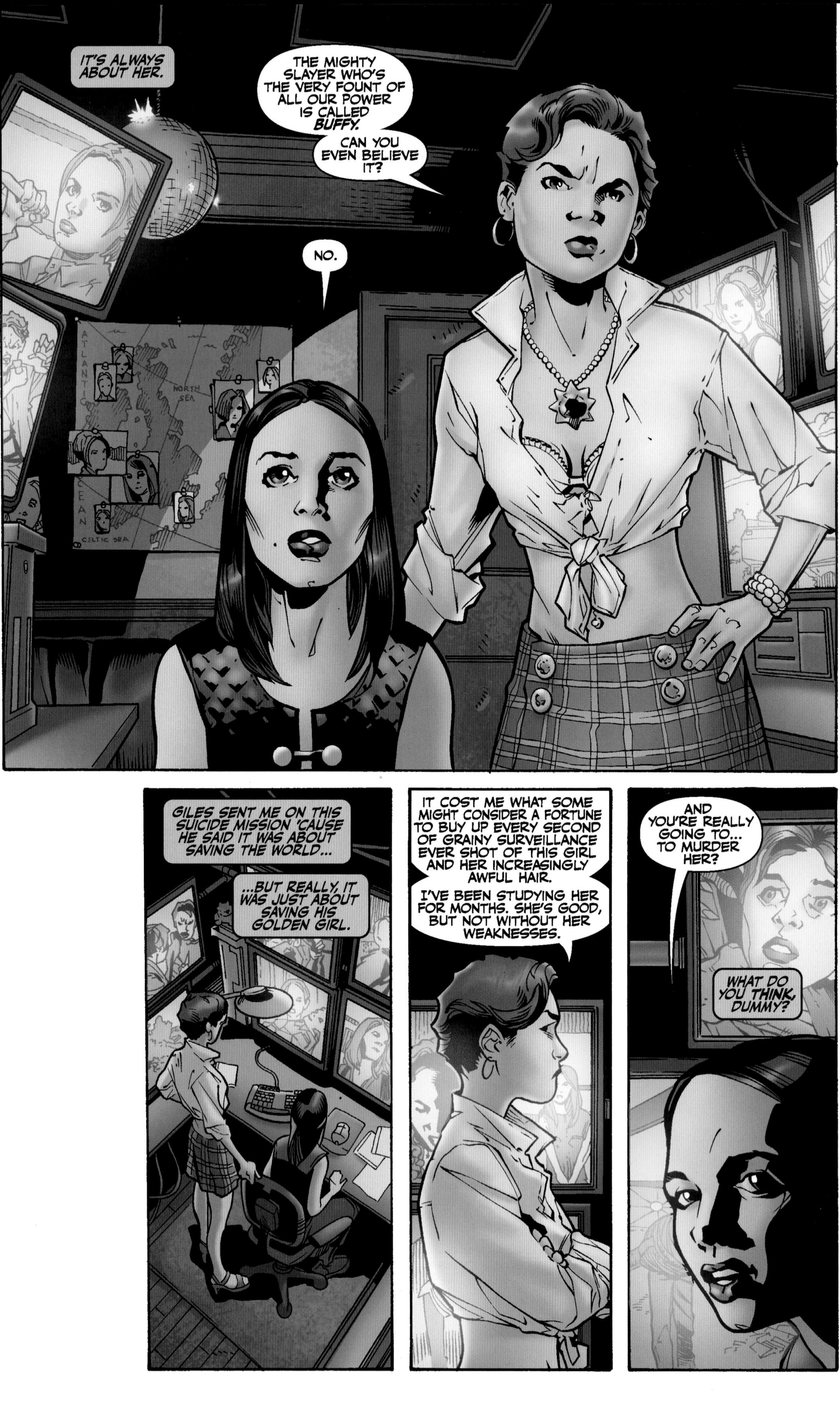
IT'S ALWAYS ABOUT HER.
THE MIGHTY SLAYER WHO'S THE VERY FOUNT OF ALL OUR POWER IS CALLED *BUFFY.*
CAN YOU EVEN BELIEVE IT?
NO.
NORTH SEA
CELTIC SEA
GILES SENT ME ON THIS SUICIDE MISSION 'CAUSE HE SAID IT WAS ABOUT SAVING THE WORLD...
...BUT REALLY, IT WAS JUST ABOUT SAVING HIS GOLDEN GIRL.
IT COST ME WHAT SOME MIGHT CONSIDER A FORTUNE TO BUY UP EVERY SECOND OF GRAINY SURVEILLANCE EVER SHOT OF THIS GIRL AND HER INCREASINGLY AWFUL HAIR.
I'VE BEEN STUDYING HER FOR MONTHS. SHE'S GOOD, BUT NOT WITHOUT HER WEAKNESSES.
AND YOU'RE REALLY GOING TO... TO MURDER HER?
WHAT DO YOU *THINK,* DUMMY?

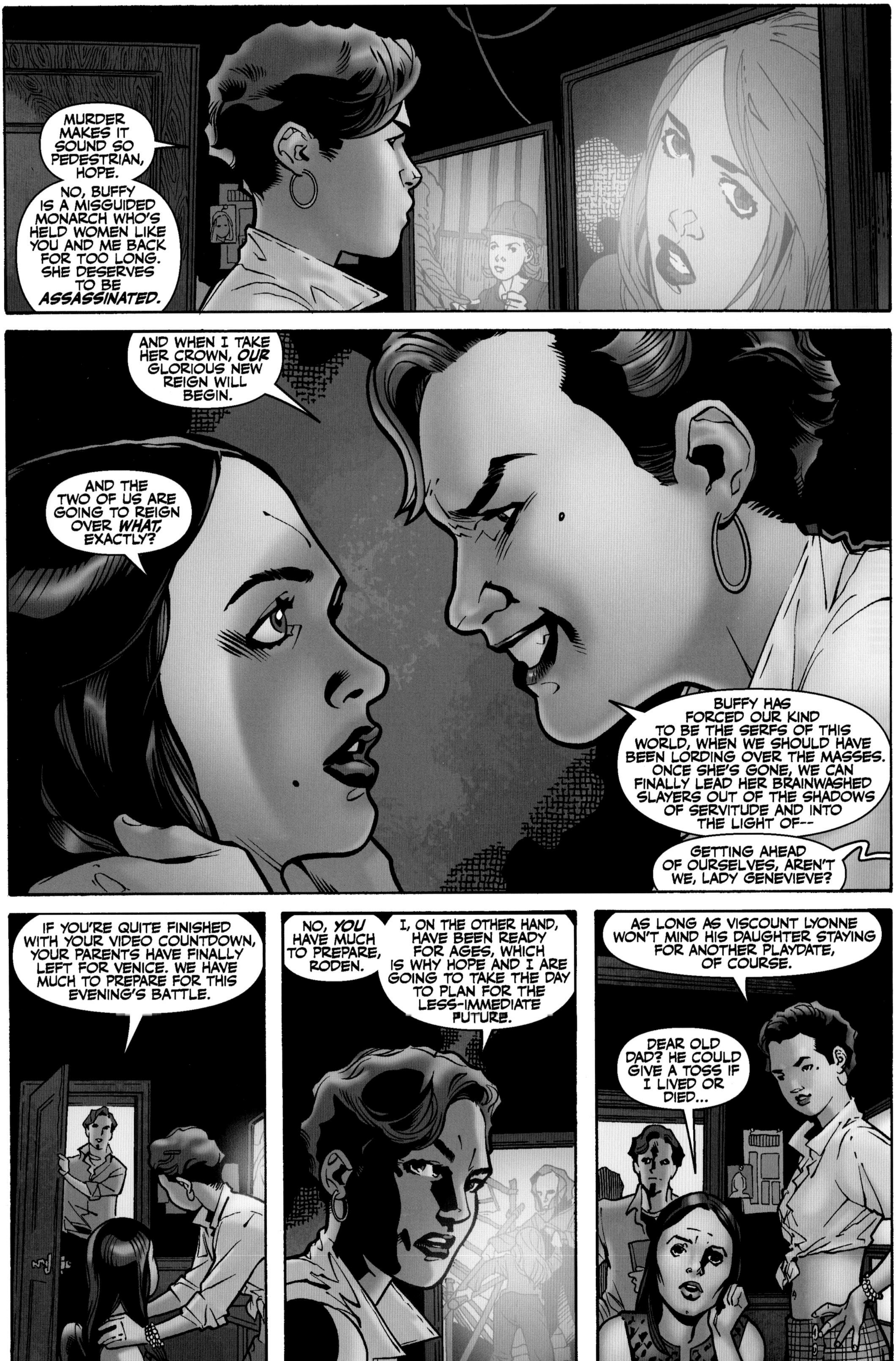
MURDER MAKES IT SOUND SO PEDESTRIAN, HOPE.
NO, BUFFY IS A MISGUIDED MONARCH WHO'S HELD WOMEN LIKE YOU AND ME BACK FOR TOO LONG. SHE DESERVES TO BE *ASSASSINATED.*
AND WHEN I TAKE HER CROWN, *OUR* GLORIOUS NEW REIGN WILL BEGIN.
AND THE TWO OF US ARE GOING TO REIGN OVER *WHAT,* EXACTLY?
BUFFY HAS FORCED OUR KIND TO BE THE SERFS OF THIS WORLD, WHEN WE SHOULD HAVE BEEN LORDING OVER THE MASSES. ONCE SHE'S GONE, WE CAN FINALLY LEAD HER BRAINWASHED SLAYERS OUT OF THE SHADOWS OF SERVITUDE AND INTO THE LIGHT OF--
GETTING AHEAD OF OURSELVES, AREN'T WE, LADY GENEVIEVE?
IF YOU'RE QUITE FINISHED WITH YOUR VIDEO COUNTDOWN, YOUR PARENTS HAVE FINALLY LEFT FOR VENICE. WE HAVE MUCH TO PREPARE FOR THIS EVENING'S BATTLE.
NO, *YOU* HAVE MUCH TO PREPARE, RODEN.
I, ON THE OTHER HAND, HAVE BEEN READY FOR AGES, WHICH IS WHY HOPE AND I ARE GOING TO TAKE THE DAY TO PLAN FOR THE LESS-IMMEDIATE FUTURE.
AS LONG AS VISCOUNT LYONNE WON'T MIND HIS DAUGHTER STAYING FOR ANOTHER PLAYDATE, OF COURSE.
DEAR OLD DAD? HE COULD GIVE A TOSS IF I LIVED OR DIED...

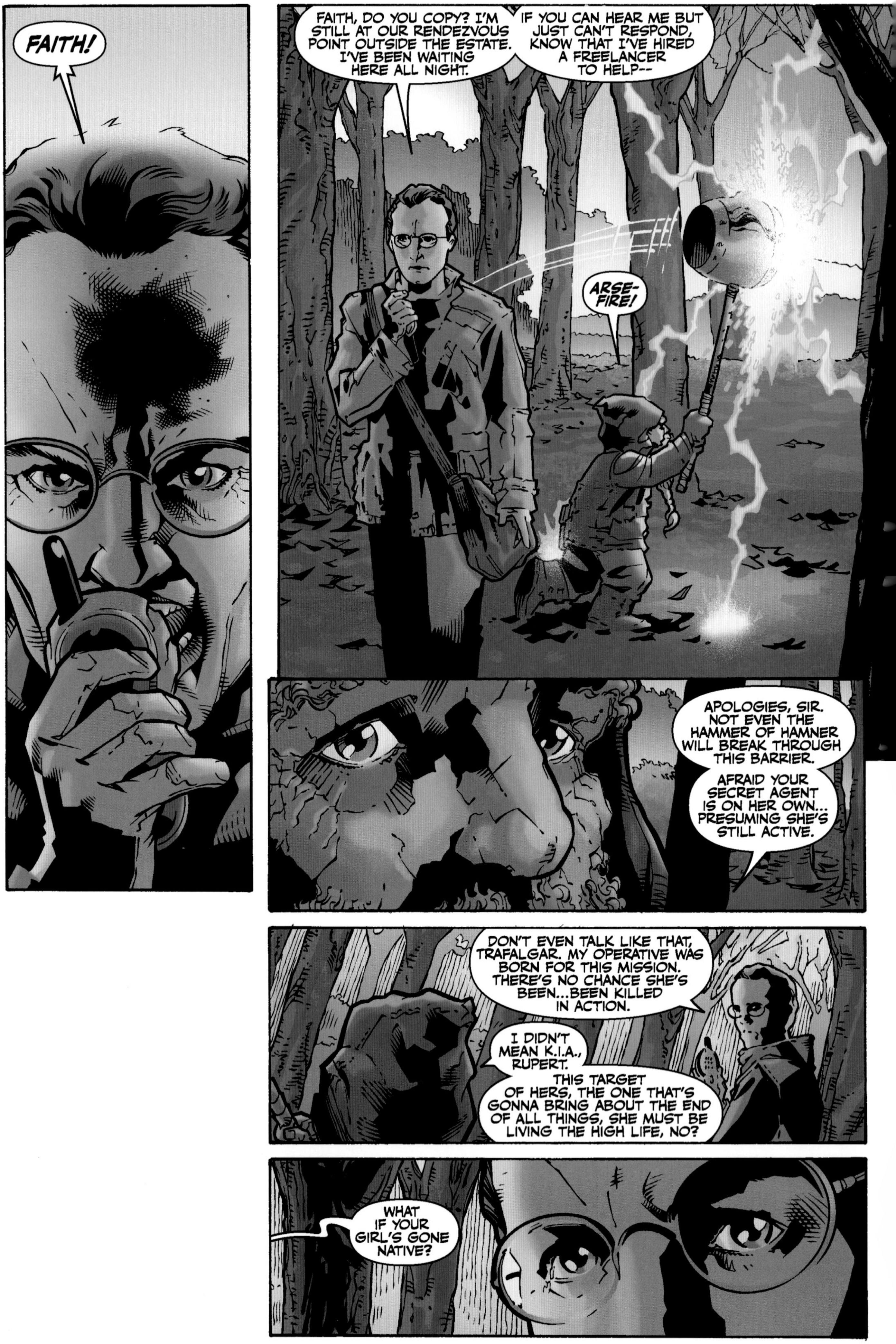
FAITH!
FAITH, DO YOU COPY? I'M STILL AT OUR RENDEZVOUS POINT OUTSIDE THE ESTATE. I'VE BEEN WAITING HERE ALL NIGHT.
IF YOU CAN HEAR ME BUT JUST CAN'T RESPOND, KNOW THAT I'VE HIRED A FREELANCER TO HELP--
ARSE-FIRE!
APOLOGIES, SIR. NOT EVEN THE HAMMER OF HAMNER WILL BREAK THROUGH THIS BARRIER.
AFRAID YOUR SECRET AGENT IS ON HER OWN... PRESUMING SHE'S STILL ACTIVE.
DON'T EVEN TALK LIKE THAT, TRAFALGAR. MY OPERATIVE WAS BORN FOR THIS MISSION. THERE'S NO CHANCE SHE'S BEEN...BEEN KILLED IN ACTION.
I DIDN'T MEAN K.I.A., RUPERT.
THIS TARGET OF HERS, THE ONE THAT'S GONNA BRING ABOUT THE END OF ALL THINGS, SHE MUST BE LIVING THE HIGH LIFE, NO?
WHAT IF YOUR GIRL'S GONE NATIVE?

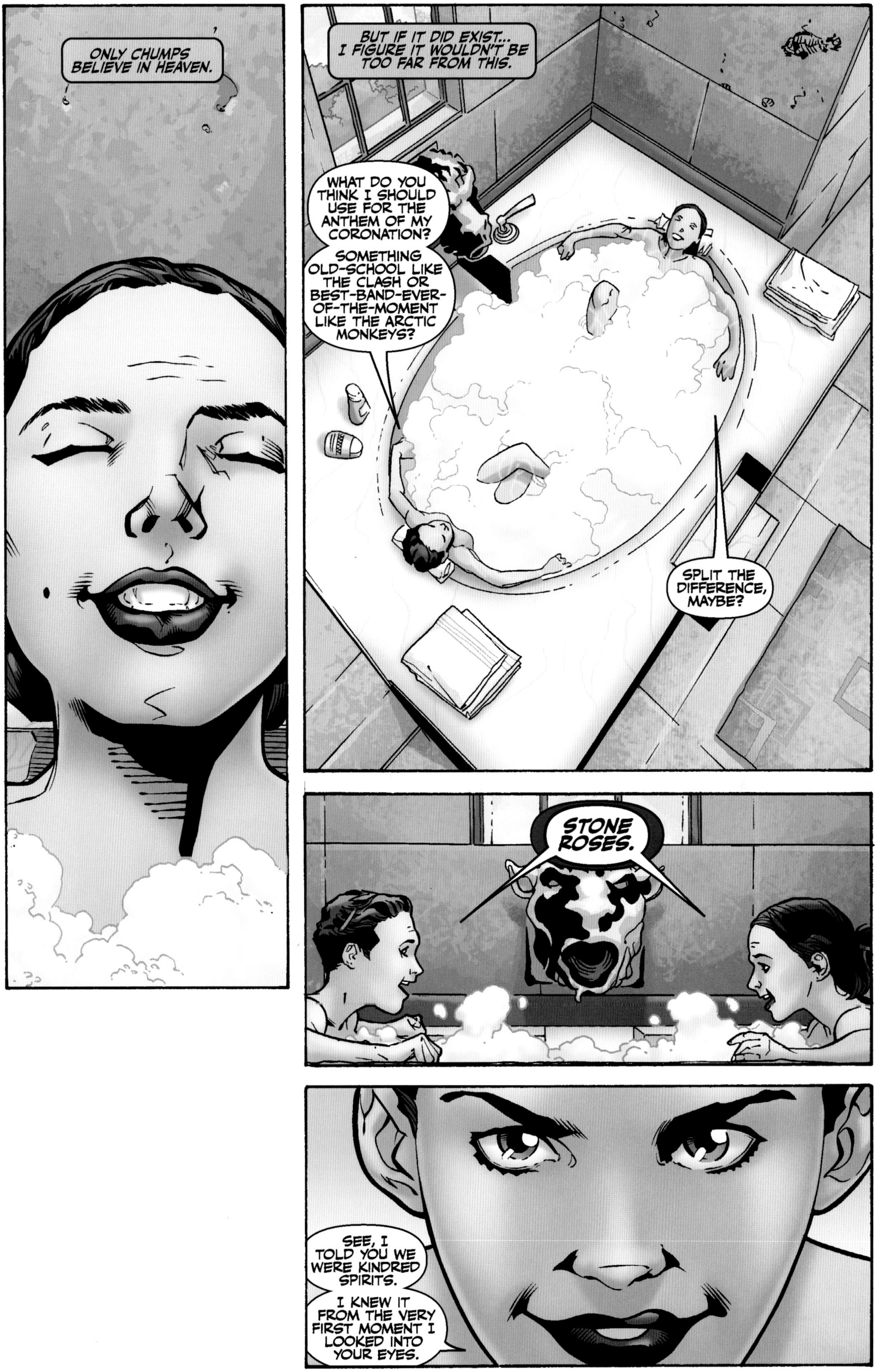
ONLY CHUMPS BELIEVE IN HEAVEN.
BUT IF IT DID EXIST... I FIGURE IT WOULDN'T BE TOO FAR FROM THIS.
WHAT DO YOU THINK I SHOULD USE FOR THE ANTHEM OF MY CORONATION?
SOMETHING OLD-SCHOOL LIKE THE CLASH OR BEST-BAND-EVER-OF-THE-MOMENT LIKE THE ARCTIC MONKEYS?
SPLIT THE DIFFERENCE, MAYBE?
STONE ROSES.
SEE, I TOLD YOU WE WERE KINDRED SPIRITS.
I KNEW IT FROM THE VERY FIRST MOMENT I LOOKED INTO YOUR EYES.

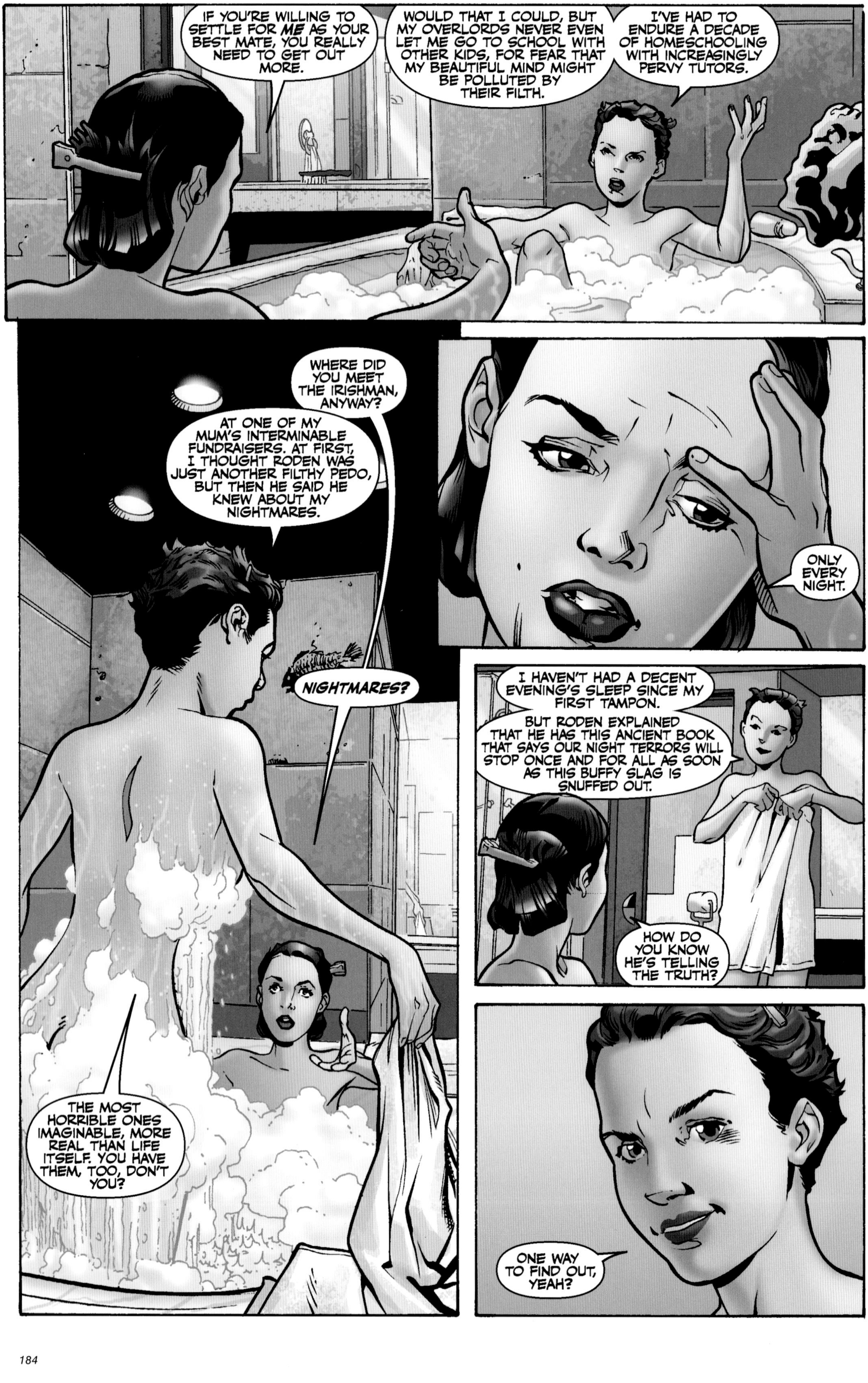
IF YOU'RE WILLING TO SETTLE FOR *ME* AS YOUR BEST MATE, YOU REALLY NEED TO GET OUT MORE.
WOULD THAT I COULD, BUT MY OVERLORDS NEVER EVEN LET ME GO TO SCHOOL WITH OTHER KIDS, FOR FEAR THAT MY BEAUTIFUL MIND MIGHT BE POLLUTED BY THEIR FILTH.
I'VE HAD TO ENDURE A DECADE OF HOMESCHOOLING WITH INCREASINGLY PERVY TUTORS.
WHERE DID YOU MEET THE IRISHMAN, ANYWAY?
AT ONE OF MY MUM'S INTERMINABLE FUNDRAISERS. AT FIRST, I THOUGHT RODEN WAS JUST ANOTHER FILTHY PEDO, BUT THEN HE SAID HE KNEW ABOUT MY NIGHTMARES.
NIGHTMARES?
THE MOST HORRIBLE ONES IMAGINABLE, MORE REAL THAN LIFE ITSELF. YOU HAVE THEM, TOO, DON'T YOU?
ONLY EVERY NIGHT.
I HAVEN'T HAD A DECENT EVENING'S SLEEP SINCE MY FIRST TAMPON.
BUT RODEN EXPLAINED THAT HE HAS THIS ANCIENT BOOK THAT SAYS OUR NIGHT TERRORS WILL STOP ONCE AND FOR ALL AS SOON AS THIS BUFFY SLAG IS SNUFFED OUT.
HOW DO YOU KNOW HE'S TELLING THE TRUTH?
ONE WAY TO FIND OUT, YEAH?

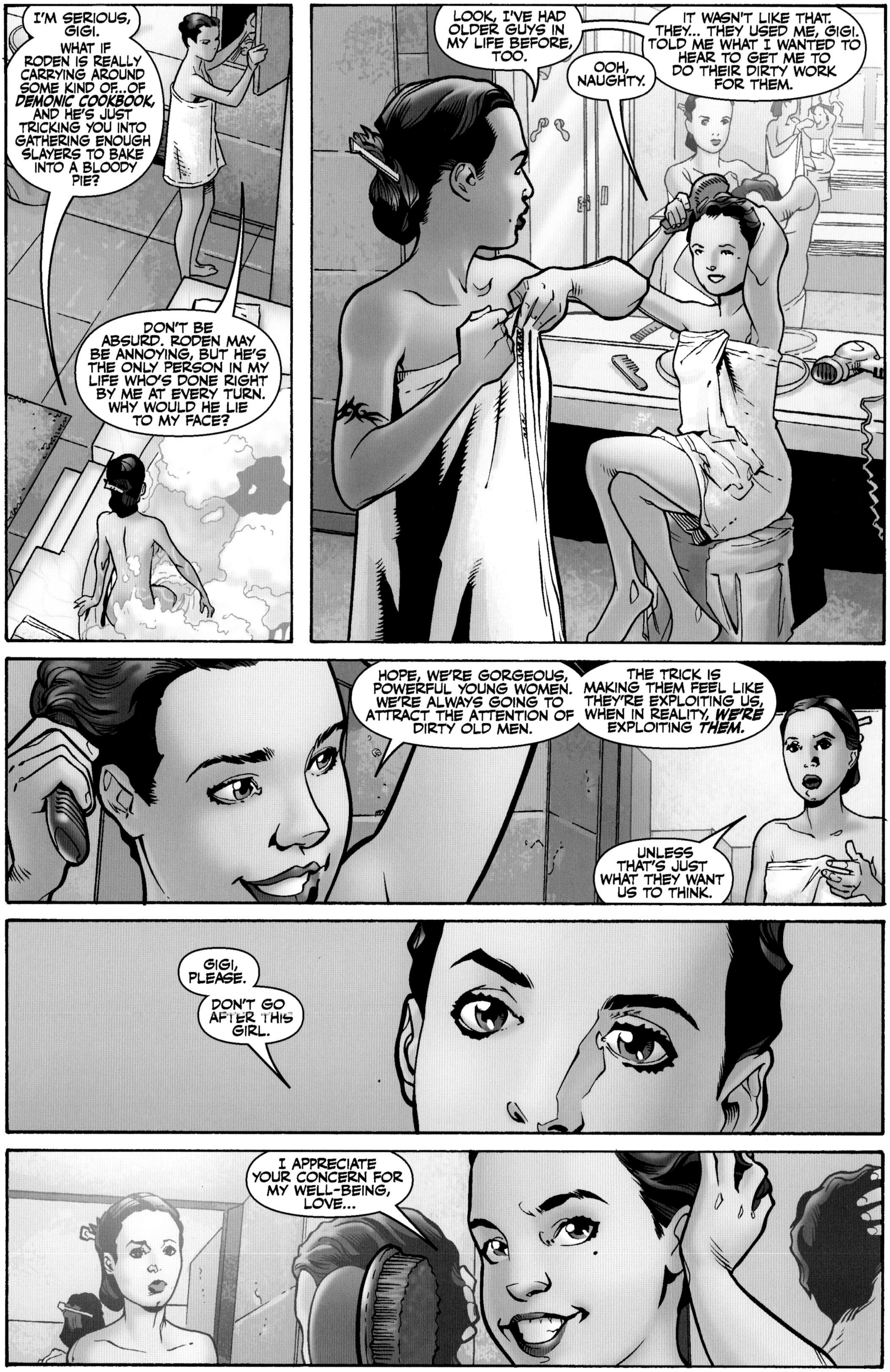
I'M SERIOUS, GIGI.
WHAT IF RODEN IS REALLY CARRYING AROUND SOME KIND OF...OF *DEMONIC COOKBOOK,* AND HE'S JUST TRICKING YOU INTO GATHERING ENOUGH SLAYERS TO BAKE INTO A BLOODY PIE?
DON'T BE ABSURD. RODEN MAY BE ANNOYING, BUT HE'S THE ONLY PERSON IN MY LIFE WHO'S DONE RIGHT BY ME AT EVERY TURN. WHY WOULD HE LIE TO MY FACE?
LOOK, I'VE HAD OLDER GUYS IN MY LIFE BEFORE, TOO.
OOH, NAUGHTY.
IT WASN'T LIKE THAT. THEY... THEY USED ME, GIGI. TOLD ME WHAT I WANTED TO HEAR TO GET ME TO DO THEIR DIRTY WORK FOR THEM.
HOPE, WE'RE GORGEOUS, POWERFUL YOUNG WOMEN. WE'RE ALWAYS GOING TO ATTRACT THE ATTENTION OF DIRTY OLD MEN.
THE TRICK IS MAKING THEM FEEL LIKE THEY'RE EXPLOITING US, WHEN IN REALITY, *WE'RE* EXPLOITING *THEM.*
UNLESS THAT'S JUST WHAT THEY WANT US TO THINK.
GIGI, PLEASE.
DON'T GO AFTER THIS GIRL.
I APPRECIATE YOUR CONCERN FOR MY WELL-BEING, LOVE...

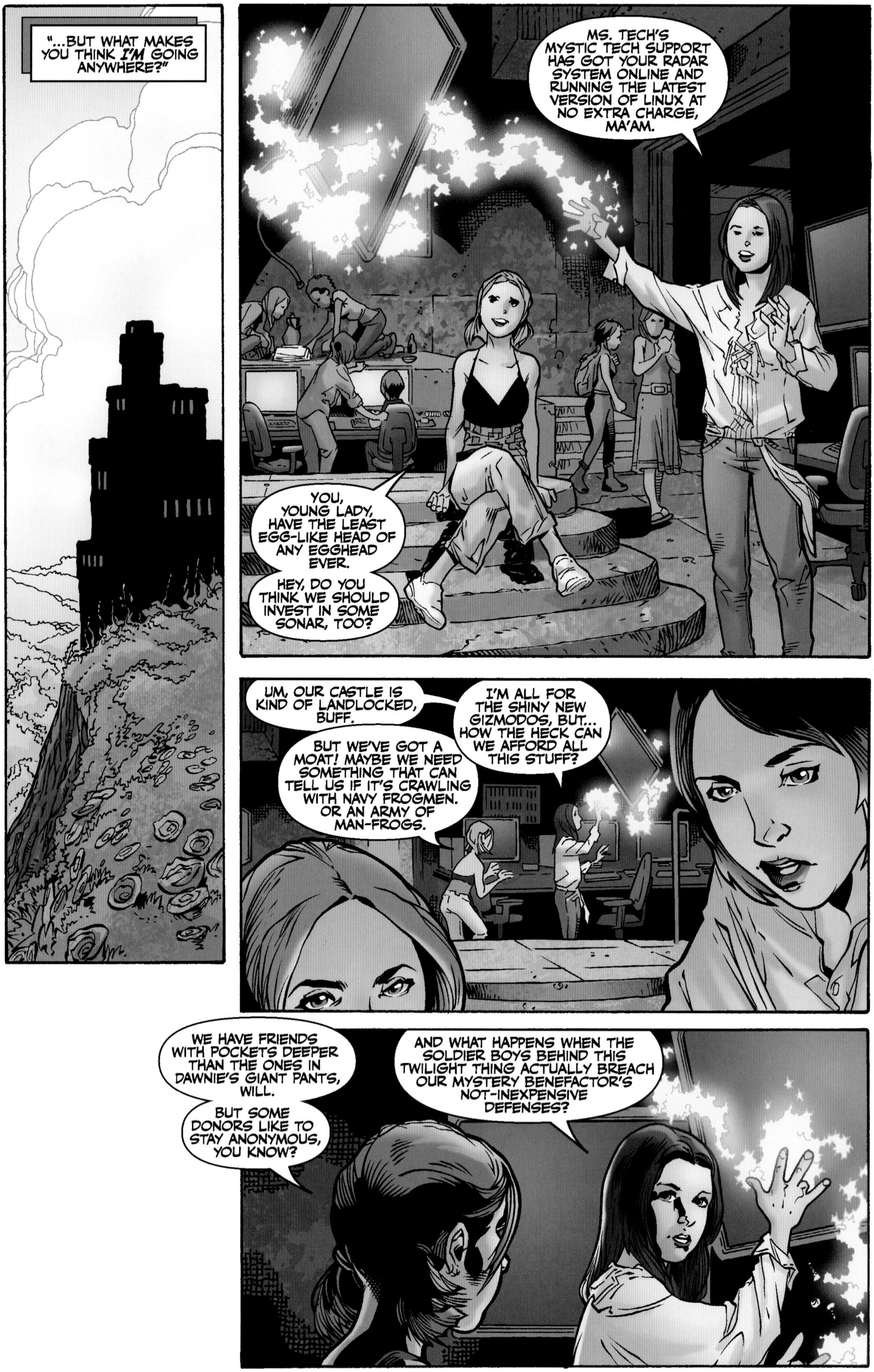
"...BUT WHAT MAKES YOU THINK *I'M* GOING ANYWHERE?"
MS. TECH'S MYSTIC TECH SUPPORT HAS GOT YOUR RADAR SYSTEM ONLINE AND RUNNING THE LATEST VERSION OF LINUX AT NO EXTRA CHARGE, MA'AM.
YOU, YOUNG LADY, HAVE THE LEAST EGG-LIKE HEAD OF ANY EGGHEAD EVER.
HEY, DO YOU THINK WE SHOULD INVEST IN SOME SONAR, TOO?
UM, OUR CASTLE IS KIND OF LANDLOCKED, BUFF.
BUT WE'VE GOT A MOAT! MAYBE WE NEED SOMETHING THAT CAN TELL US IF IT'S CRAWLING WITH NAVY FROGMEN. OR AN ARMY OF MAN-FROGS.
I'M ALL FOR THE SHINY NEW GIZMODOS, BUT... HOW THE HECK CAN WE AFFORD ALL THIS STUFF?
WE HAVE FRIENDS WITH POCKETS DEEPER THAN THE ONES IN DAWNIE'S GIANT PANTS, WILL.
BUT SOME DONORS LIKE TO STAY ANONYMOUS, YOU KNOW?
AND WHAT HAPPENS WHEN THE SOLDIER BOYS BEHIND THIS TWILIGHT THING ACTUALLY BREACH OUR MYSTERY BENEFACTOR'S NOT-INEXPENSIVE DEFENSES?

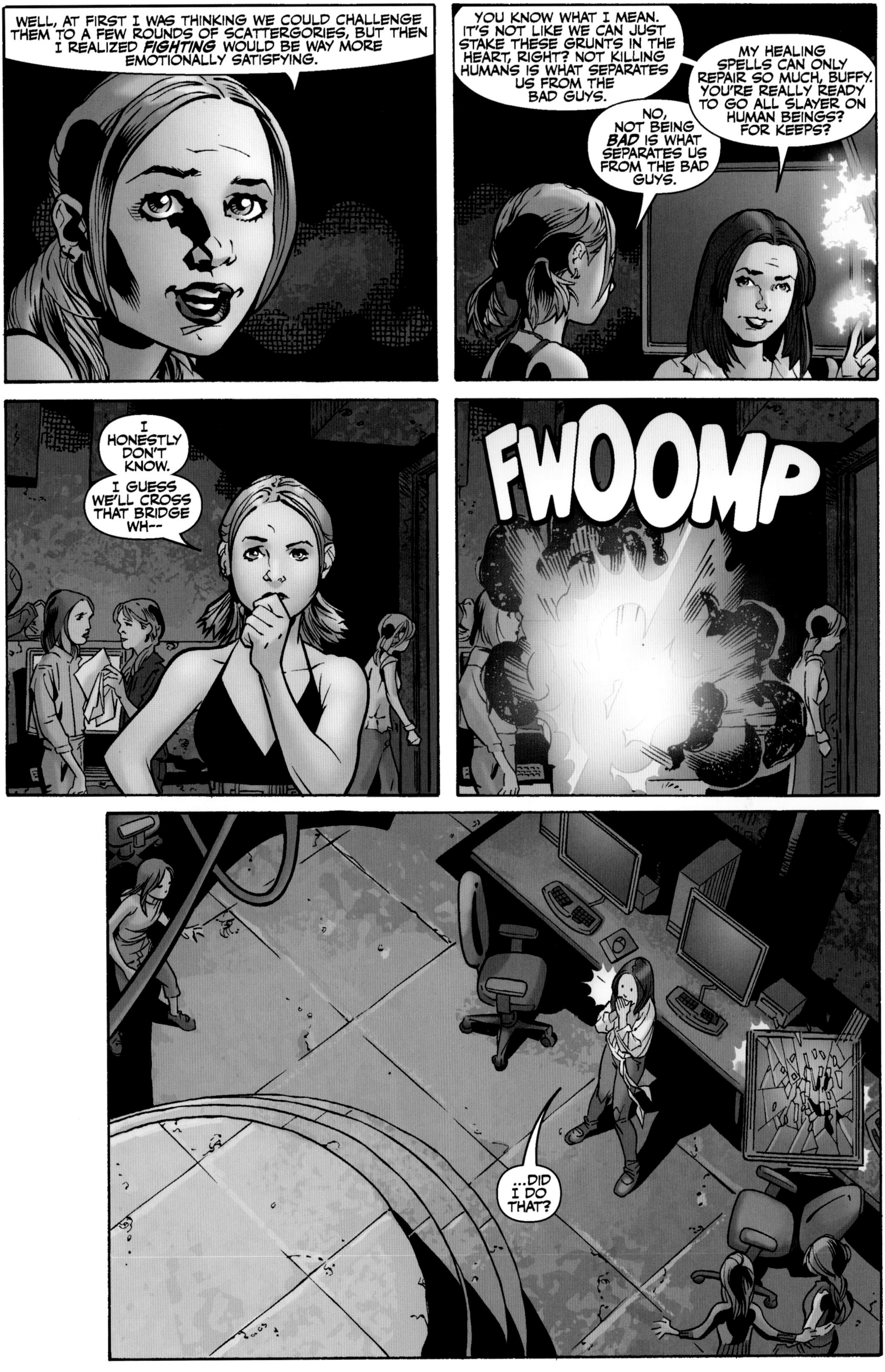
WELL, AT FIRST I WAS THINKING WE COULD CHALLENGE THEM TO A FEW ROUNDS OF SCATTERGORIES, BUT THEN I REALIZED *FIGHTING* WOULD BE WAY MORE EMOTIONALLY SATISFYING.
YOU KNOW WHAT I MEAN. IT'S NOT LIKE WE CAN JUST STAKE THESE GRUNTS IN THE HEART, RIGHT? NOT KILLING HUMANS IS WHAT SEPARATES US FROM THE BAD GUYS.
NO, NOT BEING *BAD* IS WHAT SEPARATES US FROM THE BAD GUYS.
MY HEALING SPELLS CAN ONLY REPAIR SO MUCH, BUFFY. YOU'RE REALLY READY TO GO ALL SLAYER ON HUMAN BEINGS? FOR KEEPS?
I HONESTLY DON'T KNOW.
I GUESS WE'LL CROSS THAT BRIDGE WH--
FWOOMP
...DID I DO THAT?

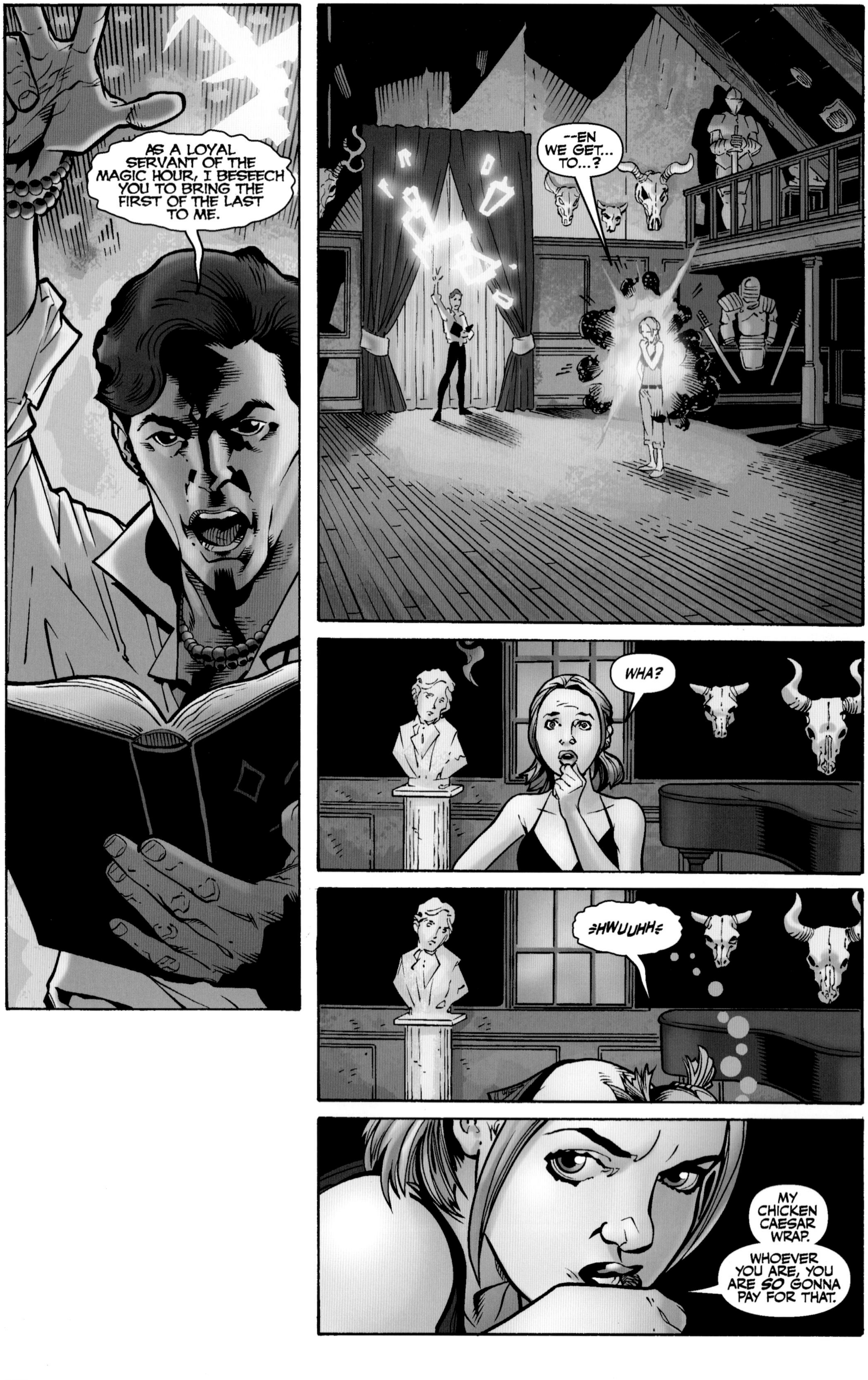
AS A LOYAL SERVANT OF THE MAGIC HOUR, I BESEECH YOU TO BRING THE FIRST OF THE LAST TO ME.
--EN WE GET... TO...?
WHA?
≈HWUUHH≈
MY CHICKEN CAESAR WRAP.
WHOEVER YOU ARE, YOU ARE SO GONNA PAY FOR THAT.

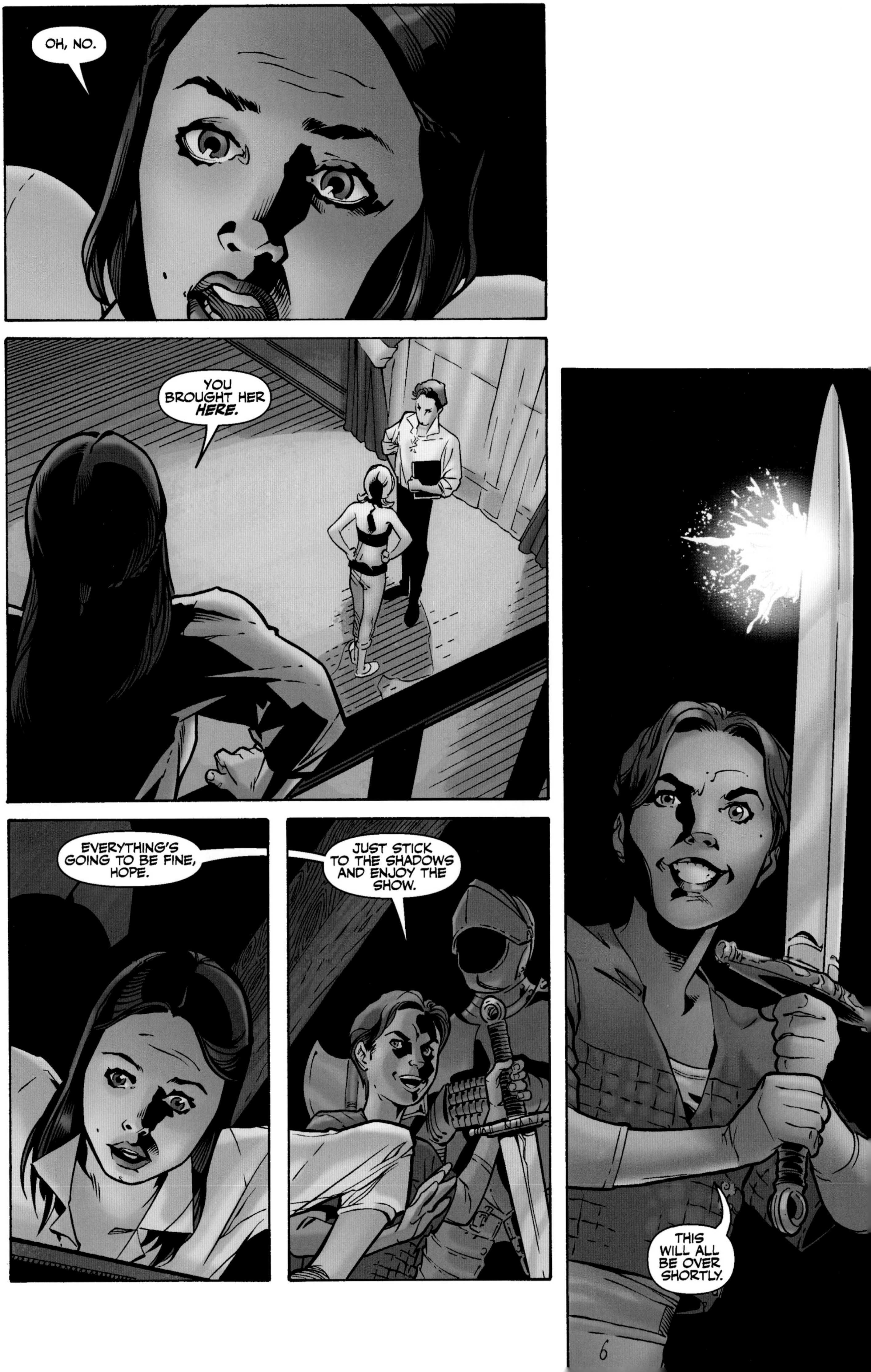
OH, NO.
YOU BROUGHT HER *HERE.*
EVERYTHING'S GOING TO BE FINE, HOPE.
JUST STICK TO THE SHADOWS AND ENJOY THE SHOW.
THIS WILL ALL BE OVER SHORTLY.

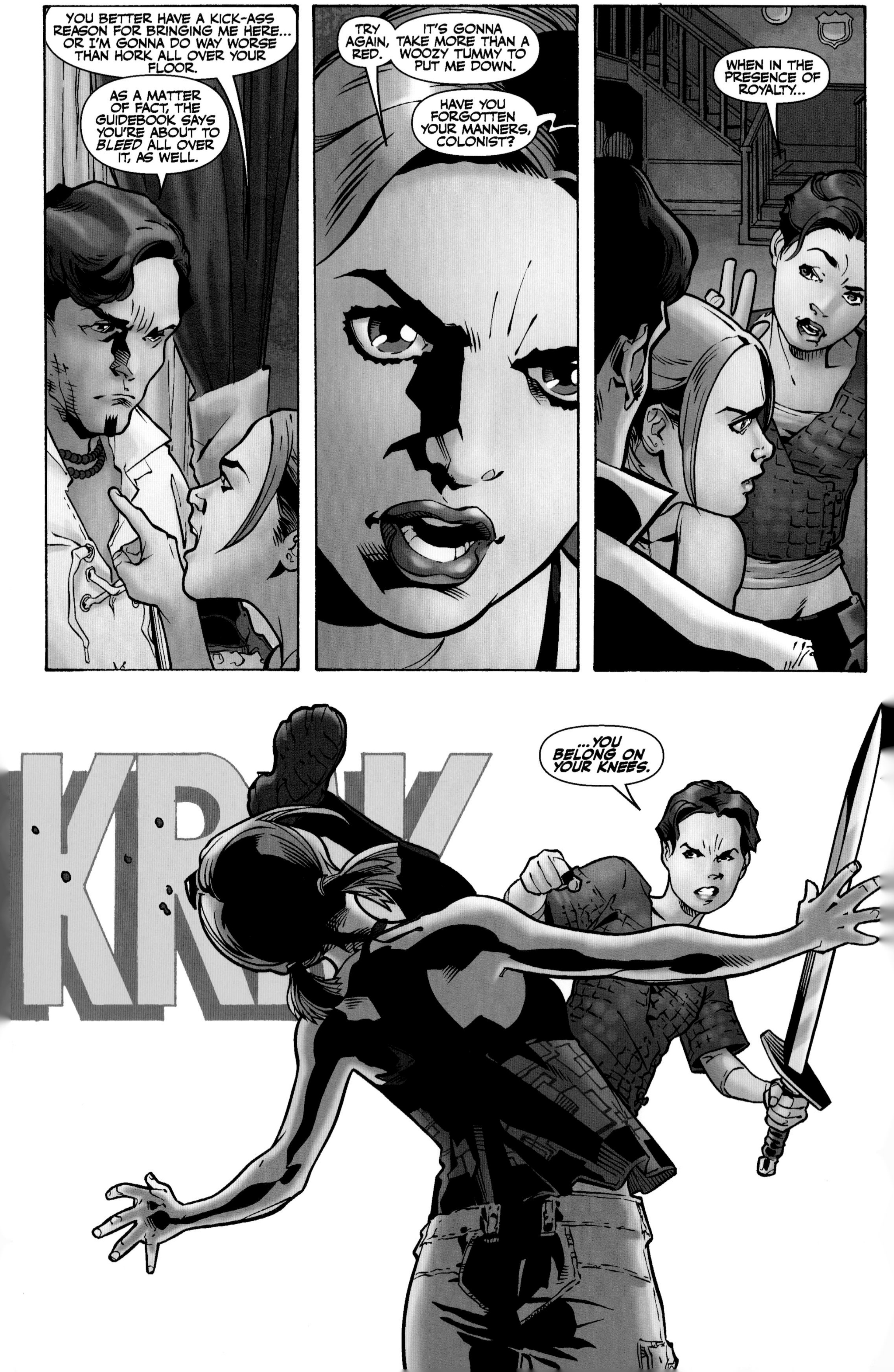
YOU BETTER HAVE A KICK-ASS REASON FOR BRINGING ME HERE... OR I'M GONNA DO WAY WORSE THAN HORK ALL OVER YOUR FLOOR.
AS A MATTER OF FACT, THE GUIDEBOOK SAYS YOU'RE ABOUT TO *BLEED* ALL OVER IT, AS WELL.
TRY AGAIN, RED.
IT'S GONNA TAKE MORE THAN A WOOZY TUMMY TO PUT ME DOWN.
HAVE YOU FORGOTTEN YOUR MANNERS, COLONIST?
WHEN IN THE PRESENCE OF ROYALTY...
...YOU BELONG ON YOUR KNEES.

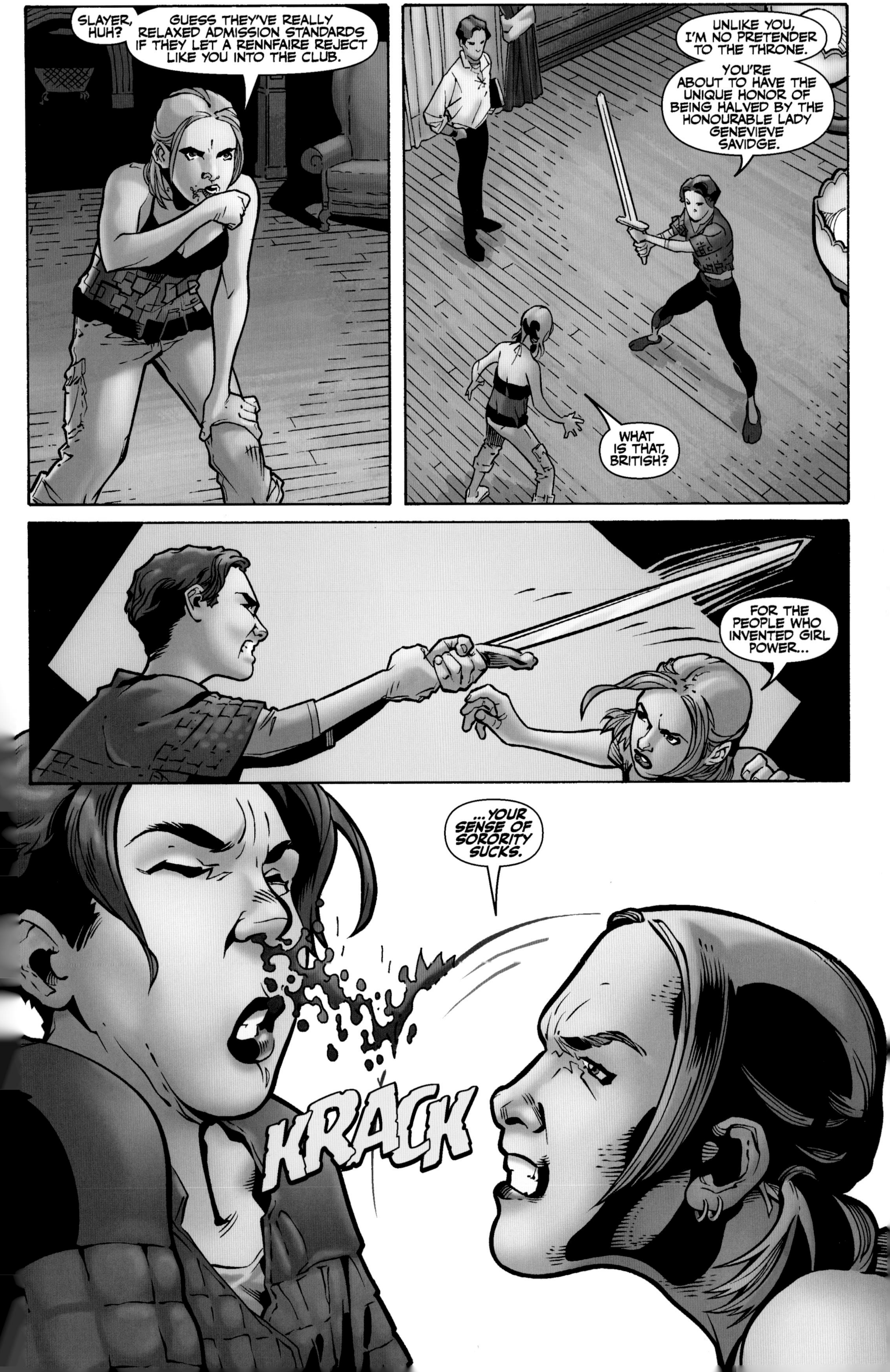
SLAYER, HUH?
GUESS THEY'VE REALLY RELAXED ADMISSION STANDARDS IF THEY LET A RENNFAIRE REJECT LIKE YOU INTO THE CLUB.
UNLIKE YOU, I'M NO PRETENDER TO THE THRONE.
YOU'RE ABOUT TO HAVE THE UNIQUE HONOR OF BEING HALVED BY THE HONOURABLE LADY GENEVIEVE SAVIDGE.
WHAT IS THAT, BRITISH?
FOR THE PEOPLE WHO INVENTED GIRL POWER...
...YOUR SENSE OF SORORITY SUCKS.
KRACK

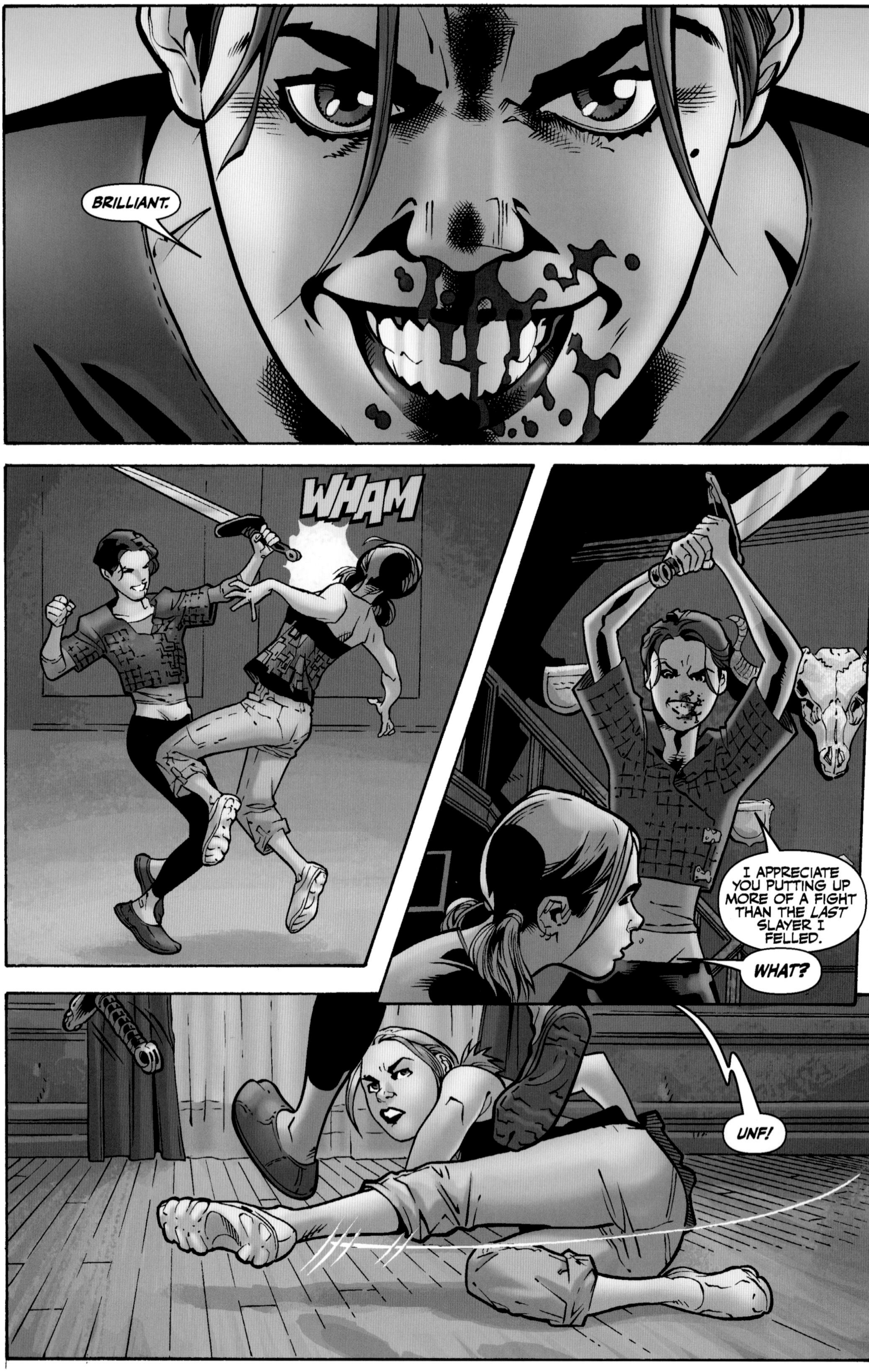
BRILLIANT.
WHAM
I APPRECIATE YOU PUTTING UP MORE OF A FIGHT THAN THE *LAST* SLAYER I FELLED.
WHAT?
UNF!

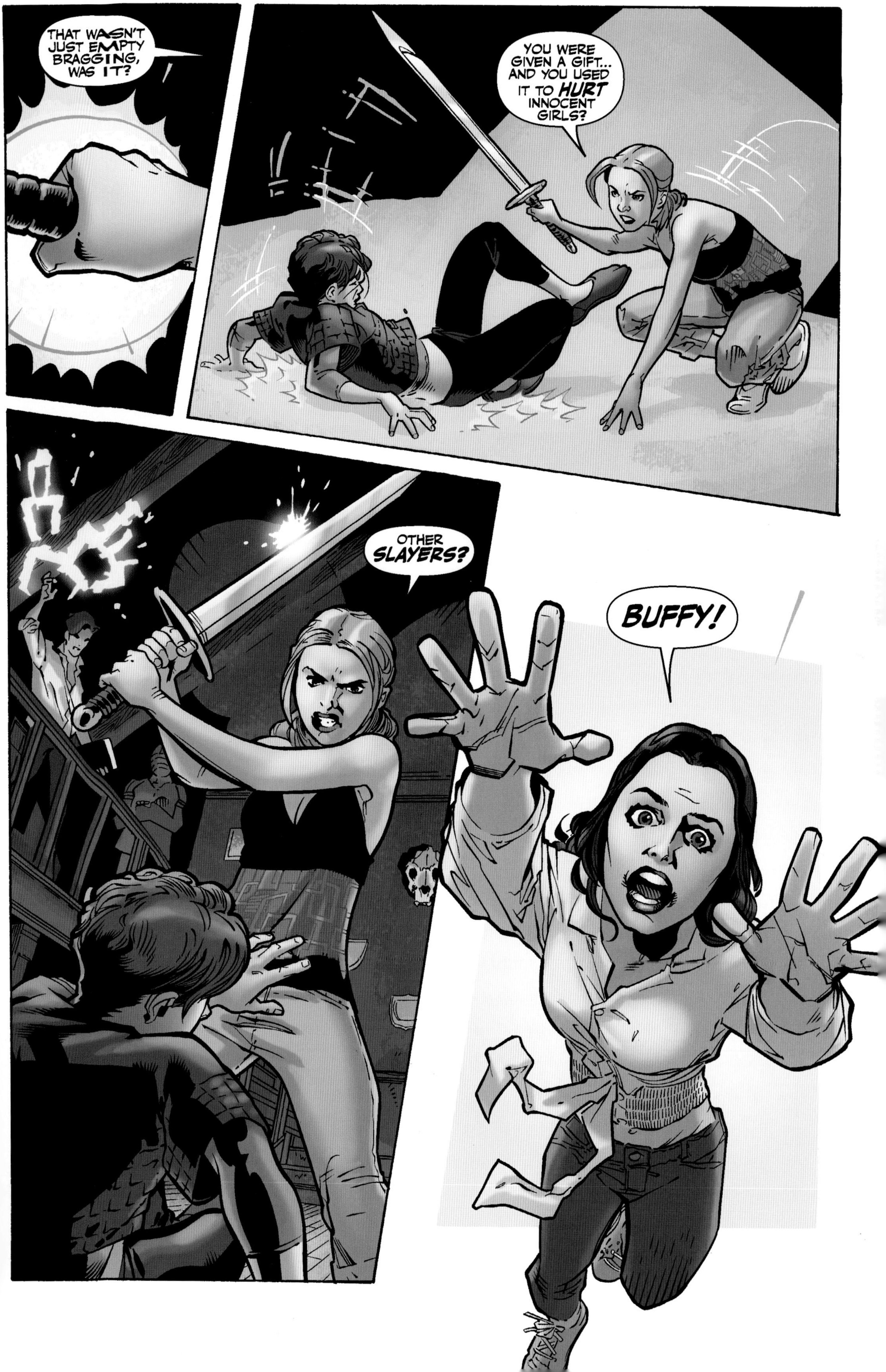
THAT WASN'T JUST EMPTY BRAGGING, WAS IT?
YOU WERE GIVEN A GIFT... AND YOU USED IT TO HURT INNOCENT GIRLS?
OTHER SLAYERS?
BUFFY!

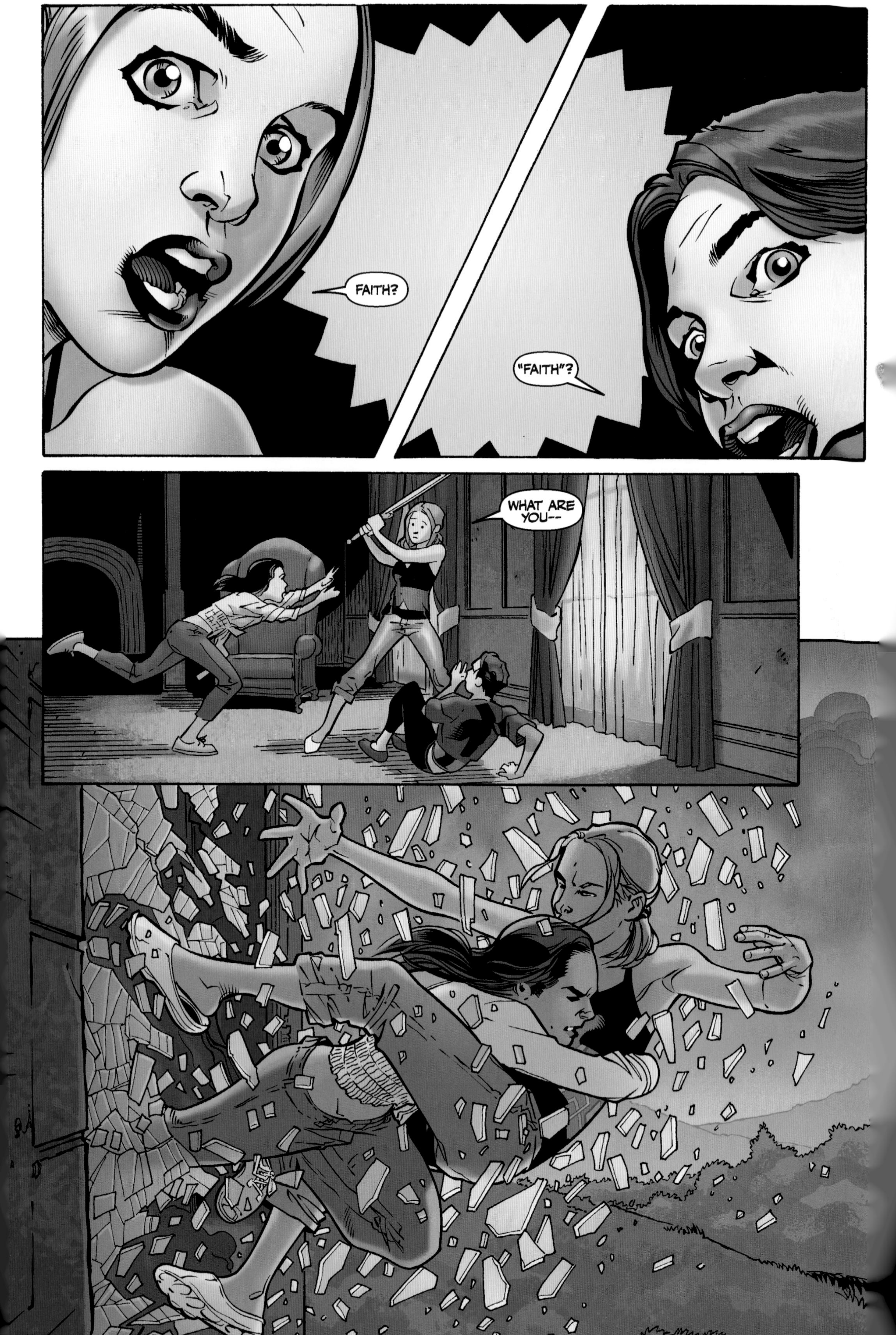
FAITH?
"FAITH"?
WHAT ARE YOU--

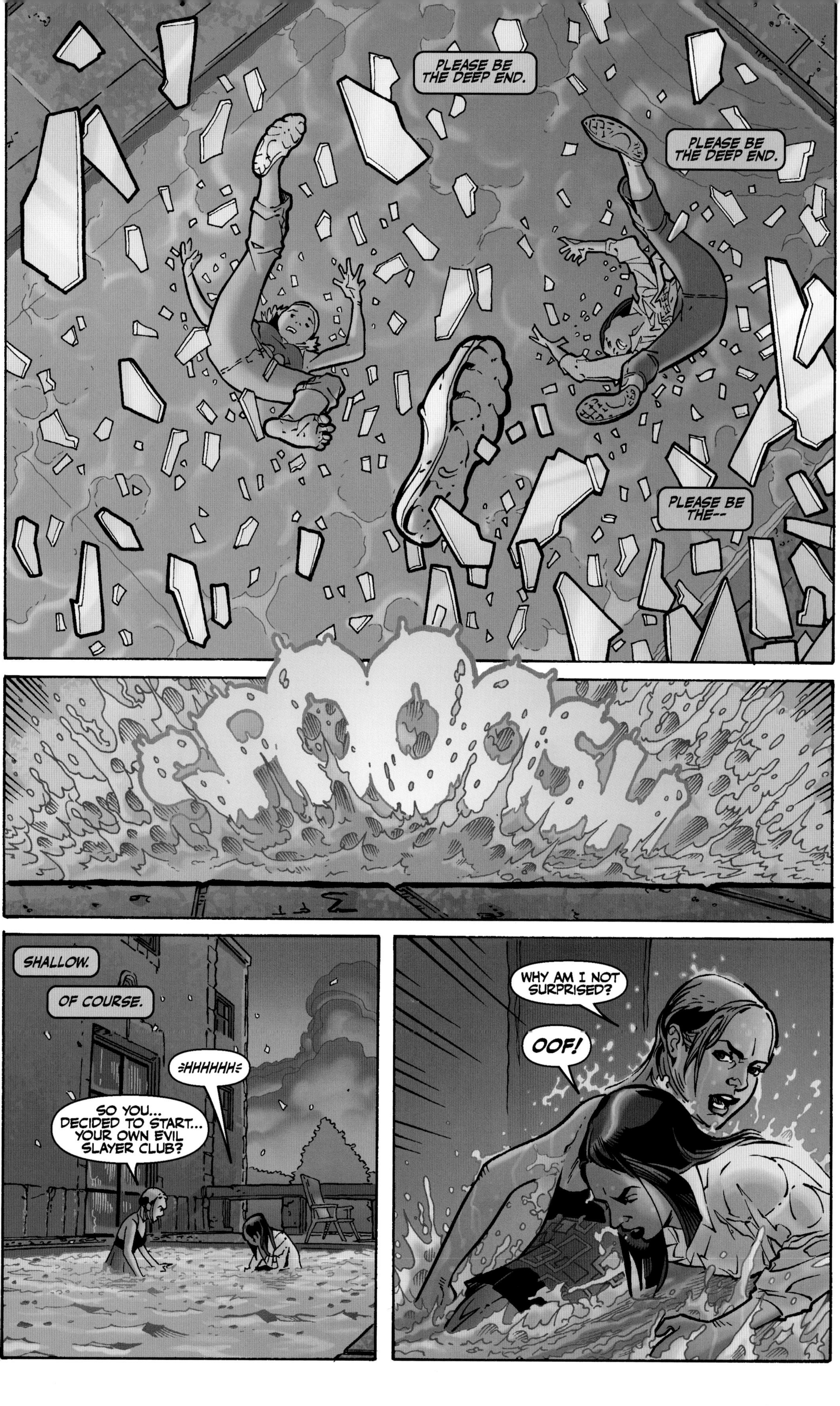
PLEASE BE THE DEEP END.
PLEASE BE THE DEEP END.
PLEASE BE THE--
SHALLOW.
OF COURSE.
HHHHHH
SO YOU... DECIDED TO START... YOUR OWN EVIL SLAYER CLUB?
WHY AM I NOT SURPRISED?
OOF!

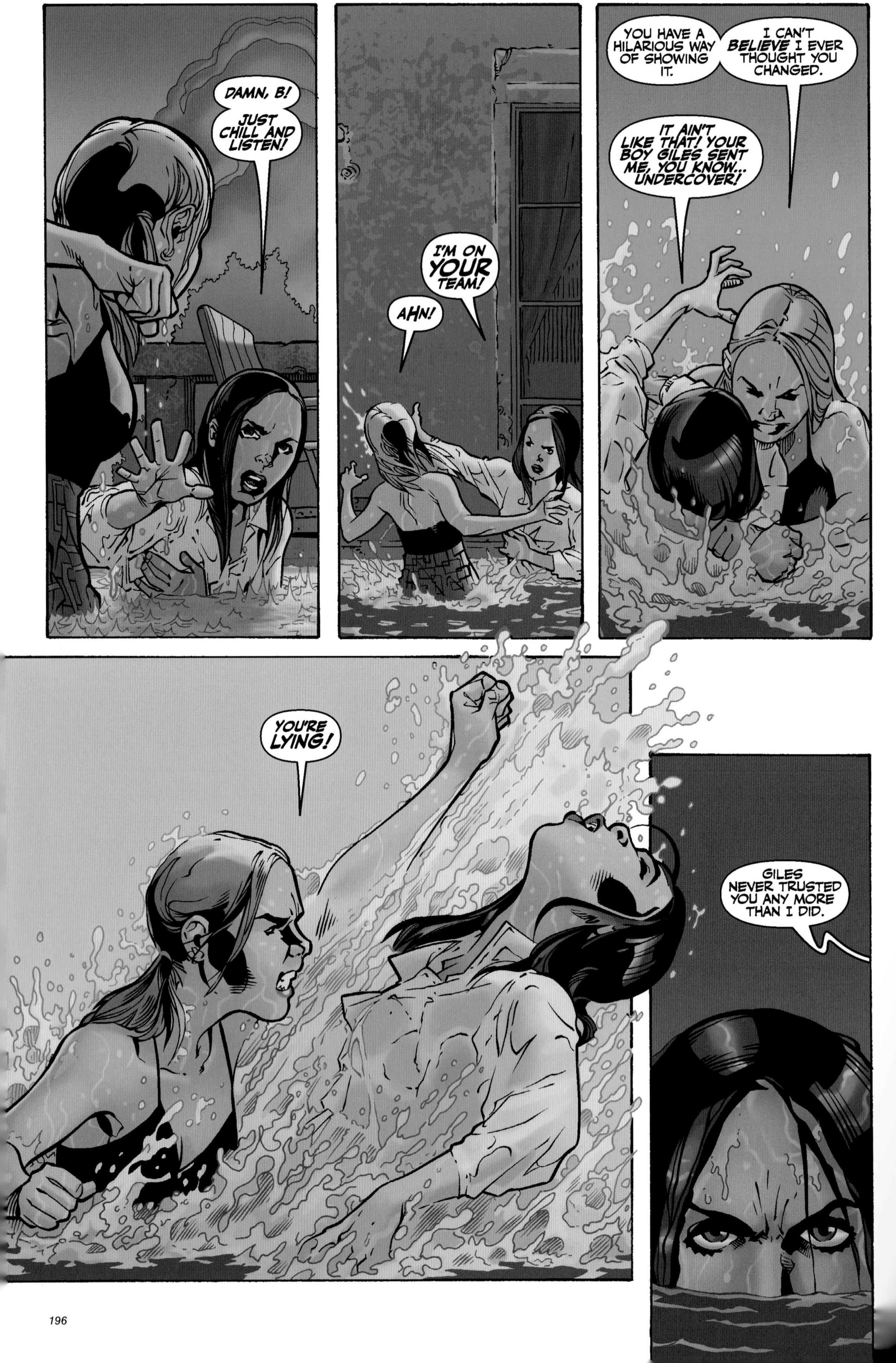
DAMN, B!
JUST CHILL AND LISTEN!
AHN!
I'M ON YOUR TEAM!
I CAN'T BELIEVE I EVER THOUGHT YOU CHANGED.
YOU HAVE A HILARIOUS WAY OF SHOWING IT.
IT AIN'T LIKE THAT! YOUR BOY GILES SENT ME, YOU KNOW... UNDERCOVER!
YOU'RE LYING!
GILES NEVER TRUSTED YOU ANY MORE THAN I DID.

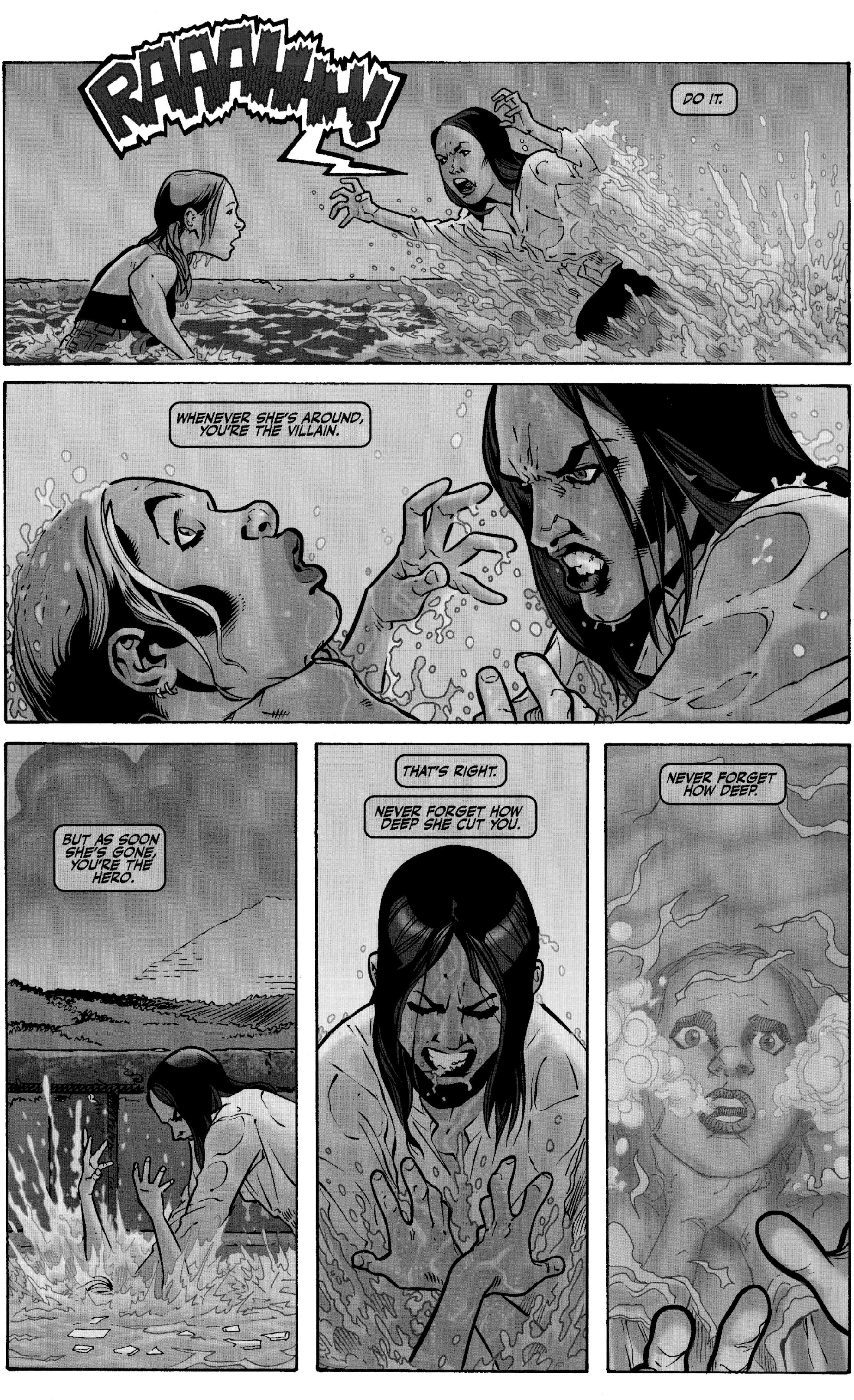
RAAAHHH!
DO IT.
WHENEVER SHE'S AROUND, YOU'RE THE VILLAIN.
BUT AS SOON SHE'S GONE, YOU'RE THE HERO.
THAT'S RIGHT.
NEVER FORGET HOW DEEP SHE CUT YOU.
NEVER FORGET HOW DEEP.

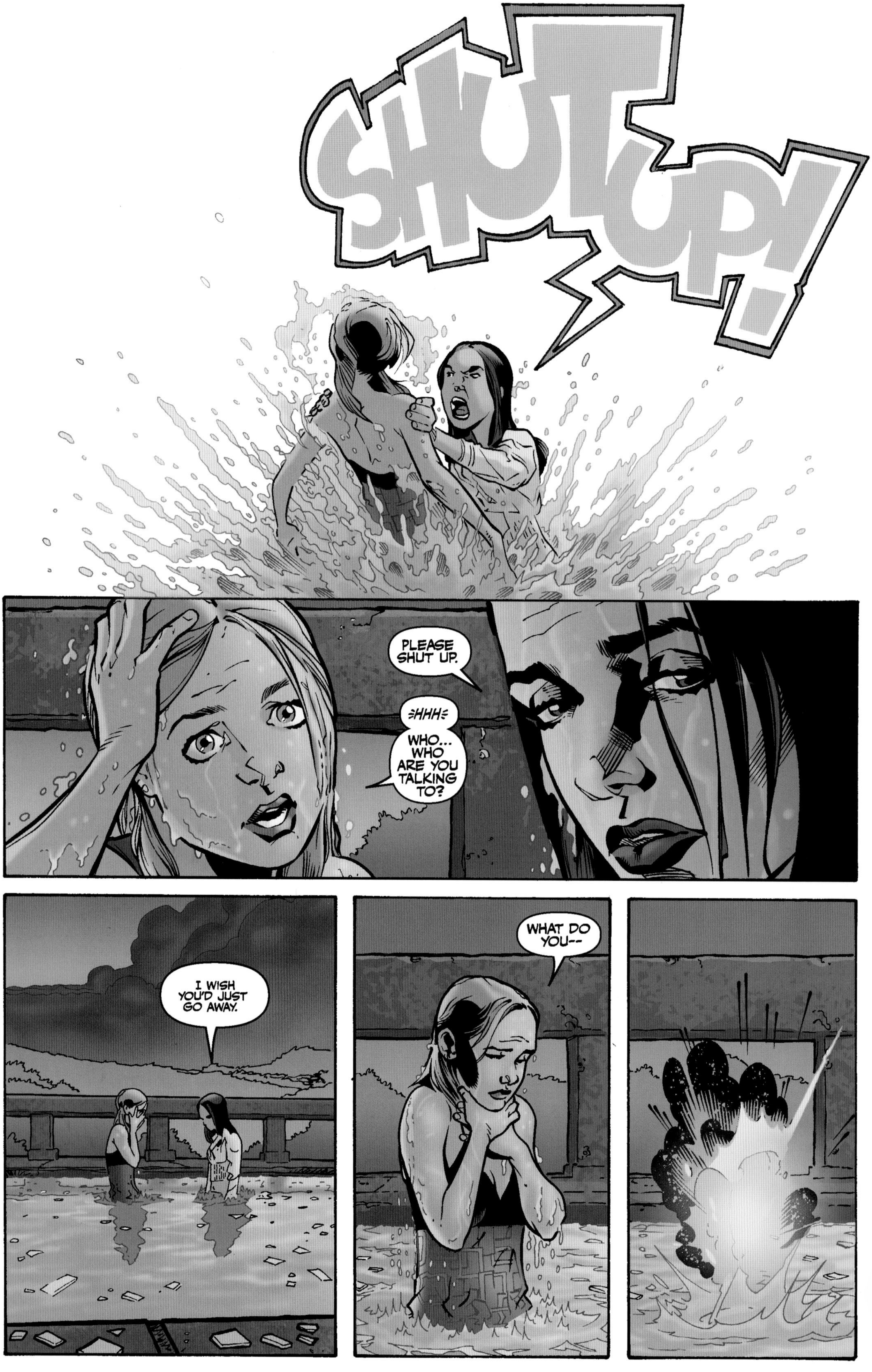
SHUT UP!
PLEASE SHUT UP.
HHH
WHO... WHO ARE YOU TALKING TO?
I WISH YOU'D JUST GO AWAY.
WHAT DO YOU--

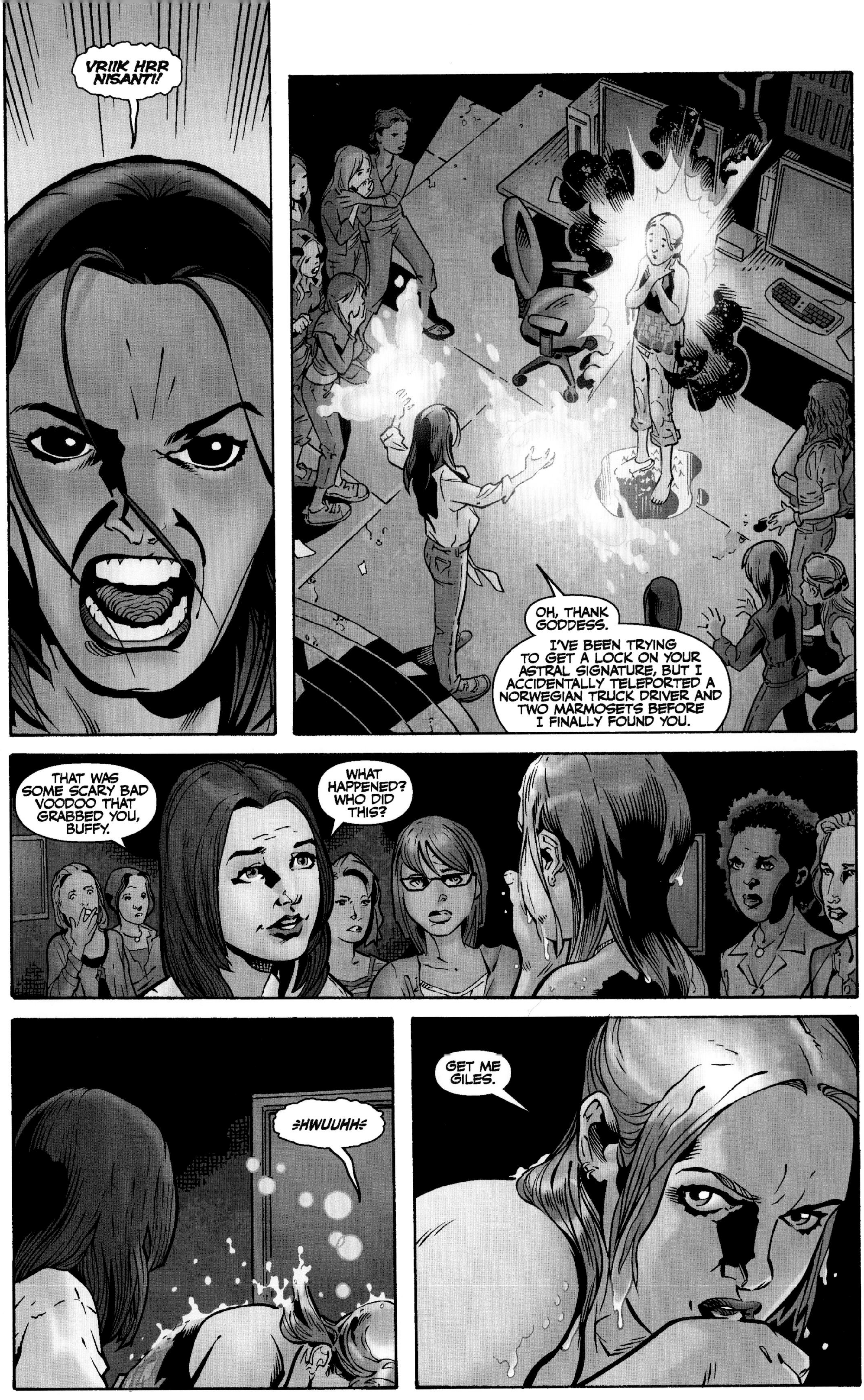
VRIIK HRR NISANTI!
OH, THANK GODDESS.
I'VE BEEN TRYING TO GET A LOCK ON YOUR ASTRAL SIGNATURE, BUT I ACCIDENTALLY TELEPORTED A NORWEGIAN TRUCK DRIVER AND TWO MARMOSETS BEFORE I FINALLY FOUND YOU.
THAT WAS SOME SCARY BAD VOODOO THAT GRABBED YOU, BUFFY.
WHAT HAPPENED? WHO DID THIS?
⚡HWUUHH⚡
GET ME GILES.

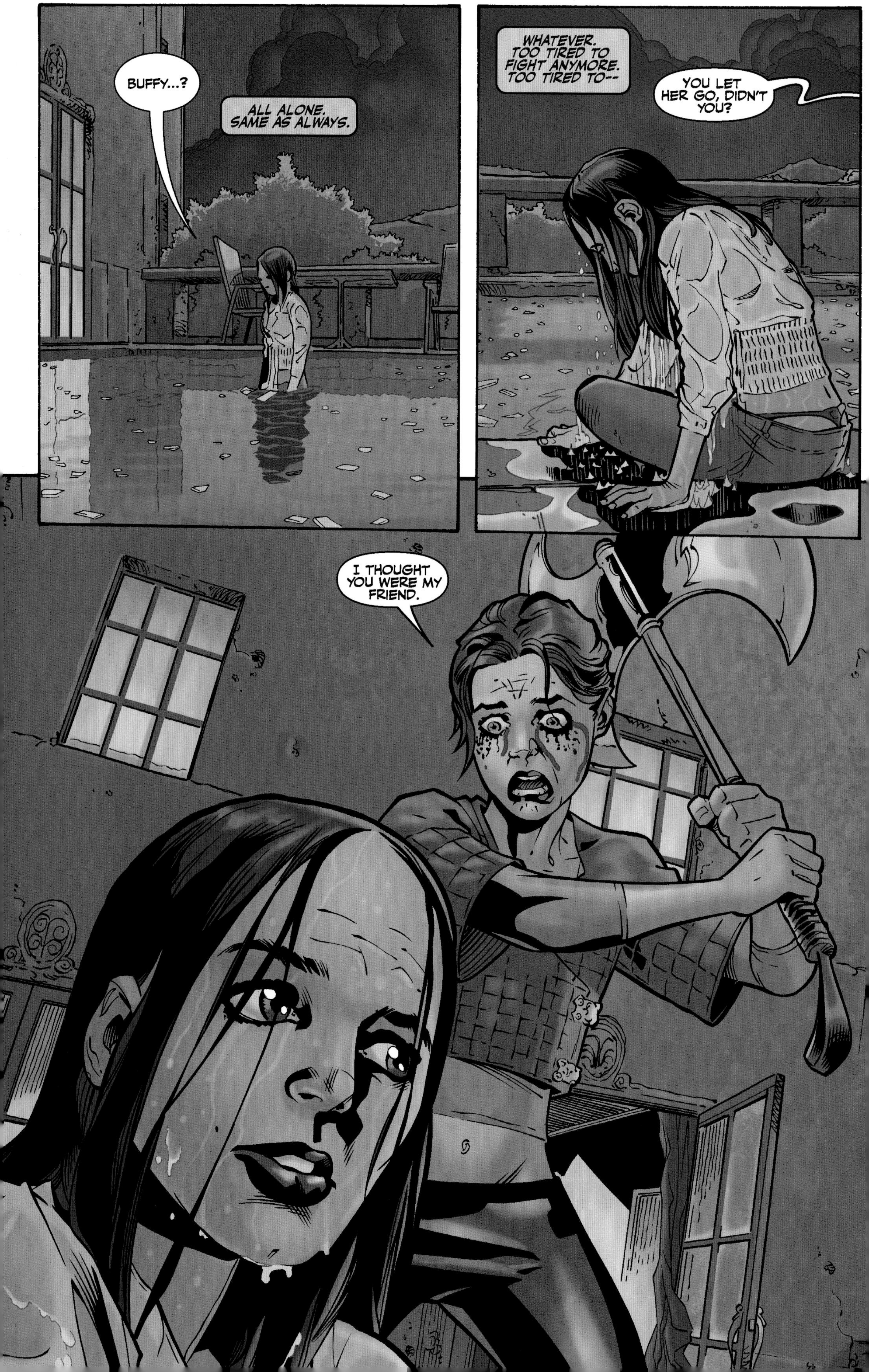
BUFFY...?
ALL ALONE. SAME AS ALWAYS.
WHATEVER. TOO TIRED TO FIGHT ANYMORE. TOO TIRED TO--
YOU LET HER GO, DIDN'T YOU?
I THOUGHT YOU WERE MY FRIEND.

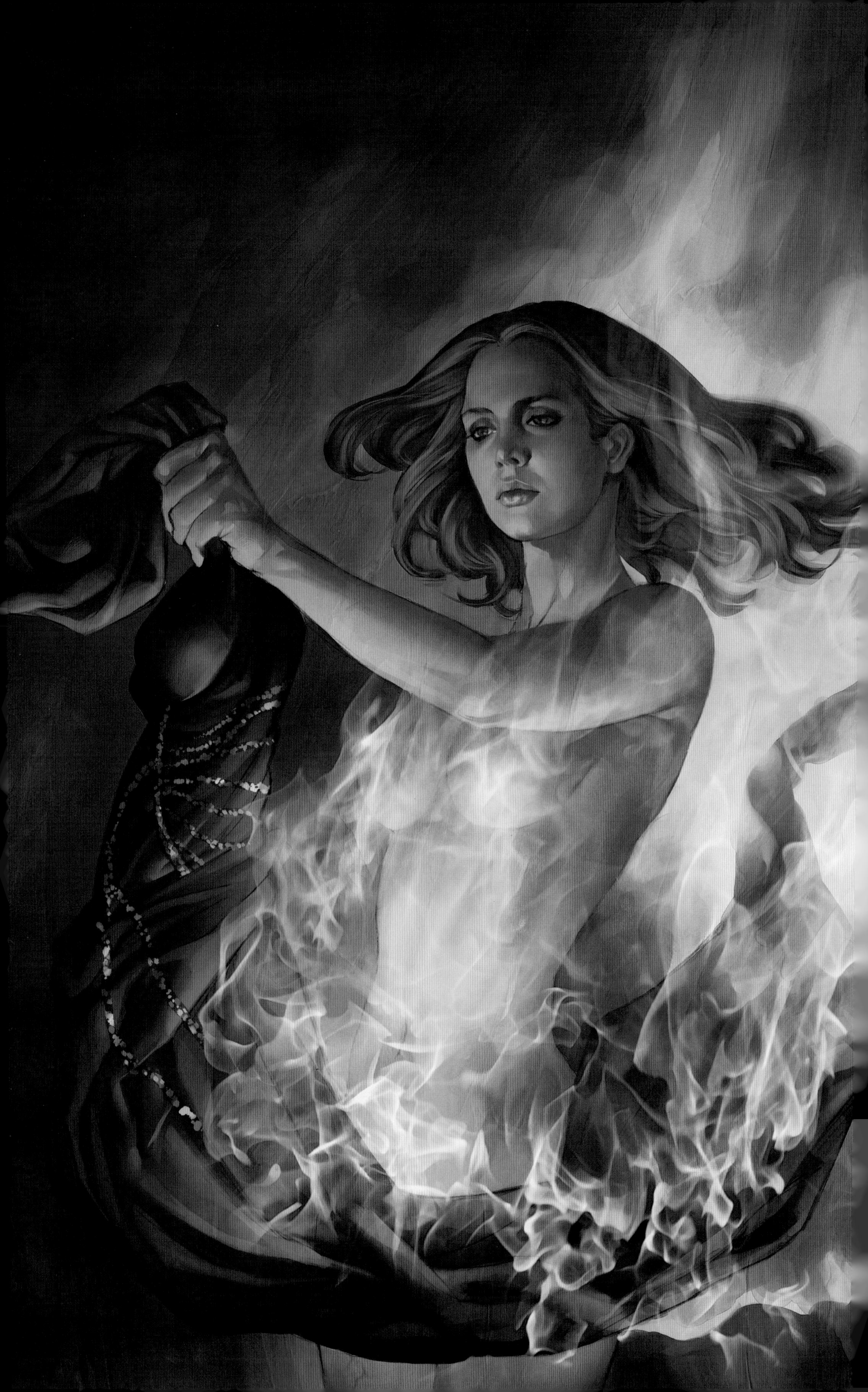

NO FUTURE FOR YOU

PART FOUR

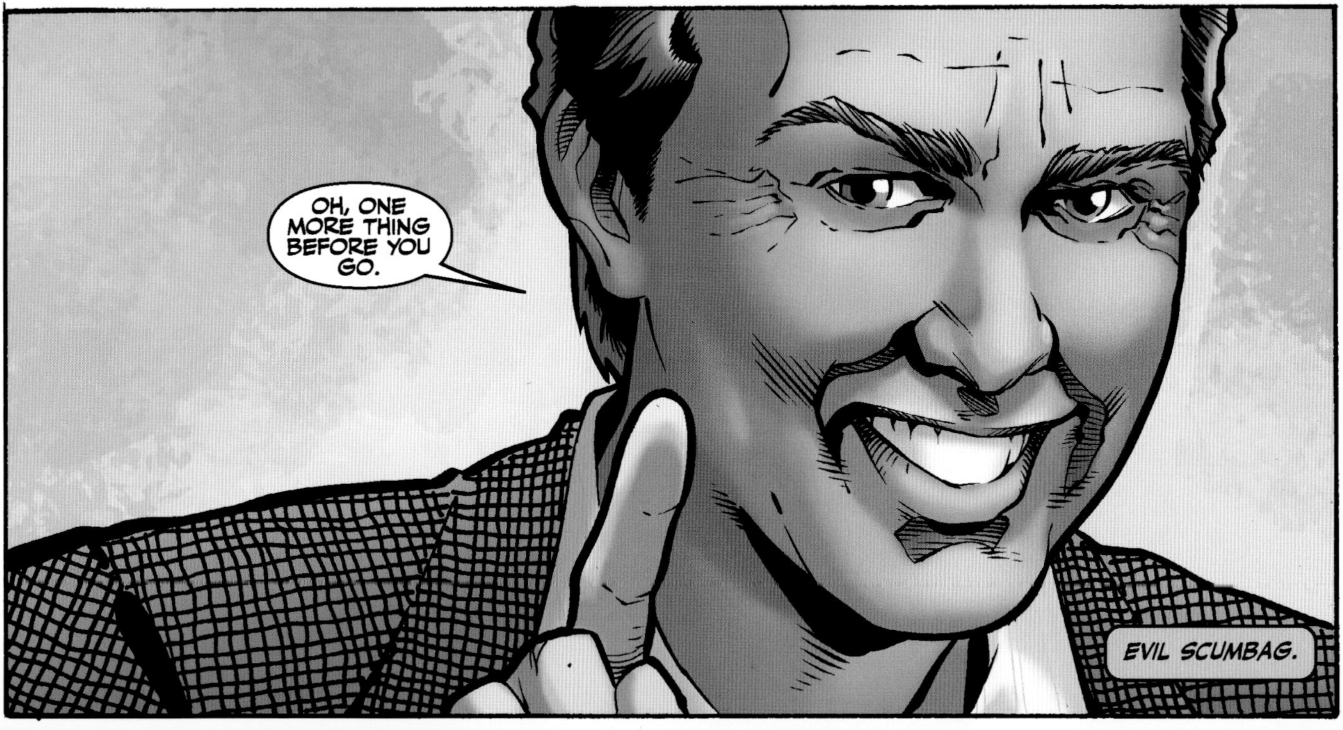
OH, ONE MORE THING BEFORE YOU GO.
EVIL SCUMBAG.

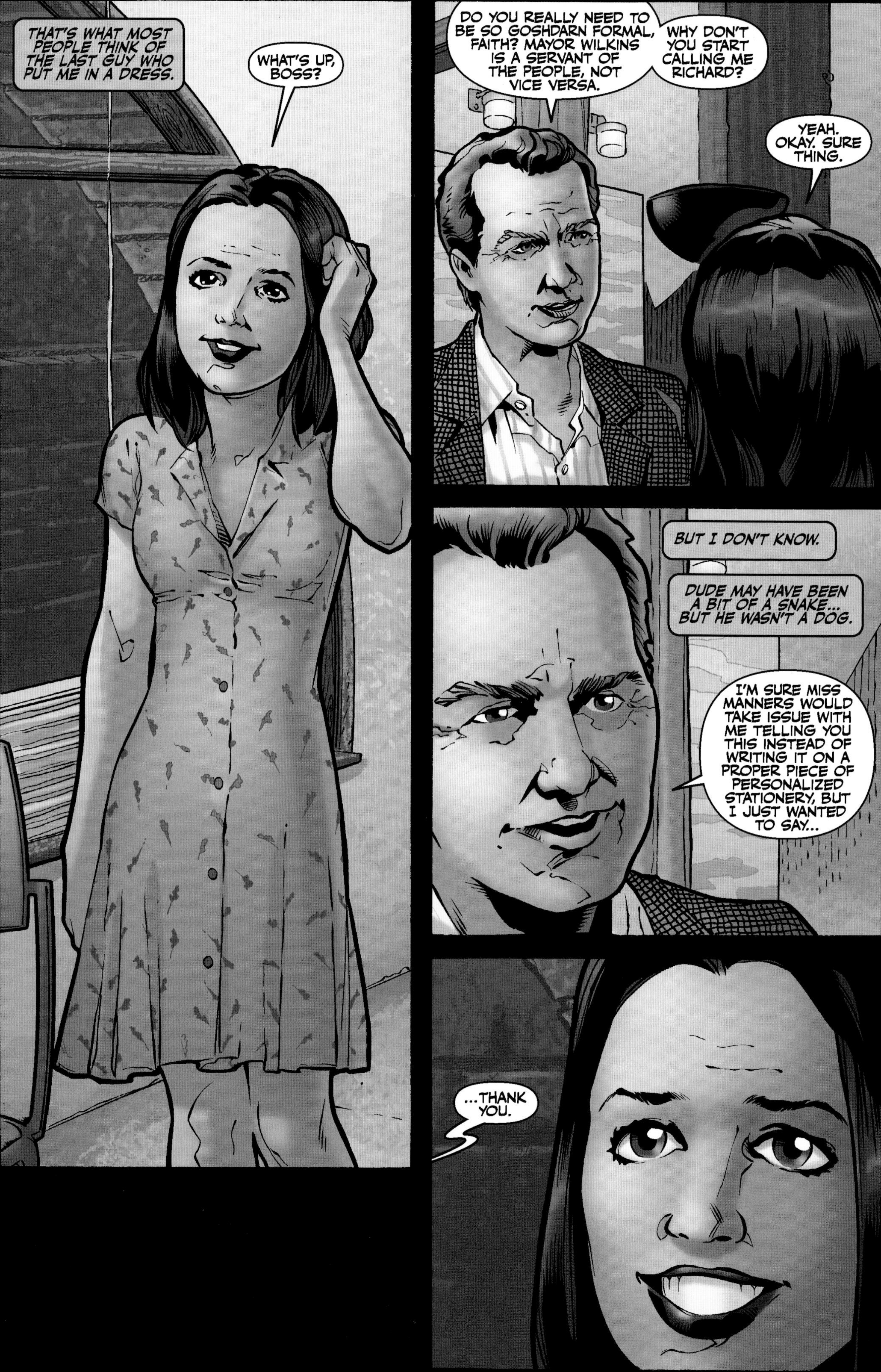
THAT'S WHAT MOST PEOPLE THINK OF THE LAST GUY WHO PUT ME IN A DRESS.
WHAT'S UP, BOSS?
DO YOU REALLY NEED TO BE SO GOSHDARN FORMAL, FAITH? MAYOR WILKINS IS A SERVANT OF THE PEOPLE, NOT VICE VERSA.
WHY DON'T YOU START CALLING ME RICHARD?
YEAH. OKAY. SURE THING.
BUT I DON'T KNOW.
DUDE MAY HAVE BEEN A BIT OF A SNAKE... BUT HE WASN'T A DOG.
I'M SURE MISS MANNERS WOULD TAKE ISSUE WITH ME TELLING YOU THIS INSTEAD OF WRITING IT ON A PROPER PIECE OF PERSONALIZED STATIONERY, BUT I JUST WANTED TO SAY...
...THANK YOU.

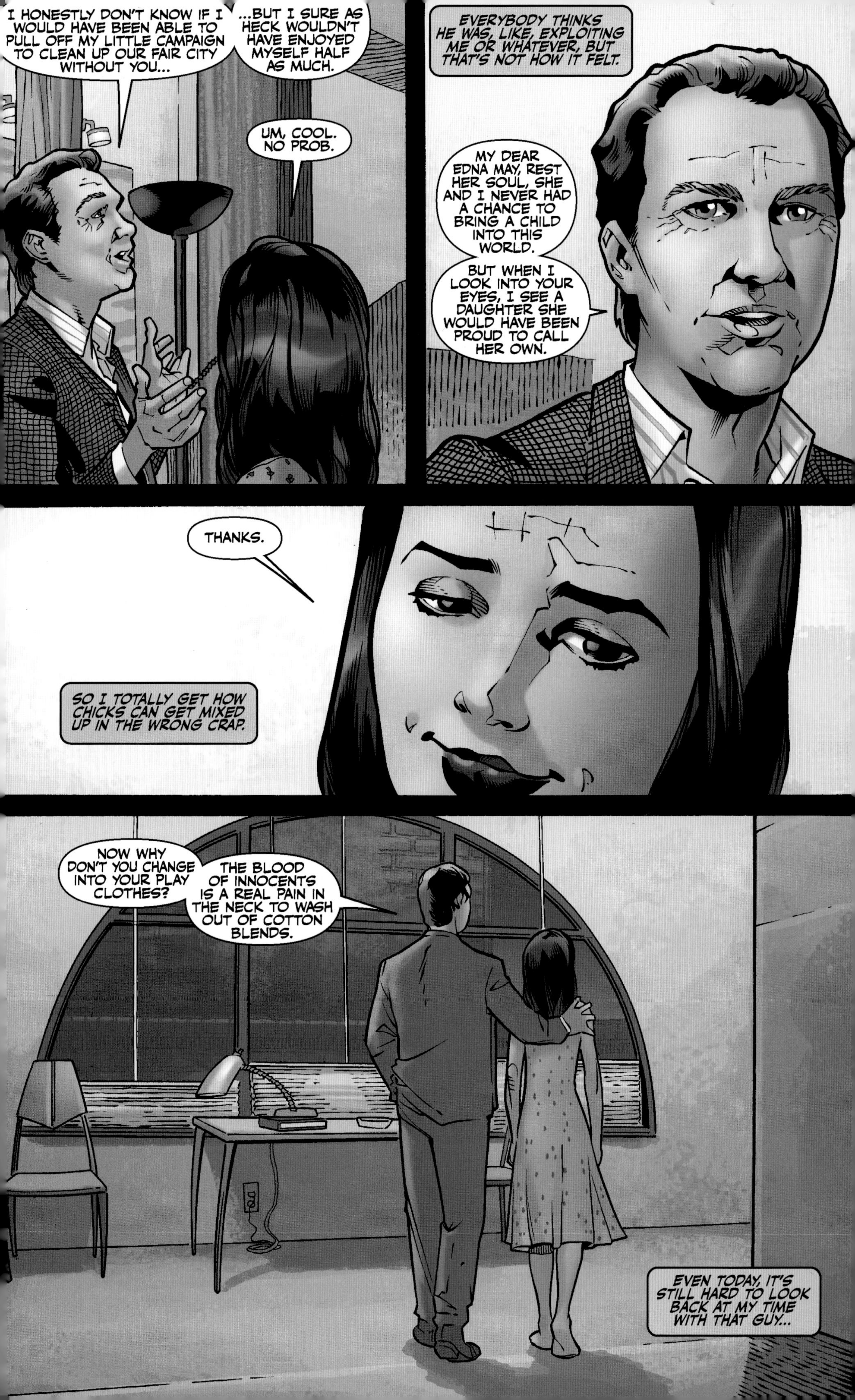
I HONESTLY DON'T KNOW IF I WOULD HAVE BEEN ABLE TO PULL OFF MY LITTLE CAMPAIGN TO CLEAN UP OUR FAIR CITY WITHOUT YOU...
...BUT I SURE AS HECK WOULDN'T HAVE ENJOYED MYSELF HALF AS MUCH.
UM, COOL. NO PROB.
EVERYBODY THINKS HE WAS, LIKE, EXPLOITING ME OR WHATEVER, BUT THAT'S NOT HOW IT FELT.
MY DEAR EDNA MAY, REST HER SOUL, SHE AND I NEVER HAD A CHANCE TO BRING A CHILD INTO THIS WORLD.
BUT WHEN I LOOK INTO YOUR EYES, I SEE A DAUGHTER SHE WOULD HAVE BEEN PROUD TO CALL HER OWN.
THANKS.
SO I TOTALLY GET HOW CHICKS CAN GET MIXED UP IN THE WRONG CRAP.
NOW WHY DON'T YOU CHANGE INTO YOUR PLAY CLOTHES?
THE BLOOD OF INNOCENTS IS A REAL PAIN IN THE NECK TO WASH OUT OF COTTON BLENDS.
EVEN TODAY, IT'S STILL HARD TO LOOK BACK AT MY TIME WITH THAT GUY...

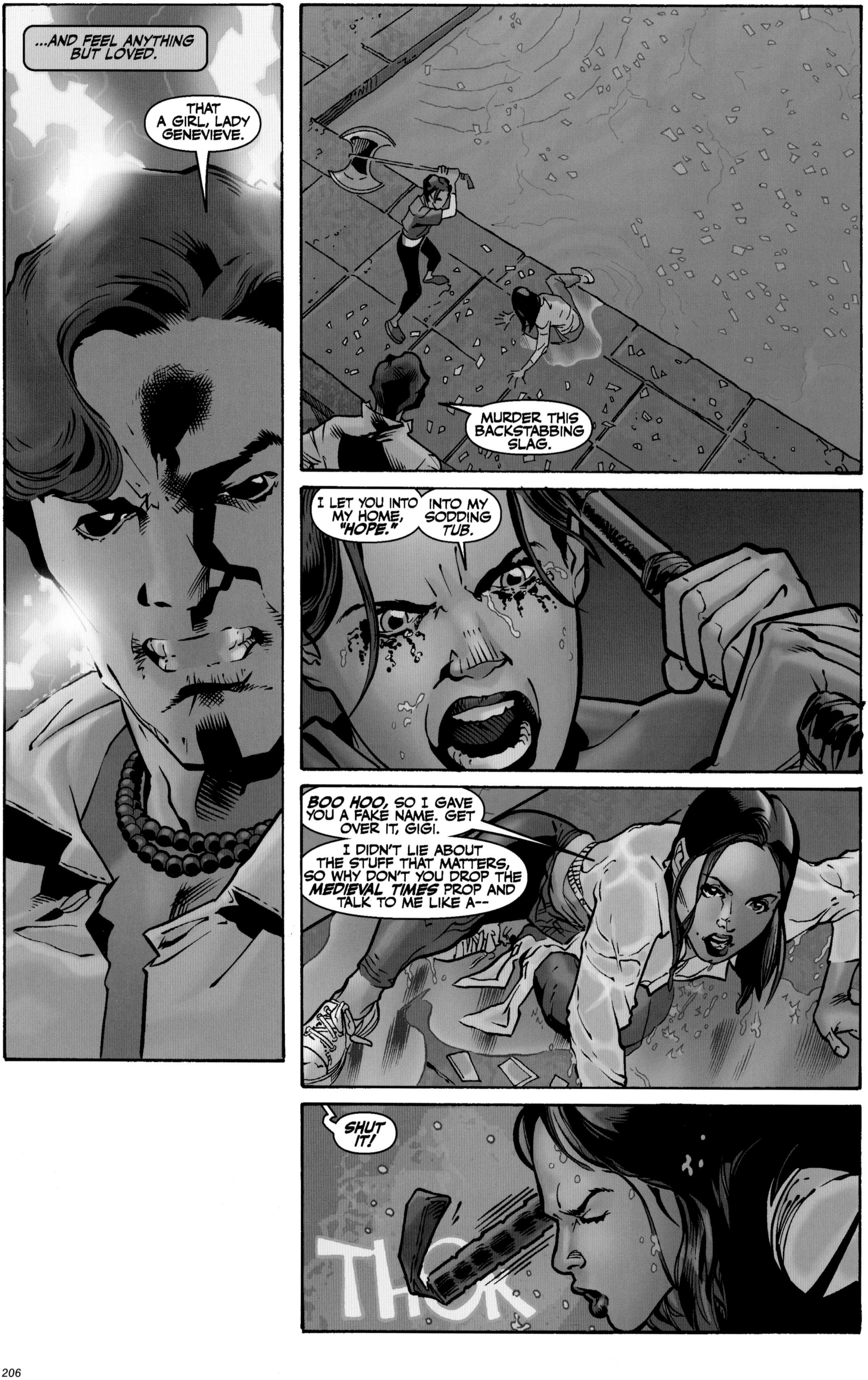
...AND FEEL ANYTHING BUT LOVED.
THAT A GIRL, LADY GENEVIEVE.
MURDER THIS BACKSTABBING SLAG.
I LET YOU INTO MY HOME, "HOPE."
INTO MY SODDING TUB.
BOO HOO, SO I GAVE YOU A FAKE NAME. GET OVER IT, GIGI.
I DIDN'T LIE ABOUT THE STUFF THAT MATTERS, SO WHY DON'T YOU DROP THE MEDIEVAL TIMES PROP AND TALK TO ME LIKE A--
SHUT IT!
THOK

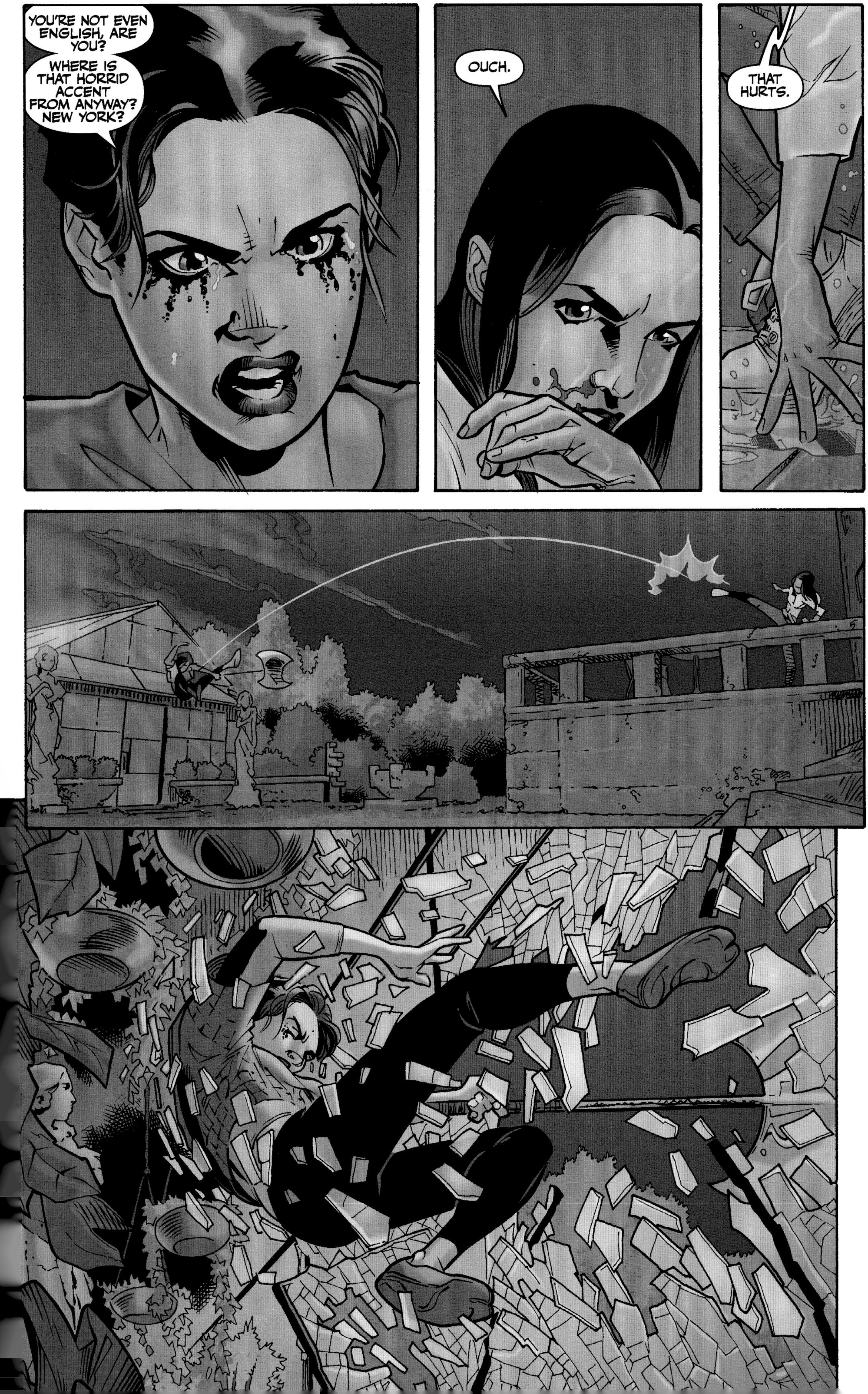
YOU'RE NOT EVEN ENGLISH, ARE YOU?
WHERE IS THAT HORRID ACCENT FROM ANYWAY? NEW YORK?
OUCH.
THAT HURTS.

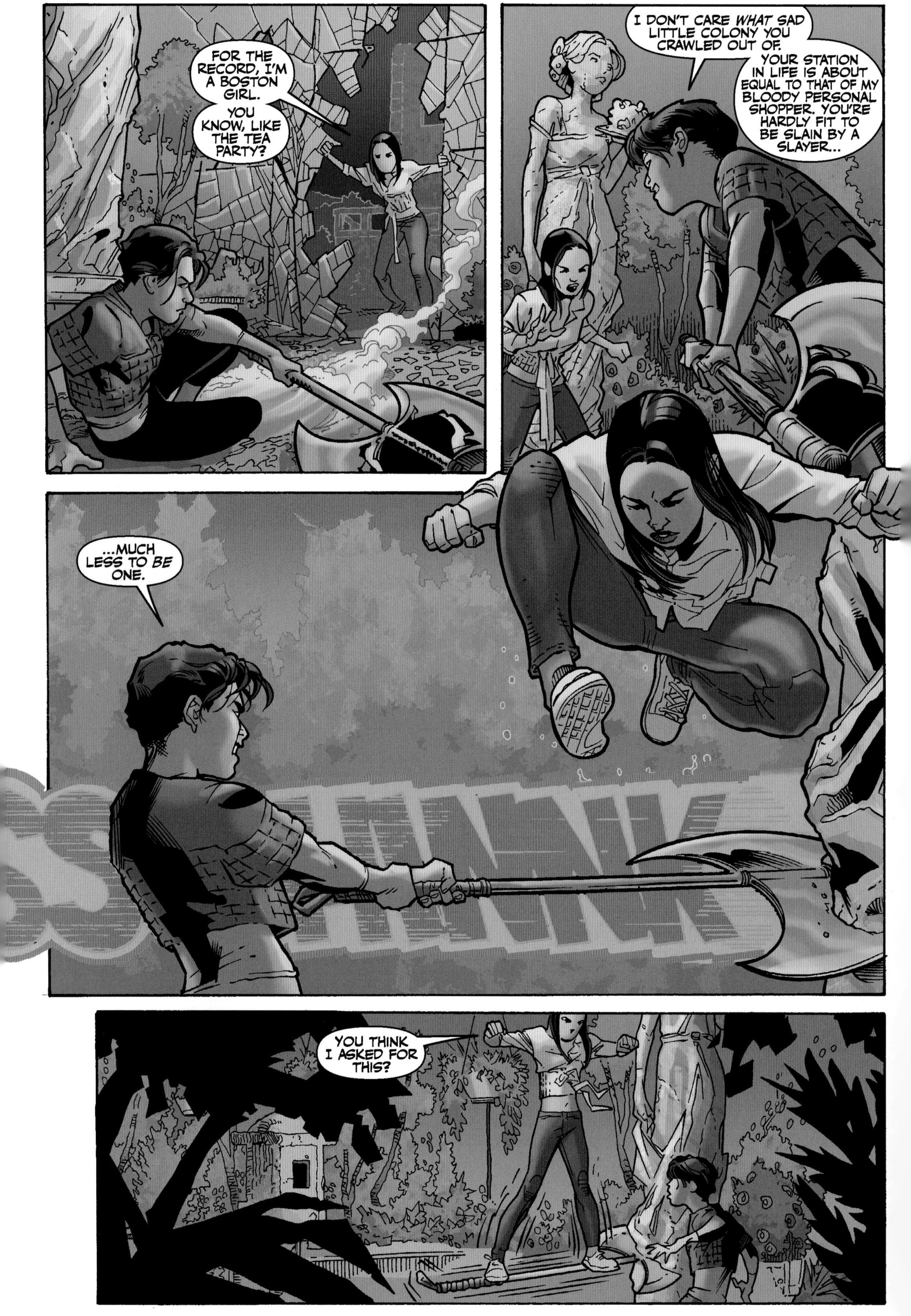
FOR THE RECORD, I'M A BOSTON GIRL.
YOU KNOW, LIKE THE TEA PARTY?
I DON'T CARE *WHAT* SAD LITTLE COLONY YOU CRAWLED OUT OF.
YOUR STATION IN LIFE IS ABOUT EQUAL TO THAT OF MY BLOODY PERSONAL SHOPPER. YOU'RE HARDLY FIT TO BE SLAIN BY A SLAYER...
...MUCH LESS TO *BE* ONE.
YOU THINK I ASKED FOR THIS?

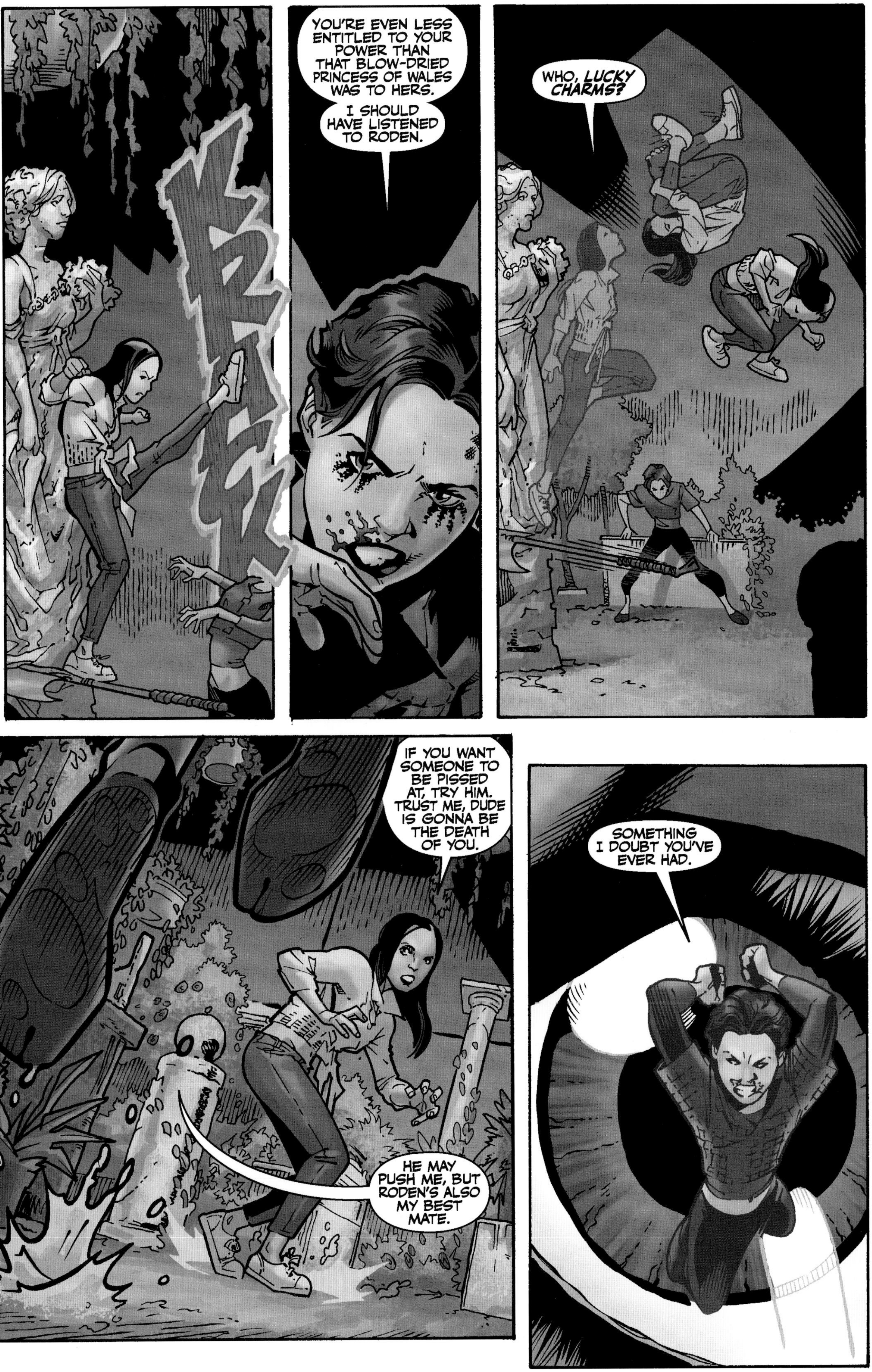
YOU'RE EVEN LESS ENTITLED TO YOUR POWER THAN THAT BLOW-DRIED PRINCESS OF WALES WAS TO HERS.
I SHOULD HAVE LISTENED TO RODEN.
WHO, *LUCKY CHARMS?*
IF YOU WANT SOMEONE TO BE PISSED AT, TRY HIM. TRUST ME, DUDE IS GONNA BE THE DEATH OF YOU.
HE MAY PUSH ME, BUT RODEN'S ALSO MY BEST MATE.
SOMETHING I DOUBT YOU'VE EVER HAD.

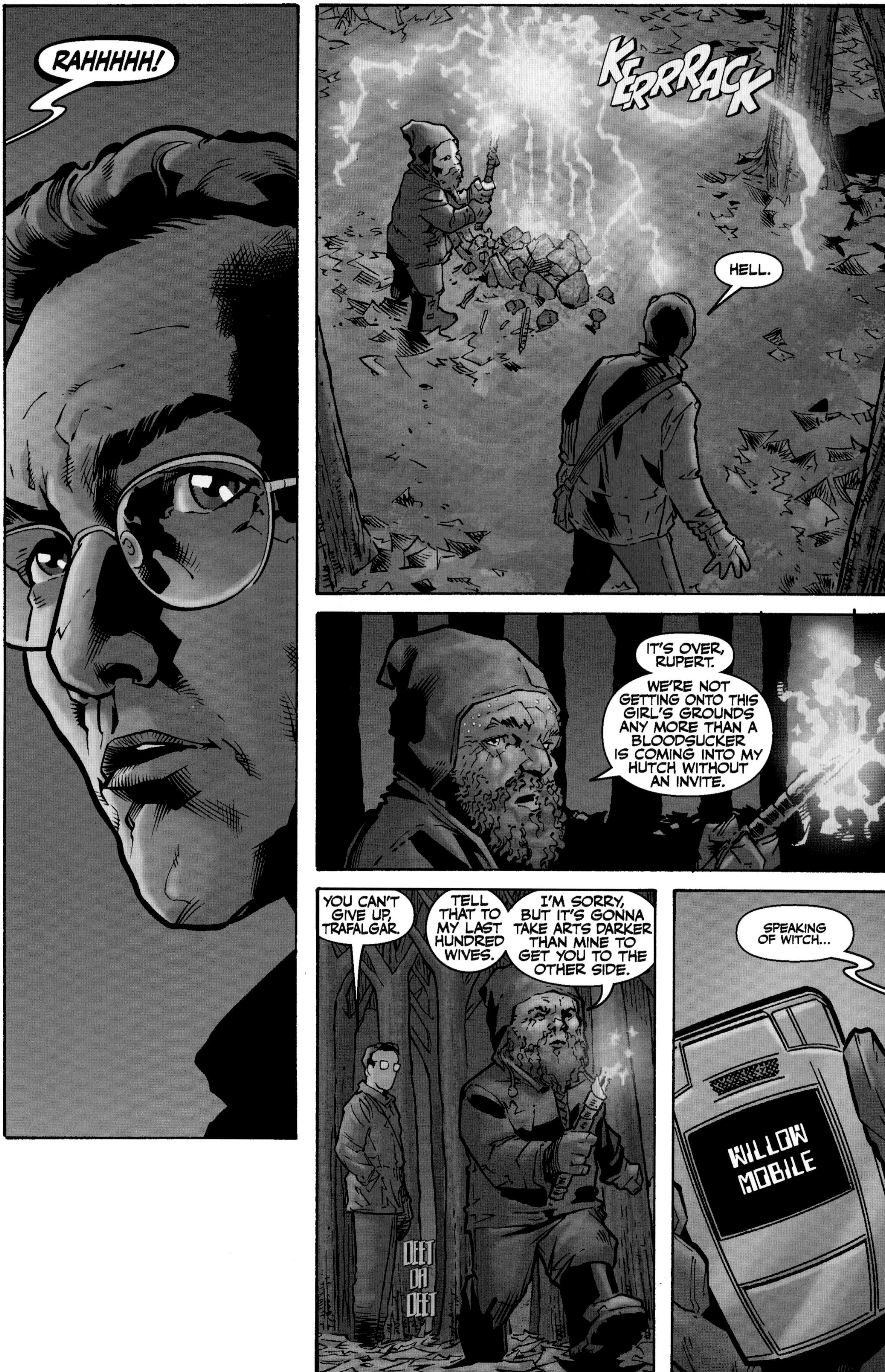
RAHHHHH!
KERRRACK
HELL.
IT'S OVER, RUPERT.
WE'RE NOT GETTING ONTO THIS GIRL'S GROUNDS ANY MORE THAN A BLOODSUCKER IS COMING INTO MY HUTCH WITHOUT AN INVITE.
YOU CAN'T GIVE UP, TRAFALGAR.
TELL THAT TO MY LAST HUNDRED WIVES.
I'M SORRY, BUT IT'S GONNA TAKE ARTS DARKER THAN MINE TO GET YOU TO THE OTHER SIDE.
DEET DA DEET
SPEAKING OF WITCH...
WILLOW MOBILE

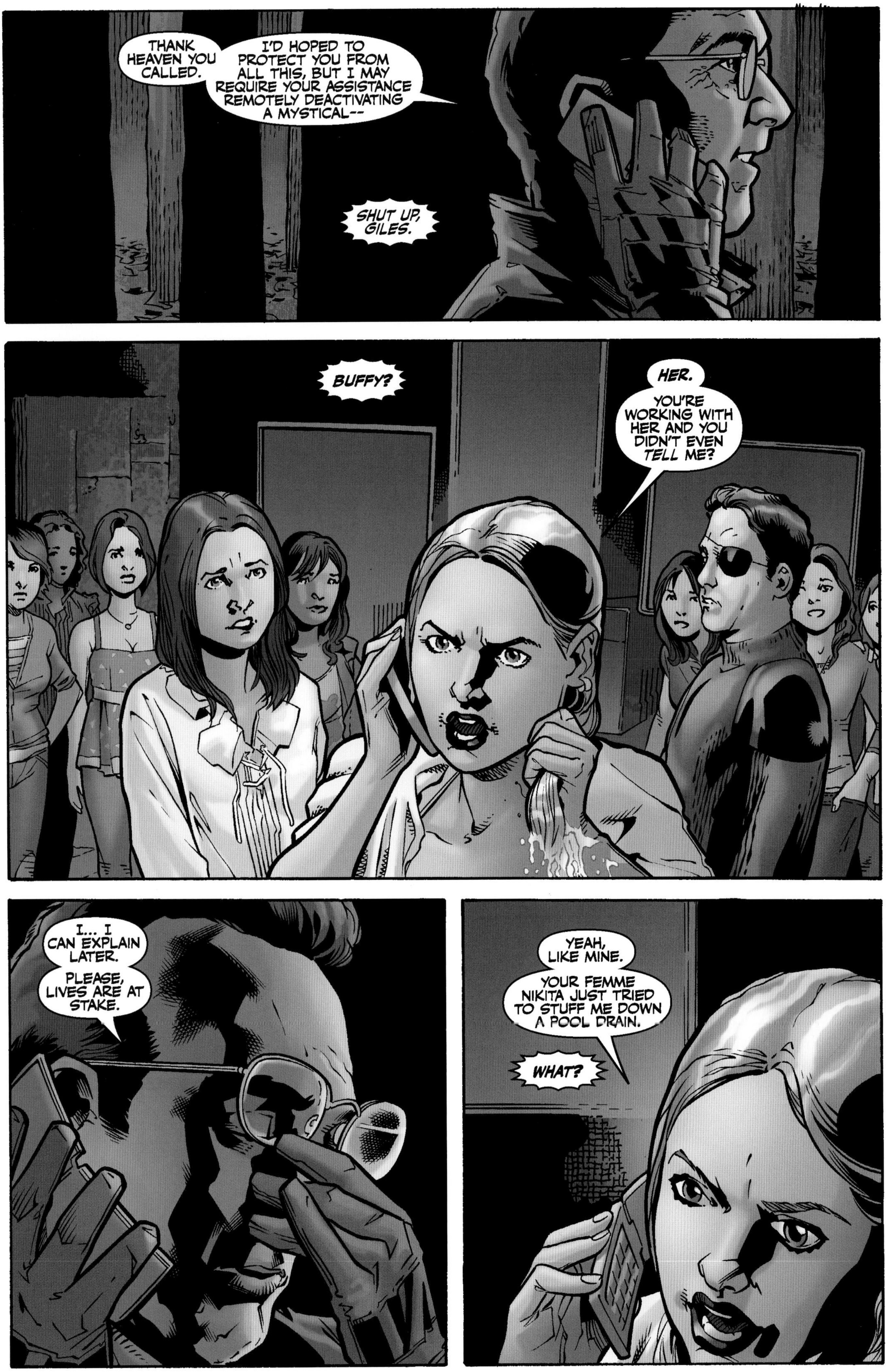
THANK HEAVEN YOU CALLED.
I'D HOPED TO PROTECT YOU FROM ALL THIS, BUT I MAY REQUIRE YOUR ASSISTANCE REMOTELY DEACTIVATING A MYSTICAL--
SHUT UP, GILES.
BUFFY?
HER.
YOU'RE WORKING WITH HER AND YOU DIDN'T EVEN TELL ME?
I... I CAN EXPLAIN LATER.
PLEASE, LIVES ARE AT STAKE.
YEAH, LIKE MINE.
YOUR FEMME NIKITA JUST TRIED TO STUFF ME DOWN A POOL DRAIN.
WHAT?

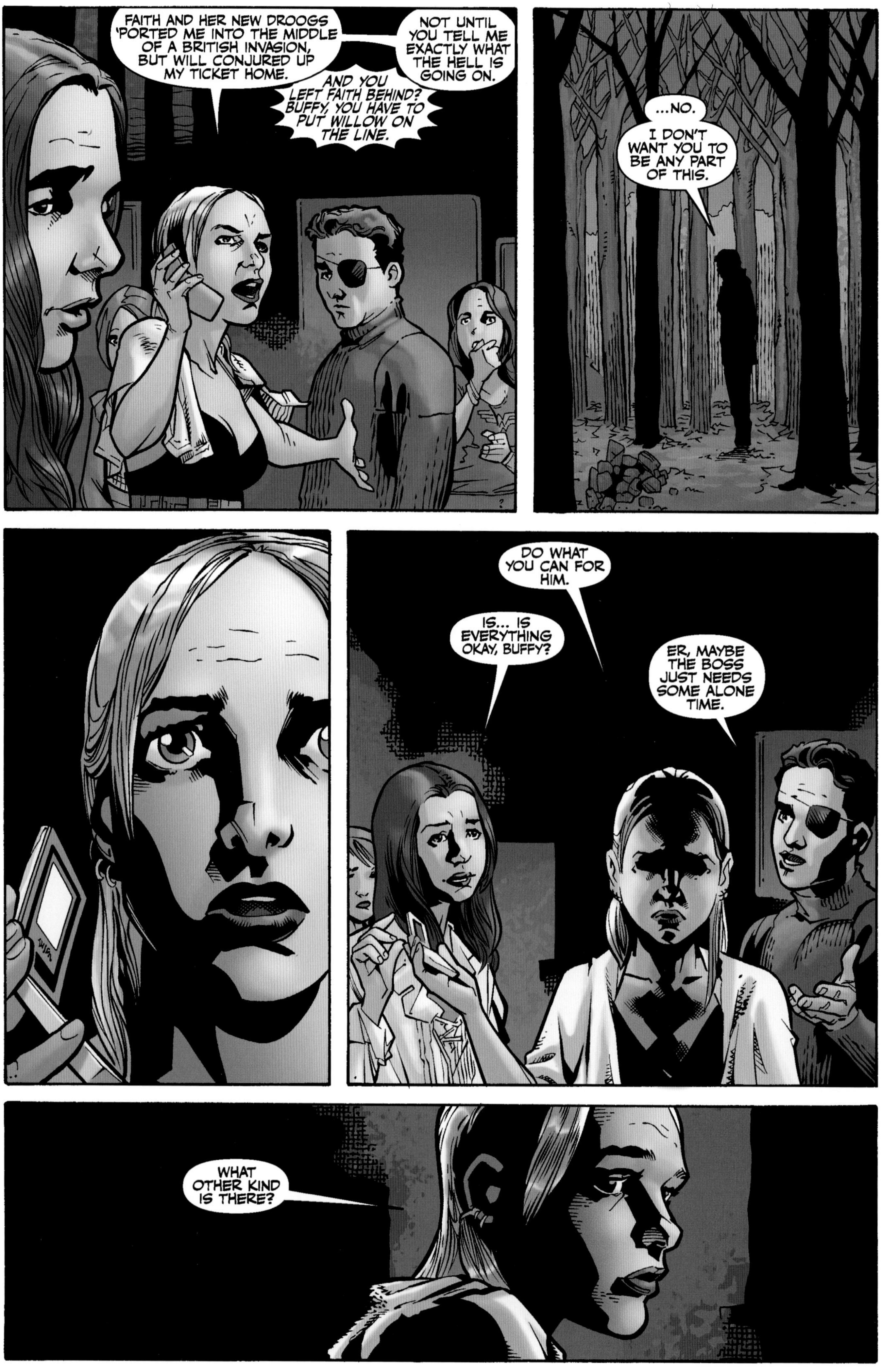
FAITH AND HER NEW DROOGS 'PORTED ME INTO THE MIDDLE OF A BRITISH INVASION, BUT WILL CONJURED UP MY TICKET HOME.
AND YOU LEFT FAITH BEHIND? BUFFY, YOU HAVE TO PUT WILLOW ON THE LINE.
NOT UNTIL YOU TELL ME EXACTLY WHAT THE HELL IS GOING ON.
...NO.
I DON'T WANT YOU TO BE ANY PART OF THIS.
DO WHAT YOU CAN FOR HIM.
IS... IS EVERYTHING OKAY, BUFFY?
ER, MAYBE THE BOSS JUST NEEDS SOME ALONE TIME.
WHAT OTHER KIND IS THERE?

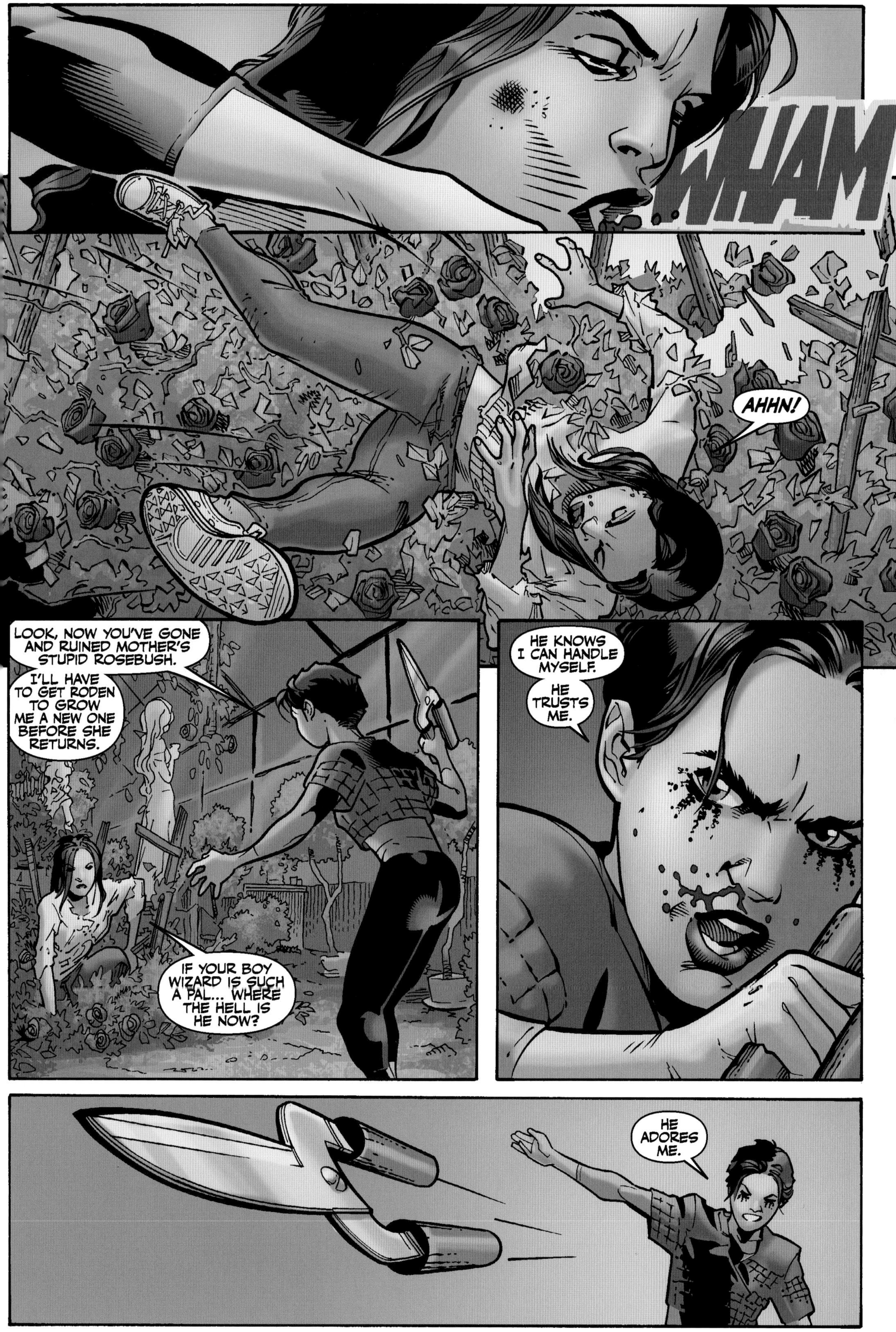
WHAM
AHHN!
LOOK, NOW YOU'VE GONE AND RUINED MOTHER'S STUPID ROSEBUSH.
I'LL HAVE TO GET RODEN TO GROW ME A NEW ONE BEFORE SHE RETURNS.
IF YOUR BOY WIZARD IS SUCH A PAL... WHERE THE HELL IS HE NOW?
HE KNOWS I CAN HANDLE MYSELF.
HE TRUSTS ME.
HE ADORES ME.

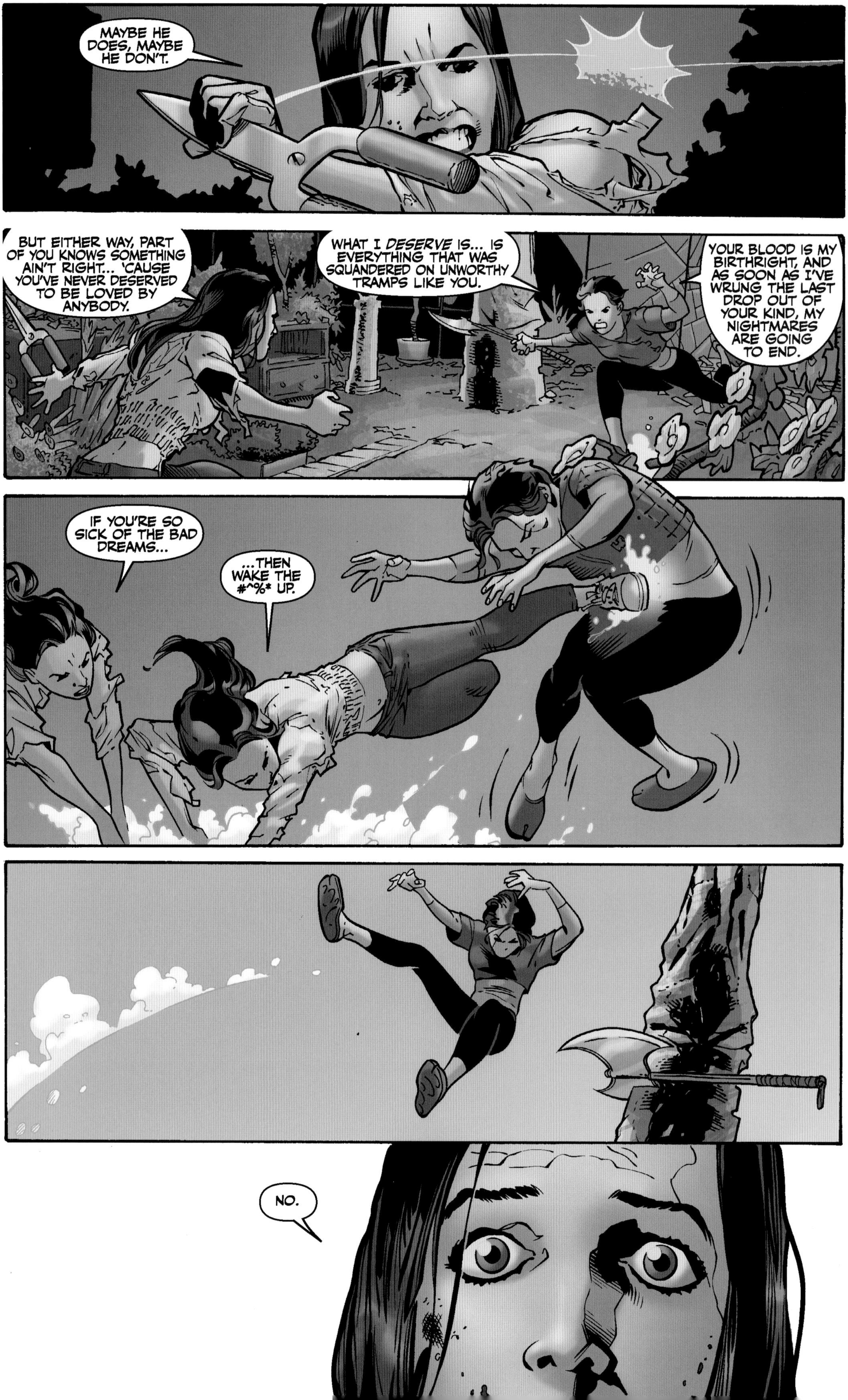
MAYBE HE DOES, MAYBE HE DON'T.
BUT EITHER WAY, PART OF YOU KNOWS SOMETHING AIN'T RIGHT... 'CAUSE YOU'VE NEVER DESERVED TO BE LOVED BY ANYBODY.
WHAT I *DESERVE* IS... IS EVERYTHING THAT WAS SQUANDERED ON UNWORTHY TRAMPS LIKE YOU.
YOUR BLOOD IS MY BIRTHRIGHT, AND AS SOON AS I'VE WRUNG THE LAST DROP OUT OF YOUR KIND, MY NIGHTMARES ARE GOING TO END.
IF YOU'RE SO SICK OF THE BAD DREAMS...
...THEN WAKE THE #^%* UP.
NO.

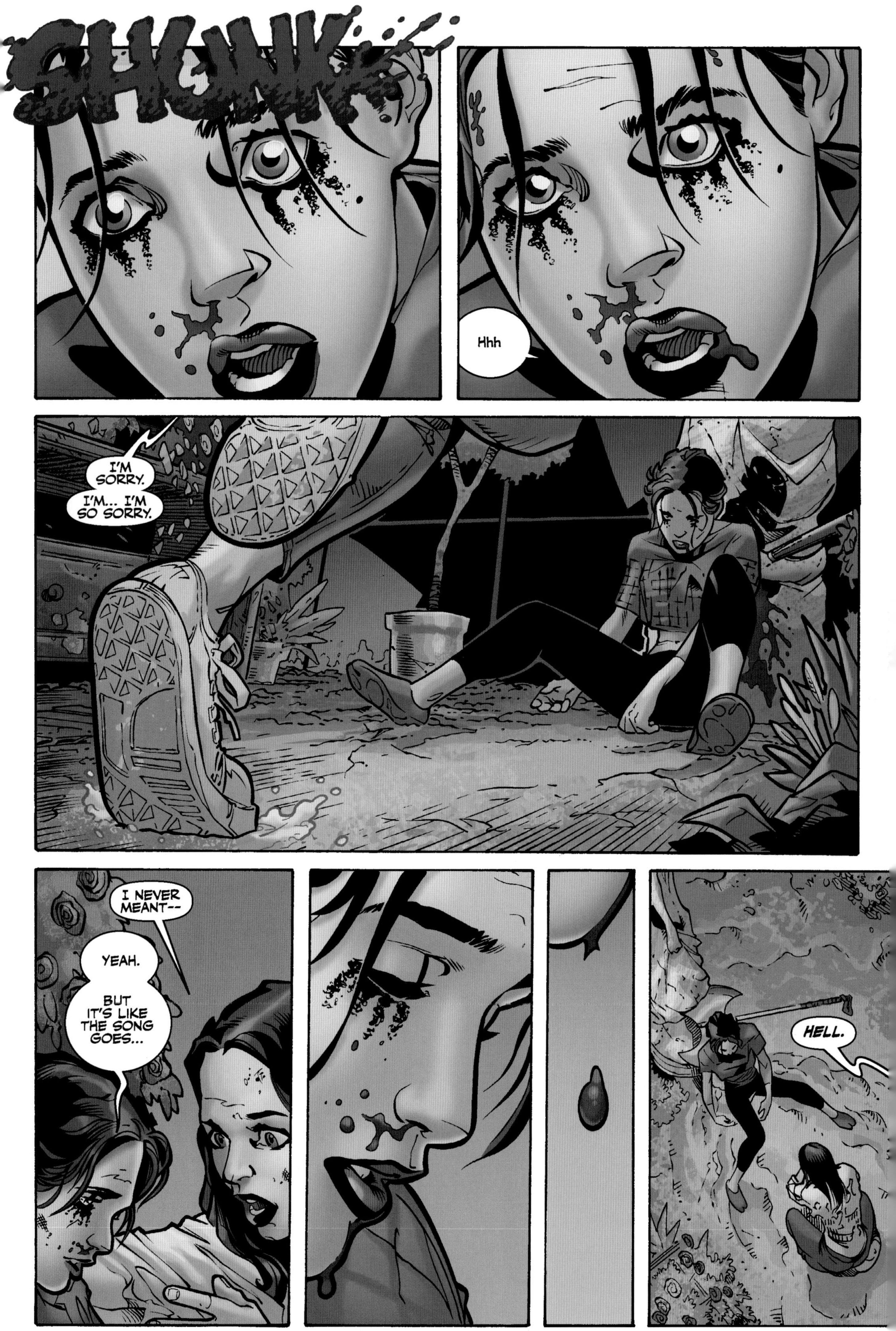
SHUNK
Hhh
I'M SORRY.
I'M... I'M SO SORRY.
I NEVER MEANT--
YEAH.
BUT IT'S LIKE THE SONG GOES...
HELL.

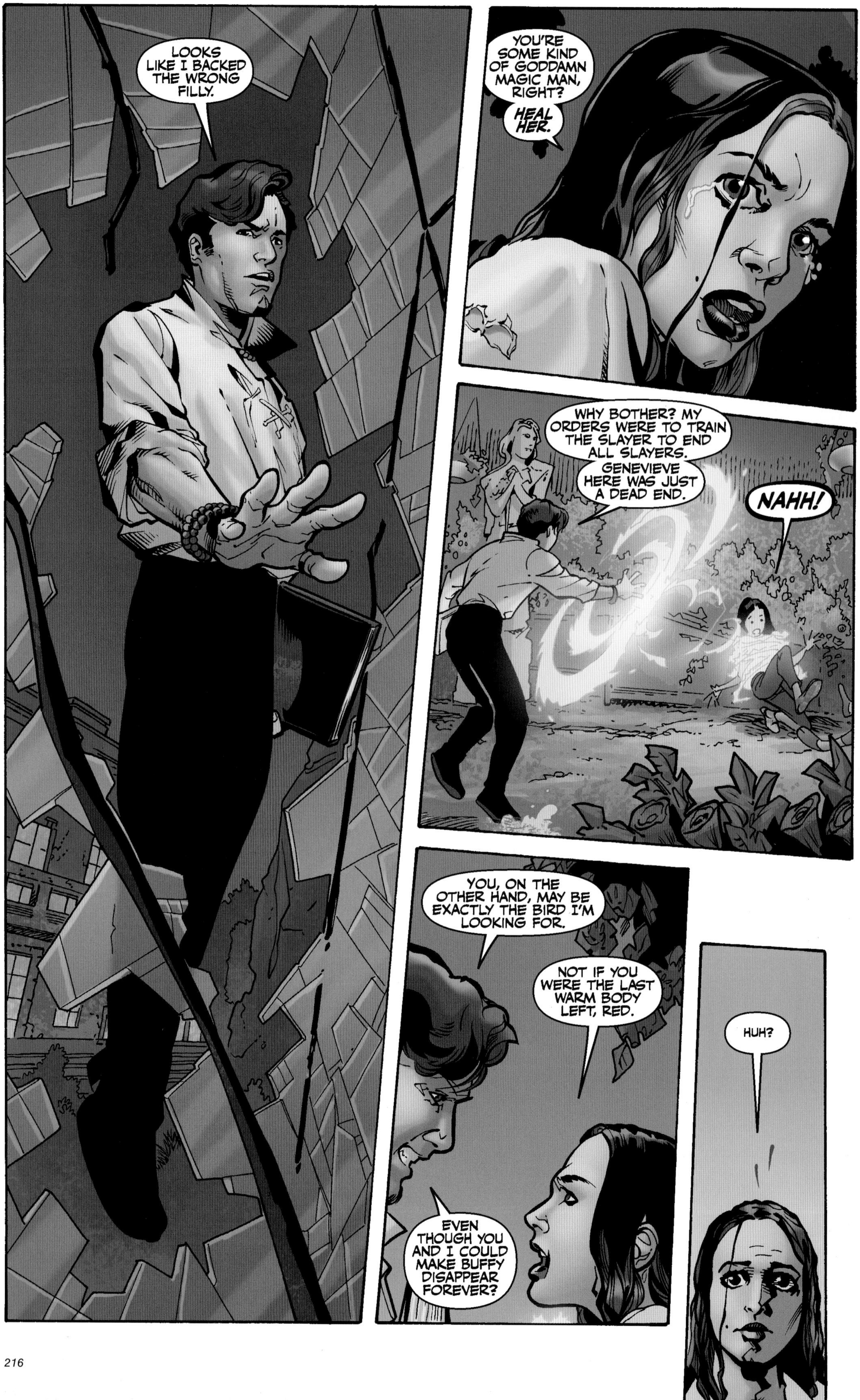
LOOKS LIKE I BACKED THE WRONG FILLY.
YOU'RE SOME KIND OF GODDAMN MAGIC MAN, RIGHT?
HEAL HER.
WHY BOTHER? MY ORDERS WERE TO TRAIN THE SLAYER TO END ALL SLAYERS. GENEVIEVE HERE WAS JUST A DEAD END.
NAHH!
YOU, ON THE OTHER HAND, MAY BE EXACTLY THE BIRD I'M LOOKING FOR.
NOT IF YOU WERE THE LAST WARM BODY LEFT, RED.
EVEN THOUGH YOU AND I COULD MAKE BUFFY DISAPPEAR FOREVER?
HUH?

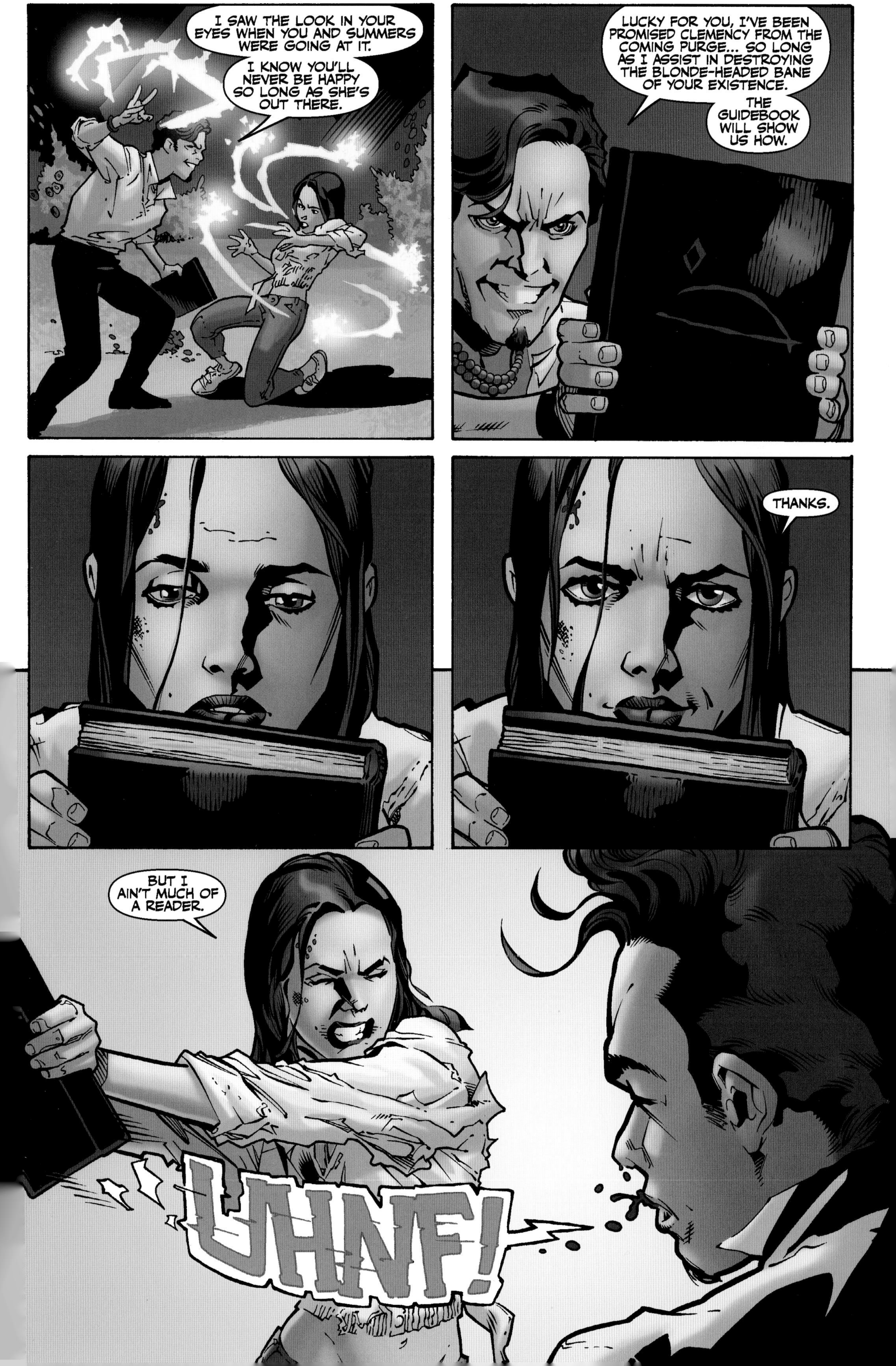
I SAW THE LOOK IN YOUR EYES WHEN YOU AND SUMMERS WERE GOING AT IT.
I KNOW YOU'LL NEVER BE HAPPY SO LONG AS SHE'S OUT THERE.
LUCKY FOR YOU, I'VE BEEN PROMISED CLEMENCY FROM THE COMING PURGE... SO LONG AS I ASSIST IN DESTROYING THE BLONDE-HEADED BANE OF YOUR EXISTENCE.
THE GUIDEBOOK WILL SHOW US HOW.
THANKS.
BUT I AIN'T MUCH OF A READER.
UHNF!

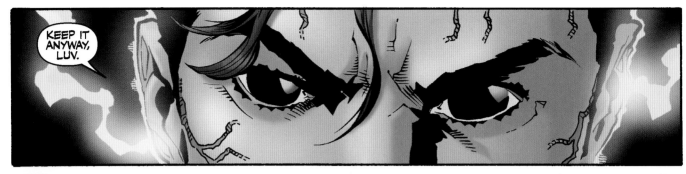

KEEP IT ANYWAY, LUV.

I ALREADY KNOW HOW IT ENDS.

KERSHRINK

LORD, NOTHING SADDER THAN AN OVER-THE-HILL SLAYER.

GIRLS LIKE YOU ARE SUPPOSED TO SHUFFLE OFF THIS MORTAL COIL WHEN YOU'RE YOUNG AND FRESH, NOT WHEN YOU'RE STARTING TO SAG A BIT.

WHA...?

AHHHHHH!

SO LONG, FAITH.

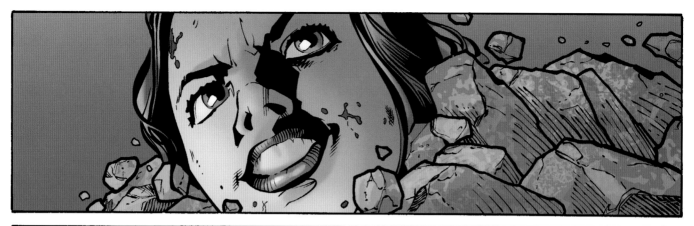

THE HELL ARE YOU SMILING ABOUT?

GAHH!

NNF!

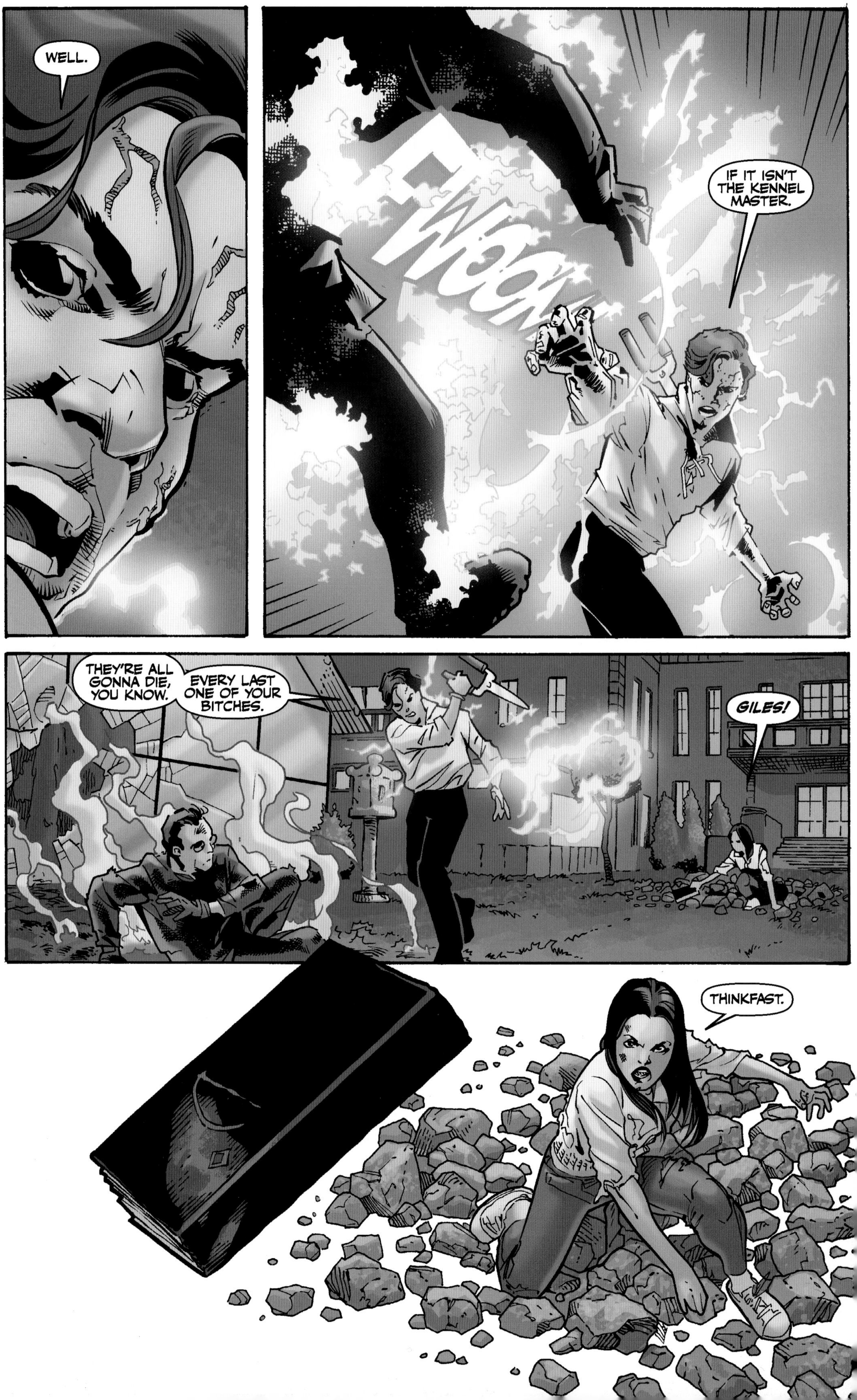
WELL.
FWOOM
IF IT ISN'T THE KENNEL MASTER.
THEY'RE ALL GONNA DIE, YOU KNOW.
EVERY LAST ONE OF YOUR BITCHES.
GILES!
THINKFAST.

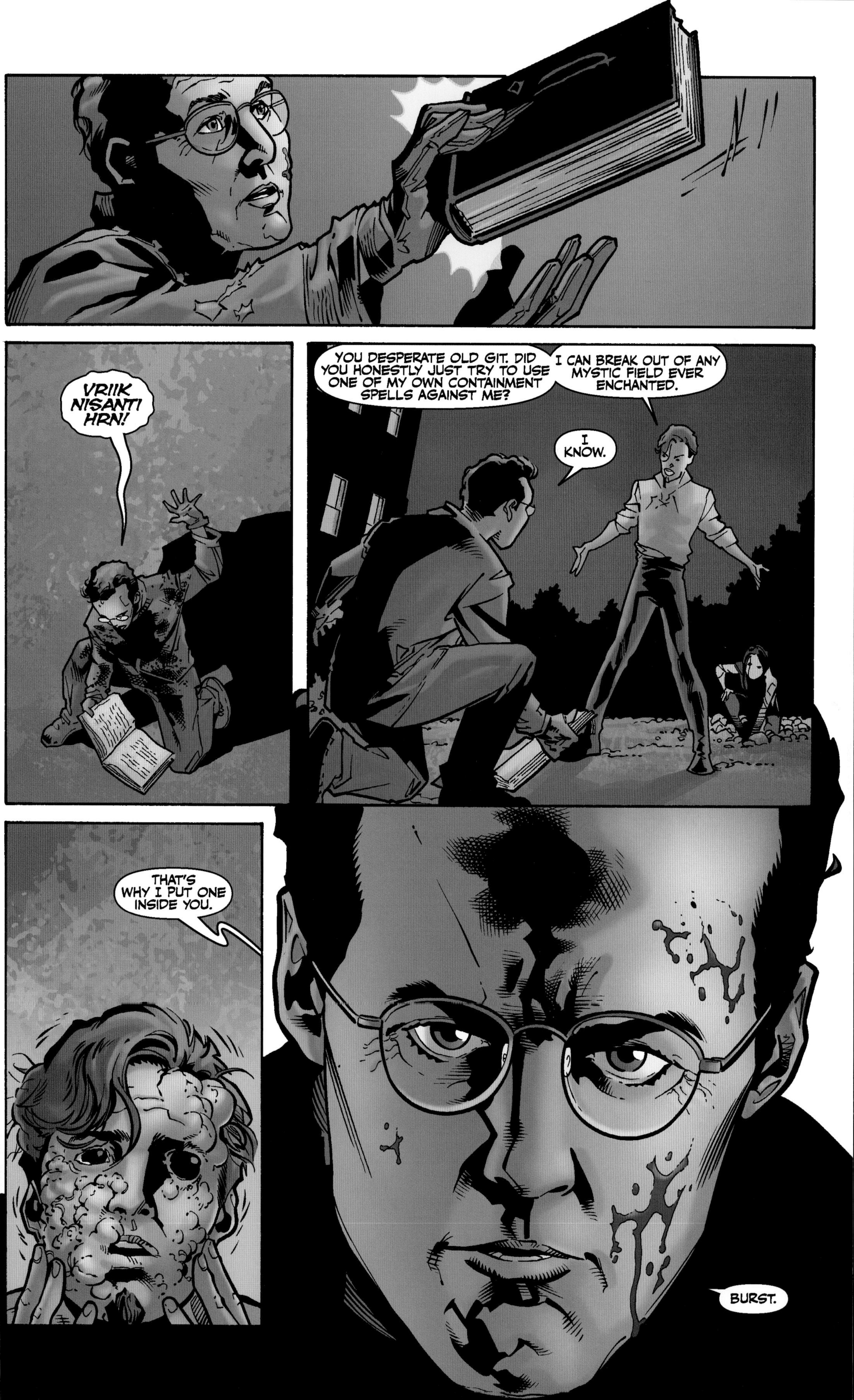
VRIIK NISANTI HRN!
YOU DESPERATE OLD GIT. DID YOU HONESTLY JUST TRY TO USE ONE OF MY OWN CONTAINMENT SPELLS AGAINST ME?
I CAN BREAK OUT OF ANY MYSTIC FIELD EVER ENCHANTED.
I KNOW.
THAT'S WHY I PUT ONE INSIDE YOU.
BURST.

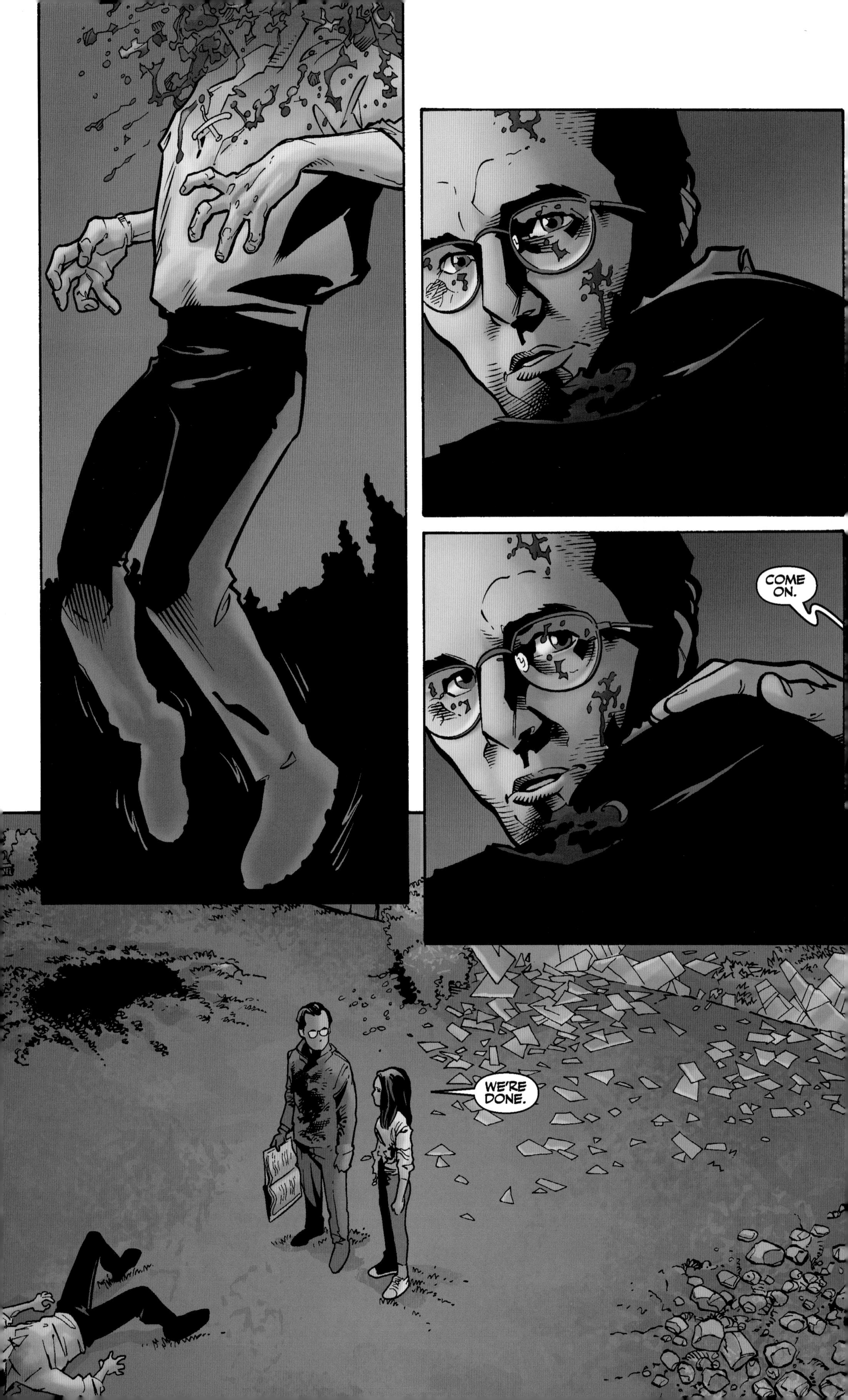
COME ON.
WE'RE DONE.

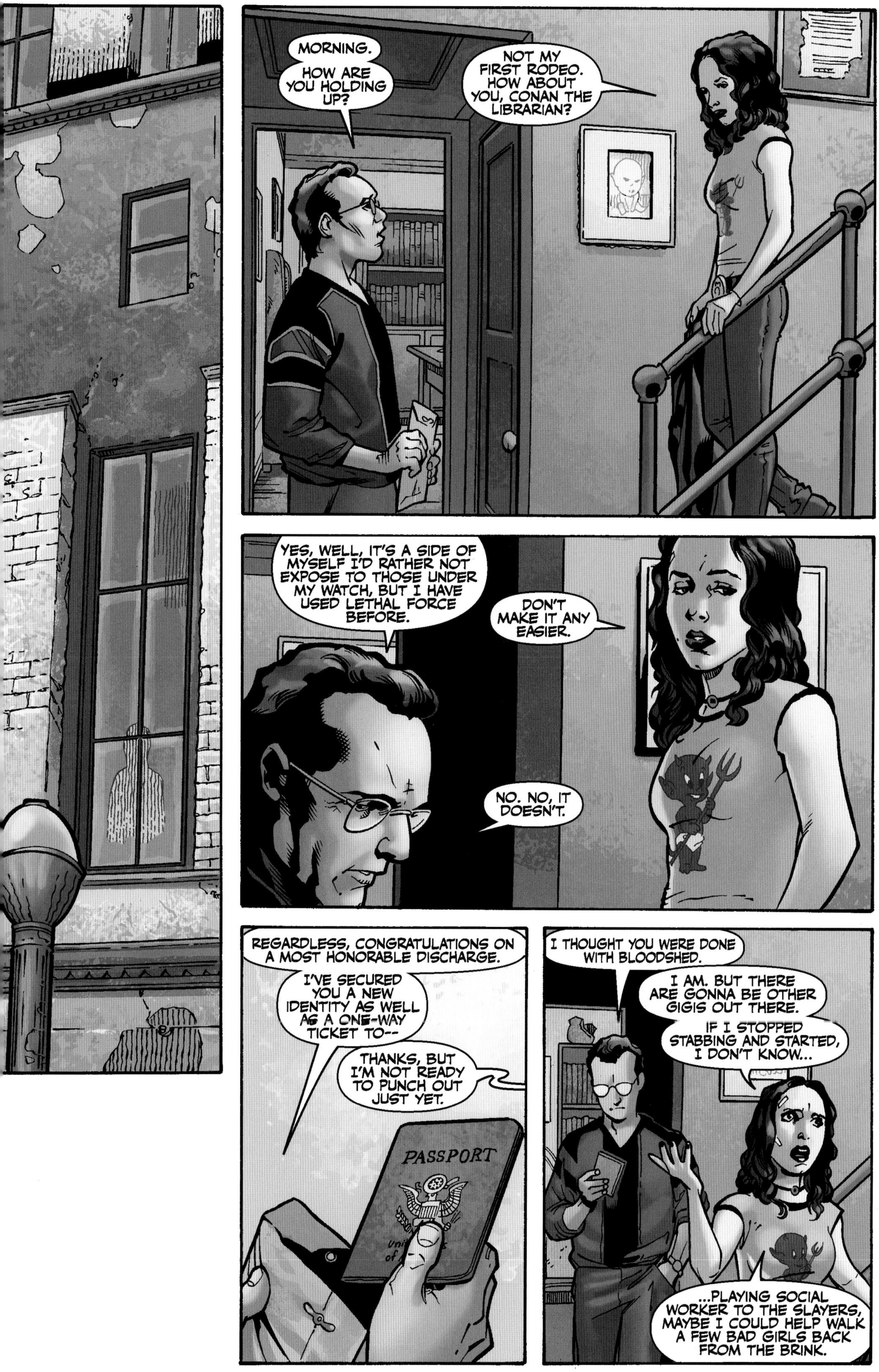
MORNING.
HOW ARE YOU HOLDING UP?
NOT MY FIRST RODEO. HOW ABOUT YOU, CONAN THE LIBRARIAN?
YES, WELL, IT'S A SIDE OF MYSELF I'D RATHER NOT EXPOSE TO THOSE UNDER MY WATCH, BUT I HAVE USED LETHAL FORCE BEFORE.
DON'T MAKE IT ANY EASIER.
NO. NO, IT DOESN'T.
REGARDLESS, CONGRATULATIONS ON A MOST HONORABLE DISCHARGE.
I'VE SECURED YOU A NEW IDENTITY AS WELL AS A ONE-WAY TICKET TO--
THANKS, BUT I'M NOT READY TO PUNCH OUT JUST YET.
PASSPORT
I THOUGHT YOU WERE DONE WITH BLOODSHED.
I AM. BUT THERE ARE GONNA BE OTHER GIGIS OUT THERE.
IF I STOPPED STABBING AND STARTED, I DON'T KNOW...
...PLAYING SOCIAL WORKER TO THE SLAYERS, MAYBE I COULD HELP WALK A FEW BAD GIRLS BACK FROM THE BRINK.

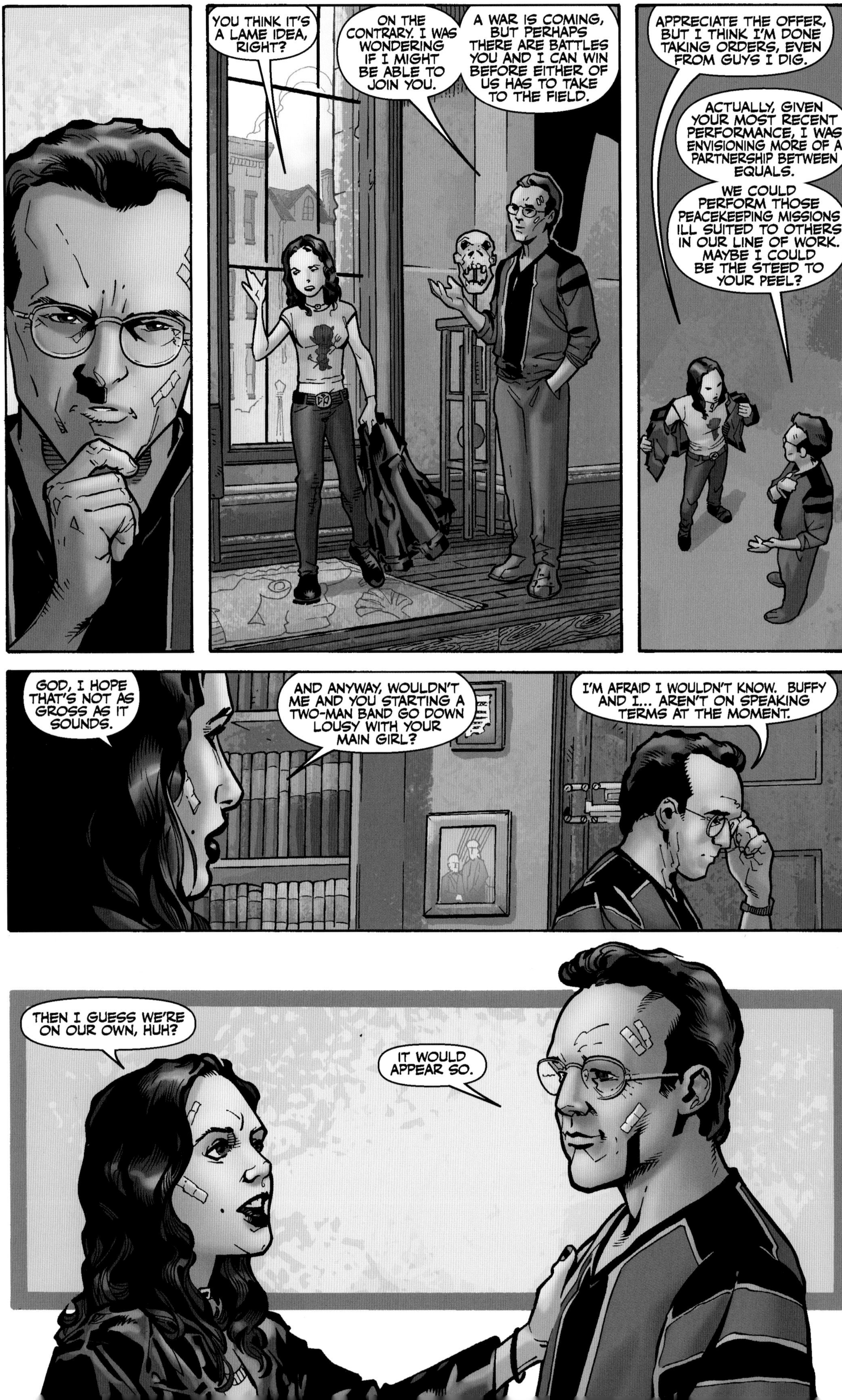
YOU THINK IT'S A LAME IDEA, RIGHT?
ON THE CONTRARY. I WAS WONDERING IF I MIGHT BE ABLE TO JOIN YOU.
A WAR IS COMING, BUT PERHAPS THERE ARE BATTLES YOU AND I CAN WIN BEFORE EITHER OF US HAS TO TAKE TO THE FIELD.
APPRECIATE THE OFFER, BUT I THINK I'M DONE TAKING ORDERS, EVEN FROM GUYS I DIG.
ACTUALLY, GIVEN YOUR MOST RECENT PERFORMANCE, I WAS ENVISIONING MORE OF A PARTNERSHIP BETWEEN EQUALS.
WE COULD PERFORM THOSE PEACEKEEPING MISSIONS ILL SUITED TO OTHERS IN OUR LINE OF WORK. MAYBE I COULD BE THE STEED TO YOUR PEEL?
GOD, I HOPE THAT'S NOT AS GROSS AS IT SOUNDS.
AND ANYWAY, WOULDN'T ME AND YOU STARTING A TWO-MAN BAND GO DOWN LOUSY WITH YOUR MAIN GIRL?
I'M AFRAID I WOULDN'T KNOW. BUFFY AND I... AREN'T ON SPEAKING TERMS AT THE MOMENT.
THEN I GUESS WE'RE ON OUR OWN, HUH?
IT WOULD APPEAR SO.

"BUT PERHAPS WE CAN BE ON OUR OWN TOGETHER."

TWILIGHT? YOU THERE? "I HUMBLY REQUEST YOUR AUDIENCE" AND ALL THAT CRAP.

I BEAR YOUR MARK, NOW GIVE ME MY DAMN AUDIENCE!

CALM YOURSELF, LIEUTENANT MOLTER.

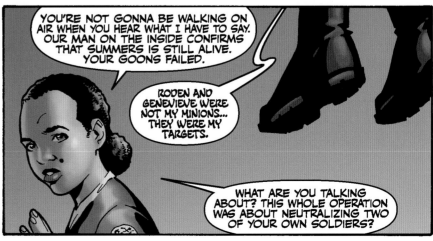

YOU'RE NOT GONNA BE WALKING ON AIR WHEN YOU HEAR WHAT I HAVE TO SAY. OUR MAN ON THE INSIDE CONFIRMS THAT SUMMERS IS STILL ALIVE. YOUR GOONS FAILED.

RODEN AND GENEVIEVE WERE NOT MY MINIONS... THEY WERE MY TARGETS.

WHAT ARE YOU TALKING ABOUT? THIS WHOLE OPERATION WAS ABOUT NEUTRALIZING TWO OF YOUR OWN SOLDIERS?

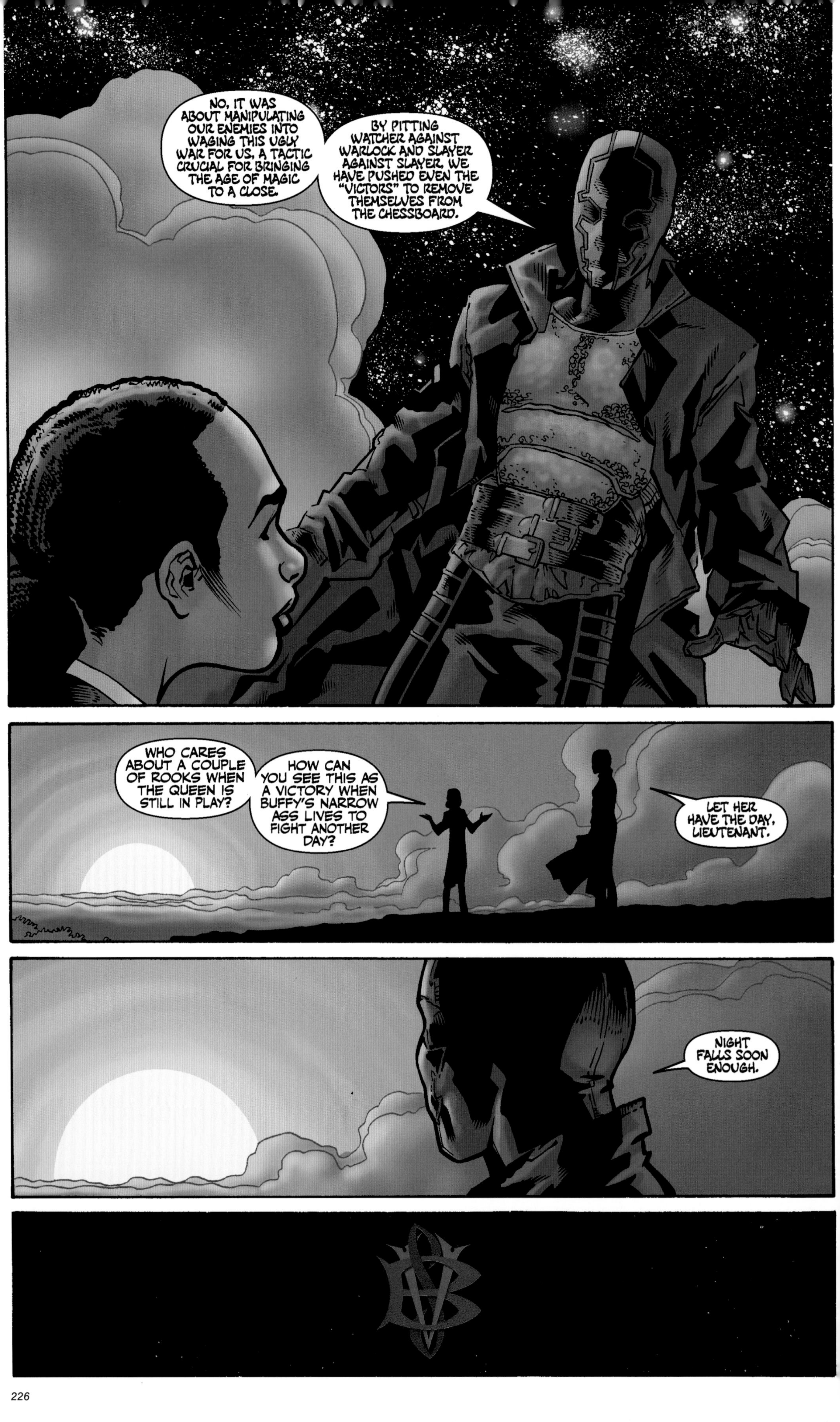
NO, IT WAS ABOUT MANIPULATING OUR ENEMIES INTO WAGING THIS UGLY WAR FOR US, A TACTIC CRUCIAL FOR BRINGING THE AGE OF MAGIC TO A CLOSE.
BY PITTING WATCHER AGAINST WARLOCK AND SLAYER AGAINST SLAYER, WE HAVE PUSHED EVEN THE "VICTORS" TO REMOVE THEMSELVES FROM THE CHESSBOARD.
WHO CARES ABOUT A COUPLE OF ROOKS WHEN THE QUEEN IS STILL IN PLAY?
HOW CAN YOU SEE THIS AS A VICTORY WHEN BUFFY'S NARROW ASS LIVES TO FIGHT ANOTHER DAY?
LET HER HAVE THE DAY, LIEUTENANT.
NIGHT FALLS SOON ENOUGH.

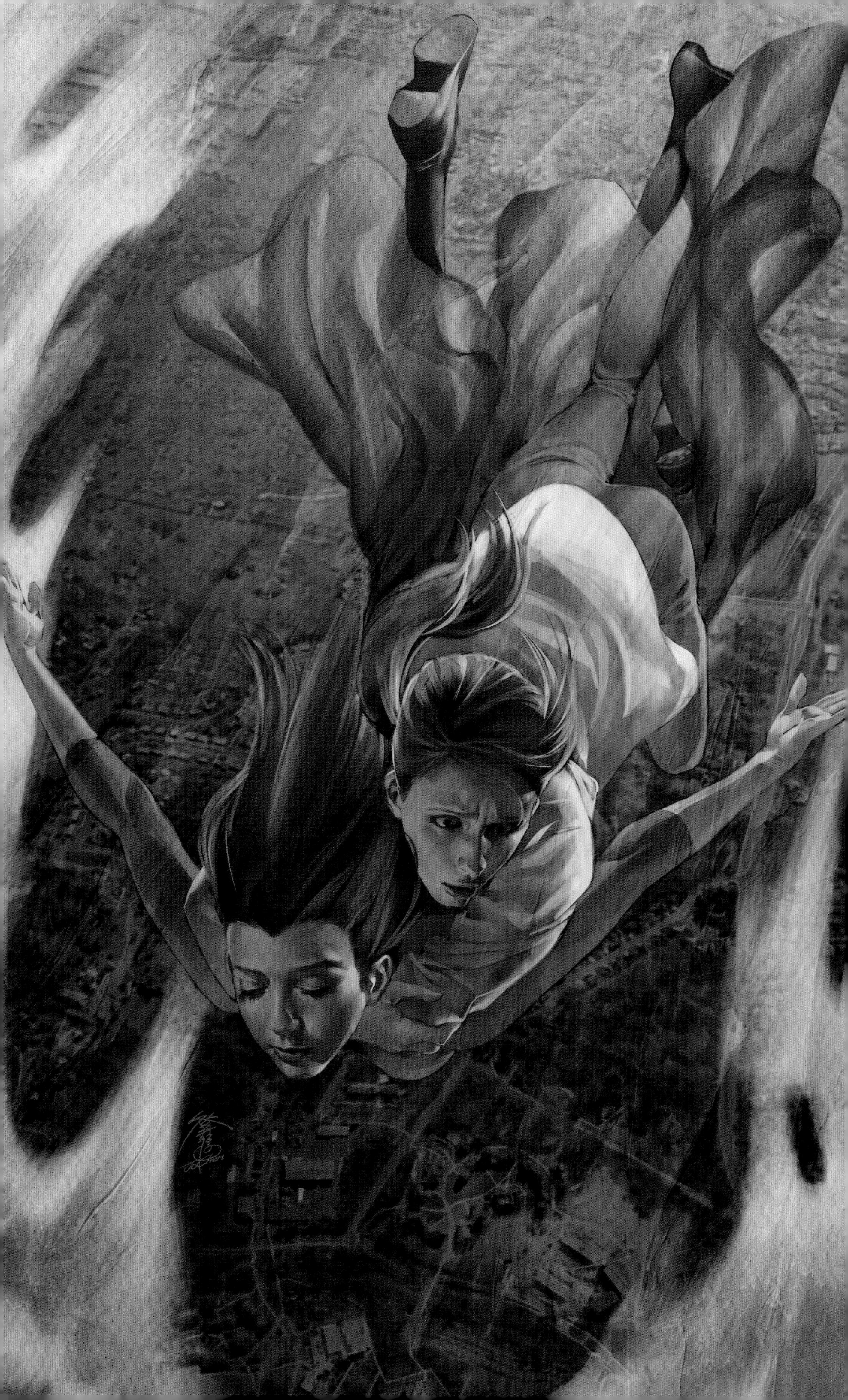

ANYWHERE BUT HERE

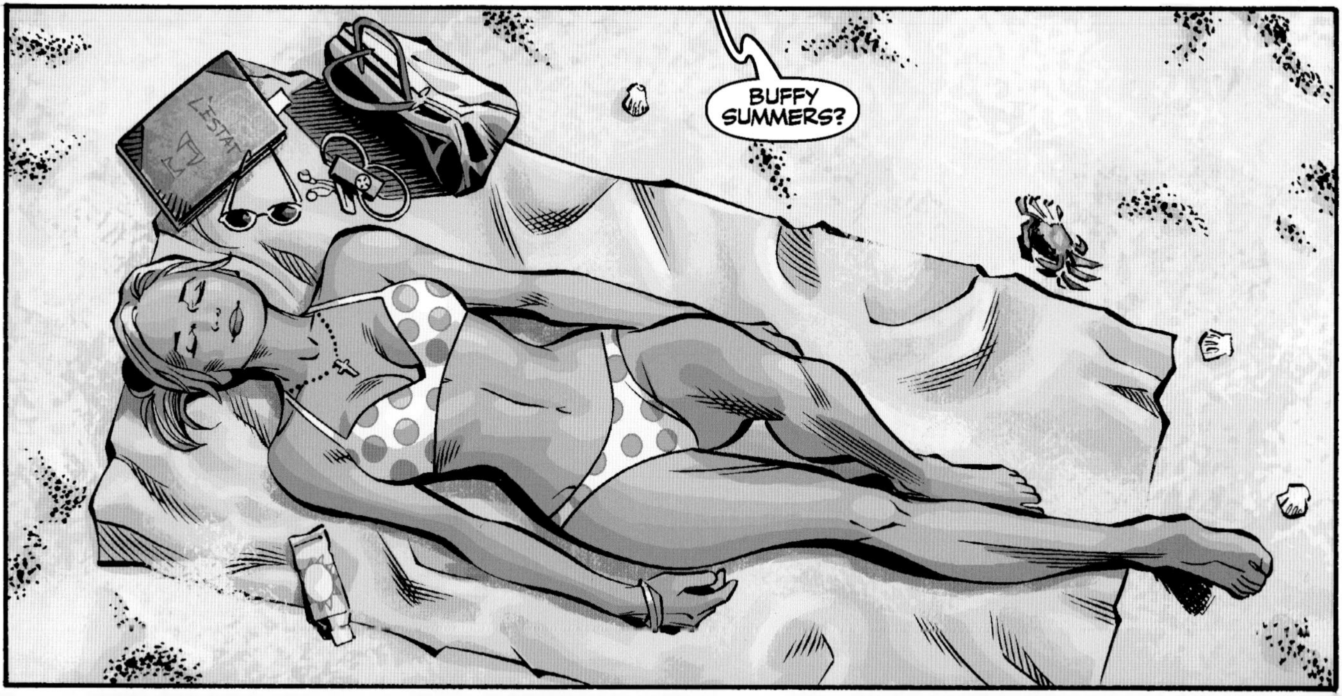
L'ESTAT
BUFFY SUMMERS?

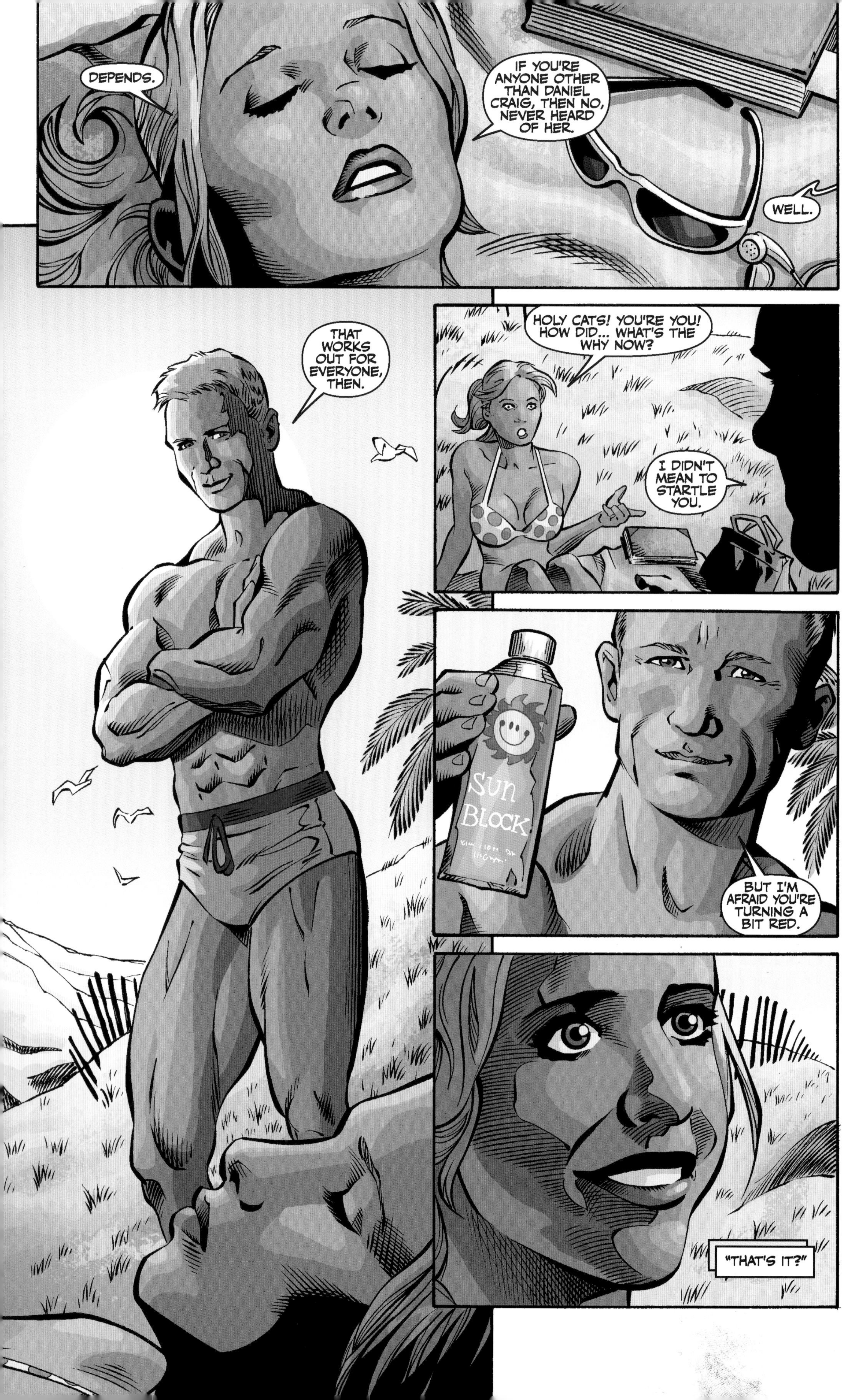
DEPENDS.
IF YOU'RE ANYONE OTHER THAN DANIEL CRAIG, THEN NO, NEVER HEARD OF HER.
WELL.
THAT WORKS OUT FOR EVERYONE, THEN.
HOLY CATS! YOU'RE YOU! HOW DID... WHAT'S THE WHY NOW?
I DIDN'T MEAN TO STARTLE YOU.
SUN BLOCK
BUT I'M AFRAID YOU'RE TURNING A BIT RED.
"THAT'S IT?"

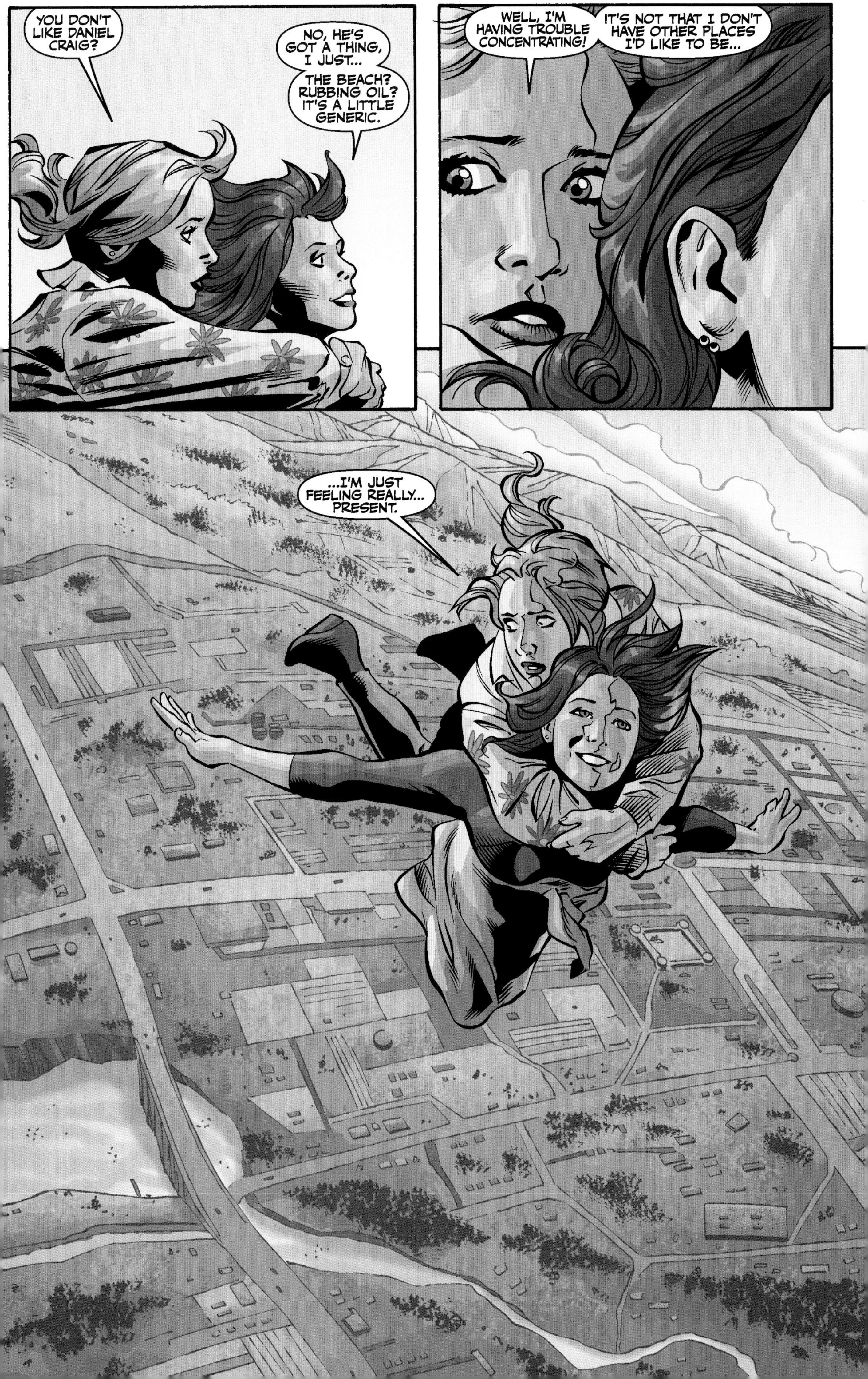
YOU DON'T LIKE DANIEL CRAIG?
NO, HE'S GOT A THING, I JUST...
THE BEACH? RUBBING OIL? IT'S A LITTLE GENERIC.
WELL, I'M HAVING TROUBLE CONCENTRATING!
IT'S NOT THAT I DON'T HAVE OTHER PLACES I'D LIKE TO BE...
...I'M JUST FEELING REALLY... PRESENT.

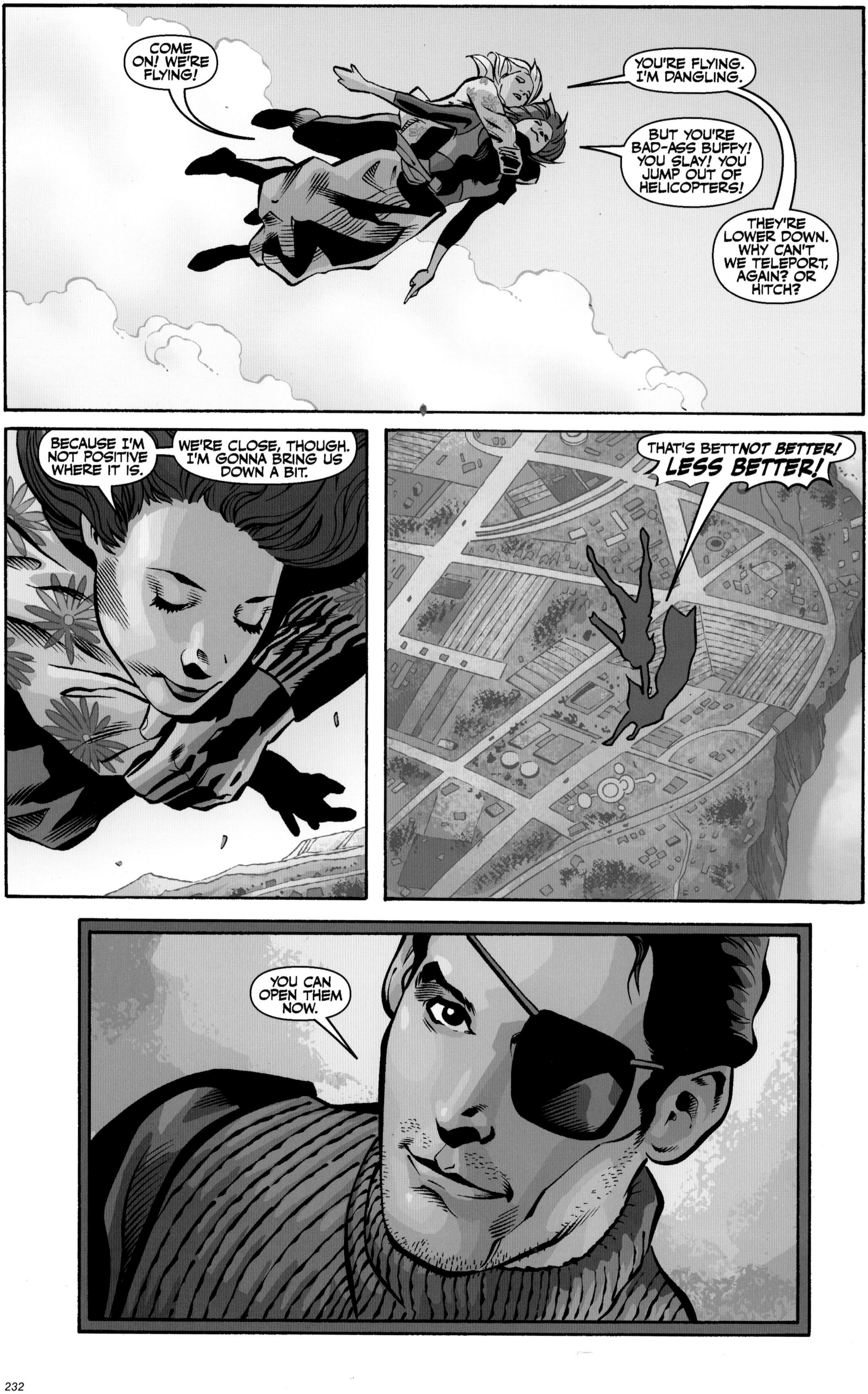
COME ON! WE'RE FLYING!
YOU'RE FLYING. I'M DANGLING.
BUT YOU'RE BAD-ASS BUFFY! YOU SLAY! YOU JUMP OUT OF HELICOPTERS!
THEY'RE LOWER DOWN. WHY CAN'T WE TELEPORT, AGAIN? OR HITCH?
BECAUSE I'M NOT POSITIVE WHERE IT IS.
WE'RE CLOSE, THOUGH. I'M GONNA BRING US DOWN A BIT.
THAT'S BETTNOT BETTER! LESS BETTER!
YOU CAN OPEN THEM NOW.

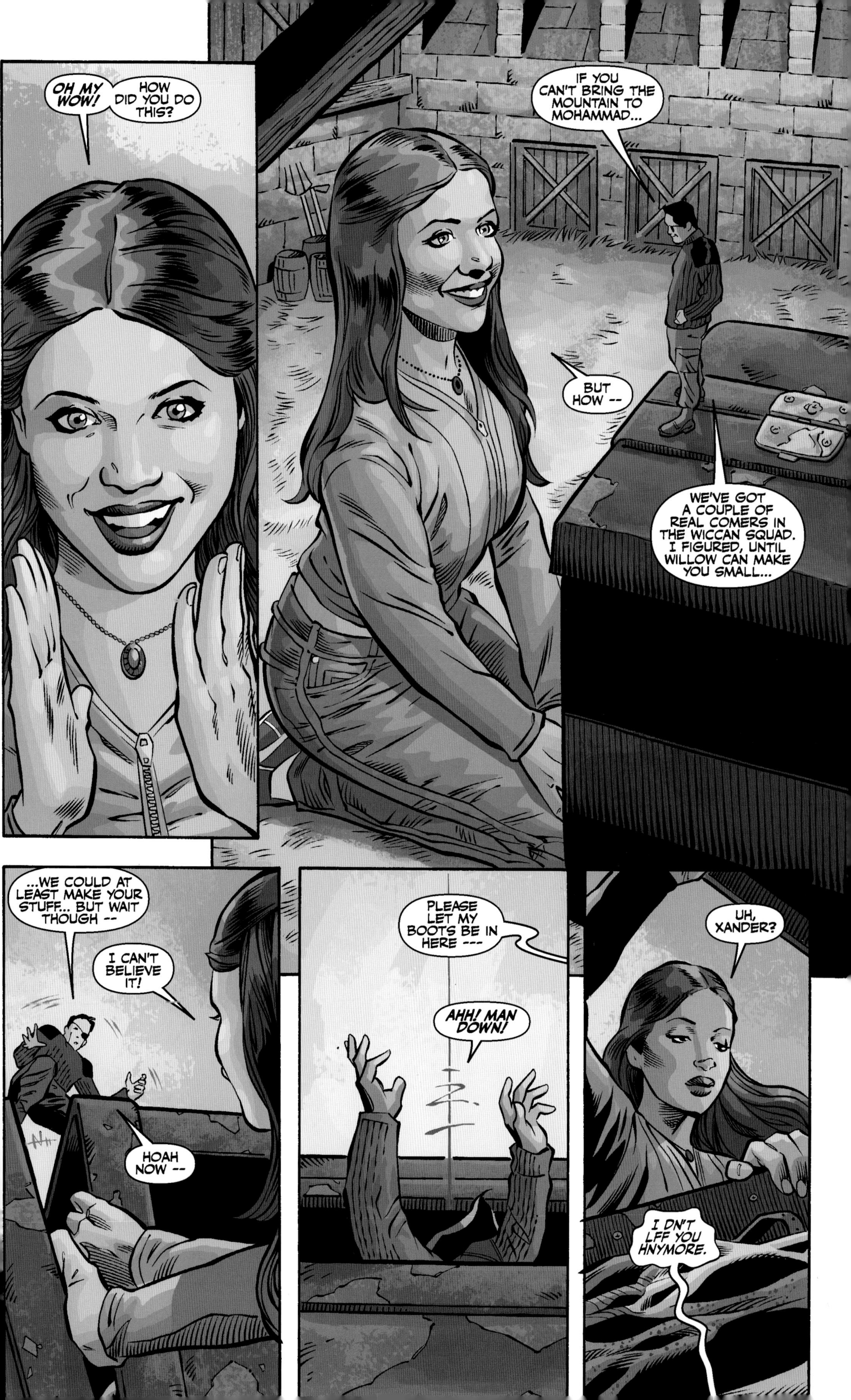
OH MY WOW!
HOW DID YOU DO THIS?
IF YOU CAN'T BRING THE MOUNTAIN TO MOHAMMAD...
BUT HOW --
WE'VE GOT A COUPLE OF REAL COMERS IN THE WICCAN SQUAD. I FIGURED, UNTIL WILLOW CAN MAKE YOU SMALL...
...WE COULD AT LEAST MAKE YOUR STUFF... BUT WAIT THOUGH --
I CAN'T BELIEVE IT!
HOAH NOW --
PLEASE LET MY BOOTS BE IN HERE ---
AHH! MAN DOWN!
UH, XANDER?
I DN'T LFF YOU HNYMORE.

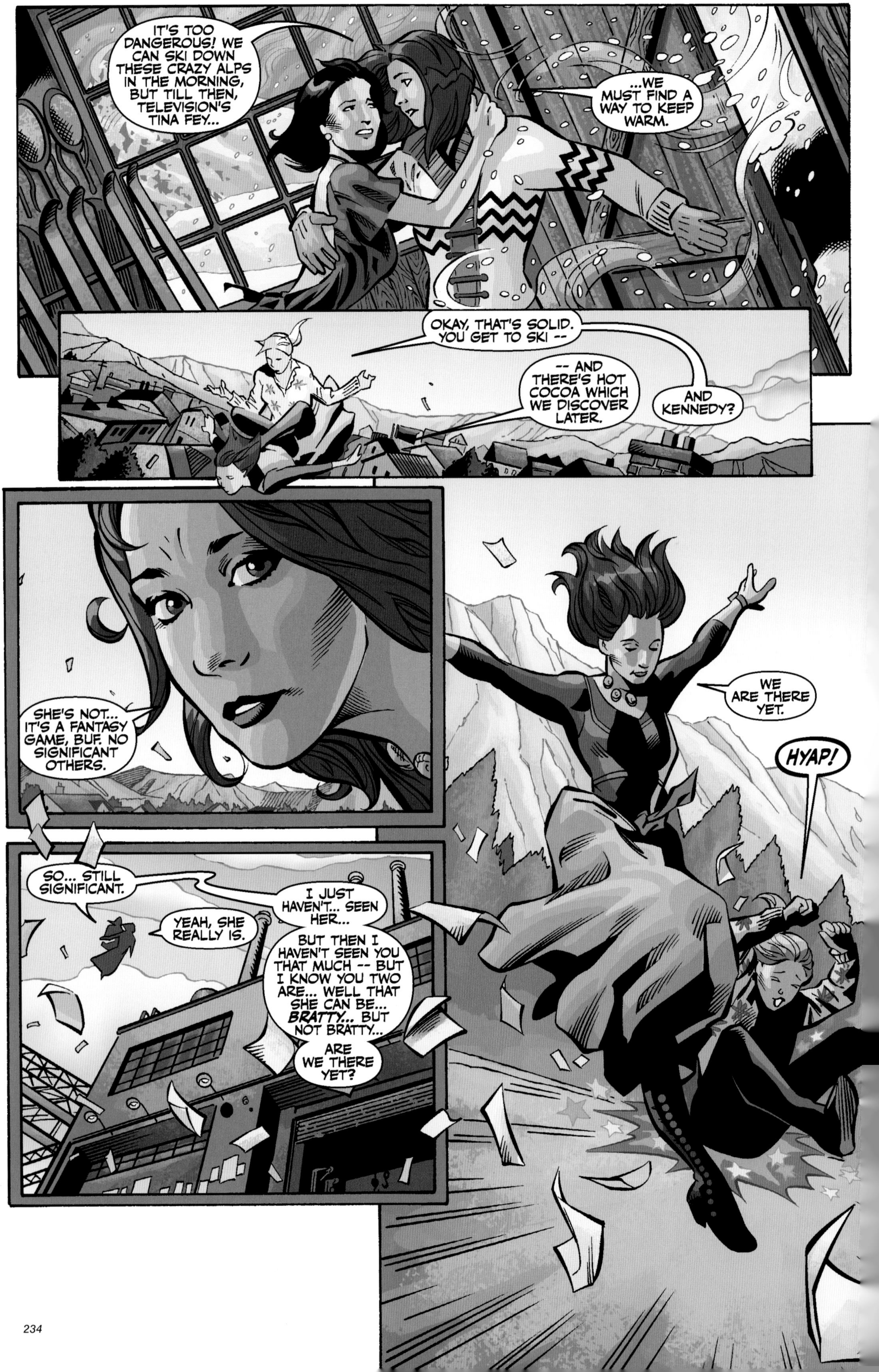
IT'S TOO DANGEROUS! WE CAN SKI DOWN THESE CRAZY ALPS IN THE MORNING, BUT TILL THEN, TELEVISION'S TINA FEY...
...WE MUST FIND A WAY TO KEEP WARM.
OKAY, THAT'S SOLID. YOU GET TO SKI --
-- AND THERE'S HOT COCOA WHICH WE DISCOVER LATER.
AND KENNEDY?
SHE'S NOT... IT'S A FANTASY GAME, BUF. NO SIGNIFICANT OTHERS.
SO... STILL SIGNIFICANT.
YEAH, SHE REALLY IS.
I JUST HAVEN'T... SEEN HER...
BUT THEN I HAVEN'T SEEN YOU THAT MUCH -- BUT I KNOW YOU TWO ARE... WELL THAT SHE CAN BE... BRATTY... BUT NOT BRATTY...
ARE WE THERE YET?
WE ARE THERE YET.
HYAP!

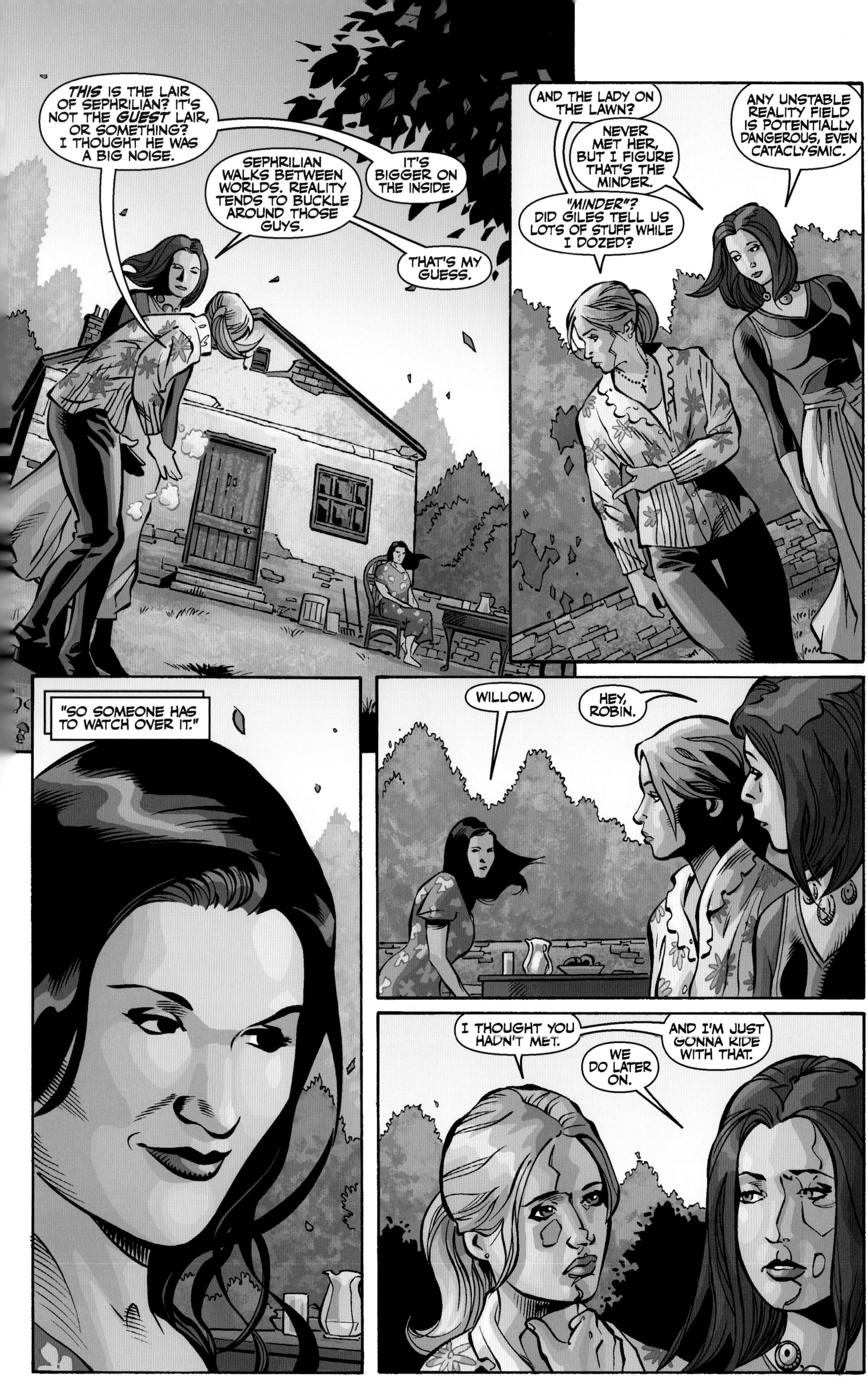
THIS IS THE LAIR OF SEPHRILIAN? IT'S NOT THE GUEST LAIR, OR SOMETHING? I THOUGHT HE WAS A BIG NOISE.
IT'S BIGGER ON THE INSIDE.
SEPHRILIAN WALKS BETWEEN WORLDS. REALITY TENDS TO BUCKLE AROUND THOSE GUYS.
THAT'S MY GUESS.
AND THE LADY ON THE LAWN?
NEVER MET HER, BUT I FIGURE THAT'S THE MINDER.
"MINDER"? DID GILES TELL US LOTS OF STUFF WHILE I DOZED?
ANY UNSTABLE REALITY FIELD IS POTENTIALLY DANGEROUS, EVEN CATACLYSMIC.
"SO SOMEONE HAS TO WATCH OVER IT."
WILLOW.
HEY, ROBIN.
I THOUGHT YOU HADN'T MET.
WE DO LATER ON.
AND I'M JUST GONNA RIDE WITH THAT.

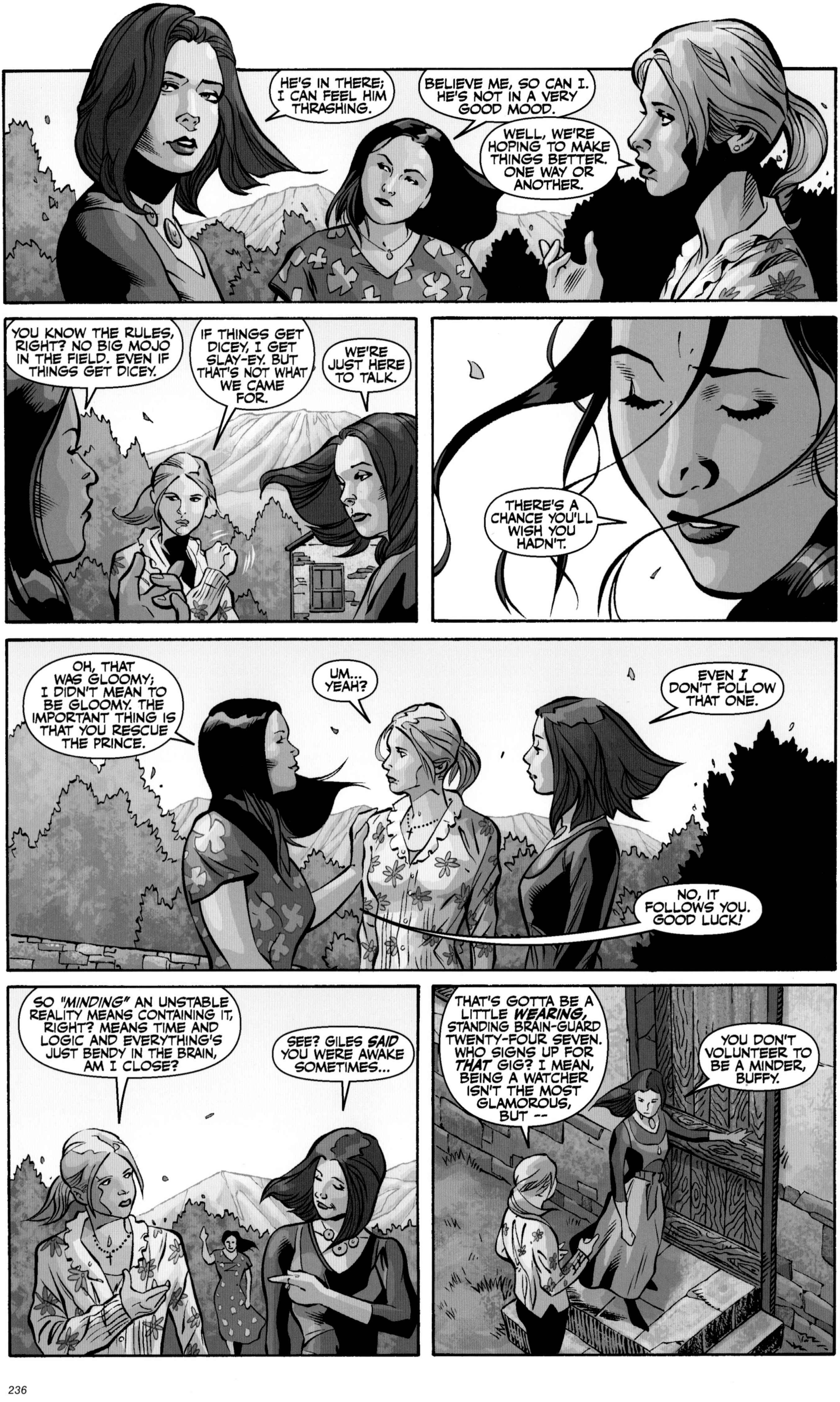
HE'S IN THERE; I CAN FEEL HIM THRASHING.
BELIEVE ME, SO CAN I. HE'S NOT IN A VERY GOOD MOOD.
WELL, WE'RE HOPING TO MAKE THINGS BETTER. ONE WAY OR ANOTHER.
YOU KNOW THE RULES, RIGHT? NO BIG MOJO IN THE FIELD. EVEN IF THINGS GET DICEY.
IF THINGS GET DICEY, I GET SLAY-EY. BUT THAT'S NOT WHAT WE CAME FOR.
WE'RE JUST HERE TO TALK.
THERE'S A CHANCE YOU'LL WISH YOU HADN'T.
OH, THAT WAS GLOOMY; I DIDN'T MEAN TO BE GLOOMY. THE IMPORTANT THING IS THAT YOU RESCUE THE PRINCE.
UM... YEAH?
EVEN I DON'T FOLLOW THAT ONE.
NO, IT FOLLOWS YOU. GOOD LUCK!
SO "MINDING" AN UNSTABLE REALITY MEANS CONTAINING IT, RIGHT? MEANS TIME AND LOGIC AND EVERYTHING'S JUST BENDY IN THE BRAIN, AM I CLOSE?
SEE? GILES SAID YOU WERE AWAKE SOMETIMES...
THAT'S GOTTA BE A LITTLE WEARING, STANDING BRAIN-GUARD TWENTY-FOUR SEVEN. WHO SIGNS UP FOR THAT GIG? I MEAN, BEING A WATCHER ISN'T THE MOST GLAMOROUS, BUT --
YOU DON'T VOLUNTEER TO BE A MINDER, BUFFY.

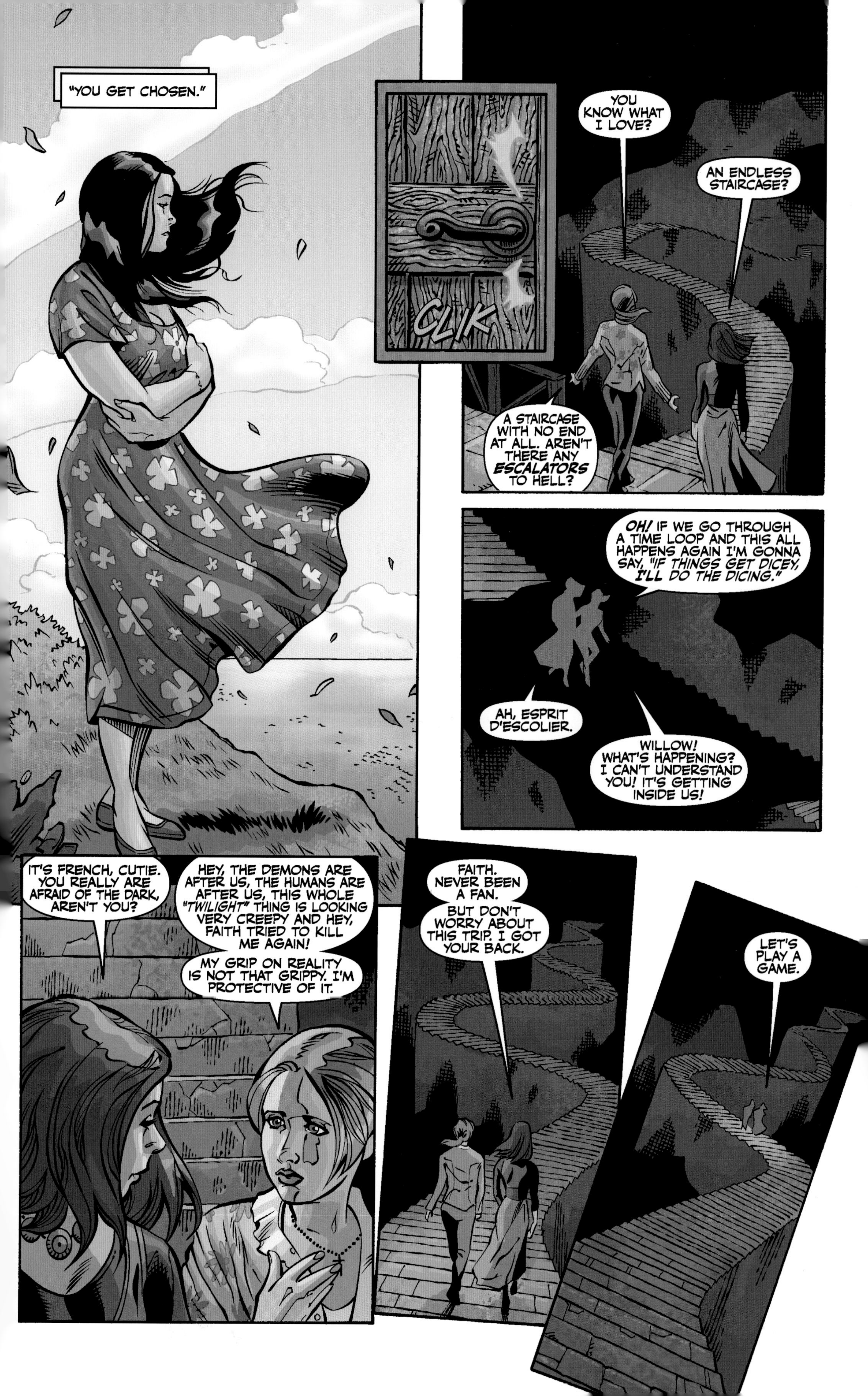
"YOU GET CHOSEN."
CLIK
YOU KNOW WHAT I LOVE?
AN ENDLESS STAIRCASE?
A STAIRCASE WITH NO END AT ALL. AREN'T THERE ANY *ESCALATORS* TO HELL?
OH! IF WE GO THROUGH A TIME LOOP AND THIS ALL HAPPENS AGAIN I'M GONNA SAY, *"IF THINGS GET DICEY,* ***I'LL*** *DO THE DICING."*
AH, ESPRIT D'ESCOLIER.
WILLOW! WHAT'S HAPPENING? I CAN'T UNDERSTAND YOU! IT'S GETTING INSIDE US!
IT'S FRENCH, CUTIE. YOU REALLY ARE AFRAID OF THE DARK, AREN'T YOU?
HEY, THE DEMONS ARE AFTER US, THE HUMANS ARE AFTER US, THIS WHOLE *"TWILIGHT"* THING IS LOOKING VERY CREEPY AND HEY, FAITH TRIED TO KILL ME AGAIN!
MY GRIP ON REALITY IS NOT THAT GRIPPY. I'M PROTECTIVE OF IT.
FAITH. NEVER BEEN A FAN.
BUT DON'T WORRY ABOUT THIS TRIP. I GOT YOUR BACK.
LET'S PLAY A GAME.

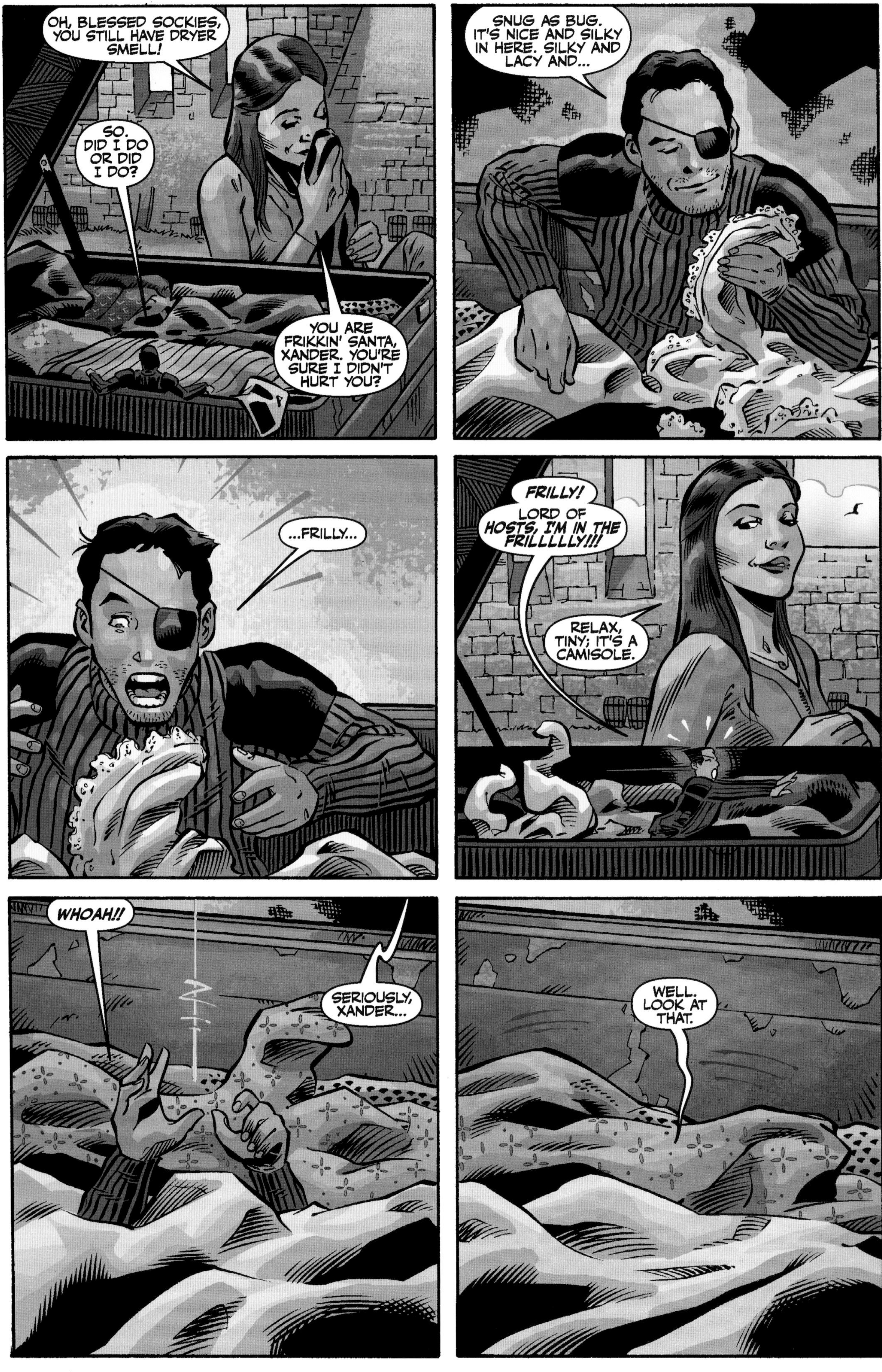
OH, BLESSED SOCKIES, YOU STILL HAVE DRYER SMELL!
SO. DID I DO OR DID I DO?
YOU ARE FRIKKIN' SANTA, XANDER. YOU'RE SURE I DIDN'T HURT YOU?
SNUG AS BUG. IT'S NICE AND SILKY IN HERE. SILKY AND LACY AND...
...FRILLY...
FRILLY! LORD OF HOSTS, I'M IN THE FRILLLLLLY!!!
RELAX, TINY; IT'S A CAMISOLE.
WHOAH!!
SERIOUSLY, XANDER...
WELL. LOOK AT THAT.

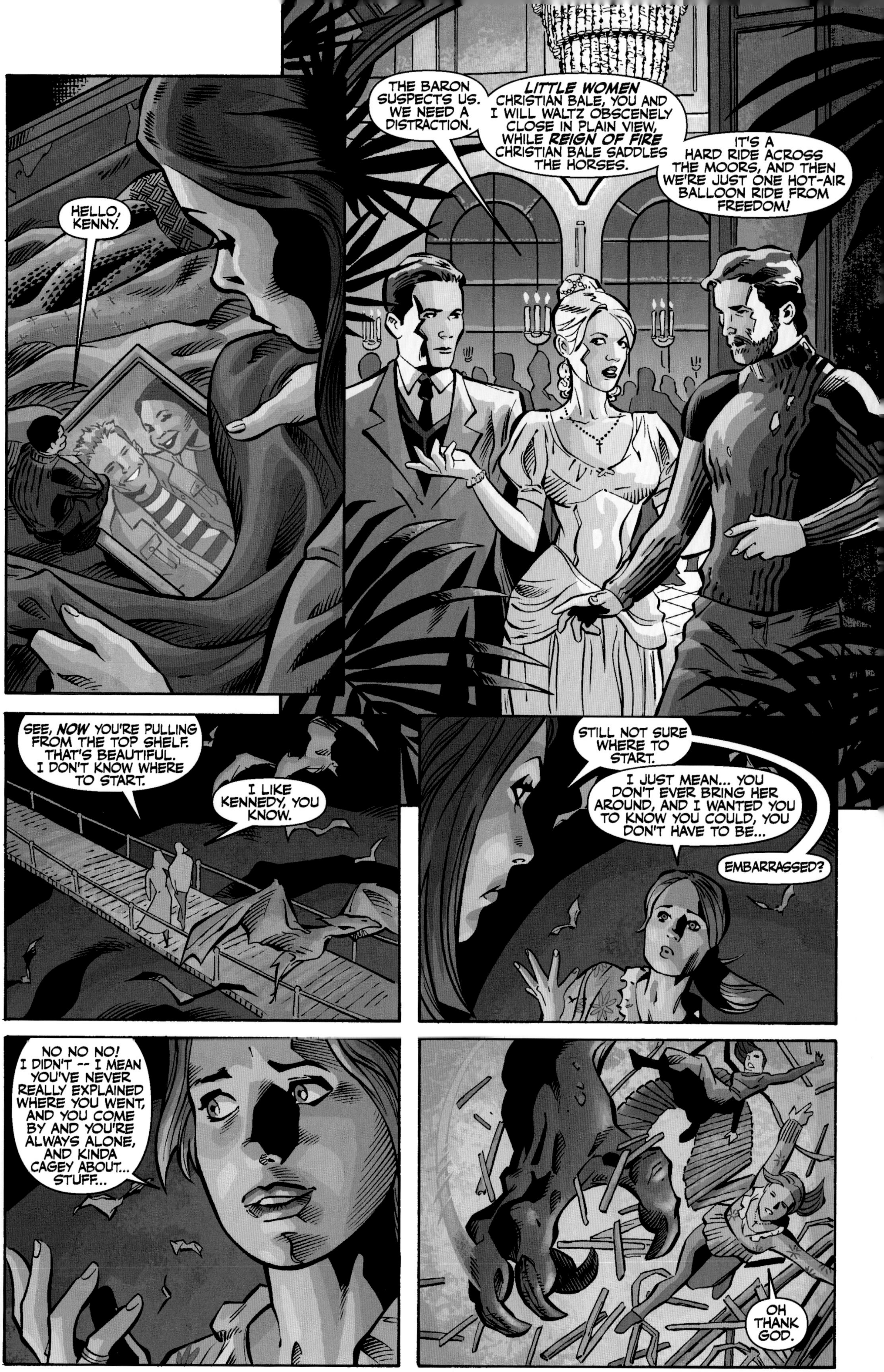
HELLO, KENNY.
THE BARON SUSPECTS US. WE NEED A DISTRACTION.
LITTLE WOMEN CHRISTIAN BALE, YOU AND I WILL WALTZ OBSCENELY CLOSE IN PLAIN VIEW, WHILE REIGN OF FIRE CHRISTIAN BALE SADDLES THE HORSES.
IT'S A HARD RIDE ACROSS THE MOORS, AND THEN WE'RE JUST ONE HOT-AIR BALLOON RIDE FROM FREEDOM!
SEE, NOW YOU'RE PULLING FROM THE TOP SHELF. THAT'S BEAUTIFUL. I DON'T KNOW WHERE TO START.
I LIKE KENNEDY, YOU KNOW.
STILL NOT SURE WHERE TO START.
I JUST MEAN... YOU DON'T EVER BRING HER AROUND, AND I WANTED YOU TO KNOW YOU COULD, YOU DON'T HAVE TO BE...
EMBARRASSED?
NO NO NO! I DIDN'T -- I MEAN YOU'VE NEVER REALLY EXPLAINED WHERE YOU WENT, AND YOU COME BY AND YOU'RE ALWAYS ALONE, AND KINDA CAGEY ABOUT... STUFF...
OH THANK GOD.

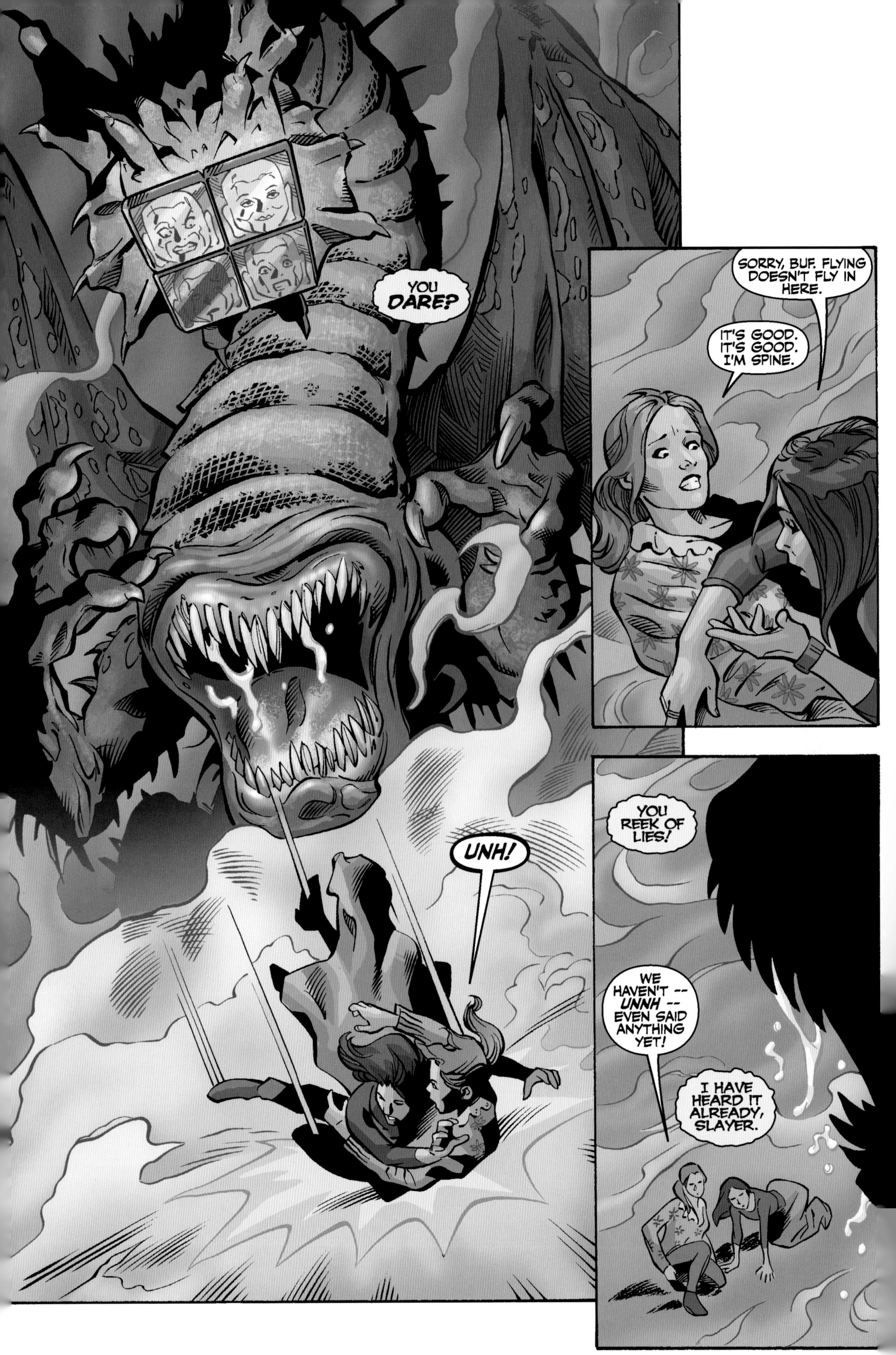
YOU DARE?
SORRY, BUF. FLYING DOESN'T FLY IN HERE.
IT'S GOOD. IT'S GOOD. I'M SPINE.
UNH!
YOU REEK OF LIES!
WE HAVEN'T -- UNNH -- EVEN SAID ANYTHING YET!
I HAVE HEARD IT ALREADY, SLAYER.

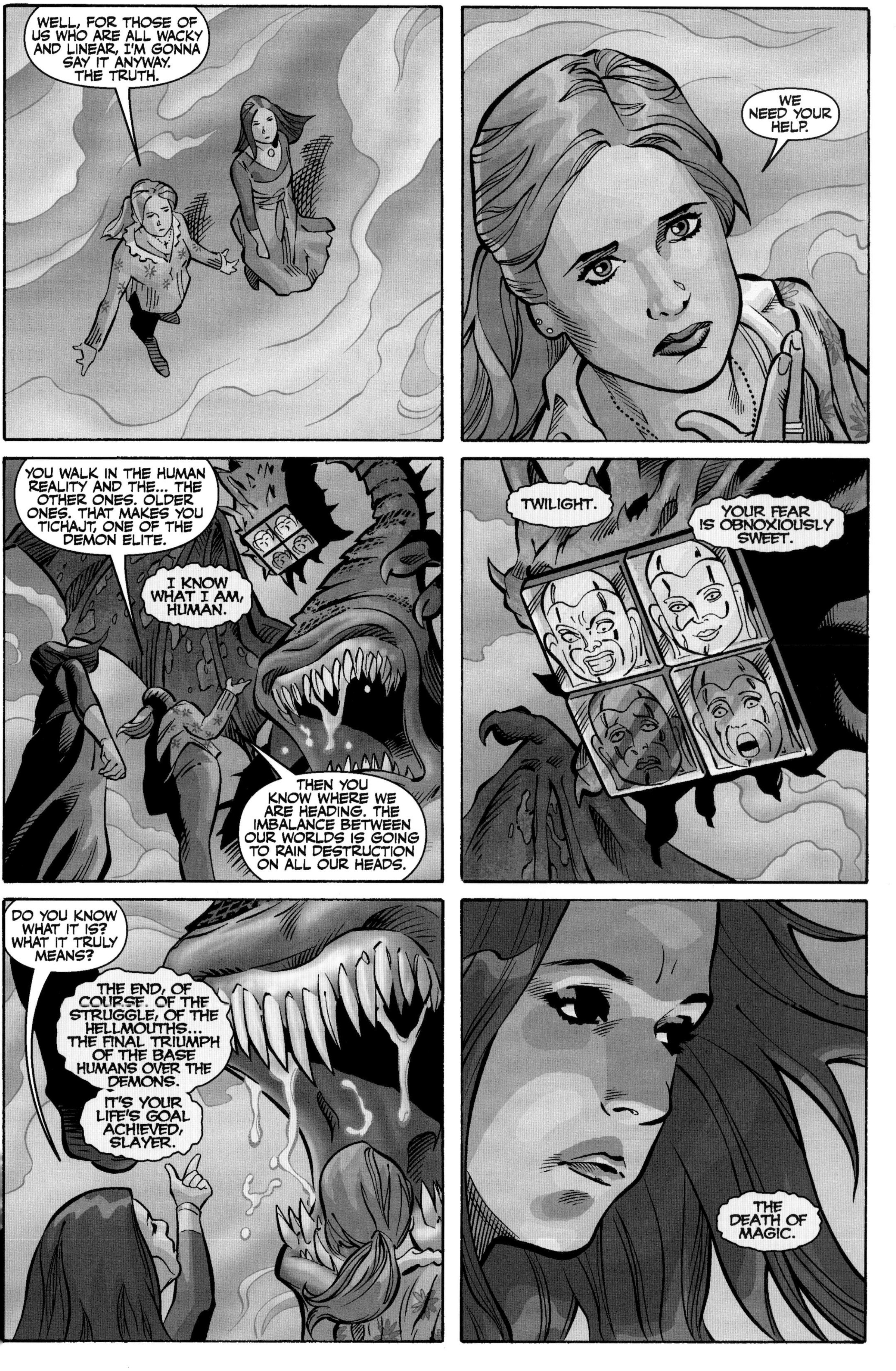
WELL, FOR THOSE OF US WHO ARE ALL WACKY AND LINEAR, I'M GONNA SAY IT ANYWAY. THE TRUTH.
WE NEED YOUR HELP.
YOU WALK IN THE HUMAN REALITY AND THE... THE OTHER ONES. OLDER ONES. THAT MAKES YOU TICHAJT, ONE OF THE DEMON ELITE.
I KNOW WHAT I AM, HUMAN.
THEN YOU KNOW WHERE WE ARE HEADING. THE IMBALANCE BETWEEN OUR WORLDS IS GOING TO RAIN DESTRUCTION ON ALL OUR HEADS.
TWILIGHT.
YOUR FEAR IS OBNOXIOUSLY SWEET.
DO YOU KNOW WHAT IT IS? WHAT IT TRULY MEANS?
THE END, OF COURSE. OF THE STRUGGLE, OF THE HELLMOUTHS... THE FINAL TRIUMPH OF THE BASE HUMANS OVER THE DEMONS.
IT'S YOUR LIFE'S GOAL ACHIEVED, SLAYER.
THE DEATH OF MAGIC.

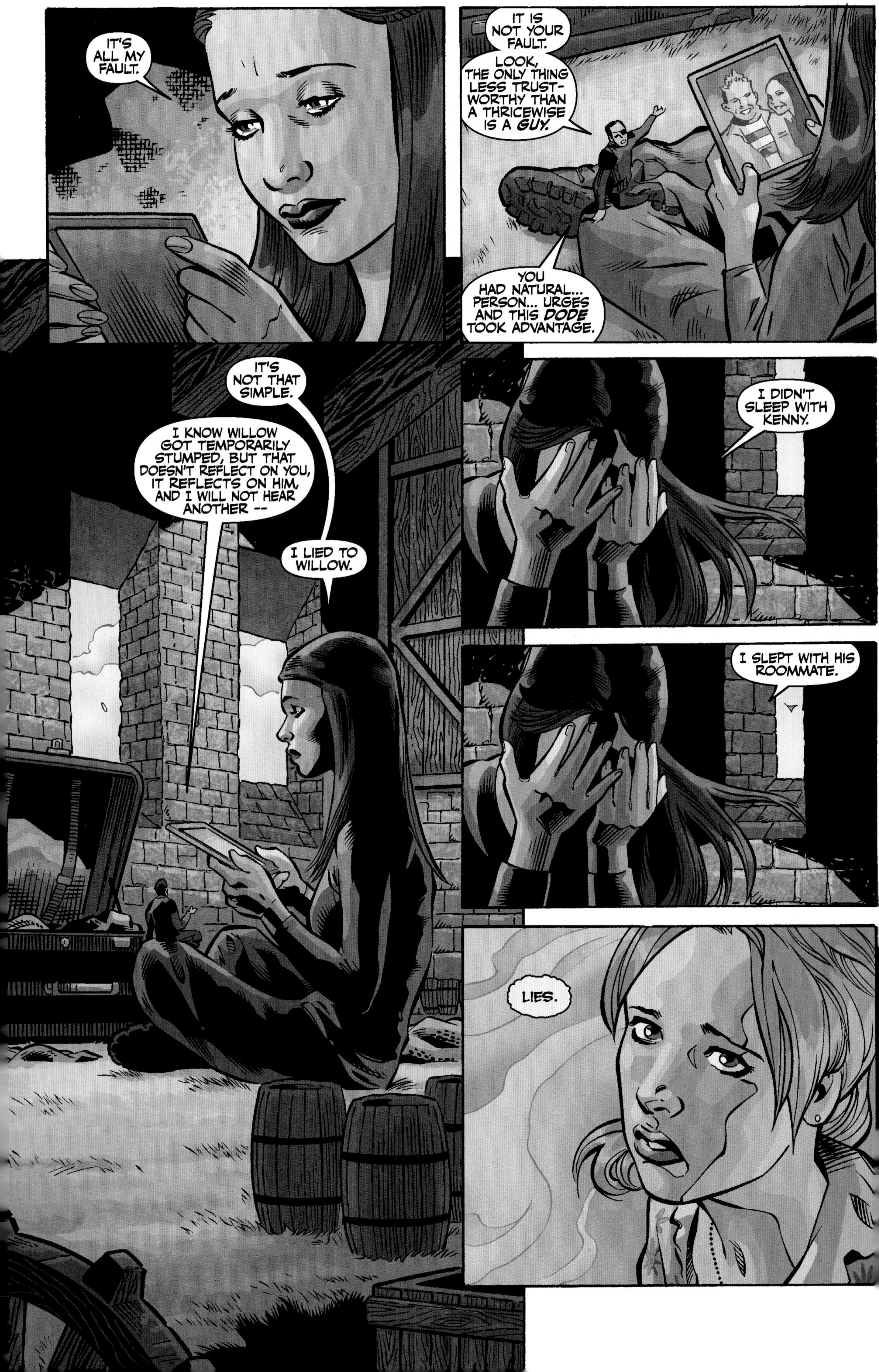
IT'S ALL MY FAULT.
IT IS NOT YOUR FAULT.
LOOK, THE ONLY THING LESS TRUST-WORTHY THAN A THRICEWISE IS A *GUY.*
YOU HAD NATURAL... PERSON... URGES AND THIS *DODE* TOOK ADVANTAGE.
IT'S NOT THAT SIMPLE.
I KNOW WILLOW GOT TEMPORARILY STUMPED, BUT THAT DOESN'T REFLECT ON YOU, IT REFLECTS ON HIM, AND I WILL NOT HEAR ANOTHER --
I LIED TO WILLOW.
I DIDN'T SLEEP WITH KENNY.
I SLEPT WITH HIS ROOMMATE.
LIES.

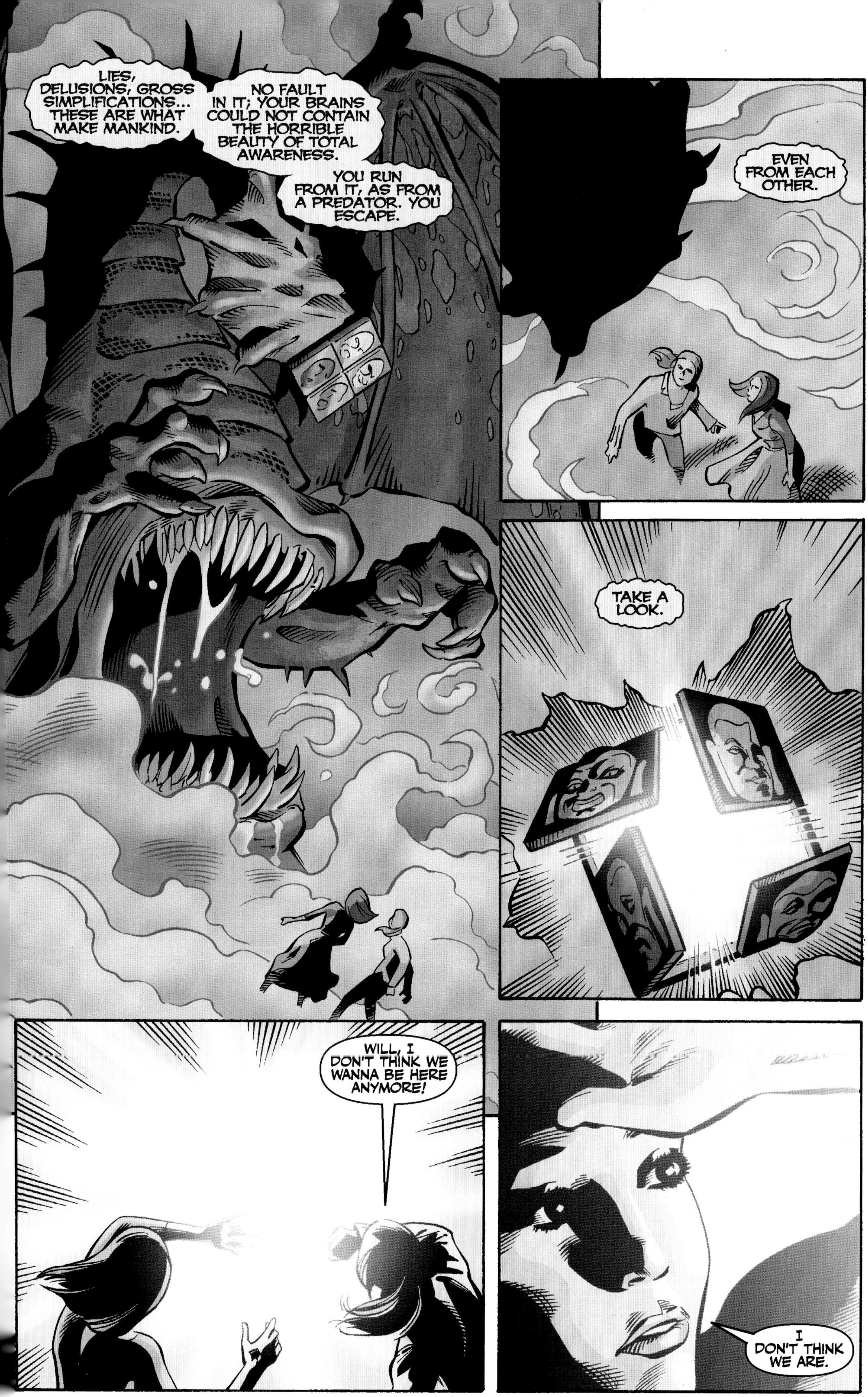
LIES, DELUSIONS, GROSS SIMPLIFICATIONS... THESE ARE WHAT MAKE MANKIND.
NO FAULT IN IT; YOUR BRAINS COULD NOT CONTAIN THE HORRIBLE BEAUTY OF TOTAL AWARENESS.
YOU RUN FROM IT, AS FROM A PREDATOR. YOU ESCAPE.
EVEN FROM EACH OTHER.
TAKE A LOOK.
WILL, I DON'T THINK WE WANNA BE HERE ANYMORE!
I DON'T THINK WE ARE.

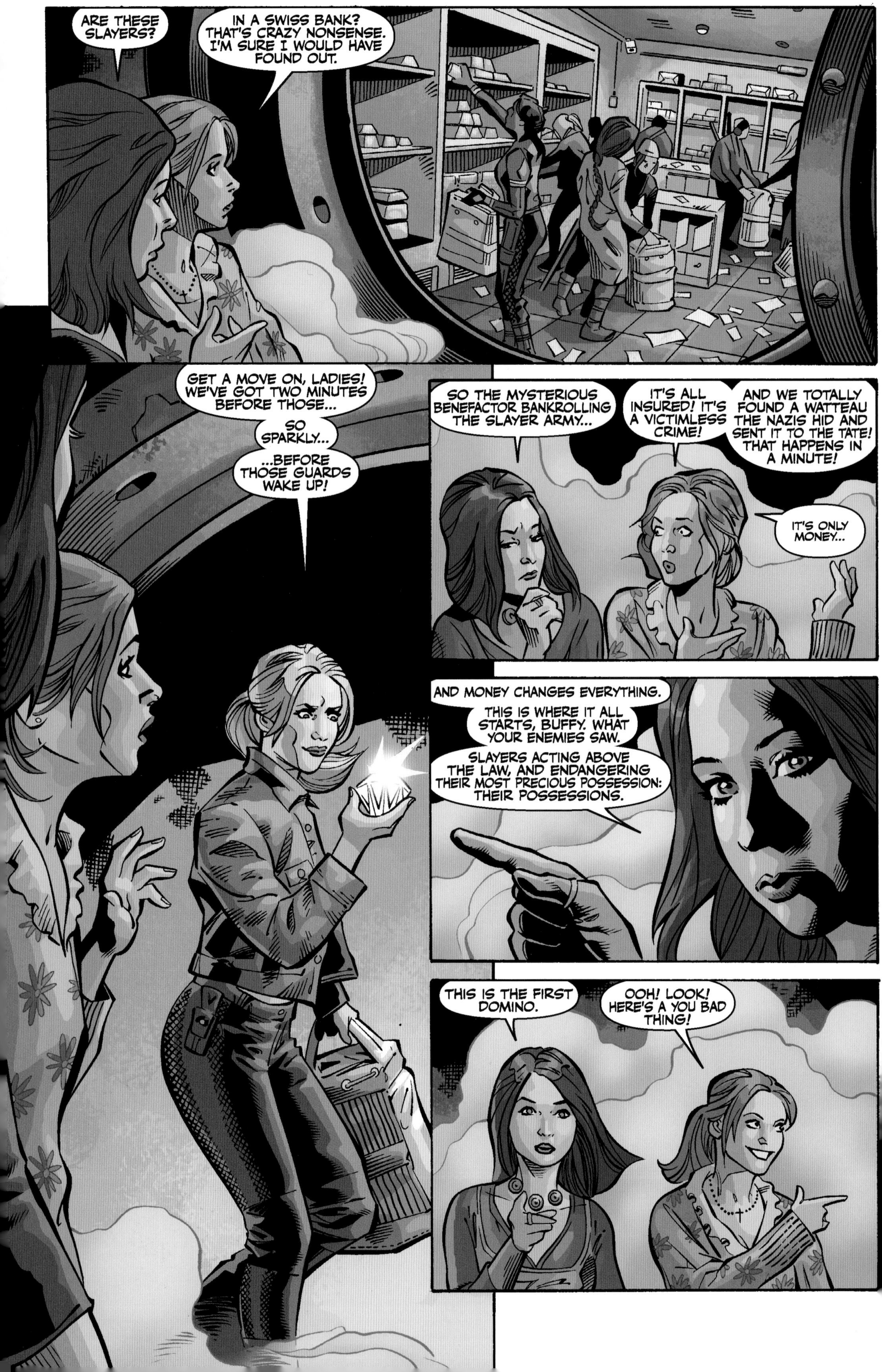
ARE THESE SLAYERS?
IN A SWISS BANK? THAT'S CRAZY NONSENSE. I'M SURE I WOULD HAVE FOUND OUT.
GET A MOVE ON, LADIES! WE'VE GOT TWO MINUTES BEFORE THOSE...
SO SPARKLY...
...BEFORE THOSE GUARDS WAKE UP!
SO THE MYSTERIOUS BENEFACTOR BANKROLLING THE SLAYER ARMY...
IT'S ALL INSURED! IT'S A VICTIMLESS CRIME!
AND WE TOTALLY FOUND A WATTEAU THE NAZIS HID AND SENT IT TO THE TATE! THAT HAPPENS IN A MINUTE!
IT'S ONLY MONEY...
AND MONEY CHANGES EVERYTHING.
THIS IS WHERE IT ALL STARTS, BUFFY. WHAT YOUR ENEMIES SAW.
SLAYERS ACTING ABOVE THE LAW, AND ENDANGERING THEIR MOST PRECIOUS POSSESSION: THEIR POSSESSIONS.
THIS IS THE FIRST DOMINO.
OOH! LOOK! HERE'S A YOU BAD THING!

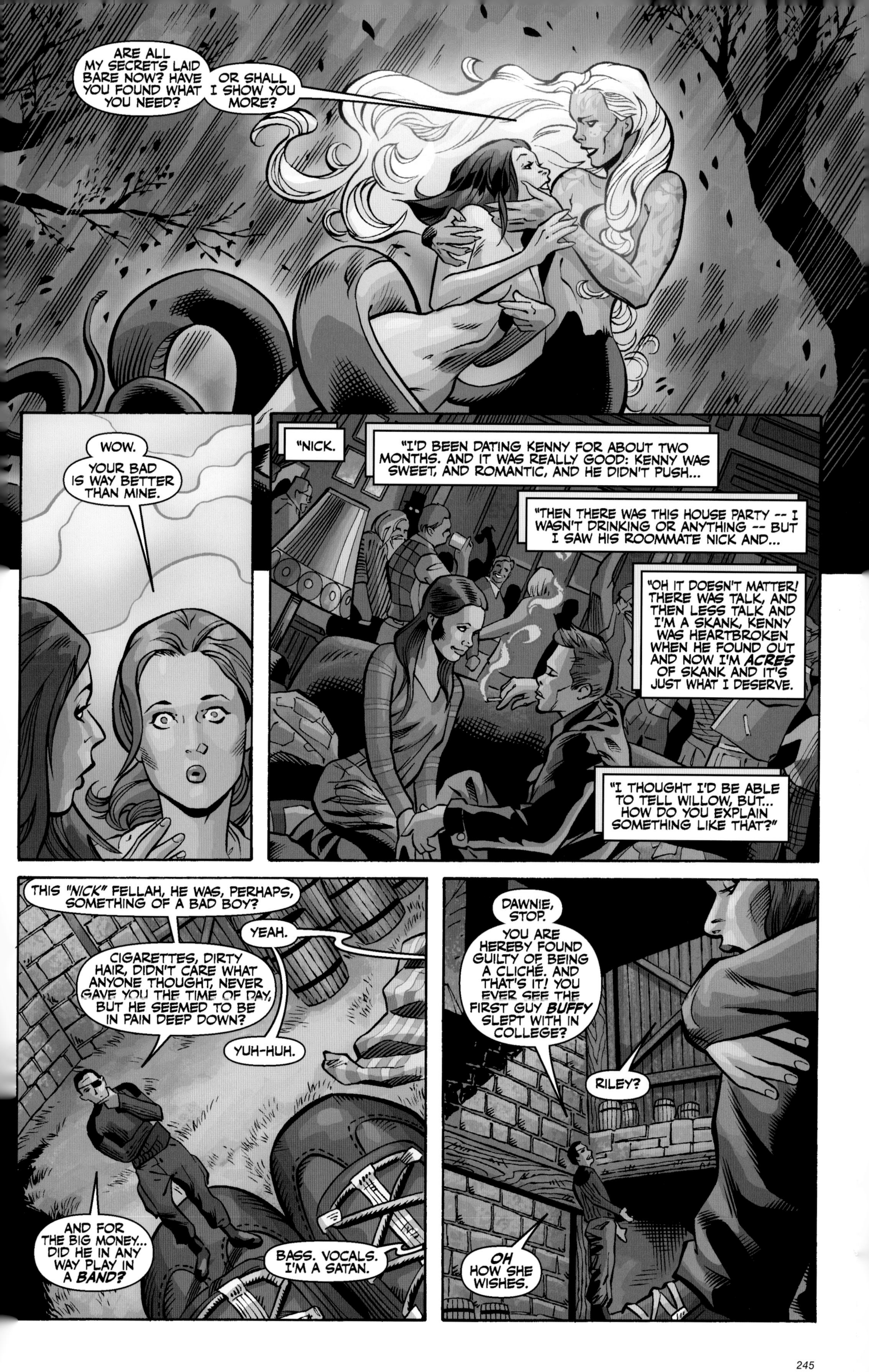
ARE ALL MY SECRETS LAID BARE NOW? HAVE YOU FOUND WHAT YOU NEED?
OR SHALL I SHOW YOU MORE?
WOW.
YOUR BAD IS WAY BETTER THAN MINE.
"NICK.
"I'D BEEN DATING KENNY FOR ABOUT TWO MONTHS. AND IT WAS REALLY GOOD: KENNY WAS SWEET, AND ROMANTIC, AND HE DIDN'T PUSH...
"THEN THERE WAS THIS HOUSE PARTY -- I WASN'T DRINKING OR ANYTHING -- BUT I SAW HIS ROOMMATE NICK AND...
"OH IT DOESN'T MATTER! THERE WAS TALK, AND THEN LESS TALK AND I'M A SKANK, KENNY WAS HEARTBROKEN WHEN HE FOUND OUT AND NOW I'M *ACRES* OF SKANK AND IT'S JUST WHAT I DESERVE.
"I THOUGHT I'D BE ABLE TO TELL WILLOW, BUT... HOW DO YOU EXPLAIN SOMETHING LIKE THAT?"
THIS *"NICK"* FELLAH, HE WAS, PERHAPS, SOMETHING OF A BAD BOY?
YEAH.
CIGARETTES, DIRTY HAIR, DIDN'T CARE WHAT ANYONE THOUGHT, NEVER GAVE YOU THE TIME OF DAY, BUT HE SEEMED TO BE IN PAIN DEEP DOWN?
YUH-HUH.
AND FOR THE BIG MONEY... DID HE IN ANY WAY PLAY IN A *BAND?*
BASS. VOCALS. I'M A SATAN.
DAWNIE, STOP.
YOU ARE HEREBY FOUND GUILTY OF BEING A CLICHÉ. AND THAT'S IT! YOU EVER SEE THE FIRST GUY *BUFFY* SLEPT WITH IN COLLEGE?
RILEY?
OH HOW SHE WISHES.

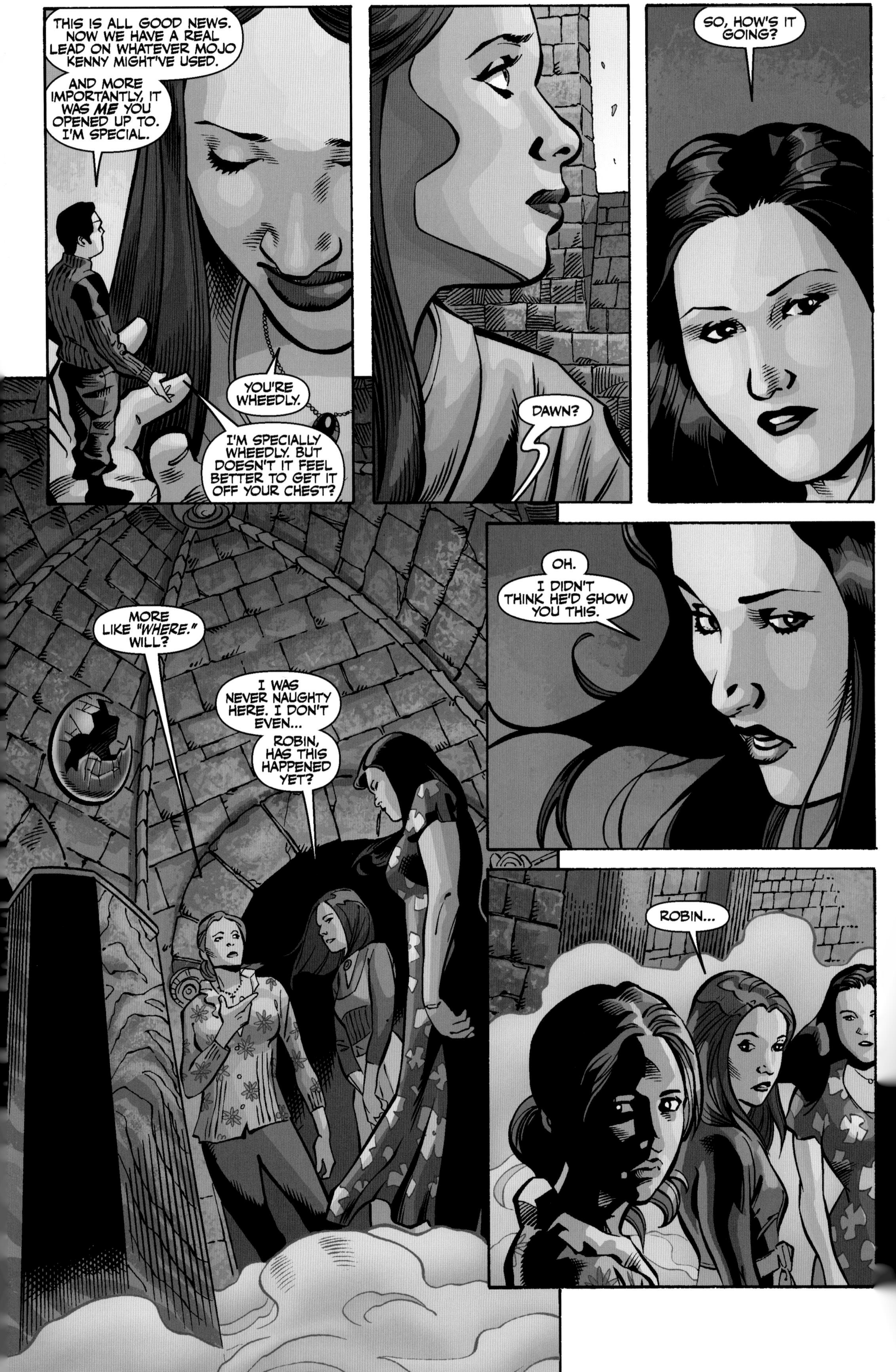
THIS IS ALL GOOD NEWS. NOW WE HAVE A REAL LEAD ON WHATEVER MOJO KENNY MIGHT'VE USED.
AND MORE IMPORTANTLY, IT WAS *ME* YOU OPENED UP TO. I'M SPECIAL.
YOU'RE WHEEDLY.
I'M SPECIALLY WHEEDLY. BUT DOESN'T IT FEEL BETTER TO GET IT OFF YOUR CHEST?
DAWN?
SO, HOW'S IT GOING?
MORE LIKE "WHERE." WILL?
I WAS NEVER NAUGHTY HERE. I DON'T EVEN...
ROBIN, HAS THIS HAPPENED YET?
OH.
I DIDN'T THINK HE'D SHOW YOU THIS.
ROBIN...

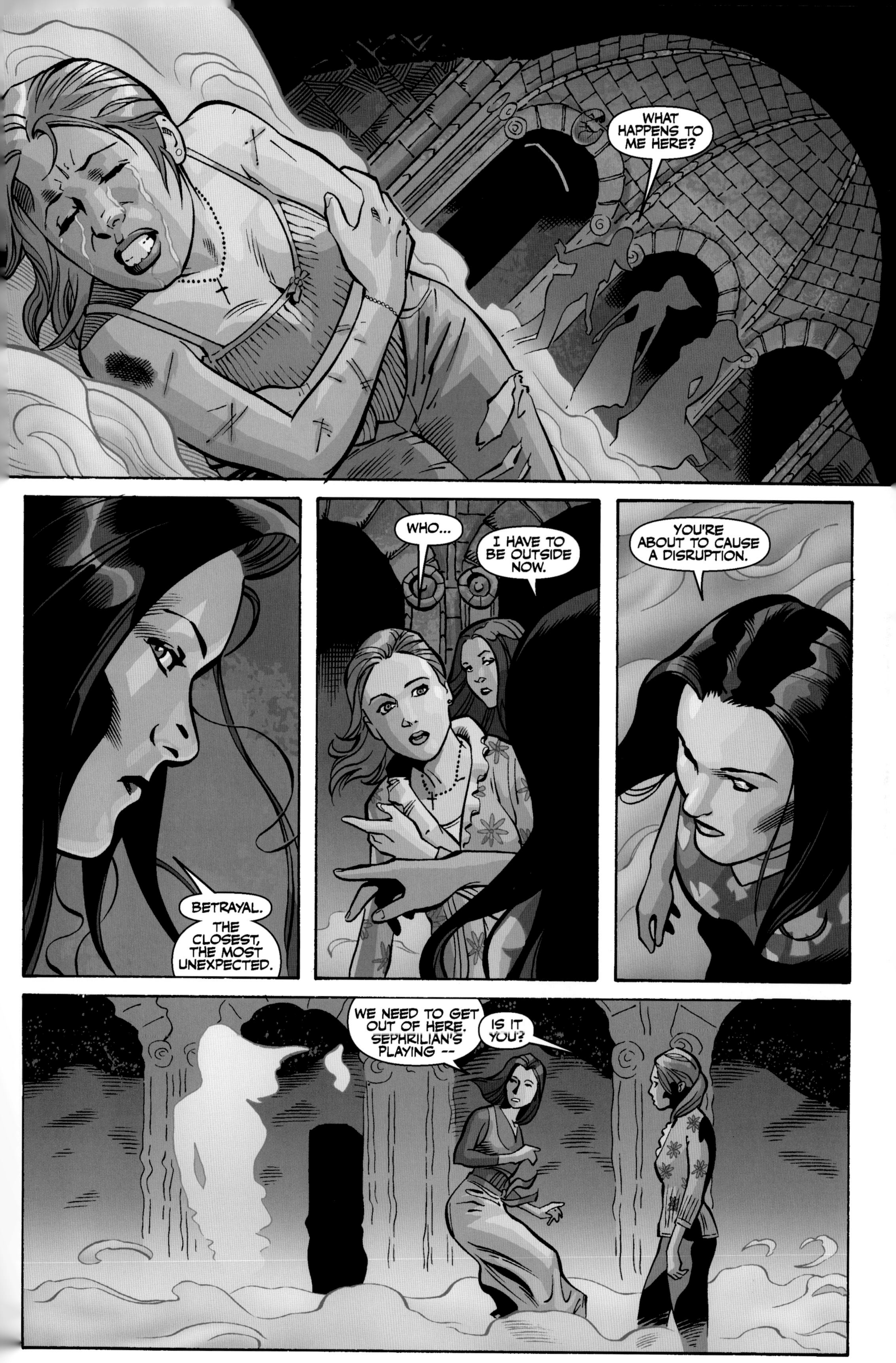
WHAT HAPPENS TO ME HERE?
BETRAYAL. THE CLOSEST, THE MOST UNEXPECTED.
WHO...
I HAVE TO BE OUTSIDE NOW.
YOU'RE ABOUT TO CAUSE A DISRUPTION.
WE NEED TO GET OUT OF HERE. SEPHRILIAN'S PLAYING --
IS IT YOU?

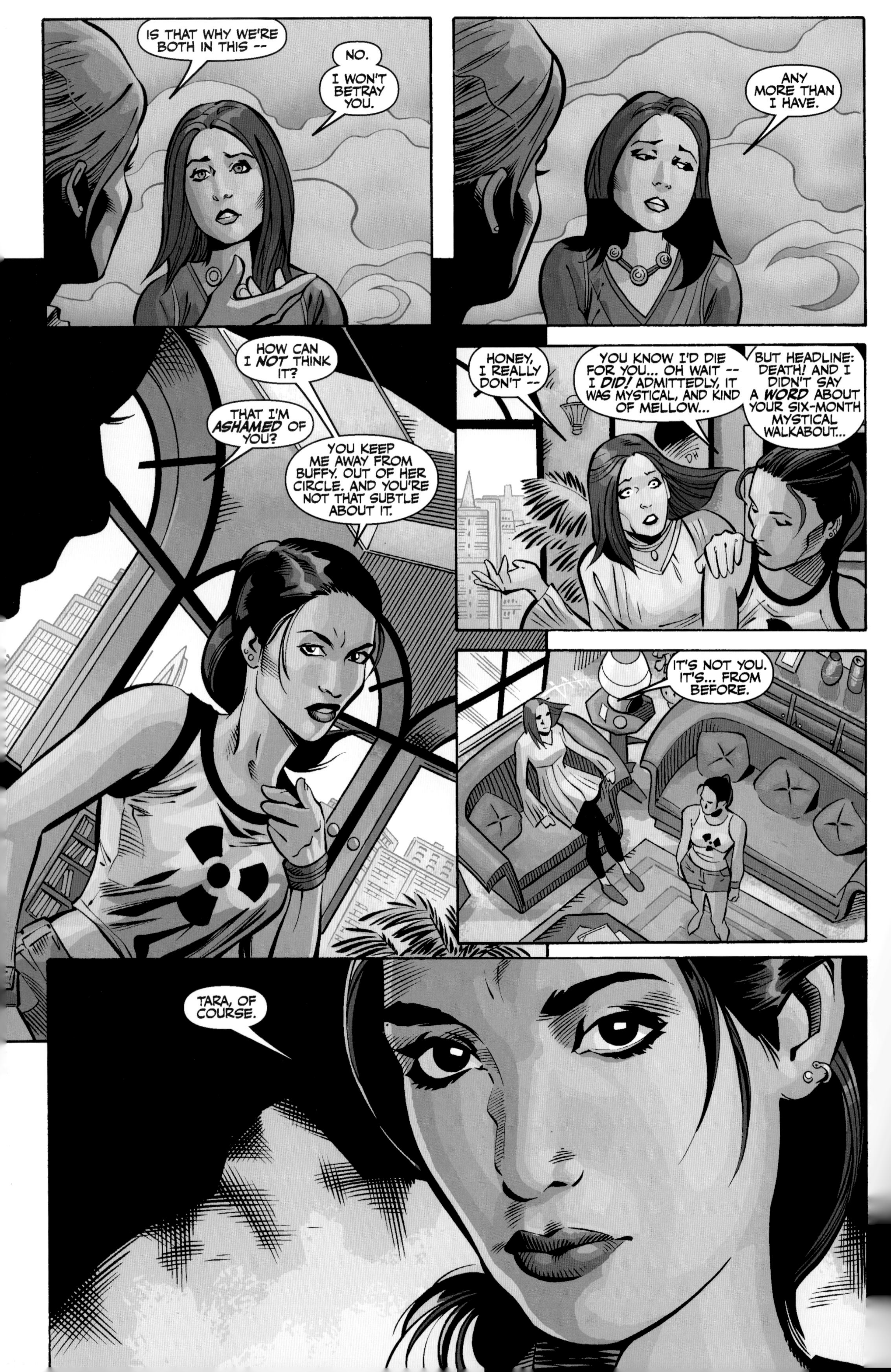
IS THAT WHY WE'RE BOTH IN THIS --
NO. I WON'T BETRAY YOU.
ANY MORE THAN I HAVE.
HOW CAN I NOT THINK IT?
THAT I'M ASHAMED OF YOU?
YOU KEEP ME AWAY FROM BUFFY. OUT OF HER CIRCLE. AND YOU'RE NOT THAT SUBTLE ABOUT IT.
HONEY, I REALLY DON'T --
YOU KNOW I'D DIE FOR YOU... OH WAIT -- I DID! ADMITTEDLY, IT WAS MYSTICAL, AND KIND OF MELLOW...
BUT HEADLINE: DEATH! AND I DIDN'T SAY A WORD ABOUT YOUR SIX-MONTH MYSTICAL WALKABOUT...
IT'S NOT YOU. IT'S... FROM BEFORE.
TARA, OF COURSE.

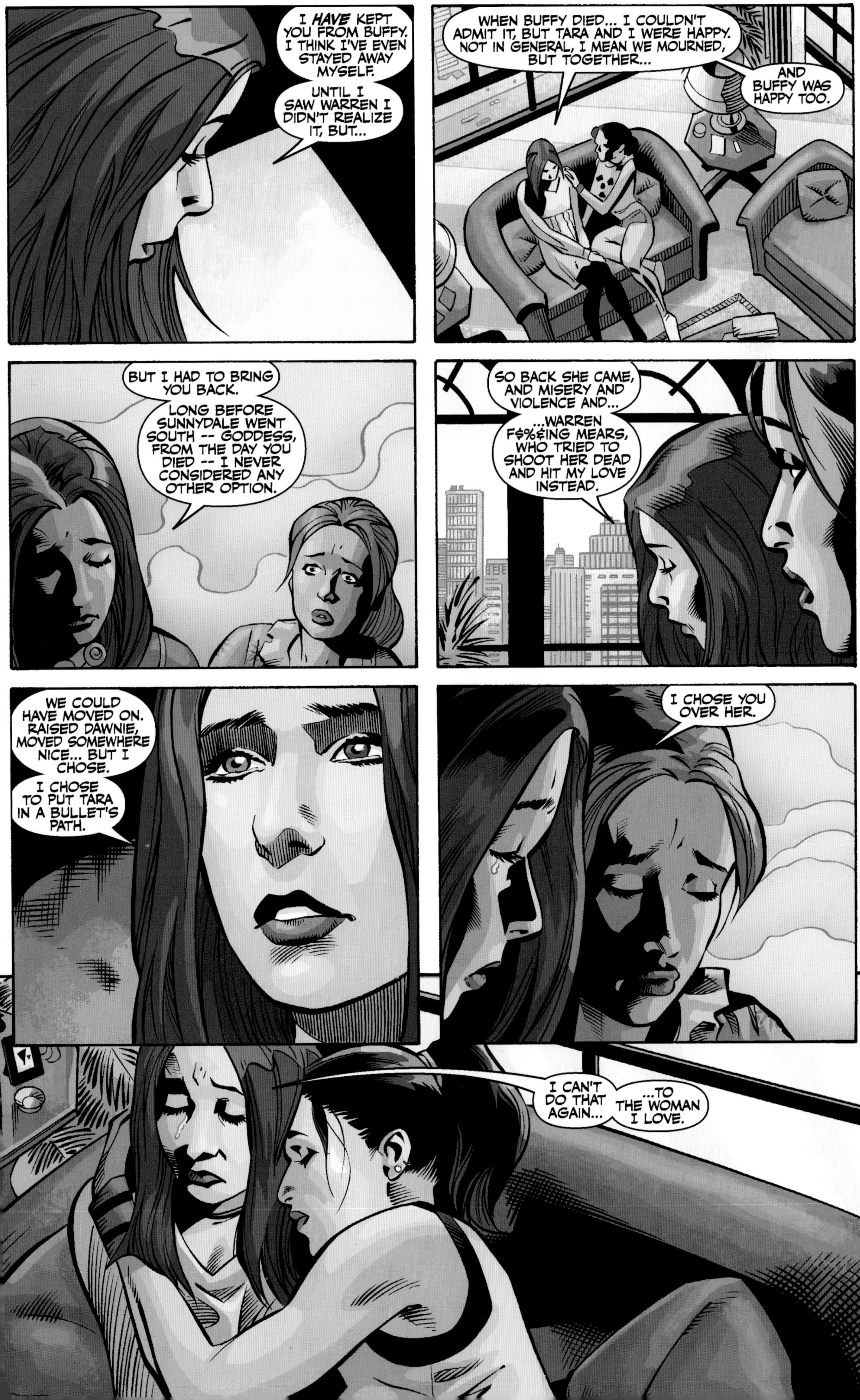
I HAVE KEPT YOU FROM BUFFY. I THINK I'VE EVEN STAYED AWAY MYSELF.
UNTIL I SAW WARREN I DIDN'T REALIZE IT, BUT...
WHEN BUFFY DIED... I COULDN'T ADMIT IT, BUT TARA AND I WERE HAPPY. NOT IN GENERAL, I MEAN WE MOURNED, BUT TOGETHER...
AND BUFFY WAS HAPPY TOO.
BUT I HAD TO BRING YOU BACK.
LONG BEFORE SUNNYDALE WENT SOUTH -- GODDESS, FROM THE DAY YOU DIED -- I NEVER CONSIDERED ANY OTHER OPTION.
SO BACK SHE CAME, AND MISERY AND VIOLENCE AND...
...WARREN F$%&ING MEARS, WHO TRIED TO SHOOT HER DEAD AND HIT MY LOVE INSTEAD.
WE COULD HAVE MOVED ON. RAISED DAWNIE, MOVED SOMEWHERE NICE... BUT I CHOSE.
I CHOSE TO PUT TARA IN A BULLET'S PATH.
I CHOSE YOU OVER HER.
I CAN'T DO THAT AGAIN...
...TO THE WOMAN I LOVE.

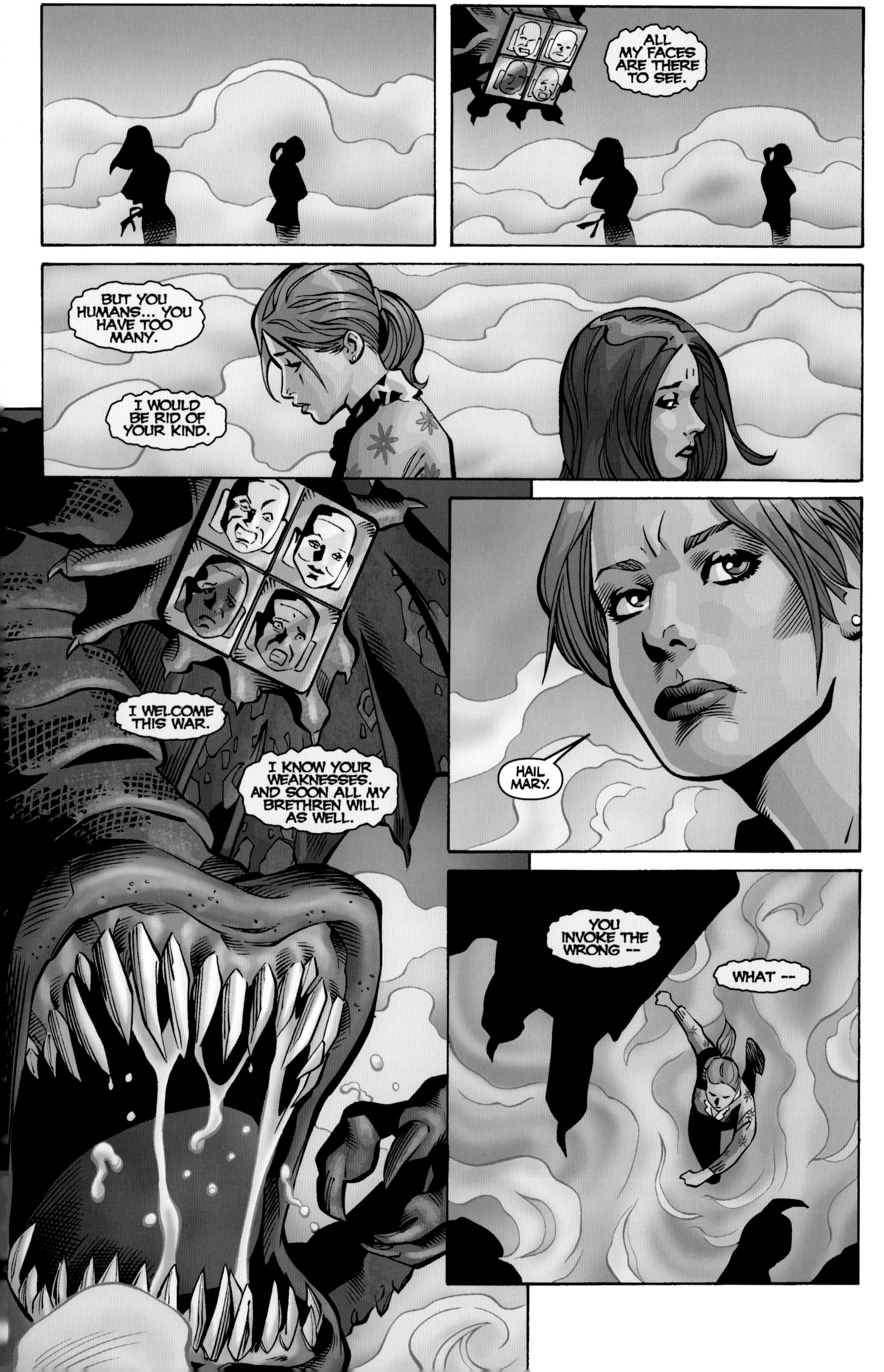
ALL MY FACES ARE THERE TO SEE.
BUT YOU HUMANS... YOU HAVE TOO MANY.
I WOULD BE RID OF YOUR KIND.
I WELCOME THIS WAR.
I KNOW YOUR WEAKNESSES. AND SOON ALL MY BRETHREN WILL AS WELL.
HAIL MARY.
YOU INVOKE THE WRONG --
WHAT --

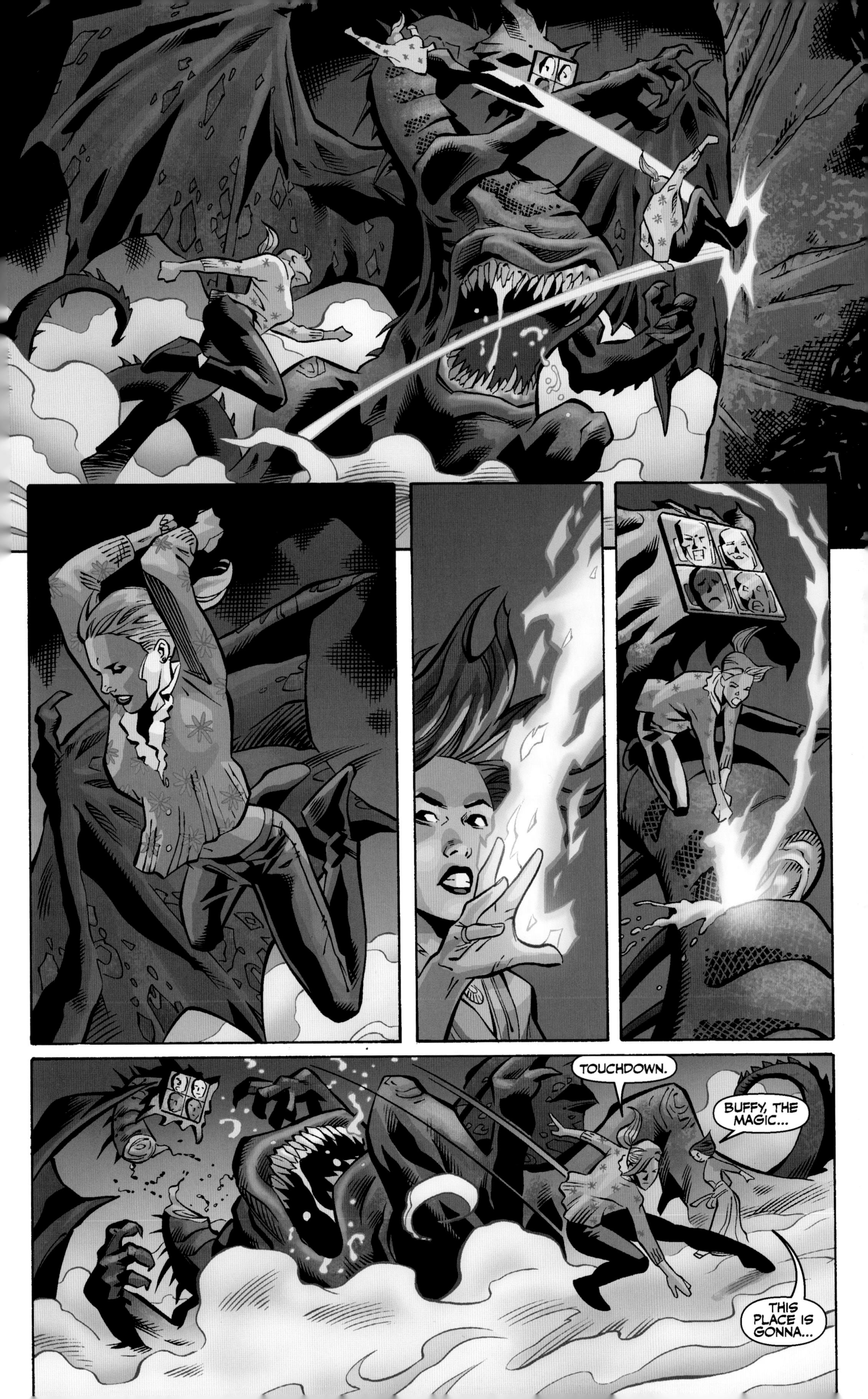
TOUCHDOWN.
BUFFY, THE MAGIC...
THIS PLACE IS GONNA...

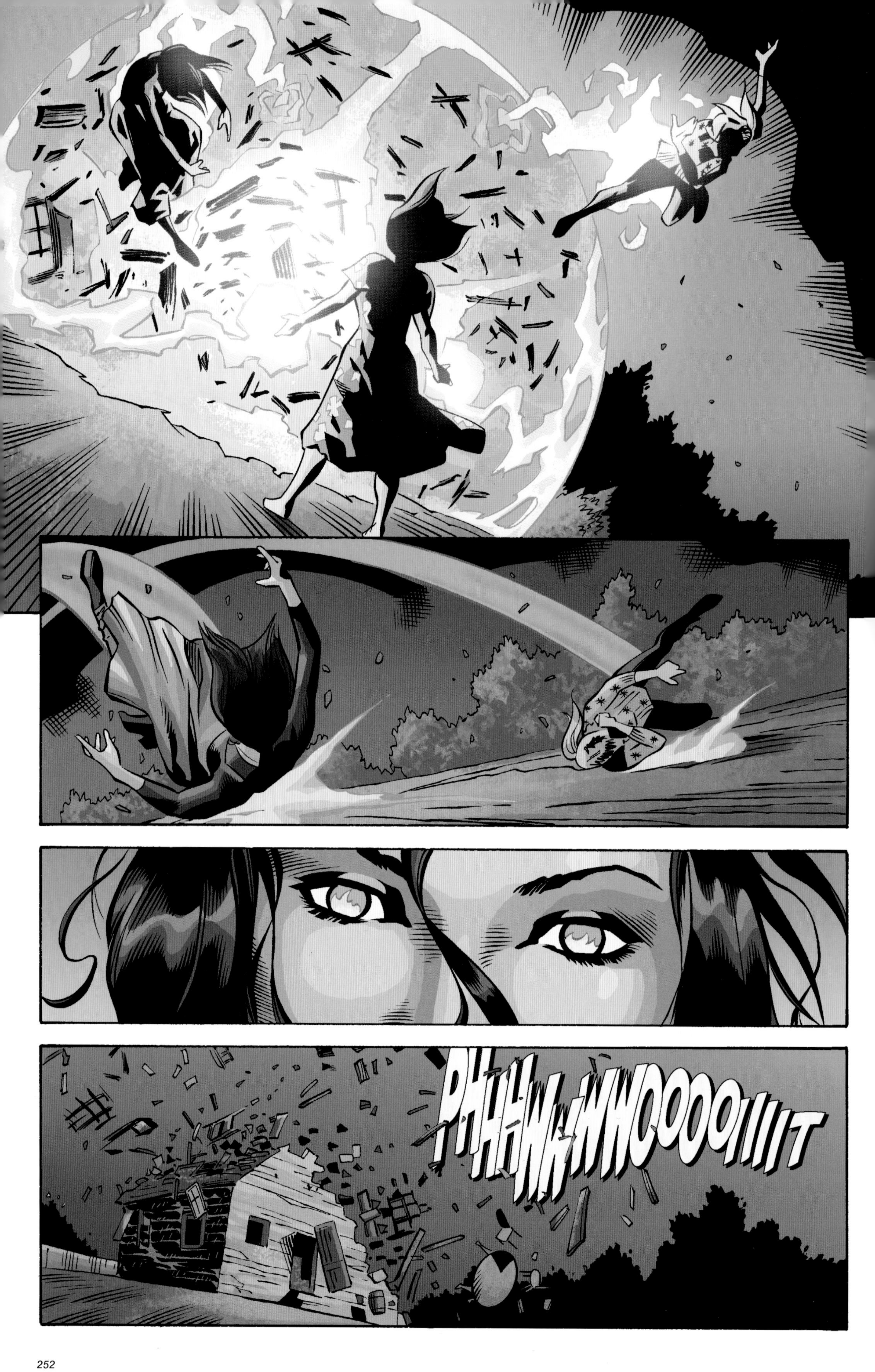
PHHHWHWWOOOOIIIIT

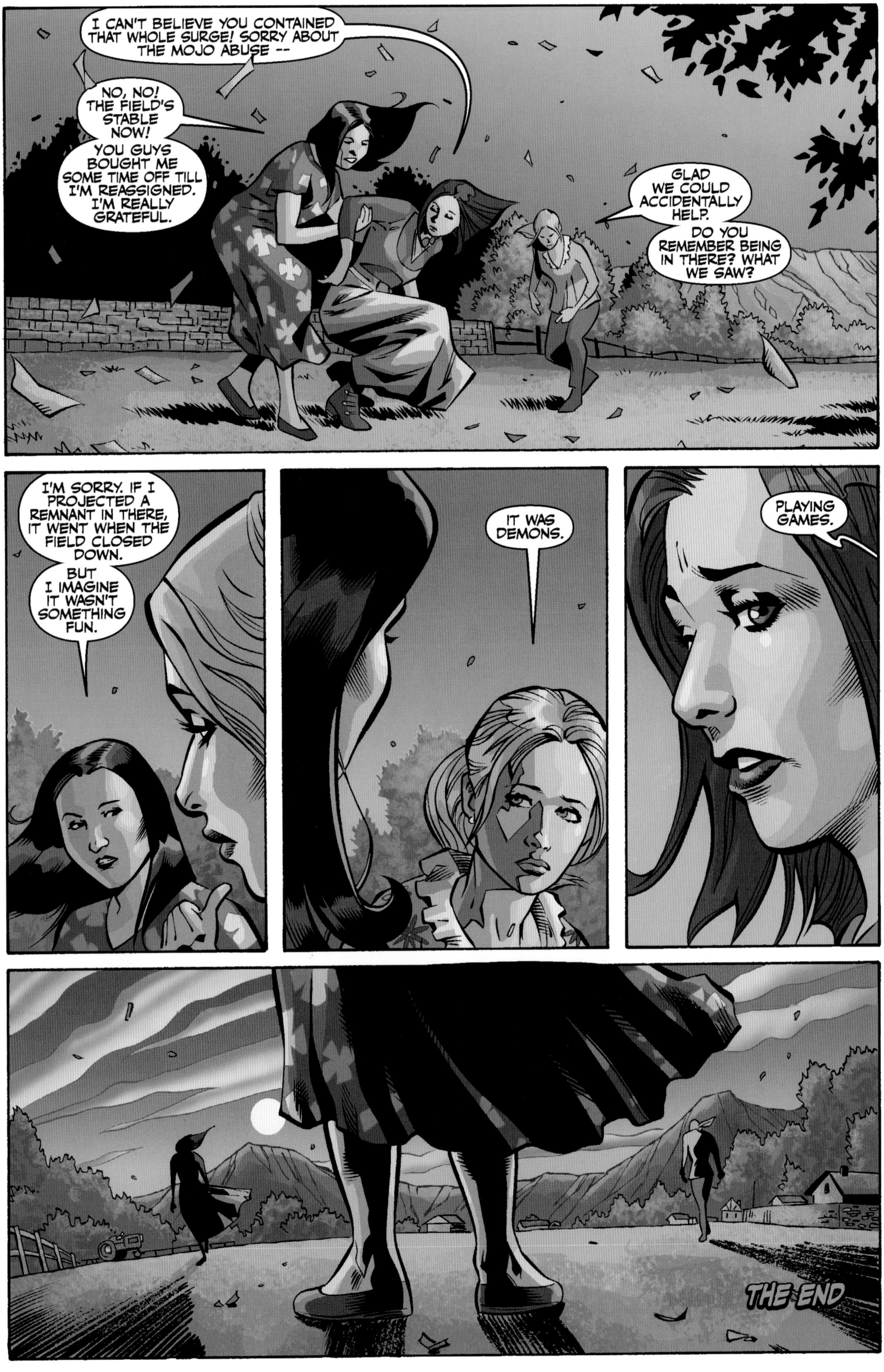
I CAN'T BELIEVE YOU CONTAINED THAT WHOLE SURGE! SORRY ABOUT THE MOJO ABUSE --
NO, NO! THE FIELD'S STABLE NOW!
YOU GUYS BOUGHT ME SOME TIME OFF TILL I'M REASSIGNED. I'M REALLY GRATEFUL.
GLAD WE COULD ACCIDENTALLY HELP.
DO YOU REMEMBER BEING IN THERE? WHAT WE SAW?
I'M SORRY. IF I PROJECTED A REMNANT IN THERE, IT WENT WHEN THE FIELD CLOSED DOWN.
BUT I IMAGINE IT WASN'T SOMETHING FUN.
IT WAS DEMONS.
PLAYING GAMES.
THE END

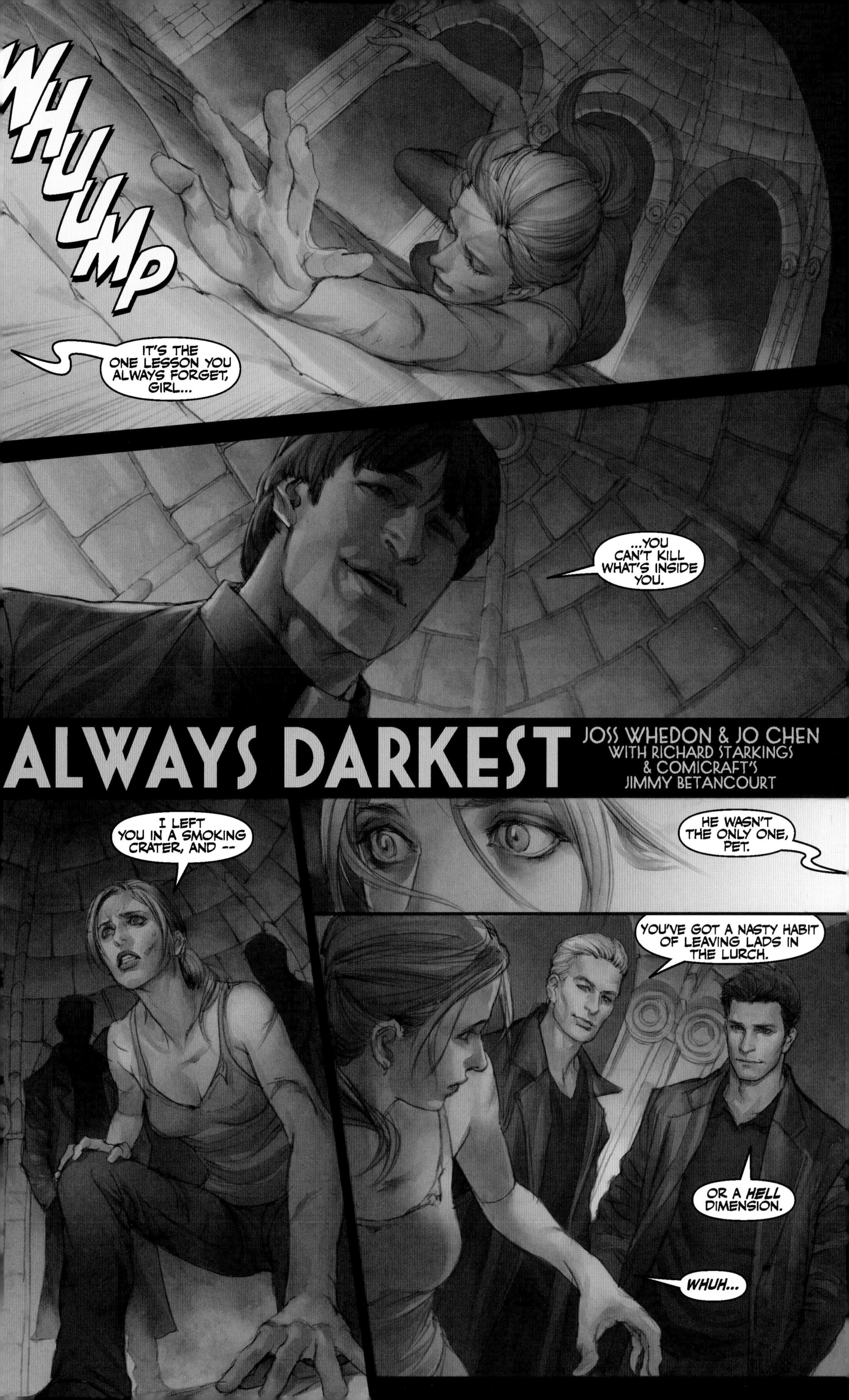
WHUUMP
IT'S THE ONE LESSON YOU ALWAYS FORGET, GIRL...
...YOU CAN'T KILL WHAT'S INSIDE YOU.
ALWAYS DARKEST
JOSS WHEDON & JO CHEN
WITH RICHARD STARKINGS
& COMICRAFT'S
JIMMY BETANCOURT
I LEFT YOU IN A SMOKING CRATER, AND --
HE WASN'T THE ONLY ONE, PET.
YOU'VE GOT A NASTY HABIT OF LEAVING LADS IN THE LURCH.
OR A HELL DIMENSION.
WHUH...

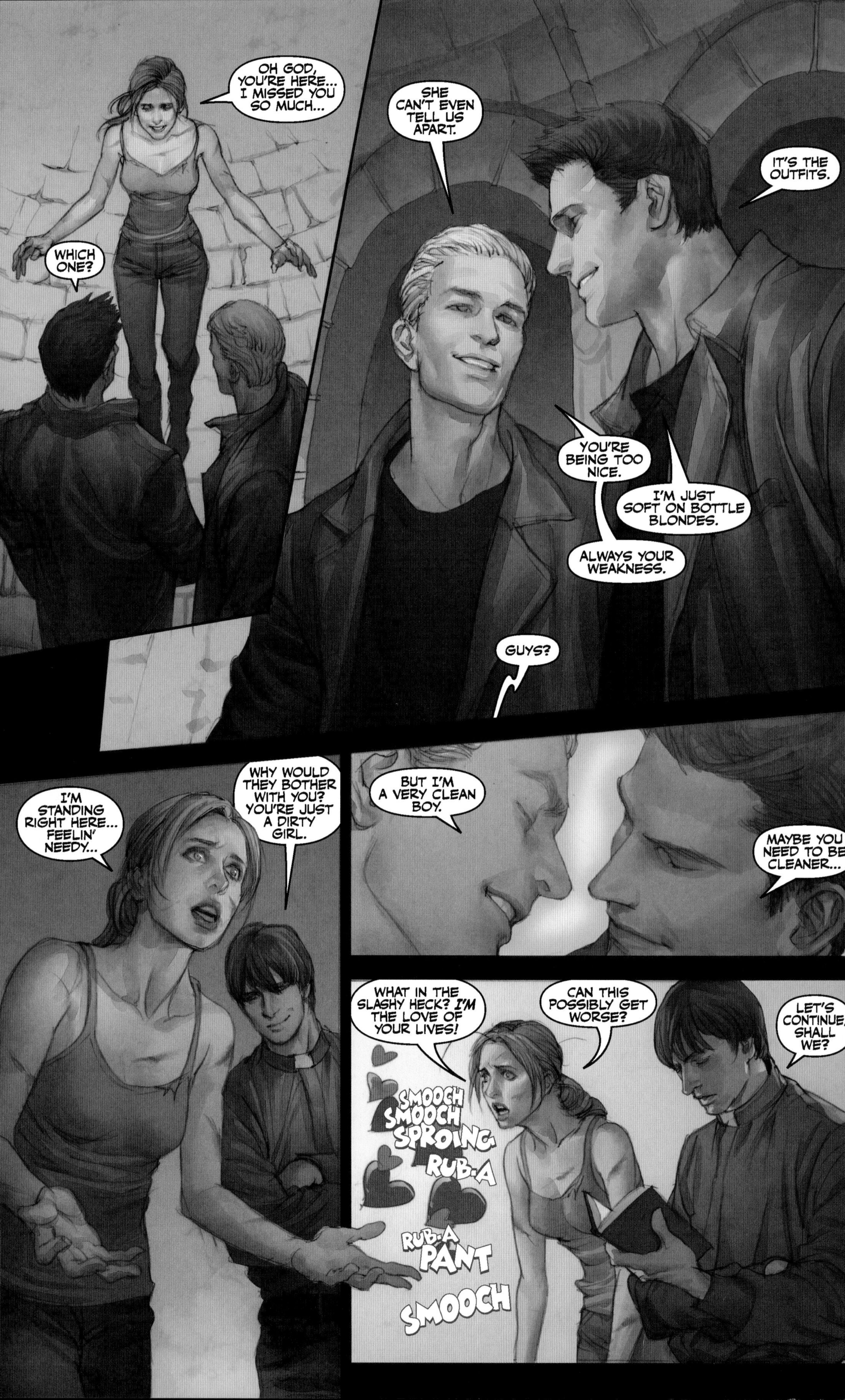
OH GOD, YOU'RE HERE... I MISSED YOU SO MUCH...
WHICH ONE?
SHE CAN'T EVEN TELL US APART.
IT'S THE OUTFITS.
YOU'RE BEING TOO NICE.
I'M JUST SOFT ON BOTTLE BLONDES.
ALWAYS YOUR WEAKNESS.
GUYS?
I'M STANDING RIGHT HERE... FEELIN' NEEDY...
WHY WOULD THEY BOTHER WITH YOU? YOU'RE JUST A DIRTY GIRL.
BUT I'M A VERY CLEAN BOY.
MAYBE YOU NEED TO BE CLEANER...
WHAT IN THE SLASHY HECK? *I'M* THE LOVE OF YOUR LIVES!
CAN THIS POSSIBLY GET WORSE?
LET'S CONTINUE, SHALL WE?
SMOOCH
SMOOCH
SPROING
RUB-A
RUB-A
PANT
SMOOCH

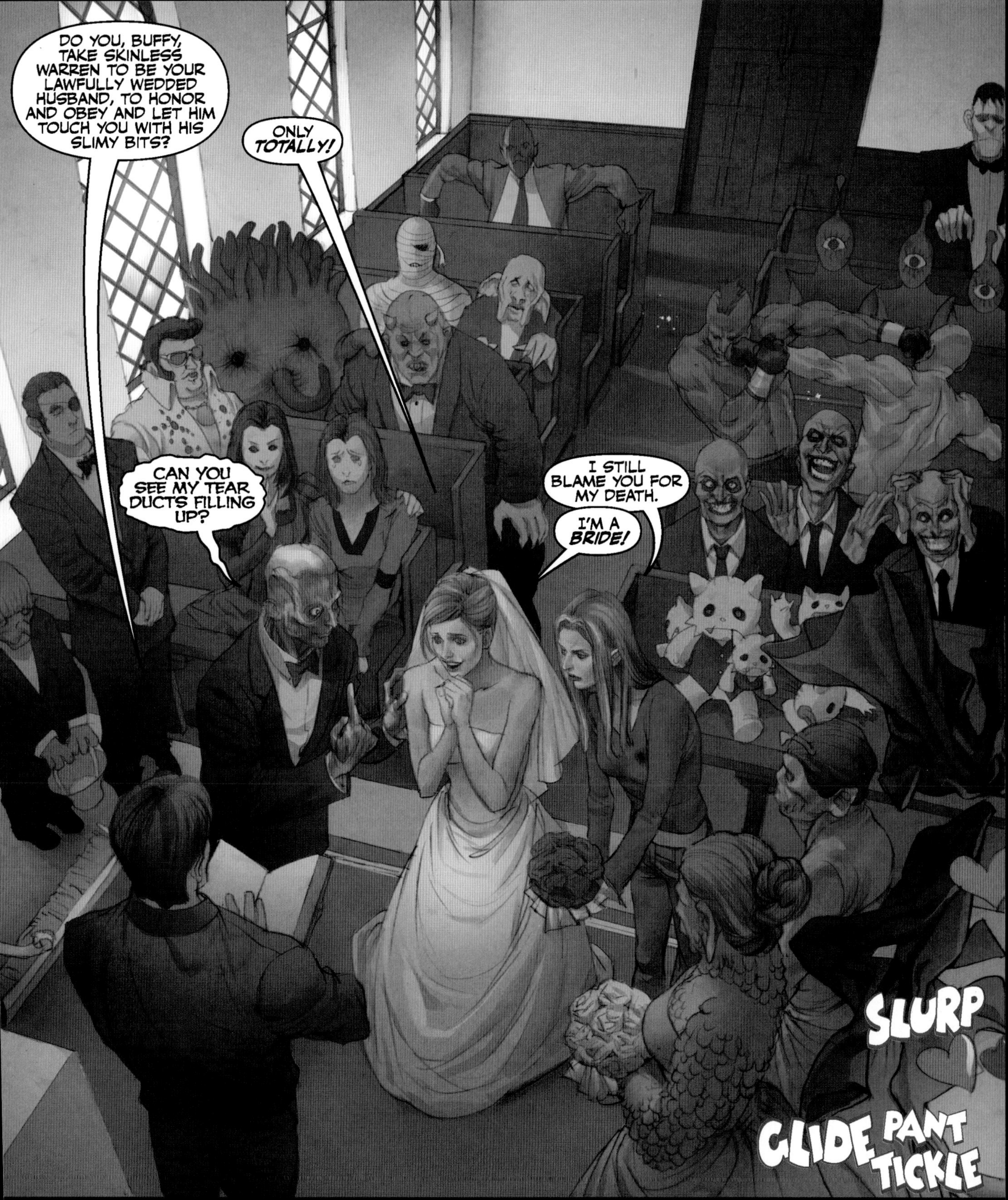
DO YOU, BUFFY, TAKE SKINLESS WARREN TO BE YOUR LAWFULLY WEDDED HUSBAND, TO HONOR AND OBEY AND LET HIM TOUCH YOU WITH HIS SLIMY BITS?
ONLY *TOTALLY!*
CAN YOU SEE MY TEAR DUCTS FILLING UP?
I STILL BLAME YOU FOR MY DEATH.
I'M A *BRIDE!*
SLURP
GLIDE PANT TICKLE

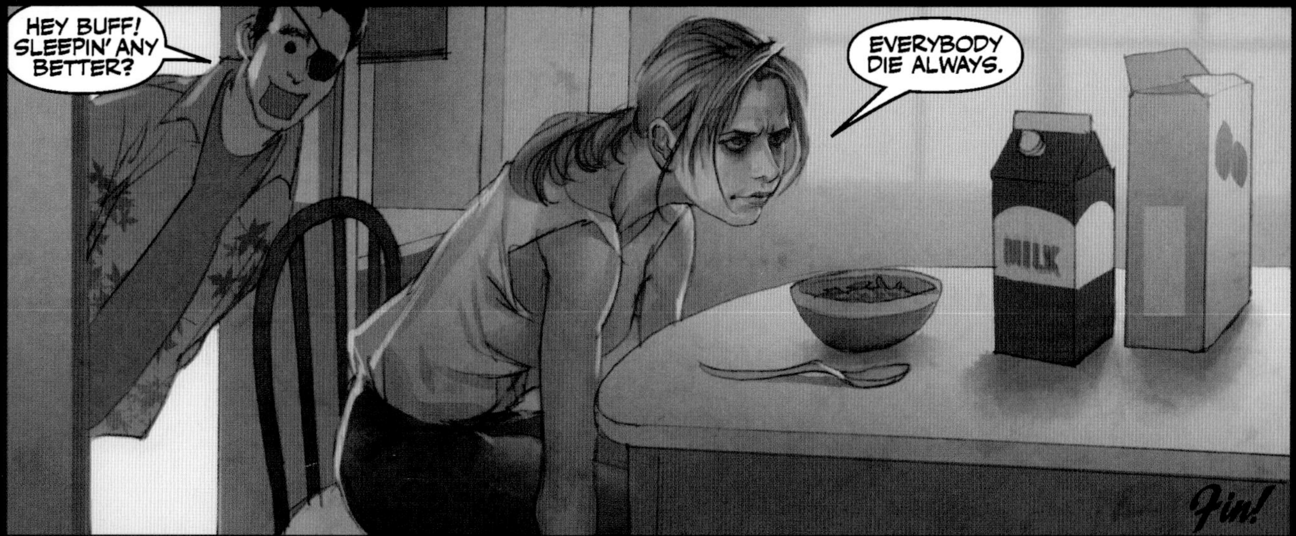
HEY BUFF! SLEEPIN' ANY BETTER?
EVERYBODY DIE ALWAYS.
MILK
Fin!

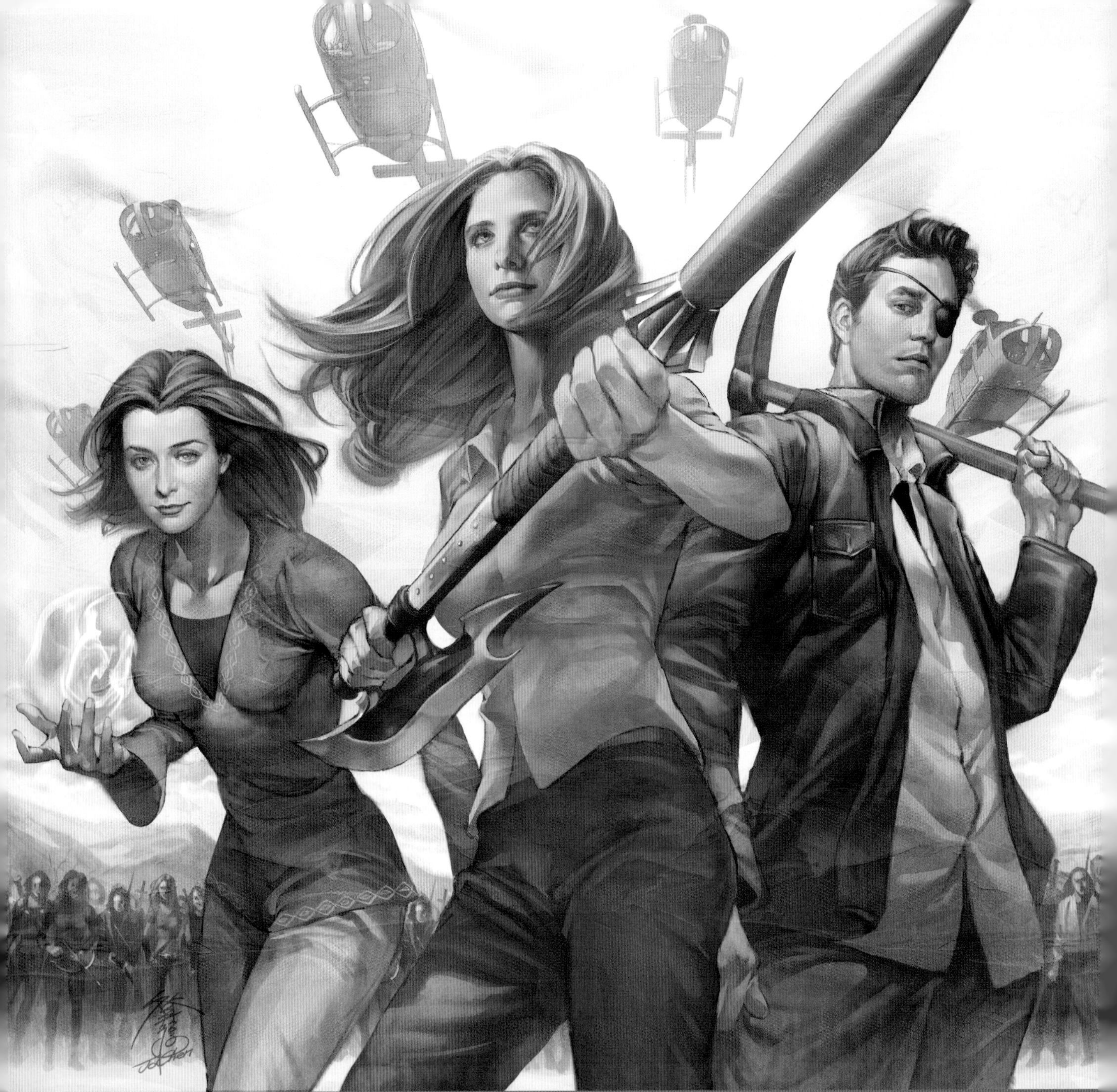

COVERS

ISSUES #1–#10

BY
JO CHEN
GEORGES JEANTY
PAUL LEE

WITH
DEXTER VINES
DAVE STEWART
DAN JACKSON
ANDY OWENS

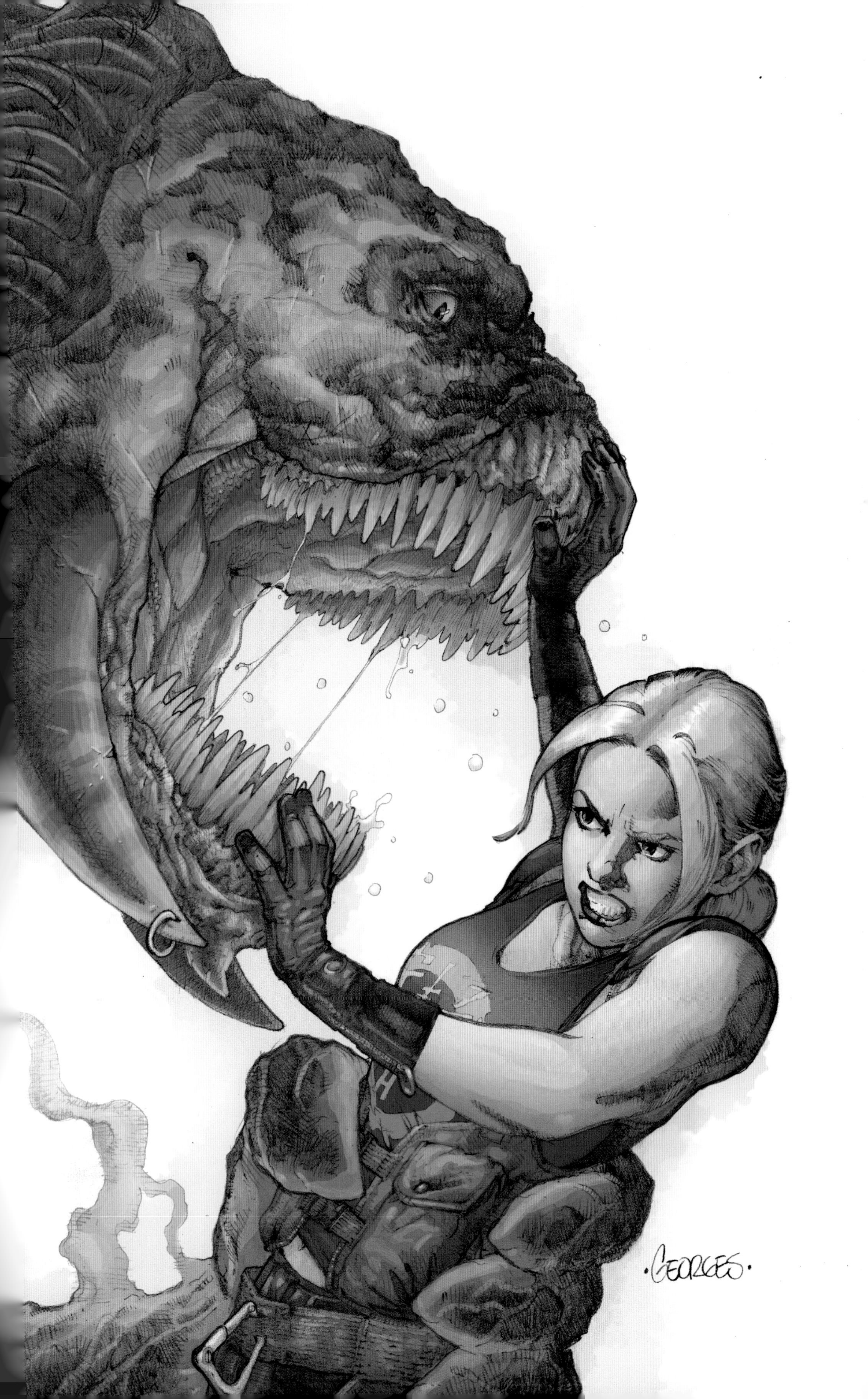
GEORGES

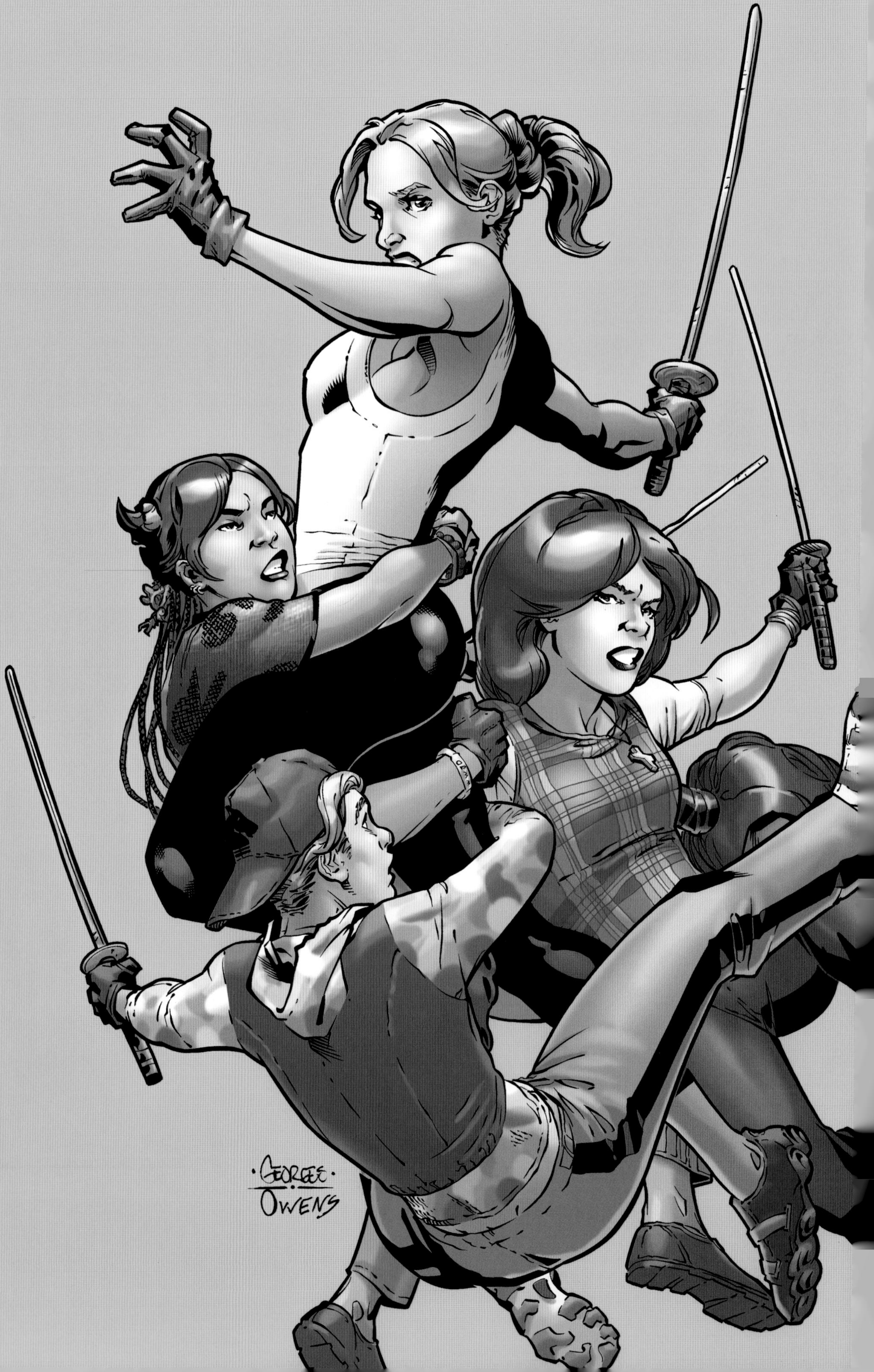
GEORGES
OWENS

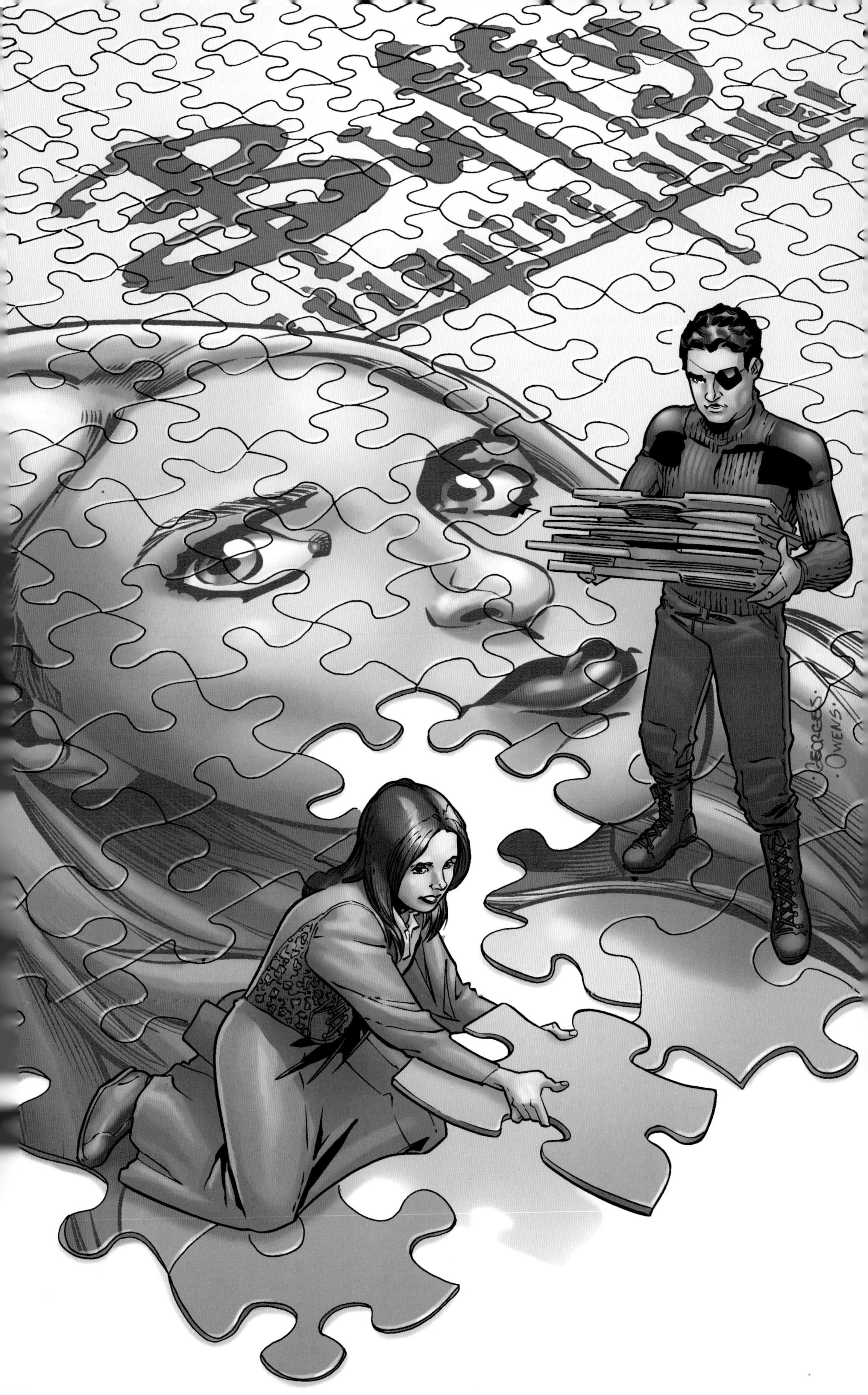
GEORGES
OWENS

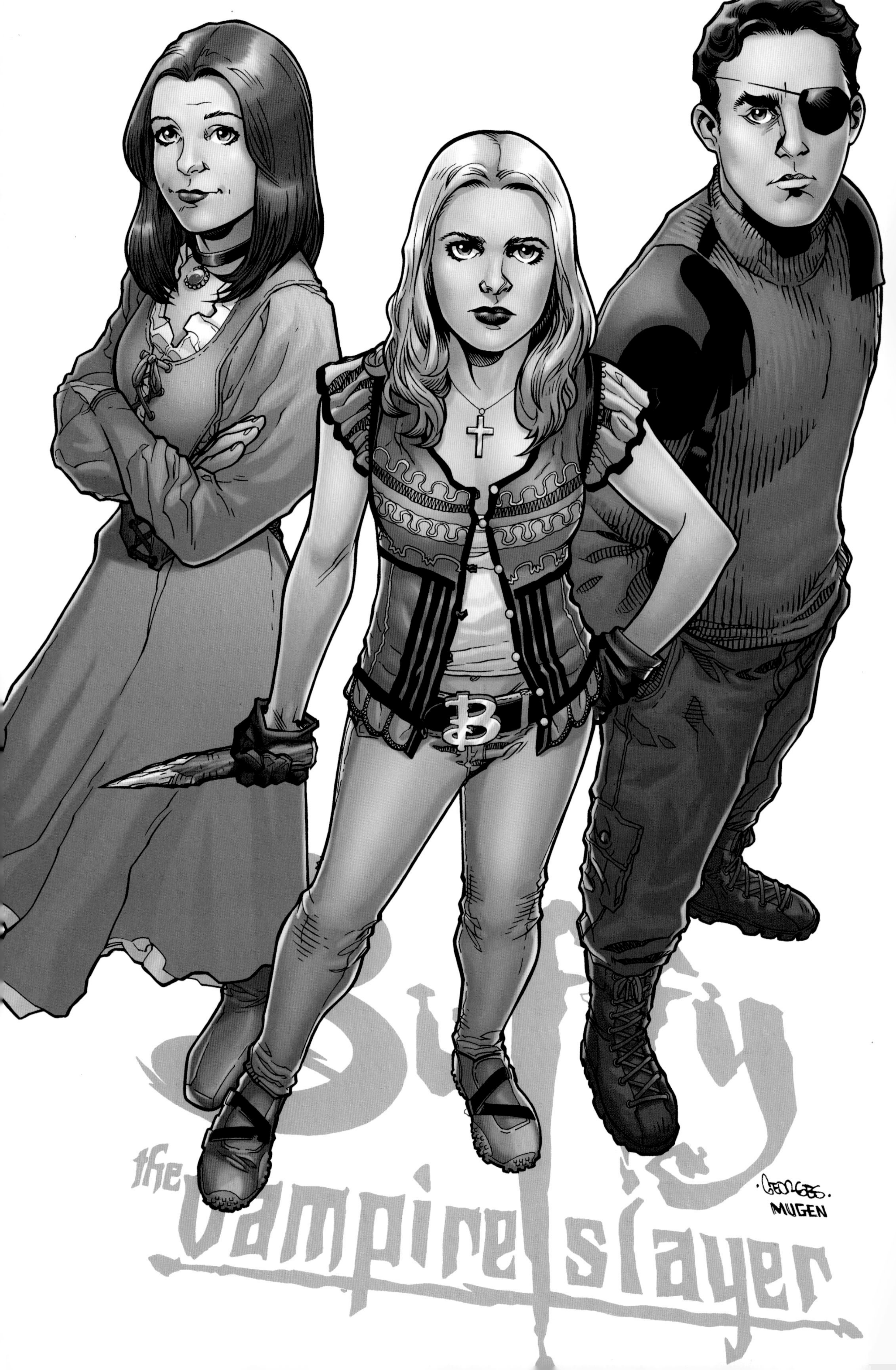
Buffy
the vampire slayer
MUGEN

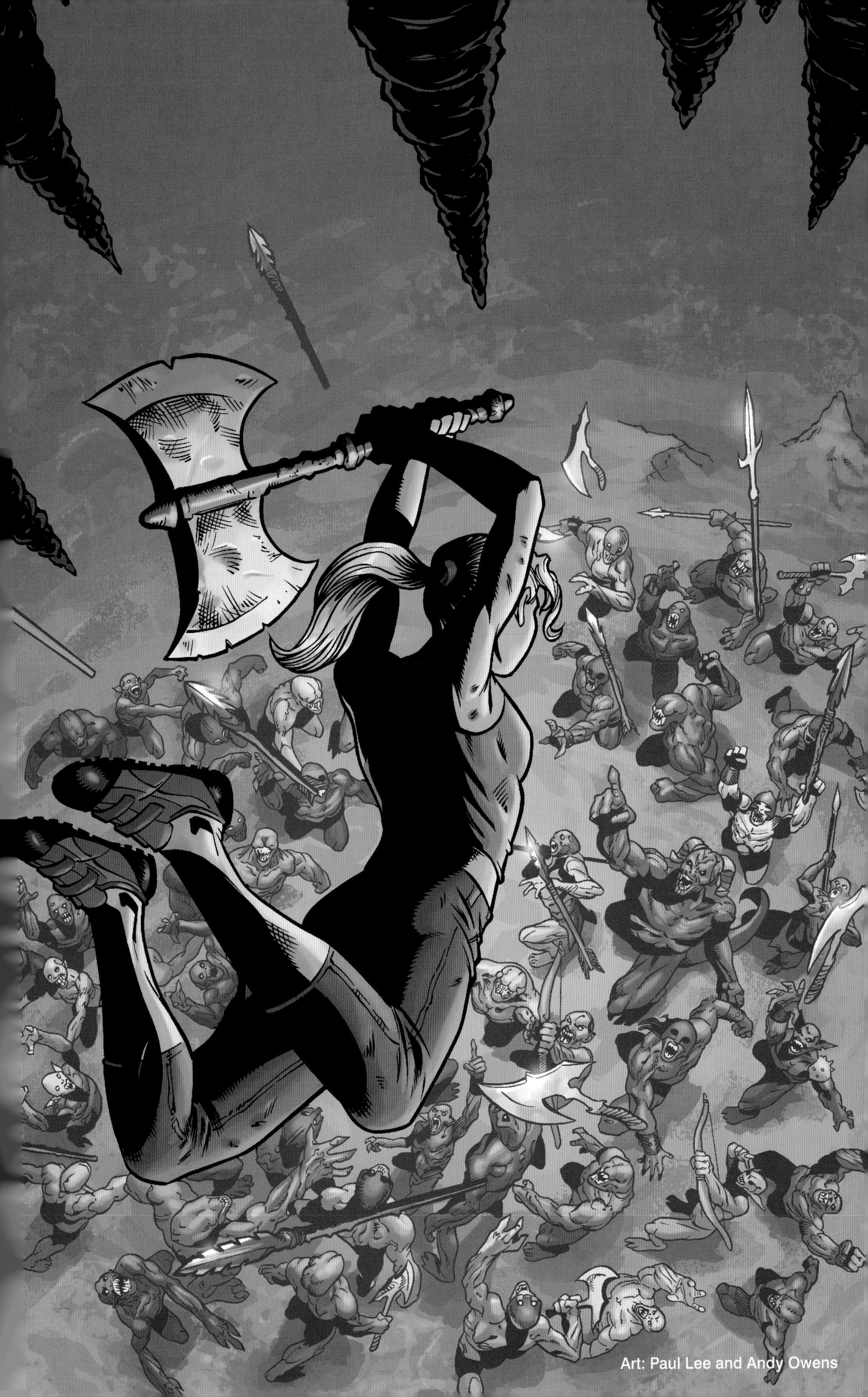

Art: Paul Lee and Andy Owens

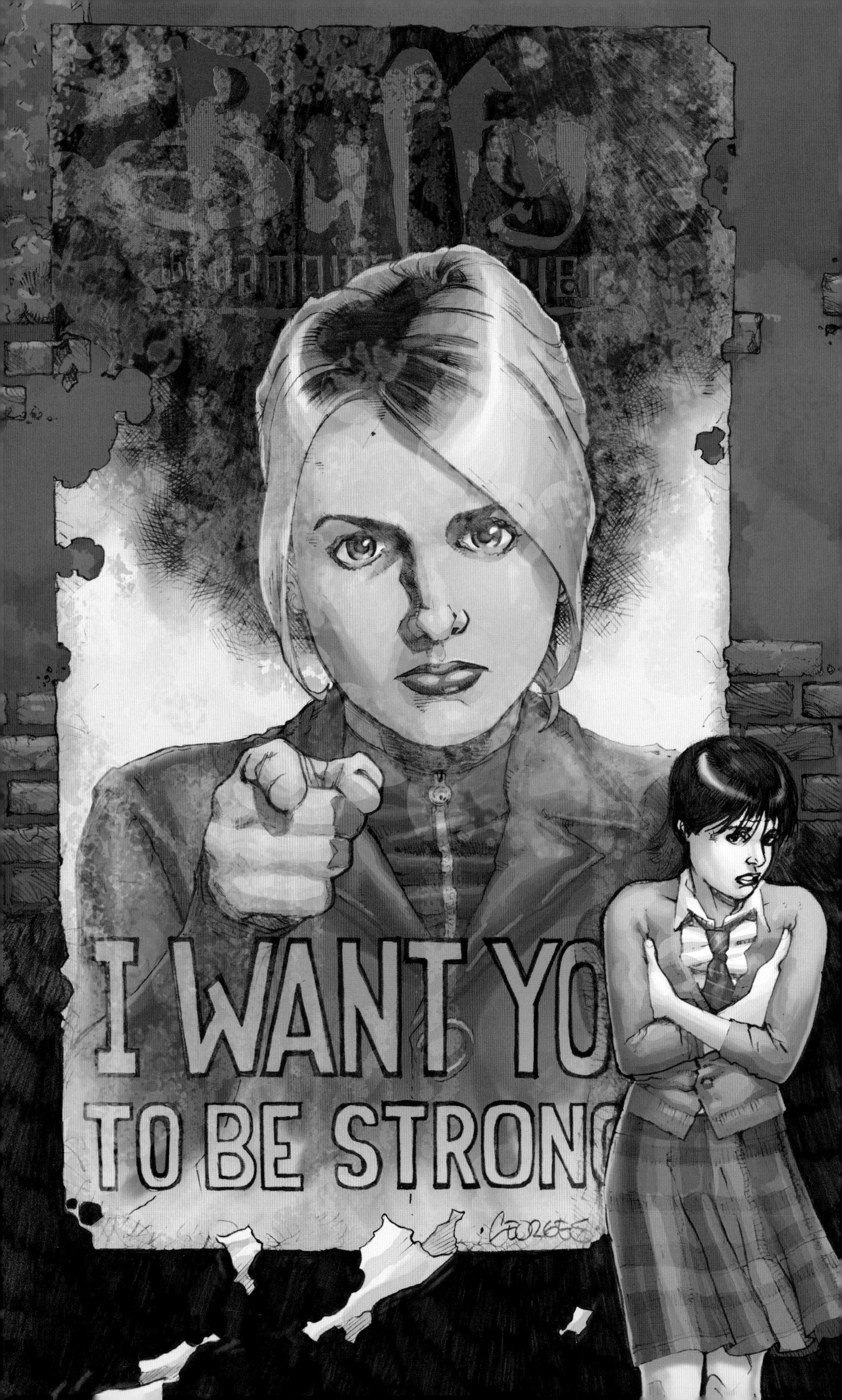

Buffy
I WANT YO
TO BE STRONG
GEORGES

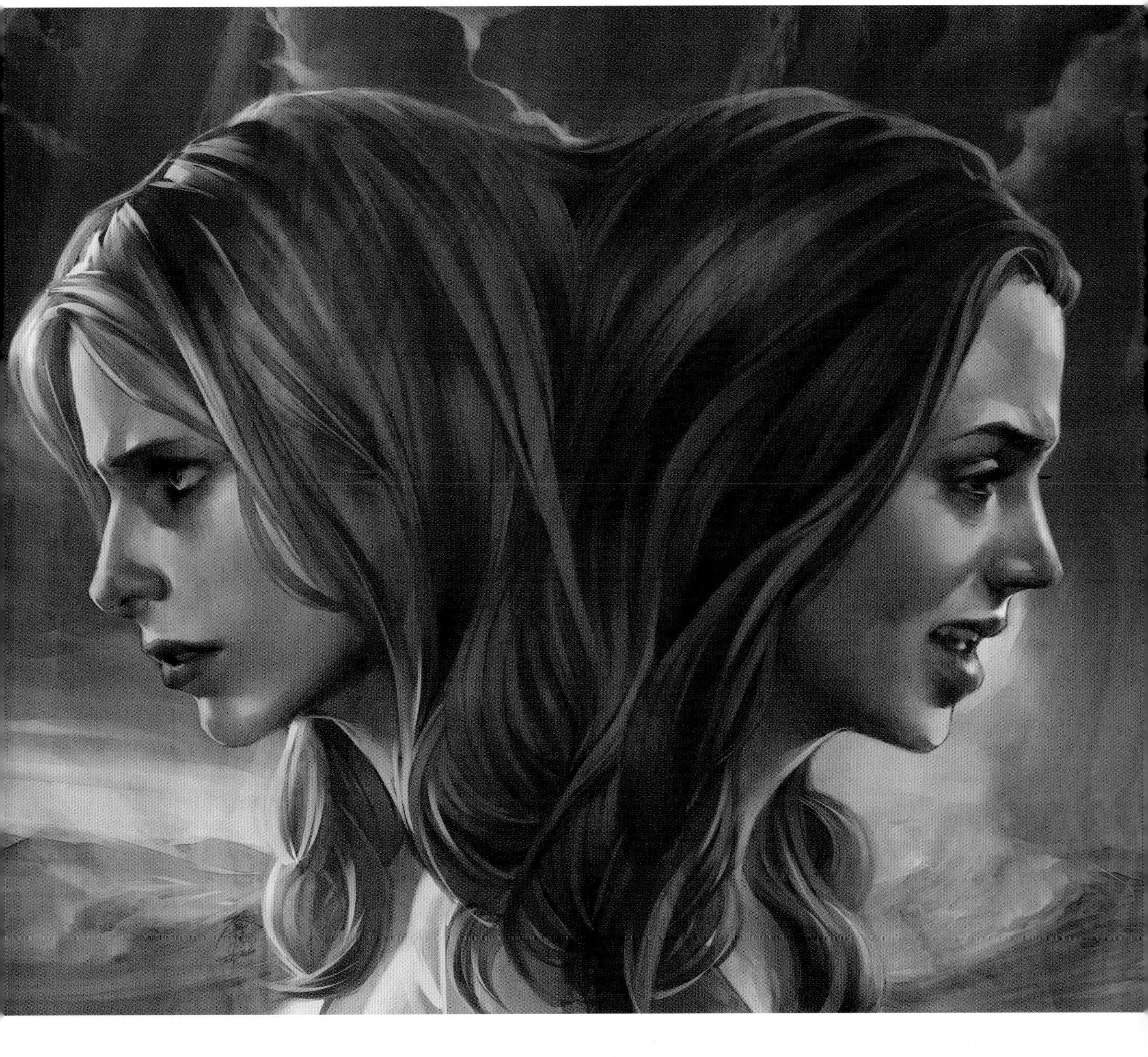

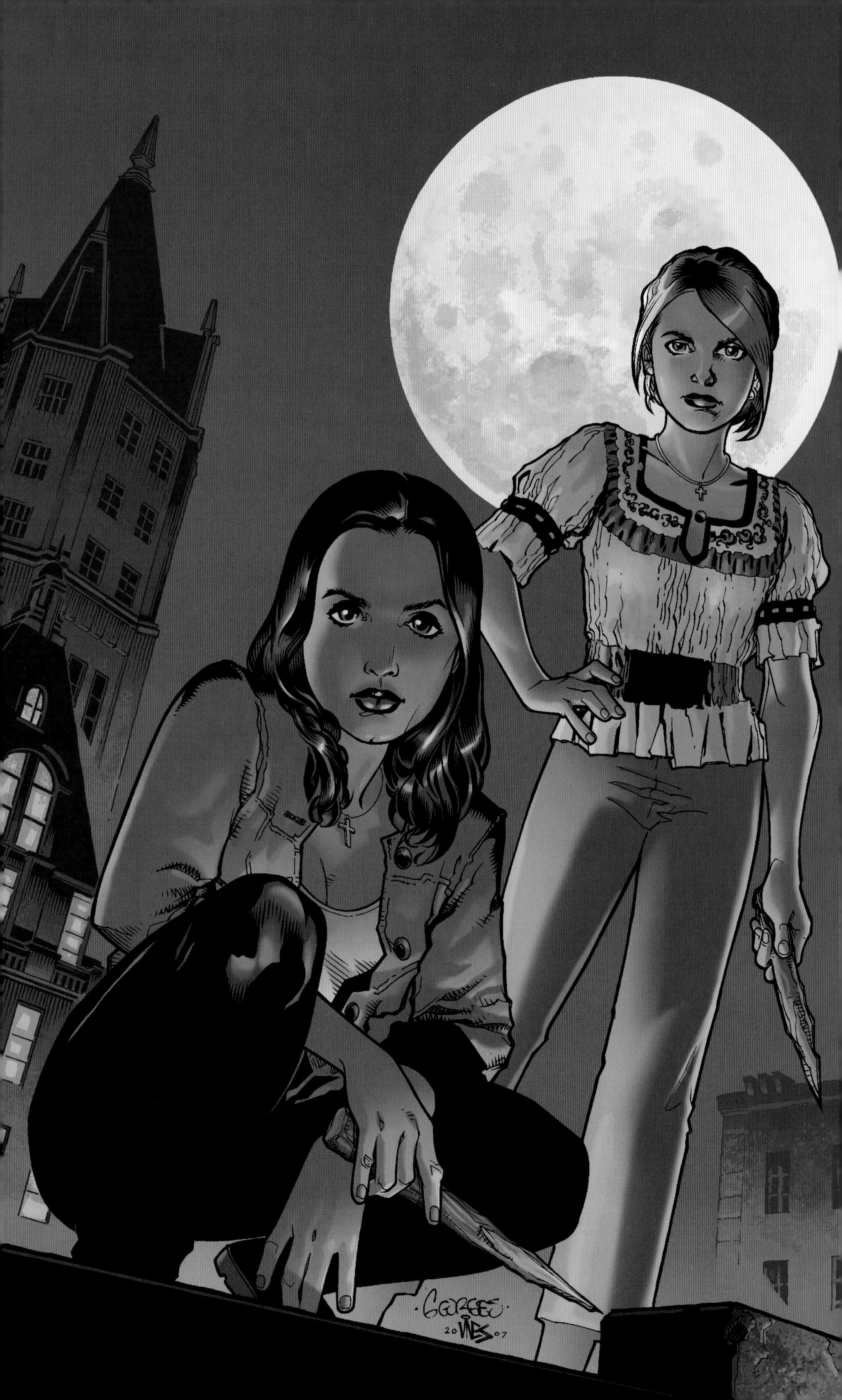

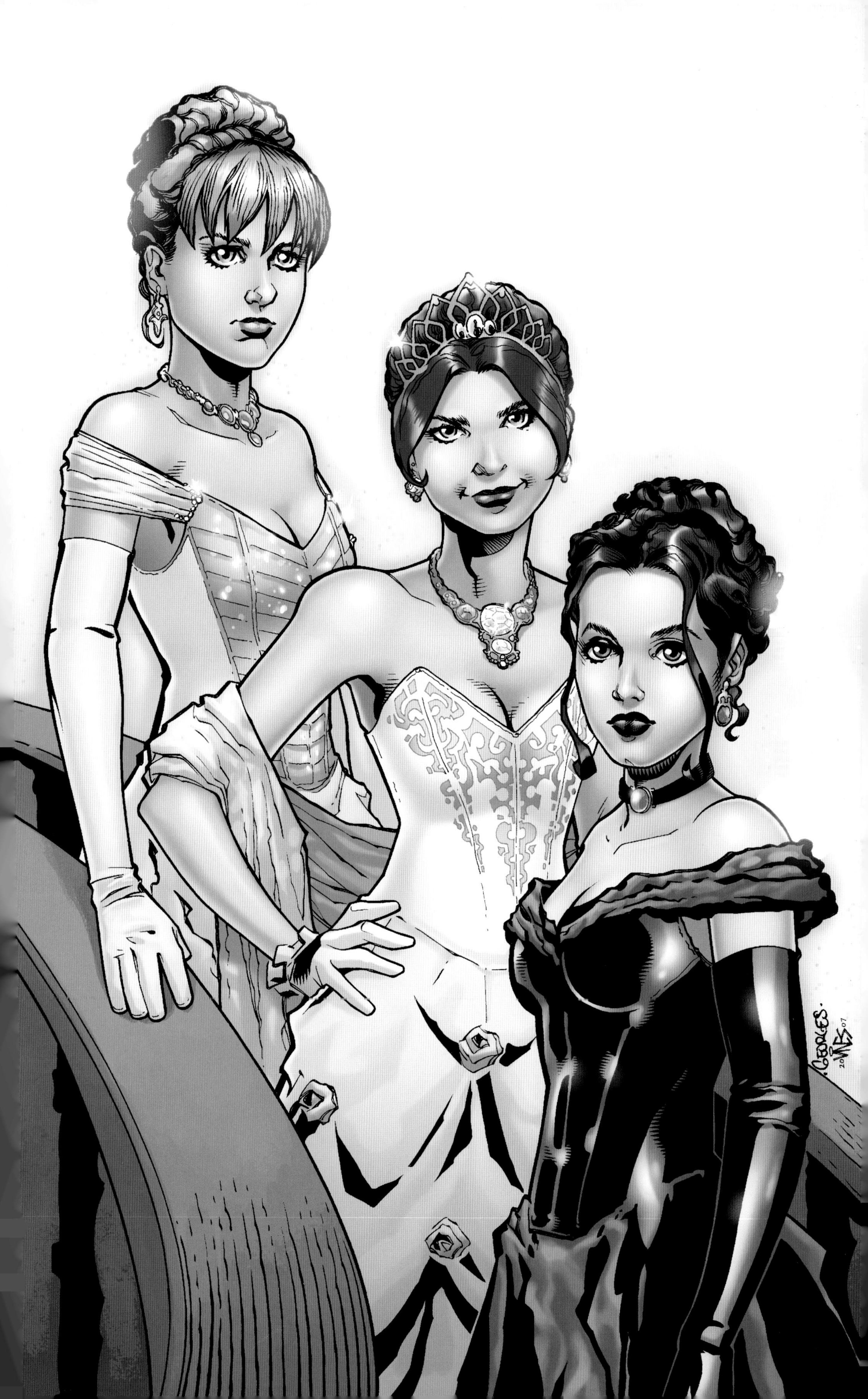

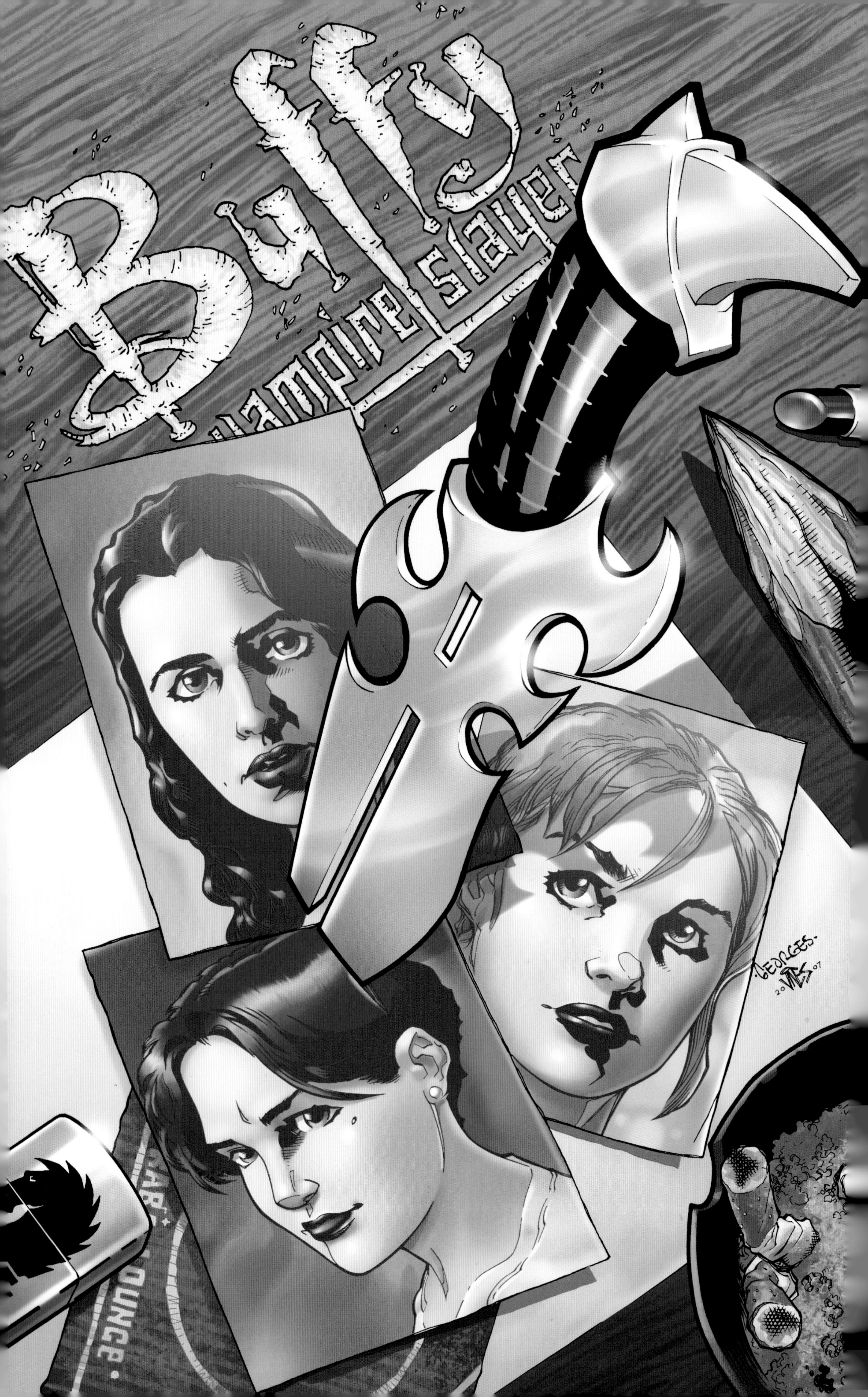
Buffy
vampire slayer

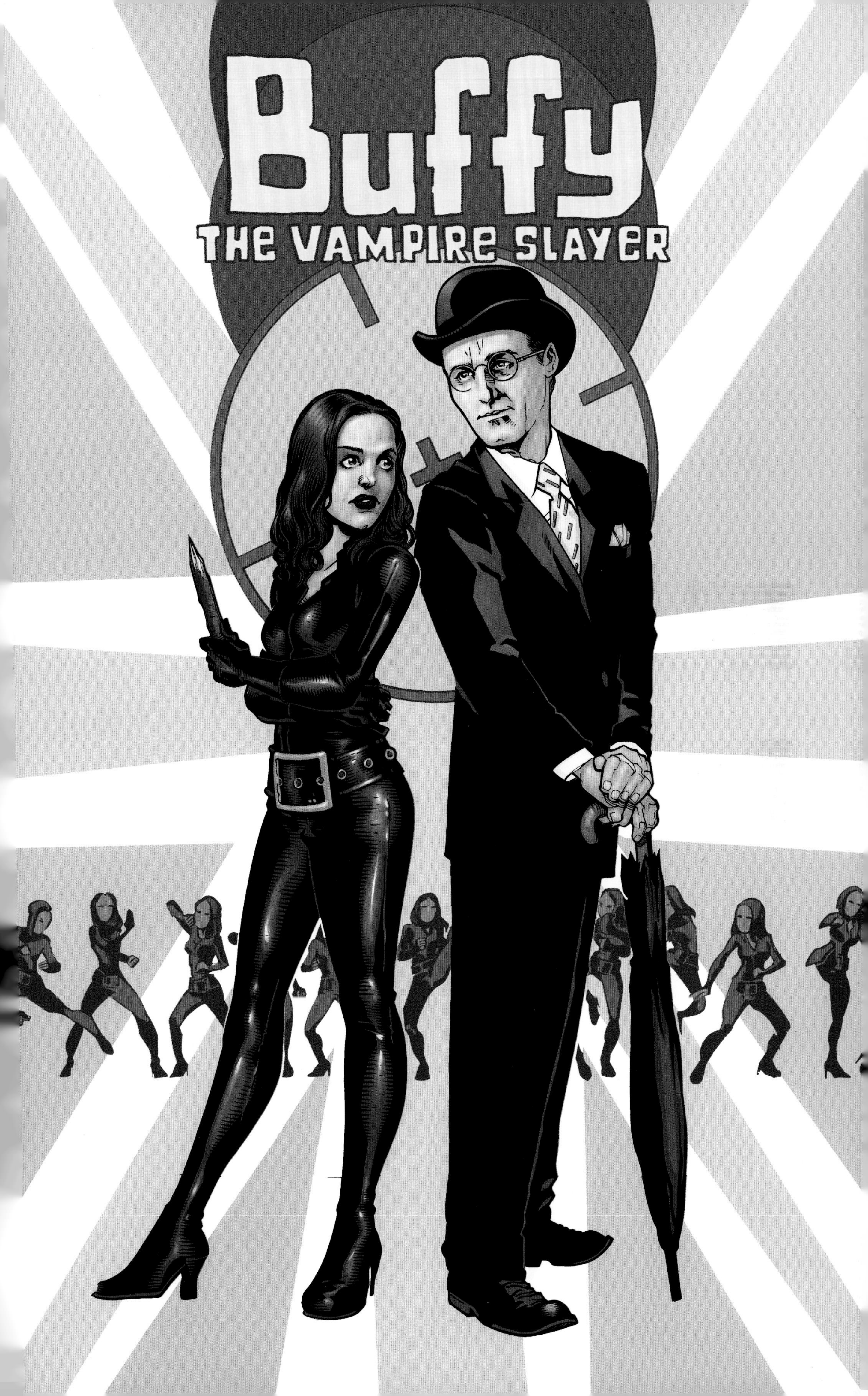
Buffy
THE VAMPIRE SLAYER

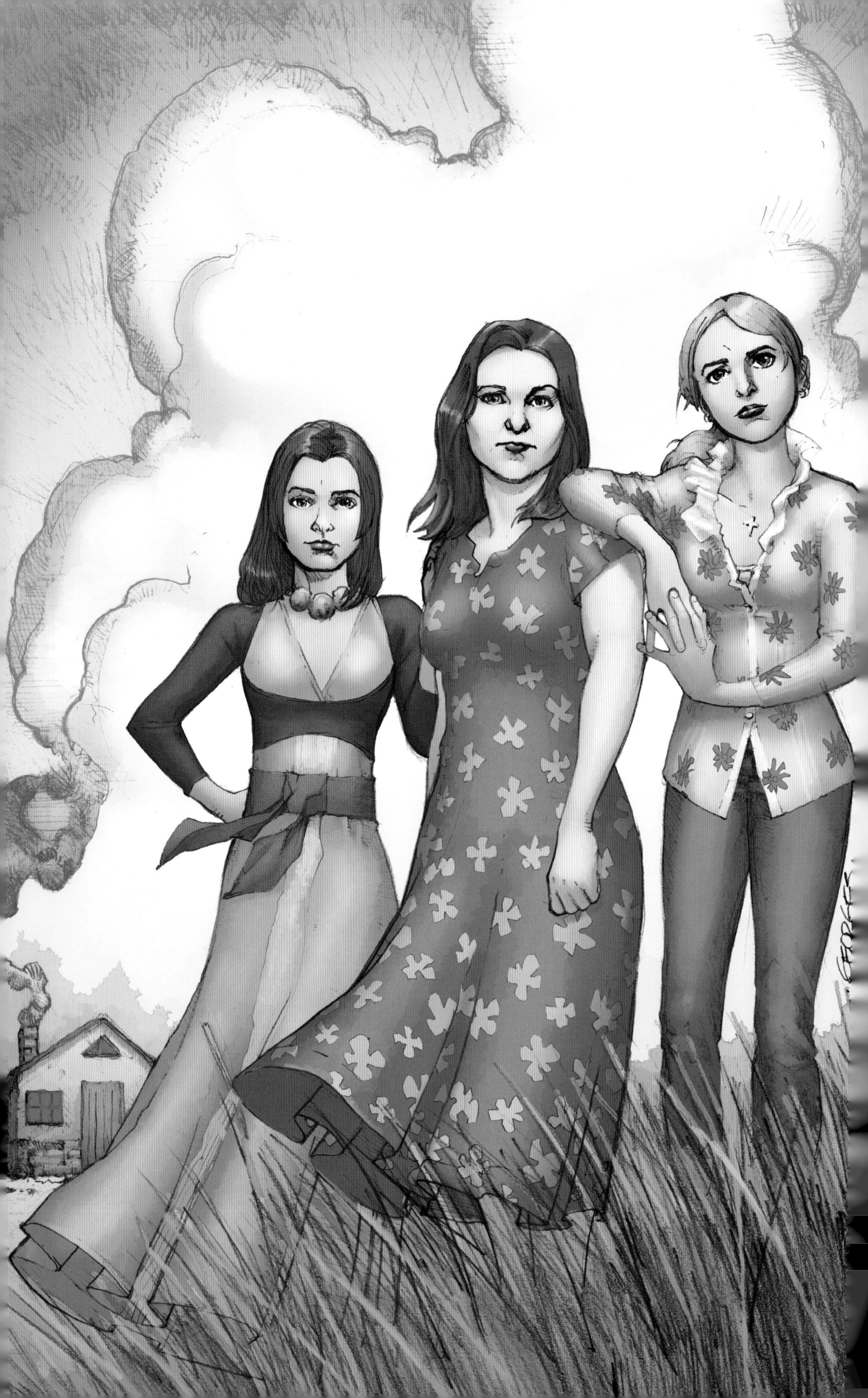

SKETCHES

TEXT AND ART BY

GEORGES JEANTY

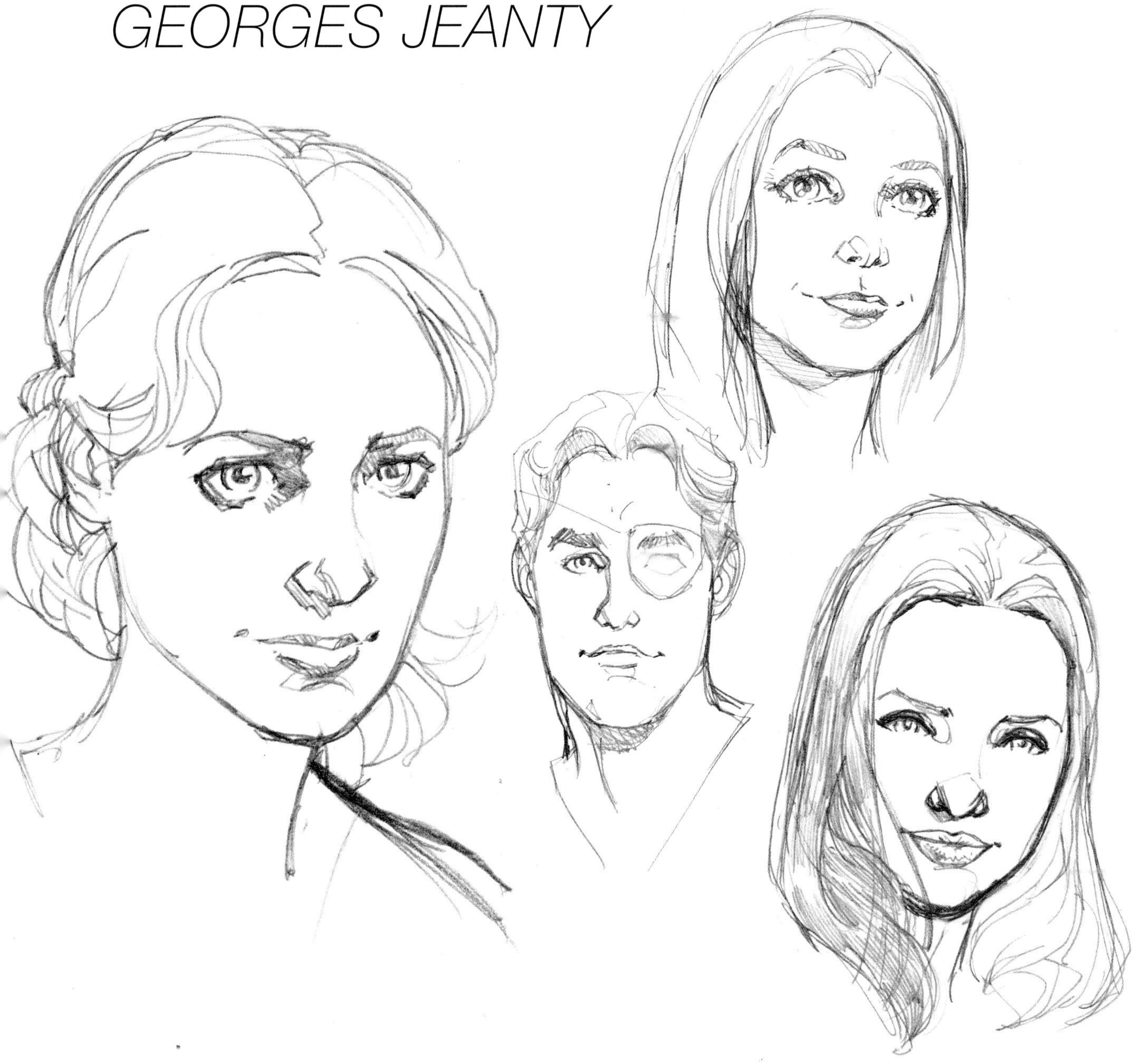

How appropriate that we start at the beginning, literally. These sketches are some of the first that I did when I was assigned to Season 8. I did the above head sketches for a print that I wanted to do like a movie poster that would encompass all the elements from the first arc. I was thinking Drew Struzan all the way here. The facing page was a cover to an issue that I didn't draw but was proud to do. There was a contest where readers had to submit an essay on how Buffy changed their lives. The winner would get to be in this issue and on the cover. This cover was colored from pencils to give it a passive feel. I had the idea of girl power going on (as with most of Joss's work) and I wanted the girls to look unified so I had them all touching in some way.

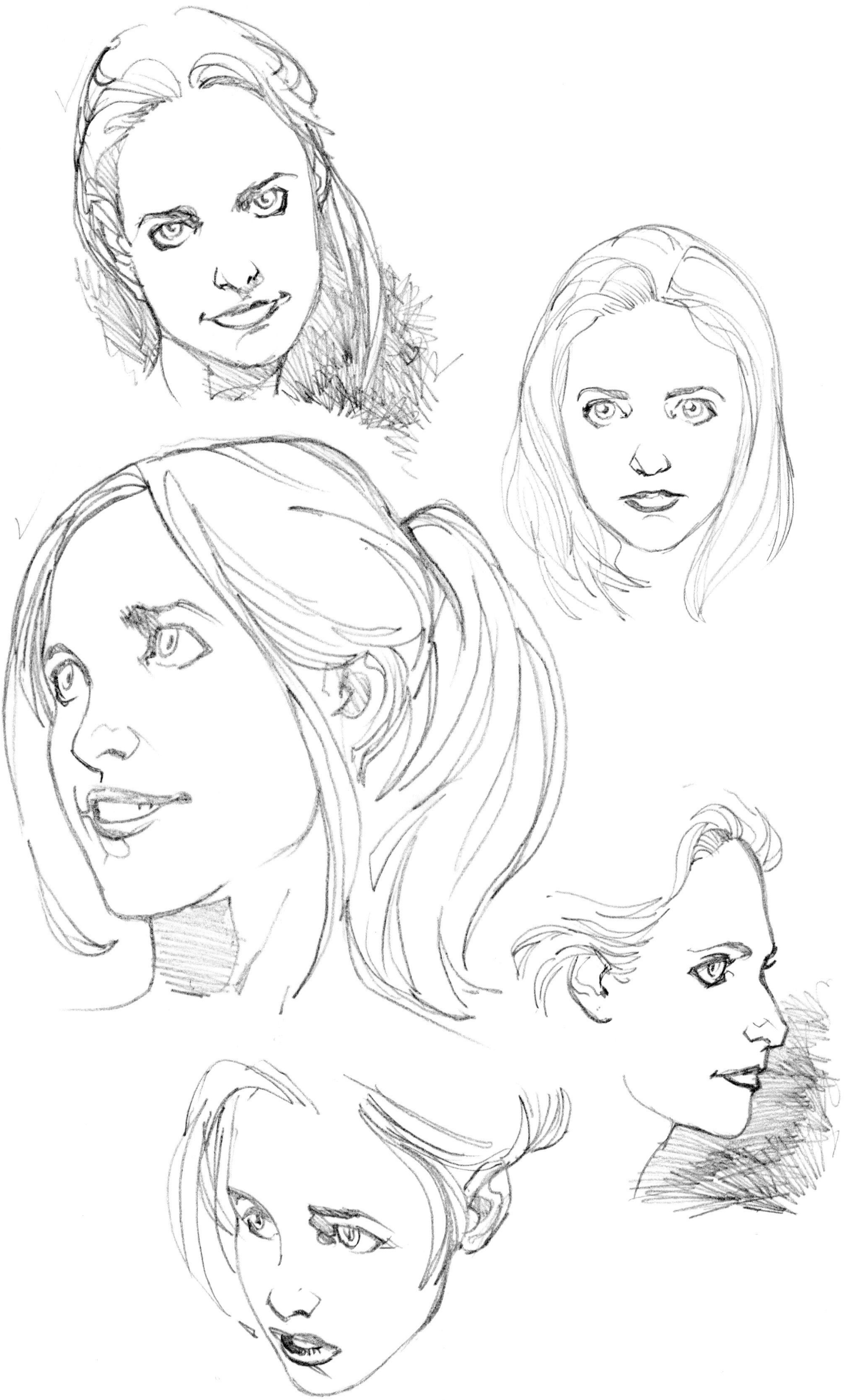

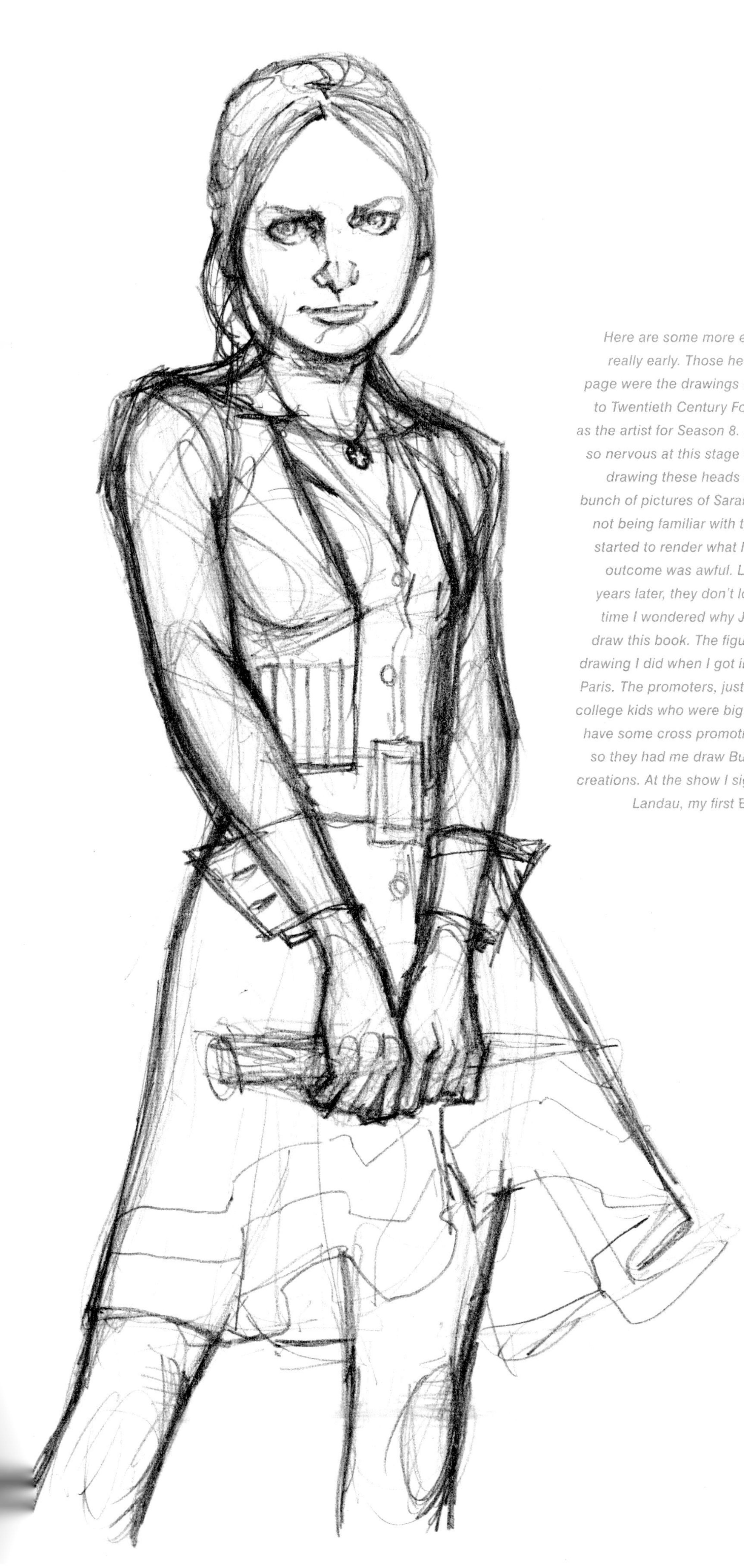

Here are some more early sketches. I mean really early. Those headshots on the facing page were the drawings Dark Horse submitted to Twentieth Century Fox to get me approved as the artist for Season 8. Needless to say I was so nervous at this stage that I don't remember drawing these heads at all! I downloaded a bunch of pictures of Sarah Michelle Gellar and, not being familiar with the show at that point, started to render what I saw, and thought the outcome was awful. Looking back at these, years later, they don't look so bad. But at the time I wondered why Joss had picked me to draw this book. The figure on this page was a drawing I did when I got invited to do a show in Paris. The promoters, just a bunch of ambitious college kids who were big Buffy *fans, wanted to have some cross promotion with a local stylist, so they had me draw Buffy wearing one of his creations. At the show I signed along with Juliet Landau, my first* Buffy*-related celebrity.*

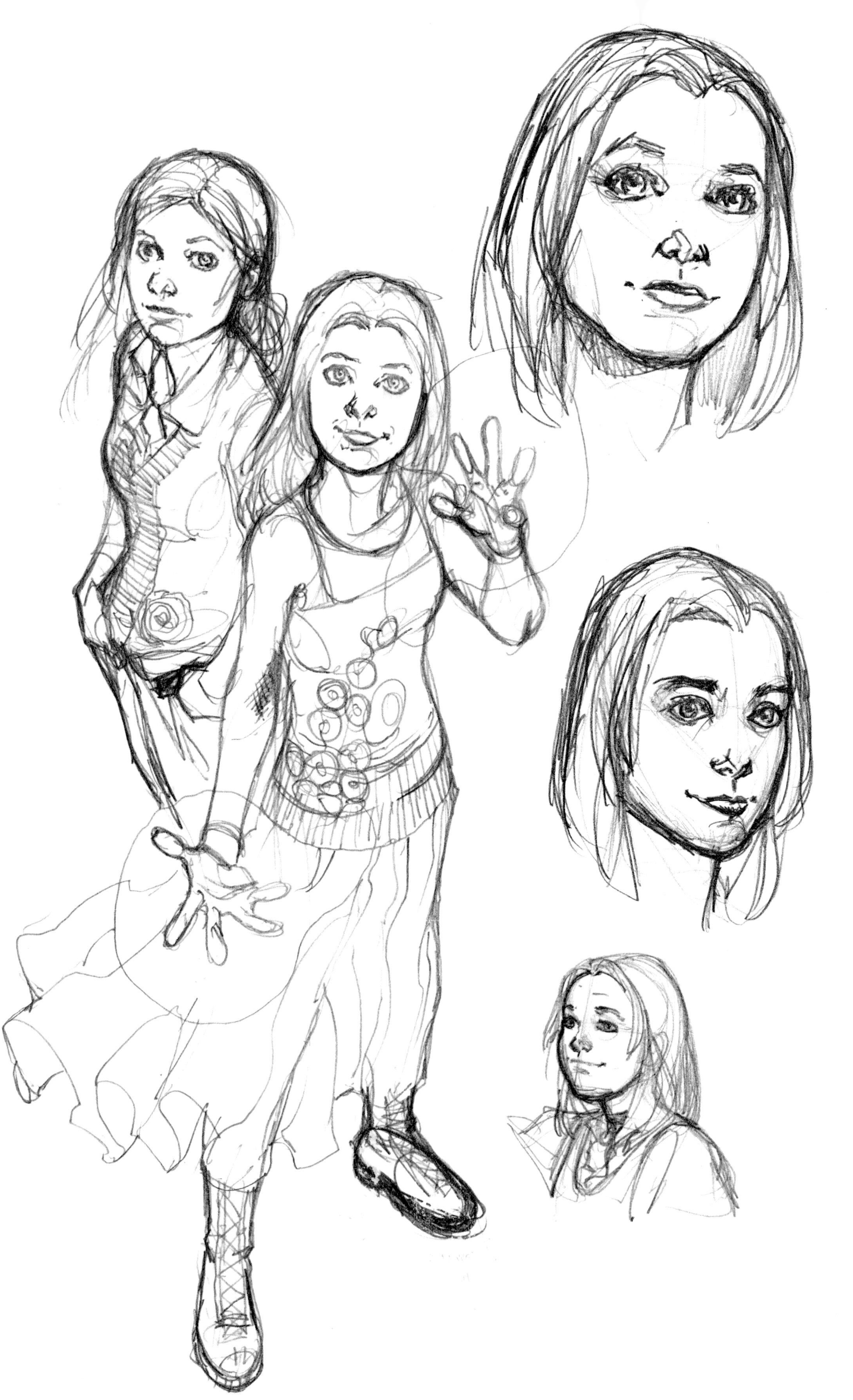

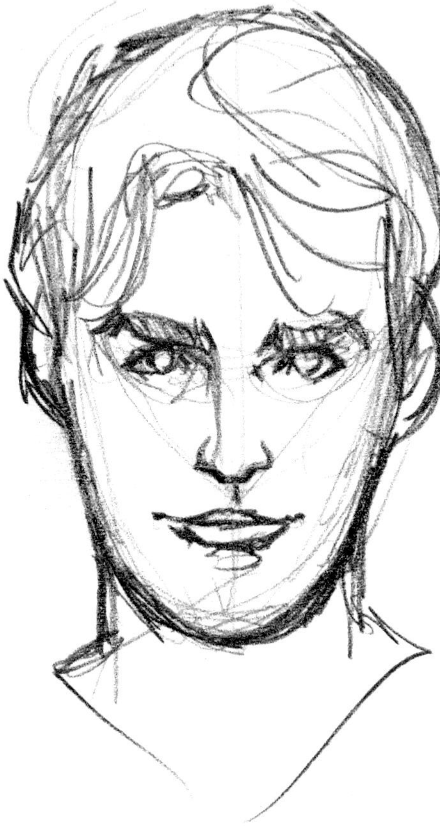

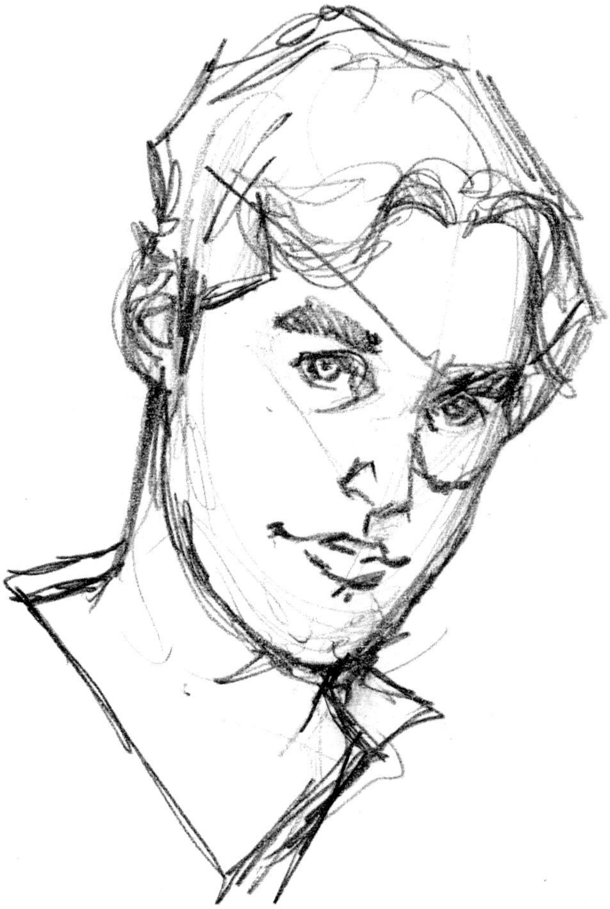

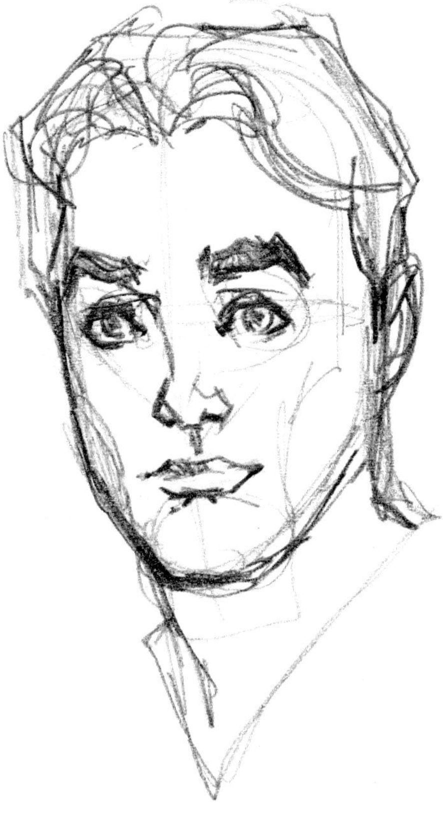

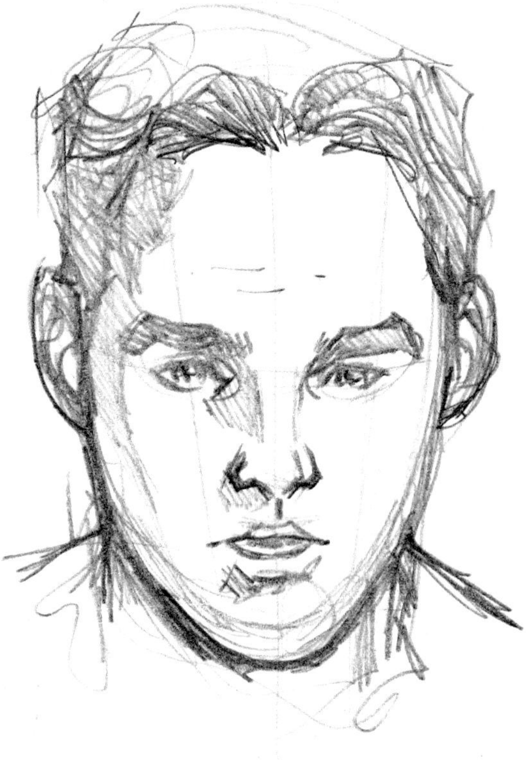

Above: More head studies. I really thought I captured Xander's likeness early on so I didn't stress over drawing him much. While it never got out, I can say now that there were a few times in the book that I drew Xander without his eye patch. I usually caught it early on but there were a few times when the pages were going out to the inker that I had to hold a page back and fill in the area for the eye patch.

Facing page: Willow was another matter altogether. Alyson Hannigan has such expressive facial features for Willow that it was (and continues to be) a challenge to find and execute that "right" kind of expression that Willow would do.

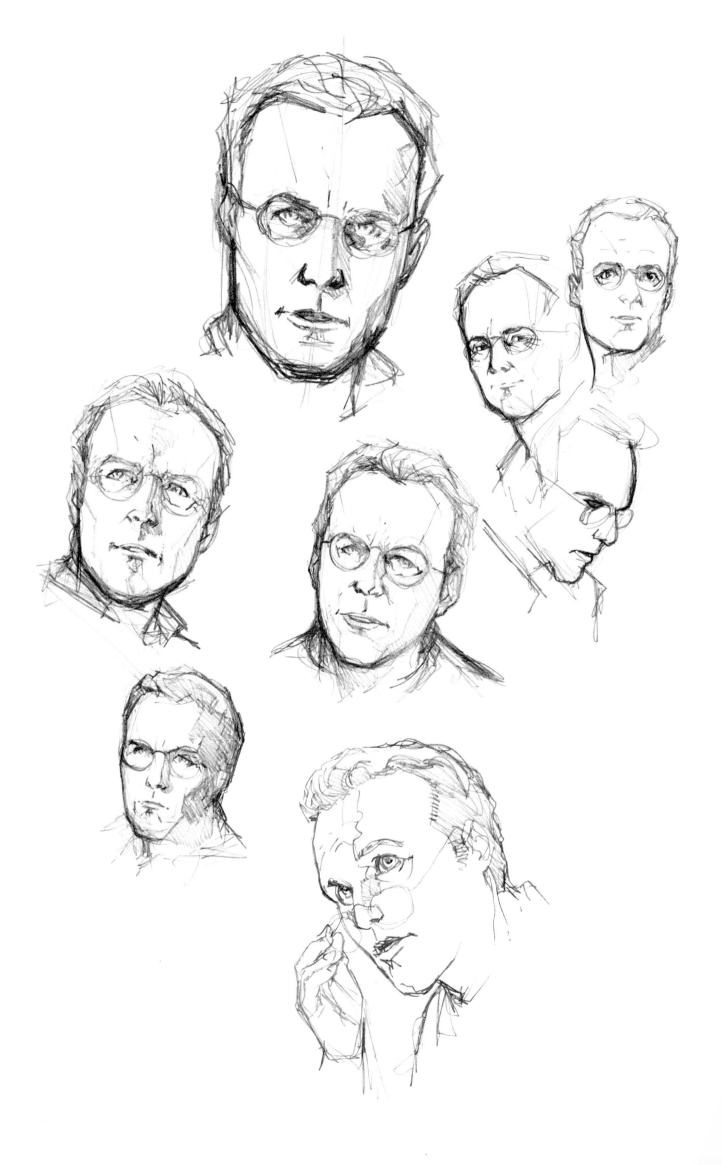

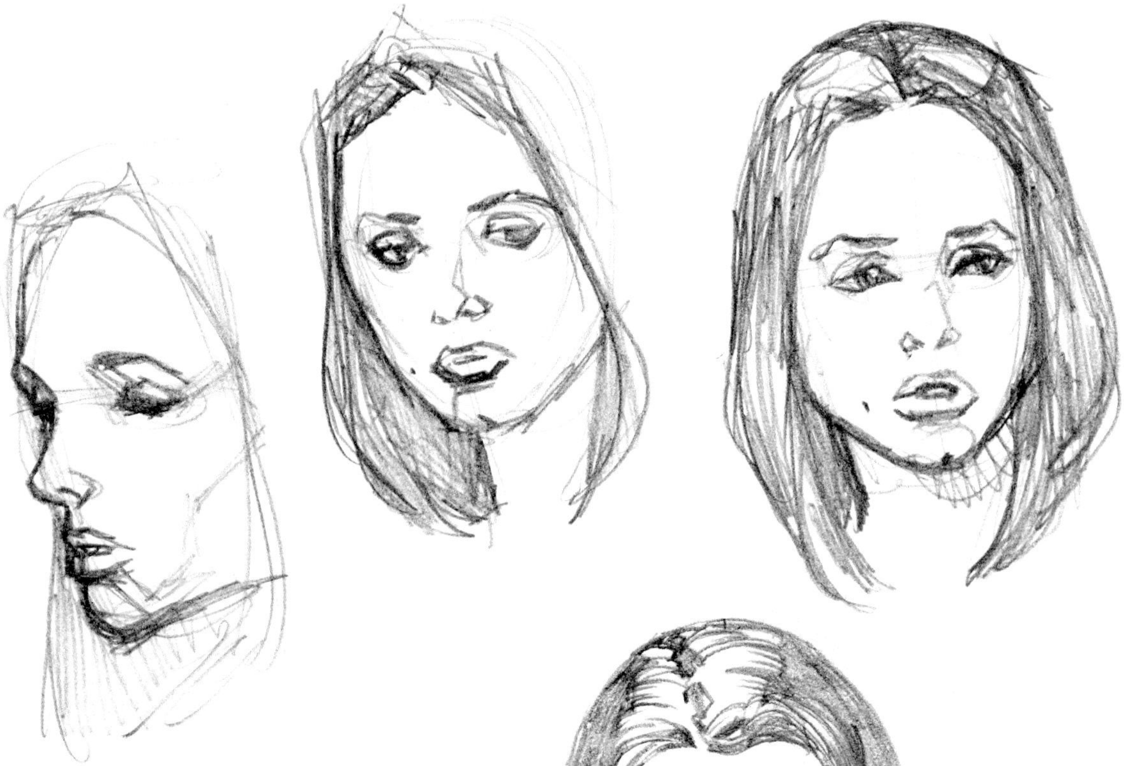

Right: *I still don't know why there's so much dislike of Dawn in the series. Sure, she was Buffy's whiny little sister, but that's what she was supposed to be. Watching the episodes in preparation to draw the comic, I enjoyed the character of Dawn. I thought she really grew up in Season 7 and was happy to see that growth continue in Season 8. This was my approval drawing for Fox.*

Facing page: *Giles was also a fun one to draw. Unlike the other characters, no matter how many lines I put in his face, it never looked bad. I had to remember to tell myself to have him clean his glasses every so often like in the series.*

Above: *Faith.*

Below: *Andrew.*

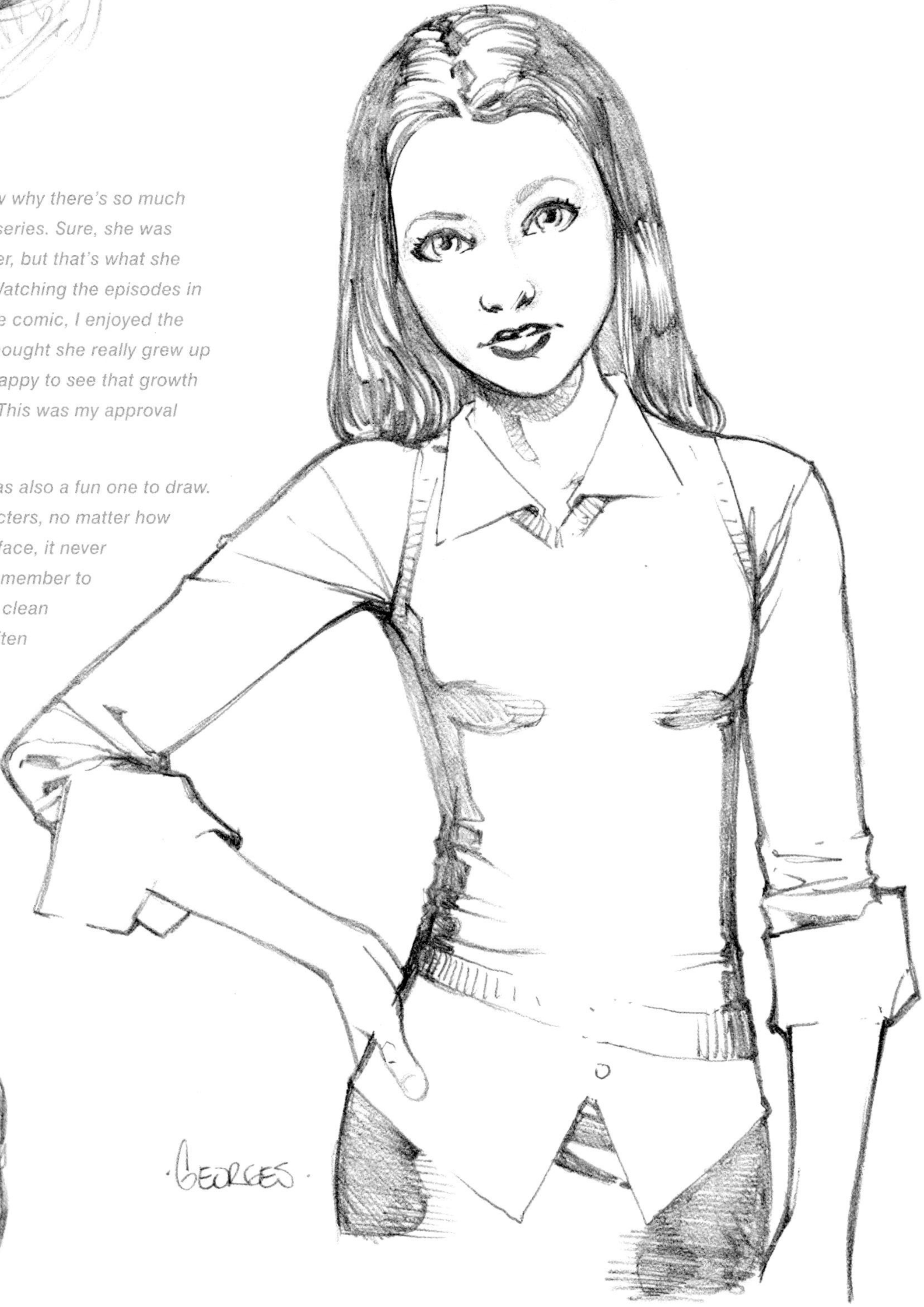
·GEORGES·

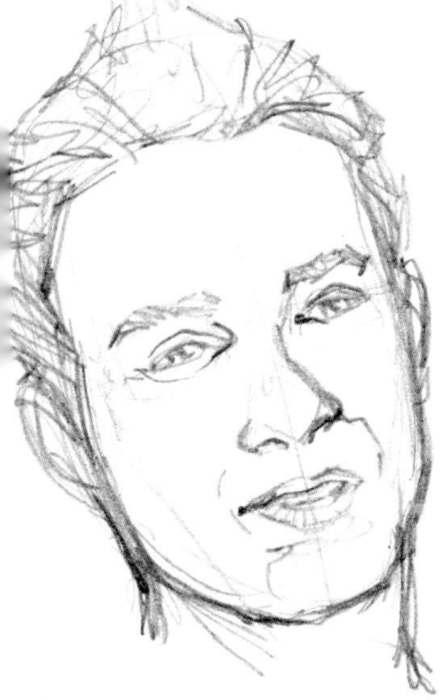

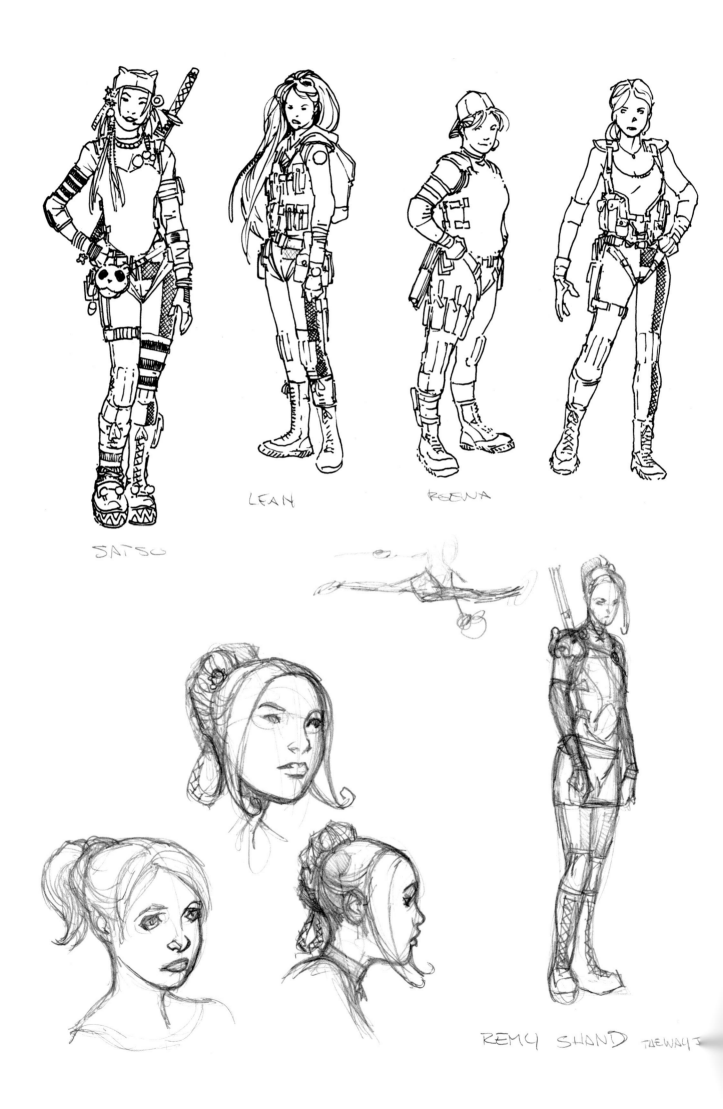

LEAH

ROENA

SATSU

REMY SHAND THEWAYS

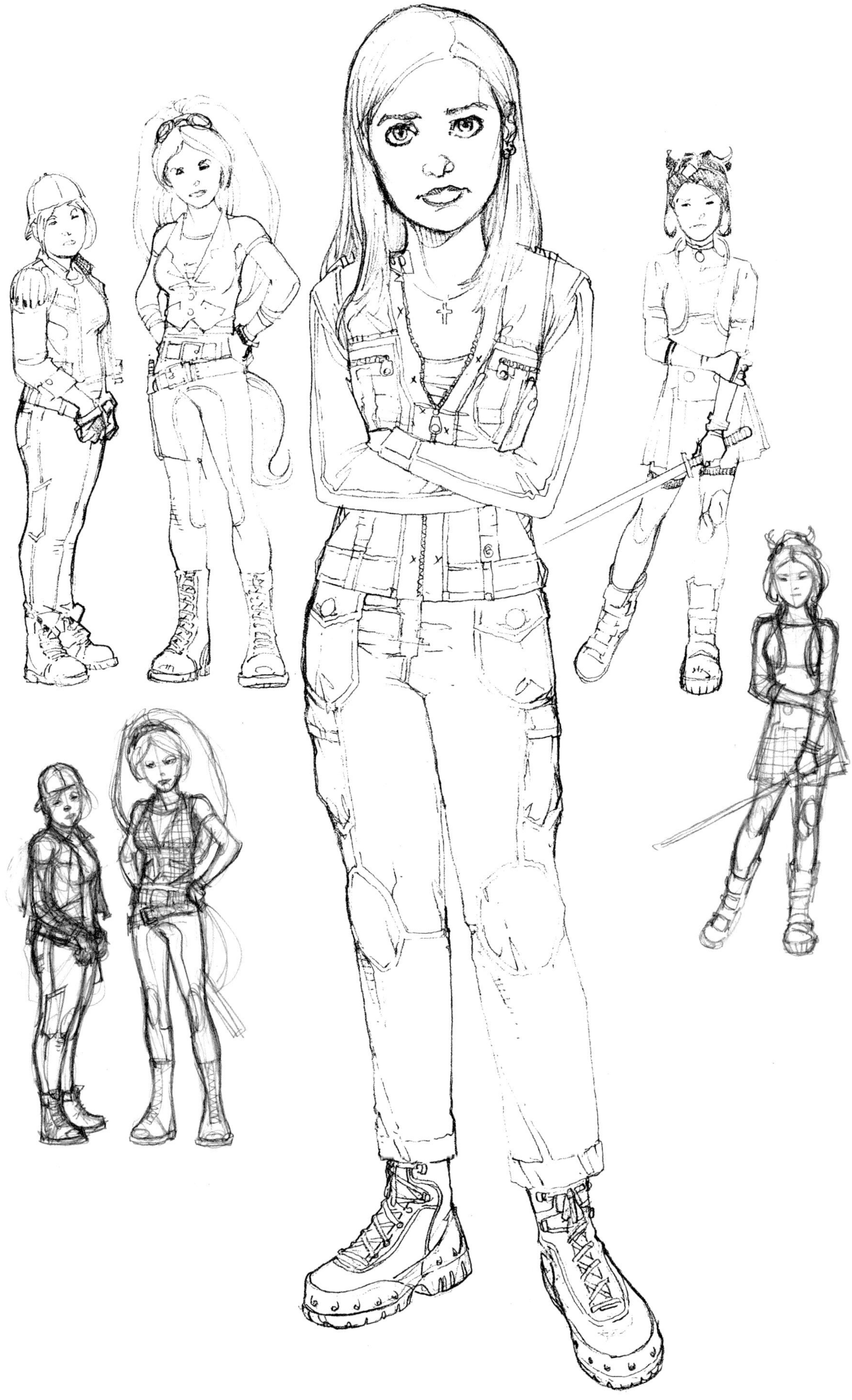

Joss really wanted the new Slayers in Season 8 to have distinctive looks and wear clothes different from one another, so I set out to do all these drawings of the main Slayers, Satsu, Leah, and Rowena, in different clothing. I'm not sure, but I think this is where Joss was really jazzed about these characters, because until these drawings, they had only been a few lines on paper that he had written. I really enjoyed Satsu. She was the genki *girl who always changed her look and that gave me free reign on how she'd dress. I spent hours looking for things she could wear.*

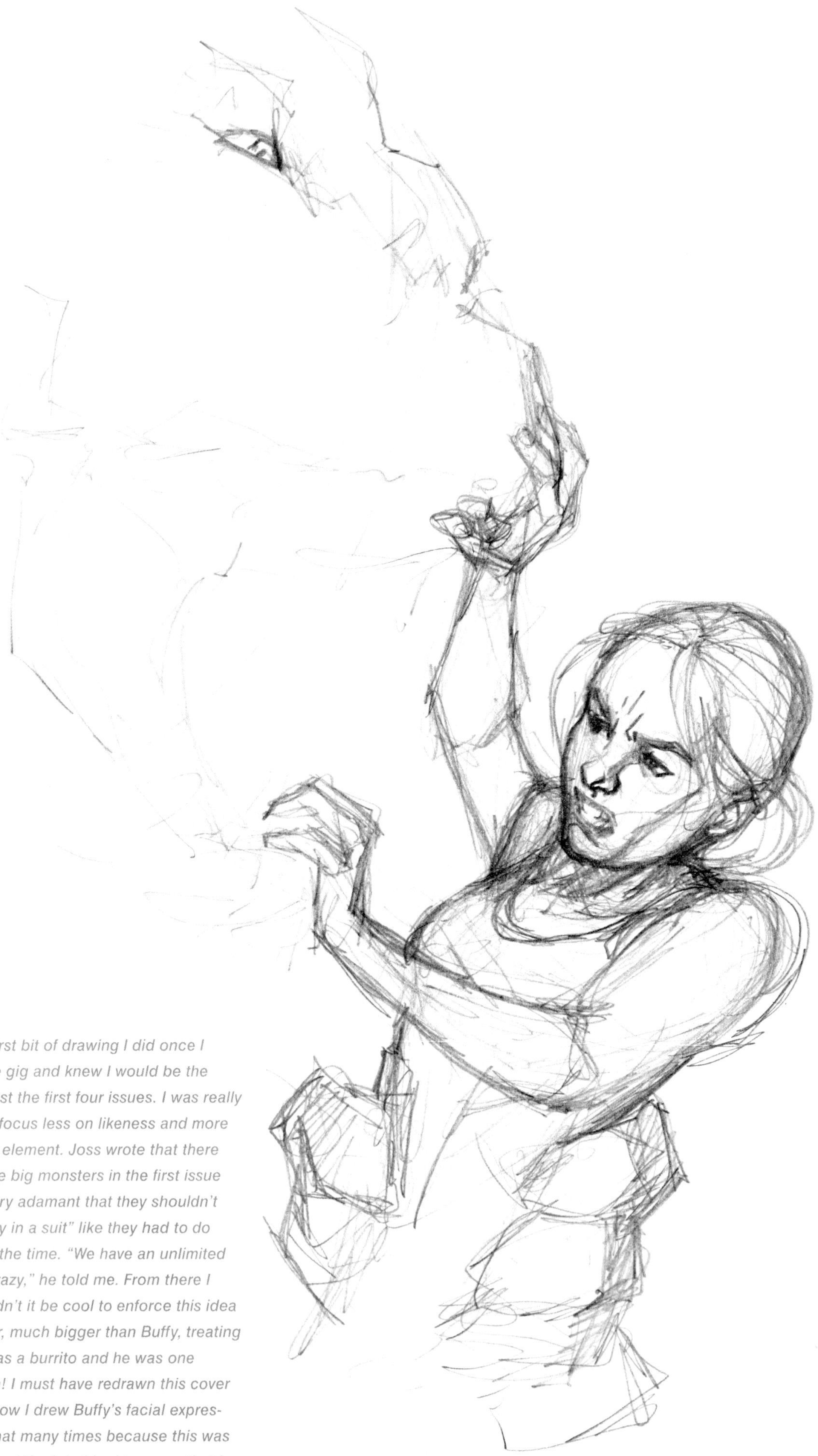

This was the first bit of drawing I did once I knew I had the gig and knew I would be the artist for at least the first four issues. I was really happy I could focus less on likeness and more on the fantasy element. Joss wrote that there would be these big monsters in the first issue and he was very adamant that they shouldn't look like a "guy in a suit" like they had to do on TV most of the time. "We have an unlimited budget—go crazy," he told me. From there I thought, wouldn't it be cool to enforce this idea with a monster, much bigger than Buffy, treating her like she was a burrito and he was one hungry demon! I must have redrawn this cover five times. I know I drew Buffy's facial expression at least that many times because this was it. Now that I had the job, I had to prove that I could do it. After it was finished, I never worried if I could draw this book again. I'm really happy with the way it turned out.

BUFFY THE VAMPIRE SLAYER 1 ALT COVER GEORGES JEANTY COVER

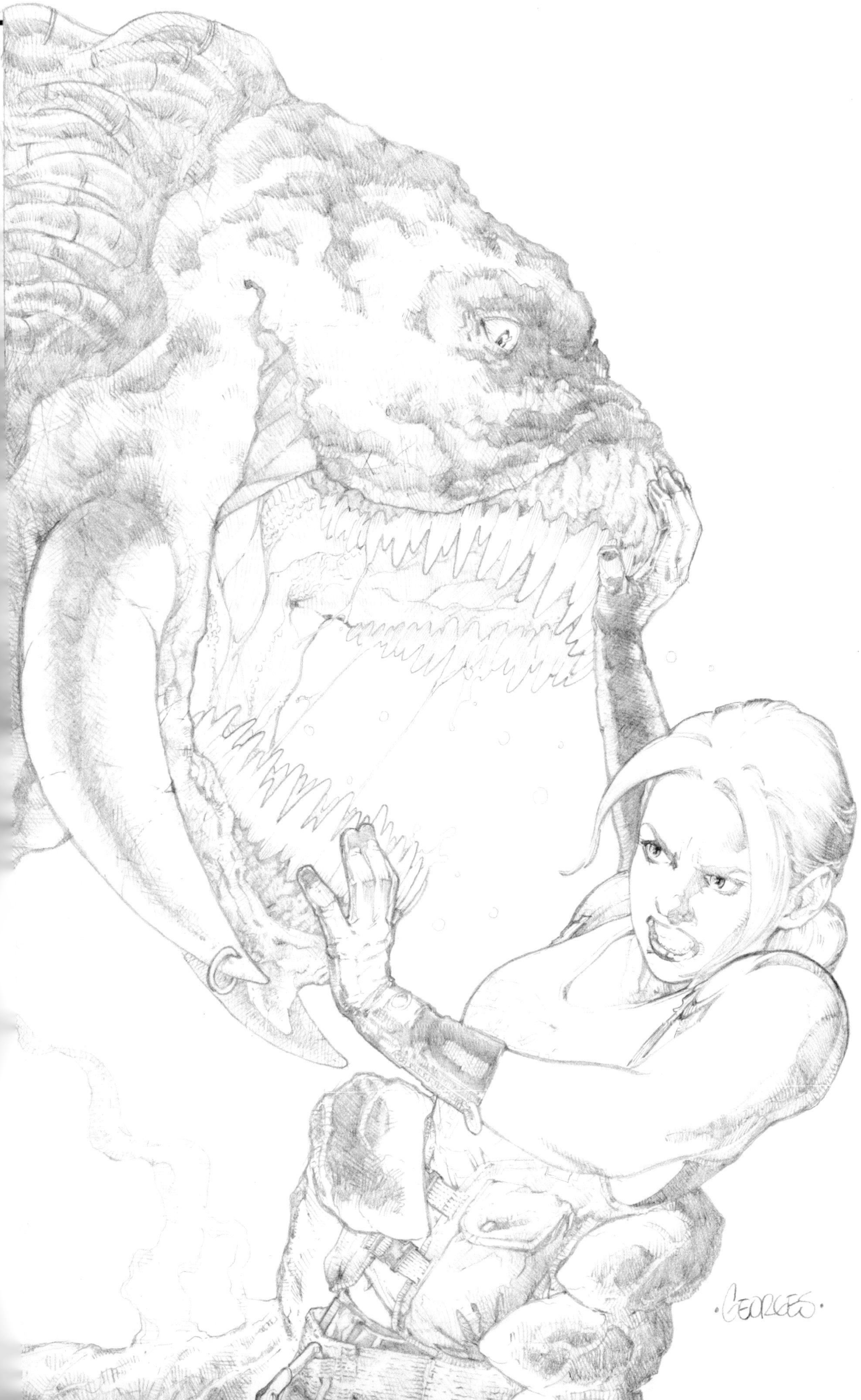
·GEORGES·

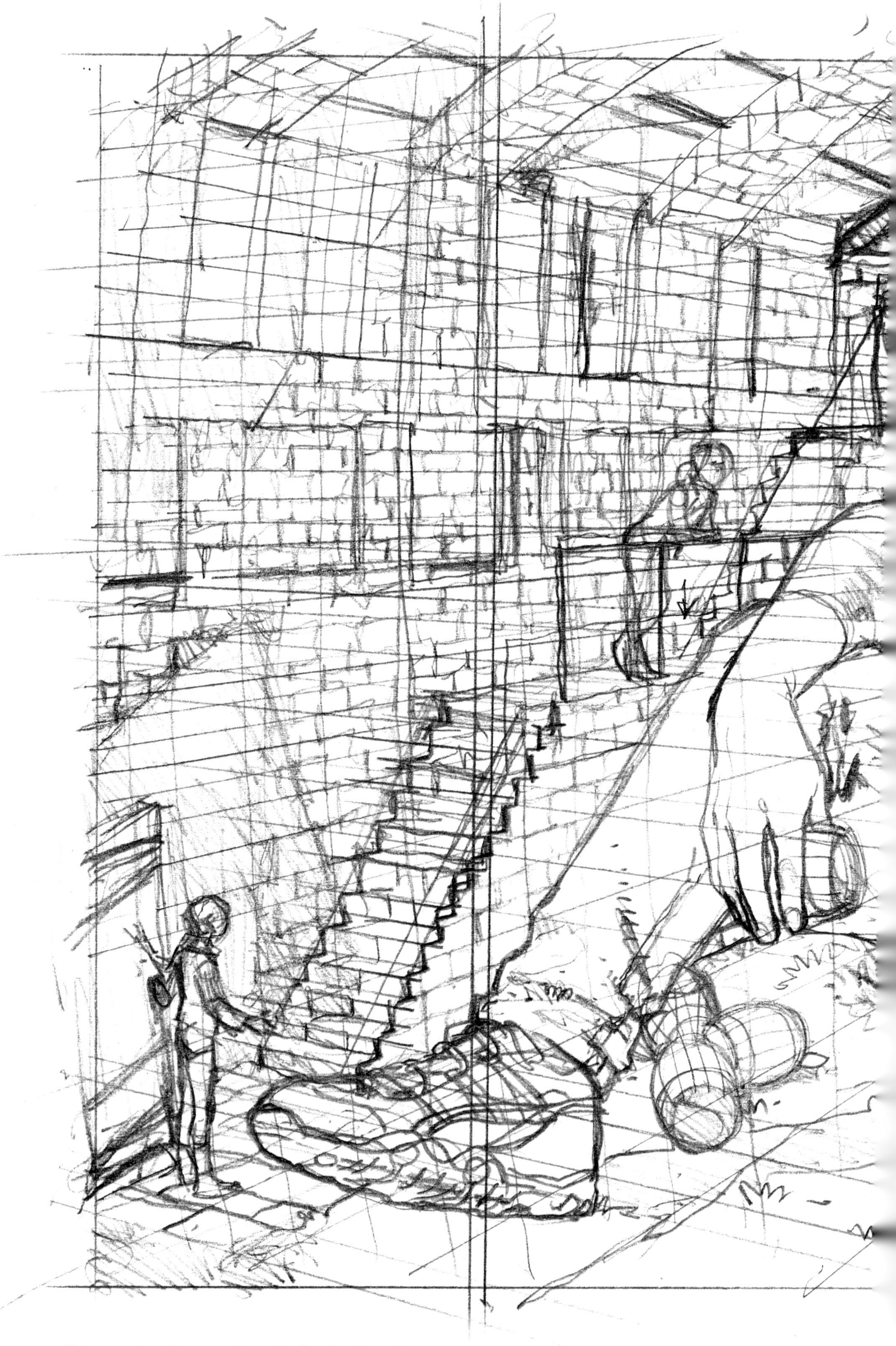

This was a daunting page. It was the first time I was drawing Dawn, and while it was the second double page of the issue, it was the most perspective heavy. I had no problem with the larger image at all. What did I have problems with? Dawn's face. I just could not get it down—so much so that I finished the piece with Dawnie's head missing.

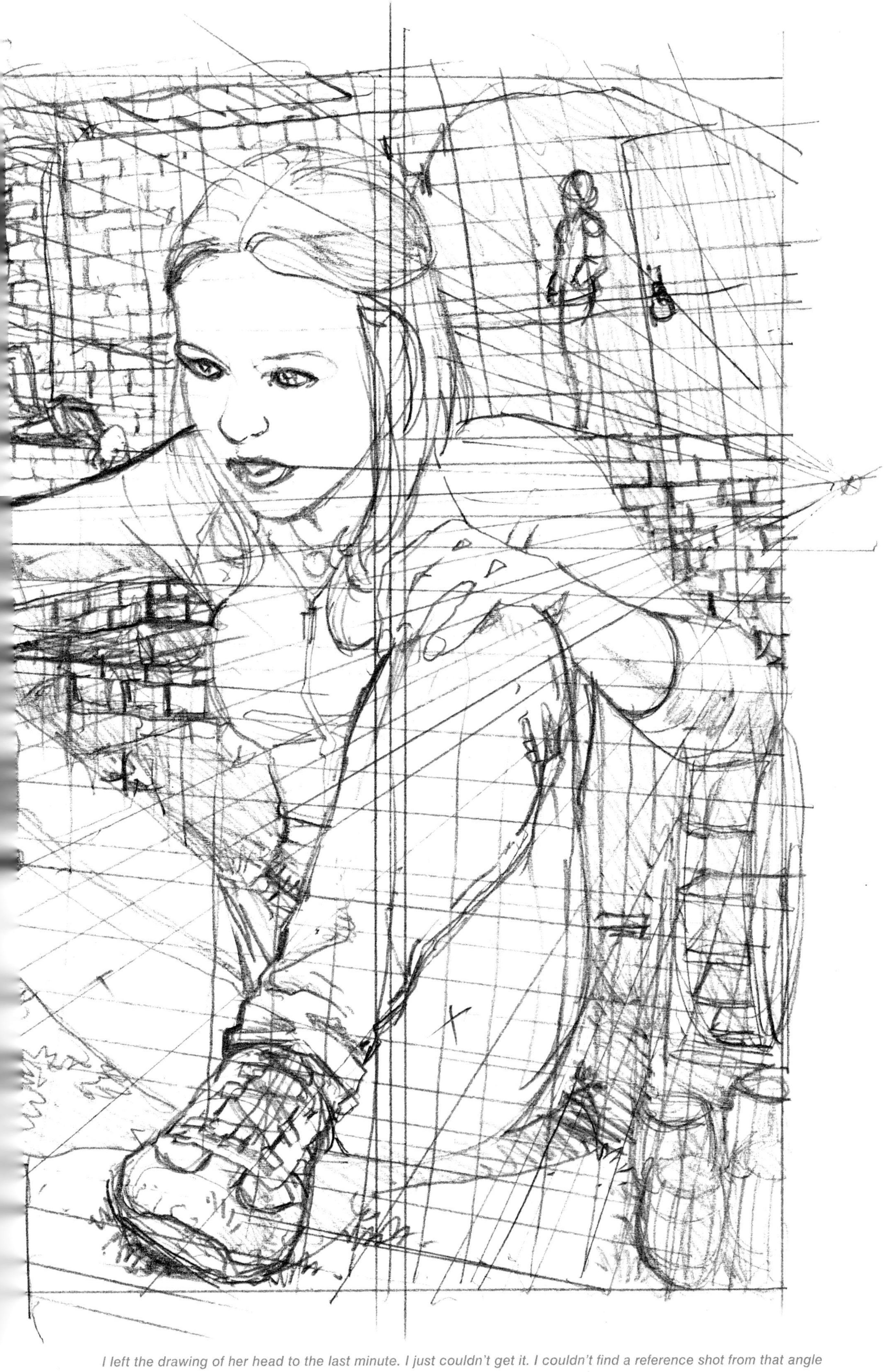

I left the drawing of her head to the last minute. I just couldn't get it. I couldn't find a reference shot from that angle that I liked and I was lost. When it came time to send out the piece to be inked, I just buckled down and drew her face as best I could. It ended up turning out pretty good.

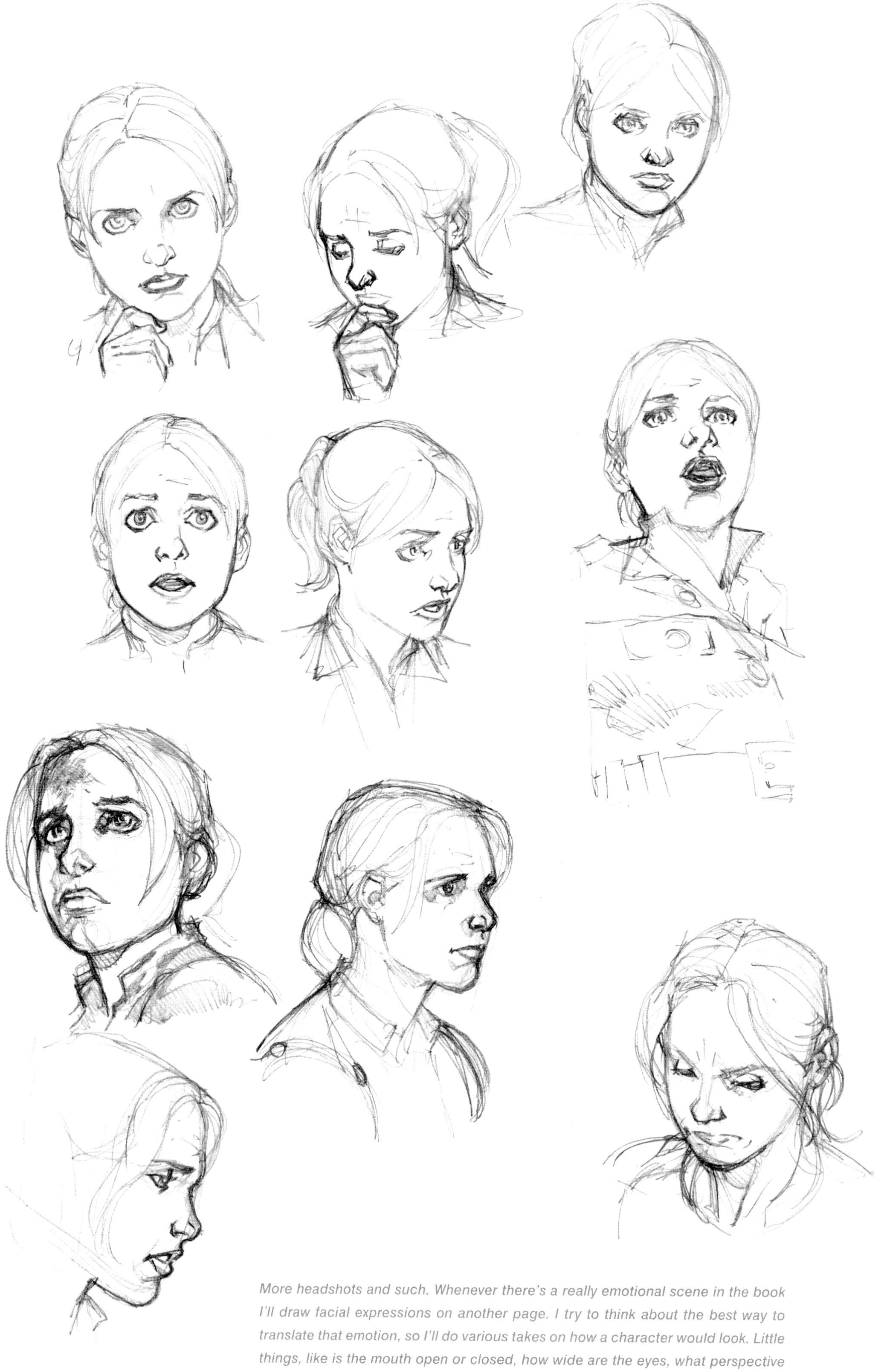

More headshots and such. Whenever there's a really emotional scene in the book I'll draw facial expressions on another page. I try to think about the best way to translate that emotion, so I'll do various takes on how a character would look. Little things, like is the mouth open or closed, how wide are the eyes, what perspective works best? Boring stuff, really, but most of the comments I hear about the book are how well the emotion is captured, so all these sketches are not done in vain!

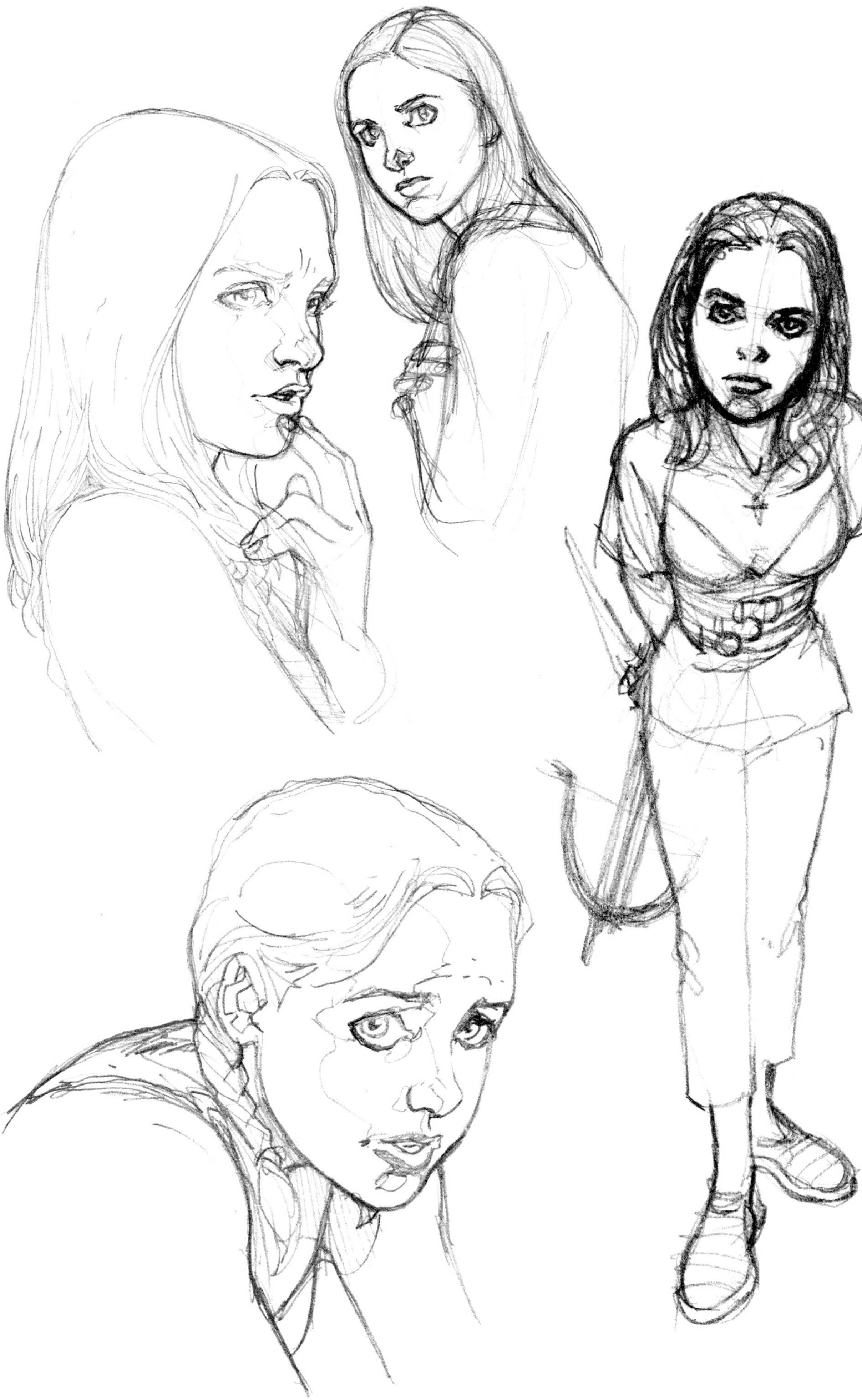

A

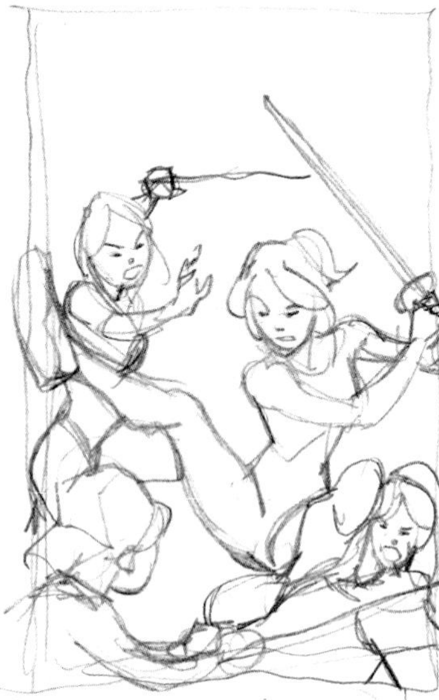

B

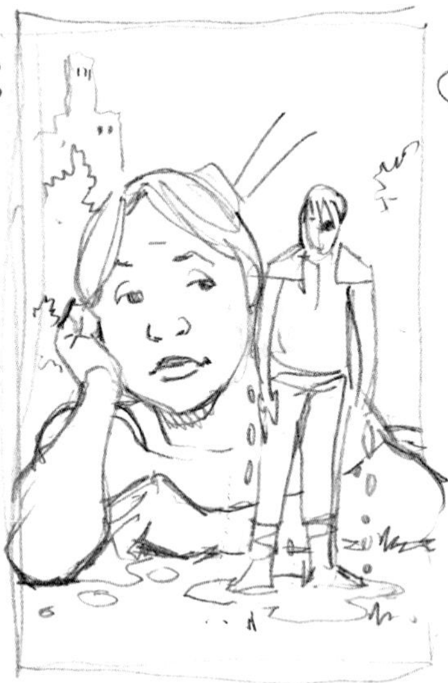

C

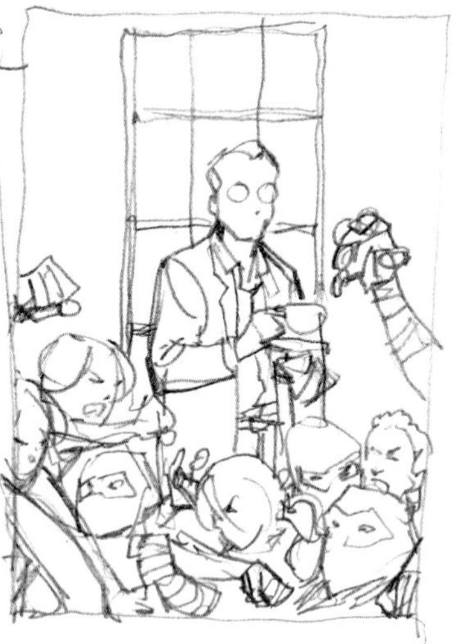

D

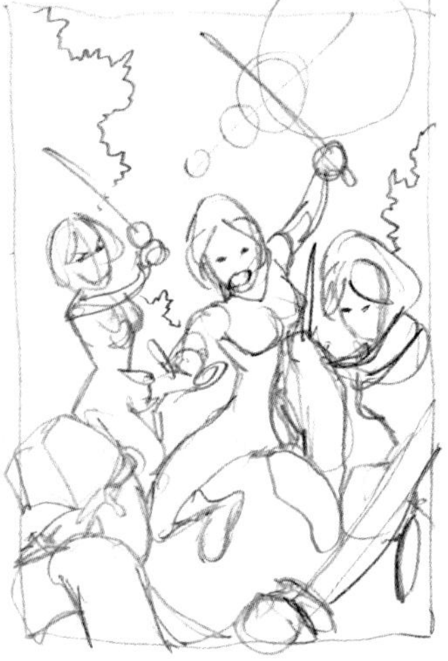

E

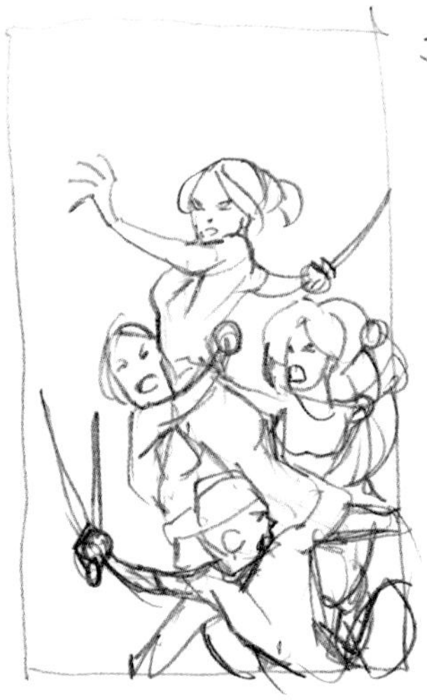

F

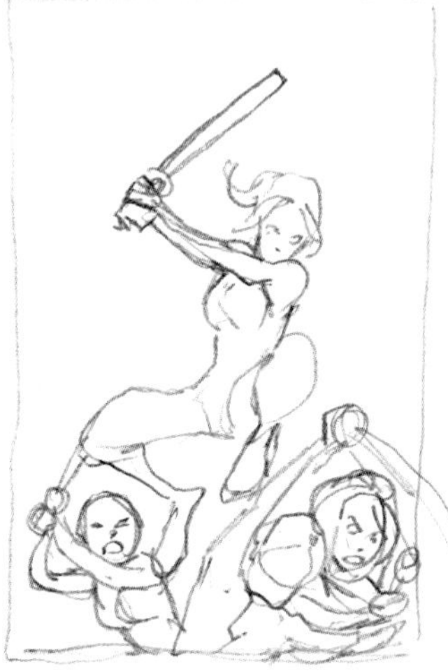

G

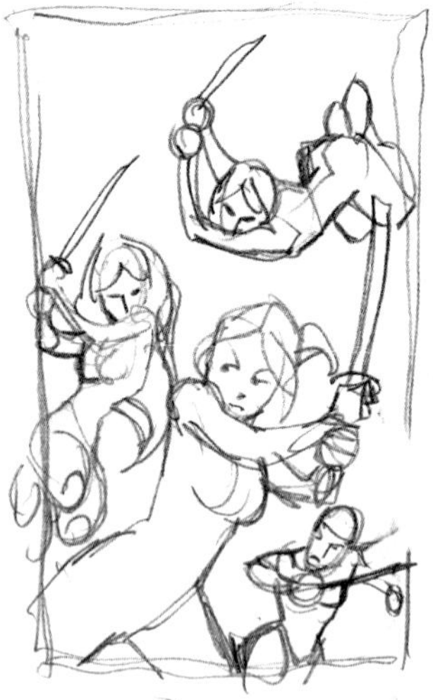

H

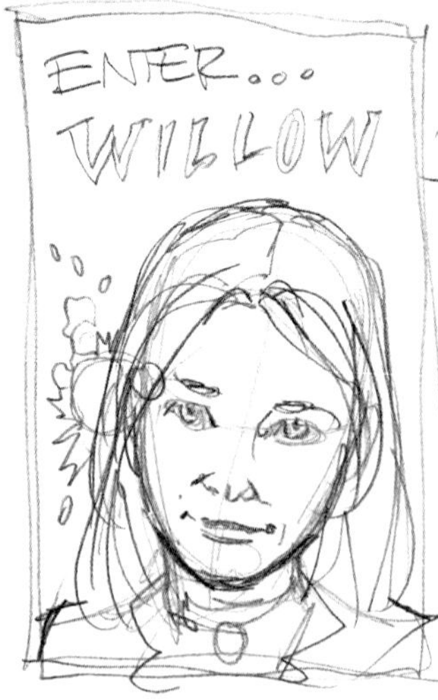
ENTER...
WILLOW

I

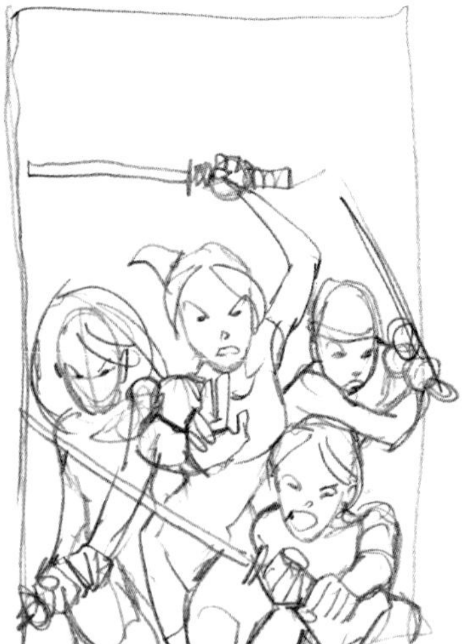

J

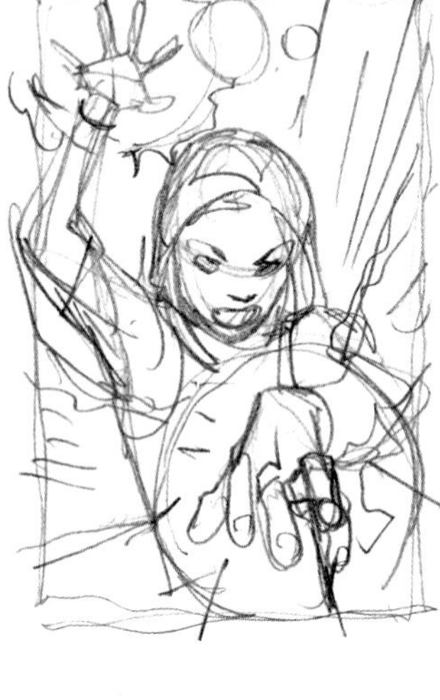

K

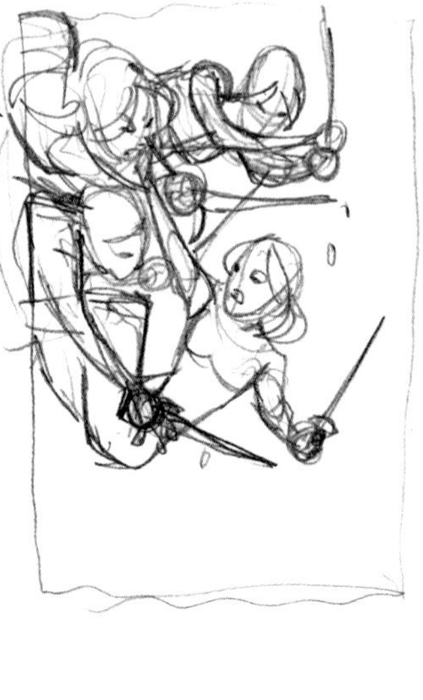

L

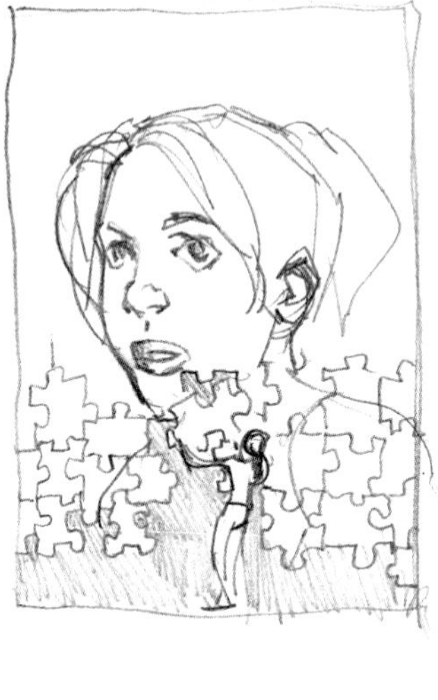

Whenever I do a cover I usually submit several ideas. I invite all involved with the issue to let me know if they have any ideas or directions they want a cover to take, then I go and sketch at least eight variations on any given theme, like the ones facing this page for the cover to issue #2. Buffy editor Scott Allie says he always looks forward to this part—looking at several ways a cover can go. These thumbnails are usually very rough and not meant for public viewing; they just have to get an idea across. Once this is done, everyone will chime in on what cover they like the most and from there I have a better idea of how to proceed. Once an idea is reached, I'll sketch it out a little more and if everyone is still in accord, we have a cover! I've done forty covers for Season 8, so I've submitted around 320 cover ideas. Some I've recycled, but I try to approach every issue fresh.

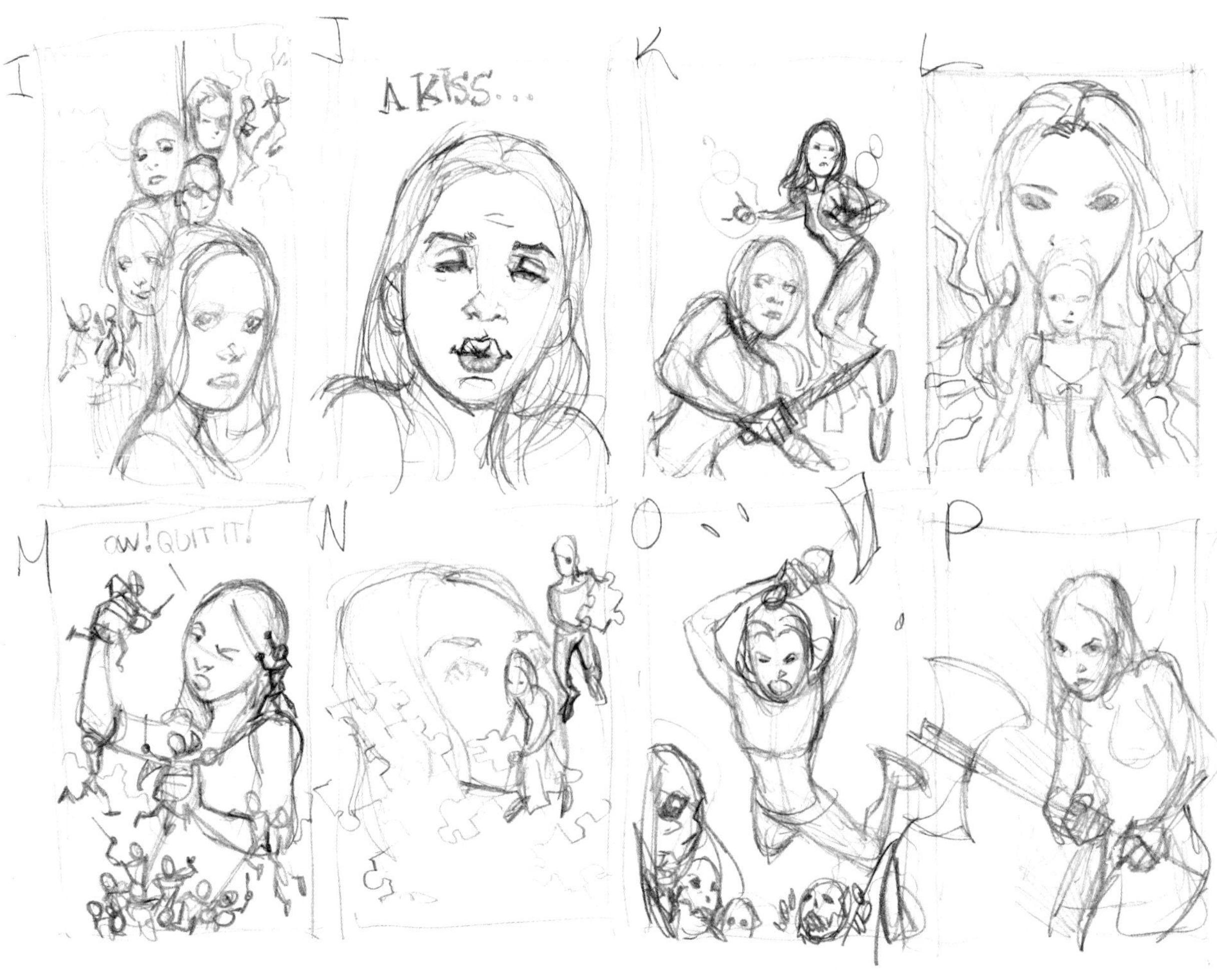
I
J
A KISS...
K
L
M
OW! QUIT IT!
N
O
P

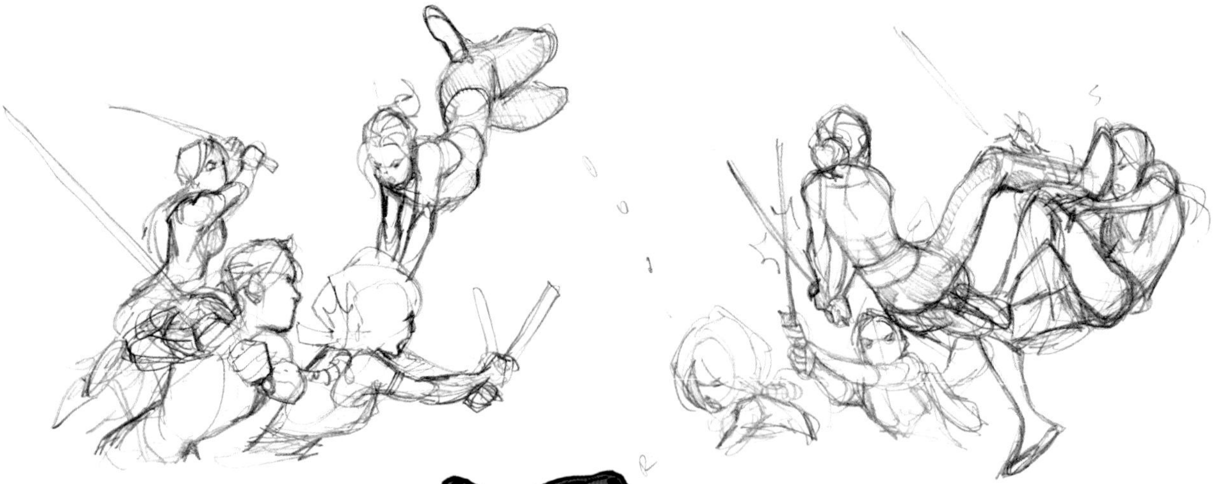

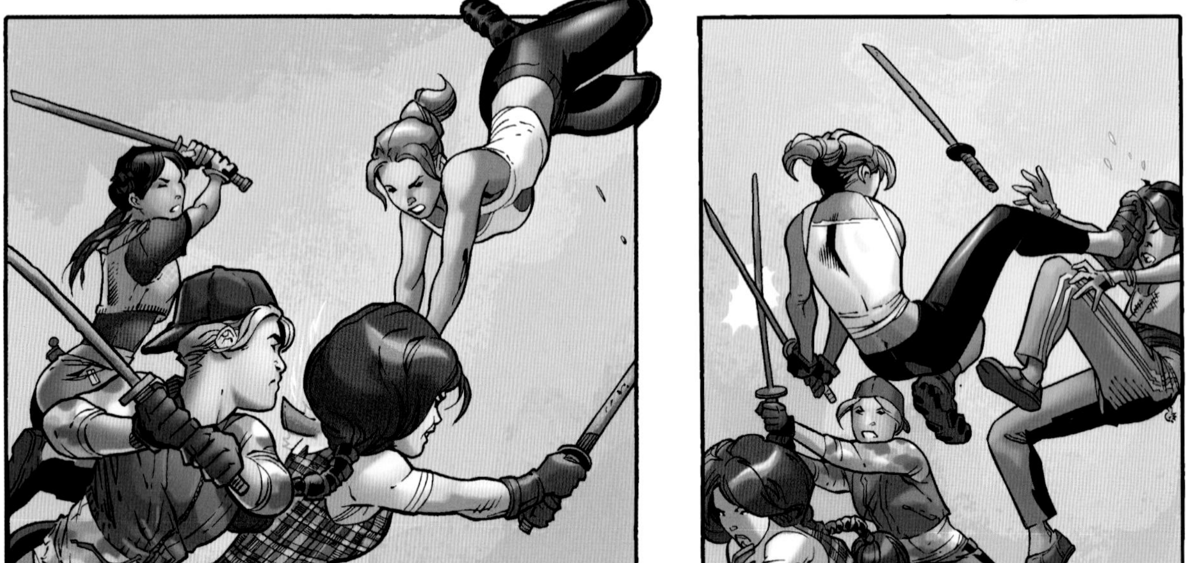

Another example of a cover process is this one for issue #3. I really liked the idea of Willow and Xander helping Buffy get back together, since that's essentially their job. I thought it would be really cool to personify that idea. But I submitted the regular crop of ideas also. I was really pulling for a cover like this; so much so, I actually included a version of it for issue #2 (go back and check; I'll wait.) From a concept, the final piece can evolve in many ways. Once you have an idea, the next step is to figure out the best way to show it. You'll notice little changes here and there from the sketch to the finished colored piece, like figures facing different ways, perspective changes, stuff like that.

Facing page: *I had to work out the fight scene on the opposite page a little more because Joss said he wanted the fight sequences to be over the top. These are Slayers, and they wouldn't fight like ordinary people, he told me. I love choreography so it was great fun to stage.*

Following pages: *When drawing the actual interior pages I do layouts. This is a typical example of how I work. I sketch everything out in two or three stages on 8 ½ x 11 inch paper, and then draw on the final big page. I think it's a great way to see the flow of the story and get a feel for what your pacing is going to be like. I'll try to get all my perspective in and any facial expressions the characters have at this point. It's a lot of fun to see what was previously in script form start to take life with pictures.*

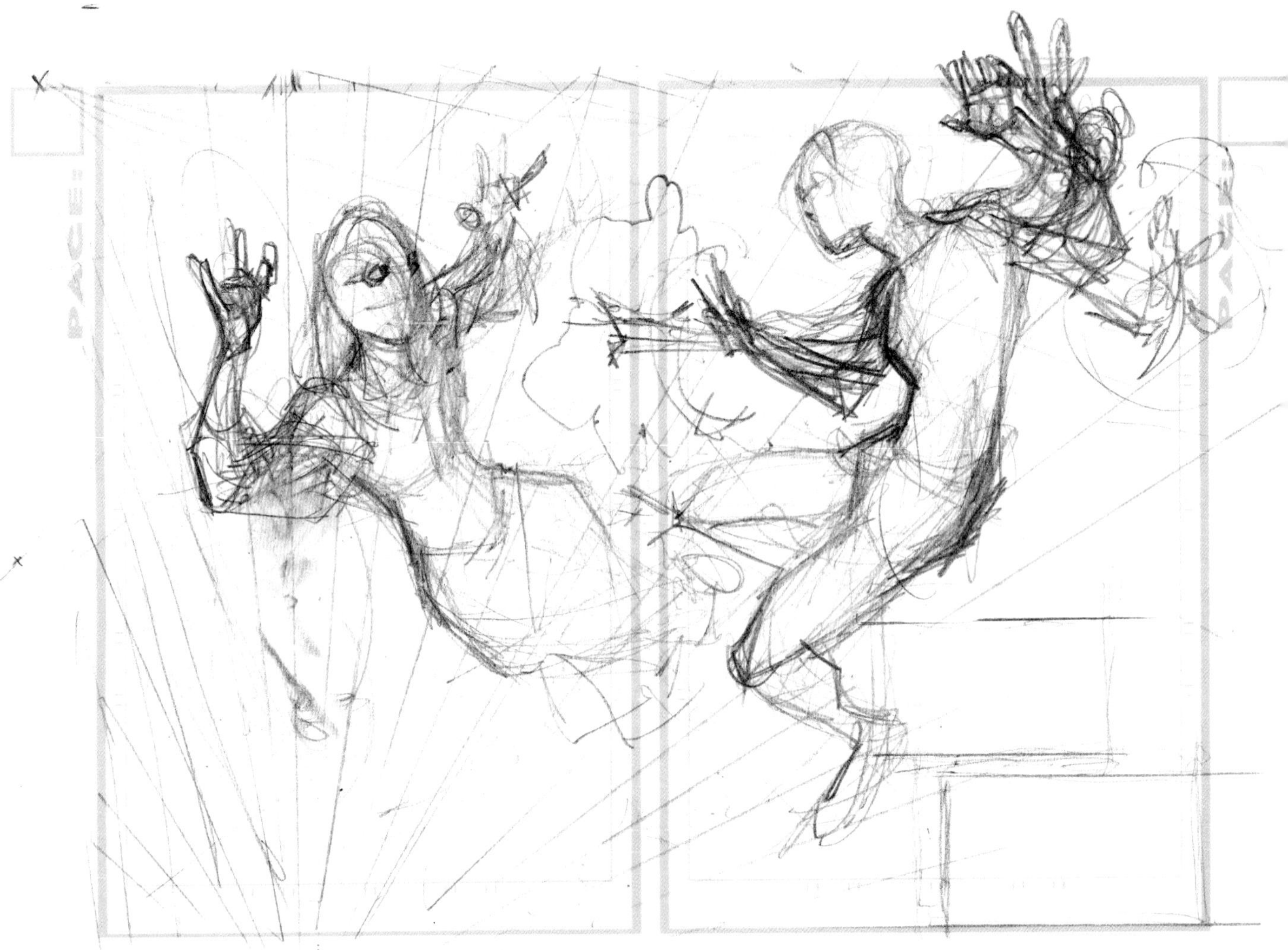

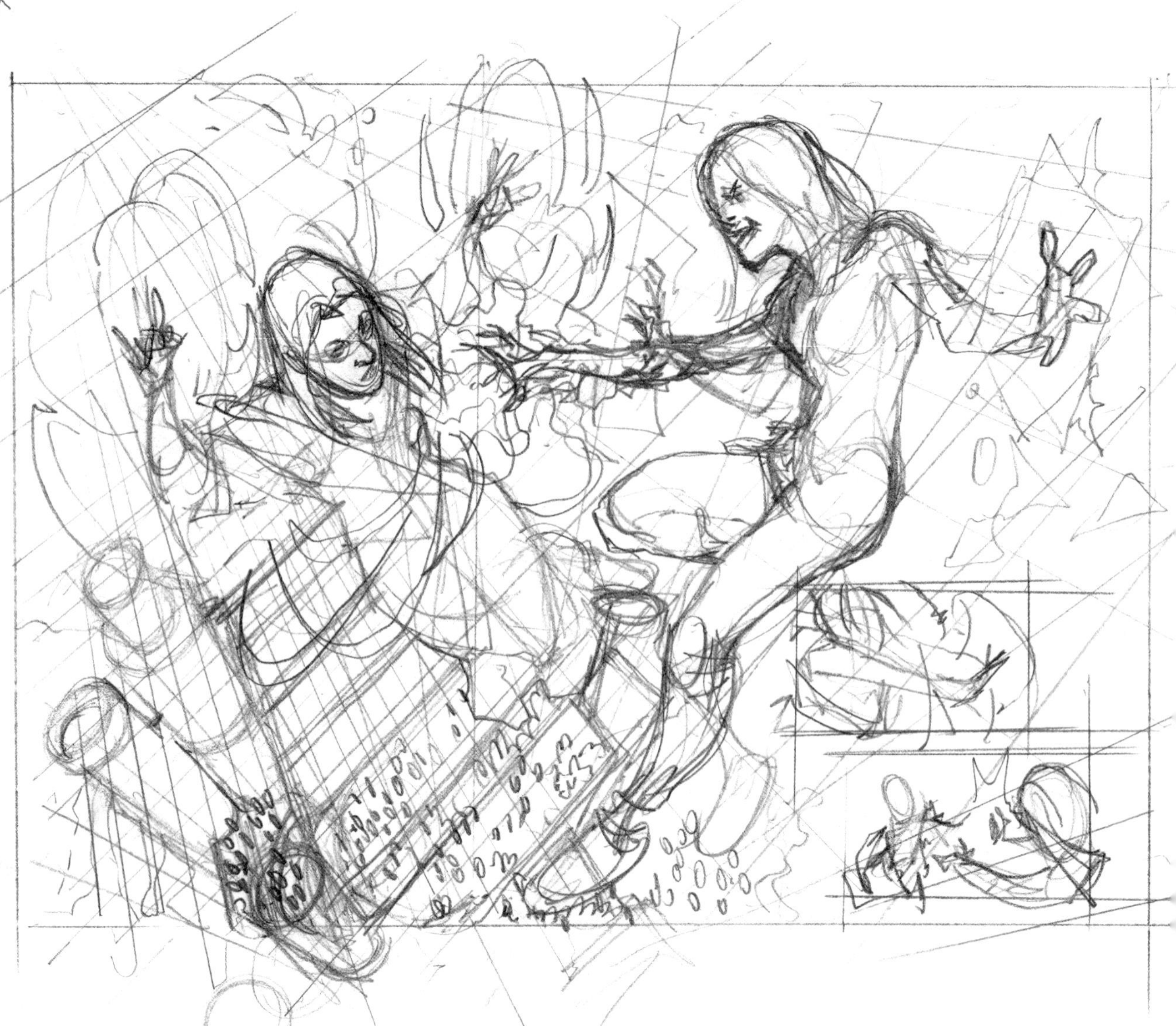

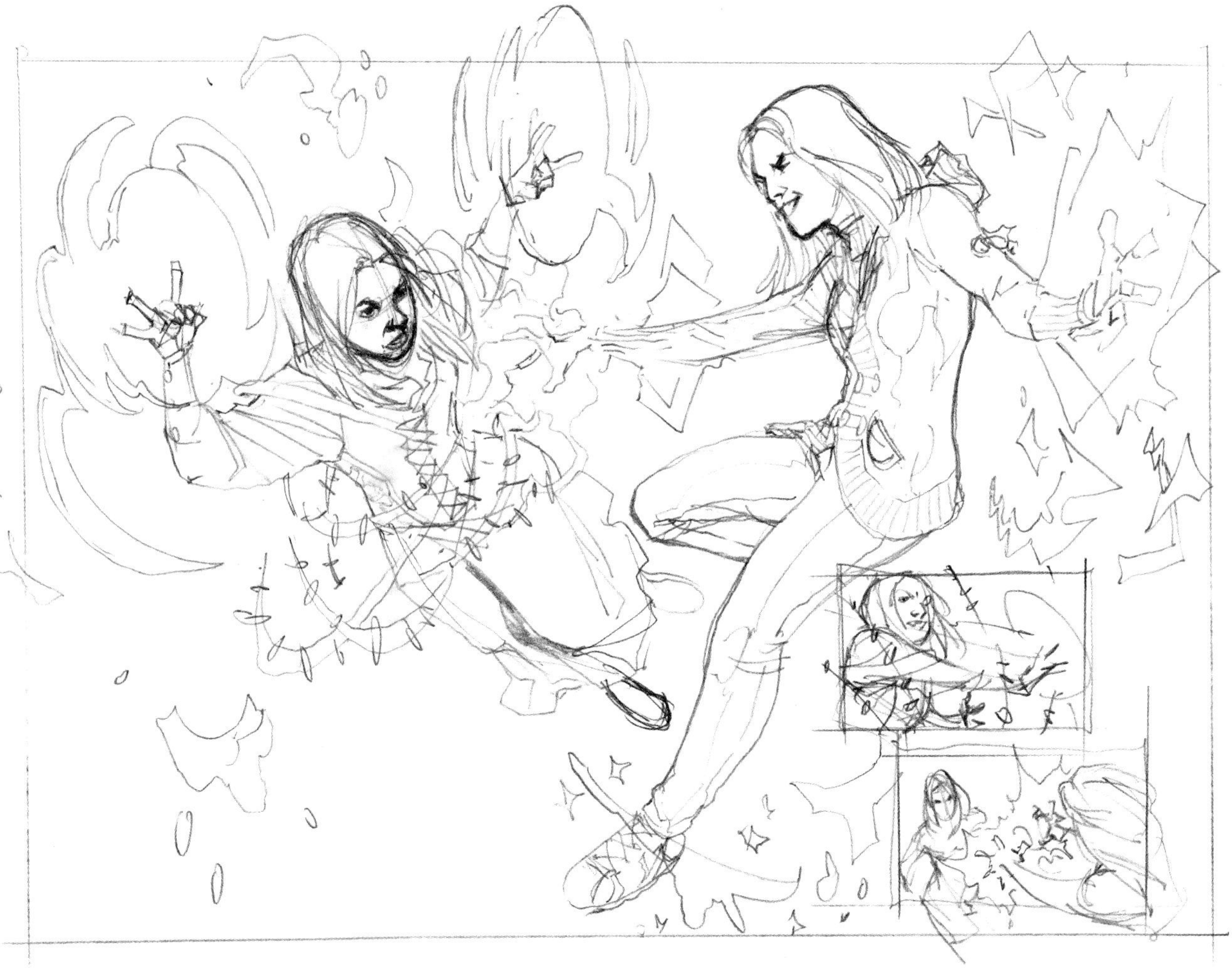

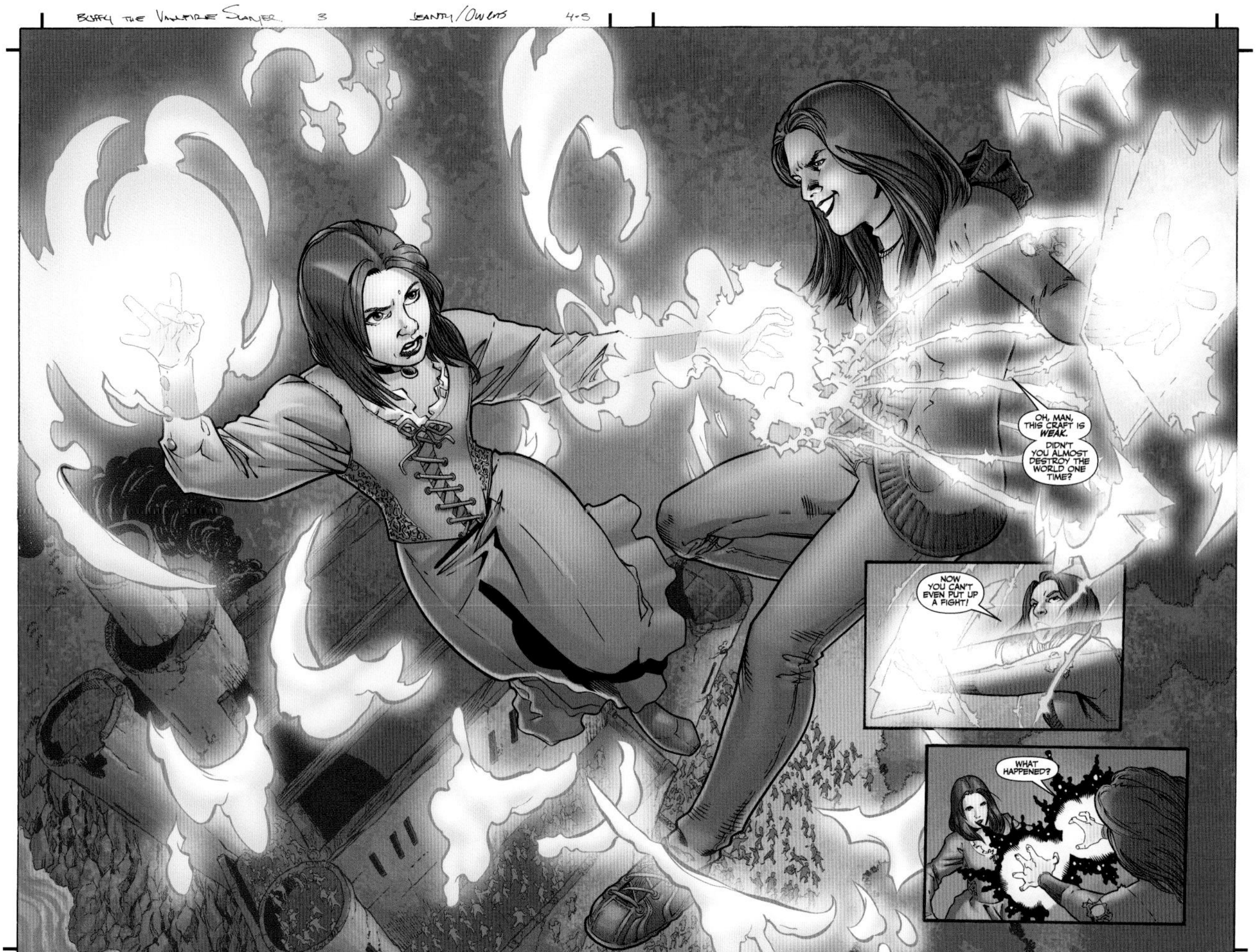
BUFFY THE VAMPIRE SLAYER 3 JEANTY/OWENS 4-5
OH, MAN, THIS CRAFT IS **WEAK.**
DIDN'T YOU ALMOST DESTROY THE WORLD ONE TIME?
NOW YOU CAN'T EVEN PUT UP A FIGHT!
WHAT HAPPENED?

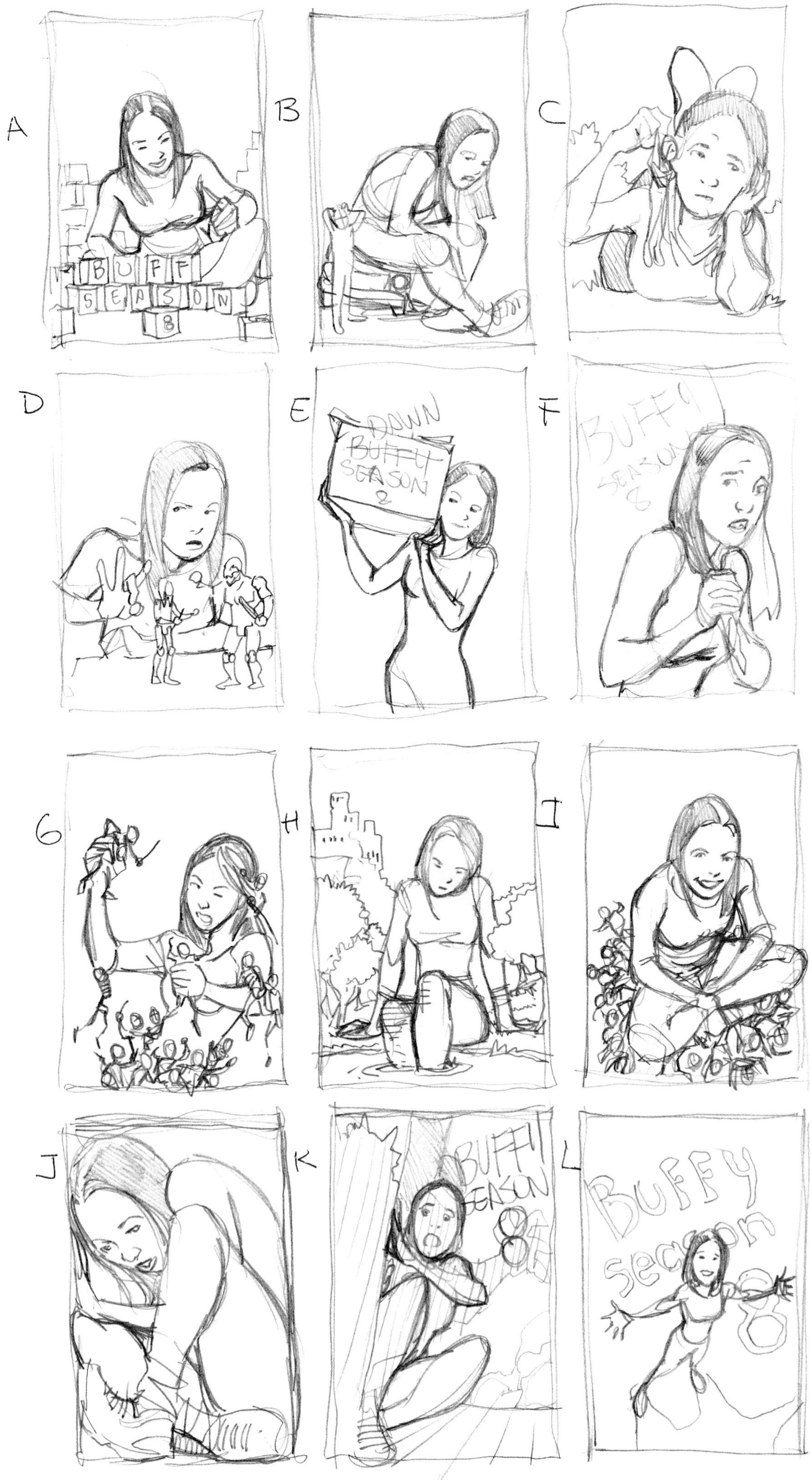
A
BUFF
SEASON
8
B
C
D
E
DOWN
BUFFY
SEASON
2
F
BUFFY
SEASON
8
G
H
I
J
K
BUFFY
SEASON
8
L
BUFFY
season
8

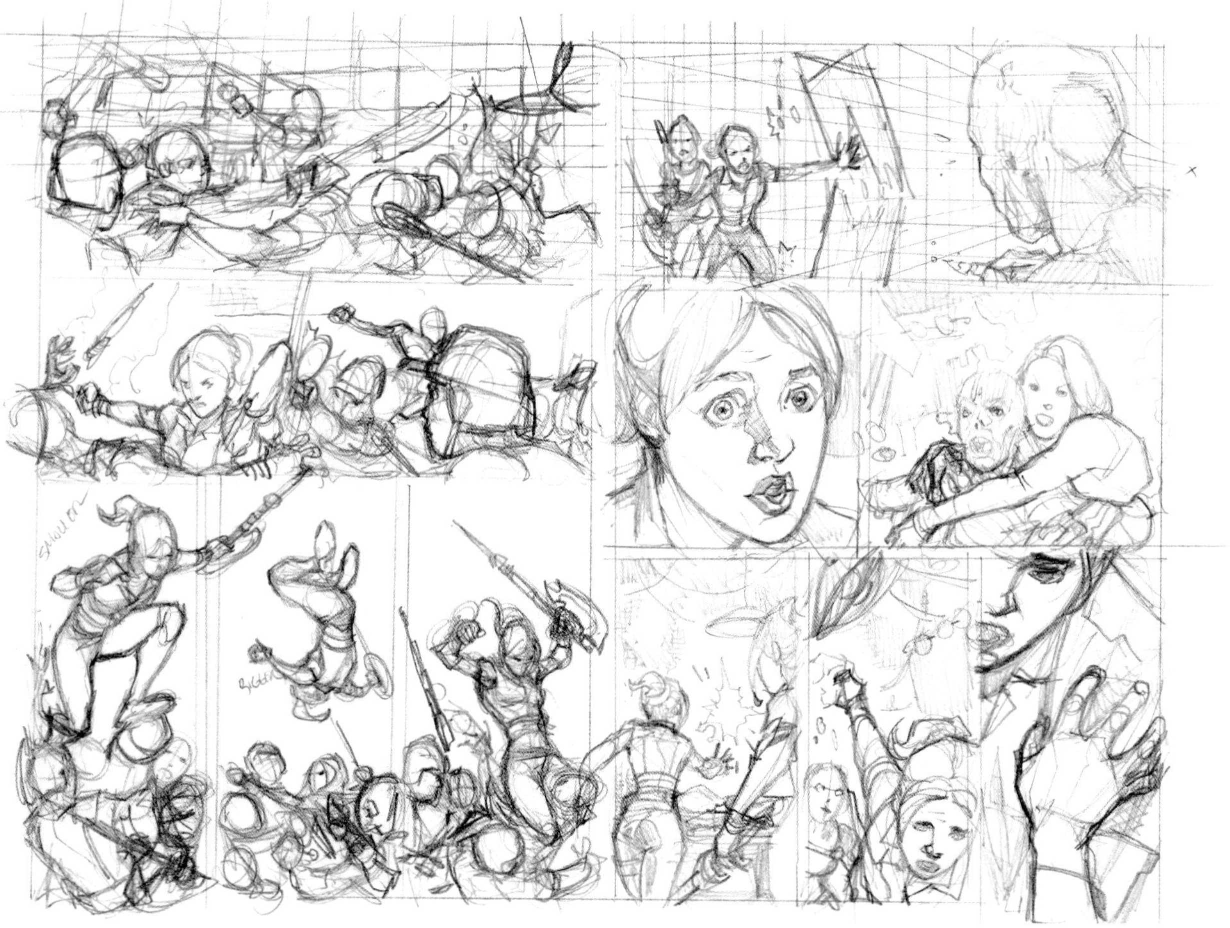

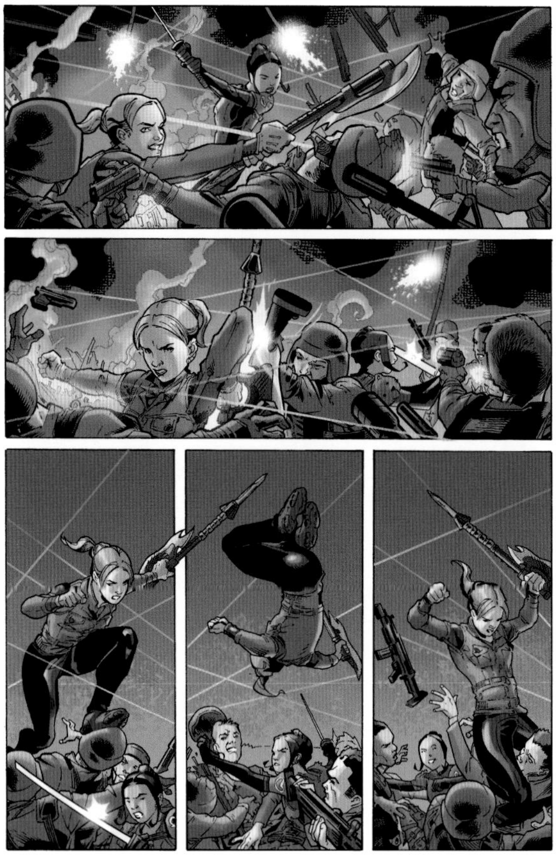

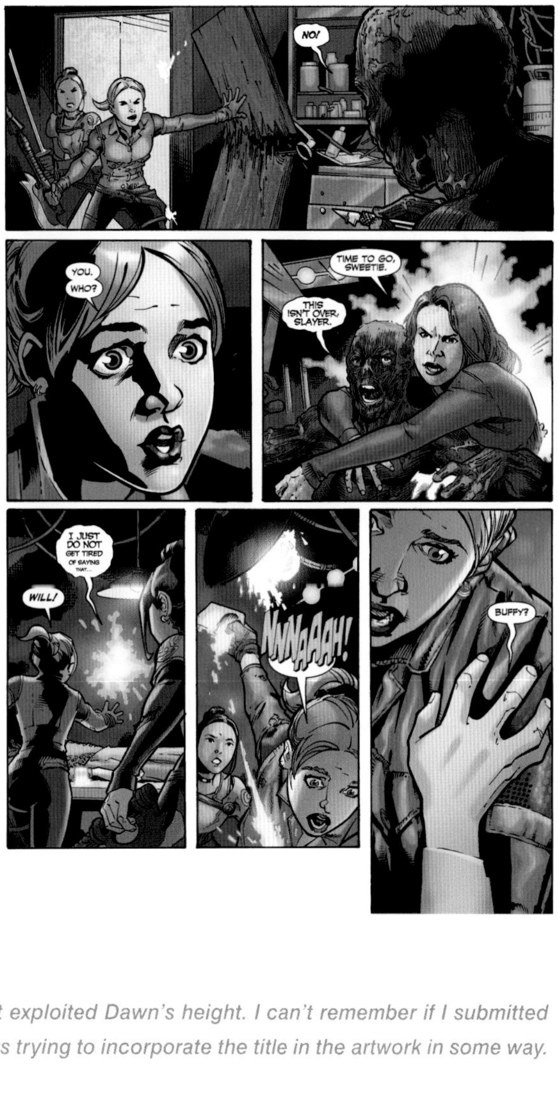
NO!
YOU.
WHO?
TIME TO GO, SWEETIE.
THIS ISN'T OVER, SLAYER.
I JUST DO NOT GET TIRED OF SAYING THAT...
WILL!
NNNAAAH!
BUFFY?

Facing page: *I was really jazzed about doing a cover that exploited Dawn's height. I can't remember if I submitted these thumbnails for the cover to issue #3 or #4. I'm always trying to incorporate the title in the artwork in some way.*

Above: *More process pieces.*

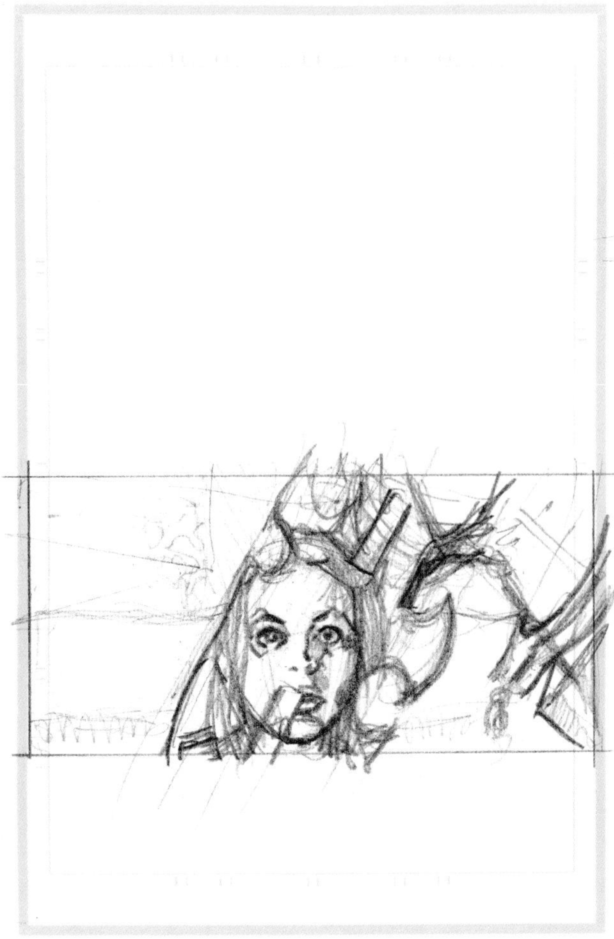

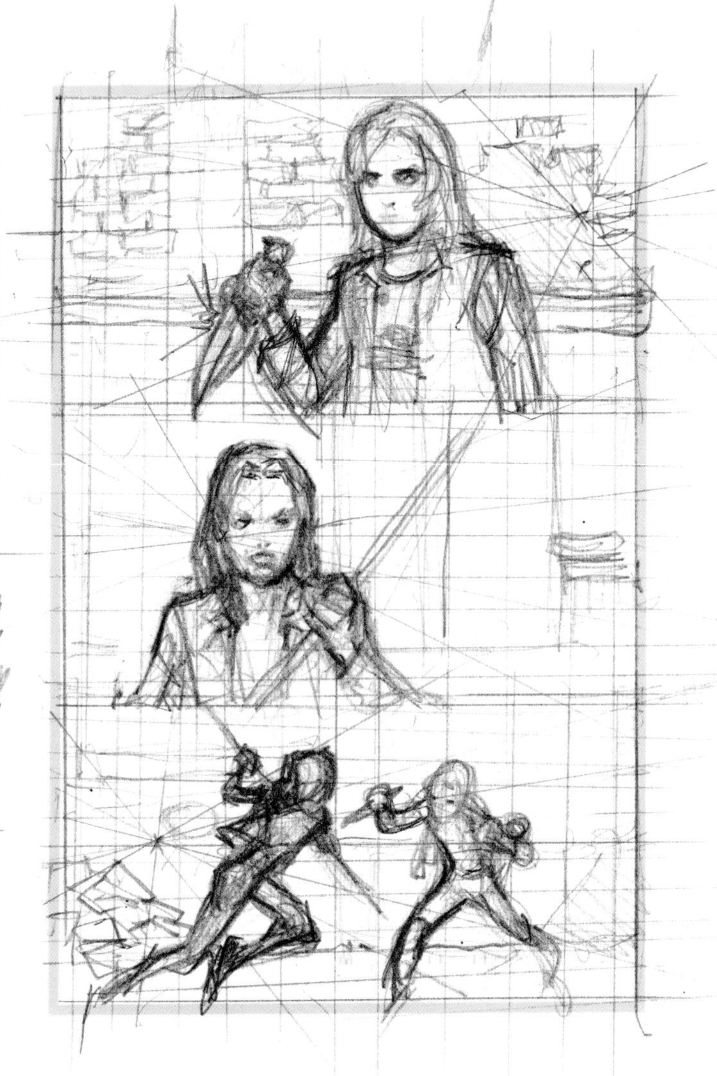

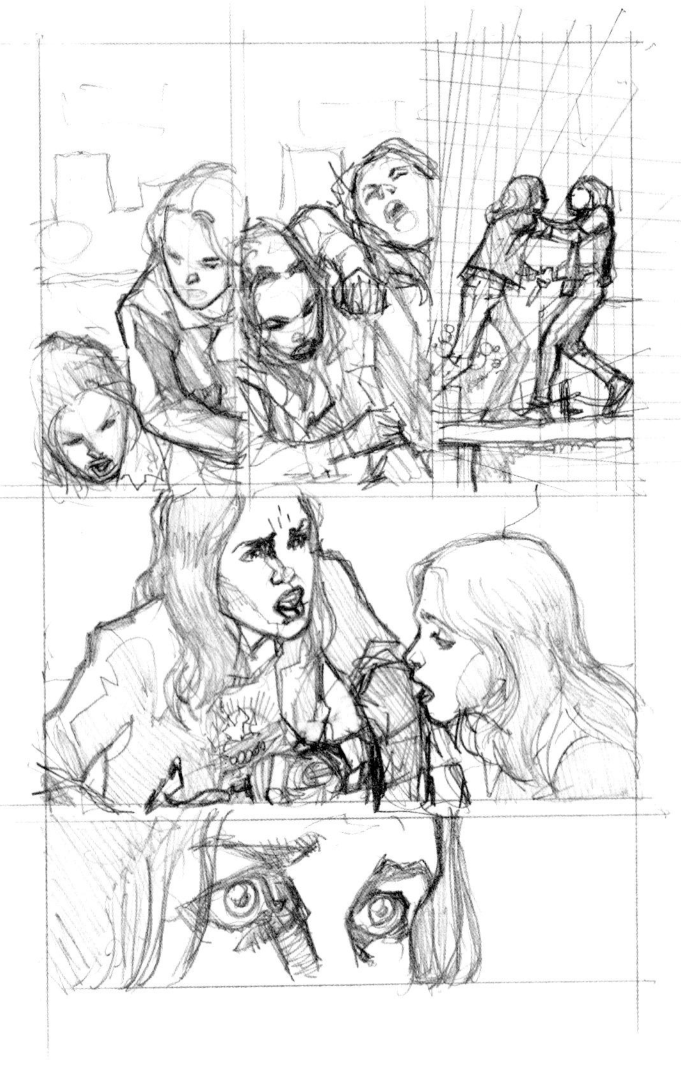

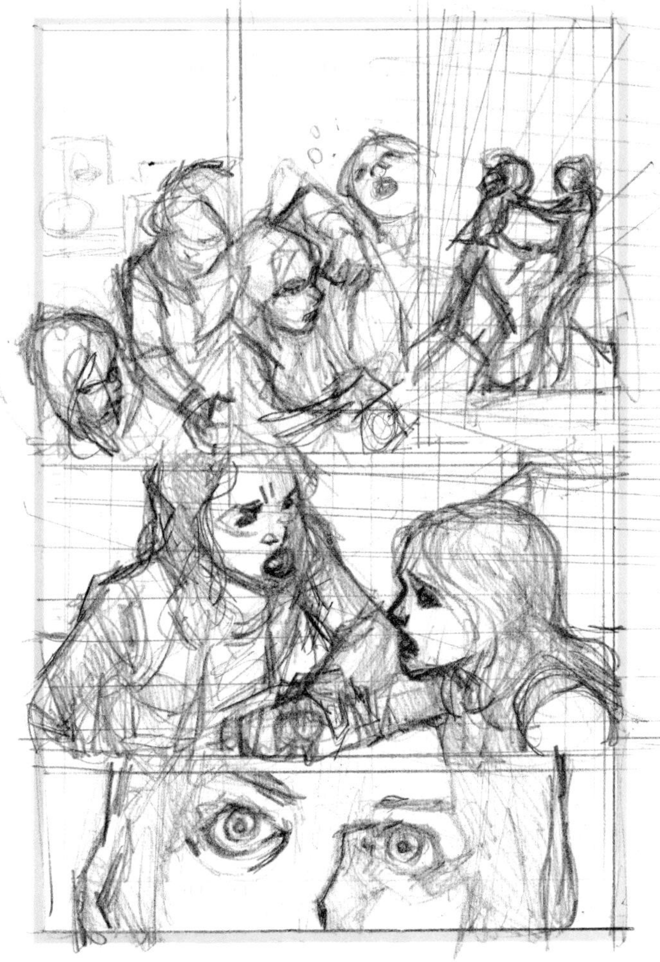

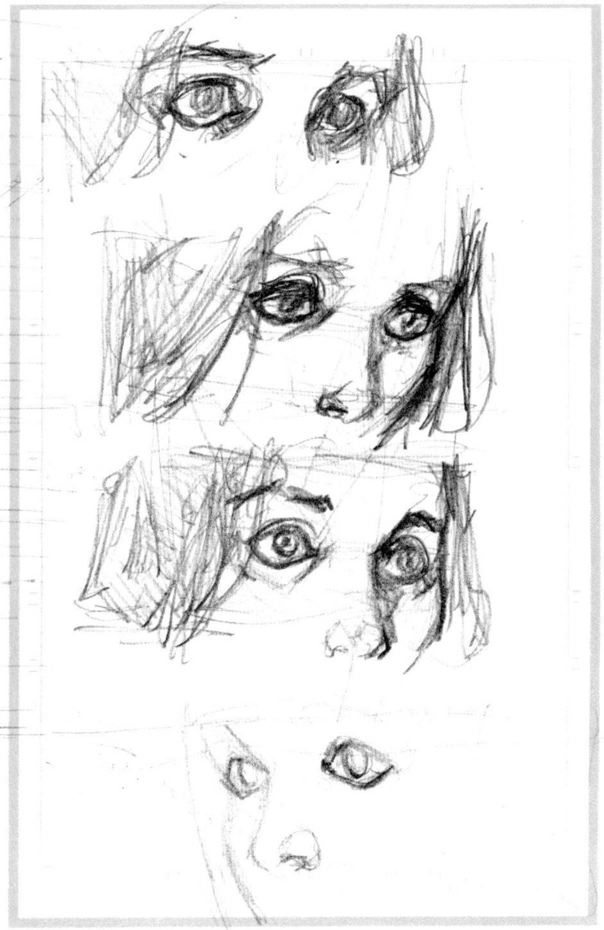

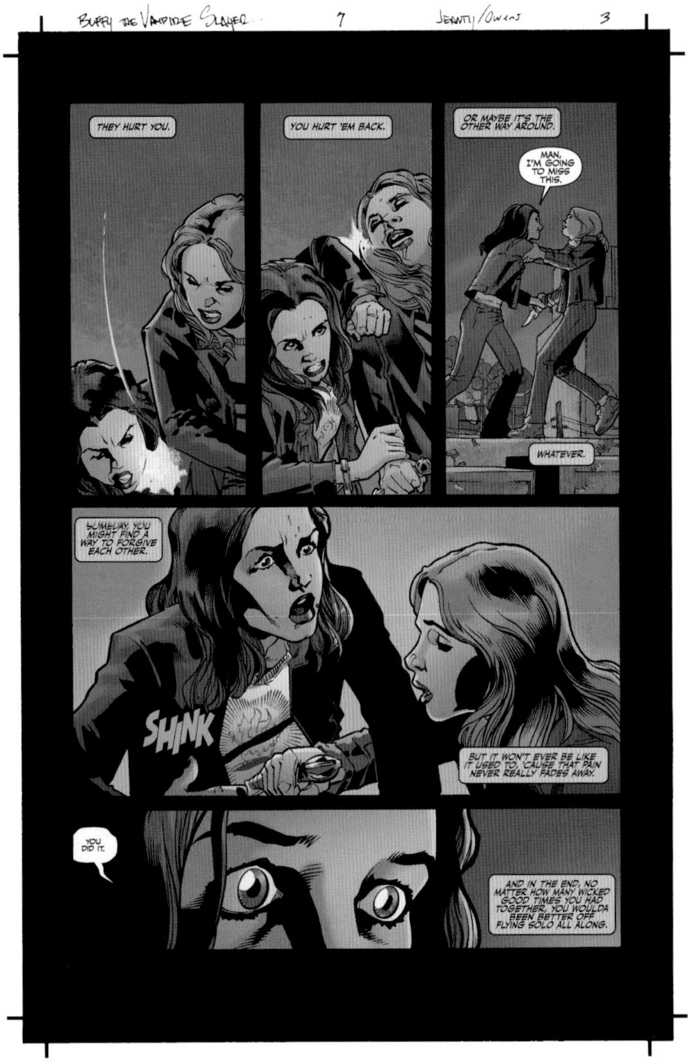

BUFFY THE VAMPIRE SLAYER
7
JEANTY/OWENS
3
THEY HURT YOU.
YOU HURT 'EM BACK.
OR MAYBE IT'S THE OTHER WAY AROUND.
MAN, I'M GOING TO MISS THIS.
WHATEVER.
SOMEDAY, YOU MIGHT FIND A WAY TO FORGIVE EACH OTHER.
SHINK
BUT IT WON'T EVER BE LIKE IT USED TO, 'CAUSE THAT PAIN NEVER REALLY FADES AWAY.
YOU DID IT.
AND IN THE END, NO MATTER HOW MANY WICKED GOOD TIMES YOU HAD TOGETHER, YOU WOULDA BEEN BETTER OFF FLYING SOLO ALL ALONG.

I have to say, I love, love Faith. I was so excited when I got the script for No Future for You. *I thought it was a tight story and it showed how the Buffyverse could thrive even though it was no longer on television. It moved the character of Faith further, and it was a good story to boot. This sequence was a flashback to Season 3's "Graduation Day." I watched and rewatched that scene to get just the right feel in these few pages. I had to choose the key moments in the fight or else it would have been ten pages long! I love how writer Brian K. Vaughan incorporated scenes from the show with what was happening in the comics. Very seldom does the work come effortlessly to me, but this arc came damn close!*

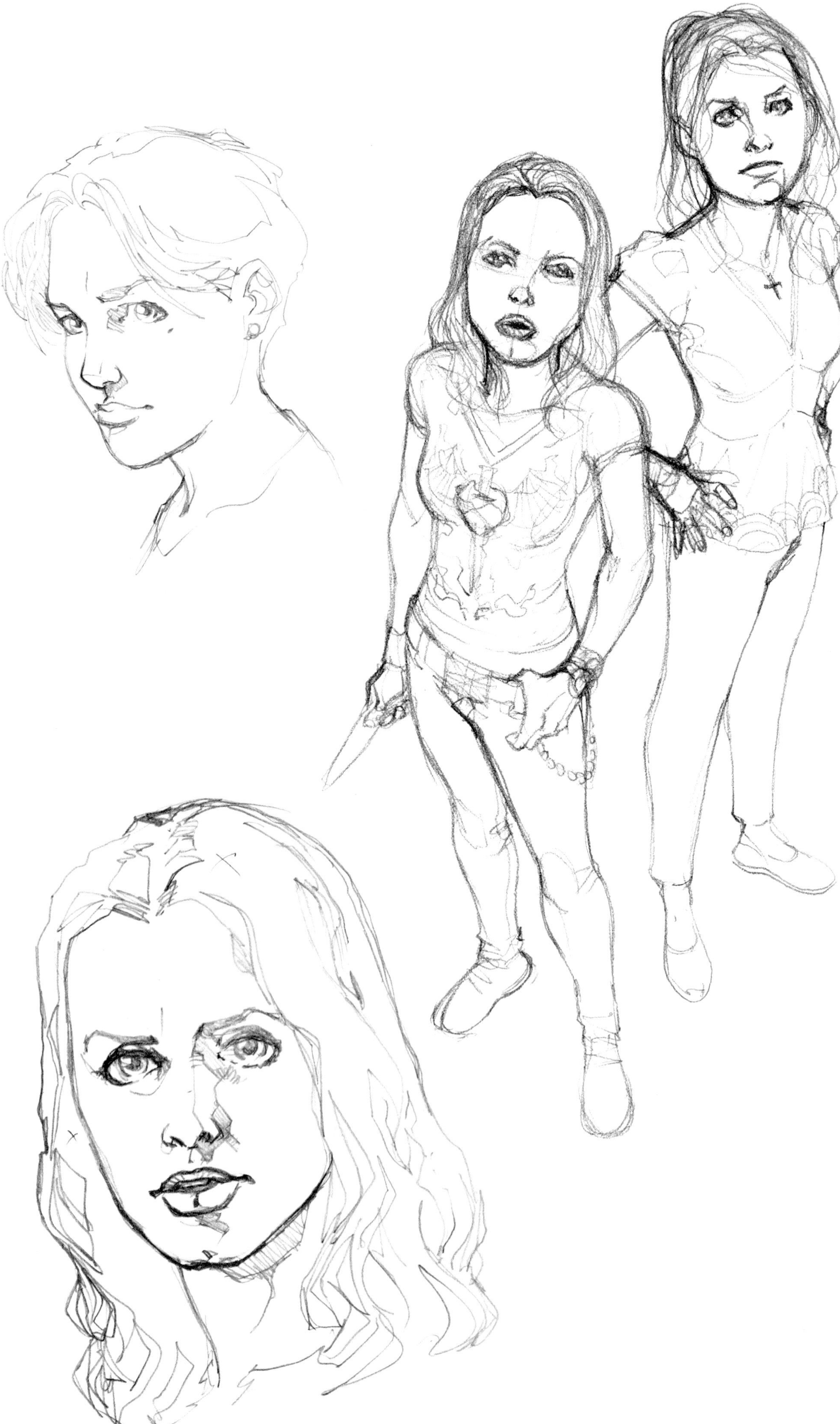

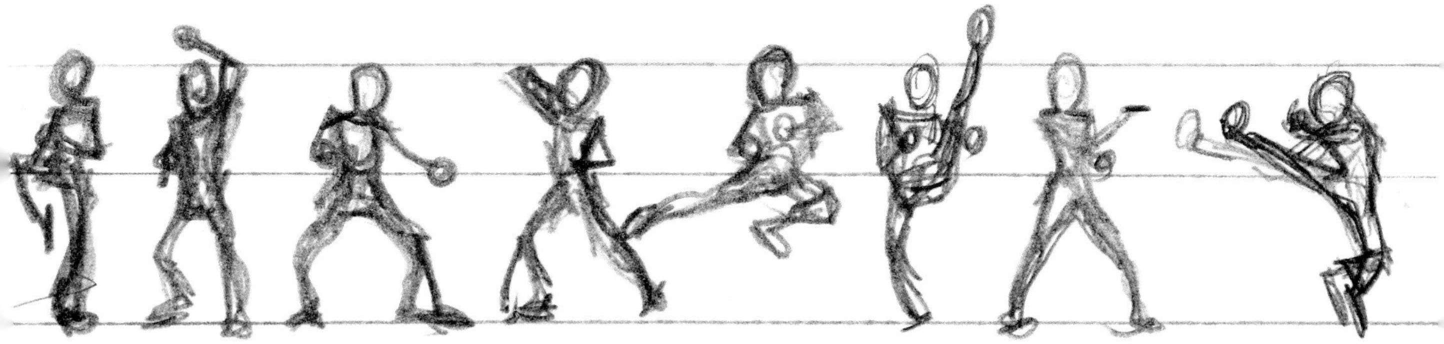

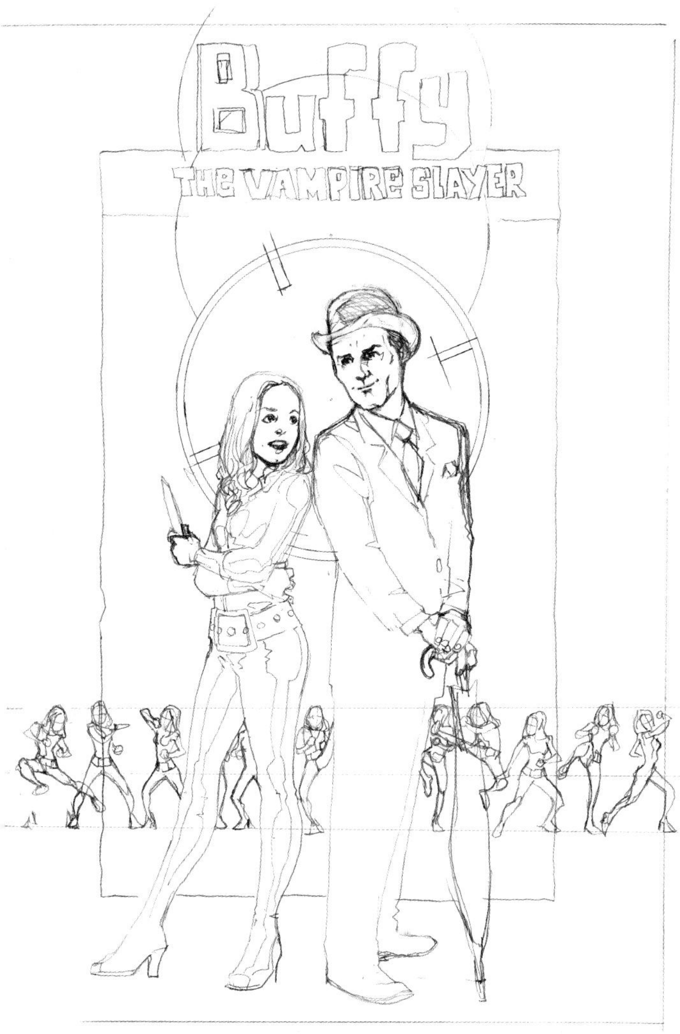
Buffy
THE VAMPIRE SLAYER

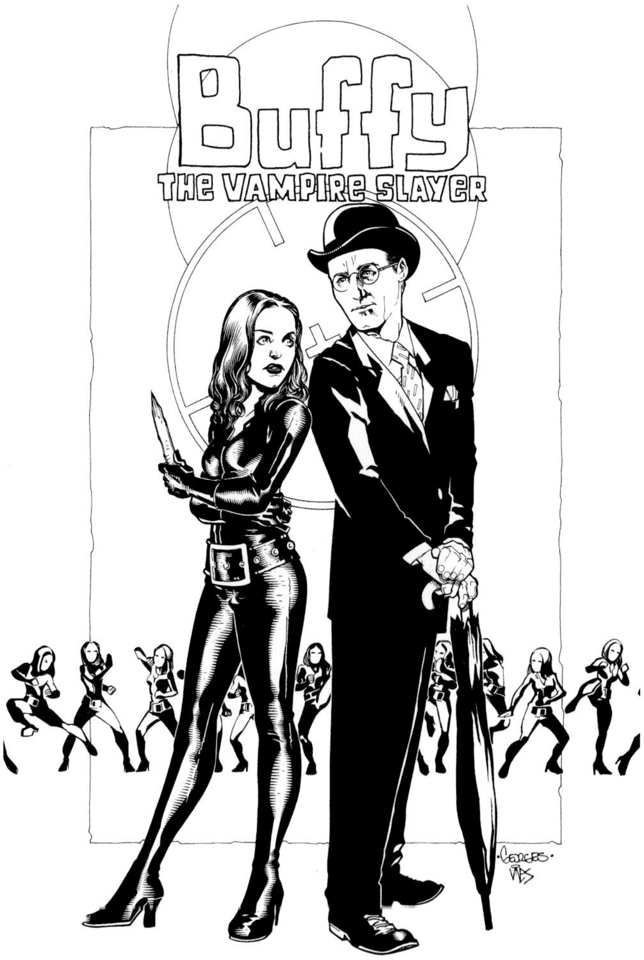
Buffy
THE VAMPIRE SLAYER

Above: *This idea for the cover to issue #9 came indirectly from the script. Giles mentions to Faith, when proposing they team up, that he could be the Steed to her Peel, which is a reference to a 1960s British television show about spies,* The Avengers. *I thought that would make a great cover. I still submitted other ideas, but I was really favoring this one. From there, I aped the poster of the movie version of the show. I wanted the cover to have a sixties feel to it and just added groovy things in. I really like the way this cover turned out. I thought this would make a great movie-poster version of the arc.*

Facing page: *These are the faces I drew for the cover to issue #8, another good cover that I've repeated several times in different ways for Season 8. I'm not as happy with the faces, but I liked the idea.*

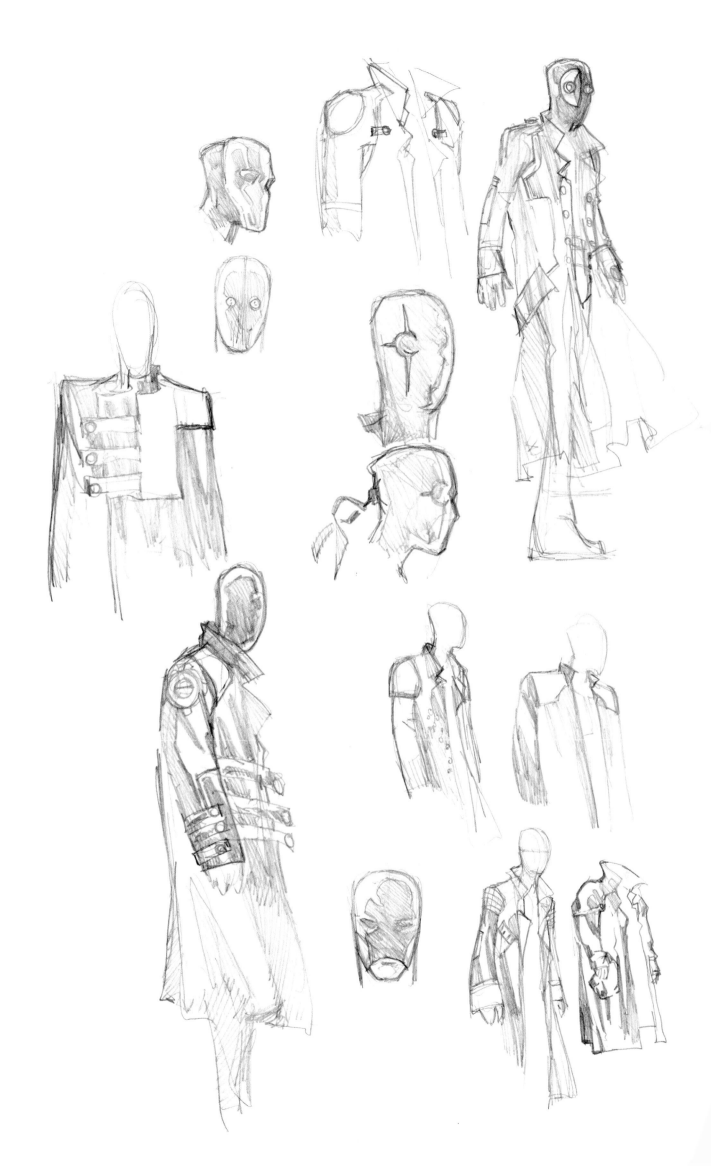

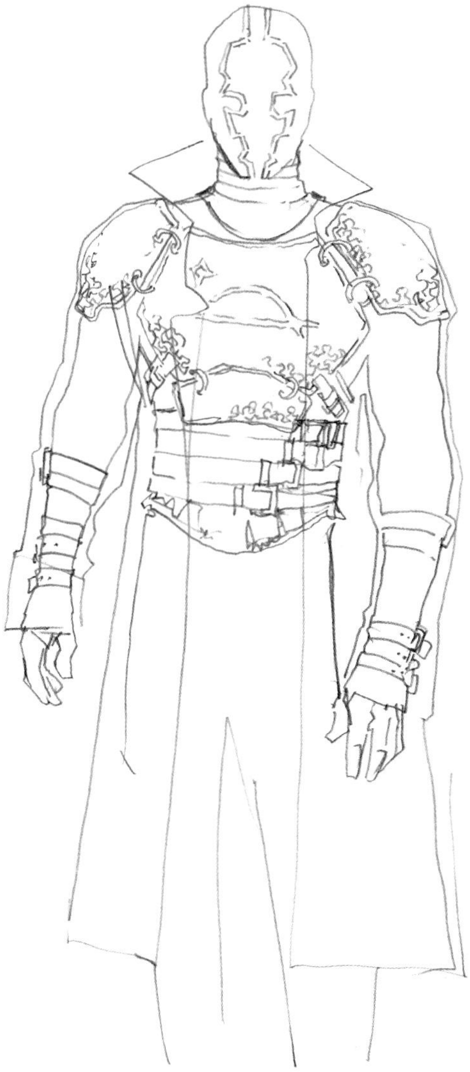

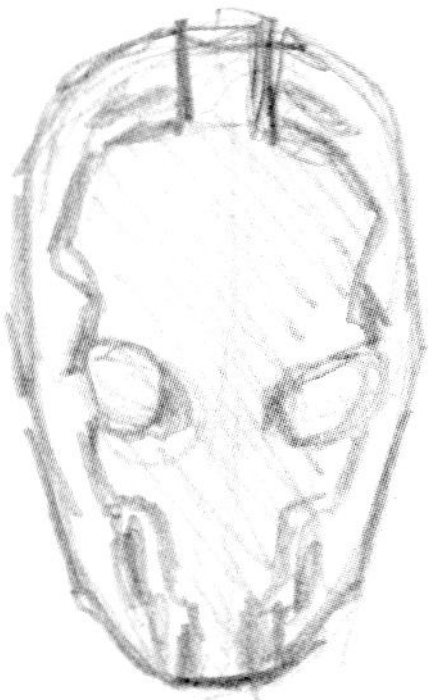

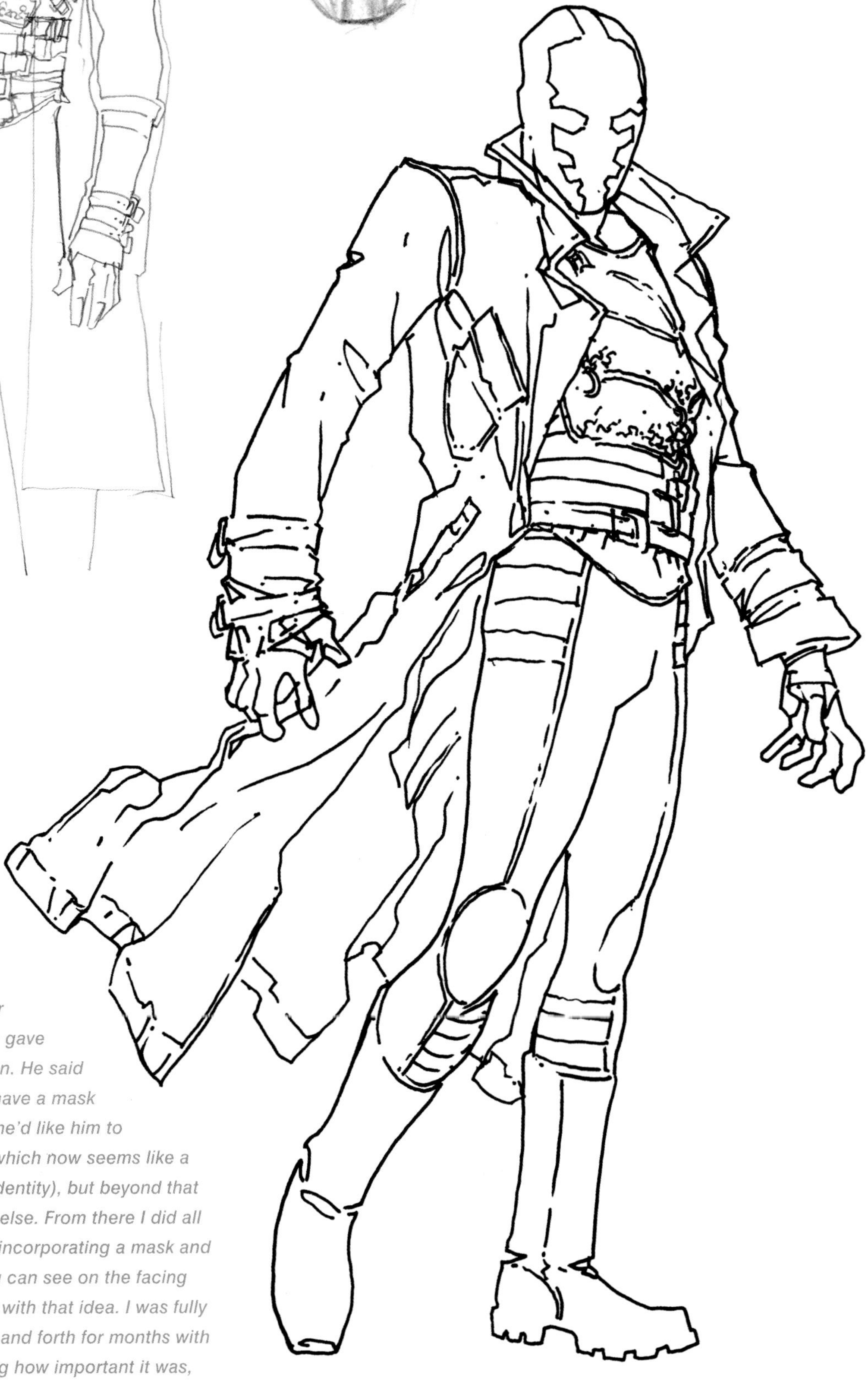

And now we come to Twilight. These two pages are but a mere fraction of all the drawings I did trying to get the Big Bad for Season 8 down. Joss gave me very little direction. He said that Twilight should have a mask to hide his face and he'd like him to have a trench coat (which now seems like a big giveaway to his identity), but beyond that he didn't have much else. From there I did all these little drawings incorporating a mask and a trench coat. As you can see on the facing page I mainly stayed with that idea. I was fully prepared to go back and forth for months with this concept, knowing how important it was, but in the end, Joss looked at the drawing above and said, "That's it." Sometimes it's just that easy!

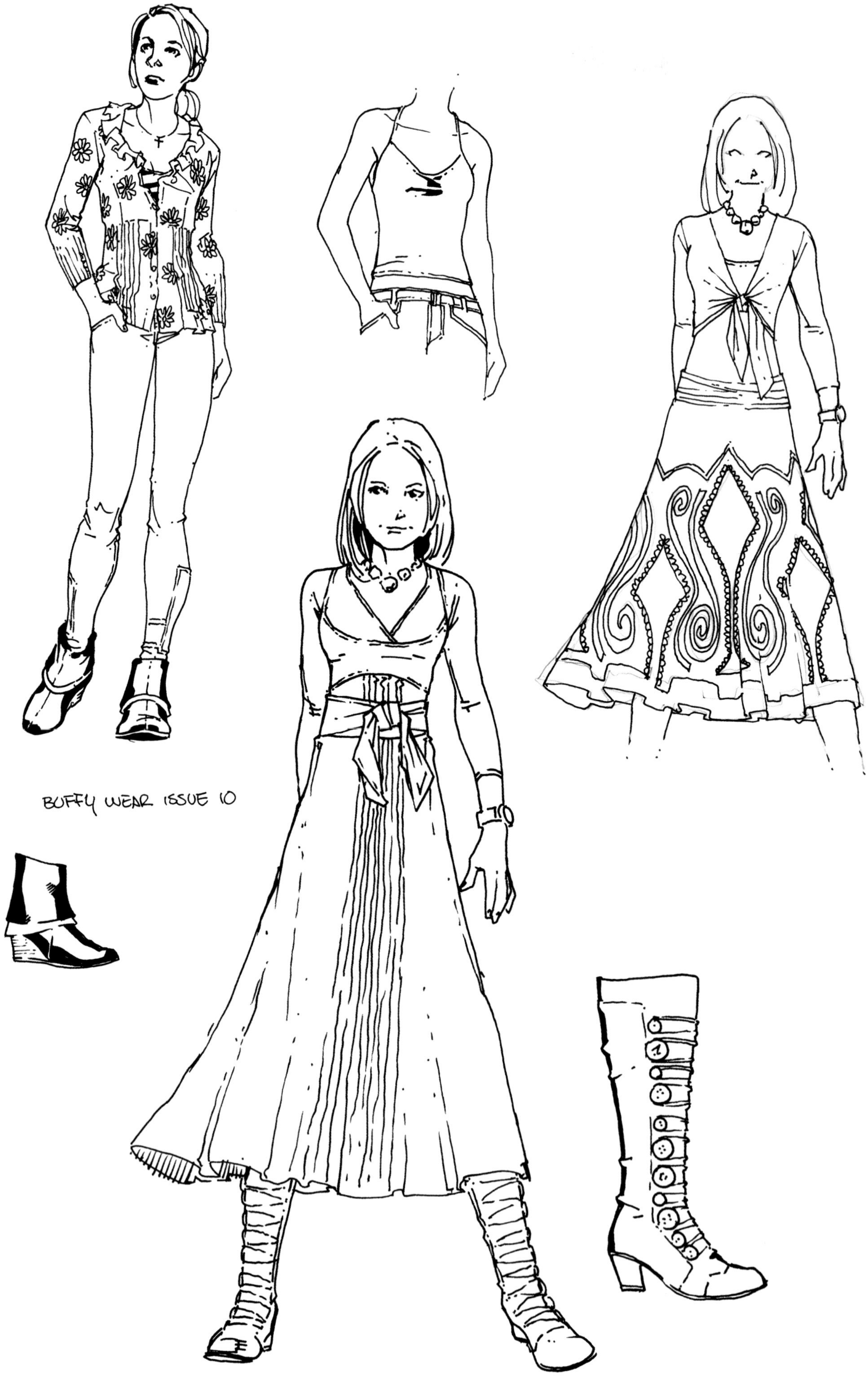
BUFFY WEAR ISSUE 10

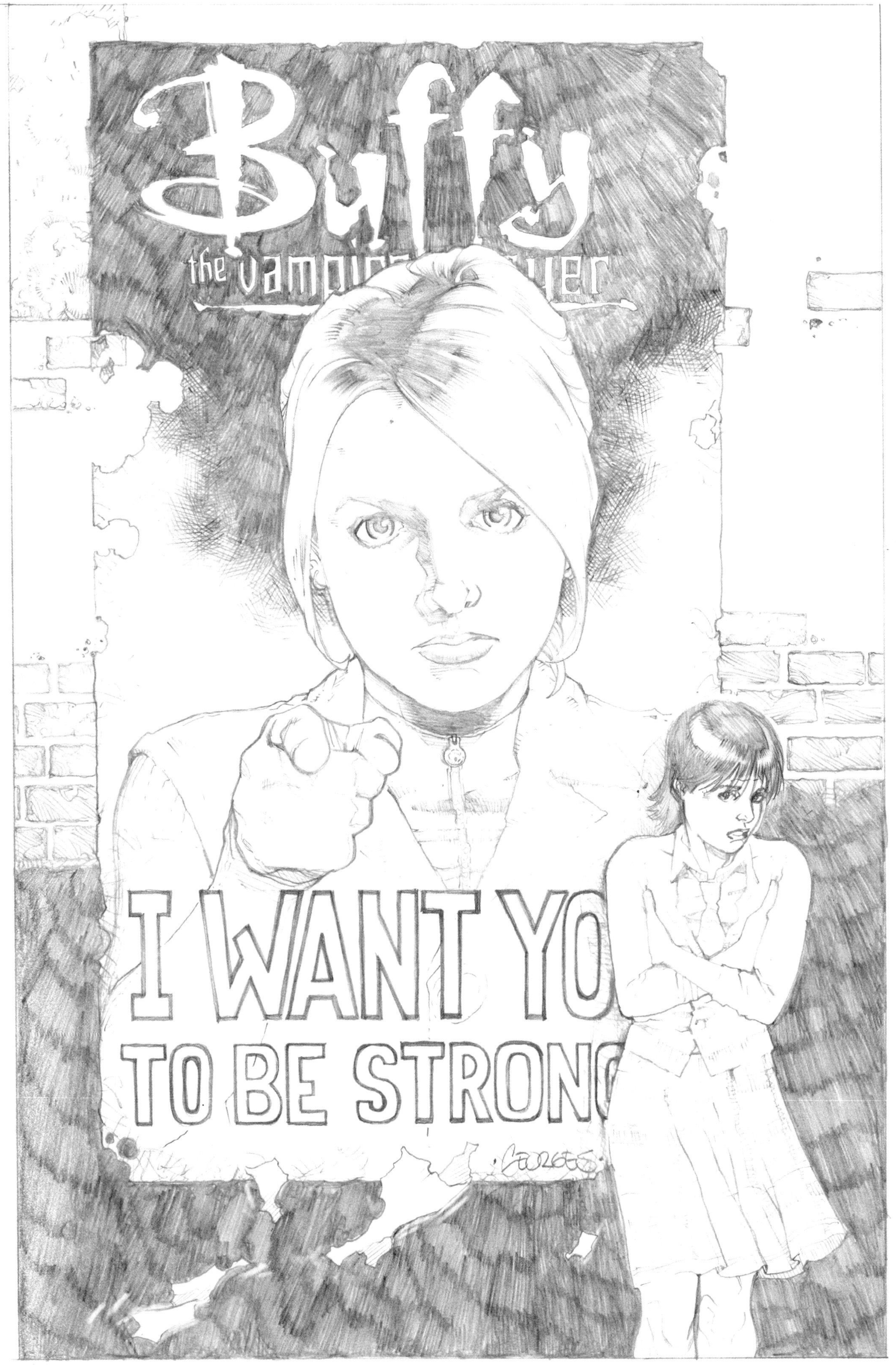
Buffy
I WANT YO
TO BE STRON

CREATOR BIOGRAPHIES

Writer, producer, and director **JOSS WHEDON** began writing feature films and acting as a "script doctor" in the 1990s. He introduced the character for which he is most well known in his script for the original *Buffy the Vampire Slayer* film (1992).

In 1997 Whedon founded Mutant Enemy Productions so that he could coproduce the television series *Buffy the Vampire Slayer*. The series ran from 1997 to 2003, giving birth to Whedon's cultlike fan following, and led to a spin-off series, *Angel*, as well as comics series based on both shows. In 2002, Whedon produced and wrote the television series *Firefly*, which eventually led to a feature film titled *Serenity* (2005), as well as more comics. In 2008, Whedon produced and cowrote, with his brothers Zack and Jed Whedon, and Maurissa Tancharoen, the Emmy-winning online series *Dr. Horrible's Sing-Along Blog*—again leading to a comics series. His most recently produced television work, *Dollhouse*, premiered in 2009. He is currently writing and directing one of the most ambitious feature films to date: *The Avengers*, based on the Marvel Comics superhero team.

Comics written by Whedon include *Fray* and *Buffy Season 8*, both based in the *Buffy the Vampire Slayer* universe, and *Sugarshock*, all for Dark Horse Comics, and *Runaways* and *Astonishing X-Men* for Marvel Comics.

Award-winning comics and television writer and producer **BRIAN K. VAUGHAN** began writing comics professionally in 1997. Since then he has written for several of Marvel's and DC's premier titles, including *Ultimate X-Men* and *Runaways*; in 2005 he won the Eisner Award for Best Writer for those titles, as well as two of his own creations: *Ex Machina* (from DC's WildStorm imprint) and *Y: The Last Man* (from DC's Vertigo imprint). In addition, *Ex Machina* earned Vaughan the 2005 Eisner for Best New Series. In 2006 he released another creator-owned property, again through Vertigo, *Pride of Baghdad*. Also in 2006, he was named Comics' Best Writer by *Wizard* magazine. While continuing to work on his own projects, in 2007 Vaughan took on scripting for issues #6–#9 of *Buffy the Vampire Slayer* Season 8 for Dark Horse Comics.

Having studied as an undergraduate film student at New York University, Vaughan made a natural segue into television writing. He was the principal writer for ABC's *Lost* in its fourth and fifth seasons, and became a producer of the show's fifth season. Both seasons under Vaughan were nominated for Best Dramatic Series (2009 and 2010) by the Writers Guild of America.

After a break from comics writing, Vaughan returned in 2012 with a new creator-owned ongoing series, *Saga*, from Image Comics.

Buffy the Vampire Slayer Season 8 and Season 9 series artist **GEORGES JEANTY** studied fine arts at Miami Dade University; the pursuit of a career in comics was a logical choice for his artistic talents. In 1993 he broke into the world of comics with *Paradigm* #1 from Caliber Comics, and soon was penciling for London Night Studios. Moving to Atlanta, Georgia, in 1994, Jeanty joined Gaijin Studios and began to work regularly for DC Comics on titles such as *Green Lantern*, *Superboy*, and *Superman*. His first ongoing series came in 1999 with Marvel Comics' *Bishop: The Last X-Man*, and was followed by work on *Gambit*, *Deadpool*, and *Weapon X*. In 2003, Jeanty left Gaijin Studios and formed Studio Revolver with fellow artists Dexter Vines, Tom Feister, and Tariq Hassan. The year 2006 brought Jeanty the critically acclaimed comics miniseries *The American Way*, a controversial sixties-era series written by screenwriter John Ridley and released through WildStorm. Soon after the success of *The American Way*, Jeanty was approached by Dark Horse Comics to be the regular series artist for *Buffy the Vampire Slayer* Season 8—for which he had been handpicked by Joss Whedon. Georges Jeanty's run as the artist for Season 8 was critically acclaimed, and the series received the 2008 Eisner Award for Best New Series. Jeanty continues as the regular series artist for *Buffy the Vampire Slayer* Season 9.

PAUL LEE is a freelance painter, comic-book penciler, and children's-book illustrator. He is best known for his cover work and interior pencils for various *Buffy the Vampire Slayer* and *Angel* comics and his contributions to *Buffy: Tales of the Vampires*, all from Dark Horse Comics. Lee's comics work can also be seen in Marvel Comics' *Amazing Fantasy Starring Spider-Man* and DC's *Batman*, as well as Dark Horse's *The Devil's Footprints*, *The Lone Gunmen*, *Star Wars Tales*, and *Conan*.

Brazilian artist **CLIFF RICHARDS** is best known for his work on the original Dark Horse *Buffy the Vampire Slayer* comics series that ran from 1998 to 2003, while the television series was still on the air. Over the years, Richards has also drawn for DC Comics' *Birds of Prey* and *Wonder Woman*, and for Marvel Comics' *Rogue*, *Excalibur*, and *New Thunderbolts*, among many other titles. Most recently, Richards was the artist for the comics series *Dollhouse*, a five-issue supplement to the television series from creator Joss Whedon, as well as a three-issue arc of *Buffy* Season 9 and 2012's *Buffy the Vampire Slayer: Drusilla* series.

'ROM JOSS WHEDON

Buffy the vampire slayer™

;UFFY THE VAMPIRE SLAYER SEASON 8

OLUME 1: THE LONG WAY HOME
ɔss Whedon and Georges Jeanty
;BN 978-1-59307-822-5 | $15.99

OLUME 2: NO FUTURE FOR YOU
;rian K. Vaughan, Georges Jeanty, and Joss Whedon
;BN 978-1-59307-963-5 | $15.99

OLUME 3: WOLVES AT THE GATE
)rew Goddard, Georges Jeanty, and Joss Whedon
;BN 978-1-59582-165-2 | $15.99

OLUME 4: TIME OF YOUR LIFE
ɔss Whedon, Jeph Loeb, Georges Jeanty, and others
;BN 978-1-59582-310-6 | $15.99

OLUME 5: PREDATORS AND PREY
ɔss Whedon, Jane Espenson, Cliff Richards, Georges Jeanty, and others
;BN 978-1-59582-342-7 | $15.99

OLUME 6: RETREAT
ɔss Whedon, Jane Espenson, Cliff Richards, Georges Jeanty, and others
;BN 978-1-59582-415-8 | $15.99

OLUME 7: TWILIGHT
ɔss Whedon, Brad Meltzer, and Georges Jeanty
;BN 978-1-59582-558-2 | $16.99

OLUME 8: LAST GLEAMING
ɔss Whedon, Scott Allie, and Georges Jeanty
;BN 978-1-59582-610-7 | $16.99

;UFFY THE VAMPIRE SLAYER SEASON 9

'OLUME 1: FREEFALL
ɔss Whedon, Andrew Chambliss, Cliff Richards, Georges Jeanty, and others
;BN 978-1-59582-922-1 | $17.99

'ALES OF THE SLAYERS
ɔss Whedon, Amber Benson, Gene Colan, P. Craig Russell,
'im Sale, and others
;BN 978-1-56971-605-2 | $14.99

'ALES OF THE VAMPIRES
ɔss Whedon, Brett Matthews, Cameron Stewart, and others
;BN 978-1-56971-749-3 | $15.99

.UFFY THE VAMPIRE SLAYER: TALES
;BN 978-1-59582-644-2 | $29.99

RAY: FUTURE SLAYER
ɔss Whedon and Karl Moline
;BN 978-1-56971-751-6 | $19.99

ALSO FROM DARK HORSE . . .

;UFFY THE VAMPIRE SLAYER OMNIBUS

'OLUME 1
;BN 978-1-59307-784-6 | $24.99

'OLUME 2
;BN 978-1-59307-826-3 | $24.99

'OLUME 3
;BN 978-1-59307-885-0 | $24.99

'OLUME 4
;BN 978-1-59307-968-0 | $24.99

'OLUME 5
;BN 978-1-59582-225-3 | $24.99

'OLUME 6
;BN 978-1-59582-242-0 | $24.99

'OLUME 7
;BN 978-1-59582-331-1 | $24.99

.NGEL OMNIBUS
'hristopher Golden, Eric Powell, and others
;BN 978-1-59582-706-7 | $24.99

.NGEL & FAITH VOLUME 1: LIVE THROUGH THIS
'hristos Gage, Rebekah Isaacs, Phil Noto, and others
;BN 978-1-59582-887-3 | $17.99

;UFFY THE VAMPIRE SLAYER: PANEL TO PANEL
;BN 978-1-59307-836-2 | $19.99

GEORGES · OWENS

DARK HORSE BOOKS®
DarkHorse.com

AVAILABLE AT YOUR LOCAL COMICS SHOP OR BOOKSTORE!
To find a comics shop in your area, call 1-888-266-4226.
For more information or to order direct: • On the web: DarkHorse.com • E-mail: mailorder@darkhorse.com • Phone: 1-800-862-0052
Mon.–Fri. 9 AM to 5 PM Pacific Time.
*Prices and availability subject to change without notice

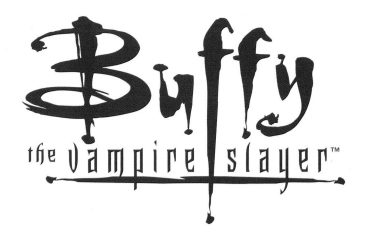

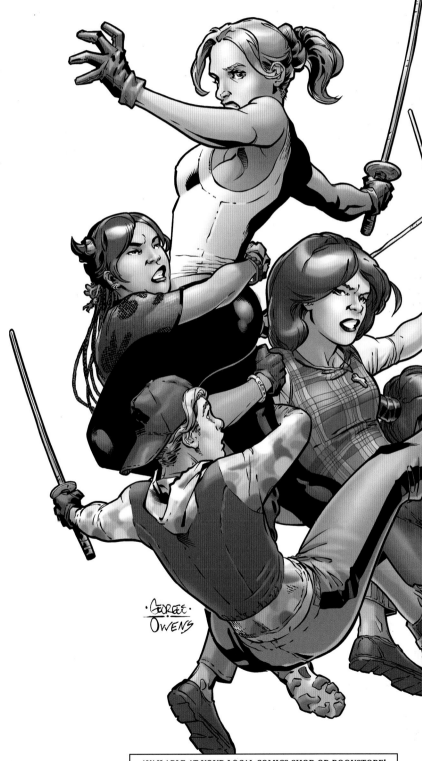

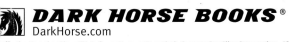

ALSO FROM JOSS WHEDON

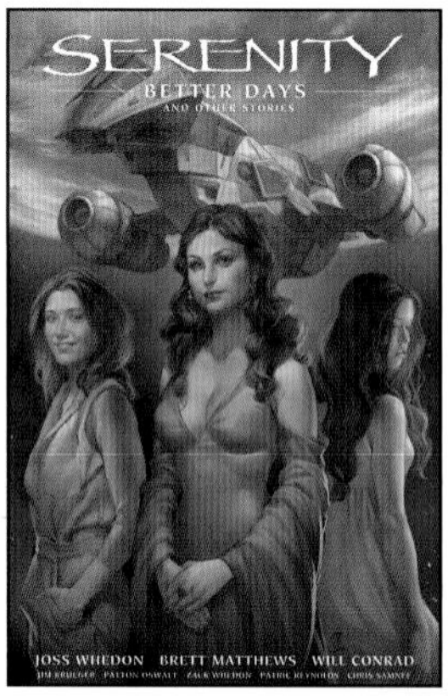
SERENITY
BETTER DAYS
AND OTHER STORIES
JOSS WHEDON BRETT MATTHEWS WILL CONRAD
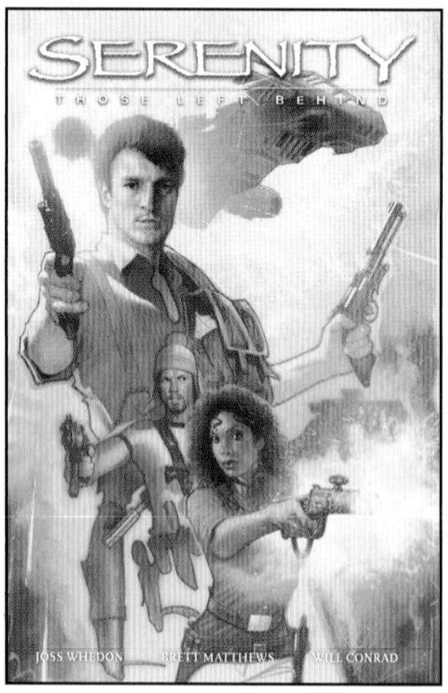
SERENITY
THOSE LEFT BEHIND
JOSS WHEDON BRETT MATTHEWS WILL CONRAD
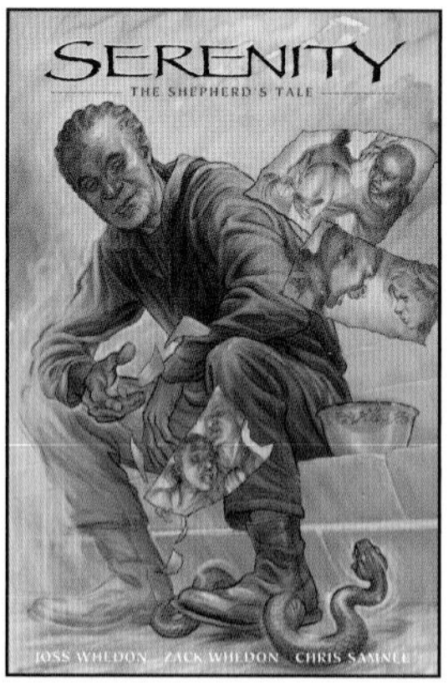
SERENITY
THE SHEPHERD'S TALE
JOSS WHEDON ZACK WHEDON CHRIS SAMNEE
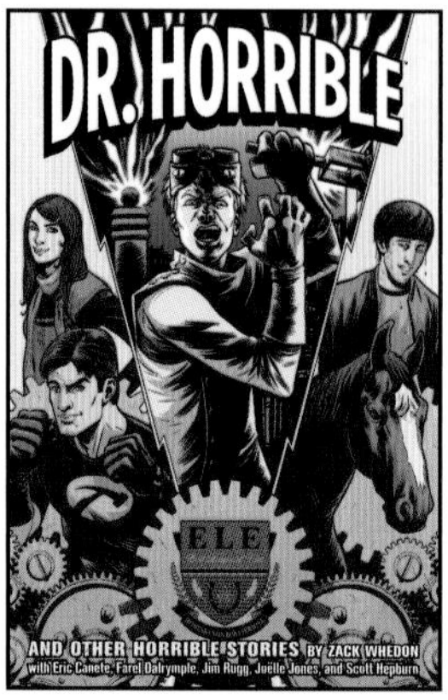
DR. HORRIBLE
ELE
AND OTHER HORRIBLE STORIES BY ZACK WHEDON
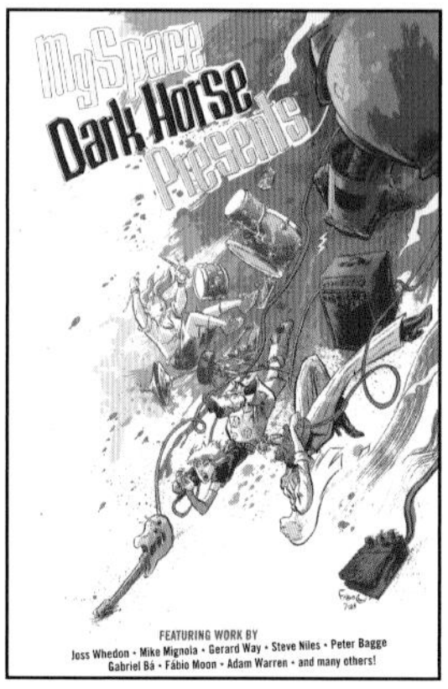
MySpace
Dark Horse
Presents
FEATURING WORK BY

SERENITY VOLUME 1: THOSE LEFT BEHIND
SECOND EDITION HARDCOVER
Joss Whedon, Brett Matthews, and Will Conrad
ISBN 978-1-59307-846-1 $17.99

SERENITY VOLUME 2: BETTER DAYS AND
OTHER STORIES HARDCOVER
Joss Whedon, Patton Oswalt, Zack Whedon, Patric Reynolds and others
ISBN 978-1-59582-739-5 $19.99

SERENITY VOLUME 3: THE SHEPHERD'S TALE HARDCOVER
Joss Whedon, Zack Whedon, and Chris Samnee
ISBN 978-1-59582-561-2 $14.99

DR. HORRIBLE AND OTHER HORRIBLE STORIES
Joss Whedon, Zack Whedon, Joëlle Jones, and others
ISBN 978-1-59582-577-3 $9.99

MYSPACE DARK HORSE PRESENTS VOLUME 1
Featuring Sugarshock *by Joss Whedon and Fábio Moon*
ISBN 978-1-59307-998-7 $19.99

DOLLHOUSE VOLUME 1: EPITAPHS
Andrew Chambliss, Jed Whedon, Maurissa Tancharoen, and Cliff Richards
ISBN 978-1-59582-863-7 $18.99

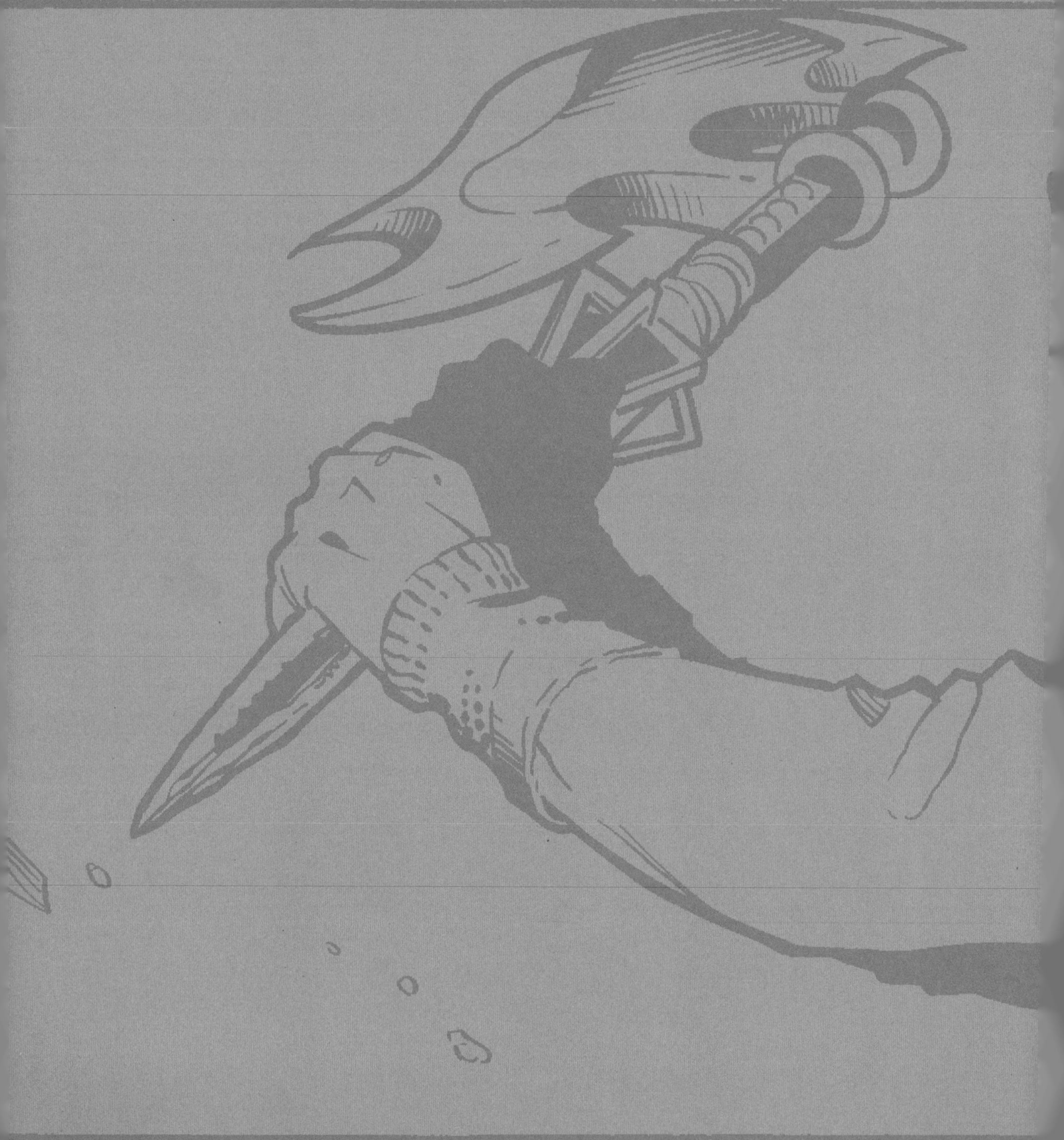

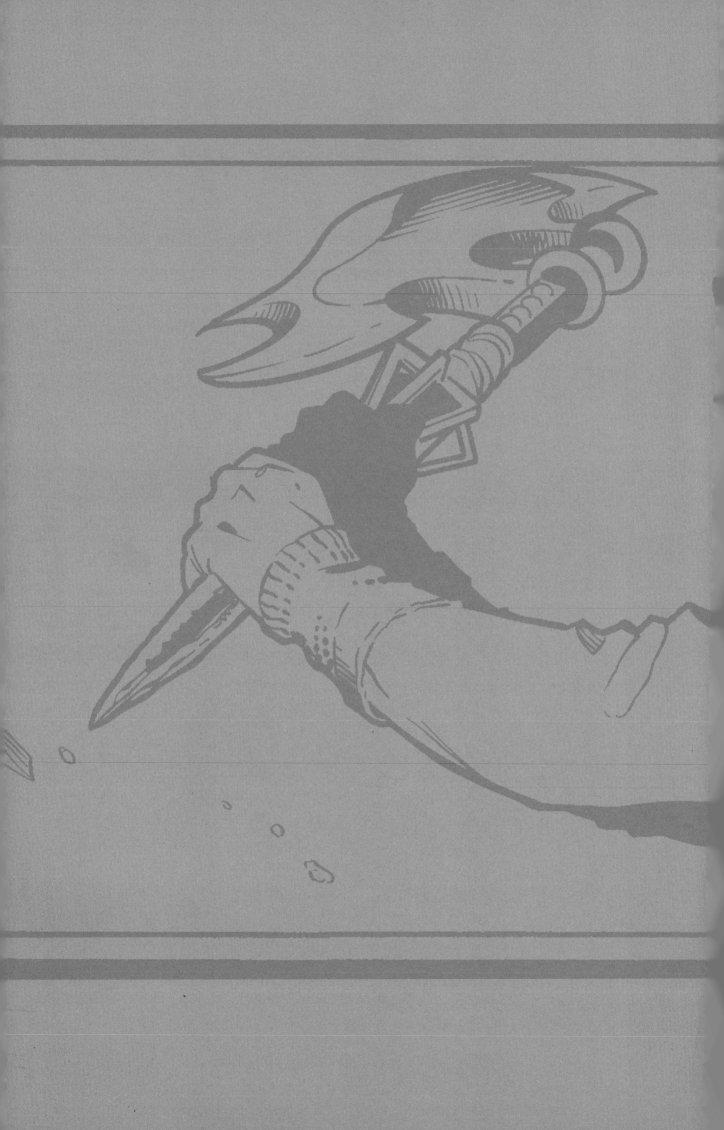